Manual of Home Repairs, Remodeling and Maintenance

Publishers · **GROSSET & DUNLAP** · New York

ISBN 0-448-01753-9

Published under arrangement with Ottenheimer Publishers, Inc.
All rights reserved under

PAN-AMERICAN COPYRIGHT CONVENTION

and the INTERNATIONAL COPYRIGHT CONVENTION

1974 PRINTING

CONTENTS

the table saw

First of the stationary tools discussed in detail, it will probably be your very first investment in power equipment

THE basic function of the table saw is to cut stock to length (crosscut) or to width (rip). There are variations of these such as miters and bevel cuts, but the miter is essentially a crosscut and the bevel is pretty much a rip. Beyond these elementary procedures, machine refinements and special techniques permit other operations that are common woodworking jobs.

Table-saw accessories such as the dado assembly and the molding head further extend the usefulness of this "first" woodworking power tool.

Since sizing stock to length and to width are the first steps in the fabrication of any project, and since follow-up steps such as the forming of simple joints (dadoes, rabbets, etc.) are easily accomplished on the

Rockwell 10-inch tilting arbor saw rips to center of a 48-inch panel, cuts stock up to 3⅛-inch thick.

8-inch bench saw from Sears offers big 17 x 20-inch table and self-aligning rip fence, cuts to 2½ inches.

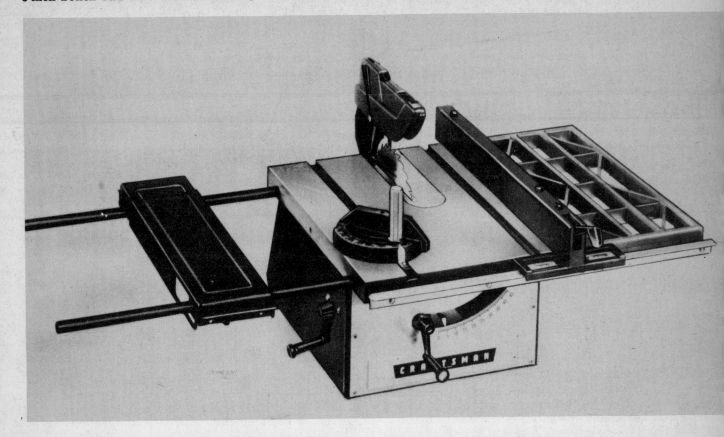

table saw, it is pretty generally conceded that this tool is the very first investment you should make in power equipment. Since, for most jobs, you'll be doing the majority of the work on the table saw, this advice makes sense, but it is not an unbreakable rule.

To understand the table saw, you should know these basic facts. It's a table with a saw blade mounted beneath it. In normal position the saw blade is perpendicular to the table surface and parallel to the table slots. These slots are for the miter gauge which is merely a guide for making cuts across the wood grain. In addition the table is so designed that a fence can be moved across its width and always parallel to the blade and to the miter gauge slots. The fence is also a guide, but for rip cuts.

Now here is why a saw does so much to make you an advanced woodworker right off. Crosscutting a board by hand is a tough job to do accurately; so is ripping. It takes a lot of skill to come up with edges that are square. On the saw you place the stock against the miter gauge and advance it against the turning blade. It will be a perfectly straight and square cut because the components of the machine handle that for you as well as supplying the power. For ripping, you set the rip fence the required

distance away from the saw blade. You know the cut will be straight and the width of the board uniform throughout its length. Again it's the machine that guarantees this. It's completely disinterested in who is flicking the switch; amateur, professional, male or female, it makes the same cut every time.

But in order for you to exploit the full potential of the machine, you must occasionally check its components to be sure they are in correct relation to each other. If they aren't you won't get the accuracy the machine is capable of, or the confidence you would gain with correct use of it. This accuracy is built into the machine with adjustment features that permit you to maintain it forever. Although all machines are basically the same, adjustment procedures may differ, so be sure to read and keep the literature that comes with the machine you buy. Before you make the first cut study it—go through the adjustment procedure detailed by the manufacturer. Only then can you be assured of accurate cuts.

Regardless of the type or make of machine, these are the component relationships:

The blade, in normal position, must be perpendicular to the table surface and

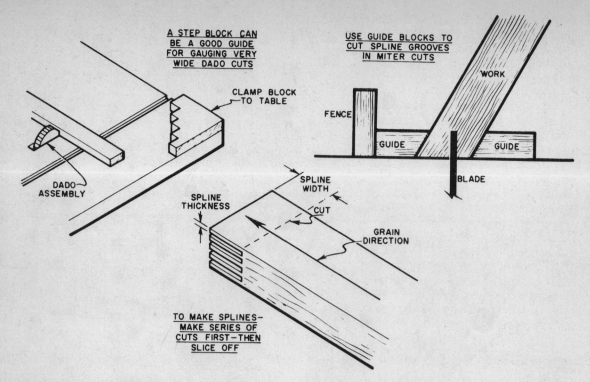

A STEP BLOCK CAN BE A GOOD GUIDE FOR GAUGING VERY WIDE DADO CUTS

CLAMP BLOCK TO TABLE

DADO ASSEMBLY

USE GUIDE BLOCKS TO CUT SPLINE GROOVES IN MITER CUTS

WORK

FENCE

GUIDE

GUIDE

BLADE

SPLINE WIDTH

CUT

GRAIN DIRECTION

SPLINE THICKNESS

TO MAKE SPLINES—MAKE SERIES OF CUTS FIRST—THEN SLICE OFF

parallel to the miter gauge slots as well.

The miter gauge, in normal position, must be at right angles to the saw blade and must move parallel to the saw blade.

The rip fence must be parallel to the saw blade and to the miter gauge slots.

If the miter gauge has automatic stops for most common miter gauge positions these stops must be perfectly set to assure correct angular cuts.

This is also true of automatic stops for blade or table tilt.

Types of Saw Blades

Most machines come equipped with a combination blade which is pretty efficient for both crosscutting and ripping. Usually you'll work with this kind of blade, but there are others and it pays to have some

on hand. Consider these when you buy.

COMBINATION BLADE is an all-purpose blade which can be used for all table saw operations.

CROSSCUT BLADE has a tooth design which is most efficient for cutting across the grain of the wood.

RIP BLADE is like the crosscut blade in that it does one job most efficiently, that is, cuts *with* the grain of the wood.

Actually it doesn't make much sense to change blades every time you make a cut. It's best to leave a combination blade on the machine. Use the other blades when you have a great amount of ripping or crosscutting to do.

HOLLOW-GROUND COMBINATION is a planer blade which gets clearance in the cut because the area between the blade

Check that the rip fence is parallel with table slot by lining it up with one slot and then passing your fingers along its base, as shown here.

Check blade alignment with allen wrench clamped so it just touches one tooth. Move miter gauge to rear, see if wrench just touches same tooth.

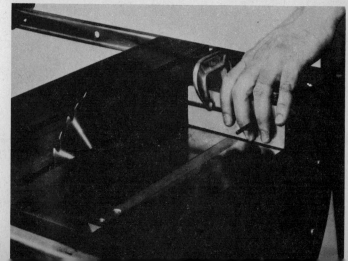

center and edge is thinner. Getting clearance this way, it requires no set in the teeth and therefore makes a smooth cut. To prevent it from burning in the cut, always give it maximum projection above the work surface, or at least ¾ inch. This is a blade you should give careful treatment to. Don't use it for sizing cuts, especially on hard, thick stock. Save it for fine trim cuts and for mitering operations.

CUT-OFF WHEEL is not a saw blade but an abrasive disc which is used for metal cutting. These should always be used with care, never under excessive pressure especially against the side of the disc. A good safety practice with such a wheel is to use arbor-mounted flanges which are at least one third the diameter of the wheel.

Any blade you use should be *sharp*. This is probably one of the most important safety rules and applies to all cutting tools.

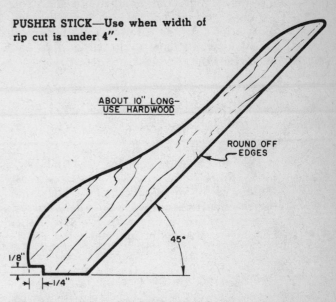

PUSHER STICK—Use when width of rip cut is under 4".

ABOUT 10" LONG—USE HARDWOOD

ROUND OFF EDGES

45°

1/8"

1/4"

Big 12-inch floor model bench saw from Sears features 4½ HP motor, see-through blade guard, miter gauge.

If a blade is dull and you must exert much pressure to make the cut, there is a great likelihood that your hand might slip. You can sharpen your own blades but it's a good idea to let a pro do it for you. With normal care you won't have to do it too often and even then the low cost is worth it.

Crosscutting

To crosscut (square an end or cut a piece to length) place the work firmly against the miter gauge and then advance both work and gauge past the blade.

The miter gauge can be used in either table slot, but the one which affords most table area for work support is the best one to use. In any case always position yourself so you are not in line with the saw blade. Don't stop the operation when the cut is complete; instead, return the miter gauge to the starting position. Most times you'll be able to make the pass with one hand. Never use the free hand to push against the free end of the work, and never lift the cut-off from the table while the blade is still turning.

Miter-gauge extensions, which are merely lengths of wood attached to the miter-gauge face, can increase work support. Many operators always work with an extension because it adds support when crosscutting long stock and safety for crosscutting small pieces. Since the extension carries a cut made by the saw blade, it's easy to cut work to a mark. Mark the piece to length, then line up the mark on the work with the cut in the extension. You know the blade will cut on that line.

Good support is essential. You should not have to strain to keep the work flat on the table.

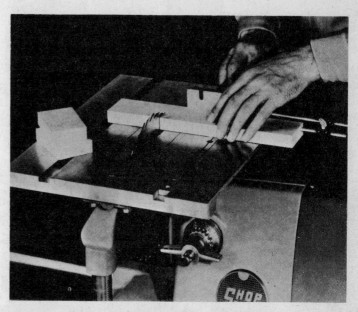

Miter gauge stop rods are economical accessory, let you cut multiple, duplicate-length pieces.

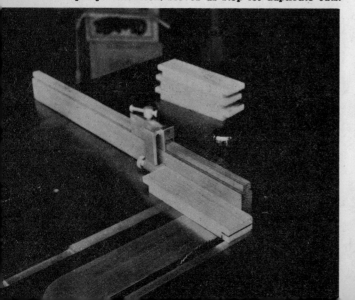

Another good accessory. It slides on simple miter gauge extension, serves as stop for duplicate cuts.

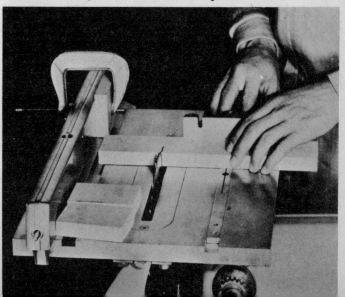

Fence will also gauge lengths; use only with a stop block clamped on. Never use only the fence.

One useful kink for extensions is to face them with sandpaper. The gritty surface acts to grip the work and keep it from moving.

A good rule for crosscutting, or any operation for that matter, is to provide maximum support for the work. When work is extra long or large, get someone to help support it, or make an extension stand that can be placed to provide help. It's a good idea to seek a better method of accomplishing the cut any time you must strain or assume an awkward position to handle the job in question.

Ripping

The rip fence acts as a control to maintain the width of the work throughout the pass. Rip cuts should be started with both

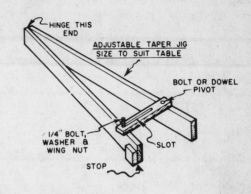

HINGE THIS END

ADJUSTABLE TAPER JIG SIZE TO SUIT TABLE

BOLT OR DOWEL PIVOT

1/4" BOLT, WASHER & WING NUT

SLOT

STOP

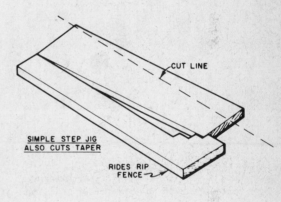

CUT LINE

SIMPLE STEP JIG ALSO CUTS TAPER

RIDES RIP FENCE

Though often omitted for clarity in these photos, remember to use the saw guard whenever possible.

When guide can't be used, feed work, well supported, slow and straight. Guide line is advised.

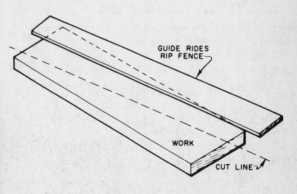

GUIDE RIDES RIP FENCE

WORK

CUT LINE

These silent helpers are self-explanatory, easily constructed, and will prove useful in your shop. You can tack-nail guide to very large work.

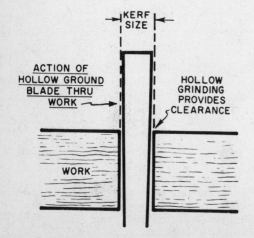

Support long panels well. Extra hands, extension for saw table are used in this commercial shop.

Good position for starting rip cut. Left hand does not move, the right feeds stock through.

Drawing below illustrates action of hollow-ground blades. Always provide at least ¾-in. projection.

ACTION OF HOLLOW GROUND BLADE THRU WORK →

KERF SIZE

HOLLOW GRINDING PROVIDES CLEARANCE

WORK

Keep good face of plywood up. Combination, fine-tooth crosscut, or special plywood blades are best.

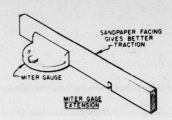

SANDPAPER FACING
GIVES BETTER
TRACTION

MITER GAUGE

MITER GAGE
EXTENSION

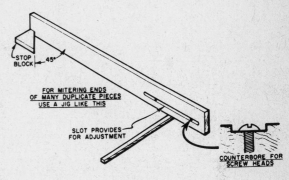

STOP
BLOCK   45°

FOR MITERING ENDS
OF MANY DUPLICATE PIECES
USE A JIG LIKE THIS

SLOT PROVIDES
FOR ADJUSTMENT

COUNTERBORE FOR
SCREW HEADS

For taper rip cuts, special jig is used. It rides
rip fence and holds work at the correct angle.

SLIDING TABLE
MITER JIG

HARDWOOD BARS
RIDE IN MITER
GAUGE GROOVES

45°

CUT
LINE

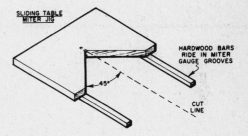

Miter cutting can be done accurately on table saw.
Guard against work movement during the pass.

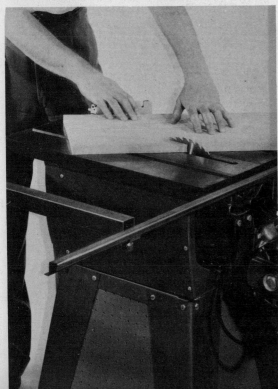

MITERING
JIG

MITER GAUGE
BAR

45°

CUT LINE
(SAW BLADE)

WORK

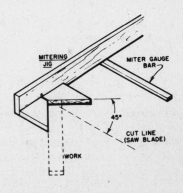

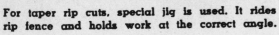

TYPICAL TABLE-SAW CUTS

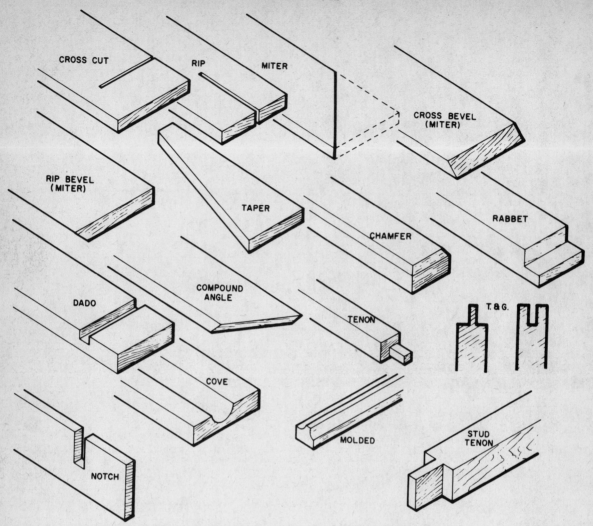

hands; the left holding the work against the fence, the right feeding the work forward. The right hand is placed with fingers straddling the rip fence so the hand is braced firmly in its safe position and is not likely to move. Anytime the width of a rip cut is less than four inches, use a pusher-stick to feed the stock through. This can be a simple stick with a notch in one end to hook over the work, or it can be a fence-straddling design. In any case, make one and have it handy. Don't reach down to the floor for scrap wood when the need for a pusher arises.

Some operators recommend that the rip fence be adjusted slightly out of line to provide greater clearance at the back of the blade. This is especially useful in ply-wood cutting since it reduces the amount of splintering as the "back teeth" of the blade continue to pass through the cut formed by the "front teeth."

Miter Cuts

Miters are accomplished by setting the miter gauge head to the angle required and making the pass like a crosscut. It's as simple as a crosscut but there is greater chance for inaccuracy, for these reasons:

When the blade hits the work it tends to pivot it around the forward edge of the miter gauge. The work tends to move along the miter gauge as you advance it. This "creeping" action plus the pivot can do enough to make accurate miter cutting pretty frustrating. A simple way to avoid these problems is to use a miter gauge extension faced with sandpaper and to hold the work very firmly against the miter gauge as you make the pass. On short work use the miter gauge in a closed position. On long work use an open miter gauge position. Any type of hold-down which attaches to the miter gauge and clamps the work firmly in position is a definite

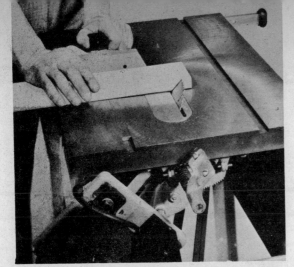

A miter cut across grain is made by tilting blade and making pass with the miter gauge, as shown.

To miter duplicate pieces, precut first to exact length, then cross-miter each end. Judge this by eye, or clamp block to table to act as stop.

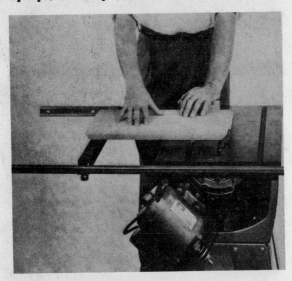

help when you're engaged in miter cutting.

Always make miter cuts slowly, even more slowly than straight cuts. If the cut is inaccurate and you've followed all the rules, check the setting of the miter gauge. Perhaps the auto-stop requires adjustment. It's a good idea to make test cuts first, before cutting into your good material.

One of the surest ways to get perfect miter cuts is to make a sliding table which has an angle guide to hold the work in correct position. The table is just a flat board with wood bars beneath it that slide in the miter gauge slots. This table can't move (except forward and back) and since the angle guide is in a fixed position, the work angle will be maintained. Another advantage of such a jig, is that often the miter gauge must be shifted from left-hand slot to right-hand slot when miter cutting stock which can't be flipped over. Having to change the miter gauge position as well

as head angle every other cut is tough to do accurately. The sliding table eliminates this chore.

Bevel Cuts

Bevel cuts call for a blade tilt (or a table tilt if you own a tilting table saw rather than a tilting arbor). A cross-bevel (one made cross-grain) is actually a miter cut. But, so you can clarify things in your own mind, identify an angle-cut *with* the grain as a "bevel" and an angle-cut across the grain as a "cross-bevel." Assuming in each case that the angle-cut is accomplished with a blade tilt.

The pass on a cross-bevel is made with the miter gauge just as if you were crosscutting. On a simple bevel, the work is passed along the rip fence just as if you were making a rip cut.

Compound Angles

These are tough—not physically tough to do—but because a great deal of accuracy is required and both a blade tilt and a miter gauge setting is required. Any frame or open structure that has sloping sides requires a compound angle cut. The most common example is the shadow box or picture frame which has sloping sides.

It's most important that you make the required settings accurately. Check on scrap stock before you cut good material. Make the pass slowly, and hold the work firmly. A procedure to follow when making a frame, that will simplify things is this. Decide the overall size of the frame and from this pick up lengths of the four pieces required. If the frame is square each piece will be the same length and width. Cut and square the stock to these exact dimensions.

If you're working to a sixty-degree work angle, you'll find from the chart that it requires a blade tilt of 21 degrees and a miter gauge setting of 49 degrees. Set the blade and the miter gauge to these exact settings. Check each with trial cuts and a protractor. Then make the cut at each end of the precut frame pieces. This is a little more wasteful than cutting the four pieces consecutively from one long board, but it is so much easier to accomplish accurately that it's worth it.

Dadoes and Grooves

Anytime you need a cut which is wider than the normal saw blade kerf you call on the dado assembly. This is a table saw accessory which consists of two outside blades and a set of "chippers" which are mounted between the blades to remove waste stock between the outlining cuts. Width of the cut is controlled by the number of chippers you place between the blades. Size range is usually from ¼ to ¾ inch. The dado assembly requires an insert with a slot wide enough to accommodate the dado at its widest setting.

A dado cut is always made with the cutter set lower than the thickness of the stock to produce a U-shaped form. Actually there are no secrets to its use, other than to feed more slowly because it removes much more material than a regular saw cut. If the dado required is very deep, it's best to make it in two passes, adjusting the dado height after the first pass. Cuts across the grain are made with the miter gauge; cuts with the grain are accomplished against the rip fence. With-the-grain cuts are often called grooves.

Dado cuts which are wider than maximum setting are accomplished in more than one pass. Wood blocks can be clamped to the saw table to gauge the width of the cuts. A good many wood joints are done using the dado assembly. Some examples are the dado, half lap, rabbet, tongue and groove and others.

Rabbeting

A rabbet is an L-shaped cut made along the edge of the stock, either with the grain or across it. Rabbet cuts across the stock are made with the miter gauge; with the stock, they are made along the rip fence.

Sears 10-inch bench saw employs 1 HP motor, cuts wood up to 3⅜ inches thick, has table extension.

9-inch bench saw from Wards offers both sliding and grid extensions, 2 HP motor, safety clutch.

Compound miter combines miter and cross-miter, requires miter gauge setting, blade or table tilt.

8-inch tilt-arbor bench saw from Sprunger gives 18 x 14-inch precision ground table, fully ribbed.

Rabbets can be cut with a conventional saw blade by making two passes, but when many of them are needed, you work faster and more accurately by employing the dado assembly. Here, too, since you are removing considerable stock, it's good practice to feed the work slowly and use more than a single pass if the cut is deep.

Molding Head

A molding head on your table saw will enable you to shape table edges, make your own sash, shape cabinet-door lips, make joints, and do many standard operations it would be time-consuming to do otherwise. In addition it can be used like a shaper to form moldings, either in standard shapes or in original designs.

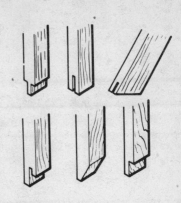

Dado can cut angled grooves. On a tilting arbor saw, dado would be set at angle, not the table.

These cuts are typical of those made safer and/or easier by use of sliding tenoning jig just below.

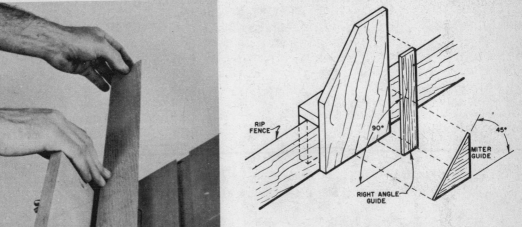

Guide of tenoning jig must slide smoothly over rip fence. Attach guides with screws for removal.

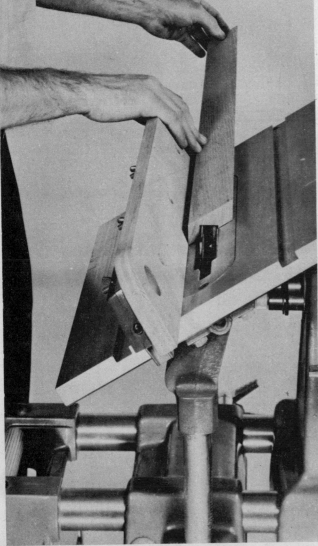

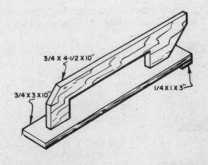

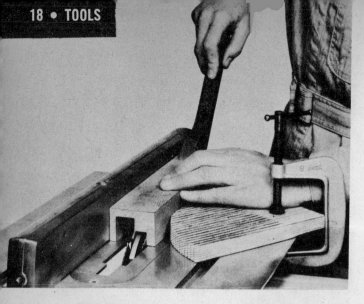

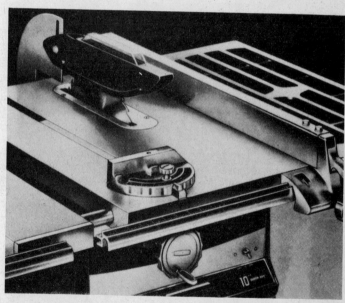

Spring holddown, made by cutting series of close kerfs, can be useful for holding stock in place.

Two-pass rabbet cutting. First cut is made with stock on edge; final cut is made as shown here.

Take no chances with molding head. Here, work's clamped to block riding rip-fence facing to keep it perpendicular, prevent its falling into opening.

Wards 10-inch saw has self-aligning ball-bearing geared rip fence, slices finished 4-inch lumber.

Molding head operations can be done on round stock, too. V-block guide permits turning work.

Coving cut. Work moves obliquely across saw blade that is raised about 1/16 in. after each pass.

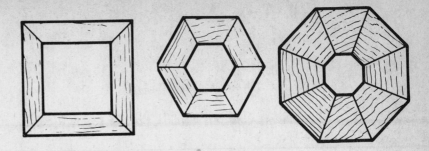

For 4-sided figure, miter cut is 45°, bevel cut 45°; for 6-sided figure, miter 60°, bevel 30°; for 8-sided figure, miter 67½°, bevel 22½°. Note chart below.

MITER CUTS FOR FLAT FRAME
(MITER GAUGE SETTING)

BEVEL CUTS FOR DEEPER STRUCTURE
(BLADE TILT)

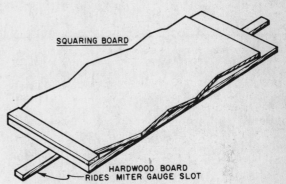

SQUARING BOARD

HARDWOOD BOARD RIDES MITER GAUGE SLOT

For straight cuts when stock has no regular edge to ride rip fence, can't be held to miter gauge.

The common molding head is a thick circle of steel, notched to receive sets of matching knives, which is locked on the arbor in place of the saw blade. Like the dado assembly it requires a special insert to accommodate it. Here is one thing to remember. Even the special insert doesn't always provide as much support around the cutter as it should. If you are doing an operation that leaves excessive gap around the cutter, spend a few minutes to make a special wood insert. Do this by using the regular insert as a template. Cut a wood blank, secure it in the table opening, then allow the molding head to form its own slot by raising it as it is turning.

By adding a wood facing, you can use the standard rip fence as a molding fence. Most table saw fences have holes in them for just this purpose.

Molding cuts should never be made too fast or too deep. Very deep cuts should be made with successive passes. This is safer and also better for the job. Be warned when the molding head slows up or if the work begins to "chatter." These are signs of feeding too fast or cutting too deep.

Cuts with the grain are always smoother than cuts made across the grain. Cuts against the grain should be avoided whenever possible. Since it's often necessary to mold cross-grain it's wise to adopt this procedure. Always make the cross-grain cuts first, then finish off with the remaining cuts that will be with the grain. This applies, of course, when molding four edges of a piece—a cabinet door, for example.

Molding knives are not always designed to cut the full profile shape. Many of them are combination cutters and are designed so you utilize just a portion of the profile shape. Usually you can tell from the name of the knife whether it's a "single-purpose" design or a combination type. A cabinet door-lip cutter, for example, is designed for just that purpose while a ¼- and ½-inch quarter-round cutter can be used to do either of the jobs in its name. •

Blade Tilt and Miter Gauge Settings for Most Commonly Used Compound Angle Cuts

Work Angle	4-Sided Figure		6-Sided Figure	
	Blade Tilt	Miter Setting	Blade Tilt	Miter Setting
15°	43¼°	75½°	29°	81¾°
30°	37¾°	63½°	26°	74°
45°	30°	54¾°	21°	67¾°
60°	21°	49°	14½°	63½°

the jointer

With it, you can quickly obtain smooth edges of guaranteed accuracy

Rockwell jointer below features 6-inch wide, ⅜-inch deep jointing, rabbeting capacity; ball bearings.

THINK of the jointer as being a mechanical planer. Remember the skill and muscle you needed to plane an edge smooth and square in manual arts? Well, the jointer is designed to do this job without effort and with guaranteed accuracy. It will do the same thing on a surface so long as the cut is light, but it should not be considered a thickness planer. There is this difference. If you plane opposite surfaces on a jointer, those surfaces will be smooth but there is no guarantee they will be parallel. The thickness planer does both jobs.

Because the jointer can smooth an edge so easily it is often set up to run together with the table saw, so that ripped edges can be immediately smoothed. Since depth of cut is adjustable on the jointer, it's just a matter of making the rip cut oversize an equal amount. Typical procedure when using a saw-jointer setup would be this:

Sears 6⅛-inch jointer planer performs smoothing, edge-aligning, surfacing, edge-squaring operations.

Rockwell 4-inch jointer boasts fully adjustable table with dovetailed ways and adjustable gibs, with ground and balanced high-speed steel knives.

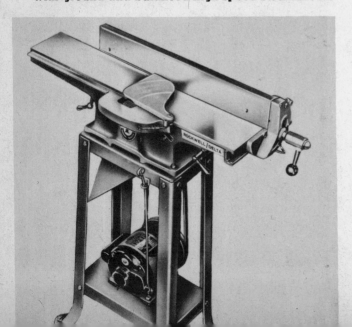

6-inch jointer planer from Sprunger provides extra long working surface of 43 inches, dial controls.

Wards 6⅛-inch jointer has built-in 1⅛ HP ball-bearing motor for powering cuts up to ½ inch.

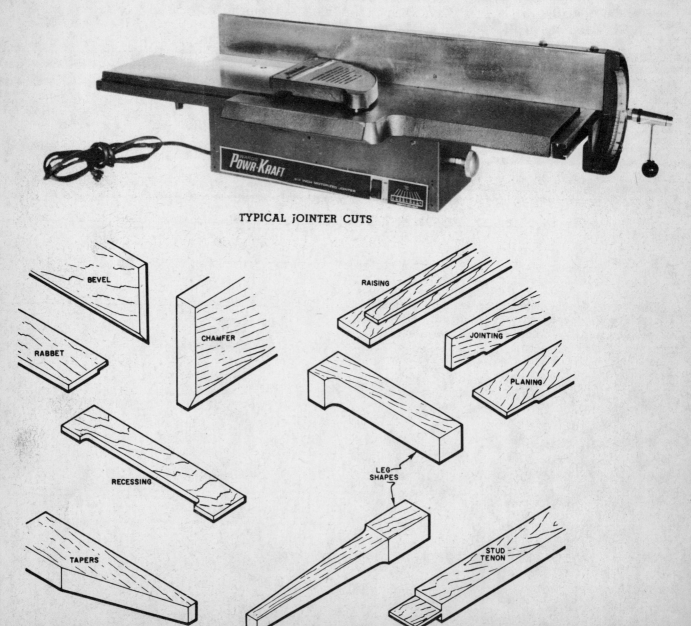

TYPICAL JOINTER CUTS

BEVEL

RAISING

RABBET

CHAMFER

JOINTING

PLANING

RECESSING

LEG SHAPES

TAPERS

STUD TENON

Joint one edge of the stock. Place that edge against the rip fence and make rip cut. Next joint second edge. Thus you have both sized and smoothed the edges of the stock so it can be assembled or glued without further attention.

The most important consideration in jointer adjustment is the relationship between knife height and the plane of the outfeed table. The rule is this: The horizontal plane of the outfeed table must be tangent to the cutting circle of the knives. How this adjustment is made and maintained is described in the manufacturer's literature. You'll know you should check when the work hits the front edge of the outfeed table (which indicates the knives are too low) or when the work drops during the cut (which indicates the knives are too high).

Depth of cut settings are usually accomplished with a handle or knob. For most jointing operations a 1/16-inch setting is good. This is not taxing the machine too much and doesn't waste a lot of wood. For surfacing, keep it even less than this,

especially when working on hardwoods.

So that the edge you joint will be square to adjacent surfaces, you'll want to be sure that the jointer fence (in normal position) forms a right angle with the jointer table. This should be checked with a square and the auto-stop (if any) adjusted if necessary.

Edge Jointing

Always joint stock so the knives are cutting *with* the grain of the wood. You'll know when you're not doing this because the cut won't feel smooth when you're making it. If you don't *feel* it, you'll *see* it because cutting against the grain seldom produces a satisfactory edge.

Make the jointing cut a smooth, easy movement. Place the stock on the infeed table and snug against the fence. Keep it this way throughout the pass. Usually it's best to use the left hand to hold the stock against the fence while the right hand moves it forward. If the work doesn't move smoothly, you'll know one of these things is happening: You're cutting

You can joint plywood, but expect some splintering at end of cut. Feed with grain of surface veneer.

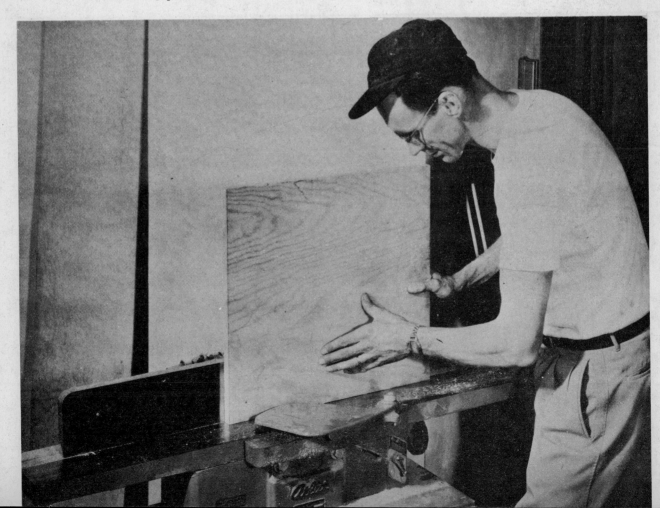

Wards 4⅛-inch jointer cuts up to ⅜-inch deep, left. It features cast-iron table to prevent vibration.

If outfeed fence is adjustable, make recess cut in one pass, A, below. If outfeed table's fixed, use two passes: first as taper cut, B; then turn stock, end for end, and make second pass like C, then sanding.

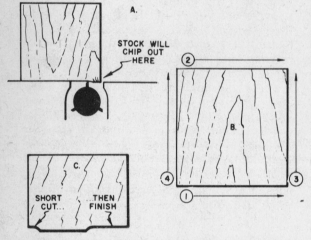

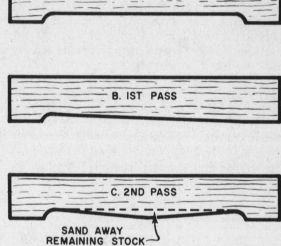

Jointing across end grain chips stock at end, as in A above. Make passes in order and direction of B, or cut an end short, turn and finish, as C.

If small pieces must be jointed, use utmost care and pusher stick. Left hand, here, is not applying pressure; it just holds stock against fence.

A pusher holddown is a good tool to make for such operations as this one. In fact, it's a good idea to use one for all surfacing operations.

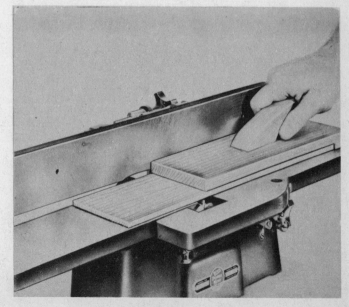

too deep; you're cutting against the grain; or the knives are dull.

To maintain the position of wide boards, it's a good idea to equip the jointer with an extra high fence. All this has to be is a wide, flat board (plywood is good) which is attached to the jointer fence with screws. Holes in the jointer fence will permit this.

When stock has an uneven edge (a dished or convex shape) it requires a little more attention. The dished edge should be jointed first. If the distortion is excessive, make more than one pass. If the other edge is also distorted, make a rip cut on the table saw (you have one jointed edge to ride the fence) to remove the unevenness before you joint the second edge.

End Grain

The problem in jointing cross-grain is that the knives will splinter the wood at the very end of the cut. If you must joint cross-grain, do it this way. Start the board across in the usual way, but stop when the cut is about an inch long. Then reverse the work and complete the cut in a second pass. If you're jointing all four edges of a piece of stock, make the cross-grain cuts first and finish off by cutting with the grain on the remaining two edges. The final cuts will remove the imperfections left by the first cross-grain cuts. It would be well to refer to the drawings in the far column on the facing page.

Surfacing

For surfacing, lay the stock flat on the table and make the pass as in jointing. On most surfacing operations it's a good idea to employ the use of a combination pusher-holddown, the same tool sketched in the table saw chapter. This will maintain pressure down on the work as you move it forward. It's most important that you use such a device on thin stock—for your sake as well as the work.

Keep surfacing cuts under 1/16 inch and make the pass very, very slowly. And, of course, it's important to work with the grain of the wood.

Don't try to surface boards which are very warped. It can be done but a small jointer is not the tool to use.

Rabbeting

Once you own a jointer you'll use it more and more, especially for rabbet cuts. To set up for a rabbet cut, move the fence across the table and lock it in position to gauge the width of the rabbet. Lower the infeed table to the depth required. Hold the stock firmly against the fence and flat down on the table. You can make a rabbet cut either with the stock flat on the table or on edge. If you're cutting a very deep or a very wide rabbet, use more than one pass to attain full depth of cut.

The same procedure can be used to form a tongue. Just cut a rabbet on one side,

Here is a good trick for surfacing extra-wide stock. Remove the fence and make the cut in two passes, each of which surfaces half board width.

Rabbet setup. Position fence to gauge its width; lower infeed table for its depth. The "rabbeting ledge," outfeed table give support after the cut.

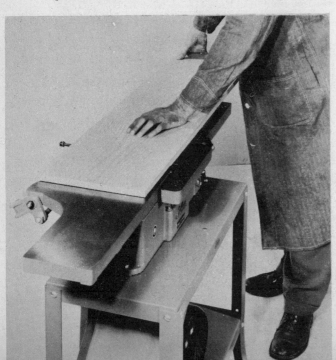

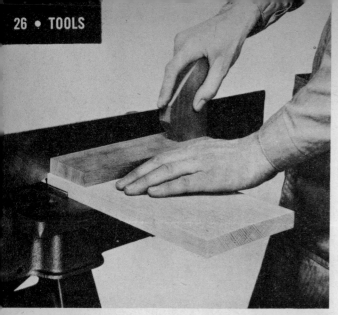

Make rabbet cut across grain this way, especially if stock's narrow. Make one rabbet this way, flip stock, rabbet opposite edge for tongue or tenon.

Starting taper cut. Work rests at front edge of outfeed table where taper is to begin. With contact made, below, work is fed across knives. This is demonstration only; use the guard on such jobs.

then flip the stock and form a second rabbet. Here, too, you can work with the stock flat or on edge.

End rabbets or tenons, especially if the stock is narrow, should be fed across the knives with the pusher-holddown. Be sure you hold the stock square to the blades and snug against the fence throughout the pass.

Tapers

You can do tapering on the jointer by proceeding as follows. Set depth of cut to amount of taper required and position the work over the cutter where the taper is to begin. Then lower the work so it makes contact with the knives and pull it across. If the amount of taper needed is more than you can accomplish with maximum depth of cut available, just make as many passes as you need.

Long work must be accomplished in steps. As an example, let's take a work piece which needs a taper 20 inches long and ¼ inch deep. Let's assume your jointer infeed table will accommodate a 10-inch long piece. Mark the taper area on the work into 10-inch divisions and set the depth of cut for ⅛ inch. Start the first cut from the first 10-inch mark. This will give

Short tapers can be made as demonstrated by this photograph. The block under the work is a height guide and also makes it easy to support the work.

you a taper 10 inches long and ⅛ inch deep. Make the second cut from the second 10-inch mark and you end up with a taper 20 inches long and ¼ inch deep. For multiple duplicate pieces, use clamped stop blocks so you can position the work for the start and end of each cut.

Angle Cuts

For cutting bevels or for chamfering, you tilt the fence to the angle required. Whenever possible tilt the fence so it forms a closed angle with the tables. This forms a snug pocket for the work with less chance of slipping.

Usually for bevels, since the entire edge of the stock must be removed you'll have to make more than one pass. Many chamfer cuts can be made in one pass.

Always work with sharp knives. Any time you have to force the stop or the cut doesn't feel smooth under your hands, you can be pretty sure that something isn't right. Dull knives are often at fault. Chipped knives may cut smoothly but will leave small ridges that run the length of the work.

The accompanying photographs and drawings should help you use this fine tool safely and efficiently. •

For bevel or chamfer cut, fence forms a closed angle with tables. This "nests" the work. Be careful to avoid slipping if you must use open angle.

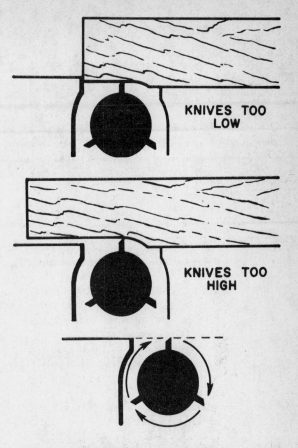

KNIVES TOO LOW

KNIVES TOO HIGH

Plane of outfeed table must be tangent to the cutting circle of knives, as indicated above. To make octagonal shape, cut away four corners with repeated passes, as shown by drawing below.

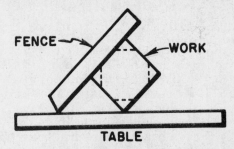

FENCE — → ← WORK

TABLE

Always feed the work with the grain, as below.

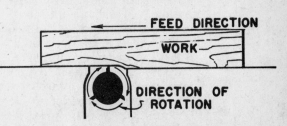

FEED DIRECTION
WORK
DIRECTION OF ROTATION

To cut tapers, make repeated passes until the full taper is reached, as drawing below indicates.

START OF TAPER
WORK   CUT
OUTFEED TABLE   INFEED TABLE

the drill press

Few shops are without this very versatile woodworking tool

THE DRILL PRESS was originally designed as a metal-working tool. As such, in the average workshop, its applications would be limited. But available accessories, plus jigs you make yourself, plus special techniques, make it one of the more versatile woodworking power tools, and few shops are without one.

Basically, it consists of a powered spindle with a chuck at the free end which grips cutting tools and turns them at speeds determined by step pulleys or by variable speed mechanisms. The chuck you get with the tool is a key-operated three-jaw chuck which is used for most common operations. When using a cutting tool which develops side thrust (router bits, dovetail cutters, and such) the standard chuck should be replaced with a special chuck designed to hold the particular tool.

You can figure drill-press capacities as twice the distance from column to spindle center. Thus a 12-inch drill press will let you drill to the center of a 12-inch diameter circle or board. Another factor is the maximum distance from chuck to supporting table. This capacity is always much less on a bench model drill press than it is on a floor model drill press. Many operators set up a bench model drill press so it can be swung to overhang the bench. Thus work may be supported on the floor of the shop to increase the tool's capacity.

Drill speeds are important, and since they relate to the tool being used, the material and the operation, it's wise to study the suggested speeds listed in the chart. On most drill presses it's difficult to achieve these exact speeds but you should get as close as possible. The general rule is this—the larger the tool, the slower the speed. Feed pressure is also important. Feeding too hard usually results in forcing the cutting tool beyond its capacity. Poor work and broken tools result. Best results are obtained by using the correct speed and feed pressure that lets the tool cut through the material easily at a steady rate.

You should retract the cutting tool frequently. This clears the hole of chips which cause the cutting tool to bind and overheat. This is one reason why a fluted drill should never be buried beyond the flutes. This prevents chips from emerging and causes excessive heat build-up. If you must drill deeper than the flutes on the drill, retract often enough to keep the hole clear.

Common Tools

There are many types of tools that drill holes. Most common are the twist drill, machine spur bit and the solid center bit. The twist drill is better for metal than wood although it's often used in wood drilling. Much better, however, are bits that have outlining spurs. These make contact with the wood before actual cutting begins, outlining the hole and cleanly severing the wood fibers to form a clean accurate hole.

Bits that have threaded tips should never be used on a powered drill press, not unless you can control the speed of the tool to match the feed of the screw. Since this isn't practical in the home workshop, it's best to avoid them. Work carefully with large tools and always clamp the job securely to the drill press table. One-side cutters (like fly cutters) can fool you into putting your hands too close to the cutting zone. Stay away from them. Clamp the work, use a slow speed, and keep your free hand well away from the work area. Don't feed too fast or tools of this type will surely bind in the cut.

Beyond this there are drill-press tools that let you cut plugs and dowels, form dovetails, countersink, counterbore, make mortise tenon joints, rout and shape, do drum sanding and many other operations.

Simple Drilling

Always place a scrap block underneath

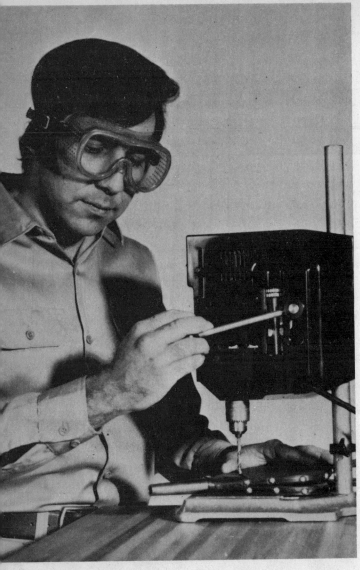

Montgomery Ward's ⅜-inch drill press includes solid state circuitry for range of even speeds.

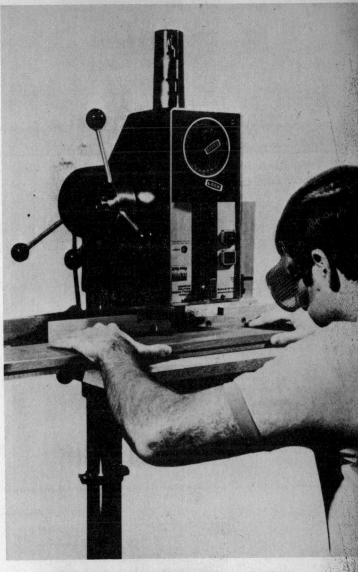

17-inch drill press from Wards has a chuck for drilling; high-speed spindle for routing, shaping.

These typical drill-press tools are, left to right at top: multispur bit; adjustable hole saw; two fly cutters. Bottom: a counterbore with pilot; stop, countersink, drill combination; solid center, double spur bit; special tool with different blades for same shank; and expansion bit.

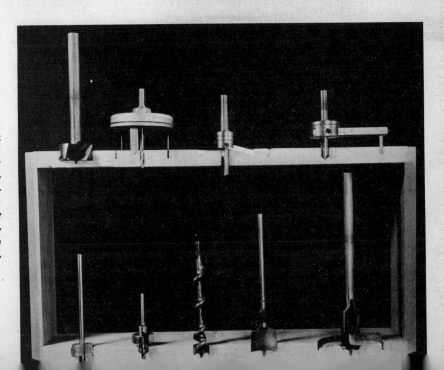

the work to protect the table and to assure a clean breakthrough. Since a drill, especially on large holes, can bind or grab in the hole, it's a good idea to clamp the work to the drill press table. Clamping also helps accuracy. Some woods have stubborn grain which can cause a drill to move off the mark. If this is the case, it's good practice to drill a small "pilot" hole and then enlarge this to correct size.

Your drill press is equipped with a quill extension stop so you can bore holes to exact depth. One simple way to use this is to mark the hole depth on the side of the stock, extend the quill until the drill point touches that mark and set the stop nuts accordingly. Thereafter every hole you drill will be to that same depth until you change the setting.

When drilling a series of holes that have a common centerline, it's best to provide a fence that will position the work to gauge the edge distance. This can be just a straight strip of wood clamped to the table or you can make or buy a special wood table with a fence.

In all cases remember that while the machine will guarantee perpendicularity of the hole to the work surface, its location on the work is up to you. That's why accurate layout is important. Make all measurements carefully; use a sharp, hard pencil to make intersecting lines at all hole centers. These intersections will be easy to hit with the brad point of the drill bit.

Screw Holes

Most times, screws will drive easier and hold more firmly if right size holes are drilled for them in advance. Usually you need a "lead" hole and a "body" hole. The lead hole is the deeper one and allows the

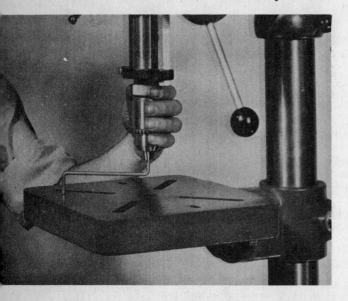

Bent rod, gripped in drill chuck, is used to test the table for squareness to the spindle center.

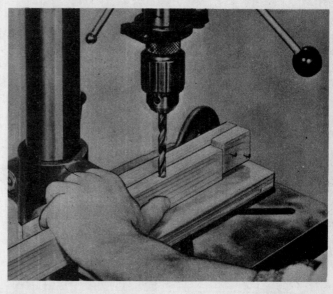

Jig clamped to table assures right hole location when drilling duplicate holes in multiple pieces.

Countersinks that slide over drill do two jobs— form the body hole and the seat for screw head.

Drill-press table tilts. With setups like this it becomes very easy to drill accurate angular holes.

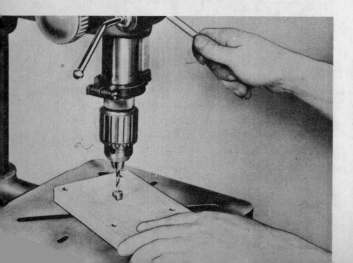

point of the screw to penetrate easily—the body hole provides clearance for the shank of the screw which does not have threads. Common procedure when screwing two pieces together is to drill the body hole through the top pieces and the lead hole into the bottom one. It's easiest to drill the lead hole first; this provides a pilot hole in the top piece which is then enlarged to the body-hole size.

Countersinking for flat-head screws is done on the body hole to establish a seat for the head of the screw. Where you want to hide the screw with a wood plug, the body hole is counterbored. This portion of the hole is then plugged with a short dowel. Sometimes these "plugs" are allowed to project slightly above the surface of the wood as decorative details. You see this quite often on furniture of early American design.

DRILLING EXTRA DEEP HOLE

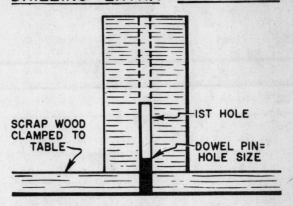

Drill first hole, then invert work. Dowel pin aligns holes. Permits drilling twice drill length.

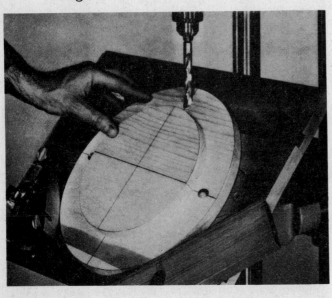

On Shopsmith, miter gauge, clamped scrap block form V-guide setup for angular drilling of discs.

Auxiliary fence mounted on drill-press table provides the guide for straight routing cuts.

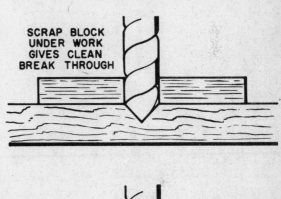

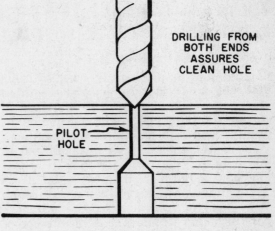

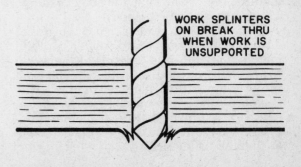

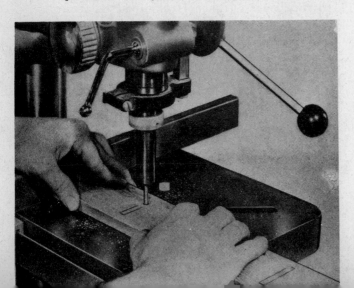

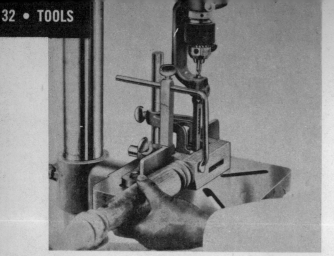

For pro mortising-tenon work, special bit that removes most of wood turns inside square chisel.

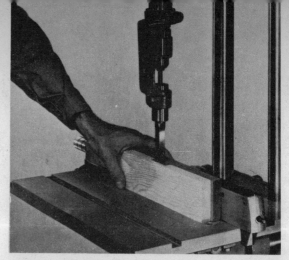

When cutting an open side mortise, use a scrap block between fence and work, as pictured here.

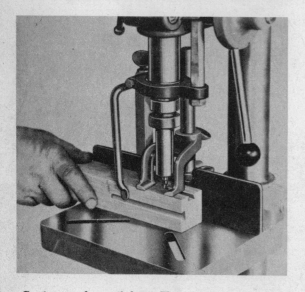

Cutting a dovetail key. The cutter is in special chuck and works in the manner of a routing bit.

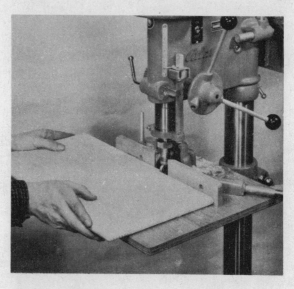

Special table and fence plus special chucks for attaching cutters make drill press a fine shaper.

Extra-Deep Holes

Maximum quill extension on most drills is 4 inches which is the average length on the cutting end of most drill bits. To drill deeper than this you need extension drills. With a long drill, you form the maximum four inches, then bottom the drill end in the hole and drill another four inches. If the work is not more than twice the maximum quill extension, you can drill through it by working from both sides. It's important here that you develop some method of aligning the two holes so they meet exactly. There are several methods.

One way is to glue a short length of dowel in a scrap board. After drilling maximum depth into one side of the work, the dowel is lined up with the spindle center and the drilled hole set over it. This positions the work concentrically so the hole can be finished from the other side. The dowel guide should equal the diameter of the hole being drilled.

Routing

Smoothest routing is done at high speeds. Special bits are used and gripped in special router chucks which can take the side thrust developed by the tool. Work feed is always *against* the direction of rotation of the cutting tool.

A router bit can be used to form round-end mortises. A fence is clamped to the table to gauge position of the cut and as a guide for the straight feed required. Stop blocks can be clamped to the fence to limit length of cut. Make deep cuts in successive passes, depressing the quill after each pass until the full depth of cut has been attained. Mortises made this way require a round-end tenon.

Unless you're doing free-hand routing (script letters or something similar) router operations usually require a fence or jig of some kind. It's wise to remember that if the fence is positioned behind the tool, the feed of the work is from left to right.

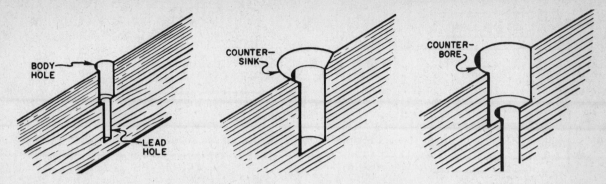

Screws will usually drive more easily and hold more firmly if right size holes are drilled in advance.

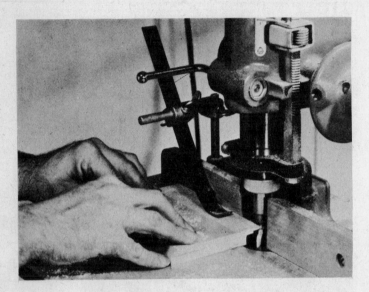

Spring holddown helps keep work snug as it's passed over cutters, hands out of danger area.

This is a drill press, too, with head inverted to put it below table just like a regular shaper.

If the fence is positioned in front of the cutting tool, then the work feed is from right to left. This assures that you'll be feeding against the direction of the tool's rotation.

Methods of routing grooves in round or curved work are shown in accompanying sketches. Guide blocks are positioned on the drill press table to make the cut where needed, and clamped firmly in place.

Work having a center hole can be pivot routed as follows: Glue a short length of dowel in a scrap board and clamp this to the drill-press table. Set the hole in the work over the dowel and then rotate the work as the router bit is cutting. This is good only for circular grooves or arcs.

Mortising

Special accessories allow you to cut "square" holes. A mortising attachment is secured to the quill to hold hollow sleeve chisels and special mortising bits. Both the

bit and the chisel are depressed together. The bit forms a hole which removes the bulk of the wood, the chisel cuts away the corners and the result is a square cavity.

Feed pressures required will vary with the hardness of the wood and the size of the chisel. For example, pine will cut easily—maple is tougher, but excessive feed pressure should never be necessary. If you must really use your muscle to make the cut, you can be reasonably sure that the cutting edges of the mortising chisel and bit require attention.

The general mortising rule is to make end cuts first and clean out stock between with overlapping cuts which should never be less than three fourths of the full width of the chisel. This can't always work out on the very last cut but keep close to it if you can. Narrow shoulders should be avoided because they inevitably result in a sloping chisel cut. If the sides of the mortise slope, there is a good possibility that

MORTISING

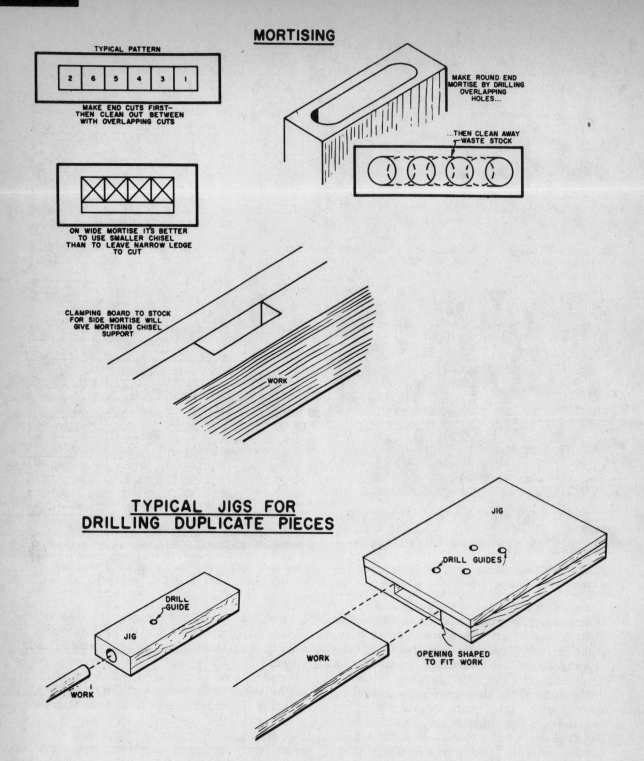

TYPICAL PATTERN

| 2 | 6 | 5 | 4 | 3 | 1 |

MAKE END CUTS FIRST—
THEN CLEAN OUT BETWEEN
WITH OVERLAPPING CUTS

MAKE ROUND END
MORTISE BY DRILLING
OVERLAPPING
HOLES...

...THEN CLEAN AWAY
WASTE STOCK

ON WIDE MORTISE IT'S BETTER
TO USE SMALLER CHISEL
THAN TO LEAVE NARROW LEDGE
TO CUT

CLAMPING BOARD TO STOCK
FOR SIDE MORTISE WILL
GIVE MORTISING CHISEL
SUPPORT

WORK

TYPICAL JIGS FOR DRILLING DUPLICATE PIECES

JIG

DRILL GUIDES

DRILL GUIDE

JIG

WORK

WORK

OPENING SHAPED
TO FIT WORK

ROUTING IRREGULAR SHAPES

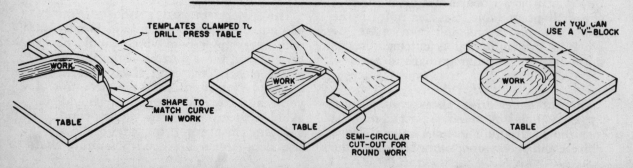

TEMPLATES CLAMPED TO
DRILL PRESS TABLE

WORK

TABLE

SHAPE TO
MATCH CURVE
IN WORK

WORK

TABLE

SEMI-CIRCULAR
CUT-OUT FOR
ROUND WORK

OR YOU CAN
USE A "V"-BLOCK

WORK

TABLE

Rotary planer used on drill press to form tenon. It does good, fast job reducing stock thickness.

Compound slide that bolts to table is accessory that will facilitate most metal-working chores.

Good Drill-Press Speeds

Material	Operation		Speed
Wood	Drilling	Up to ¼"	3800
Wood	Drilling	¼"-½"	3100
Wood	Drilling	½"-¾"	2300
Wood	Drilling	¾"-1"	2000
Wood	Drilling	Over 1"	Slowest
Wood	Using expansion or similar bit		Slowest
Wood	Routing		Highest
Wood	Cutting plugs		3000
Wood	Carving		4-5000
Wood	Using fly-cutter		Slowest
Wood	Using dowel cutter		1800
Hardwood	Mortising		2200
Softwood	Mortising		3300
Metal	Wire brushing—fine		3300
Metal	Wire brushing—coarse		1200
Wood	Wire brushing—coarse		2200
Soft Metal	Buffing (cloth wheel)		3800
Hard Metal	Buffing (cloth wheel)		4700
Plastics	Buffing (cloth wheel)		2300
Metal	Using fly cutter		Slowest
Metal	Grinding		3000
Glass	Drilling w/metal tube		Slowest

the work will split when the tenon is forced into place.

Shaping

Most home workshops lack a regular shaper simply because the drill press does such an efficient job as one. One of the basic differences between a regular shaper and the drill press is that the former has the spindle under the table, while the drill press spindle is above the table. Most time this doesn't mean much but headstock interference on the drill press can limit operations that would otherwise be easy to handle.

Do drill-press shaping at high speeds and always make the cut *with* the grain of the wood. For more details on shaping see the chapter pertaining to the shaper.

Other Jobs

In addition to the basic jobs described this versatile drill press can be used as a drum sander, buffer, surface planer and even as a grinder. It's only a question of mounting the correct accessory and operating at the best speed.

The speeds of the chart atop this page are good for the operations indicated. We suggest you study them carefully. ●

Screw Hole Chart

Screw Size	Body Hole	Lead Hole
0	53	—
1	49	—
2	44	56*
3	40	52*
4	33	51*
5	⅛	49*
6	28	47
7	24	46
8	19	42
9	15	41
10	10	38
11	5	37
12	7/32	36
14	D	31
16	I	28
18	19/64	23

* Required in Hardwood Only

the lathe

It is regarded by many owners as the most enjoyable tool of the shop

THE MODERN LATHE is a very flexible machine that lets you handle work in many sizes. You can turn things smaller than a cigarette lighter in wood, or in nonferrous metals by using carbide-tipped tools; and you can make good size salad bowls or turn heavy, long columns. Long pieces can be handled beyond the capacity of the machine merely by turning them in sections and joining them together with dowels.

To get the most from a lathe, you do have to know how to use the lathe chisels, but this is no particular trick. Anyone who wants to do a little practicing will quickly acquire the skill needed to manipulate the tools that do the forming.

You can mount some wood on the lathe

and come up with a complete project, such as a lamp base or fruit bowl, or you can use the lathe as an accessory tool to form parts for projects, table or chair legs for example. Most people who own lathes are not hesitant to claim it as one of the most enjoyable tools in the shop. There is a lot of fascination in watching the raw wood take shape as you apply the cutting tools. It's somewhat akin to shaping or molding, except that with the lathe you control the shape and it is applied to the circumference of a part.

There are two ways to mount work on a lathe. One way is between centers—this is called spindle turning. The other method involves a flat plate which screws or otherwise attaches directly to the head-

Above, Rockwell lathe gives precise wood turning.

In spindle turning, left, work is mounted between centers. Work which can't be placed between centers is mounted on faceplate, as above. Position tool for maximum support at cutting edge. Tool rests are designed so they can readily be swung around to front of work.

stock spindle and to which work is secured —this is called faceplate turning. The maximum diameter of face-plate work is determined by twice the distance from lathe bed to spindle center. Spindles are limited by the maximum distance available between headstock and tailstock.

Some lathes permit you to mount a face plate outboard of the headstock—then the diameter of faceplate work is limited only by the distance from spindle to floor—if you can provide a safe speed relative to the size of the work.

Generally speaking, the larger the work, the slower the speed. Too many rpm's on large work is dangerous. The speed chart gives you some idea of good and safe lathe speeds. Keep as close to them as possible.

Lathe Chisels

Lathe chisels are usually sold in sets which consist of one of each of the following: Skew, Roundnose, Large Gouge, Small Gouge, and Parting Tool.

Larger, more expensive sets will include a squarenose, different size skews and roundnose. An ordinary butt chisel, if kept sharp, can be used in place of a squarenose lathe chisel.

When feeding the lathe chisel into the work, always move it slowly and steadily; never jab it in suddenly. Your hands should be firm on the chisel but not so tight as to be fatiguing. Usually, the left hand is on the blade with the thumb resting on top. The back of the left hand abuts the finger ledge on the lathe-tool rest. The left hand can control depth of cut and also gauges the cut when the chisel is moved parallel to the work. The right hand grips the handle of the tool and does the moving which determines the cut. Figure the point at which the chisel rests on the tool rest as a kind of pivot around which the right hand moves the tool point.

THE GOUGE is usually used for initial roughing operations, those cuts which reduce the cylinder to near project size. In addition it is used for heavy stock removal, forming coves, and for smoothing.

THE SKEW has considerable use for detail forms as well as general smoothing operations. With it you can form tapers, trim ends and square shoulders, make V-cuts, and form beads.

THE ROUNDNOSE is a good forming tool for long curves and coves and is the tool to use for forming cavities in face-plate-mounted stock. In the latter operation it is the safest tool to use so long as the tool rest is positioned to provide support near the cutting edge.

THE PARTING TOOL is most often used for sizing cuts, but after some experimenting you'll find it useful for detail forms such as small V's, shoulders and slight tapers. It's also good for cleaning the

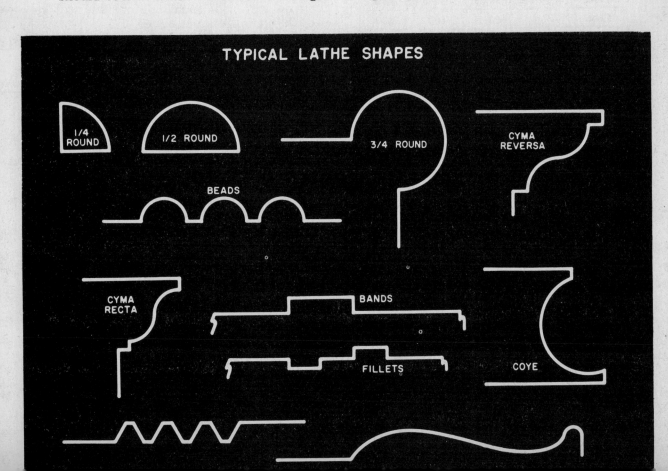

TYPICAL LATHE SHAPES

1/4 ROUND

1/2 ROUND

3/4 ROUND

CYMA REVERSA

BEADS

CYMA RECTA

BANDS

FILLETS

COVE

ends of your stock and for cutting off, too.

THE SQUARENOSE is a very easy tool to use and, if kept sharp and fed slowly into the work removes material fast while leaving a reasonably smooth surface. The wider the chisel the faster it works. It's also used for squaring shoulders and forming tapers, making V-cuts, forming recesses and bands and for smoothing convex forms.

Cutting Actions

Lathe chisels will scrape, cut or shear, depending on how they are held against the work. The easiest action and the one all beginners should start with, is the scraping action. Even experienced wood turners advance no further than this action by choice, because results are good and there is less likelihood of bad cuts. The tool is held on a horizontal plane and moved di-

rectly forward to make contact with the work. The position is maintained as you move the chisel along the stock to make the cut. The depth of cut should never be excessive; it's better to go over the area several times than to try making the form in one pass.

The *cutting* action is similar to the cut made with a hand plane. The handle of the tool is slow to bring the cutting edge up. This action is more difficult to master than scraping—keep cuts light for it's easy for the chisel to dig in and be jerked from your hand by the work. Trying to cut too deep can also remove large chunks from the project and so ruin the stock.

The skew and the gouge can be used in a *shearing* action. This is a cutting action with the edge of the tool being moved parallel to the work, cutting throughout the stroke. A shearing action with the skew, done properly, will leave a surface smoother than you can get with sandpaper, but it isn't something you can master right off. It takes practice.

Best bet is to use all tools in the simple scraping action and proceed further, if you wish, when you've become more proficient. Each of the different types of lathe chisels does some jobs best, but each of them is very versatile and you'll find, after you have accomplished a few projects, that there is considerable overlap between them. Most operators eventually develop their own uses for each tool and this will probably happen to you, too.

Lathe Speed Guide

Material and Size		Roughing Cut	Shaping Cut	Finishing Cut
Wood	Up to 2"	900	2500	4200
Wood	2-4"	800	2300	3300
Wood	4-6"	650	1800	2300
Wood	6-8"	600	1200	1800
Wood	8-10"	Slowest	900	1000
Wood	10"+	Slowest	600	600
Plastics	Up to 3"	2200	3000	3700
Plastics	3"+	1000	1200	1700
Nonferrous Metal Up to 3"		600	1300	3000

Carbide-Tipped Tools

These are special lathe chisels used for free-hand turning of nonferrous metals. They are similar in shape to ordinary

After the stock has been reduced to basic dimension, parting tool is used to make dimensional cuts. The calipers gauge the correct diameter.

The gouge is often used to form coves. Note the proper hand positions, that fingers of left abut the ledge on the tool rest in order to gauge cut.

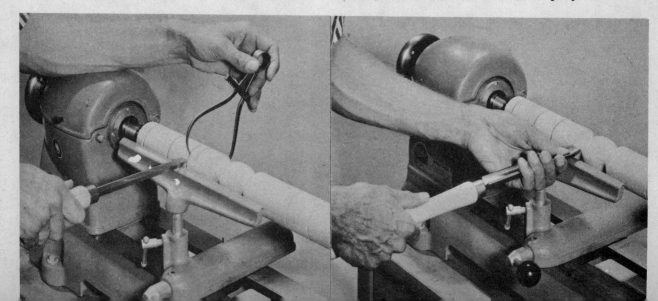

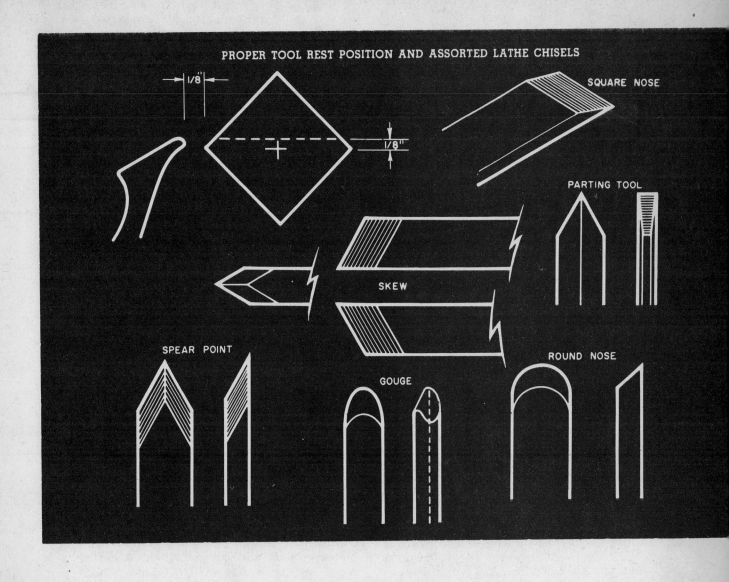

PROPER TOOL REST POSITION AND ASSORTED LATHE CHISELS

SQUARE NOSE

PARTING TOOL

SKEW

SPEAR POINT

GOUGE

ROUND NOSE

Parting tool is also a cut-off tool. When section's thin, cup a hand around free end to catch it. The work here is mounted on a screw center.

Skew used in shearing action. It does require skill to do a good job in this application, but results are smoother than sandpaper would yield.

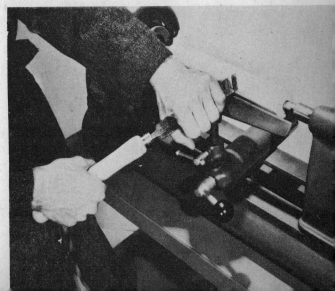

Drilling concentric holes. Chuck and drill are on tailstock; work is spindle-fed forward. Conventional lathe's tailstock moves to form hole.

Correct tool rest position for starting cavity in stock mounted on screw center or faceplate. The round-nose tool is always used for this job.

MAKE A CENTER FINDER

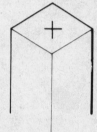

Easily constructed, it will be useful for finding the center of either round or square stock, as indicated.

lathe chisels but are tipped with tungsten carbide, an extremely hard material which holds a cutting edge for a long time. But the edges are also pretty brittle so you should use them with care and store them so as to prevent damage. They also do a good job on wood and since the cutting edges are smaller than conventional tools, you'll find they do a good job on fine details.

Use slow speeds for metal turning. If you find that the work begins to chatter as you cut, it's a sure sign that the work is turning too fast or that you are cutting too deep, or maybe both.

Spindle Turning

Stock to be mounted between centers should be squared at both ends and marked so the spur center (at the headstock end) and the dead center (at the tailstock end) can be placed on a common line that runs through the center of the work. On square stock you can find the centers by drawing intersecting diagonals at each end. If the work is round, you'll need a center finder. You can make one easily (see sketch, this page) which can be used on square stock as well as round. After the centers are found, make saw cuts at one end for the spur cen-

ter. These are just shallow cuts on the intersecting diagonals you originally drew to find the center. Tap the spur center into place gently with a mallet to seat it firmly. All the dead center needs is a shallow hole you can form with an awl. If the wood is very hard, you may drill the hole. When you mount the stock don't tighten the dead center too much. Since this doesn't turn with the stock, it develops friction and can burn. Best bet is to tighten it, then back off just a bit. A drop of oil will help it turn freely.

Once the stock has been turned down to the basic dimension, mark it off to locate design details. Use the parting tool to cut to the depth required at each point and applicable tools to form the shapes between dimensional cuts.

If you are turning just one piece, it's okay to lay a ruler on the stock and mark off from that, but if you are making a set of parts (chair legs) it pays to make a profile template first. This is a cardboard cutout which is the reverse of the actual part. The template is then used to mark dimension lines and also to check the shapes as you do the turning. Using a template makes it more likely that each piece you turn will closely resemble its neighbor.

Make fancy "inlays" by turning glued up blocks of contrasting woods such as maple and mahogany.

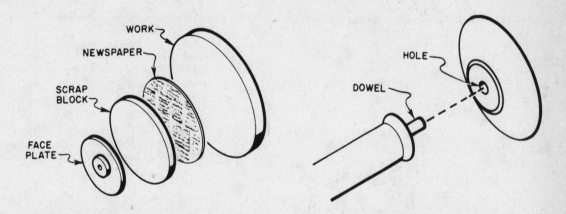

Here's how to avoid mounting holes in work. After forming work, split apart on the newspaper joint.

Here's a very good and simple way to make extra long spindle turning or to attach post to base.

Faceplate Turning

Flat projects such as trays and bowls or bases for spindle turnings must be mounted on a faceplate. Screws are used to do this after the stock has been centered on the faceplate. If the stock is square use diagonals to find the center, then scribe a circle which is just a bit larger than the diameter of the faceplate. By centering the faceplate in the larger circle on the stock, you'll be pretty sure that it is centered.

Be careful with the screws you use to attach the work. Note how long they are so you'll avoid cutting into them when you are turning. To save time and effort, it's a good idea to precut the stock to shape on a band saw or jig saw before you mount it on the faceplate.

The lathe chisels are handled as they would be for spindle turning except that the scraping action is used almost exclusively. You can use marking templates and profile templates here, too. It's definitely recommended when you are turning several pieces which should match exactly.

The Screw Center

Work which is too small to mount on a faceplate and not long enough to mount between centers, can be turned by mounting it on a screw center. This is nothing but a device which is attached to the lathe spindle. It has a projecting screw which holds the work.

On faceplate and screw-center work it's often necessary to follow a special technique if you want a project that does not reveal the screw-mounting holes. The work is mounted on a scrap block that can take the screw holes. Best way is to glue the work blank to the scrap block but with a sheet of newspaper between. After the project has been turned, it is easy to remove the scrap-wood mounting block by splitting them apart on the newspaper joint.

Sandpaper Is a Tool

Even if you don't end up with smooth cuts on your lathe work, you don't have to worry, for sandpaper will do the job for you, fast. In fact, so fast that you have to be extremely careful on small details to be sure they don't get sanded away. Best bet for a super smooth finish is to start with rough paper and slow speed and end up with fine paper and high speed. For a glass-smooth finish, dampen work before final sanding and then end up with steel wool. •

the band saw

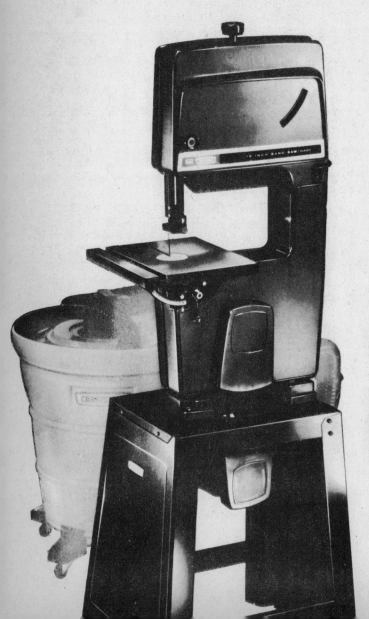

12-inch band saw from Sears cuts wood up to six inches thick, contains a sawdust ejector system.

10-inch band saw from Sprunger features a double trunnion table for rigidity. It tilts 45 degrees.

14-inch band saw from Wards cuts to 6½ inches deep, to center of 28-inch circle. 14 x 14-in. table.

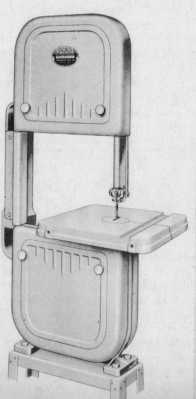

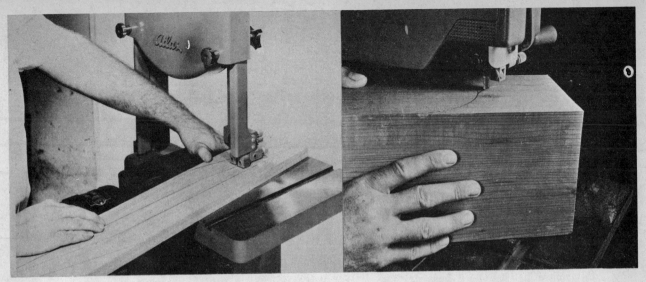

In normal cutting, right hand is the guide, left turns and feeds the work. Note that blade guard is almost on work. No part of blade is exposed.

It is this kind of cutting that makes the band saw particularly impressive and useful. Slicing through a six by six is routine task for band saws.

THE BAND SAW has the greatest depth-of-cut capacity of any woodworking machine, and it's also the fastest cutting. That's how it will amaze and impress you—the speed and ease with which it can cut through a six by six in curved, circular or straight lines. Among the things you can do on it that would be very difficult or impossible to do on other power tools are these:

RE-SAW . . . Cutting available stock into thinner boards.

COMPOUND CUTTING . . . Cutting on more than one surface to create special shapes. The cabriole leg is a prime example.

STOCK REDUCTION . . . Reducing stock thickness in limited areas; especially useful when preparing stock for lathe turning.

PAD SAWING . . . The business of temporarily joining a number of pieces of wood so all of them can be cut simultaneously.

Since you can use a fairly narrow blade on the band saw (⅛-inch), it's possible to make some cuts that rival the intricate turns of the jig saw, but it can't do the extremely fine work that is the jig saw's exclusive. But the jig saw doesn't compare when it comes to real heavy cutting. With a ½- or ¾-inch blade mounted on the band saw you can easily cut heavy timbers. If you had glued up a 6-inch thick blank for turning a bowl on the lathe, you could precut it to circular shape with no strain or effort.

The band saw has an endless, flexible blade which turns over two (sometimes three) wheels. One of the wheels is powered, the other is idle. Various methods of adjusting the wheels (relative to the particular machine design) assure that the blade will "track" on the wheels. Some band saws are designed so the blade tracks automatically. On these you worry only about blade tension. Most machines have built in scales which advise the proper amount of tension for each blade size. This is important for it affects blade life. Most of us tend to provide too much tension.

Blade guides, one set above the table and another below, are provided to keep the blade cutting straight. These should never be adjusted to cause excessive friction as the blade rubs them. Actually, when setting them, it's good practice to keep them away from the blade the thickness of a sheet of bond paper.

A tell-tale sign of poor blade-guide adjustment is called "lead." This is the tendency of the blade to pull to one side when you are cutting. Normally, if you feed the stock easily, the blade cuts straight and the kerf is parallel to the side of the table. If you have trouble, check the blade guides for adjustment. If you find the guides okay, then look for incorrectly set teeth on the blade. Maybe you've cut through a nail; this can dull one "side" of the blade and cause "lead." When excessive and not caused by the guides, the fault can be corrected only by discarding the blade or having it sharpened and reset. If lead is slight, try this. Back up the good side of the blade (the side from which the blade tends

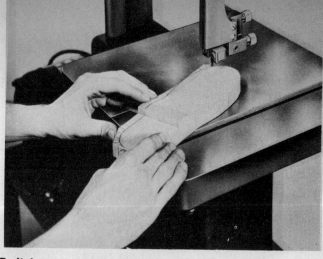

Try to visualize cut before starting. Here work has hit throat, halting the cut. Started at other end it would have required but a single pass.

Radial cuts make it possible to turn corners with wider blades. (See diagrams below.) Often, they save trouble of blade-changing for just few cuts.

Tilting table makes bevel cutting possible. This deep-bowl lathe project is being precut to minimize stock removal to be done with lathe chisels.

An improvised fence setup for resawing is pictured here. The resaw fence should be as high as possible. Widest, heaviest blade should be used.

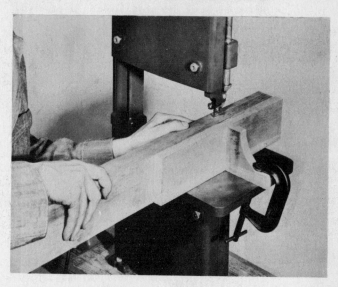

RADIAL

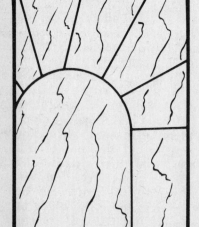

Radial or tangent cuts, as indicated left and right here, help a blade to turn a corner it couldn't normally, simplify job.

TANGENT

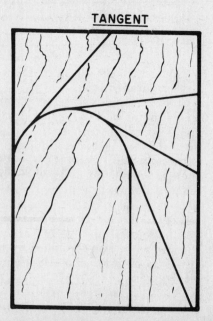

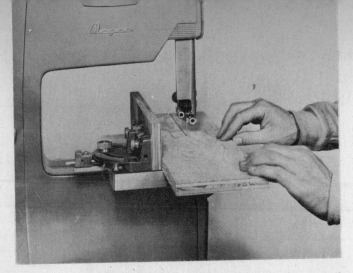

Straight cuts can be accomplished by the use of a fence. When engaged in this operation be very careful to keep work from moving off the fence.

Compound-cutting trick. Nail supports work after first side has been cut. Keep work down firmly on table doing this and don't force the cut.

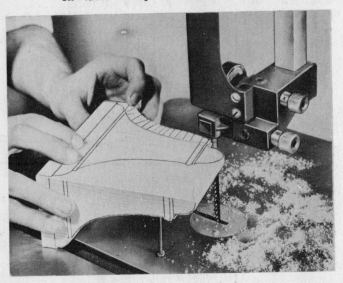

to travel) with some scrap wood and apply a honing stone very lightly to the lead side. Actually what you're trying to do is equalize the fault on each side of the blade, but it works and can save a blade.

Speeds

Good speed for general cutting ranges from 2,000 rpm to 2,500 rpm. Faster speeds with a fine blade produce a smoother cut. Slower speeds with a heavy blade are good for heavy-duty work. Best bet, regardless of the job and the speed, is to feed the work no more than the cutting teeth can handle. Beyond this, you're forcing the cut, trying to get the blade to cut more than it was designed to do.

Blades

"Narrow" blades are generally used on home workshop band saws. These run from ⅛ inch to ½ inch wide. Thin blades with a minimum set give the smoothest cuts but are most easily broken. You can't manipulate them so easily because the kerf they cut is so fine. Heavier blades with more set, cut faster and cooler, but, of course, don't cut as smoothly. One good blade style is the "Roll-Chip" blade which does an excellent job on wood cutting but also can be used on plastics and nonferrous metals.

To prolong blade life, don't try to turn corners too tight for the blade width. The turn radii in the chart is good for average blades, but blade thickness and the amount of set in the teeth has some bearing on the facts. With two blades of equal width, the one having the most set in the teeth will be more easy to maneu-

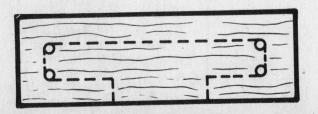

Good planning can result in saving stock. Cut above and glue joint result in figure at right.

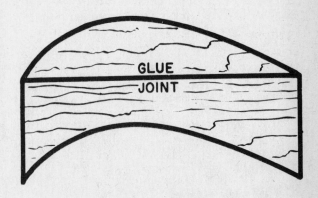

GLUE JOINT

Relief holes, as indicated at the left, help on internal cutouts, are also good for sharp corners.

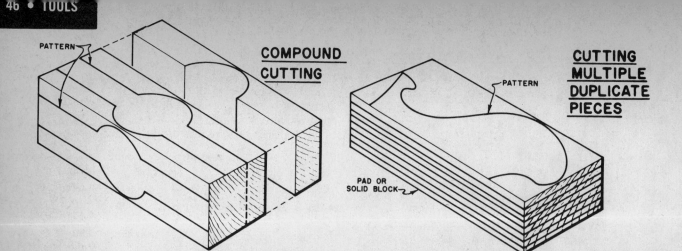

COMPOUND CUTTING

CUTTING MULTIPLE DUPLICATE PIECES

Mark pattern on two adjacent faces of stock. Cut out pattern on one face. Replace cutoffs by tack-nailing, taping; then cut out on second face.

Tack-nail or tape pieces together. Make cut and then separate. Alternative is to draw pattern on solid block, make cutout, resaw for separates.

ver around tight turns. This is because the kerf is wider.

Simple Cutting

The band saw is a fairly safe tool to use, so long as you keep from feeding with your hand directly on the cut line. Since you'll be doing a lot of curve cutting and the work must be moved around the blade, there is no set position for the operator. Most common practice is to use the left hand as a guide for keeping the blade cutting on the line and the right hand for turning and feeding. If you've never used a band saw before, a brief practice period during which you cut circles, curves and straight lines will give the feel of how the band saw cuts and works.

It's important to try to visualize the travel of the cut before you start. This, mostly to minimize backtracking, the business of having to move out of the cut so you can approach from another angle. This is best done on short cuts, so when

laying out the design, plan how you will make the cuts. Sometimes, since there is throat limitation on the band saw, a curve will swing the work so that you can't complete the cut. Often, if the cut had been started from the other end of the work, it could have been completed in one pass without backtracking.

Heavy Cutting

Although the band saw does a great job of heavy-duty cutting, it's unwise to force the work beyond the cutting capacity of the blade. Feed slowly; let the blade cut. Forcing will usually result in a "bowed" cut; the blade will not remain perpendicular in the cut but will bend.

For resawing, use the widest blade available. Use a fence, or clamp a straight piece of wood to the table to serve the same purpose. The higher the fence the more support it will provide for the work. Be especially careful here to keep the blade on the line. Anytime you use a fence as a

A special all-purpose blade can be used on your band saw to cut plastics, wood, and nonferrous metals, as is demonstrated in this photograph.

Special blades and speed reduction unit let you cut steel, other ferrous metals. Most common home workshop band-saw blades are ⅛ to ½ inch wide.

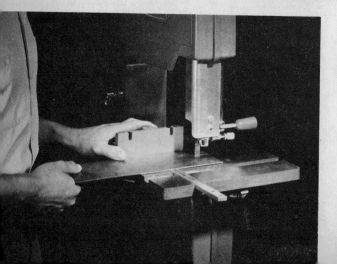

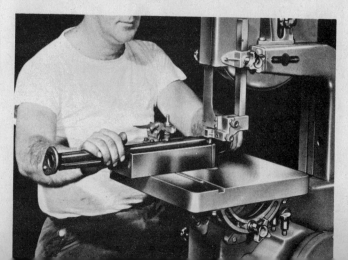

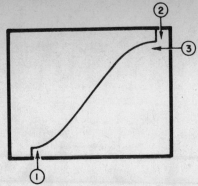

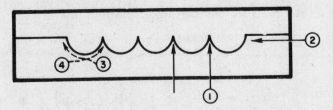

Make short cuts first, as indicated here. By doing so, you ease job and minimize backtracking.

TURNING RADIUS OF VARIOUS BLADES

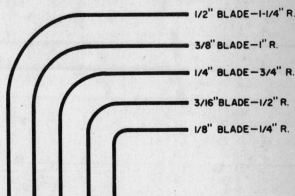

1/2" BLADE—1-1/4" R.

3/8" BLADE—1" R.

1/4" BLADE—3/4" R.

3/16" BLADE—1/2" R.

1/8" BLADE—1/4" R.

guide on band-saw work, you'll find that the work tends to creep away from the fence. Feed even more slowly than you normally would; be sure the blade is sharp and in good condition.

To thin out stock—that is, reduce a limited area, mark out the section to be cut on one edge of the stock. Make the two end cuts first. Then, starting anywhere between them, make an oblique approach to the straight line and carry the cut forward to meet one of the first in-cuts. Then turn the work end for end and complete the operation.

Compound Cutting

Always work with a pattern, since you have to mark two adjacent sides the same way. After the work is cut out on the one side, the scrap pieces are tack-nailed or taped back in place again. Then the stock is turned and the adjacent side cut. Then all the waste pieces are removed to reveal the shape planned for. Compound cutting

is a good way to prepare the stock for lathe turning, in addition to the preparation of fancy shapes for furniture projects.

Multiple Cutting

Since the band saw can cut through heavy stock, you can make many exact duplicates from one block. First, draw the shape needed on one face of the block and cut it out. Then turn the block to the next adjacent side and resaw the block into as many pieces as you need. Each one will be identical.

Pad-sawing means temporarily putting together a cutting block that consists of multiple layers of thinner stock. For example—the band saw has a 6-inch cut capacity. You can make a pad of 24 pieces of 1/4-inch plywood. By the one cutting operation you develop 24 duplicate pieces. Be sure to tack parts together in waste areas. If this is impossible you can always use some wood dough to hide the tack-nail holes. •

Special guides for this machine let you offset blade 45° to permit crosscutting of stock that is too long to be crosscut in the normal manner.

Band saw is probably safest machine for cutting dowels. Clamped block assures correct length of each piece. Hold dowel firmly to prevent turning.

the jig saw

It is the ideal tool for fine cutting in various materials

THE JIG SAW uses a straight, short blade which travels straight up and down. This is generally provided for through a kind of crankshaft arrangement much like an automobile piston rod. Like the band saw, it cuts curved and straight lines. In fact, the two machines are very similar with the basic advantage of the band saw being heavy-duty operations while that of the jig saw is flexibility and fine cutting. One other notable advantage of the jig saw has to do with difference in blades. As you've noted, the band-saw blade is endless. It can be broken and re-welded but this is not a home-workshop chore. But the jigsaw blade is held independently at each end. The big advantage here is that you can insert the jigsaw blade through a hole in the work, before you lock the blade in its chucks. Thus you can make internal cutouts with a lead-in cut from any edge of the work. This operation is called "piercing."

The jig saw, because it can handle extremely fine blades, is an ideal tool for intricate, fine cutting in many materials. Scrollwork, fretwork, intarsia, marquetry, intricately pierced designs in soft metals, are routine jobs on the jig saw. Because of its ability in these areas, the machine is often thought of as a strictly fun tool, a hobbyist's machine. While this is true, it shouldn't be limited to those areas. Since depth of cut on most machines is at least 2 inches and since you can mount fairly heavy blades, it's possible to cut pretty heavy stock. So the jig saw can be used to shape furniture legs and do other similar operations.

Without doubt, the jig saw is the safest power tool there is. It's the logical first tool for a youngster and even friend wife can have an enjoyable time at practical projects on the jig saw.

Blades

Jigsaw blades are identified by physical dimensions. Most of them are 5 inches long and have blank ends. The chart does not list all the different types and sizes of blades available, but you could spend a lifetime in the shop and never have the need to go beyond these. Try to work as close as possible to the speeds recommended for each blade and each operation. Step-pulleys supply different speeds, and variable speed changers, available as accessories on some machines, do an even better job.

The general rule is the heavier the material, the heavier the blade and the slower the speed. As the cut gets finer, the finer the blade should be and the faster the speed. Heavy blade, slow speed, rougher cut. Fine blade, fast speed—smooth cut.

There are two general blade classifications: the "jeweler's" blades which are locked in chucks at each end, and "saber saws" which are locked in the lower chuck only. The latter are heavy, usually coarse blades and intended for heavy cutting when curves are not too severe. They're also used for cutting large panels (with machine arm removed) when the arm on the machine is removed to eliminate interference. When this is done, it also removes the upper chuck, so the blade can be gripped at one end only.

Blade position between chucks should be either perpendicular to the table or with the top end leaning just a little bit forward. This can be checked by eye or with a square.

The jig saw has a built-in tensioning device so you can hold the blade tight and straight. Tension is adjustable so you can apply more tension to fine blades, where it is needed, and less to heavier blades, which are more rigid and do not require as much.

Friend wife is taught the rudiments of jigsaw work on the Delta machine. A word of warning: the jig saw is fun and it may prove difficult for you to reclaim machine from the better half.

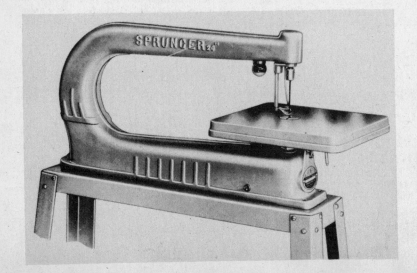

Left, 20-inch jig saw from Sprunger is designed to handle 2-inch thick wood.

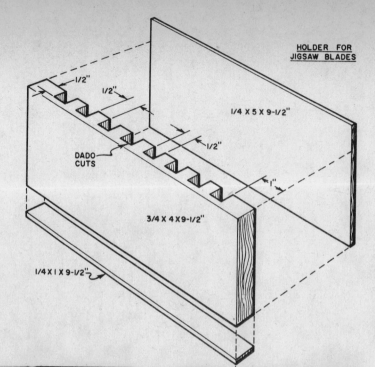

HOLDER FOR JIGSAW BLADES

1/2"

1/2"

1/4 X 5 X 9-1/2"

1/2"

DADO CUTS

1"

3/4 X 4 X 9-1/2"

1/4 X 1 X 9-1/2"

Chuck beneath table. The back-up guide is most useful for saber sawing. Slot in chuck tube permits "indexing" chuck to turn the blade 90°, eliminate arm interference on long work.

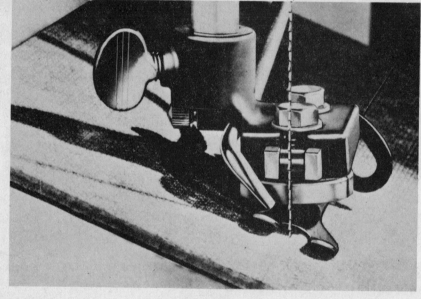

Blade guide and spring hold-down on the Delta. Spring hold-down can be tilted when doing bevel cutting. The modern jig saw is not a toy, does heavy duty in pro shops.

This is the correct setup for good cutting. The blade guide is in place, blade is under proper tension, spring hold-down just on work's surface.

A good hand position for most cutting is demonstrated in this photograph. Keeping blade tangent to the cut line assures you of smooth curves.

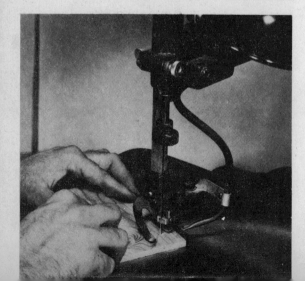

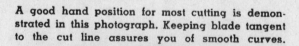

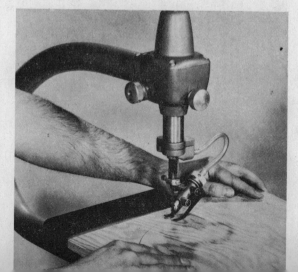

SALVAGING JIGSAW CUTOFFS

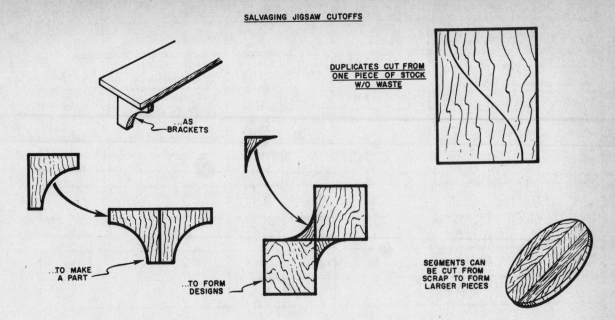

...AS BRACKETS

DUPLICATES CUT FROM ONE PIECE OF STOCK W/O WASTE

...TO MAKE A PART

...TO FORM DESIGNS

SEGMENTS CAN BE CUT FROM SCRAP TO FORM LARGER PIECES

But excessive tension should never be applied to any blade. This will only help it break more quickly. Be sure to adjust the blade-guide mechanism as directed in the machine's owner's manual.

The spring hold-down, a device which combines with the blade guides, should be adjusted so there is just enough pressure to keep the work down on the table. Excessive hold-down pressure will make it difficult for you to move the stock when cutting and may also mar the surface of the work.

Work Position

Take a position that lets you stand comfortably. Normal hand position is like that for the band saw; the left hand keeps the work on the line, the right hand feeds it forward and moves it to line up the cut. Actually, there is no set rule. It depends on the job. Many times both hands will be feeding the work forward and often you'll shift from right to left hand for feeding.

As always, let the blade do the cutting. Don't try to speed up the job by forcing the cut. It doesn't work that way but does help to break blades. Your big job is to keep guiding the work so the cut is accurate. The blade will do the cutting nicely if you feed slowly and evenly.

Patterns

If you are creating the pattern, you can draw it full size on the stock to be cut; or you can draw it on paper and then cement the paper to the stock. If you want to save the original pattern for future use, transfer it to the wood by means of carbon paper.

The enlarging-by-square method is commonly used to make a pattern from a picture or drawing. The original is "graphed off" in convenient size squares. On a clean sheet of paper another graph is drawn but with squares that are proportionally larger than those on the original. Then, points where the drawing crosses lines are picked up and marked on the larger sheet. Thus points are connected to duplicate the original art in larger form. A french curve, a draftsman's tool is useful when transferring or enlarging illustrations this way.

Simple Cutting

The jig saw is not a fast cutting machine. Any attempt you make to speed up the action (except by increasing speed and/or changing to a coarser blade) can only harm the blade or work. Feed pressure should always be forward, never from the side. If the blade width is always kept tangent to the cutting line (in the case of curves) the cut will be true and the line easy to follow. Almost always, when a jigsaw blade runs off the line, it's the operator's fault.

Piercing

Anytime you have an internal cut-out to make, drill a hole somewhere in the waste area of the work, insert the blade through this hole and then secure it in the chuck. When the cut is complete, loosen the blade from the chuck and remove the work. Many times, when the corners of the internal cutout are round, it's possible to drill blade insertion holes at each corner. The drilled hole takes care of cutting away the

Blade Selection Guide

BLADE DESCRIPTION			OPERATION				SPEED
Thickness	Width	Teeth Per Inch	Stock Thickness	Turn Radius	Kind of Cut	Best Used For	
.028	.250	7	¼" and up	Large	Rough	All Woods Hard Boards	745
.020	.110	15	⅛"-½" in metal ⅛"+other mat.	Med.	Med.	Metal—Wood Fiber—Bone	1175
.010	.040	18	1/16"-⅛"	Small	Very Smooth	Wood—Plastics	1600
.012	.023	20	Up to ⅛"	Tiny	Smooth	Plastics—Fiber Bone	1050
.020	.070	7	Up to ¼"	Med.	Med.	Plastics Hard Rubber	1400
.010	.070	14	⅛"-½"	Med.	Very Smooth	Wood—Plastics Bone—Hard Rubber	1525
.020	.110	20	1/16"-⅛"	Med.	Med.	Nonferrous Metals— Mild Steel	940
.028	.250	20	3/32"-½" ¼" max. in steel	Large	Rough		830

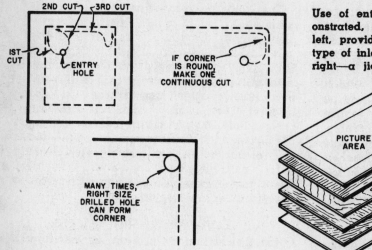

Use of entry holes for internal cutouts is demonstrated, left. Pad sawing of veneers, lower left, provides parts for inlay pictures. Another type of inlay is shown by drawing at the lower right—a jig-sawed design set in routed cavity.

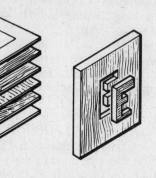

Lead-in cuts are a good idea for jig-saw work, too. Note in this picture the amount of backtracking avoided by use of short preliminary cuts.

Blade-insertion holes permit internal cuts without lead-in. Try pasting illustrations right on the work, jig-sawing around them for a pattern—it's fun.

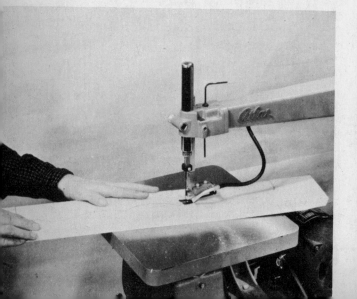

corner. If the corners are square, then you have to approach the corner from the blade-insertion hole, backtrack to the hole and re-approach the corner from another side in order to cut it away square and clean. Circular cutouts and similar shapes are easy. You just approach the line from the blade insertion hole and then continue around in one pass until you have completed the cut.

Beveling

Bevel cutting can be accomplished in such a way that any internal piece will jam tightly when it's pushed through the piece from which it has been cut. This is much like the action of a collapsible picnic cup. The bevel must range between 1 and 10 degrees and is obtained by adjusting the table accordingly.

To test this technique, draw 3 or 4 concentric circles on an 8-inch square of ¾-inch stock. Draw a diameter, and where the lines cross each circle drill a hole just large enough to get the blade through. Tilt the table, insert the blade through the first hole and then cut on the line as you would any other work. *Always keep the work on the same side of the blade.* Otherwise, you'll change bevel direction and the pieces won't mesh as they should. Make the cut on each of the circles drawn and when you're finished you'll find the cut pieces extend beyond the plane of the next piece and that you've created a deep shape from the original flat board. By gluing the pieces in the extended position, you can make a hollowed-out blank for a lathe turning.

The technique is very good for preshaping hulls for model boats.

Inlaying

This type of inlay is like pad sawing. A set of contrasting veneers is assembled into a pad with the pattern or picture on the top layer. Since all the veneers are cut at the same time, any piece from one veneer will fit the corresponding hole in any other piece. Thus if the original pad consists of seven different veneers, you can have seven different wood inlay pictures.

The job will be easier if, as you cut, you place each cutout on a board in the position it occupied in the pad. To assemble the wood picture, you assemble the pieces on gummed paper. Then glue the assembled picture, paper side up, to a backing board. When the glue is dry, remove the paper, and sand the exposed picture.

Metal Cutting

Metal cutting doesn't differ from wood cutting, except that you use a metal-cutting blade. Beeswax, used as a lubricant, will make cutting easy and prolong blade life. Metal cutting is most efficient, especially on thin sheets, if you clamp an auxiliary table to the regular jigsaw table. The hole through the wood table should just accommodate the blade. This gives maximum support right around the blade and prevents it from burring the metal.

Another technique for smooth sheet-metal cutting is to either sandwich the sheet between scrap wood or cement the sheet to a scrap block. •

A setup such as this one with the multipurpose Shopsmith is good for jig-saw work. With it, you can smooth curved lines right after cutting them.

There are special files available that can be gripped in the lower jig-saw chuck to put super-smooth edges on metal work, as shown here.

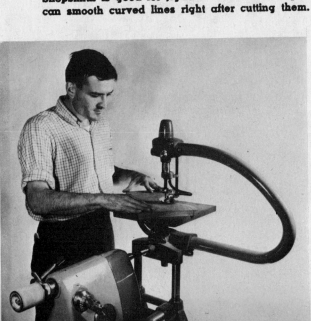

the belt and disc sander

With them, and today's fine abrasives, sanding's a simple task

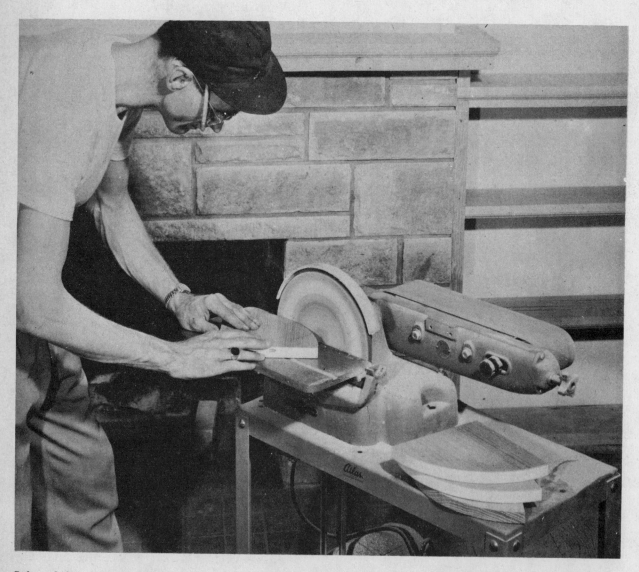

Belt and disc of this combination run off the same motor. It's handy on the job as well as in the shop.

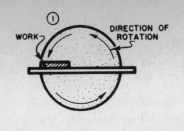

SANDING TO EXACT WIDTH

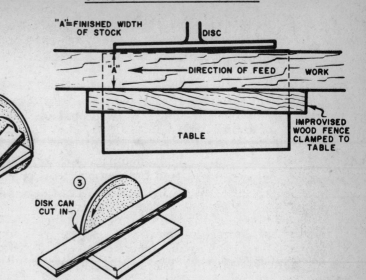

With care, you can sand perfect circles freehand. To do so you should keep the work moving and constantly tangent to the disc surface, as shown.

Combination 9-inch disc and 6 x 48-inch belt sander from Wards. Belt works either level or upright. Table tilts to 45 degrees. Belt tension adjusts.

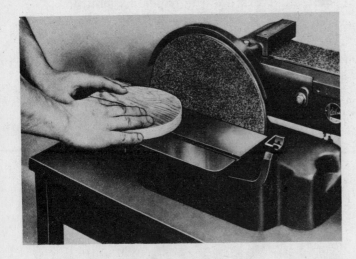

YOU can buy a disc sander or a belt sander as individual machines or you can buy one unit which is both tools. Other machines in the shop can be used as disc sanders. You can mount a sanding disc on a lathe, or a drill press, even on a table saw, but it's difficult to improvise a belt sander.

A disc sander is a flat plate to which adheres a flat circular sheet of sandpaper. It is not a good tool for surface sanding since the action is constantly cross-grain. The belt sander employs an endless abrasive belt which travels over two drums. With it you can sand parallel to wood grain and come up with super-smooth surfaces.

Both of these tools can be used for fine dimensional sanding and for finishing. The disc sander is very good on end grain.

Abrasives

Time was when sanding was pretty tough to do. It wasn't just lack of machines, but inferior abrasives. It's much different today. There are many good, long-lasting sandpapers available today and the machines to use them on.

Consider three things when choosing an abrasive for a job.

1. *OPEN OR CLOSED COAT?* Closed-coat sandpaper has the abrasive particles very close together. This produces the smoothest surface because you have many more abrasive "teeth" doing the cutting. Just as a saw blade with many teeth will cut smoother than one with a few teeth.

Open-coat sandpaper has the abrasive particles spaced further apart. Not as many cutting particles and not so smooth a surface, but one that will not clog as easily as the close-grain paper. This in an advantage when doing rough sanding or when removing an old finish.

2. *WHAT ABRASIVE?* Flint paper is

very common and very cheap. Rely on it for jobs you know will clog the paper quickly. Use it for paint removal and the like.

Garnet is the abrasive most wood-workers depend on. It costs more but lasts longer and in the long run is probably cheaper to use.

Aluminum oxide is excellent for both wood and metal. It is tougher than garnet and has excellent cutting action. An excellent material for power sanding.

Silicon carbide is harder than any of them. It's especially good in finer grits for sanding undercoats and for smoothing finishes between applications.

3. *WHAT GRIT?* There are numerous classifications but to make things easier see accompanying charts which break them down into understandable terms like coarse, medium, and fine. The finer the paper, the smoother the finish. For rough sanding, where you want to remove a lot of material use a rough, coarse paper. General rule is to work from coarse paper through to fine paper but because the wood you buy is usually S4S, it is necessary to start with very coarse paper. Judge the surface you have, and the smoothness you need—then select the grit accordingly.

Using the Disc Sander

Always sand on the "down" side of the disc's rotation. If the disc rotates counter-clockwise, you place the work on the left side of the table. Placing it on the other side would cause the "up" action of the disc to lift the work from the table.

Hold the work flat on the table as you move it into the turning disc. If you're sanding a flat edge, you move the work directly forward. If the edge is curved or if the work is circular, you sand lightly and "turn" the work as you sand. The disc surface should be tangent to the curve or arc of the work.

Don't force! Remember that abrasive particles are cutting teeth. They can only remove so much. If you feed beyond this point, the work and the paper may burn; the paper will become clogged and useless long before it should. When sanding long edges, longer than the diameter of the disc, you can cut into the work at the disc edges

Abrasive Selection Guide

Abrasive	Use	Grit		
		Rough	Medium	Fine
Alum. Oxide	Hardwood	2½-1½	½-1/0	2/0-3/0
Alum. Oxide	Aluminum	40	60-80	100
Alum. Oxide	Copper	40-50	80-100	100-120
Alum. Oxide	Steel	24-30	60-80	100
Alum. Oxide	Ivory	60-80	100-120	120-280
Alum. Oxide	Plastics	50-80	120-180	240
Garnet	Hardwood	2½-1½	½-1/0	2/0-3/0
Garnet	Softwood	1½-1	1/0	2/0
Garnet	Comp. Board	1½-1	½	1/0
Garnet	Plastics	50-80	120-180	240
Garnet	Horn	1½	½-1/0	2/0-3/0
Silicon Carbide	Glass	50-60	100-120	12-320
Silicon Carbide	Cast Iron	24-30	60-80	100
Flint	Remov. Paint— Old Finishes	3-1½	½-1/0	——

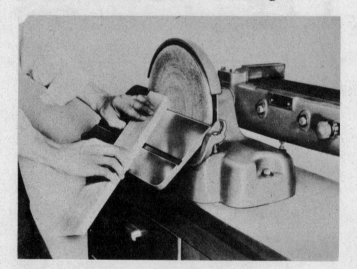

Odd angles can be smoothed freehand, but for greater accuracy use miter gauge. Sanding compound angle, below, takes miter gauge and table tilt. Note protractors on table, miter gauge.

if you try to work too fast or feed too strongly. Hold the work lightly against the disc and move it parallel to the disc surface.

You can sand to exact width on a disc sander by using the technique shown in the sketch Clamp a board to the table just slightly off line. The distance from the front end of the board to the edge of the down side of the disc should equal the required width of the work. Then pass the work easily between the improvised fence and the disc. Remember this is essentially a smoothing operation; you're just using it to get an exact width at the same time. So don't try to remove a lot of material. About 1/16 inch on coarse paper and less than 1/32 inch on fine paper are the limits.

Angles

Most disc sander tables can be tilted and are equipped with a slot so you can use a miter gauge. This expedites sanding of miters and bevel cuts. Use the miter gauge whenever a miter is sanded. This will assure accuracy.

Cross-bevels call for tilting the table to the angle required. Here, too, the miter gauge should be utilized to hold the work square to the disc. You can sand bevel-cut pieces to exact width by using the technique described for square edges. The only difference is that you tilt the table to match the bevel angle.

Curves to Exact Width

One or many curved pieces that must be of uniform width throughout their length can be done this way. Point a guide stick at one end and then smooth that end into a nice radius. The guide stick can be of ¾-inch stock and about 2 inches wide. Clamp this to the disc sander table at right angles to the disc and with the point a distance away from the disc that is equal to the

Combination belt-disc sander from Sears features cast iron frame. Work table tilts to 45 degrees. It has push-pull, on-off switch and lock-out key.

Rounding off corners is done by resting an edge of the stock against the disc, then turning the corner and coming to rest on next side, as shown.

When sanding edges on large work, such as this Formica-covered table top, be sure to provide adequate support to keep stock in level position.

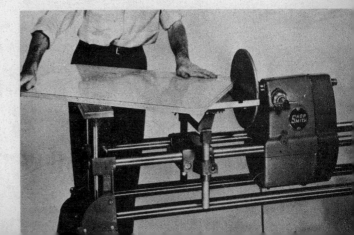

width required for the work. Then pass the work pieces between the guide and the disc. The secret to getting uniform width is to keep the curve of the work tangent to the disc at all times during the pass.

Using the Belt Sander

The belt sander is a more flexible machine than the disc and since the abrasive moves in a straight line it's particularly useful for sanding with the grain of the wood. Belt width doesn't limit the stock that can be sanded, because you can make repeat passes to smooth boards that are wider than the belt itself.

One thing to watch for on a belt sander: make sure the belt tracks evenly over the drums. If you see the belt move to left or right, make the necessary adjustment to center the belt. The machine's instruction book will reveal how this is done. Methods may vary from machine to machine but you can be sure that the adjustment is there.

Like the disc sander, the belt sander may have a table which can be tilted and which has a groove for the miter gauge. Some machines don't have a table but do have a stop, which is important; otherwise, the belt travel would carry off the work.

Surface Sanding

A belt sander can be positioned in a vertical or horizontal position. The horizontal position is best for surface sanding; the vertical position is best for edge and end sanding.

If the work is short leave the table or stop in place and use it to hold the work in position. If the work is too long for this, remove the stop. Then you must be careful not to apply too much pressure. The belt can really grip the work and pull it from your hands.

Most surface sanding on the belt is done in line with the grain of the wood, but when you want to remove a lot of material fast, it's possible to sand across the grain. Just

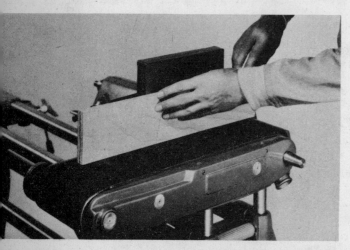

Sand edges like you would make a jointing cut. Use table or stop to keep work perpendicular.

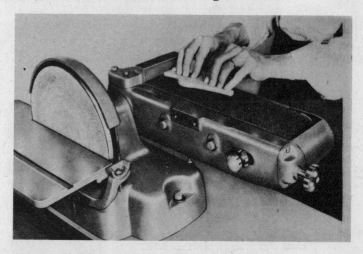

Don't sand small pieces with a stop. Belt can pull work from under hands, injure fingernails.

Cross-grain sanding removes stock fast. If possible set up table to guide, help support work.

For long curved work, such as this, machine is used in the horizontal position, as picture shows.

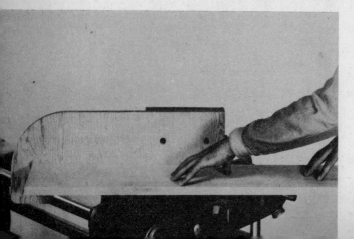

pass the work diagonally across the belt. Remember this is for stock removal; it does that but also leaves cross-grain marks in the wood. You must follow up with in-line sanding in order to obtain a really smooth finish.

Edge Sanding

Short or long pieces of stock are edge-sanded with the machine in vertical position. If you're sanding a long edge, the table or stop should be positioned parallel to the sanding belt and the pass made as if you were working on a jointer. The stop or the table helps to keep the work vertical so the sanded edge will be square to the adjacent surfaces. If you're sanding a short edge or end, then the stock can be moved directly forward into the belt as you would do it on a disc sander.

Curves

One drum on the belt sander can be used for sanding inside edges on curved work much as you would do it on a drum sander. This is the idler drum. If it is covered, the cover must be removed for sanding operations. The sander may be in either vertical or horizontal position—whichever is more convenient for the job being done. In order for the sanded edge to be square, it's a good idea to attach an auxiliary fence to the table or stop, to act as a guide for the work. Shape the auxiliary fence so it wraps around the sanding drum.

Since the back side of the sanding belt is not supported by a back-up plate, it has enough slack in it so you can use that area to smooth irregular shapes and round knobs. This is a particularly handy feature of the belt and disc sander. •

When the work is relatively small, your sander can sometimes be best employed in the vertical position, as demonstrated in photo at the left.

Grit Size and Number Equivalents

8/0=280
7/0=240
6/0=220
5/0=180
4/0=150
3/0=120
2/0=100
0=80
1/2=60
1=50
1 1/2=40
2 = 36
2 1/2=30
3=24

Classes of Abrasives Assorted into Grit Numbers

Abrasive	Very Fine	Fine	Medium	Coarse	Very Coarse
Flint	4/0	2/0-3/0	1/0-1/2	1-2	2 1/2-3 1/2
Garnet	6/0-10/0	3/0-5/0	1/0-2/0	1/2-1 1/2	2-3
Aluminum Oxide Silicon Carbide	220-360	120-180	80-100	40-60	24-36

the radial arm saw

It's now as popular in the home workshop as on the construction site

IT USED to be called the "contractor's tool" because you found it wherever a house was being built. It was there because it was so easy to lay a board down on its table and pull its blade through for the cut. For notching, for sizing studs, for myriad home construction operations it couldn't be beat. It still can't, but home-craftsmen have come to recognize its impressive versatility so that today, in applicable sizes, the radial arm saw is as popular in the home garage workshop as it is on a home construction site.

There are different types available. The DeWalt, which is famous in this field, is representative of what a radial arm saw is generally pictured to be. Its motor is encased in a yoke which is carriaged to travel to and fro in an overhead arm. The arm turns on a rigid column and can be adjusted up or down. Since the motor, too, can be turned and tilted, the whole relationship of components affords a flexibility of movement that can't be stymied by any woodworking operation. In fact, the true potential of the tool has finally been recognized and exploited so that it no longer is considered just a saw, but is used for routing, shaping, sanding, drilling and other chores. Refinements, modifications, different features distinguish one make from another. The latest entry in the field features a built-in variable speed changer so you can select a suitable speed for the job being done. The latest DeWalt has a built-in brake so the saw blade stops in a few seconds after the switch is turned off. An admirable feature since the blades used to turn too long a time after the cut.

You don't need much space to house a radial arm. The machine itself doesn't require more than a square yard of floor space, but you'll limit its usefulness if you don't provide space at either side of it. This is because, whether you rip or crosscut, the work is placed laterally across the table. The radial arm makes it easy to

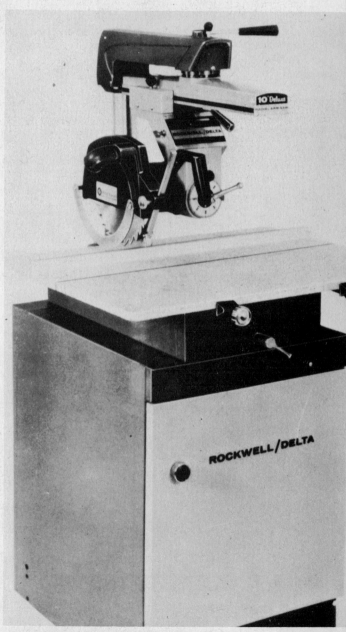

Rockwell 10-inch radial arm saw has leaf, upper guard; anti-kickback device; 3-inch cut capacity.

12-inch radial arm saw from Sears cuts wood up to 4 inches thick, has 4½ HP motor, ball bearings.

10-inch radial arm saw from Wards can shape, mold, drill, sand and polish with various accessories.

A special setup like this, easily constructed and affixed, provides you with a power saw that can be used in the shop or out in the field.

When you're working close to end of the stock, so there's no room for your left hand, keep it off table. Normal blade thrust keeps work positioned.

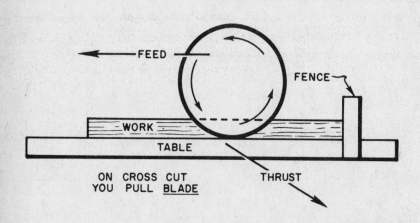

ON CROSS CUT
YOU PULL **BLADE**

These drawings show movements of blade or work in ripping, crosscutting operations. If blade is moved, always return it to its original position.

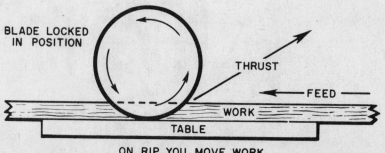

ON RIP YOU MOVE **WORK**

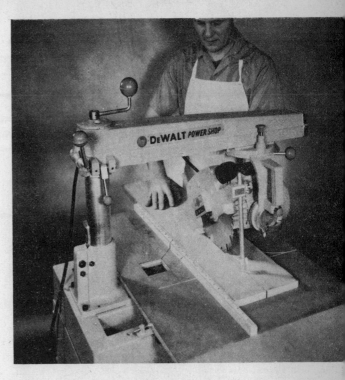

When cutting duplicate pieces to length, use a stop on the fence. The one pictured here can be purchased; it slides in grooves cut in fence.

Simple ripping operation with blade "in rip." Note guard, anti-kickback fingers. Use pusher stick unless room's ample between blade, fence.

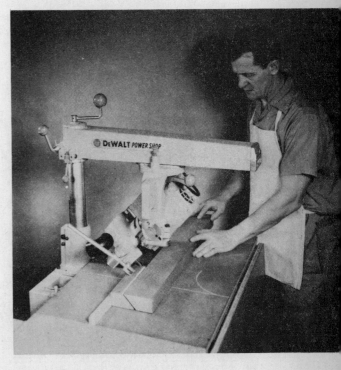

Rip operation with blade in the "out rip" position. Note direction of feed has been changed; work is being fed against rotation of saw blade.

Bevel rip is accomplished like a normal rip except that the blade is tilted to the desired angle. You can do this in inboard or outboard position.

square the end of a very long board, but if you don't provide room for the board, you've defeated the purpose. Actually to reap the benefits you should allow 5 to 10 feet at each side of the machine; the more the better.

The machine can be backed against a wall and you don't need a lot of space in front. You can make a stand to use it on or you can buy a ready-made one. Or you can use it on a specially made cabinet that will house other workshop tools as well as any accessories you may buy for the saw. DeWalt is one of the manufacturers that will furnish plans for a specially designed cabinet that is ideal for the saw and almost a workshop in itself.

An obvious difference between the radial arm and a conventional table is that in the former the saw blade is *above* the work,

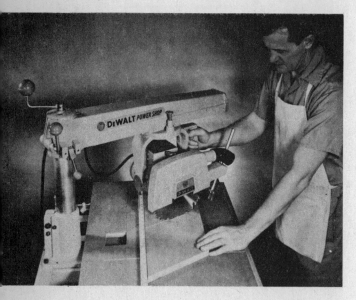

A simple miter cut is demonstrated in this photograph. In making such a cut, you must guard against "creep." Keep work firmly against fence.

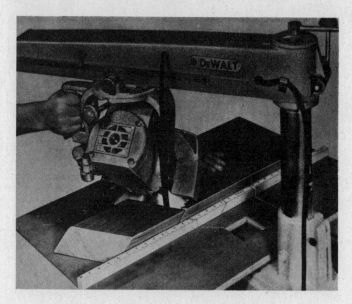

A compound-angle cut requires moving arm, as for miter cut, and tilting of blade. The blade of saw is also tilted when you make a cross-bevel cut.

For dadoing, you mount a dado assembly instead of the saw blade. Don't pull the dado through too fast or it will have tendency to "climb" work.

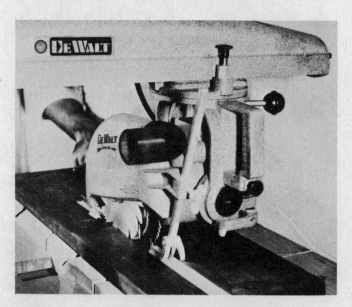

"Ploughing" is merely a dado cut that is made with the grain of the wood. The radial arm is set up and work fed through as for a rip cut.

and that you move *the blade* to make the cut; the work stays put, flat on the table with cutting marks in plain view. Rotation of the blade, when you face the arbor, is clockwise. This means that thrust against the work is down and to the rear. Material placed against the fence is held there by the action of the blade. An effective demonstration of this, is to place a 1-inch square piece of ¾-inch stock on the table and against the fence. Pull the blade through and you make the cut through that tiny piece easily and without having to hold it.

Like any power tool, the radial arm will function efficiently and accurately only if you assure that all components are in correct relation to each other. You can't expect a square crosscut if the auto-stop which positions the blade is not accurately

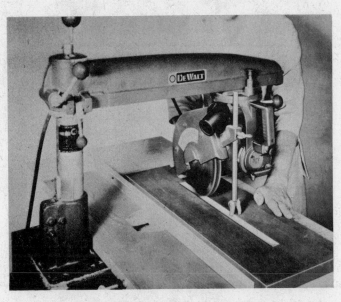

"Stopped" dado. Lower blade where cut is to begin, feed work full length of cut and raise the blade. Stops on fence assure right length of dado.

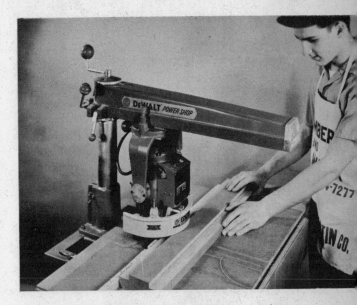

Demonstrated here is machine position for making a rabbet cut using a dado assembly. You will note that a special guard replaces regular saw guard.

With this power tool, dadoes can also be cut using the regular saw blade. To do so, you merely make enough repeat passes to achieve wanted width.

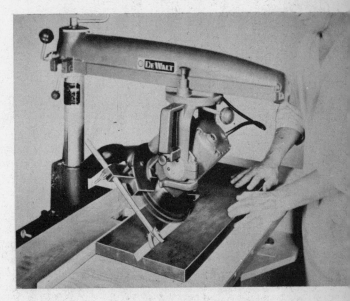

"V" cuts such as this are easily made with dado assembly. Just tilt blade and set up machine in this manner as you would to make a rip bevel cut.

You can actually surface stock with a regular saw blade, with a dado assembly, or even with a molding head so long as the cuts are kept light.

With the radial arm saw, off-angle rabbets are accomplished in this manner. The guard is adjustable so it can be set to accommodate depth of cut.

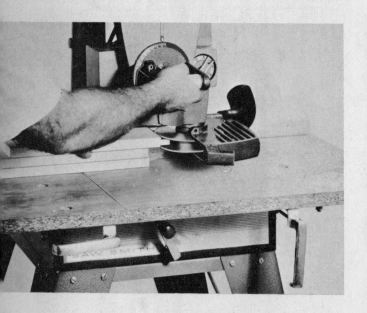

Special setups such as this one are simple and routine on the modern radial arm saw. Spaced blades are cutting a tenon in just one pass.

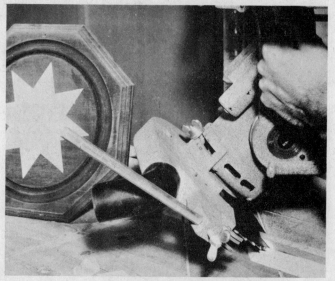

Fancy small shapes are possible without special setups as action of the blade helps keep work in position. Your hands can be kept safely away.

set. While the relationship of parts is basically the same on all machines, adjustment procedures may vary, so study the literature that comes with your machine. Check the machine as per instructions the first time you set it up; check it periodically thereafter.

Crosscutting

This is what you should do first. Place a board on the table against the fence. Place your left hand to the left of the saw blade travel. Turn on the switch and pull the blade gradually through the work. Then return the blade to starting position.

The *cut* is complete when the blade has passed across the board width, but the *operation* is *not* complete until you have returned the blade to the rear of the arm

Grooving is perfect as the work is flat on the table and fed against the fence. Thin grooves are cut with saw blade; heavier ones with dado.

You can make this or similar cuts in the end of a 2x6, 20 or more feet long—which points up one of the decided advantages of this fine tool.

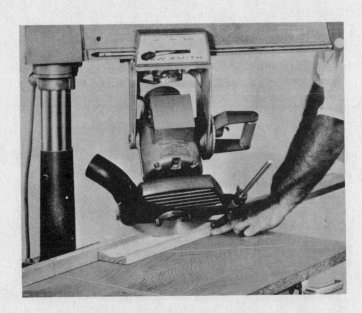

Coving can be accomplished by setting up arm and saw blade as if for compound miter cut. Pass work through as if ripping. The cuts should be light.

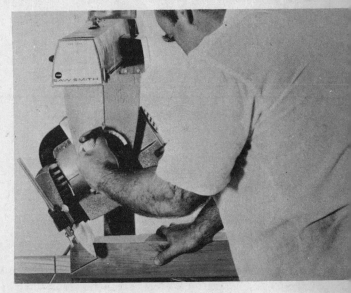

The notching of studs, as demonstrated in this photograph, is routine with the radial arm saw, thanks to flexibility of machine's components.

travel. This is important: *Always return the blade to the starting position.*

In normal cutting the blade height is set so it cuts into the table about ⅛ inch. The blade, of course, passes through the fence. The kerf in the fence is a cutting guide. Line up the cutting mark on the work with the kerf in the fence and you know the blade will cut exactly where you want it to. If you have a number of pieces to cut

to the same length, clamp a stop block to the fence to gauge the length of the cutoff.

Mitering

Mitering is basically a crosscut action except that you adjust the arm to the angle required. Then you pull the blade through as before. For common angles such as a 45-degree miter, the machine probably has automatic stops. If you have set these cor-

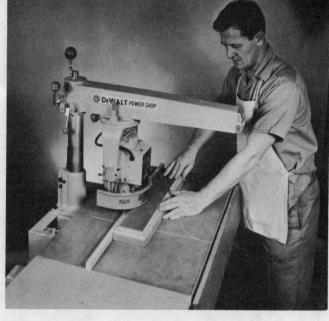

The radial arm saw is no longer just a saw, but is used for routing, shaping, sanding, etc. Here is shaper fence accessory of one make of tool.

Bead and cove cut. Since you can move cutters in or out, raise or lower them, tilt them to any angle, you get multiple shapes from one cutter.

rectly the cut should be right on the button. Hold the work firmly when mitering for "creep"—the action present on the table saw, is also present here—and it can spoil the accuracy of the cut. One way to get away from it is to face the fence with fine sandpaper or drive short nails through the back of the fence so they protrude slightly at the front. These will anchor the work in place when you press against the fence.

This can be done to the regular fence or you can equip a special fence for the purpose and save it for making angular cuts in the future.

Compound angle cuts require two settings. You swing the arm for one; you tilt the blade for the other. They can be accomplished on the radial arm machine with great facility because the work is flat on the table and stays put during the pass.

Here craftsman is cutting a cabinet-door lip. Work is elevated on scrap block for full profile cut. Tool used in this photograph is Saw Smith.

The Saw Smith radial arm saw has two arbors so that tools can be mounted at either end of the motor. A molding head setup is demonstrated here.

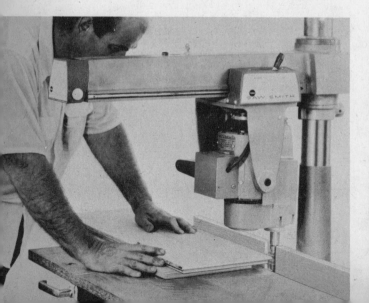

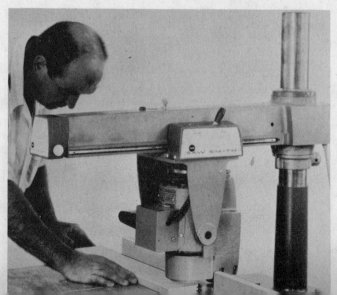

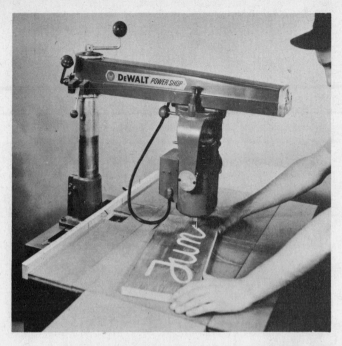

Freehand routing. Depth of cut is easily controlled by raising or lowering the arm. Flexibility of the radial arm saw is virtually unlimited.

Disc sanding. Here work is held still and the disc is moved across it. The power of the machine's motor can be used to run other tools.

Ripping

Ripping is one operation where you lock the blade in position and push the work through for the cut. Never feed the work in the direction of rotation of the blade. You must always feed against the rotation. Most saws are marked with arrows and warnings to help you remember correct feed direction for rip cuts.

Since the motor can be turned a full 360 degrees, you have a choice of either "in-ripping" or "out-ripping." The choice is one relative to cut capacity. Most times the "in" position will do. For extra-wide cuts the "out" position is employed.

One edge of the work rides against the fence, as it would on the table saw, so parallelism between blade (in rip position) and fence is important. This is a question

The radial arm saw again serves as a disc sander in this photograph, but in this application the disc itself is locked in place and work moved.

Drum sanding. Broad table surface makes it possible to keep any size work level. Note drop-shelf to provide even more table surface when needed.

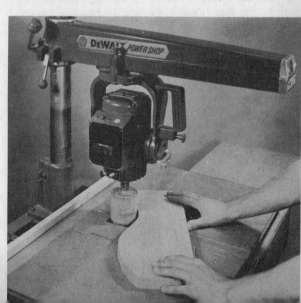

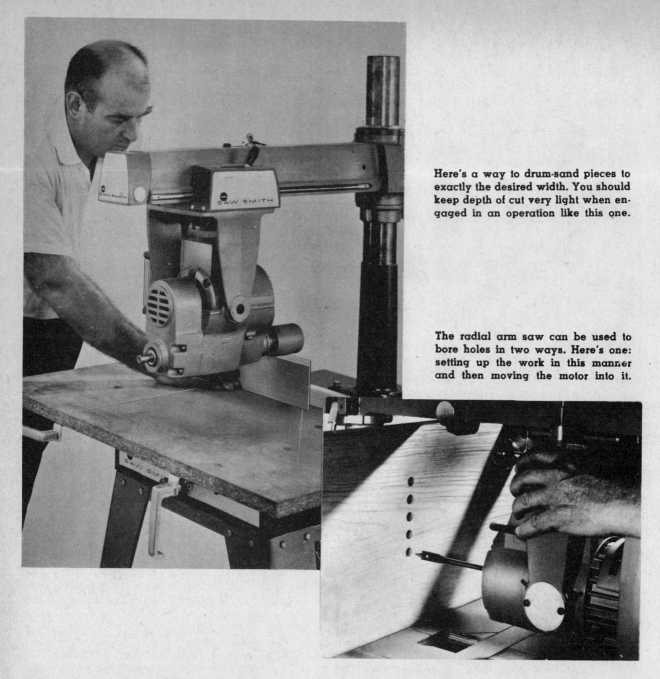

Here's a way to drum-sand pieces to exactly the desired width. You should keep depth of cut very light when engaged in an operation like this one.

The radial arm saw can be used to bore holes in two ways. Here's one: setting up the work in this manner and then moving the motor into it.

Second way of boring holes is to position work in this manner and lower the arm. An added recommendation for this tool: it needs little space.

Regular saw blade can be used on such metals as Do-It-Yourself aluminum. Special metal-cutting blades can be had for use with harder stuff.

of machine adjustment. And binding action is a good sign that you should check alignment. Use the guard and the anti-kickback device at all times. Keep the hand that is doing the feeding well away from the cutting area. When the cut is complete, turn off the switch and *then* remove the work that is between the blade and fence. Never do this while the blade is turning! If the work is narrow, use a push stick to feed it, just as you would on a conventional saw.

Bevel ripping is accomplished the same way, except that the blade is tilted to the angle required. Either the inboard or the outboard position can be used.

These are just the basic operations. The machine is capable of dozens of others, not only with the standard saw blade, but with many other tools you can mount in its place. A dado, for example, by using it in a normal crosscut setup or in a rip setup. With accessories you can do excellent shaping—a really efficient use since you can tilt the cutting tool to any angle. Routing, sanding, drilling—many other standard woodworking procedures are available. In addition you can use the power of the motor to run other tools that will do jobs the basic machine can't—lathe work and jigsaw work are just two examples.

Study the accompanying photographs for techniques involved in accomplishing many power woodworking chores. •

Need a buff? Planning a wire-brush operation? With the radial arm saw, you're in. Just use it as pictured here—as if it were a polishing head.

How are you fixed for a grinder? This special accessory for the remarkable tool permits you to do a real pro job of sharpening your tools.

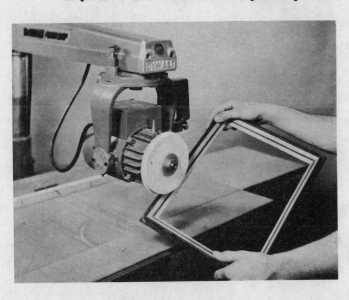

This special lathe is designed for mounting as pictured on the DeWalt. It has its own flexibility, too; it can be used as a separate tool.

This saber-saw accessory has sufficient power to cut 2-inch stock, so you are not limited to straight cuts with the modern radial arm saw.

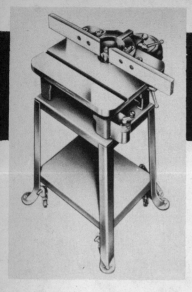

the shaper

It lets you exploit this phase of woodworking to the utmost

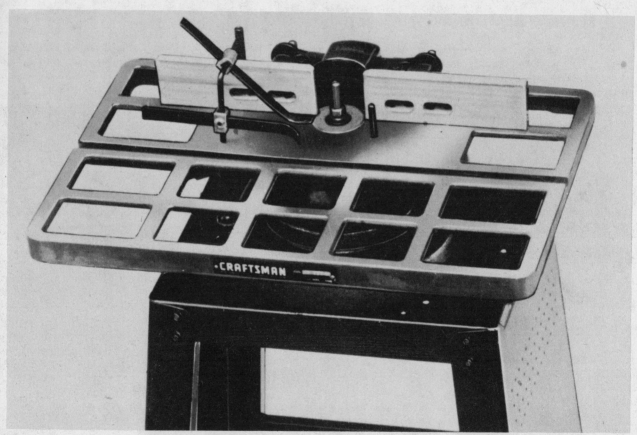

Sears shaper hits speeds up to 9,000 rpm for smooth finish. Table is 27 x 19 inches. Spindle reverses.

BASICALLY, the shaper is a vertical spindle. It's designed to withstand considerably more side thrust than a drill-press spindle and is located under the table rather than over it. The spindle is adjustable up or down and can be locked at any height. The average home-workshop shaper operates on ½-hp reversible motor and at a speed which is up around 10,000 rpm. Interchangeable spindles allow use of a wide variety of shaper cutters. So here is a machine specifically designed for shaping operations and with built-in flexibility to exploit this phase of woodworking to the utmost.

The two shaping methods you'll be using most frequently are shaping against guides (or fence) and shaping against collars. The first is essentially for straight shaping while the other is for freehand shaping of curved or circular shapes.

A fence is usually supplied with the shaper. It's a two-part deal, adjustable so it can be used to control depth of cut. With

SPECIAL SETUPS FOR SEGMENTS AND CIRCULAR PIECES
(The guides are clamped to the table.)

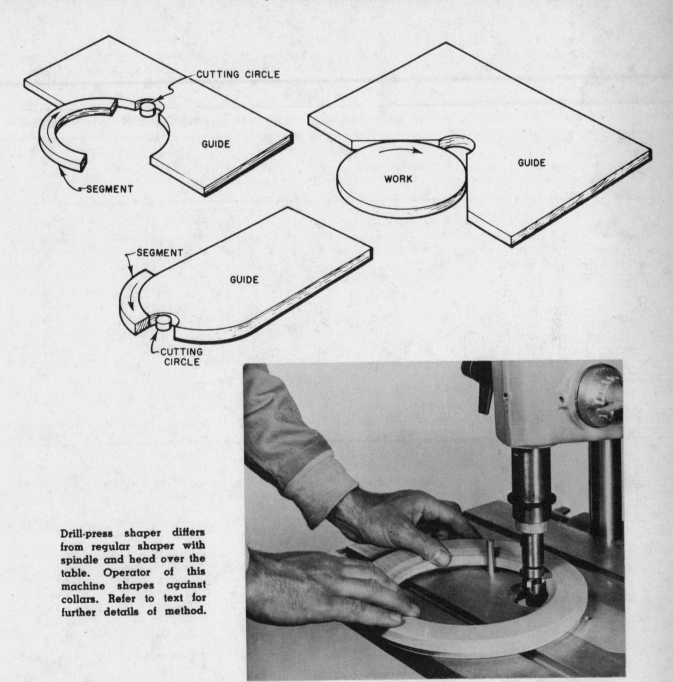

Drill-press shaper differs from regular shaper with spindle and head over the table. Operator of this machine shapes against collars. Refer to text for further details of method.

a fence—remember this—when the cutter removes only part of the edge, the fences are in line. When the cutter removes the entire edge, the outfeed fence is moved forward to supply support for the work after the cut.

Collars can be used (in freehand shaping) only with partial edge removal. The remaining edge of the stock rides the collar and this is what controls depth of cut. Since collars are available in various diameters, you select the size you need for the cut

wanted. Collars are also used as spacers when more than one cutter is being used.

Work feed is always against the direction of rotation of the cutters and, whenever possible, with the grain of the wood. There are times when you can't obey the latter rule, but the first one is always in order. When you cut all edges of a work piece, make the first cut on the end grain and follow through so that the last cut is made with the grain of the wood.

Sometimes because of the nature of the

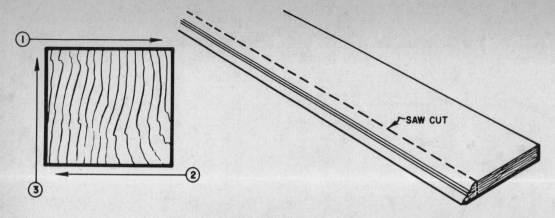

SAW CUT

Always make cross-grain cuts first, as indicated by the drawing at left here. When a slim molding is required, shape the edge of a large, easily-handled piece; then rip off molding, as indicated.

work, it's advisable to replace the standard table with an extra-long or extra-high fence—sometimes even a fence that will hold the work at any angle. You shouldn't hesitate to make this special equipment because, chances are, you'll have use for it again later on.

Special guides that take the place of the regular fence are made to suit the shape of the work. Prime examples are circular pieces and curved segments. This is a good rule to follow when many duplicate pieces require shaping. It's easy and faster to work this way when the job has a custom-made guide.

When you work with collars you may position them above, below or between cutters. Generally, it's best to have the collar under the cutter, for this setup does not obscure the cutting area. But it requires

more care, for accidental lifting of the stock during the pass will cause the cutter to dig in and mar the work. If the cutter is under and the collar above, lifting the work won't cause any damage at all.

When you work with collars, you generally start the work against a fulcrum pin. This is but a support point which enables you to start the feed into the cutter without danger of kickback. When you start work this way, let the wood follow a line that runs from the fulcrum pin to the outside engage of the collar. Feed it in slowly until it rests firmly against the collar of the machine.

Correct use of the shaper will not only let you put decorative edges on any kind of cabinet work, but also lets you produce many standard shapes and forms of moldings and castings. •

Shaping a cabinet-door lip. Note that work is held down firmly on table, snug against fence. Feed is controlled so that cutter bites smoothly.

The use of spring holddowns is a sensible way to keep your fingers out of the cutting zone. Machine in this photograph is an Atlas model.

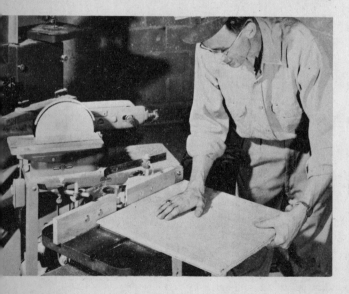

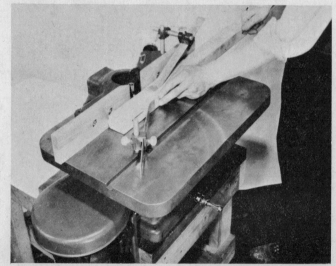

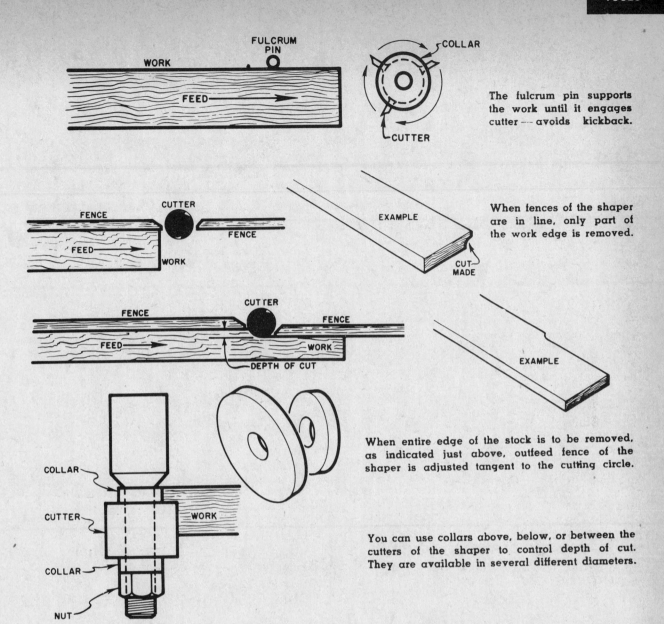

FULCRUM PIN

WORK

FEED

COLLAR

CUTTER

The fulcrum pin supports the work until it engages cutter — avoids kickback.

FENCE

CUTTER

FENCE

FEED

WORK

EXAMPLE

CUT MADE

When fences of the shaper are in line, only part of the work edge is removed.

FENCE

CUTTER

FENCE

FEED

WORK

DEPTH OF CUT

EXAMPLE

When entire edge of the stock is to be removed, as indicated just above, outfeed fence of the shaper is adjusted tangent to the cutting circle.

COLLAR

CUTTER

WORK

COLLAR

NUT

You can use collars above, below, or between the cutters of the shaper to control depth of cut. They are available in several different diameters.

Table slot of the shaper enables you to use holddown jigs or a miter gauge, as demonstrated in this photograph, for smooth, safe operation.

Wards shaper develops speed of 18,000 rpm with 1 HP motor, shapes plywood cross-grain without splintering. Cutters are alloy steel with 3 lips.

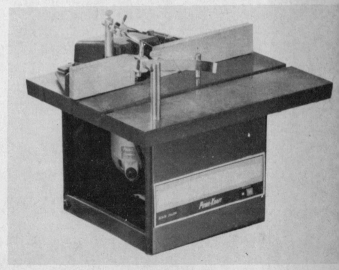

the grinder

It is your assurance of sharp tools for efficiency and safety in the shop.

Bench grinder, like this Delta model, bolts to bench top. Pedestal type has built-in floor stand.

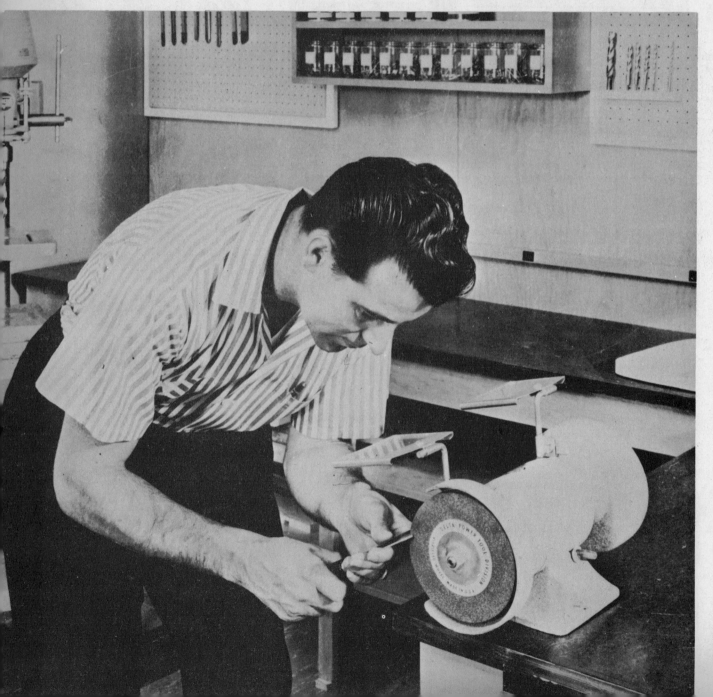

Rockwell grinder has 6-inch diameter wheels with heavy duty motor, ball bearings. Spark deflectors are adjustable. And eyeshields are unbreakable.

WOOD CHISEL CARE

APPLY HOLLOW-GROUND EDGE TO CHISEL...

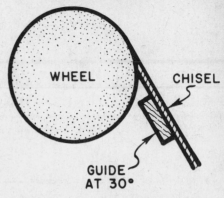

WHEEL

CHISEL

GUIDE AT 30°

...REMOVE BURRS FROM BACK

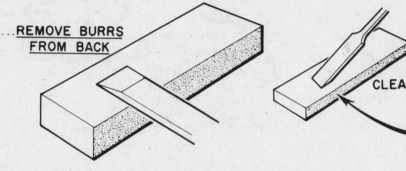

...THEN HONE ON A STONE...

CLEARANCE

THINK of the grinder as a double-shafted motor on which you can mount a couple of abrasive wheels. If you go out and buy a "grinder" you get a setup like this equipped with one medium-grain and one fine-grain abrasive wheel, plus shields for the wheels and rests on which tools being sharpened can be placed. You can buy a bench grinder, which you bolt to a bench top or you can buy a pedestal grinder which is fully equipped to stand on its own.

Many craftsmen just buy grinding wheels and use another shop tool to turn them. That's okay but such setups usually lack the guards a regular grinder is equipped with. You must also be careful to operate the wheels at the recommended speeds. Slower is okay, but never, never faster. Recommended speeds are printed on the paper flanges of the wheels so remember to check them and obey them.

Other craftsmen buy a polishing head. This is a bearing-mounted horizontal shaft with arbors at each end. You run it by motor and V-belt. On the shafts you mount the grinding wheels or buffs or wire brushes.

Whichever arrangement you use, remember the recommended speeds of whatever tool you put on the shaft. Always work with goggles to protect your eyes.

Some grinders are equipped with eye shields but even so it's usually recommended that you also wear safety goggles.

It's easy to operate a grinder. The basic rule is to use the coarser stone when you want to remove a lot of material; the finer stone for the actual sharpening. For super-keen edges, the fine-stone stage is followed by honing—either by hand, or with a power hone.

Position the tool rests as close as possible to the wheel to provide maximum support for the tool being sharpened. Grinding wheels, no matter how fine, have pores which become clogged during use. They also lose their original shape and dimensions, because as you remove metal from the tool you also remove abrasive particles from the wheel. Every so often, and you can judge by the appearance and the action of the wheel, they must be "dressed" to their original shape and efficient working condition. This is accomplished with a specially designed dressing tool which employs diamonds to cut the abrasive; this is an expensive tool. A more economical tool that can serve the purpose is equipped with replaceable wheels that are studded with hard sharp points of metal. These turn rapidly as you hold them against the grinding wheel and can reshape the wheel and open its pores.

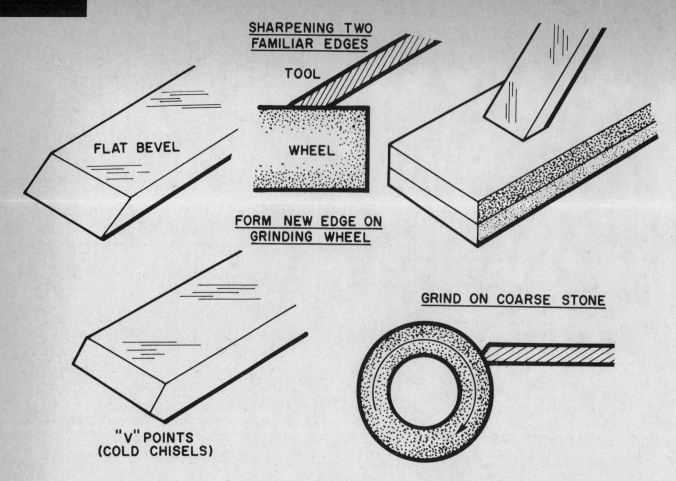

SHARPENING TWO FAMILIAR EDGES

TOOL

FLAT BEVEL

WHEEL

FORM NEW EDGE ON GRINDING WHEEL

GRIND ON COARSE STONE

"V" POINTS (COLD CHISELS)

Skip wheel when new edge is unneeded. Just use hone stone's coarse side and then its fine side.

The story of the grinder is not so much one of the tool itself but one concerned with sharpening. That's the big reason for having a grinder and it's certainly a good one. Nothing is more important in the shop —for work and safety—than sharp tools. A professional can quickly repoint a tool without too much concern. He knows the angles and how to accomplish them free-hand. Most of us have to be a little more cagey. Whenever possible it's a good idea to buy or make a jig or fixture that will hold the tool against the wheel exactly right for the correct edge angle.

Sometimes you can buy these jigs. One example is the drill-grinding jig. The dull drill is clamped in the tool and held against the grinding wheel. The angle and motion are controlled by the jig. You get a factory-new edge every time. Doing it by hand is not so simple. You must hold the drill at exactly the right angle, turn it and at the same time adjust the angle to maintain the shape of the point. This must be done on each side of the drill and both sides must match exactly. It isn't easy but it's certainly not impossible. Practice is the answer.

Lathe chisels, hand-plane blades, butt chisels—all of them are sharpened better and more easily if you make a jig to hold them correctly. Time spent making the jigs is not wasted for you will be using them often if you realize the important advantages of sharp tools. Some ideas relative to common tools are sketched in the accompanying drawings. These convey the idea.

Other tools may be substituted for the grinding wheels, buffs, wire brushes among them. Some grinders will even accommodate a sander. A wire brush is useful for giving soft metals a satin finish and for removing dirt, oxidation and grit from soft or hard metal surfaces. A buffing wheel will let you put a lustrous finish to metal projects.

One tool in this area which certainly deserves mention is the Atlas Grinder-Hone which combines a grinding wheel with a horizontally-mounted honing wheel. Speeds are controlled through a gear mechanism. Since the unit is double shafted you have an extra spindle for mounting other sharpening tools or for a drum sander or similar items. •

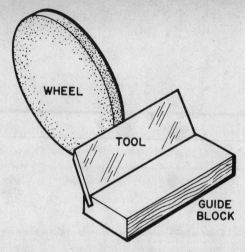

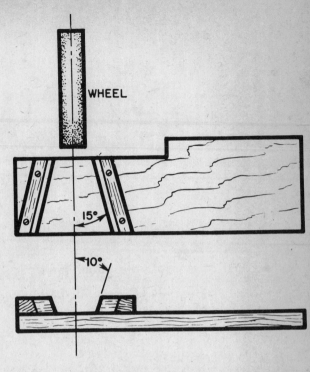

By making special guide blocks, you automatically hold angle on cutting edge of item sharpened.

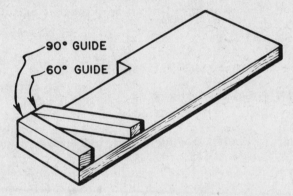

90° GUIDE
60° GUIDE

You can easily construct a special guide such as
the one above for use in grinding skew bevels.

The 60-degree guide at left can be used for skew,
parting tool, etc.; 90-degree for straight edges.

Buffing wheels "load" with polishing compounds
for high-luster finish on metals. They also take
emery particles for smoothing metal surfaces.

A number of devices that are easily constructed
will help you maintain your tools. Use this one
to square the edges on chisels, plane blades, etc.

SMALL TABLE WITH
"MITER GAUGE"

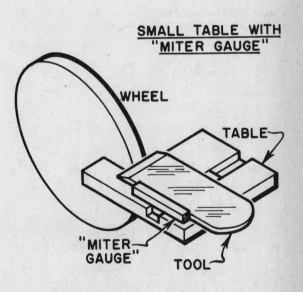

the cut-off saw

First of the portable power tools considered, it is available in many models, can be used to cut a variety of materials besides wood, and is as useful in the workshop as outside it

IT'S OFTEN called a "cut-off" saw but this is not truly descriptive of its functions. Like the radial arm saw, its value was first recognized by construction men for whom it's usually more convenient, if not absolutely necessary, to bring the tool to the job. The tool first used was the hand saw but then someone put the cutting teeth on the perimeter of a disc and secured it to a motor that was light enough to be hand-held but powerful enough to cut through 2x4s and 2x6s. So industry replaced hand saws (not entirely) with electric saws and soon after, inevitably, home craftsmen discovered them.

At first they rented them for very special jobs that merited the particular talents of this power tool. But after a taste of it, they wanted them for keeps and manufacturers obliged by developing special models that could be handled easily by the average homeowner. Today there are numerous models available with blade sizes ranging from 4- to 12-inch diameters. You can even buy an accessory to hook up with a portable electric drill. The big fellows are not the home workshop tools. You don't need the capacity and the weight that goes along with it. A 7- or 8-inch blade should be considered maximum for convenient home workshop use.

With the many special blades available,

7½-inch Rockwell cut-off or circular saw has safety blade clutch, double insulation, accurate blade depth and angle scales plus breakproof housing.

Inner workings of portable electric cut-off saw. Blades range to 12 inches in diameter, but 8 inches should be considered maximum for home shop.

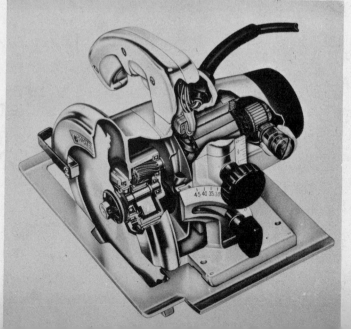

Simpson Logging Co. photo

When cutting large panels, a guide strip clamped to work like this assures you of a straight cut.

portable electric saws can be used to cut many other materials in addition to wood; in fact, almost any building material from slate and corrugated metal sheets to fiberglass.

Since the saw is so versatile, it is as useful in the shop as out. Many shops built around a good floor model table saw also boast a portable cut-off saw. The portable is used when the work can't be brought to the tool and also for many preliminary sizing cuts that reduce raw material to dimensions that can be more easily handled on stationary equipment. Two examples

are cutting long pieces of lumber into shorter lengths and reducing plywood panels to smaller dimensions.

Types Available

Weights differ widely, from as low as 4 or 5 pounds to as much as 40 pounds. This is an important factor when you choose one for yourself. Since you are the one who must handle it on the job, take plenty of time in the store, "hefting" the unit and simulating actual operations. If at all possible make a few actual cuts while the dealer stands by. The tool must feel right

The Stanley 7-inch heavy-duty builder's saw seen in this photograph blows a stream of air ahead of the cut to clear chips away from the cutting line.

Portable electric cut-off saws manufactured by Disston differ from most other models with this feature: a cord that plugs in right at the tool.

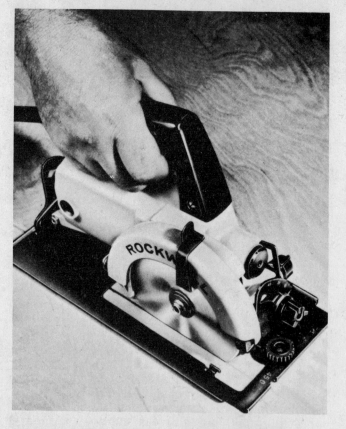

Craftsman saw is sturdy looking and comes equipped with a ripping guide. Available as accessory is a table that converts it for use as table saw.

Unique Rockwell 4½-inch trim saw was designed for problem cuts such as trim, composition boards, paneling, laminates, plexiglass, non-ferrous metals.

A marked cut line is easily followed with the cut mark in shoe of the tool, as demonstrated here.

Correct positioning of a crosscutting guide enables you to cut accurately without penciled mark.

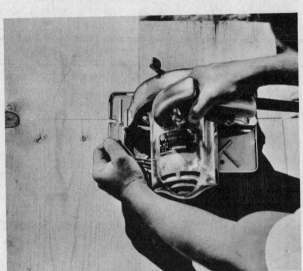

in your hands. Test it as you would a hammer. The right one for you will feel like it belongs in your hand. Chances are the one you choose will weigh between 5 and 12 pounds.

Most of these tools are equipped with universal motors that will operate on either AC or DC current and require 115 voltage which is common in most houses.

A trigger switch is the usual method of turning the tool on and off and this is conveniently located on the underside of the tool's handle so that when you grip the handle for cutting, your index finger wraps neatly around the switch. Before you do any cutting, it's a good idea to practice turning the tool on and off, getting the feel of the switch and of the tool when it is running.

Cutting depth is regulated by a hinge shoe. This is the plate on which the tool rests when you are cutting. The higher you adjust the plate, the deeper the cut will be. While professionals will often set theirs for quite a bit of blade projection under the work, it's a pretty good safety practice for you to start off with a minimum, say about ¼ inch. Always be sure, after adjusting the depth of cut, that the locking device is secure. This is usually some kind of winged nut arrangement conveniently located for easy manipulation.

These tools are equipped with two-piece blade guards. The top is fixed, being a permanent part of the housing; the lower portion is arranged so it will "telescope"

back when the blade is in the cut and then return after the cut to enclose the blade. Remember during cutting all blade you can see is covered but blade projection— that is, the portion of the blade that is under the work—is not. There are teeth down there and they are exposed. Always be aware of that. A good many saws are now equipped with clutches that cause the blade to stop turning as soon as they can't cut. Ordinarily, when the blade begins to bind, the saw will "kick back"— tend to move out of the cut in your direction. The clutch is designed to prevent this.

Using the Tool

Regardless of whether the saw you select has this safety device or not, it's definitely poor and dangerous practice to ever force a portable saw. It's wise to remember that every saw blade functions most efficiently when feed is matched with the blade's capacity to cut. You don't have to figure this out; you can feel it. You'll know when the cut is smooth; you'll know when you are forcing. Let the blade do its own cutting. The tool will last longer and you will work easier because it's less fatiguing. Above all, keep the blade sharp. If it is you won't be tempted to force to compensate. Cuts will be cleaner and smoother.

Unless the cut is to be a rough one, it's good practice to mark a pencil line across the work which indicates the cut line. Somewhere at the front of the shoe is a

The protractor accessory, demonstrated in photograph at the left, is a big help in making angular cuts.

To cut notches, make two limited parallel cuts, then knock away material left between them, as shown above.

On extra thick stock, make a cut on one side, then flip work, make second. Do same for chamfering, bevels.

When appearance is unimportant overcut slightly where cuts intersect so as to remove waste entirely.

mark which tells you the cut line of the saw blade. By keeping this mark traveling on the pencil mark you'll know the cut will be true. If you find that you are traveling off the line, don't attempt to force the blade back into line again. It's best to back out the blade a bit and make a new approach.

At the start of the cut, be sure the blade is not making contact with the work. Rest the tool on the work, line up the cut guide, turn on the switch, and when the blade has attained full speed, then start cutting. Wood does not have uniform density. The blade will cut easier in some places than in others. This, of course, is especially true when you are cutting through a knot. If the blade, at any time, begins to labor, slow up the feed pressure. Many professionals advise not to release the switch when the blade stalls or approaches a stall. Keep the switch depressed and back out the blade until it regains its maximum speed, then continue the cut, slowing the feed pressure to compensate for the ad-

ditional density you are cutting through.

One important general rule is not to work with the tool resting on the portion of the work which is being cut off. If you do this the tool will have no support at the end of the cut. Always position the tool on the main side of the cut. Position *yourself* so that your body favors this side. Always try to stay out of the line of cut. The cut itself should be just outside the pencil mark. Remember that the saw cut (kerf) has width and that if you cut exactly on the line, you will be reducing the dimension you need by at least half the width of the kerf, which can be as much as 1/16 inch.

Stock you are cutting should always be securely anchored. If you are cutting off a long piece, be sure the work rests on saw horses and that it is held down firmly. If you feel that the work does not have sufficient weight to keep it stable *during* and *after* the cut, take time to clamp it. This is especially true when the work is small.

In using the cut-off saw, good side of the material should always be down, which is just the opposite to the procedure used with a table saw.

The cut-off saw enables you to limit the depth of the cut so as to cut through surface material without damaging what's below it, as shown here.

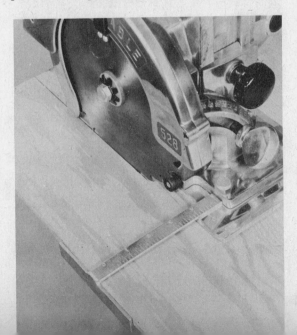

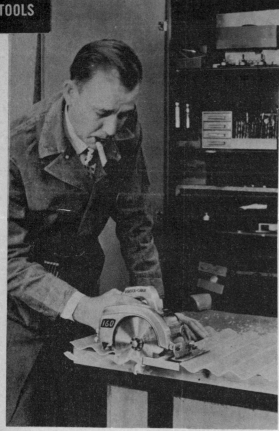

With special blades, the portable cut-off saw will cut almost any building material in existence, even slate, corrugated metal, fiberglass.

Always stand off to the side of the tool, placing hands well away from the cut line. Note how guard is "telescoping" as the blade enters stock.

Don't be careless when you reach the end of the cut. Blade guard at the bottom of the cut-off saw won't return until blade is clear of material.

Long cuts can be made freehand, by following a penciled line, but you'll find it easier to maintain accuracy if you provide some kind of guide. When cutting across the width of a panel, clamp a straight stick to the panel for use as a guide. When ripping the length of a board, use the ripping guide with which most modern cut-off saws are equipped.

When the work has a good "face" side, position it for cutting with this side *down*. This is exactly opposite correct procedure on a table saw, but so is the cutting action. A table saw cuts "down"—the portable saw cuts "up."

"Plunge" Cuts

You can make "plunge" cuts, that is, make an internal cutout in a panel without a lead-in cut from any edge, by following this procedure. Clearly mark the boundaries of the cutout. Then rest the tool on the front of the shoe so the blade clears the surface of the stock. Make sure the blade is on the cut line. Turn on the switch and slowly lower the blade until it makes contact with the wood. Continue to lower slowly until the blade is through the work and the tool rests solidly on the shoe. Then cut the length of the line as you would any other cut. Repeat the procedure

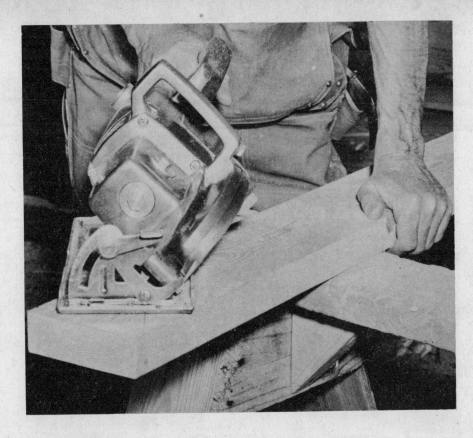

Compound cuts are a combination of miter cut and blade tilt. Great accuracy is required if the cut parts are to mate accurately.

for all four sides. Approach each corner carefully. Since the saw blade does not cut square, you'll have to finish up at each corner with a hand saw.

Rabbets and Dadoes

Since you can control depth of cut, it's possible to use a cut-off saw to make rabbets and dadoes, although these are not considered particularly convenient operations; certainly you can't do them as easily with a cut-off saw as you can on a table saw.

To make dadoes, first mark the width of the dado in pencil. Clamp a guide strip to the work, and after adjusting the blade for correct depth, make a cut which outlines one side of the dado. Readjust the guide block to make the other outlining cut. The stock between is removed by successive passes with the saw—freehand or by readjusting the guide for each new pass. You can do this type of cutting by working either across the grain of the wood or with the grain.

A rabbet, which is an L-shaped cut, can also be accomplished with guide blocks. In this case two single cuts are needed with blade projection adjusted so the two cuts meet to remove the wood which leaves the L-shape. Since, many times, one of these cuts will have to be made with the tool riding a narrow edge, great care is required. It's a good idea when making the edge cut, to clamp a piece of stock to the work so the tool will have greater support than the edge alone could provide.

If you use your tool beyond simple wood cutting you'll find that an assortment of blades will be a great help. Chances are, the blade you get with the machine will be a combination blade which will function adequately for both crosscutting and ripping, but there are special crosscut and rip blades available as well as hollow-ground blades which leave a smooth edge on the work. When special materials must be cut, consult the dealer from whom you purchased the tool for the correct blade to use. He'll have a blade for any material, and you may be able to rent one for that special job rather than buy one for very infrequent use.

Special guides are available for use with the tool in addition to the ripping guide already mentioned. You can get crosscut guides, beveling attachments, even a protractor device which is useful for miter cuts. And if you want to go all out, you can buy a special table which permits you to mount your portable for use as a table saw.

the portable drill

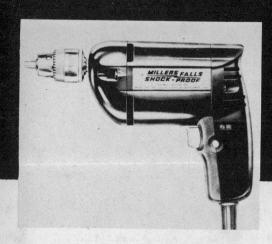

It has developed into a hand-held motorized shop

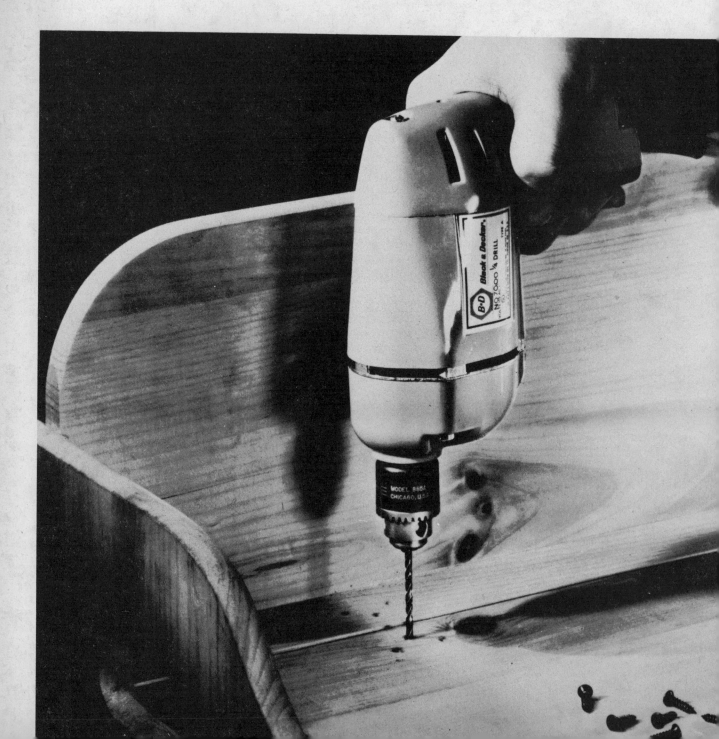

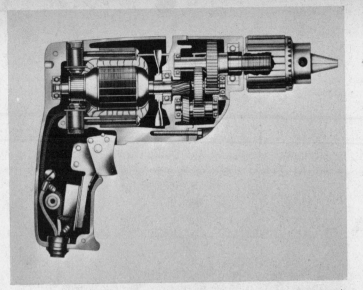

Cutaway view of typical tool shows how electrical energy is converted into rotary mechanical motion. Note built-in fan which cools the motor.

Rockwell ½-inch drill can be preset and locked in any speed, forward or reverse, from 0-700 rpm. Drill and remove screws quickly. Auxiliary handle.

WHY was the portable electric drill invented? For speed and ease in drilling holes—obviously. But today it has developed into a motorized shop you can hold in one hand! It's true. There are so many types available with so many diversified accessories you can add, that this little bundle of power can be exploited to do almost any woodworking operation you can imagine. Sanding, sawing, buffing, polishing, screw-driving, wire brushing, paint mixing—these are just a sample of possible uses. Of course, you may want a drill just to drill holes. Which is fine; even for just this basic use, it will pay off to invest a bit of the "ready" in a good electric hand drill.

Choosing Your Drill

Before you part with your money, spend a little time checking the features of various models. Some drills have a slow rpm and a lot of oomph. Others will turn a cutting tool at great speed. They differ in horsepower. Most are the pistol-grip type. Many have a handle plus provision for an additional projecting bar which can be mounted for applying added feed pressure. Most important are rpms and power. You'll find that speed decreases with increase in power rating, primarily because the stronger units are designed to turn larger cutting tools or to drill in heavy materials and both these factors rule for slower

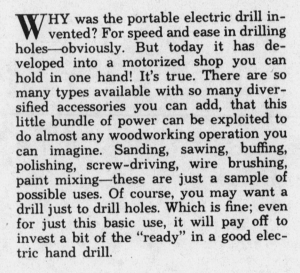

Left, Black & Decker drill performs one of the basic portable drill functions, pre-drilling of screw holes for neat fit, non-splitting of wood, accurate position.

Right, Montgomery Ward ⅜-inch drill can handle metal, wood, masonry, plastic, ceramic materials. It can also sand, polish, drive and remove screws.

speed. Example:—A cutting tool that will drill a large hole through a steel plate at about 400 or 500 rpm would be completely inadequate turning at 2,000 rpm. While a flat blade "bit" would drill through wood at the slower speed, it would produce a much cleaner hole, faster, when operating at the higher speed.

If you are continuously doing heavy work, drilling in masonry or steel, then you'll want to think in terms of a ⅜-inch drill at least; and probably a ½-inch drill would be even better. If the test of your drill will be forming holes in wood and small holes through sheet metal, then a ¼-inch drill will probably be perfectly adequate.

A ¼-hp drill doesn't actually deliver ¼ hp at the tool. It merely means that it takes ¼ hp of electrical energy and uses it as a mechanical force. Between "this" and "that" there are a few losses which considerably reduce the actual power de-

livered at the business end. All of which means that if you want a drill that really *delivers*, its rated hp is very important.

Chances are, unless you have a very specific use for the drill, you'll end up making a compromise with maximum consideration for those jobs you will be doing most frequently. A medium-speed, ⅜-hp drill is a good choice for all around use. If you want to go whole-hog, then buy two; a high-speed, low-horsepower model and a slow-speed, high-horsepower companion. Then you will be set for just about everything.

Another consideration is the chuck on the tool; this is what is used to grip the cutting tool that will be turned by the motor. A *hand* chuck, one which you tighten by hand, is really an economy venture. It will take punishment, but only for simple drilling. If the loads you apply are unbalanced, any bending load at the business end will cause the chuck to run

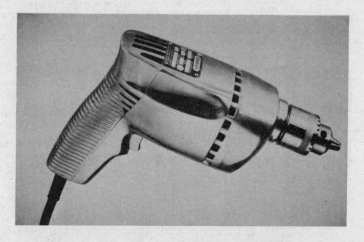

Desired speed is inversely proportional to hardness of material drilled. Bit, left, would drill cleaner hole, faster, in wood at high speed. Stanley's 130 series includes ¼'s, ⅜'s, stand duty and heavy duty, up to a model that turns at 800 rpm and can handle ⅜ inch in steel and 1 inch in wood.

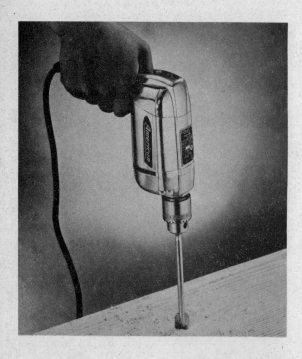

The heavy-duty drill, such as Porter-Cable type shown here, often has an extra "arm," so that additional pressure can be applied to cutter.

Fingertips can twist this ball-bearing chuck to lock tools firmly. Introduced by Sears, Roebuck on Craftsman electric drills of 5/16 to ½ inch.

off so that it will cease to grip firmly or run true. It's perfectly fine for straight-line drilling and if you limit its functions to that, it will last a satisfying time.

An in-between chuck is the *hex-key* chuck and is so called because you use a hexagonal key to tighten the cutting tool in place. It will adequately grip heavier tools and will take some side thrust.

But the real work horse is the *geared* chuck which is operated with a geared key. This will stand up under continual load and takes a lot of abuse. Most quality drills are equipped with this type of chuck.

Using the Tool

Before drilling in any material, even wood, it's a good idea to center-punch the

A good set of power bits like these are, naturally, important. Sizes usually run from ¼ up to 1 inch.

At right, adjustable hole saw. Other accessories drill in masonry, drive screws, even trim hedges.

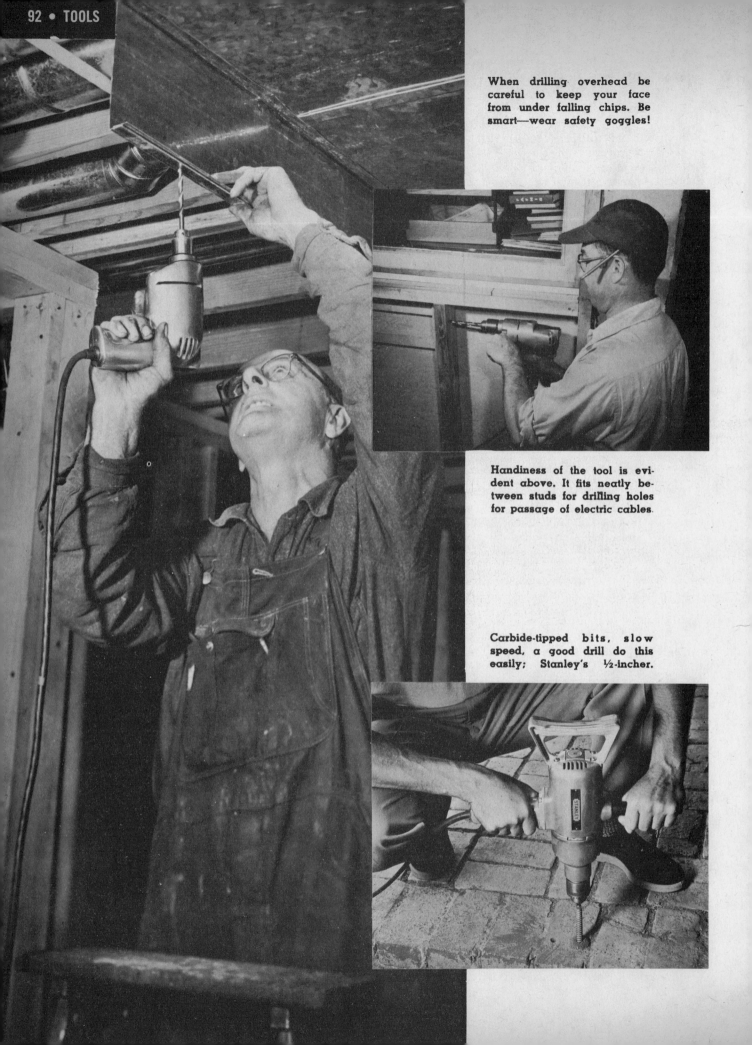

When drilling overhead be careful to keep your face from under falling chips. Be smart—wear safety goggles!

Handiness of the tool is evident above. It fits neatly between studs for drilling holes for passage of electric cables.

Carbide-tipped bits, slow speed, a good drill do this easily; Stanley's ½-incher.

exact location of the hole. This forms a seat for the drill point and assures accuracy. It's especially important in metal since, without the mark, the drill could "walk off" before it begins to bite into the material.

When drilling sheet metal, place the sheet on a flat surface to prevent the pressure you apply from buckling the sheet. Small pieces, wood or metal, should be securely clamped. The drill exerts a twisting force which is most apparent on break-through and this can twist a lightly-held piece of material from your fingers.

Always apply pressure on a line which goes right through the axis of the drill. Keep the drill steady and apply enough pressure to keep the tool cutting. Too much pressure will overload the tool, too little pressure will merely cause the cutting tool to polish instead of cut. This will quickly dull cutting edges. You'll know pressure is correct, when the cutting tool bites continuously and without loading the drill.

Once you've lined up the hole, keep the drill straight. Side pressure or swaying off the line will enlarge the hole and can break small bits. Back up the underside of the hole with some scrap wood to minimize splintering and jagged edges when the drill breaks through.

When drilling large holes, do it in stages, especially if you are using a low-power drill. A pilot hole, in any case, is a good idea, since it serves as a guide for the larger drill and helps to increase accuracy. Above all, keep drills and bits sharp.

There are many items on the market which can make electric drills function more easily. A good example is the combination drill and countersink. This is a special gadget available in various sizes which is perfect for forming holes for flat-head wood screws. The one bit in one operation drills the correct size lead hole, the correct size body hole, both to correct depth, and also provides the countersink that allows the screw to be driven flush with the surface of the wood. Ordinarily, you would have to drill a lead hole, then the body hole and then do the countersinking—and depth of each would be controlled by you. The combination tool makes all operations automatic.

Lubrication is a big help when drilling in heavy metals. Kerosene is good for drilling in steel and some other metals while paraffin is better for soft metals like aluminum and brass. Metal work should always be firmly clamped and the hole started in a center-punch mark. For real accuracy, locate the hole by using intersecting lines. Tap the center punch exactly on the intersection. Drill a pilot hole before forming the actual size hole needed. If the hole is very large, open up the pilot

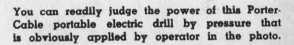

Black and Decker's Scru-Drill, shown here, needs but a turn of the spindle collar to convert from ⅜-inch drill to a positive-clutch screwdriver.

You can readily judge the power of this Porter-Cable portable electric drill by pressure that is obviously applied by operator in the photo.

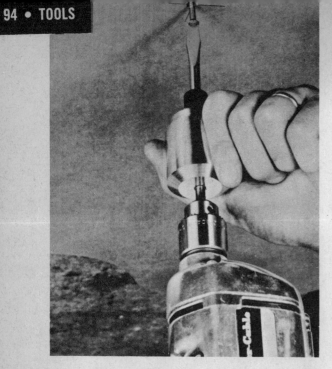

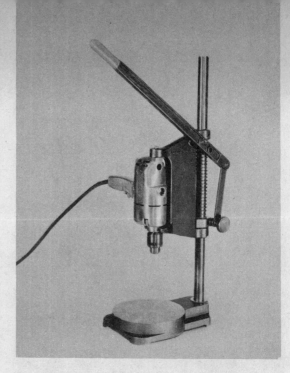

A screwdriver attachment, such as this one, enables you to seat screws easier and faster than you could by hand. For boatbuilders, it's a must.

Among the accessories you can purchase to extend the usefulness of your drill is this special stand that converts it to a kind of drill press.

Why not let the drill polish your car for you? Mount a lamb's-wool pad over flexible rubber disc.

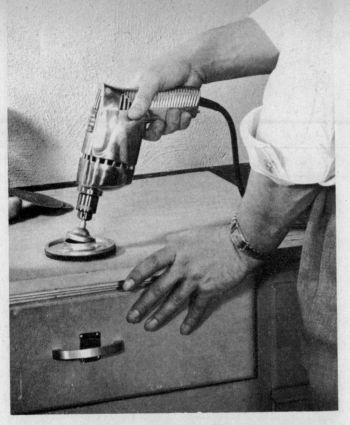

Stanley's "Swirlaway" disc-sanding attachment has a universal swivel which enables the sanding pad to be flat against work surface at any angle.

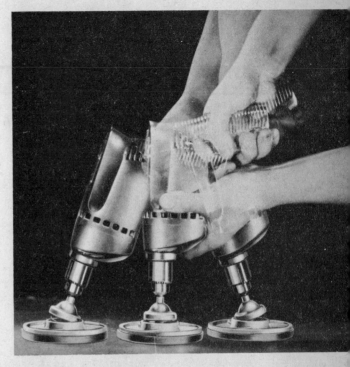

The way the ball-jointed disc sander works is perhaps best demonstrated by this multiexposure. Polishing bonnet over it boosts its usefulness.

hole with an intermediate drill or two. This will help produce cleaner, more accurate holes and will reduce the strain on the electric drill.

Drilling in masonry calls for special carbide-tipped drills. These are available in various sizes and will form holes in cement, cinder blocks, brick, tile and other masonry units. The operation calls for slow speed and good power. Even though the bits will handle the job, using a small, light drill to turn them is just deliberately trying to burn them out. Keep steady pressure on the tool so the bit will be cutting constantly. Just letting it turn in the hole without actually cutting is a sure way to dull the cutting edges quickly. All you do is use them to polish the bottom of the hole.

Accessories

One very handy accessory for a portable drill is a screw-driver attachment. This is a tool which is gripped in the drill chuck and which, in turn, grips the screwdriver bit. This bit is removable so you can turn various sizes and types. The purpose of the attachment goes beyond holding the bit—it slows the turning relative to the force needed to turn the screw. When the screw is firmly seated, the bit stops turning. It's important when using this attachment that you first drill correct-size lead holes and body holes for the screw. In very soft wood it's possible to eliminate the countersinking, for the drill will be strong enough to turn the screw into making its own seat. But if the wood is hard—if you find the drill laboring—then take time to countersink the holes before driving the screws.

A word about other accessories. There is one rule that can be generally applied to all drills. Any tool turned by chuck with pressure application in line with the spindle is a very safe attachment to use. In this area lie tools like small end grinders, drills (of course), files, plug cutters, hole saws. Any cutting tool which does not extend too far out (a large fly cutter, for example) so as to make a bending force possible, won't hurt the drill.

Side thrust or pressure applied to a light drill spindle isn't the best thing in the world for it. •

the sander

It is the real work horse of portable power tools

Work through progressively finer abrasives with the belt sander for a really glass-smooth finish.

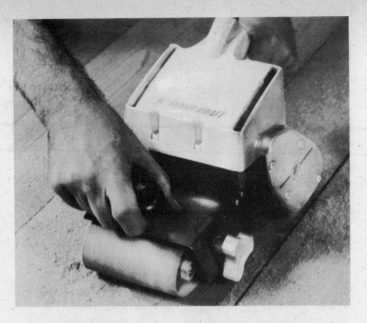

4-inch belt sander from Wards tackles heavy-duty sanding jobs. It can sand flush to vertical and horizontal surfaces. 8-amp motor develops up to 1 HP.

Stanley Electric Tool's 3-inch portable belt sander is a heavy-duty machine. Its 3 x 24-inch belt provides plenty sanding surface for most any job.

POWER SANDING has brought great finishing within the reach of any craftsman. There are wonderful finishing materials on the market these days, though none will compensate for an improperly prepared surface. This is an area where a good many craftsmen fall down. It's not neglect, not really. Most of us honestly intend to do the final chores of a project correctly. But a few hours of hand sanding soon blind you to surfaces that require further attention. But power sanders, especially the **kind** you can hold in your hand and apply to the work, bless them, can minimize time and effort and produce a surface as it should be for maximum effect.

Now you can take down the roughest surface, smooth it, and further smooth it between coats of the finishing material. With today's sanders you can even buff and polish the final coat to produce a hand-rubbed effect that used to be, literally, a hand-rubbed effect. Even if you can't own a power sander, you can rent one so there is no longer any reason not to have the kind of finish a well-executed project deserves.

Belt sanders are the work horses in this group of power tools. Like the stationary models, they employ an endless belt which turns over two drums, one powered the other idle. Since the belt runs in a straight line, you can sand in grain direction which always produces the smoothest surfaces.

Most popular size is 3 inches, although belt size also includes the belt length. The 3 inches indicate the width of the belt.

The machines are designed to simplify belt changing and this procedure usually involves depressing the forward drum, slipping off the old belt and putting on the new, thus releasing the forward drum so it pulls the belt taut. The only other adjustment is the turning of the screw which keeps the belt "tracking," that is, maintaining its alignment with the drums.

Using the Sander

It's almost always good practice to switch on the machine *before* you make contact with the work. Your hands should be firm on the tool. If you were to rest the machine lightly on the work, it would travel on its own, using the abrasive belt like a tractor tread. To make contact with the work, lower the tool slowly while holding it firmly. One procedure is to make contact with the rear of the belt first, or to rest the tool on the back edge of its housing and then tilt it forward until it rests horizontally. Many professionals just bring it right down. It's best to use the former method until you are thoroughly accustomed to the feel of the working tool in your hands. Once complete contact is made it's a question of moving the machine around so it can do its job. One positive rule: Don't allow the machine to rest in

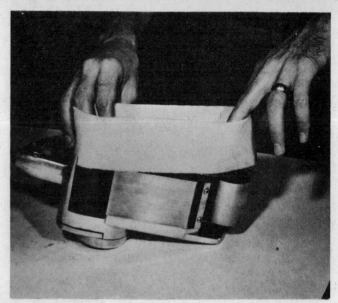

Replacing or changing belts on the belt sander is easily accomplished. Pressing down on forward drum causes it to catch in retracted position. Be sure arrow on belt back points in direction of rotation. Belt "tracking" is adjusted with screw on side of machine. Do this while belt is running.

one place; keep it moving continuously. If you must stop for one reason or another, lift it from the job. An abrasive belt removes material fast and if you keep it in one spot, it will surely create a depression.

When you are going to remove a lot of wood, work the machine cross-grain to start. Then as you approach the finish you want, bring the tool back into line with the grain of the wood. The same rule applies to portable-sander work as to any other abrasive chore. Start with heavier grits of paper and work through progressively finer grits until you have achieved the desired finish. When removing old paint use a cheaper grade of paper and one with an open grain. In fact all the rules concerning types of abrasives and uses for

abrasives outlined in the Belt and Disc Sander chapter apply here as well.

When working on very broad surfaces, you can sand quite fast by holding the tool diagonally across the grain of the wood but moving it parallel to the grain. This has the effect of working cross grain but allows you to move in a straight line.

Be extremely careful when sanding a surface veneer as on plywood. These veneers are usually quite thin and excessive sanding can work right through them, ruining the panel. In fact it's a good idea when sanding any plywood, to limit the machine to very fine abrasive belts and to limit the sanding. Take care of the panels as you work and you won't have to rely on sanding to smooth them or to remove work

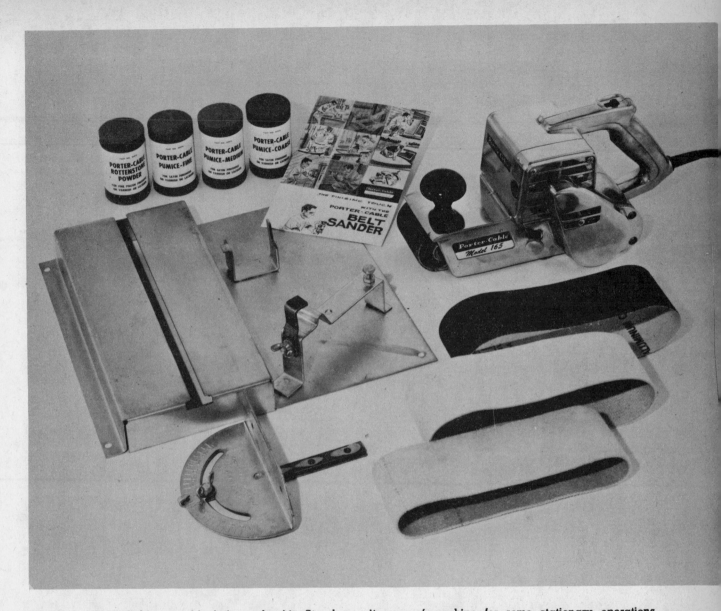

Porter-Cable portable belt sander kit. Stand permits use of machine for some stationary operations.

marks. This is a rule that applies to craftsmanship generally. It's best to regard all sanders as finishing tools. Do your construction work as if sanders didn't exist and you minimize the amount of sanding you have to do.

When sanding vertical surfaces, hold the machine at such an angle that you can see the right edge of the belt. Stand so you won't get the dust in your face. Don't work so long that you become fatigued. Even though portable belt sanders designed for use by home craftsmen are light enough for easy handling, you can tire quite quickly when you must support the machine with your arms extended.

There are many other uses for your portable belt sander besides smoothing

Contact work first with rear of belt. On full contact, keep tool moving—parallel to grain for smoothest finish, cross for fastest stock removal.

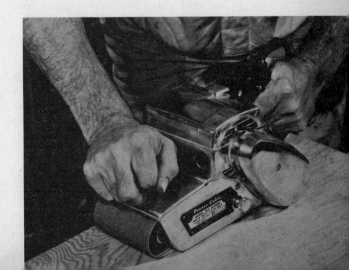

Seen here is the Stanley orbital pad sander. It "orbits" 4500 times per minute. For an abrasive it uses half of a standard sheet of sandpaper.

Rockwell finishing sander delivers 4,500 orbits per minute with 2.3 amp motor. Uses ⅓ standard sandpaper sheet. Flush sides get you into all corners.

Orbital sanders are for final finishing, with or across the grain. Pressure you apply should be sufficient to keep abrasive particles of pad cutting.

These sanders get into tight places, eliminate need for final smoothing before assembly. Front knob comes off for work against vertical surface.

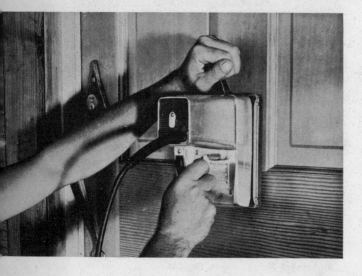

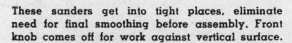

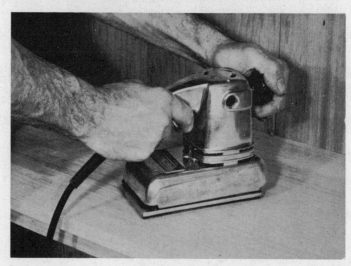

wood. You can smooth down rough spots on concrete by using a No. 3½ belt. Work the tool in all directions until the area is smooth. For removing rust or to sharpen garden tools, fit the machine with a No. 1 belt and lock the tool in a vise. If you are removing rust, first coat the tool with kerosene or a light oil. If you are sharpening the tool, tilt the sander to create the edge and use light strokes to prevent burning the metal and/or tearing the belt.

To get particularly smooth, satin finishes on projects, you can equip the belt sander with a canvas belt and use it with different grades of powdered pumice between applications of the finishing material. A common procedure is to mix paraffin oil with kerosene (one part oil to two of kerosene) and to apply it to the surface with a brush. Mix the pumice with enough oil to make a paste and spread this over the project surface. Then use the canvas-belt-equipped belt sander to rub the surface until it is smooth and finely polished. Don't use very heavy pressure during this operation and keep the machine moving constantly. When the surface is smooth to your satisfaction, wipe it clean. Be sure to clean

In working outside, be sure cord is heavy enough. Minimum gauge should be No. 14; No. 12 is even better.

the machine thoroughly after a job like this.

Pad Sanders

Pad sanders (or finishing sanders as they are often called) do a great job of smoothing surfaces but don't work as fast or remove as much material as the belt sanders. Actually it isn't their purpose, although with heavy paper they aren't to be scorned in this area. However, it's safe to say, they are the sanders to rely on for super-smooth surfaces. If you owned both a belt sander and a pad sander, you would soon be using the belt sander for rough, preliminary work, and the pad sander for the final touches.

An *orbital* sander is so named because of the action of the pad. The pad moves in a tiny orbit with a motion that is hardly discernible, so that it actually sands in all directions. This motion is so small and so fast that, with the fine paper mounted, you would need a microscope to see any cross-grain scratches. The pad, around which the abrasive sheet is wrapped, usually extends beyond the frame of the machine so it's possible to work in tight corners and against vertical surfaces—a handy feature.

The sheets of paper it uses are not too large which is an economy; many operators cut standard sheets of sandpaper for use on these machines. Manufacturers size them so this can be done without waste. It's very important that you pull the abrasive sheets tightly across the pad when mounting them; otherwise the action will not be transferred to the abrasive and the pad will be moving inside the sheet without accomplishing anything.

You must exert just enough pressure on these tools to keep the sandpaper cutting. Too much pressure will slow the action and reduce the smoothness of the finish. Too little pressure and the machine will hardly work at all.

One trick to use before the very final passes with the pad sander, is to pass a damp cloth over the surface of the wood. All you want is to "raise" the grain and just a little moisture will do this. Allow the wood to dry or help it along artificially with a photoflood or similar item. Then do the final sanding moving the machine in

In sanding similar edges, clamp them together and work on them simultaneously. You can do several at once—and gain added support for tool.

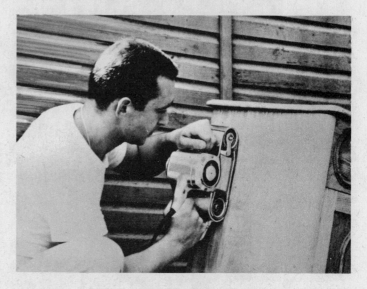

Taking your project into the great outdoors is one way to prevent sanding dust from covering the remainder of the equipment in your workshop.

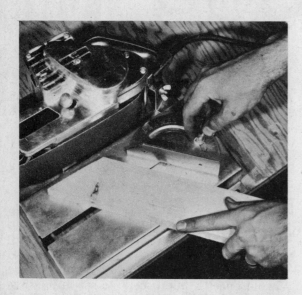

Porter-Cable 165 in its stand. The simple miter gauge, being set by operator, is helpful when you're squaring stock ends, truing miter cuts.

With the correct abrasive tool installed in your belt sander, you can use it to sharpen chisels and similar tools, as demonstrated in this photo.

the grain direction. The result will be glass-smooth.

Disc sanders are like portable drills with an abrasive disc attached. Regardless of how you apply them to the work, they are constantly cutting across the grain. Only high speed and extremely fine paper will produce a really smooth surface. To a great extent this is related to the backing used for the abrasive disc; the harder the backing, the coarser the cut.

Usually, the perimeter of the disc is kept in contact with the work and is moved constantly. If you placed the disc flat on the work and held it in one place you would discover a dead spot at the center. A closer examination would reveal just a series of concentric circles formed by the abrasive particles on the sanding disc.

Constant motion of the tool causes the cuts made by individual abrasive particles to criss-cross and overlap and this results in a smoothing action.

Study the accompanying photographs carefully. It will help you to get top mileage from this portable work horse.

You can clean or sharpen garden equipment with the machine. To remove rust, first coat metal with kerosene. Clean sander afterward.

You can handle vertical surfaces this way, but take a break frequently. Don't reach so high that it forces you to stand right below sander.

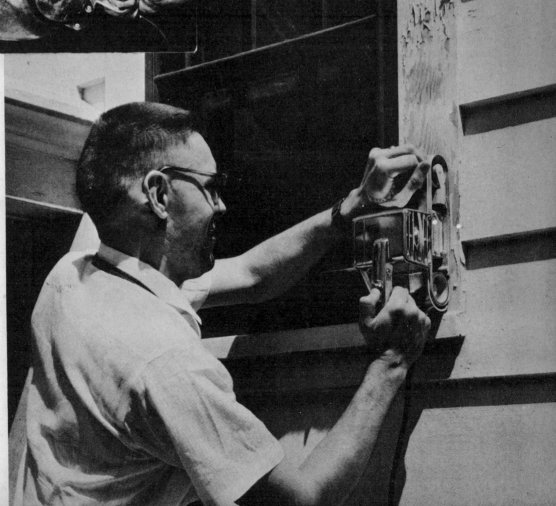

the router

It is extremely versatile, a wise buy for most

Here the router trims edge of plastic-lamination counter top. Light and easily handled, this tool of many uses has a fascination much like the lathe's, can add pro decorative touches to any project.

MOST of us regard the router as a kind of portable shaper, but this flexible tool is much, much more than that. It's a very versatile tool, capable of hundreds of woodworking operations that can add decorative professional touches to any woodworking project. But in addition, it can help in dozens of practical ways.

Because it is essentially a high-speed machine (22,000 rpm idling speed is not uncommon) it produces extremely smooth machined surfaces which require no further attention. Despite its smoothness and power it is a lightweight machine (or should be) and easily handled. Available accessories include template guides for special cuts as well as special tools which utilize the power and speed of the router to do power planing, spindle shaping, hinge mortising and dovetailing just to name a few.

The router, even in its simple cuts, has a special kind of fascination not unlike that associated with shaping and lathe turning. You apply the tool to the work and miraculously a square sterile edge acquires an intricate and super-smooth contour. Even complicated inlay work, where you must incise a surface preparatory to gluing down fancy inlays, becomes pleasantly simple. Dovetails which are tedious and tough to do accurately by hand become routine so you can up-grade the quality of your craftsmanship and projects. There's little doubt that the router is an all-around tool; money invested here is well spent.

Construction and Use

All routers are basically the same. They consist of an enclosed power unit (115-volt, universal motor) and a base. The outside of the motor housing and the inside of the base are threaded so that by turning the base up or down on the housing, you adjust for depth of cut. A thumb-screw-type clamping arrangement locks the two units together after depth-of-cut adjustment. The chuck on the routers intended for the home craftsman has a capacity of ¼ inch and is wrench-tightened. When the manufacturer says use the wrench to secure cutting tools in the chuck, he means it.

Simple cutting is just a matter of securing the cutting tool in the chuck, adjusting for the correct depth of cut and moving the tool along the work. Shaped router bits are designed with an extending central pilot which rides the uncut portion of the edge being shaped and controls the width of the cut. Router bases are designed to take guides so that if you want to rout a groove or a dado parallel to an edge, you can lock in a special accessory which controls edge distance through the operation.

We repeat this for all tools, but it's important—the quality of the cut you make *and* the "health" of the tool depends on your realizing that cutters are designed to remove just so much material. When you feel or hear the motor begin to slow or stall, when you see the wood begin to dis-

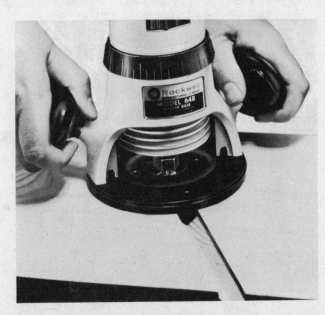

Rockwell double insulated ½ HP router delivers 28,000 rpm speed for super smooth cutting. Full ball bearing construction and breakproof housing.

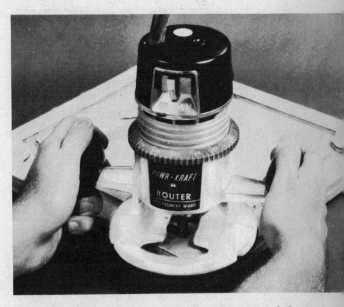

Powerful 1 HP router from Montgomery Ward does beading, inlaying, makes rabbet and dado cuts on all woods and plastics. Accurate depth adjustment.

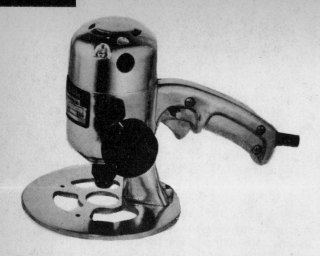

The Routo-Jig, made by Porter-Cable, is in reality, a multipurpose tool. Here it appears as a router.

When set up as shown in this photo, Routo-Jig serves as jig saw. This is maker's model 140.

With special table, the same tool is converted into a spindle shaper, as is demonstrated here.

When the special accessory pictured here is added, the versatile Routo-Jig becomes a sanding tool.

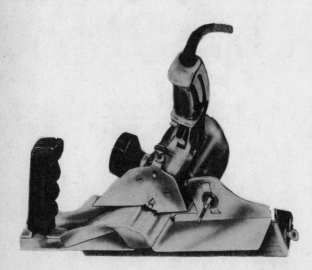

Also available is this planing attachment for the Routo-Jig. It is sometimes wise to buy the basic accessories for your router in kit form.

Basic power unit is in router category, but can be many tools. Sears, Roebuck offers some 49 accessories to extend versatility of basic unit.

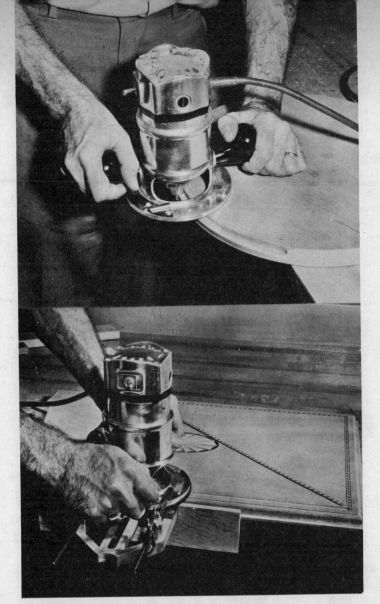

Curved or straight edges, the router handles them all. In use in this photograph is Black and Decker's ¾-horsepower model.

Beautiful, intricate inlays are possible with this tool. Note block that makes possible use of straight gauge on shaped edge.

color, you know that you are forcing the cut. The control you have is the pressure you apply to the tool. When that pressure is correct, the tool will hum along smoothly. When it's excessive, the tool will react accordingly. It's something you see and feel. Feed pressure must be adjusted according to the density of the wood and the amount of material you are removing (depth of cut). A light cut in hardwood can be done faster than a heavy cut in hardwood. A heavy cut in soft wood is easier to do than a heavy cut in hardwood. It's that simple. If you are routing deep grooves and the motor slows and/or the sides of the cut show burn marks, then reduce the depth of cut and do the operation in two passes. Remember this for all router operations, whether you are working with a simple cutter on the router or with an accessory tool.

Direction of feed should be opposite the direction of the motor. To understand the reasoning behind this merely try this simple experiment. Make a cut on the edge of a piece of stock—first in one direction and then in the opposite direction. You'll be able to judge by the cut and by the feel of the router which direction is best—and it will be opposite the direction of the cutting tool's rotation. If you move the tool along with the turning of the cutter, the cutter will tend to "walk" as well as cut.

Grooves and Dadoes

Grooves and dadoes are best done with a guide. Most routers come equipped with an accessory that will control edge distance and this should be used where edge distance permits. If the cut is too far from the stock's edge for the guide to be usable, then clamp a straight board to the work and allow it to be the guide. Do this whether you are cutting with the grain (grooves) or across the grain (dadoes). If a "stopped" dado is called for (one that does not extend the full width of the work), make a pencil mark where the dado is to end. If the project calls for a series of such dadoes, then clamp a block across the

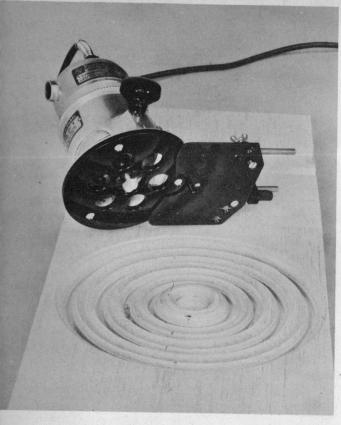

Here's a photo to gladden the hearts of meticulous craftsmen. A special guide permits precise circular travel of router to make such fancy cuts.

Router mounted with special sharpening attachment to keep cutting tools keen. Even plywood edges cut smoothly with router and sharp bits.

Use a clamped board as straightedge for cutting dadoes, as shown. If a "stopped" dado is called for, make a pencil mark where dado is to end.

There are few cutting tools available today that could make such a cut as this one in a plastic surface and leave an edge that's 100% unscarred.

work which will act as a stop and automatically control the length of each cut.

Cutting a groove in an edge calls for special care since a narrow edge does not supply much support for the router. Your best bet here is to clamp extra pieces along the edge which provide a wider base for the router to sit on. Another way, if possible, would be to clamp the work to a bench or table with the top edge flush. This then does the job of providing needed support.

For perfect circular grooves, you can use a special jig, or improvise with a length of dowel. Insert the dowel in one of the holes used for the straight gauge and lock it in place. At a suitable distance from the center of the router, drive a small nail through the dowel and into the center of the circular groove. You then merely rotate the router around that pivot point.

For circular grooves which are parallel to a circular edge, you use the straight gauge. The gauge is reversible, having one V-shaped side which can ride a curved edge.

Freehand use of the router can provide script lettering for name plates and plaques. The secret is to move the cutter slowly and to be especially careful when moving cross-grain for it will be especially easy here to move off the cutting line. A similar technique is used for recessing or carving. When the outline of the figure is drawn on the wood, the router is used to remove the material around it.

You can use templates to make exactly matching duplicate cuts or parts. This is especially useful when you are cutting your own part for inlay in another piece. Both the inlay and the recess that will receive it must be perfect. One way to do this is to make a pattern of the shape (template), using either plywood or tempered Masonite. You can cut this by hand and depend on sanding to perfect it, or you can rely on your skill with the router by making depth of cut just slightly more than the thickness of the material. A special template guide which is attached to the router base in combination with the pattern, then assures that recess and inlay will be identical. What a break to be able to do duplicate work in such fashion; knowing that each part you cut will be an exact duplicate of the pattern!

These are just a few, a very few of the jobs possible with a good router. Accompanying photos show some others. •

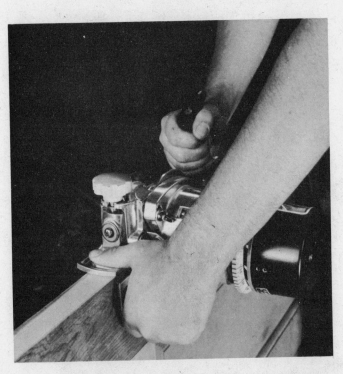

Portable router, used with plane attachment as in this photograph, makes quick work of reducing door dimensions and leaves slick, square edges.

One rule in using the high-speed router is to keep its base perfectly flat on the surface of the work. Tilting into work results in gouge.

the saber saw

Actually a portable jig saw, it is capable of fairly heavy duty

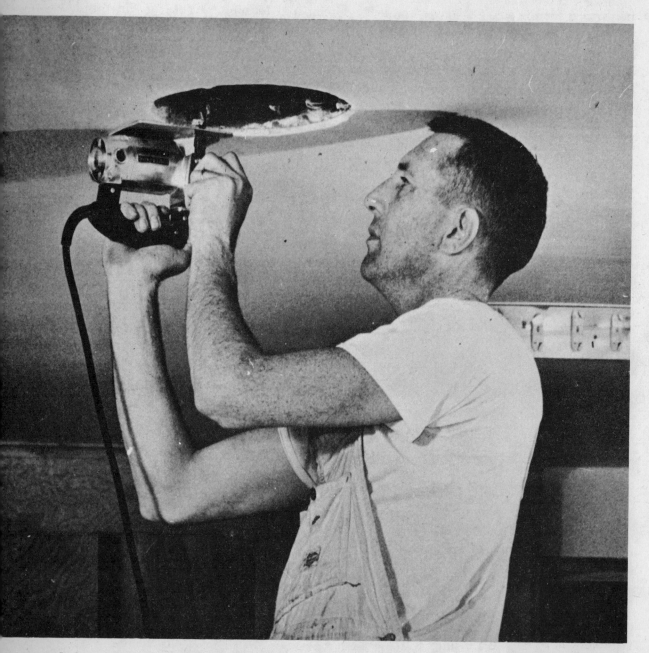

Light weight of the machine makes this an easy task. In cutting overhead, keep eyes from under tool.

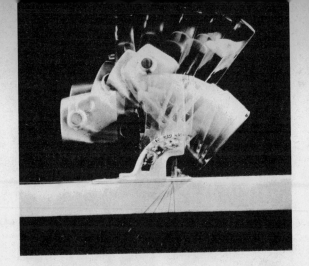

Disston's multi-exposure effectively demonstrates the capacity and tilting action of saber saw.

The Stanley saber saw enables you to cut flush against a perpendicular, as shown in this photo.

HAVEN'T you often wished you could pick up a jig saw and apply it to a job? Or longed for an electric tool that would allow you to be less dependent on a keyhole saw? That's exactly what a saber saw lets you do. Actually it's a portable jig saw that will let you cut smooth and decorative curves, yet is powerful enough to do some fairly heavy-duty work. Unlike the stationary jig saw, it is a self-contained unit without a limiting arm and can be used on any size stock.

The important thing to learn about a saber saw, and this seems to be true of all powered tools, is that the cut should never be forced. The saber saw is not designed for extremely fast cutting, and any forcing you do to try to speed up the operation will only result in blade breakage. When you start the cut, rest the forward edge of the shoe on the work, line up the blade with the cut mark, turn on the switch and then approach the stock to make contact.

This type of tool, especially when heavier blades are used is not the smoothest cutting tool in the world. The smaller the teeth on the blade, the smoother the cut will be. Since the blade cuts on the "up" stroke the good side of the material should be down. Some tricks used to get smoother cuts, especially on plywoods, are to use transparent tape over the cut line, or to coat the wood with shellac. Both these techniques tend to hold together the wood fibers to help prevent splintering and tearing as the saw blade works.

The best way for you to learn the handling of this type of tool is to actually cut with it. Clamp down a piece of scrap plywood and draw some lines to follow, curved ones as well as straight ones. You'll develop your own way of gripping the tool, and this will be affected somewhat by the particular tool you are using. On some tools, for example, you'll find guiding

easier if you apply some downward pressure on the tool as you move it forward. You'll find that if you are not firm with your grip the tool might tend to vibrate excessively and this will tend to roughen the cut. You'll definitely find that the saw won't cooperate if you force it to cut more than the blade is designed to take. All you'll do is break saw blades, as we said. If it happens don't blame the tool.

Like the jig saw, one of the features of the saber saw is its ability to do "piercing." This is the business of making internal cut-outs in a piece of stock or plywood without a lead-in cut from any edge. Not only will it accomplish this but you can even eliminate the insertion hole for the saber saw can pierce through the material on its own. This is simply a matter of resting the tool in a tilted position on the forward edge of the shoe, then lowering it slowly until contact with the work is made. Hold the tool firmly and start the cut slowly until the blade goes through and the tool rests solidly on its shoe. Of course, you *can* drill a blade insertion hole if you want to. In some cases, where the cut-off may have round corners, it might pay to drill holes at each corner, not just to let the blade through but actually to form the corner.

The saber saw is such a flexible machine that it would take a whole book to describe all its uses. Not only will it do the intricate cutting of the jig saw to produce decorative scroll work and fancy curved edges, but it is husky enough so that many contractors and electricians and plumbers include one in their kit of tools for making cut-outs for pipes, electrical cables, stud notching and flooring cut-outs for duct inserts. Special blades let you cut metal. Thin metal sheets should be sandwiched between layers of scrap plywood. This will produce smoother, less jagged edges. Metal cutting will be easier if a stick of beeswax is rubbed on

Saber saw shows its muscle in slicing a 2 x 4. As with other power tools, never force the cut.

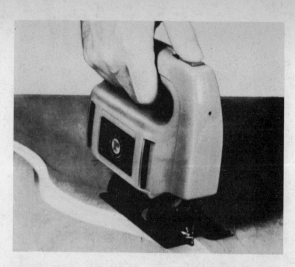

Rockwell saber or jig saw offers variable speeds from 900 to 2,900 strokes per minute. Base tilts.

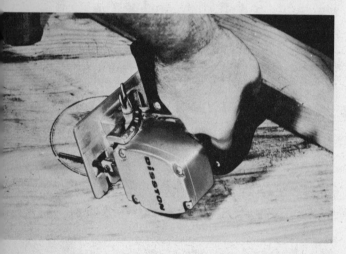

Starting plunge cut for pipe hole. Tip of blade makes contact. Lift saw back slowly to deepen cut.

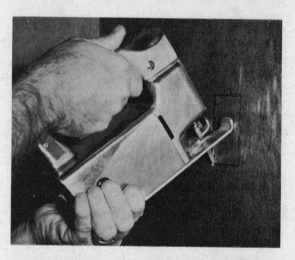

Plunge cutting for electrical switch. Starting cut in this manner assures you of square corner.

Ripping guide lets you cut long, straight pieces. This model is Wen Products' heavy-duty 909.

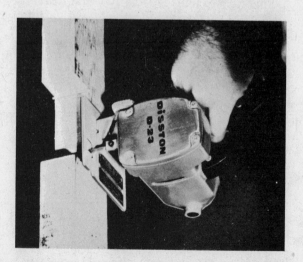

Notch 2 x 4 stud in 3 cuts (previously marked). Make parallel cuts first; third removes stock.

the blade of your saber saw before cutting.

Guides can be helpful for straight cutting. Like the electric cut-off saw, the saber usually comes equipped with a ripping guide. If this can't be used to guide the tool on some operations (ripping down the center of a large panel) substitute a straight piece of wood clamped to the work. The shoe of the tool will ride against the guide to keep the cut straight.

Some manufacturers have designed the machine's shoe so it will take a special insert to minimize the opening around the blade. This is especially useful on plywood cutting because it comes down decidedly on splintering and produces a smoother cut.

Another helpful accessory for this saw is a small table to which the saber saw can be attached for use as a table model jig saw. However, since the tool's blades are gripped at one end only, they must be large enough to have rigidity which precludes blades fine enough to duplicate the very intricate cuts a table-model jig saw can perform. •

A fun tool for the whole family! Saber-saw kits usually include accessory shoe for tilting, small "table," special insert, ripping guide and several blades. Blade changing can be done in seconds.

Tools and Materials

Hand tools should be stored in a cabinet of this type to make them instantly available. Leaving tools lying about on workbenches will result in dulling many of the fine cutting edges.

Before attempting a carpentry project, be sure you know how to handle tools and how to select materials for the job

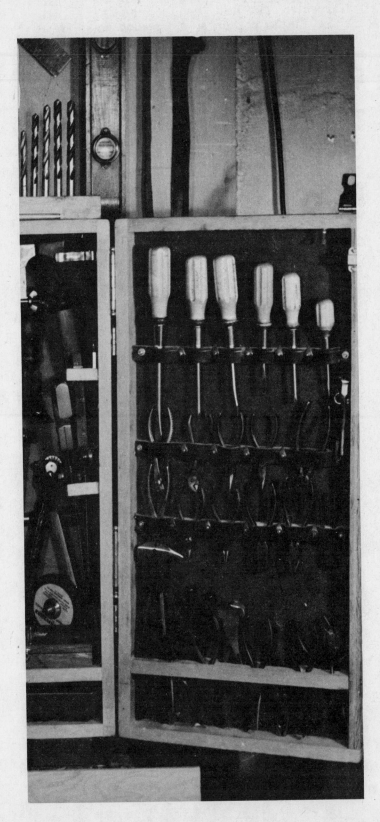

FOR GOOD WORK to be done quickly, it is necessary to have good tools and the right material for each purpose. This is especially true for a new carpenter. Ordinarily on the rough work for a new house the tool box should have at least a hammer, a rip saw, cross cut saw, 24 inch level, square, six foot folding rule, wrecking bar and a steel tape. Finish work will require a few more, a nail set, adjustable bevel square, a small adjustable and combination square, brace and bits, a short block plane and especially a miter saw to make angle cuts exactly correct. If electric power is available, a power saw is a necessity for both rough and finish work. These last are against union regulations in some localities. Other forms of carpentry work like bridges or form work require a few other special tools which can be purchased later but the above are always required.

Hammer: The correct use of this tool is almost entirely a matter of physical skill. The most important factor is to be able to hit the nail on the head with a strong stroke every time. In rough work like the subfloor or frame work of a building a few hammer marks are not important, but on inside or outside finish, carpenters are careful not to miss. A workman not accustomed to swinging a hammer, unconsciously grasps the handle only a few inches from the head instead of back on the handle where the head will have a good swing. A good carpenter can drive a 6d (penny) nail with a tap and two strokes. While making the two strokes with the right arm, the left hand should be bringing a second nail from the pocket to its proper position. A man with a strong arm ought to learn to hit the nail in a few hours of practice but if the swing muscles must be developed it will require several minutes each day for several weeks. The apprentice should also learn to drive nails at knee level, above the head, on the left side of the body and overhead in the ceiling. The apprentice should make it a habit to never lay the hammer down. Always hang it in the strap on the leg of the carpenter trousers. Otherwise, in actual construction much valuable time is lost either going for the hammer or hunting for it.

Crosscut hand saw: Outside of the square this is probably the most difficult tool to handle properly in the carpenter's chest. Saws are divided into classes by the number of teeth to the inch. A saw for coarse work is usually a No. 7 or 8 point, meaning 7 or 8 teeth to the inch. It will cut fast and comparatively wide with a tendency to tear the wood on the under side. A saw with 9 or 10 teeth to the inch is called a finish saw. It cuts slower, smoother, and the cut is narrow. A 12 point is still finer and is called a panel saw.

How to saw to a line: On a large stick, like a 6x6 or larger, most carpenters square and mark across the top, down the front and the far side. Smaller pieces like 2x12's are marked on the top and usually on the near side. Three-quarter inch stuff is only marked across the top. The most important factor in the cutting is to stay on these lines. All that this requires is to keep the back of the saw and the teeth in line with both the vertical and horizontal lines on the board being sawed, which does not change

the fact that even the best of carpenters run off the lines occasionally.

Carpenters cut into the stick half an inch on the far corner, stop a second and line up the saw, cut a couple of inches more and line up again. On a large, important piece they may line up the saw six or eight times. On sheeting they line up as the saw cuts. With such a procedure carpenters are frequently off the line and it is necessary to bring the saw back. Usually the lumber lays fairly level and the saw must be held vertical during the stroke. For a beginner this is awkward. The natural position for the hand to assume is not vertical but slanting with the thumb turned toward the body and the cut will have a similar slant. The top of the cut may be on the line and straight but the bottom of the cut will be outside of the vertical line. This is especially noticeable when the novice tries to cut a thick piece, like a 4x4.

A is a wooden mallet; B—lightweight plastic-tipped type; C—hard-faced plastic hammer with leaded head; D—heavy rubber-tipped hammer; E—light peening type; F—lather's half-hatchet; G—two-faced peening hammer; all are designed for a specific job.

Hammers 1 and 3 are the claw type; 2 is a machinist's hammer; 3 is termed a ripping tool because of straight jaws.

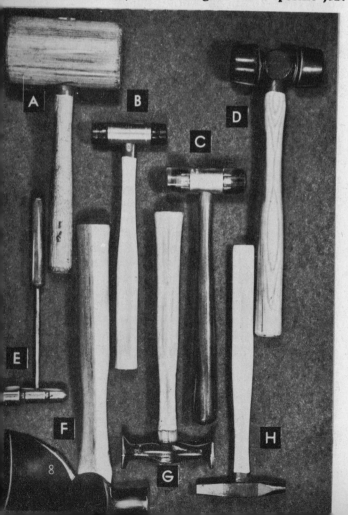

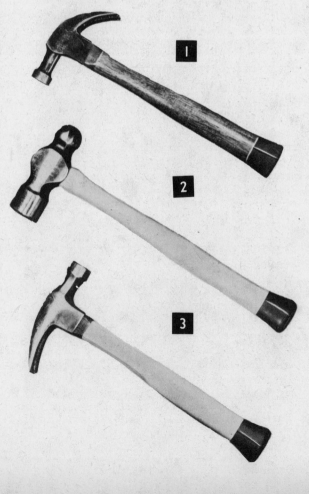

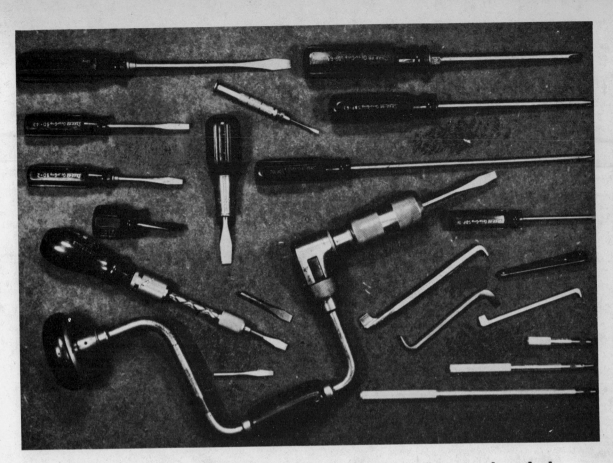

Largest tool is a hand brace; above it, a push-pull screwdriver; top left, several standard screwdrivers; lower right, screw starters; above them, offset screwdrivers; top right, Phillips-head screwdrivers. All of them are useful and some are indispensable to the handy man.

The stroke of the saw as it is shoved away from the body (the cutting stroke) must also be in line with the horizontal line on the board or square across the stick. The natural stroke of the arm is not straight forward but from the shoulder slantways to a line in front of the center of the body and the tendency of the saw is to have this same slantwise cut. To overcome this, carpenters place the cutting line even with the shoulder and not even with the center of the body so that the feet are well to the left of the cut. Another thing a novice is apt to do is to swing his stroke. That is, the hand on the cutting stroke instead of going straight toward the line, starts toward the center of the body and then straightens so the hand makes a small arc on each stroke.

If the saw is sharpened or filed so the teeth are a little longer on one side than on the other this will make the saw run off the line even with experienced carpenters. In this case, have it fixed if you have to hire it done.

The teeth of all crosscut saws have a set or a flare so the width of the saw across the teeth is wider than the back of the blade. This allows the back of the saw a little play sideways in the cut, and a carpenter by twisting the handle and the blade during the cutting stroke can steer the cut to a considerable extent. Thus if the cut is running outside of the *vertical* line or to the right, twist the back of the saw hard against the outside of the cut which will force the teeth back toward the line. If the saw is running outside of the *horizontal* line start the stroke with the hand more toward the center of the body even if it bends the saw a little. Both of these movements can be emphasized by stepping back a step from the work and leveling the saw. The back teeth of the saw can then be practically set on the line for the cutting strokes. Occasionally a carpenter may suddenly realize he will be away off on the *vertical* line and will turn the plank over and make a few strokes with the plank upside down, pulling the cut back to position as much as possible. When the plank is turned back the saw will follow the bottom cut until it begins to cut new wood. The best method is not to get off the line in the first place. Another trick the carpenters

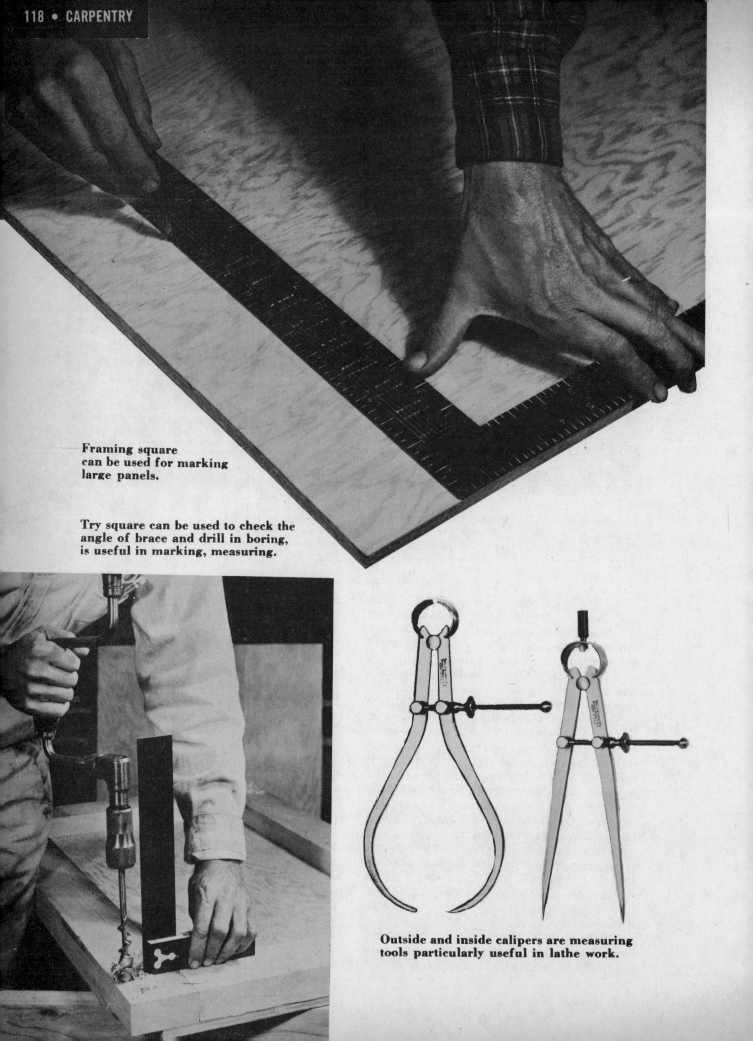

Framing square
can be used for marking
large panels.

Try square can be used to check the
angle of brace and drill in boring,
is useful in marking, measuring.

Outside and inside calipers are measuring
tools particularly useful in lathe work.

use to get back on the line is to twist the saw and the stroke without cutting any deeper. Thus, the cut is widened and they saw themselves back to the line with the side or set of the teeth.

Some carpenters can cut a 2x12 to within a 16th of an inch of square both ways time after time without any lines at all. It takes practice.

Rule and tape: Every carpenter must carry a six-foot folding rule and a carpenter's pencil and many have a 50-foot steel tape. A beginner must even learn to measure. Give the ordinary person a two-foot rule to measure off exactly 16 feet and the chances are he will have 16 feet and half an inch or more. This is because the pencil will make the mark at least $\frac{1}{16}$ of an inch beyond the end of the rule and the workman does not allow for this when the rule is laid down the next time. In fact, it is difficult for anyone to measure exactly with a short rule so most carpenters carry the long folding six-foot rule. There are two forms, one reading 24, 25, 26 inches and so on and the other reading 2 feet, 1 inch, 2 inches, 3 inches and so on. The last are often misread. A very common error is to read 4 feet 11 inches as 5 feet 11 inches because the large red or black 5 is directly beneath the eyes. Carpenters usually prefer the straight reading rules and speak of a measurement as 34 inches and not 2 feet

10 inches or 56 inches instead of 4 feet 8 inches. For longer measurements with a 6-foot rule carpenters will say 6 feet and 33 inches instead of 8 feet 9 inches. It saves the mental calculation and the possibility of an error.

Steel tapes, however, are made and read as feet and inches. Measurements are taken from inside of the ring.

Do not let the mind wander when measuring. Measure accurately where the piece is to go and measure the piece carefully and mark it. Then stop and think a moment what has been done so as to be positive that everything is right.

Planes: See the illustrations regarding planes in this chapter.

Levels: These may be aluminum, iron or wood in various lengths, but the 24-inch wood level and plumb with adjustable bulbs is as good as any. The level is a simple and very efficient tool to indicate plumb and level surfaces.

Sometimes through rough usage one of the glass bulbs in a level will shift and the level is useless until the bulb has been re-adjusted.

If there is any doubt about a level, test it at once by laying it on a timber or the floor and note the position of the bubble. Then turn it end for end and again note its position. If the bubble is right, *both* readings will be the same. If the level is out of ad-

Top to bottom: a framing square; a combination square with three heads; under that a sliding T-head for locating angles; at bottom left, a four-square for measuring 90° and 45° angles; a try square.

Top left is a zig-zag extension rule; then a two-foot folding rule; top right, a caliper rule; also shown are sliding steel tapes, various small rules, marking gauges, dividers and scribers.

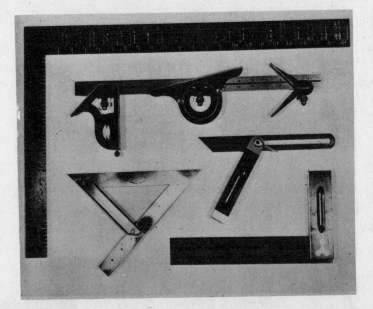

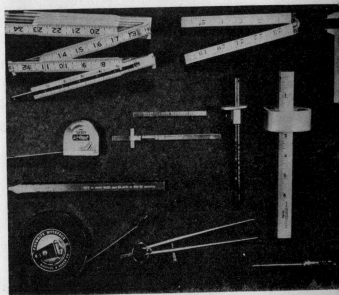

Nail size	Length in inches	Wire gauge size	Approx. No. per lb.	Where Used
3d	1½	14	568	Shingles, lath, ⅜ battens.
4d	1½	12½	316	Shingles, lath, ⅜ battens.
6d	2	11½	181	¾" forms and temporary work.
8d	2½	10¼	106	Sheeting, sub-floors, roofs, etc.
10d	3	9	69	Same as above.
12d	3¼	9	63	Not used a great deal.
16d	3½	8	49	Studding, rafters and other 2x4's and 2x6's.
20d	4	6	31	Plank flooring, etc.
30d	4½	5	24	Plank braces.
40d	5	4	18	Same as above.
50d	5½	3	14	Three inch planks.
60d	6	2	11	Mostly to toenail large timbers temporarily before bolting.

justment the bubble will indicate the timber is out of level twice as much as it really is on one of the readings. For adjustment remove the cover plate over the glass bulb and it will be observed that the glass is set in plaster of paris which in turn is set in a metal frame with a screw at each end. One of these screws is fixed but the other passes through a small spring and this end of the bulb can be raised or lowered with this screw.

Nails: There are two forms of nails commonly used in house construction. Common wire nails and finish nails. The common nails have a larger head than the finishing nail and are driven flush with the wood. They are used for all general rough work. Finishing nails have a smaller head and are driven below the surface of the wood about an eighth of an inch with a nail set. They are used for inside and outside finish.

The accompanying table gives the different sizes, length, and number of nails per pound and size of lumber each is best fitted for.

Finish or casing nails vary in size from 2d to 40d. Six penny (6d) is usually used for lap siding and inside finish and 8d is used for outside finish, window and door jambs.

In sheeting, roofing, rough flooring or six-inch pine flooring, two nails should be placed in each board at each stud or joist about an inch from the edge of the board. Some carpenters put three nails in a 12-inch board. Battens, finish trim and four-inch lumber fastened flat are usually nailed with one nail every two feet on each side. The nails are staggered so there is a

A necessary tool in any shop is the carpenter's bench vise. Temporary faces may be attached to it with wood screws; these protect work in vise.

You may find occasion to use all of these units: top, pipe or pony clamps; at left are wooden hand-screw clamps (toolmaker's type in center); the others are all C-clamps.

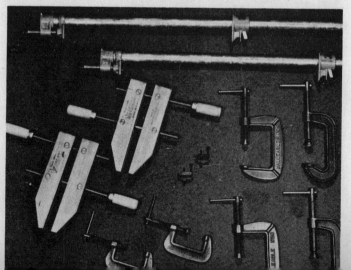

nail every foot in the board. Where two 2x4's or two 2x6's cross each other flatways carpenters normally drive three 16d nails: one in the center of the intersection and the other two in opposite corners of the intersection. Nails should never be driven close together or near the same grain as they may split the wood in time. The slant of a nail is generally set to accommodate the stroke of the hammer. Occasionally it is necessary to drive a large nail in a piece too small for it. In this case, set the slant of the nail to cross the grain of the wood as much as possible in order to lessen the splitting action.

The Square: Much has been written on the square. It is true that it has many varied and important properties but the fact remains, its most important feature is to indicate square and angle cuts.

It is necessary that the apprentice learn to handle a square in a workmanlike manner and not like a rule. It should be grasped with the left hand near the center of the larger arm, or blade, between the fingers and the palm of the hand so the right hand is free to mark with the pencil. To measure for a certain length, place the blade of the square against the farther edge of the board with the smaller arm, or tongue, to the right and across the piece. Start at the left end of the board and mark the first two feet with the pencil against the outside of the tongue. The square is then moved right and another mark made for another two feet. If the distance required is 4 feet and 11 inches, the next step is to place the 11-inch mark on the inside edge of the blade even with the 4-foot mark

on the board and mark the length square across the board on the *inside* of the tongue and remember to make allowance for the mark at each step. It is also natural to mark on the wrong side of tongue at some point in the operation and the measurement will be wrong the width of tongue.

If it is not necessary to square the last mark, experienced carpenters much prefer to measure with a six-foot folding rule. It is more accurate and quicker.

Power tools: For several years, and particularly since the end of World War II, power driven hand tools have been bringing about a major revolution in the work of the carpenter. Houses which formerly were put together entirely with hand tools and manual labor can now be erected in less than half the time by fewer men and almost entirely by machine operations. Home carpentry and repairs have been greatly speeded up and made more accurate by electric power tools. Today there is a motor-driven tool for almost every job the carpenter has to do.

One of the greatest advantages of these modern tools is their portability. A professional carpenter can now put his electric saws, sander, drills, planer and nailer into the back of his car and take them right to the job. Where electricity is not available, the contractor can now provide a portable generator giving DC or AC current for any of the power tools.

Another great advantage of these new tools is the range of work they will do. New steels have provided saw blades that will cut anything from fiberboard to drain tile. Sanders will work on metal, masonry, wood or glass. Hand drills can also saw wood or metal, do sanding jobs, sharpen

A variety of fixed-jaw pliers and assorted nippers are a useful adjunct to the carpenter's tool kit and may be used for holding, bending and cutting operations as needed.

When sawing, the job will go much easier if you adopt the correct stance for crosscut sawing. As illustrated, balance the body directly over line of cut.

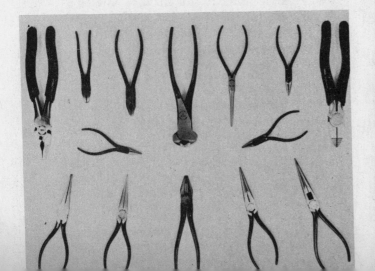

Above, the entire family of hand planes used by the carpenter: l to r, block, smoothing, jack, fore, and finally, the jointer.

Left, at top is small dovetail saw, then the 24-inch 12-point crosscut type, the 5½-point rip saw and the back saw.

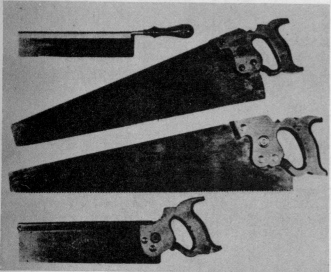

Below, a metal handscraper is a handy tool for removing excess burr from lumber, or as a paintscraper; use as illustrated.

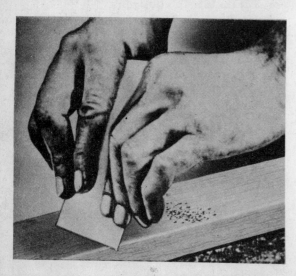

saws, polish surfaces and drill holes in almost any material. Other tools will do fancy routing work, cut out intricate figures and dig holes in the ground. The more commonly used power tools—the saws, drills and sanders are now almost essential to the home craftsman. Whether they are portable or fixed table type is a matter of personal choice and need. The general principles of operation and the over-all flexibility are about the same.

Power saws: Those for the shop are of several types—the common circular saw, the band saw, jig saw, scroll saws and the saber type for keyhole and veneer work. Most people think of the circular saw as a tool for cutting lumber to length and width. To the modern carpenter, the circular saw is more than that. It will cut almost every type of angle, grooves, joinery work, and elaborate cabinet construction. What is more, it does all this work about ten times faster than could be done with the hand saw.

The table-type shop saw is generally more adaptable to different types of work than the portable. Extension arrangements are available or can be rigged to the table for ripping long stock or for cutting large plywood and fiberboard sheets. The saw

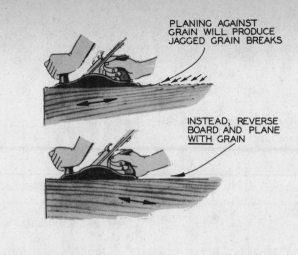

PLANING AGAINST GRAIN WILL PRODUCE JAGGED GRAIN BREAKS

INSTEAD, REVERSE BOARD AND PLANE WITH GRAIN

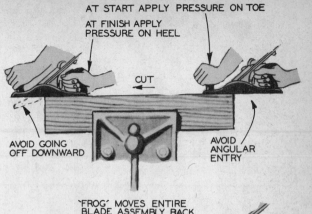

AT START APPLY PRESSURE ON TOE

AT FINISH APPLY PRESSURE ON HEEL

CUT

AVOID GOING OFF DOWNWARD

AVOID ANGULAR ENTRY

ON LONG WORK SMALL PLANES WILL FOLLOW DIPS AND RISES ON SURFACE ~

~WHILE LONG PLANES WILL BRIDGE THE DIPS AND SHAVE DOWN THE RISES

'FROG' MOVES ENTIRE BLADE ASSEMBLY BACK AND FORTH TO WIDEN OR NARROW MOUTH

FROG SET SCREW

CAP IRON DEFLECTS SHAVINGS

MOUTH IS WIDENED FOR DEEP CUTS IN SOFT WOODS

MOUTH IS NARROWED FOR HARD, CROSS GRAINED WOODS

BLADE WILL CUT TO WITHIN ¼" OF ANY JOINT

BULL NOSED PLANE IS USED FOR PLANING AREAS ALREADY ASSEMBLED

NEVER RUSH PLANING OPERATIONS ~ STROKE PATIENTLY AND PLANE WILL TAKE DOWN ANY JOB TO ANY SIZE

COMBINATION PLANE IS FOR EXPERTS ~ GIVES RABBETS DADOS AND MANY VARIETIES OF MOLD DESIGNS AND SIZES

Above are tips on use of the plane; below, two views of the Stanley Sureform tool, new on the market. Cutting teeth (right) fit into plane or wood rasp holder; it's easy to use.

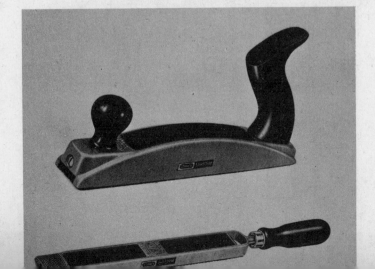

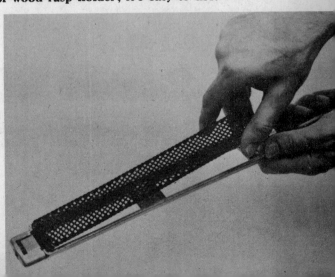

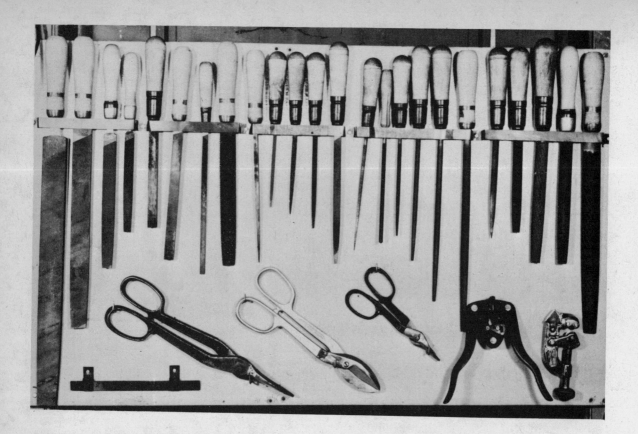

Increase the life of your files and snips by using a convenient wall rack to keep them from touching each other. Large assortment of sizes and cuts assure right file for every job.

blade must be adjusted so that the tip of the highest teeth will extend about ¼ inch above the work. In ripping, the fence can be adjusted to the scale at the front of the table for the required width and the stock held against the guide. Measurements should be checked and the saw turned on to reach maximum or normal speed before the sawing is started. The user should stand a little to one side so that he can hold the work firmly against the guide fence as it advances and so that he will be clear of the direct line of the saw blade. Before starting any cut with the circular saw, a trial cut should be made and checked for accuracy of measurement.

The blade of the circular table saw can be changed for different types of cutting. There is a dado head available for making wide grooves or dadoes, cut-off wheels for tubing and metal, shaper heads and knives, and sanding and abrasive discs for many types of operations. Several of the portable saws also have some of these adjustable features and guide attachments for special jobs.

The radial arm type: Another very useful and versatile saw that is becoming more popular with the home craftsman is the radial arm circular saw. This type of power

machine is made in many sizes and varieties of heads which are suspended over the cutting table and the work. The saw moves as required on a support arm. The better type of radial saws will do five or six different types of operations and have several advantages over either the table saw or the portable. It takes up little space in the shop and can do drilling, sanding, routing, planing and mortising as well as drive many other tools in the shop. Another big advantage of this type of saw is the minimum of movement and the ease of cross cutting. The board is set on the horizontal table so that the mark is in line with the saw blade. The head assembly is moved forward and the cut is made accurately without any movement of the work. The depth of cut is adjusted by raising or lowering the head assembly.

Band saws: They are another very useful and popular type of time-saver. These saws are made for a great variety of uses, and range from the large machines of the sawmill to the ripping and resawing blades of the lumberyard and the small ¼-inch blade of the cabinet shop. The big machines may have blades from 3 to 6 inches wide for cutting through thick material parallel to an edge. The smaller machines with

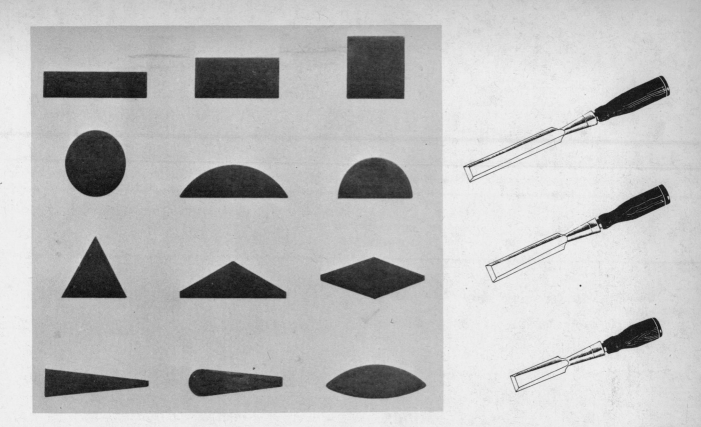

Wood files take name from shape; above, flat, square, round, half-round, triangular, etc.

At top, bevel-edge 6-inch wood chisel; center, bevel-edge 4½-inch pocket; bevel-edge butt.

narrow blades are more suitable for the home carpentry shop. Various widths of blades and types of teeth can be used for different purposes. The band is supported and driven by two large wheels, one above and one below the work table. The blade runs through two guides that keep it from turning and give it support from the back. The slot in the table through which the blade runs is located near the center of the working area. The endless band and the room available make the band saw particularly useful for cutting several pieces at one time where exact duplicate shapes are needed. In cutting several pieces of work at one time, the best procedure is to nail the layers together, putting the nails through the waste portions of the work. Another satisfactory method of holding several pieces together consists of making two or three slots into the waste portions of the whole pile and driving hardwood wedges into the slots. Good technique with the band saw requires that the guides be kept as close together as possible and that the widest blade which the curvature of the work will permit is used. The wider the blade, the easier it will be to cut to a line. Narrow blades are necessary for sharp curves and angles.

Advantages of the jig saw: The jig saw is a smaller relative of the band saw but is better for more intricate patterns and sharp curves. Inside cuts that cannot be reached from the edge of the wood are easier to do because the blade can be quickly removed and inserted through a hole on the inside of the work. The jig saw base and driving mechanism is similar to the circular saw table except that the rotating motion of the drive shaft is converted into a reciprocating motion of the blade. The table can usually be tilted to almost any degree for angle cuts up to about 45 degrees.

The jig saw uses fine blades and is an excellent tool for intricate and exacting cut-outs. Some of them are made in a small vibrator type of drive and others are made with a large table and reciprocating cam that moves the blade up and down very rapidly. Different blades are used for different materials and, with the jig saw, it is generally advisable to limit the number of pieces cut at one time. A total thickness of ½ inch is maximum for the small vibrator saws. Larger saws can take up to about 1½ inches with accuracy.

Electric drills: The handy man-carpenter will probably find that the first electric tool he will want to buy is the ¼-inch

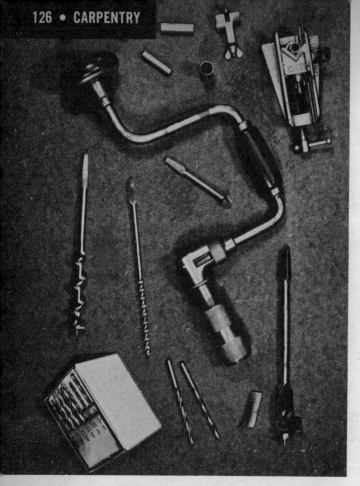

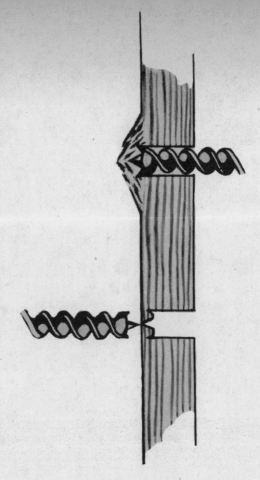

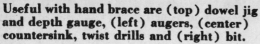

Useful with hand brace are (top) dowel jig and depth gauge, (left) augers, (center) countersink, twist drills and (right) bit.

To avoid splintering wood when drilling, do not bore completely through; rather, stop short of completion and drill from other side.

hand drill. The size designation denotes the maximum size of drill that the chuck will hold. A good small drill with various attachments will do more work for the dollars invested and will take more of the hard labor out of work than any other tool he can buy. This little "Paul Bunyan" will drill holes in wood, metal, cement, plastic and almost any object. It will grind and sand almost any material, will polish the car or the floors, drive screws into wood, turn nuts, cut metal, stir paint, trim the hedge, wax floors, grind tool edges and the kitchen knives, and will saw metal up to ¼ inch in thickness as well as wood up to about 1½ inches. With a fixture to hold the body of the drill, it can be used as a table sander and as a small lathe for turning small stock.

In selecting and using the electric hand drill, it is important to estimate the type of work to be done and choose the machine that will do the job without being overloaded. Remember that a heavier and stronger tool will also do the light work but a small tool will not do the heavier and continuous jobs such as floor sanding or grinding. An overloaded motor will burn

out on heavy jobs. The little ¼-inch drill with a pistol grip can safely handle drilling up to its maximum drill capacity in steel or will do ½-inch holes in wood (with small shank drills) without overloading. This is assuming that the work is intermittent.

Useful accessories: By all means, buy a sanding head and sanding discs, a Jacobs chuck, a few wood boring bits, a horizontal stand, a few small rotary mounted grinding bits, a wire brush, a polishing and buffing head, and a small circular saw attachment for your hand drill. These accessories will make your investment worth a great deal more and will make your work much easier for a great many jobs.

Another very useful tool of the same nature is the small "Handee" type of grinder and drill. This is a tiny motor that can be held in one hand for carving, grinding, very small sawing and intricate work in model making, patterns, wood carving and small machine work.

Electric sanders: Finishing carpentry work before the painting is done is a very tiresome and exacting job if it is done by hand. One of the first power tools invented for the woodworker was the motor sander.

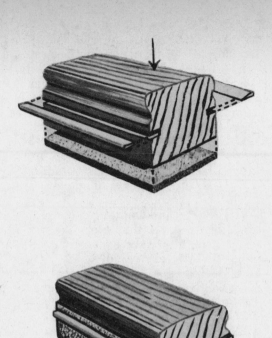

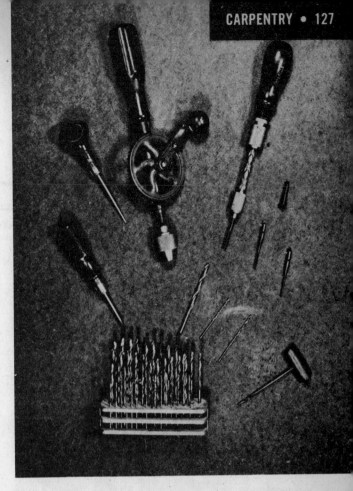

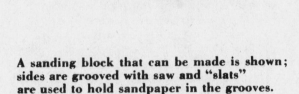

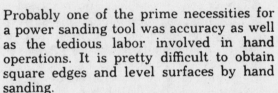

A sanding block that can be made is shown; sides are grooved with saw and "slats" are used to hold sandpaper in the grooves.

For small holes use (top) hand drill, (right) a push drill, (left) prick punch and punch for leather, twist drills or the hand auger.

Probably one of the prime necessities for a power sanding tool was accuracy as well as the tedious labor involved in hand operations. It is pretty difficult to obtain square edges and level surfaces by hand sanding.

There are five types of electric sanders available and all of them are especially adaptable for particular uses. The disc type has been mentioned previously in connection with the hand drills. This type of pad is also used with the flexible shaft drive, the bench saw attachments and the combination tools with direct drive and rotary motion. The other types are the belt sander, the revolving drum, the vibrating pad and the oscillating machines.

Belt sanders: The belt sander is by far the best major sanding device for good finishing. In the first place, the portability of this tool allows it to be used almost anywhere and in almost any position. It can be fastened to the bench for surface or edge sanding where accurate work is required. The most important feature of the belt sander is the movement of the belt which is entirely in a lengthwise direction. This movement does its sanding with the grain

of the wood and produces excellent finishing in a very short time. The belts can be quickly changed for finer work and with special grits the sanding can be done on metal, glass, stone, or composition materials. When clamped vertically in a vise, the belt sander can be used on curved surfaces and in close corners of the work.

Disc sanders: The round sanding pads of the hand drill and the flexible shaft are made of rubber so that the edge can be pushed to the work at an angle. This allows the actual sanding to be done fairly close to the direction of the grain. Long sweeping motions with fairly light pressure will produce the best results. The flat disc sanders of the table saw variety have a firm base and will do very accurate work if the table guides are used to feed the material and if only one side of the wheel is utilized.

Vibrator type: The vibrator type of sander moves a small sanding pad forward and backward at a rate of about 14,000 strokes per minute. This type of machine is usually the lowest in cost and does excellent work on light jobs such as furniture, small cabinets and joint finishing. This tool

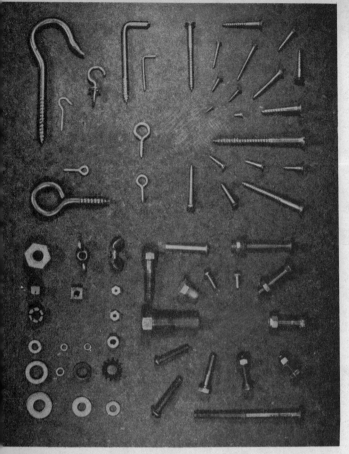

Screw and other threader fasteners above include (lower left) common wood screws, (upper left) bolts and screws, (lower right) hooks, eye screws, (top right) washers, nuts.

Common nails are the principal fastening tools used for general woodworking; this size range includes 2d, 4d, 8d, 10d, 16d, and 20d.

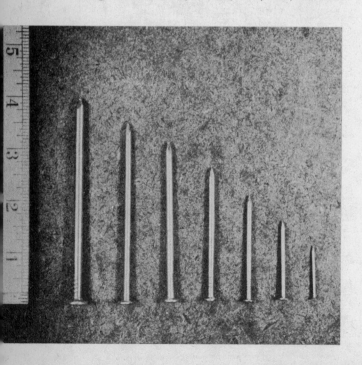

also cuts in the direction of the grain and with extra pads which can be quickly attached, will do waxing and buffing as well.

Revolving drum sanders: Revolving drum sanders are usually extra attachments for the flexible shaft drives. They are about 2½ inches in diameter and 4 inches long. This tool can be used in many places where other sanders will not work and is very handy for inside sanding of cut out sections, the inside of legs, drawers and cabinet sections. Since they are of small diameter, these drums run at a high surface speed and will bite into the work very rapidly.

Oscillating type: The reciprocal or oscillating sander moves a pad back and forth in an oval motion. This type of machine is good for work on floors, boat decks, large surfaces such as plywood panels, walls and painted surfaces. The units are usually small and can be operated with one hand. They will work entirely into close corners and up to edged borders on shelving.

Other power tools: Two other power tools are becoming more popular today for the home carpenter. These tools were formerly used solely by the millwork and professional cabinet shops. The router-shaper and the jointer-planer are basically tools for bench operations, but the lightweight models now available can be easily moved to the job and used wherever needed. These tools will do a varied job of grooving, edging, shaping and surfacing all types of material. The router-shaper-carver is an excellent tool for cabinet and furniture work where intricate and precise joints and shaping is required.

Drill press: The drill press is not a portable tool, but it is highly adaptable to other types of operations than just drilling holes. Adapters are available for most drill press machines which will permit routing, carving, boring, sanding, mortising, shaping, dovetailing, countersinking, planing and many other general carpentry tasks. The machine drive is usually set up with a multiple-step pulley device which will permit changing the drive to other speeds for drilling and adapter operations on several types of material.

Grinder: The grinder is a bench necessity in every carpenter shop for keeping tools sharp. Many types of materials can be shaped and finished on the grinding wheel as well as tool edges. The grinder wheels themselves can be easily changed for wire brushes or buffing heads for various cleaning and finishing jobs. The grinder usually has a coarse wheel set at one end under an enclosed wheel guard and a fine grit

Brush care and use are graphically outlined below; read the chapter on Finishes on page 130.

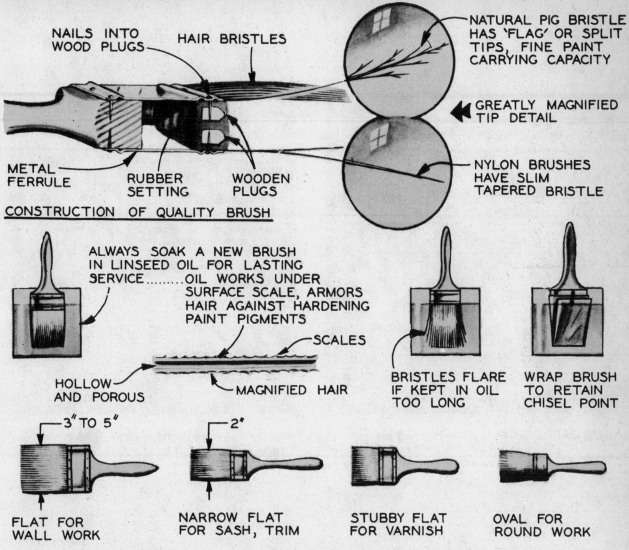

NATURAL PIG BRISTLE HAS 'FLAG' OR SPLIT TIPS, FINE PAINT CARRYING CAPACITY

NAILS INTO WOOD PLUGS

HAIR BRISTLES

GREATLY MAGNIFIED TIP DETAIL

NYLON BRUSHES HAVE SLIM TAPERED BRISTLE

METAL FERRULE

RUBBER SETTING

WOODEN PLUGS

CONSTRUCTION OF QUALITY BRUSH

ALWAYS SOAK A NEW BRUSH IN LINSEED OIL FOR LASTING SERVICE.........OIL WORKS UNDER SURFACE SCALE, ARMORS HAIR AGAINST HARDENING PAINT PIGMENTS

SCALES

HOLLOW AND POROUS

MAGNIFIED HAIR

BRISTLES FLARE IF KEPT IN OIL TOO LONG

WRAP BRUSH TO RETAIN CHISEL POINT

3" TO 5"

2"

FLAT FOR WALL WORK

NARROW FLAT FOR SASH, TRIM

STUBBY FLAT FOR VARNISH

OVAL FOR ROUND WORK

BRUSHES ARE DESIGNED FOR SPECIFIC JOBS ~ CHOOSE WISELY

45°

A FINE BRUSH SHOULD BE HELD AND STROKED PROPERLY ~

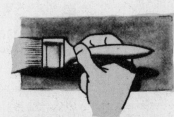

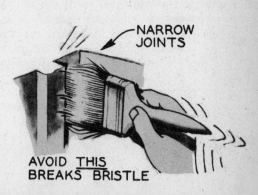

NARROW JOINTS

~TOO LARGE BRUSH TIRES HAND AND ARM

~TOO SMALL MEANS TOO MUCH STROKING

AVOID THIS BREAKS BRISTLE

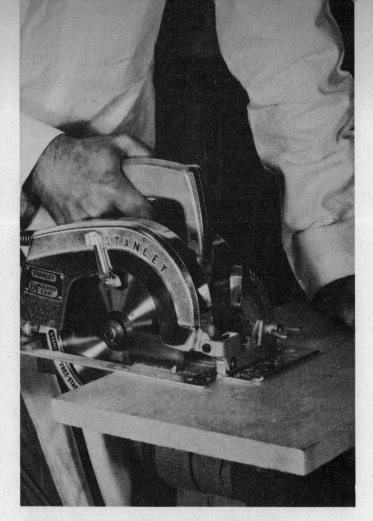

Router is ideal for grooving and mortise work; the one pictured is a Stanley, has safety features and adjustable guide for close work.

Stanley 6½-inch builder's saw is ideal for fast performance of heavy work, can be adjusted to cut at an angle for miter joints.

wheel set at the other end under a similar protective device.

Flexible shaft: Flexible shaft tools are the general work horses of the shop and will do several types of operations. The motor is usually fixed on a movable table or an overhead fixture that allows some freedom of movement. The shaft itself can be turned at almost any angle to the work and can also be attached to other tools for driving power. The combinations of tools available for this type of arrangement are practically unlimited.

Materials: One of the prime factors in the success of a carpenter is his knowledge of the material with which he works. He must be able to identify any particular piece of wood, recognize its characteristics, grade, working qualities and also know the limitations which will affect his work.

No two kinds of wood are identical in structure or other characteristics. Indeed, the same kind of tree may grow in different localities and have different color, grain defects or other important characteristics. The uses of woods will be affected by the

differences in texture, strength, resistance to warping, shrinking or rot, hardness or softness, ease of working and so on. All wood is composed of fibers and the size, closeness, shape and arrangement of these fibers give the wood its identifying character and determine its usefulness. Carpentry is very much concerned with these things.

The word timber is used in two different ways by the wood harvesting and handling trades. In the forest, the word refers to the standing trees before they are cut. In the building trade, the word refers to the large beams which are used for supports. The word lumber is generally used to designate the boards which are sawed from logs of forest timber.

There are only two broad classifications of woods which are useful to the carpenter, the hardwoods and the softwoods. From the evergreen, or coniferous trees having needle-like leaves, we get a great variety of softwoods. From the broadleaved trees which shed their leaves each year, we get the hardwoods. One word of caution here—

SOFTWOODS

easy to work		medium		hard to work	
Alaska cedar	31	Eastern cedar	33	Longleaf pine	41
Ponderosa pine	28	Cypress	32	Shortleaf pine	36
Idaho white pine	27	Port Orford cedar	29	Larch	36
Sugar pine	25	Lodgepole pine	29	Douglas fir	31
Northern pine	25	Western hemlock	29		
Incense cedar	24	Eastern hemlock	28		
Engelmann spruce	23	Redwood	28		
Western red cedar	23	Eastern spruce	28		
Southern cedar	23	Sitka spruce	28		
Northern cedar	22	White fir	27		
		Balsam fir	25		

HARDWOODS

Chestnut	30	Black walnut	38	True hickory	51
Red alder	28	Paper birch	38	Black locust	48
Yellow poplar	28	Magnolia	35	White oak	47
Butternut	27	Tupelo gum	35	Beech	45
Basswood	26	Black gum	35	Pecan hickory	45
		Red gum	34	Red oak	44
		Sycamore	34	Birch	44
		Cottonwood	26	White ash	41
				Maple	40
				Cherry	35
				Elm	35

these terms are not to be taken as indicative of the softness or hardness of the wood of the tree. The terms, hardwood and softwood, refer strictly to a botanical classification and we will find that there are several instances where a "softwood" is harder than a "hardwood" and vice versa.

Wood comparison: In general, the hardwoods are more durable and more beautiful for furniture, paneling, plywood cores, and more expensive cabinet work. The hardwood trees grow very slowly and are not nearly as abundant as the softwoods. The softwoods grow much faster, are more abundant, and have a much wider application in both house construction and general carpentry. The softwoods are the most important to the beginner in woodworking because they are cheaper, generally easier to work with and have a better range of usable qualities.

A comparison is presented above which will give some idea of the relative weight and working qualities of various commonly used woods. The weights show pounds per cubic foot of air-dry wood with 12 per cent moisture content. The working qualities are based on the general reputation of the wood among workmen and wood users.

As to the working qualities of woods, it will be seen that the above tables show the majority of softwoods in the easy and medium classes of working qualities and the majority of hardwoods in the medium and hard to work classes. Again we should point out that this is not necessarily due to softness or hardness of wood but is affected by grain structure, splitting qualities and other important characteristics.

Softwoods: The pine trees of North America produce the royalty of woods for the carpenter. The pines are not only the major lumber product, but are the most abundant in growth and are the most widely useful of all woods. There are about fifteen different varieties of commercial pines, but the two chief classes are the Southern yellow and the white or soft pines from the Northern and Western states.

White or soft pine woods are very easy to work with hand tools, keep their shape very well and are ideal for craft projects, pattern making and general cabinet work. Most of the lumber of this group is made into millwork products such as doors, sash, interior and exterior trim. The principal commercial woods of this group are Ponderosa pine, Western white pine, sugar pine and Northern pine.

Ponderosa pine is not classified botanically as a true white pine, but it has the soft texture, close and uniform straight grain of the white pines and is unexcelled for smooth and lustrous finishing. Ponderosa pine ranks high in strength qualities and is an outstanding wood for light construction requiring close-fitting joints and high dimensional stability. This wood nails easily and has far less tendency to split than the harder and denser softwoods of the Southern group.

Idaho white pine is one of the few true white pines and is also one of the principal building woods. It is a little more difficult to work than the other white pines and is not quite as stable, but has a straight grain and a soft, even texture which makes it highly useful for general woodworking. The wood is light in color, varying from nearly white to pale reddish brown, finishes with a smooth silky grain, and has excellent nail and screw holding qualities.

Pines: Sugar pine, because of its magnificent stature in the forest and its excellent working qualities in the shop, is truly the "King of the Pines." It is the largest of the white pine trees and produces high quality lumber in large sizes. The wood is a soft-toned creamy white which darkens with age and despite the rapid growth of the tree, it produces a grain texture that is indistinct, uniformly soft and lustrous. The sugar pine is not a structural wood, but it is strong for its weight and has the least shrinkage factor of all the pines. It is exceptionally resistant to splitting when nailed and holds all types of fasteners very well. Sugar pine is a number one choice for wood carving, cabinet work and pattern making. It is also ideal for table tops, picture frames, high quality woodwork, doors and any work where neat and close-fitting joints are required.

Northern pine is also one of our finest

DeWalt radial arm saw has many uses (see the illustrations at right), can be used for delicate sawing operations such as grooving (below) to allow "bending" of lumber. This particular tool is among the handiest and most versatile of the multi-purpose power tools, is ideal for shop.

soft pines, but is now becoming rather scarce. It is a close grained wood of fine texture and is white to pale ivory in color. This pine is not much affected by atmospheric changes which makes it a good pattern wood. It is used commercially for doors, sash, blinds, and matches.

Longleaf vs. shortleaf: Southern yellow or pitch pine woods are heavy and hard to work. They split easily when nailed and are highly resinous. This wood is very strong and is used mostly in the construction industry.

Longleaf pine produces large timbers for heavy construction work. It is a straight grained, highly resinous wood which checks easily and does not hold paint well. It is good for floor joists and wall sheathing in house construction, but it has little use to the shop wood workers.

Shortleaf pine is less dense than the longleaf variety, is softer and more easily

worked with hand tools. It is yellow in color, straight grained and only moderately resinous. It is used chiefly for millwork, doors, flooring and trim.

Other softwoods: Cedars are a group of easily worked softwoods that are light, stiff, brittle, fragrantly scented, produce a beautiful finish but are not very strong. Cedar has a very desirable quality of being durable and resistant to decay which makes it useful for log cabin construction, boat planking, fence posts, railway ties, utility poles and many other exposed applications. All the cedars are non-resinous and take a great variety of stains and painted finishes. Its nail holding qualities are good, but care must be taken in driving nails or screws near the board ends. Cedar is a very good material for the home craftsman for a great many uses.

Spruce is an important lumber tree, but is not nearly as abundant or productive of

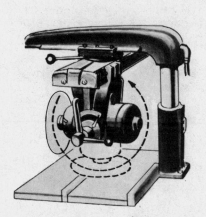

SAW MOTOR ROTATES ON A TRUNNION SET IN THE YOKE, GIVING SAW BLADE ANY BEVELING ANGLE THROUGH 360°

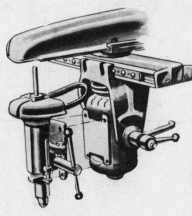

DRILL PRESS UNIT IS EASILY BOLTED ONTO MOTOR FOR FURTHER VERSATILITY - PULLEY SPEEDS ARE FROM 1200 TO 10,000 R P M

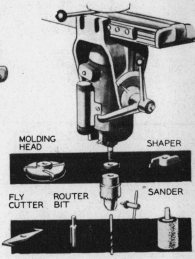

MOLDING HEAD   SHAPER

FLY CUTTER   ROUTER BIT   SANDER

THESE ARE A VERY FEW OF THE MANY TOOLS ADAPTABLE FOR MOUNTING ON MOTOR SPINDLE

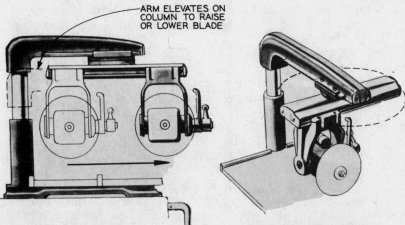

ARM ELEVATES ON COLUMN TO RAISE OR LOWER BLADE

BACK AND FORTH MOTION BY PULLING MOTOR YOKE ALONG BALL BEARING TRACK

TRACK BEAM ALSO ROTATES ON ITS HANGER, THEREBY PERMITTING CUTS OF ANY ANGLE THROUGH 360°

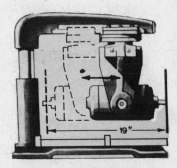

TRACK BEAM HANGER SLIDES ALONG SUPPORT ARM, FOR RIPPING OF WIDE PANELS

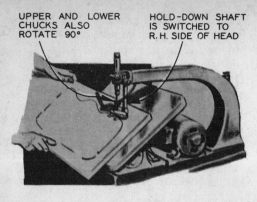

UPPER AND LOWER CHUCKS ALSO ROTATE 90°

HOLD-DOWN SHAFT IS SWITCHED TO R.H. SIDE OF HEAD

TABLE ROTATES 90° TO PERMIT CUTTING LONG STOCK EVEN WHILE TILTED TO 45°

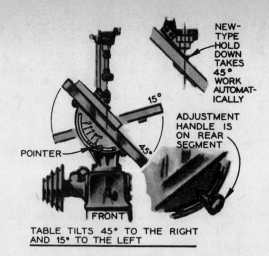

NEW-TYPE HOLD DOWN TAKES 45° WORK AUTOMATICALLY

15°

ADJUSTMENT HANDLE IS ON REAR SEGMENT

POINTER

45°

FRONT

TABLE TILTS 45° TO THE RIGHT AND 15° TO THE LEFT

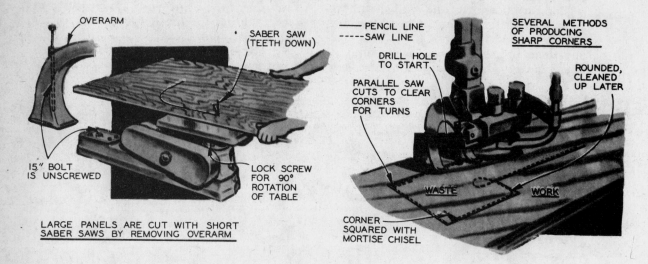

OVERARM

SABER SAW (TEETH DOWN)

15" BOLT IS UNSCREWED

LOCK SCREW FOR 90° ROTATION OF TABLE

LARGE PANELS ARE CUT WITH SHORT SABER SAWS BY REMOVING OVERARM

—— PENCIL LINE
----- SAW LINE

SEVERAL METHODS OF PRODUCING SHARP CORNERS

DRILL HOLE TO START

PARALLEL SAW CUTS TO CLEAR CORNERS FOR TURNS

ROUNDED, CLEANED UP LATER

WASTE

WORK

CORNER SQUARED WITH MORTISE CHISEL

Adjustable jig saw can be used for many operations; always follow manufacturer's tips.

good grades as the pines and firs. The two principal varieties on the market are the Eastern group—the white, black and red spruces, and the Western group, which includes the Sitka and Engelmann spruce. Both are fairly strong and straight grained and easy to work, but are not very resistant to decay. The Western spruces produce better lumber grades in large sizes and are excellent for cabinetwork, built-in furniture, sporting goods, aircraft structure, auto trailers, stepladders and general household articles. The Eastern group is extensively used for pulp wood, framing lumber, sub-flooring, boxes and crates, and, in the better grades, for sounding boards in pianos. Both are very useful to the handy man carpenter.

Firs are a major lumber product although the wood is not very strong and is of a coarser quality than the spruce. White fir is used in building, crating, plywoods,

and millwork. It has a soft, fine texture, straight grain, and good whitish color with slight red-brown tinges. Its lack of resin gives white fir a high rank among the softwoods in painting and finishing qualities.

Balsam fir is somewhat lighter in weight than white fir, but has similar qualities and uses.

Douglas fir: This is a highly resinous wood and is almost as hard to work with hand tools as the Southern pine. The tree is found in diameters up to seven feet and heights of 200 feet. Its supply and production probably exceeds all other commercial woods. In color, the Douglas fir is pure white to orange red and is straight grained, moderately heavy and normally dense. In proportion to its weight, this wood is one of the strongest ever tested. This quality accounts for its wide use in structural timbers, posts, rafters, beams and house framing. Generally, it is not as useful to the cabinetmaker or wood craftsman as the white pines because of its tendency to check and split easily. Where strength is the chief requirement, however, you couldn't find a better wood. When properly seasoned and given a good priming coat, Douglas fir will take and hold paint or enamel very well for outdoor use. Although it is subject to some shrinkage and swelling with weather changes, it is a good commercial wood and is sturdy and long lasting for many building purposes. Its use for plywoods greatly enhances its general value and its usefulness to the carpenter.

Other softwoods collectively play a major role in the lumber market and some of them are very useful to the craftsman and handy man carpenter. Cypress, hemlock and redwood are the principal varieties and are very useful for special purposes.

Cypress, for instance, comes from the swamps of the deep South and is widely recognized as the most resistant to weather and rot of any wood in this country. It is reddish in color, close grained and resinous. Its decay resistant qualities make it desirable for gutters, water tanks, shingles, siding and other outdoor uses. The hemlocks are beautiful as trees, but for general purposes, are not very useful to the carpenter except in house construction.

Redwood (not to be confused with the giant Sequoia) grows in very large sizes and is another good outdoor lumber. It is a very handsome wood in texture and color, is straight grained, medium-easy to work, and very resistant to both decay and termites. Redwood is good for all outdoor uses, shelving, furniture, and is frequently used for fancy boxes and chests. Larch is another of the softwoods hard to work, but has unusual strength and is good for commercial building, outdoor benches, ladder steps and freight car decking.

Hardwoods: The wood of the broadleaved trees is more porous in cell structure and the lumber is more subject, generally, to warping and twisting than that of the coniferous trees. The hardwoods provide more beautiful and serviceable material for the carpenter and craftsman, but the wood is usually more expensive. The hardwoods are too scarce, expensive and hard to work with to be used in general building work, but do provide first rate flooring lumber, interior trim, furniture wood, paneling and cabinet material. All of the hardwoods are useful and valuable to the craftsman-carpenter because of the more interesting textures, grain patterns, color and finishing qualities. The hardwoods are also more rigid and generally have more durability than the softwoods.

Hickory is the heaviest, hardest, toughest

Bandsaw attachment on Shopsmith is particularly useful for decorative sawing of large panels for use in valances.

Close-up shows proper method of guiding lumber through bandsaw; hands are kept clear but lumber is held with firm grip.

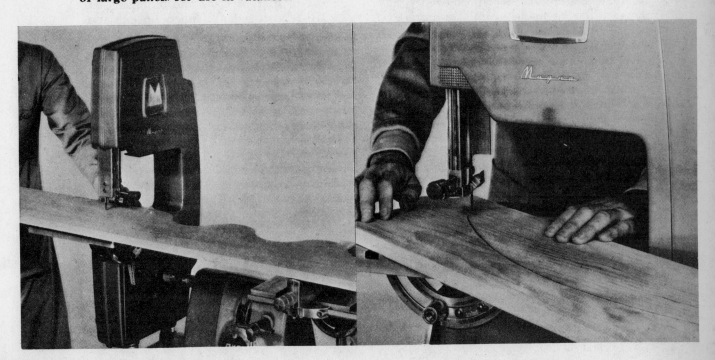

and strongest of all woods grown in this country. It is brownish in color and very flexible which makes it desirable for bentwood construction of furniture, tool handles, skis, etc.

Chestnut was formerly used extensively in house construction, but due to blight which killed most of the native stand, the wood is somewhat scarce. It is light brown in color, light in weight, and easy to work. Chestnut has a very straight and open grain and requires a filler before finishing. It is an excellent wood for furniture, flooring, trim, shingles and veneers.

Alden, poplar, butternut, and basswood are all very easy to work with hand tools because of their straight grain and soft texture. They are all light in color and take natural as well as imitative stains and paint very well. These woods are not as strong as the tougher varieties and are subject to some checking and shrinkage. When well preserved, however, with varnish or paint, they are good material for cabinetwork and joinery.

Black walnut is about the finest cabinet wood available in the United States. It is rich brown in color, straight grained, hard and stiff. It works very well with hand tools and takes an exceptionally good finish. Walnut of several types is highly valued for fine furniture and the more expensive types of cabinetwork.

Red gum is another strong and fine textured wood that is highly valued for interior paneling and fine table tops. Its grain is somewhat twisted and interlocking, however, which makes it difficult to plane easily. Red gum takes a stain so evenly that it can often be made to imitate more expensive mahogany and walnut. Gum will warp and check badly when exposed to weather and is not durable at all for outdoor use.

Popular cabinet woods: Oak is the chief hardwood product of North America and is one of the most useful woods for the carpenter-craftsman. It is available commercially as white oak and red oak. The white variety is best for furniture, flooring and cabinetwork. Oak is an extremely hard, stiff and strong wood and is useful for furniture frames, particularly the upholstered types of furniture, dresser and bureau frames, boat construction, farm implements, children's toys and many objects which take hard and rough usage. Red oak has the same general qualities of the white variety, but is coarser and less desirable for exterior finish on furniture.

Beech and birch are both very strong woods, hard and stiff, and are used widely for furniture of all types, flooring, woodturning projects and for fancy veneers in expensive paneling and interior finishing. Both of these woods are very light in color and take a beautiful finish.

Maple is commercially available in almost every lumberyard. The hard sugar maple and the well-known black maple are two of our most important furniture woods. Both are used for flooring, woodturning, shoe lasts, pianos and many objects which must withstand considerable wear. Maple lumber is both heavy and strong, has a fine texture and finishes very well with a wavy, twisting and satiny grain.

Cherry is also a heavy, hard and strong wood, but is obtainable only in small sizes of lumber for molding, trim, small craft projects and as veneer for fine furniture finishing.

Common wood defects: Wood being a product of nature, it is subject to many natural defects, some of which cannot be corrected. Some faults can be eliminated or avoided in cutting, selecting and grading lumber and this effort accounts for considerable loss in the harvesting of timber and the marketing of usable lumber products. Technically, a defect is an irregularity that impairs the strength, use or durability of a wood. A blemish is a mark or imperfection which affects only the appearance of the lumber. Common defects are known as heartshakes, windshakes, starshakes, holes, knots, decay, checks and warps. The common blemishes are stains, pitch pockets, bark pockets, skips in dressing, and machine burns.

Some of these defects and blemishes are readily recognized and need no explanation here. Some of them are peculiar to the trade and are not easily recognized by the layman. The heartshakes, for instance, are actually splits which originate in decay occurring in the pith and extending through the heartwood, sometimes out into the sapwood. Windshakes are circular or curved splits in the wood which follow one or more of the annular rings. These are said to be caused by the twisting and bending of the trunk in the wind. The starshakes are very similar to the heartshakes, but without the rot at the pitch center. Just what causes the starshakes is not certain, but they are usually associated with discoloration and the beginning of decay. Stain, usually bluish in color, is caused by a mould-like fungi and does not affect the strength of the lumber.

Why wood warps: Warping is a distortion or twisting of lumber out of its original plane and is caused by evaporation of the

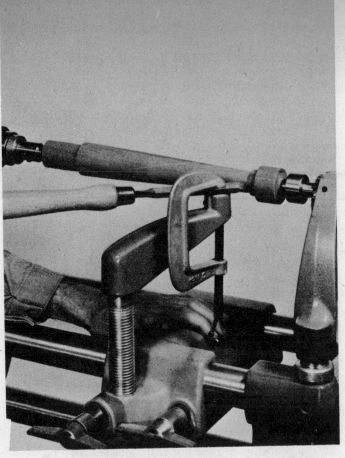

Wood lathe can be used for a number of decorative carving effects; here, a wood chisel is held in place with C-clamp.

Right, drum sander attachment on wood lathe can be used for shaping and sanding, is particularly useful for work on table legs.

Grooving of interior of a circular piece is accomplished by holding wood chisel in place by hand over lathe's metal support.

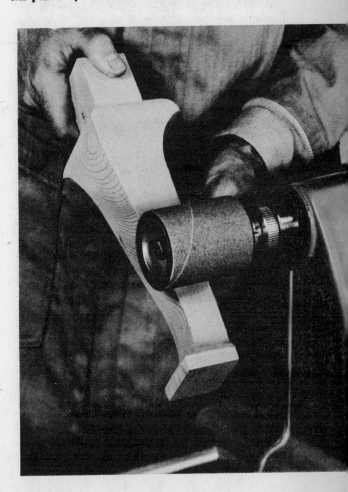

moisture in the cells of the wood and subsequent shrinkage of the cell structure. The wood cells and fibers are of different sizes in any piece of lumber and a particular board may contain some heartwood and some sapwood. Since the wood fibers are interlocked, one of them cannot shrink without causing some effect upon the others. The softwoods have a more even and uniform structure and tend to dry and shrink more evenly and with less warping than the hardwoods.

Another defect of wood of importance to the carpenter-craftsman is that of checking. If wood shrinks more rapidly around the growth rings than in the direction of the medullary lines, checks or small cracks will appear around the outside of the board.

How lumber is cut: The cutting of trees for lumber and the manufacture of wood products out of the rough logs is a job that requires considerable skill and knowledge of woods. Good cutting will obtain the greatest amount of usable material out of a timber stand or out of a given log with a minimum of waste. Proper cutting of the log will avoid cuts which are likely to result in excessive warping and checking of the finished lumber. The method used in cutting the log into lumber will also determine the appearance of the wood as well as affect its strength and other qualities.

The simplest method of cutting a log into lumber is that of straight slicing to various thicknesses. This method results in boards which will certainly warp when dry. The better cutting methods are known as quarter-sawing since the log is cut directly into quarters and various sizes of planks are cut from each quarter-segment. The best method of quarter-sawing is that which cuts along radius lines to the center.

Sizes, measure and grading: Lumber dealers in various sections of the country will carry stocks of various woods that are in greatest demand for general building and construction purposes in their service area. A yard in the Eastern states may have on hand in several grades and sizes of lumber: native pine, Douglas fir, eastern spruce, hemlock, white pine, Ponderosa pine, cypress, yellow pine, oak, maple and walnut in smaller quantities. All lumber manufacturers and dealers throughout the country use a standard size and grade system which greatly simplifies ordering, but which must be understood by the customer if he expects to get the right sizes and quality of material for his particular job.

Rough lumber at the sawmill has three principal designations. "Dimension stuff" is cut 2 inches thick and from 4 inches to 12 inches in width. "Timbers" are cut 4 inches to 8 inches thick and from 6 inches to 10 inches wide. The "common boards" are 1 inch thick and from 4 inches to 18 inches in width. When this material is cut down for the yard, it becomes "strips" which are less than 2 inches thick and 8 inches wide, "boards" that are also less than 2 inches thick, but over 8 inches wide, and "dimension" lumber, which is 2 inches to 5 inches in thickness and is cut to any specified width.

Dressed lumber: When these lumber sizes are "dressed" by the planing machines, the rough surfaces are removed from one or more sides to a depth of about ⅛ of an inch on each dressed side. This finishing process is sometimes called "surfacing" and a particular lumber will be designated as D1S or S1S, meaning that the piece has been dressed on one side or surfaced on one side. D1E will mean that the piece has been dressed on one edge. Naturally, this dressing or surfacing of the finished product will reduce the actual size of the lumber. Each common size will retain its original size designation, however. A 2x4 S4S, for instance, is dressed on all four sides and is sold as a 2x4, but actually measures 1⅝ inches by 3⅝ inches. This system must be remembered when lumber is ordered for any particular purpose which requires specific sizes of material.

How lumber is sold: Lumber is generally sold by the board foot which is a standard measure 1 inch thick by 12 inches wide by 12 inches long. Any size of lumber can be converted to board feet by the following formula:

B. F.=Thickness (in.) x width (in.) x length (ft.)

Grading rules: Small pieces, trim, siding, 2x4, and other standard lumber will be quoted at a price per running foot. This price is always derived from the board foot price of the specified quality and type of lumber. Plywoods, siding, veneer, and composition material are always sold at a square foot price.

The National Bureau of Standards has set up grading and classification rules for lumber selection to insure uniformity throughout the industry. The actual grading of lumber products from a particular log is done largely by inspection. "Select" is the top quality material which is suitable for natural finishing and is graded into two classes, A and B. The B grade allows a few small blemishes or defects. "Finish" material is the second classification and is of good appearance and suitable for paint surfacing, graded C and D according to the number and size of defects. "Common" is the lumber that is suitable for general utility and construction purposes. Numbers 1 and 2 common must be usable without any waste. Numbers 3, 4 and 5 common contain the coarsest defects.

The handy man-carpenter, when working on home projects and building small articles can often "upgrade" his material by selecting better or clear sections from a lower grade yard piece of wood. A number 3 or 4 common, for instance, may contain sections which are entirely free of the knots and splits which give the standard yard size that classification. For any particular purpose, therefore, the carpenter will need to consider only the actual size of the piece he needs and find a section that will produce what he wants.

Plywood and composition material: Many years of effort and a great amount of money have been spent in the development of products which would utilize the by-products of the sawmill and create useful

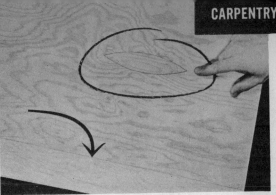

In plywood, Grade B Veneer is smooth and paintable, similar to Grade A Veneer, but permits circular plugs, up to 1-inch knots.

Grade A Veneer may be of more than one piece, well-joined, but there should be no open defects in this type of plywood.

materials for various types of construction. The result is a great variety of useful materials which are made in various ways from sawdust, wood pulp, scrap and types of wood that would otherwise be useless. Another reason for this development is the search of strong materials which are lighter and thinner than regular lumber and which can be made in larger sheet sizes than the usual wood products. These materials are also much more stable than lumber and are not subject to shrinking and swelling and warping and decay.

The principal material to come out of this development is plywood. Plywood is such an important material to the carpenter that an entire chapter will be devoted to this subject later in this book. There are a great many woods made up in plywood besides the well-known fir stock that is often seen in house building and partitioning. In addition to fancy veneers and expensive woods, many plastic materials are now added to the plywood face for interesting and useful building for the home.

Fiberboard materials are available in thin sheets that are tough, easy to work with, very strong for their thickness and weight and very useful around the home in many faces and finishes. These boards are made from various substances such as sawdust, waste paper, corn stalks, limestone, wheat straw and many others. The raw material is mixed with some type of bonding material, poured out on a paper machine to form a wet mat. It is then run through rollers and pressed into sheets of different thicknesses and to different degrees of hardness. These materials are excellent for general building use, wall finishing, backing of cabinets, drawer bottoms, and so on, depending on the strength and hardness and wearing qualities of the particular material. All such products are usually sold in sheets measuring 4 feet by 8 feet and since they have no grain, can be used in any type of cut. •

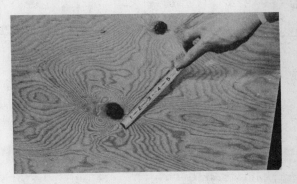

Grade C Veneer plywood permits knotholes up to 1-inch, small borer holes and various repair patches. Good for backing, etc.

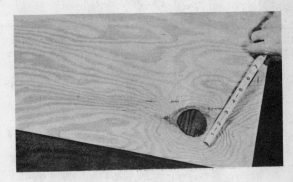

Grade D Veneer plywood is used only for interior panels, permits up to 2½-inch knots and limited splits. Prices are relative to grade.

Here, a cutaway section of plywood shows cross-graining of layers for strength, secret of why plywood is as tough as metal.

Closing-in is speeded up with large plywood panels for decking, siding, flooring.

Wood Types and Sizes

What you should know about this basic material, and how to choose it.

KNOWING something about wood and related materials can save you time and money and gain you much satisfaction in terms of better, easier-to-make, more durable projects. For wood in itself is a most versatile product and what is done to it by manufacturers after it has been taken from the tree, vastly increases its potential and degree of usefulness. Plywood, for example, as opposed to high-grade cabinet woods, is economical, generally available, and made with surface veneers of almost any hardwood (and non-wood materials) you can name. Because of this, it has be-

come the most popular form of wood for the homecraftsman and, for that matter, industry.

You can get it in various thicknesses for either indoor or outdoor use and in grades that assure the most economical application. And finishing is not different from finishing the same wood with which it has been surface-veneered. And when you consider that you get it in big 4′x8′ sheets from which, for example, you can cut good size table tops in one piece, that are flat and warp-free, it isn't hard to understand why it's so popular.

Good sound timber is important in piers which literally support the entire weight.

Make a roof look solid with short false beams tied in to supporting rafters.

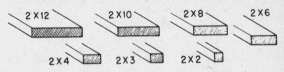

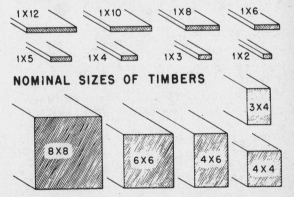

Roof decking, 2" thick, combines finished ceiling, vapor barrier, and rigid insulation.

The hardboards, when first introduced, were considered by the week-end carpenter to be great stuff for fast, economical drawer bottoms, case backs and the like. But they have come more and more into their own; now being available with embossed or otherwise decorated surfaces that are attractive and applicable to many interesting uses.

Wood is either hard or soft, a designation which has nothing to do with the actual density of the wood itself. These are botanical terms which indicate that the wood has come either from a broad-leafed deciduous tree (hardwood) or a cone-bearing or evergreen tree (softwood). Some popular hardwoods are birch, maple, walnut, mahogany, oak—some popular softwoods are pine, fir, redwood, cedar.

Check a piece of wood under a microscope and you will discover that it is composed of myriad tube-like fibers. The walls

NOMINAL SIZES OF LUMBER USED FOR STRUCTURAL AND FRAMING PURPOSES

2 X 12   2 X 10   2 X 8   2 X 6

2 X 4   2 X 3   2 X 2

NOMINAL SIZES OF LUMBER USED FOR SHEATHING, FURRING AND TRIM

1 X 12   1 X 10   1 X 8   1 X 6

1 X 5   1 X 4   1 X 3   1 X 2

NOMINAL SIZES OF TIMBERS

3 X 4

8 X 8   6 X 6   4 X 6   4 X 4

HOW TO MEASURE AND FIND COST PER BOARD FOOT OF LUMBER*

Example:—

You need a 10 foot length of 2 x 8 which costs 30 cents per foot.

Use chart to find contents in one *lineal* foot;

———— one lineal foot of 2 x 8 = 1.33 board feet

———— 10 (1.33) = 13.3 board feet

————
$$\begin{array}{r} 13.3 \\ \times\quad .30 \\ \hline \$3.990 \end{array}$$ = cost of 10 foot length of 2 x 8 @ 30 cents per board foot.

Width (Inches)	Thickness (Inches)											
	1	2	3	4	5	6	7	8	9	10	11	12
2	.17	.33										
3	.25	.5	.75									
4	.34	.67	.1	1.33								
5	.42	.83	1.25	1.67	2.08							
6	.5	1.	1.5	2.	2.5	3.						
7	.59	1.17	1.75	2.33	2.92	3.5	4.08					
8	.67	1.33	2.	2.67	3.33	4.	4.67	5.33				
9	.75	1.5	2.25	3.	3.75	4.5	5.25	6.	6.75			
10	.84	1.67	2.5	3.33	4.17	5.	5.83	6.67	7.5	8.33		
11	.92	1.83	2.75	3.67	4.58	5.5	6.42	7.33	8.25	9.17	10.08	
12	1.	2.	3.	4.	5.	6.	7.	8.	9.	10.	11.	12.

*For example: If you need a 10 foot length of 2 X 8 which costs 30 cents per board foot—find 2 X 8 on chart which is 1.33 board feet—10 X 1.33 = 13.3 board feet X .30 cents = $3.99

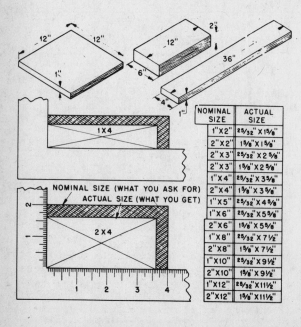

NOMINAL SIZE	ACTUAL SIZE
1"X2"	25/32"X1⅝"
2"X2"	1⅝"X1⅝"
2"X3"	25/32"X2⅝"
2"X3"	1⅝"X2⅝"
1"X4"	25/32"X3⅝"
2"X4"	1⅝"X3⅝"
1"X5"	25/32"X4⅝"
1"X6"	25/32"X5⅝"
2"X6"	1⅝"X5⅝"
1"X8"	25/32"X7½"
2"X8"	1⅝"X7½"
1"X10"	25/32"X9½"
2"X10"	1⅝"X9½"
1"X12"	25/32"X11½"
2"X12"	1⅝"X11½"

NOMINAL SIZE (WHAT YOU ASK FOR)
ACTUAL SIZE (WHAT YOU GET)

of these "cells" vary in thickness from species to species. It is this characteristic or the degree of it, which determines the porosity of the wood or, as far as the home-craftsman is concerned, whether it is an "open-grained" wood or a "close-grained" wood. Oak is a good example of porous wood which results in a surface requiring a filler if it is to be really smooth. Maple is about as opposite as you can get, being very dense with tiny, close cells.

These tubes or cells are the blood vessels of the tree and it is by their growth that new layers of wood are added each year. Speed of growth, most rapid in the spring, results in different degrees of hardness and color in the tree itself. A cut through a tree trunk reveals concentric circles which are these "annual growth" rings. By counting them you can tell the age of the tree,

BASIC LUMBER GRADES

Select	Generally, lumber of SELECT grade is lumber of good appearance and with good finishing qualities. It is usually clear but does have defects that are limited both to size and number		Remarks
A	these grades are suitable for natural finishes.	practically clear wood—sometimes combined with B grade and sold as "B and better."	high quality lumber—can be used in fine cabinetwork, interior & exterior trim
B		a few very slight imperfections, defects, blemishes, permissible	Cabinetwork, paneling, trim, flooring. Grade between "A" and "B," very slight.
C	high quality lumber for painted finishes	A limited number of small defects & blemishes—about twice the number that are allowed in "B"	all defects easily hidden with paint—all jobs where high quality paint finish is required.
D		any number of defects or blemishes but these must not detract from a finish appearance under paint	millwork, moldings, short-length clear lumber, painted built-ins and fixtures
Common	Generally suitable for construction and utility purposes. Number, size and type of defects and blemishes do not make it very suitable for quality finishes.		Remarks
1	lumber may be used without having to cut out unsuitable waste	has knots but must be sound and tight. Size of other defects and blemishes limited	good general purpose wood—low cost for siding, shelving, paneling.
2		tight-grained but with large and coarse defects	sheathing, concrete forms, subfloors are typical uses—select pieces have good "knotty" effect
3	includes areas of waste	larger and coarser knots than number two and often has knot holes.	temporary construction—often used as cheaper substitute for #2
4		very low quality—coarsest defects—even decay	sheathing, subfloors and roof boards in cheap construction
5		if it holds together under ordinary handling its #5 common	so poor its not even shipped far from the mill—rough and temp. bld'g. coverage, boxes, crates

but more important—as far as use is concerned—these rings are what contribute the wood "grain" when the tree is cut up into boards. The grain is more obvious in some woods than others, in fact it can vary in the same species or even in different sections of the same tree, yet each is characteristic enough so that a wood could be identified by its grain pattern.

Grain pattern is also affected by the way the log is cut up into boards. Flat cutting, which is just a question of slicing the log lengthwise into boards, produces wide stock with prominent grain patterns. There are some disadvantages here, among them greater shrinkage and more tendency to warp, but it is the least wasteful and less costly of the techniques used and so produces most of the "yard" lumber. Quarter-sawing is more expensive but the boards produced have a more attractive, more even grain pattern and so the technique is usually reserved for the rarer and more expensive hardwoods. Quarter sawing consists of first slicing the log lengthwise into four wedged-shaped pieces. Boards are then cut from the flat sides of each wedge.

Lumber is wet or "green" when it is first cut; its moisture content is high. This must be considerably reduced before the material is fit to use to frame a house or make a table. Air-dried lumber, which is fresh boards that have been very carefully stacked to assure adequate air circulation around all surfaces, is rare today, probably because demand is great and air-drying takes time. If it is air-dried stuff, chances are it's been rushed a bit and moisture content isn't as low as it should be.

Moisture content can also be reduced artificially—hence the term "Kiln-dried." One method used is to house the green lumber in huge storage rooms and to dry it by artificially controlling the temperature therein:—as you might dry a small piece of wood in your own kitchen oven. You can reduce the weight of almost any piece of wood in your shop merely by "baking" it in the oven. What you accomplish, of course, is reduction of its moisture content.

It's the reduction, or rather, the irregular reduction of this moisture content that causes wood distortions. Most of us have experienced what happens when we lay a dry piece of wood down on a concrete floor. The side of the wood touching the concrete will pick up moisture from it. This stretches the fibers, or cells, so that, actually, the one surface becomes longer than the opposite surface; the opposing forces causes the wood to warp. If this happens irregularly over the board, you get "warp" and "wind" and "twist" and so on.

This goes on all the time, no matter how carefully the wood is prepared for you. The humidity in your workshop or garage is not the same as the lumberyard where you bought the stock. This will affect the wood if you store it for long periods unless your workshop is really, really dry. That's why finishing, what you do to the wood after your project is complete, is more than

KINDS OF SIDING

	DROP SIDING 1"X6" LAPPED
	DROP SIDING 1"X6" TONGUE & GROOVE
	DROP SIDING 1"X6" CENTER V-GROOVE
	DROP SIDING 1"X6" LAPPED
	DROP SIDING 1"X6" TONGUE & GROOVE
	BOARD & BATTEN
	CLAPBOARD 4", 5", 6", 8", 10"
	SHIPLAP 4",6", 8", 10", 12" TONGUE & GROOVE
	SHIPLAP 4" 6" 8" 10" 12" STANDARD

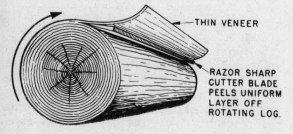

WOODED IS PEELED OFF LOG ON HUGE WOOD LATHE.

—THIN VENEER

RAZOR SHARP CUTTER BLADE PEELS UNIFORM LAYER OFF ROTATING LOG.

VENEER SHEETS ARE CROSS-GRAINED DURING THE BONDING PROCESS TO OBTAIN STRENGTH ACROSS PANEL AND ALONG PANEL.

TYPICAL HARDBOARD CORNERS

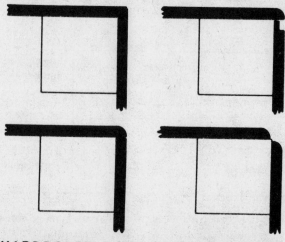

HARDBOARD SHELVES & COUNTERS

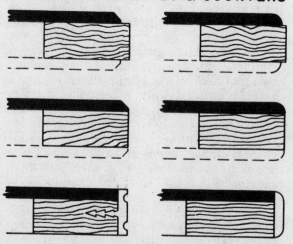

just enhancing the natural beauty of the wood. It's sealing it, keeping out outside influences that might cause distortion after you've put your cut parts together into a finished project.

Many times it's wise to stock your lumber where the project will ultimately be. For example, if you are going to put cabinets in your garage for a workshop, store the lumber in the garage for awhile before cutting it up and making the cabinets. It will tune itself to the garage conditions *before* and not *after* your cabinets are made. The same holds true if you are about to remodel an attic or basement.

Always buy the cheapest lumber that's adequate for the project you need. You don't need a fancy, clear stock for a painted storage bin. Be imaginative. A knotty, inexpensive wood can often be turned into an attractive and distinctive wall paneling. Don't be too hasty about throwing cut-offs into the fireplace. If you've done a job that produced many similar, apparently unsalvageable short lengths, consider form-

Big sheets of plywood do a fast job of covering an old ceiling for tile base.

A new high density plywood has a hard, smooth surface, is completely waterproof.

MECHANICAL FASTENING OF HARDBOARD

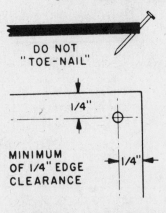

DO NOT "TOE-NAIL"

1/4"

MINIMUM OF 1/4" EDGE CLEARANCE   1/4"

COUNTERSINK HOLES FOR FLATHEAD SCREWS

NAILING HINTS -- NAIL THE CENTER OF PANELS FIRST, EDGES LAST. DRIVE NAILS PERPENDICULAR TO PANEL.

SCREW FASTENING -- DRILL PILOT HOLES FOR WOOD SCREWS. USE WASHERS UNDER SCREW HEADS AT HIGHLY STRESSED POINTS.

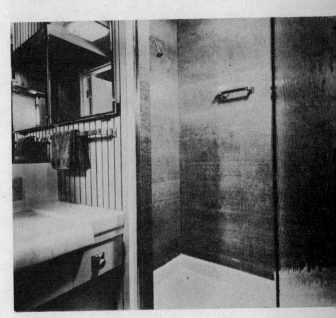

HOW FIR PLYWOOD IS GRADED
STANDARD STOCK SIZES AND GRADES OF EXTERIOR-TYPE

GRADE—TRADEMARKS®	Face	Back	Widths (Feet)**	Lengths (Feet)**	Thicknesses (Inches)**
EXT-DFPA · A-A For permanent outdoor uses where appearance of both sides is important. Outdoor furniture, certain fences and enclosures, signs, marine uses.	A	A	4	8	¼, ⅜, ½, ⅝, ¾
EXT-DFPA · A-B Uses similar to Exterior A-A panels but where appearance of one side less important. Alternate for EXT-DFPA · A-A.	A	B	4	8	¼, ⅜, ½, ⅝, ¾
EXT-DFPA · PLYSHIELD Siding of homes and buildings of all types. Also for soffits, breezeways, gable ends. For store fronts, highway stands. The versatile "one side" grade of Exterior plywood with waterproof bond.	A	C	4	8	¼, ⅜, ½, ⅝, ¾
EXT-DFPA · UTILITY As grade name indicates, a utility outdoor panel. Farm buildings.	B	C	4	8	¼, ⅜, ½, ⅝, ¾
EXT-DFPA · SHEATHING Unsanded grade with waterproof bond. Backing or rough construction.	C	C	4	8	⅜, ½, ⅝
EXT-DFPA · PLYFORM This is the grade of plywood specified when panels with waterproof bond are desired so concrete forms may be re-used and re-used until wood is literally worn away.	B	B	4	8	¾

Wall treatment of wire-brushed rustic wood makes a dramatic background when stained and rubbed in two contrasting tones.

STANDARD STOCK SIZES AND GRADES OF INTERIOR-TYPE

GRADE—TRADEMARKS®	Face	Back	Widths (Feet)**	Lengths (Feet)**	Thicknesses (Inches)**
INTERIOR · A-A For all interior applications where both sides to be in view. Cabinet doors, built-ins, furniture, displays, booth partitions.	A	A	3, 4	8	¼, ⅜, ½, ⅝, ¾
INTERIOR · A-B For all inside uses requiring one surface of highest appearance and opposite side solid and smooth. Alternate for A-A.	A	B	3, 4	8	¼, ⅜, ½, ⅝, ¾
PLYPANEL The many-purpose, "one side" material for interior uses. Wall and ceiling paneling, built-ins, wainscoting, backing and underlayment, counters, fixtures, displays, cut-outs.	A	D	2½, 3, 4	8	¼, ⅜, ½, ⅝, ¾
PLYBASE A base and backing material for interior use. Face also is solid, paintable.	B	D	4	8	¼, ⅜, ½, ⅝, ¾
PLYSCORD The unsanded sheathing or structural grade of fir plywood. Wall and roof sheathing, subflooring. Temporary enclosures, backing; containers, temporary partitions and construction barricades.	C	D	4	8	⅜, ⁵⁄₁₆, ½, ⅝
INTERIOR PLYFORM The re-usable concrete form plywood for ease of form construction, smooth concrete surfaces. Glue bond is highly moisture resistant but NOT waterproof.	B	B	4		⅝, ¾

ing them into blocks with chamfered edges that could be applied over a sheet rock wall with a mastic to make a wood-tile paneling. Of course, this is just an illustration. But wood is expensive and *can* be utilized, even to the sawdust.

When you buy lumber don't expect to get stock that measures exactly 2″ by 4″ when you order a 2x4; not unless you order it in the rough. The stock you get will be reduced in its thickness and width by the amount of material removed when it was surfaced and by natural size reduction due to drying, climatic conditions, etc. But the nominal size (2x4) is always used in buying and selling. You always ask for a 1x6 or a 2x8 or a 1x12 even though what you take home will be reduced in those two dimensions by as much as ½″. If you owned a planer you could buy lumber in the rough and get every inch you pay for, but you would have to reduce its dimensions anyway if you wanted to surface it.

Lumber can be dressed (surfaced) as follows:

S1S—surfaced one side
S2S—surfaced two sides
S1E—surfaced one edge
S2E—surfaced two edges
S1S1E—surfaced one side and one edge
    —other similar combinations of surfaces and edges
S4S—surfaced 4 sides

You usually buy it S4S, but suppose you needed some redwood headers that were going to set off a concrete patio in squares? Then you could order S1E because that one surfaced edge would be the only side exposed after the concrete had been poured.

WORKED lumber has been dressed and further machined in some way; maybe into a molding or some other form of millwork. If it's MATCHED it means it has a groove formed along one edge and a tongue along the other so that pieces can be fitted snugly against each other for a good joint. It can be matched and end-matched which would mean that the tongue and groove apply to

The particle board shown at left has a dense, hard surface which in this case has been embossed in a basket weave pattern.

At right is a hardboard which has been perforated. It can be used to allow some light and air to pass through, or with hooks as a peg board.

Above is a typical example of the grain brought out by wire brushing which removes the softer part of grain and leaves the hard.

THE RIGHT HARDBOARD TO USE

PROJECT	THICKNESS								Material
	Solid Backing				Open Backing				
	⅛	³⁄₁₆	¼	³⁄₈	⅛	³⁄₁₆	¼	³⁄₈	
DOORS	X				X	X	X		C E G*
DRAWER BOTTOMS					X	X	X		B C F* G*
FLOORS	X	X							C**
EXTERIOR CEILINGS	X	X			X	X	X		A** C**
EXTERIOR SIGNS	X	X	X		X	X	X		C** G*.**
EXTERIOR WALLS	X	X	X⁻		X	X			C**
INTERIOR CEILINGS	X	X			X	X			A B C
INTERIOR WALLS (ORDINARY)	X	X			X	X			A B C D E
INTERIOR WALLS (SEVERE COND.)	X	X			X	X			C** D** E**
UNDERLAYMENT	USE SPECIAL UNDERLAYMENT ONLY								
WAINSCOTS	X	X			X	X			C D E
DIVIDERS					X	X			F* G*
CASE-BACKS	X	X			X	X	X		A B C E F* G*
CASE-ENDS	X	X			X	X	X		A B C E F* G*
COUNTER AND BENCH TOPS	X	X				X	X		C E

A . . . Panelwood E . . . Leatherwood
B . . . Standard Presdwood F . . . Standard Duolux
C . . . Tempered Presdwood G . . . Tempered Duolux
D . . . Temprtile

* when both sides are exposed
** when applied for existing conditions

both the ends as well as to the sides.

If it is rabbeted, or has a similar shape along the sides, then it is SHIPLAP which is designed to provide a close, lapped joint.

In the area of WORKED lumber we could include "ready-mades," like moldings, trims, baseboards, door jambs, etc. You don't have to make these items; you buy them in a lumberyard all set to install. Door jambs for example can be purchased in correct width for standard openings dadoed for the top member and kerfed along the back (hidden) side to guard against warpage after installation. Once purchased, it's just a matter of cutting the pieces to correct length right on the job, setting them in place plumb and square, and securing them. The gap or joint, which will exist between the jamb and the finished wall, is covered with trim which is another worked lumber you buy ready made. It's a good idea to get acquainted with these products if only to know how they are shaped. Should it ever be necessary to make a special one, you'll be pre-

pared to come up with something professional.

It does happen. For example, you panel the walls in a room. If you use ¼" paneling and ¾" furring strips, you increase the thickness of the wall by 1". When you get to a door, you either make special arrangements to recess back to the existing jamb or you replace the jamb with a wider one to meet the new wall thickness. You could order a special jamb, but this is expensive. If you make your own, you save more than half the cost and lots of time, for you don't wait for the special order.

This goes for trimming, too. Most jobs result in "waste" cut-offs and slim strips that can be readily utilized to form moldings for finishing doors, windows and the like. The fact that moldings are sold ready-made doesn't mean you must buy it so. If you make your own you can accomplish two things, especially if you make it from remnants. You save money and you can end up with something different and distinctive. •

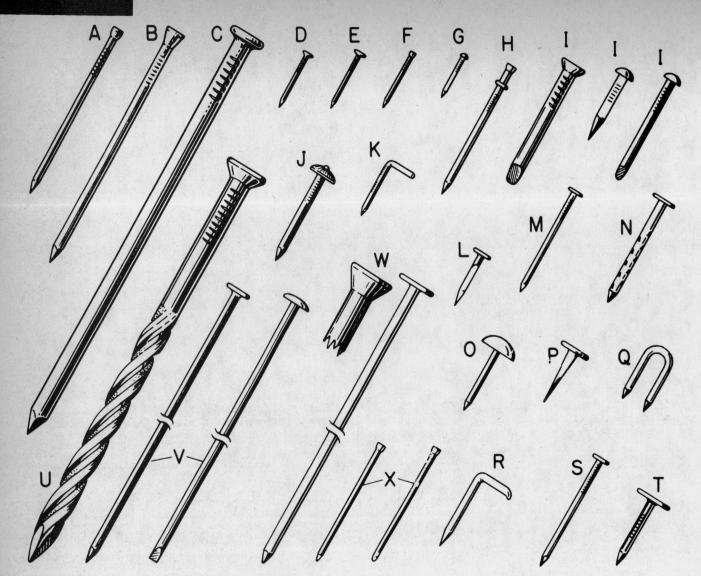

Fastenings

What you should know about . . .

THE variety in nails is staggering, but encouraging, because there is a type and size which is exactly right for the job you want done and the material you are working with. It's not likely you'll need to keep a complete supply on hand. Best bet is to buy nails as you need them, selecting the right type and size for the job, but buying more than you need. Thus you'll have a quantity remaining which you can add to your shop supplies for use when a similar job comes up. These you can store in small drawers made for the purpose, in open top bins, or—as many people do—in Mason jars.

In addition to various types and sizes, nails are available in different degrees of hardness and finishes. Etched, barbed or adhesive-coated nails do a good job where vibrations or continuous strains and stresses may tend to cause joined parts to separate. Where a nail is subject to discoloration or rust, or where a combination of weather and nail material may cause the work itself to stain, nails are supplied in copper, bronze, aluminum, stainless steel—or they may be cad-plated or galvanized. Galvanized nails are used extensively outdoors. For example, if you were going to build a wooden planter box, it would be wise to select galvanized nails for the job because they would not rust and would not stain the wood. Wooden siding is best attached with aluminum nails for these will resist the weather forever and do not require any special treatment to prevent discoloration of any covering paint. Especially designed for attaching corrugated roofing or similar materials, are leak proof nails; the heads so shaped that

A — Finishing Nail
B — Casing Nail
C — Common Nail
D — Box Nail
E — Blued Lath Nail
F — Brad
G — Escutcheon Nail
H — Scaffold or Duplex or Double Head
I — Hinge Nails
J — Nail for Corrugated Roofing
K — Nail for Metal Lath
L — Upholsterer's Tack
M — Shingle Nail
N — Asbestos Shingle Nail (Barbed)
O — Upholsterer's Nail (Plain or Fancy)
P — Tack (Flat-Head)
Q — Staple
R — Electrician's "Staple"
S — Sheetrock Nail (Cement Coated)
T — Asphalt-Roofing Nail
U — "Screw" Nails
    (For Every Purpose — Available In Different
    "Thread" Designs)
V — Flat-Head and Round-Head Gutter Spikes
W — Round Wire Spikes
X — Flooring Brads

Toenailing is easier if a pilot hole is drilled slightly smaller than nail shank.

Nail is driven almost completely in with hammer, taking care not to dent the wood.

nails, screws, bolts, and special devices.

water will flow off them like it would off a roof.

Where a nail is used as a temporary fastener (you may be building a scaffold that you want to tear down when the job is done), you can buy them with double heads. The nail is driven in to the depth of the first head which does the holding job required, but the second head is there so you can pull the nails easily later on.

More often than not, the name of the nail describes its use. For example, shingle nail or sheetrock nail or siding nail and so on. If you are ever puzzled about the right nail to use, merely give it the name of the job you are going to do or the material you are working with and your supply dealer will know exactly what you want. Also let him know the thickness of the materials you are going to join for this will determine

Finish with a nail set the same size or smaller than the nail head, then putty.

NAIL SIZE REFERENCE CHART

Size	Lgth.	FINISHING		CASING		COMMON		BOX	
		Size	Ga.	Size	Ga.	Size	Ga.	Size	Ga.
2d	1"					x	15		
3d	1¼"	x	15½			x	14	x	14½
4d	1½"	x	15	x	14	x	12½	x	14
5d	1¾"					x	12½	x	14
6d	2"	x	13	x	12½	x	11½	x	12½
7d	2¼"					x	11½	x	12½
8d	2½"	x	12½	x	11½	x	10¼	x	11½
9d	2¾"					x	10¼		
10d	3"	x	11½	x	10½	x	9	x	10½
12d	3¼"					x	9		
16d	3½"			x	10	x	8	x	10
20d	4"					x	6	x	9
30d	4½"					x	5		
40d	5"					x	4		
50d	5½"					x	3		
60d	6"					x	2		

NUMBER OF NAILS PER POUND (APPROXIMATE)

Nails are bought by the pound, the symbol —d— (penny) indicating the size, by length and gauge. The length is the same for all nails, the gauge will differ.

SIZE	COMMON	CASING	FINISHING	CLINCH	FINE	BRADS
2d	800		1100		1000	
3d	480		720		760	
4d	290	400	525		370	
5d	200		410			
6d	170	225	270	95		125
7d	125		190	75		100
8d	90	130	145	60		75
9d	70	110	130	55		65
10d	60	90	100	45		55
12d	45	70	75	40		40
16d	35	55	60	36		
20d	25	40	55	33		
30d	20	35		20		
40d	15	30				
50d	10					
60d	8					

the size and length of the nail. The general rule is for the nail to be three times as long as the thickness of the material you're going to nail through.

A nail holds because the wood fibers tend to return to their original positions and thus wedge against the nail. When the fibers are broken or otherwise distorted by excessively heavy hammer blows, the holding power of the nail is not as great. Thus it's best not to try to *smash* a nail home but to hit it firmly and without arm strain. This is best anyway because hitting too hard will only cause the hammer head to bounce or slide off with damage to the work—or your finger.

Nails near the end of a board or along its edge require special consideration especially as regards the wood being nailed. Hard, strong-grained woods will split easily whereas soft, grainless wood will not. If you discover from experience, or feel, that the wood you're working with splits easily, do one of two things. First try blunting the point of the nail by setting the head down on a hard surface and tapping the point with a hammer. Destroying the original, sharp nail point will reduce splitting tendency. If this doesn't work, drill small holes before you hammer the nails. *Don't* use a lot of nails on the same line; this will almost surely split the wood. *Do* use fewer nails, but stagger them, to spread out strain over grain lines.

If a nail bends, use a pair of pliers to straighten it *at the bend,* and continue driving. If it bends again, remove it. Sometimes a bent nail will do a better job. On some kinds of the toenailing and butt-nailing, bend the end of the nail slightly. This will direct it as you hammer so that it curves in the wood and draws the two parts more tightly together. You can also file the point to a chisel-like edge. This bevel will deflect the point of the nail in the direction you want it to go.

Don't hammer any more than it is necessary to drive the nail flush with the surface of the wood. Pounding beyond this will only mark the work. On finish work, where the nail head will be concealed, drive it in until it projects about ⅛ or $\frac{1}{16}$" and then use a nail set to sink it about ⅛" below the surface. You can do this with common or box nails by using a flat-face punch instead of a nail set. Nail sets come in various sizes so choose one which more closely matches the head diameter of the nail. Nail heads are usually hidden with wood dough or putty or, in really fine cabinet work, by lifting a chip of wood and then gluing it back down again after the

FLAT-FACED PUNCH CAN BE USED TO SET FLAT-HEAD NAILS UNDER WOOD SURFACE.

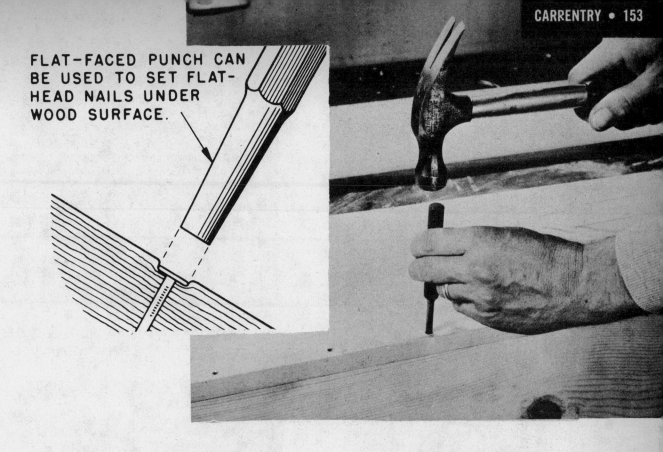

A FEW STAGGERED NAILS (A) ARE BETTER THAN MANY IN A LINE (B).

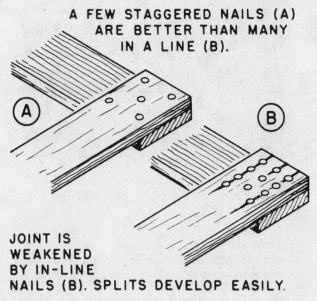

JOINT IS WEAKENED BY IN-LINE NAILS (B). SPLITS DEVELOP EASILY.

NAILS CLINCHED WITH THE GRAIN ARE WEAKER.....

...THAN NAILS CLINCHED ACROSS THE GRAIN

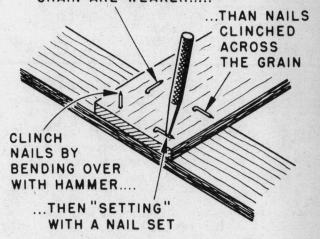

CLINCH NAILS BY BENDING OVER WITH HAMMER....

...THEN "SETTING" WITH A NAIL SET

V-NAILING ON EDGES AND ENDS GIVES MORE STRENGTH.

CONCEAL NAILHEAD BY LIFTING CHIP --- THEN GLUING DOWN AGAIN AFTER NAIL IS DRIVEN IN.

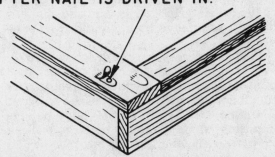

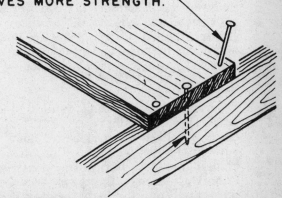

NAIL SHOULD BE THREE TIMES THICKNESS OF PIECE BEING NAILED

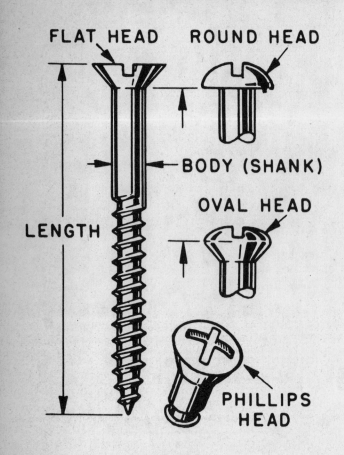

FLAT HEAD   ROUND HEAD

BODY (SHANK)

OVAL HEAD

LENGTH

PHILLIPS HEAD

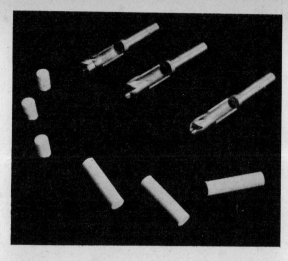

Plug cutters are used in a drill press to cut plugs of the same wood as the workpiece.

Plugs can be cut with end grain, but more often they are cross grain to match the work.

Screws, properly driven, have great holding power, and can be removed and replaced.

nail has been driven home and firmly set.

Not too far back, nails with threaded shanks were introduced. Actual tests indicate these are much improved fasteners which are screw-like in the way they work. Some of them actually drive easier, don't split wood easily, and all of them have greater holding power. They are made in a type to fit almost every building need, even to fence and electrician's staples.

SCREWS

Screws provide the greatest holding power, yet are easily removed. This combination makes them ideal for many jobs where nails just won't do. For example, a hidden glue block in furniture construction is best attached with screws because the screws will pull the parts together providing the same kind of action you get from

clamps. Screws are also more decorative than nails and many times can be left exposed where a nail would look bad or amateurish.

Like nails, screws come in types that are well-suited for outdoor work. They are available in brass, stainless steel, aluminum, galvanized steel or plated in chromium or cadmium. These will not discolor, or rust which would make them unsightly, reduce their gripping power, and make it difficult to remove them should it ever be necessary.

Except for very small screws where an awl or ice pick can be used to start it, a pilot, or lead hole is drilled to avoid splitting the wood and to make it easier to drive. The size and depth of the pilot hole is important since it should be large enough to permit driving the screw but not so

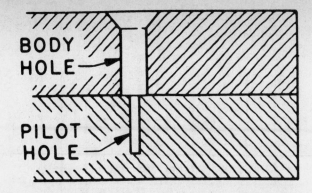

Above shows the proper drilling for screws. Pilot hole is the diameter at base of threads.

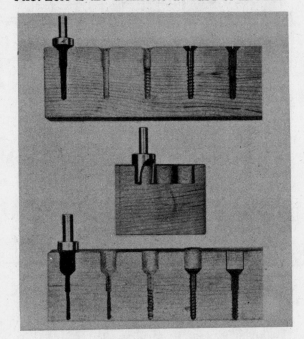

All-in-one drill makes pilot hole, shank hole, and countersinks flush or deep for a plug.

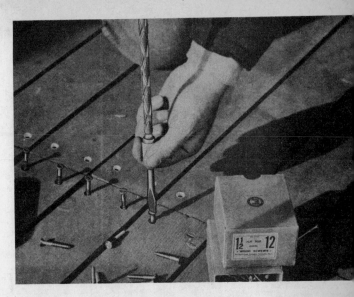

A ratchet drill does a fast job after the holes are formed. All you do is push.

Attachments are available for power drills that reduce the speed for driving screws.

For better holding power in end grain, drill a hole at right angles and insert dowel.

large that the screw will lose its efficiency. The shank, or body hole is always the same size as the screw gauge. The countersink, when needed, is the same dimensions as the screw head. A good procedure to follow, for holding two boards together with screws would be this: First drill the pilot hole through the first and second board to the depth required. Enlarge the hole through the first board in order to grip solidly in the second, thus pulling the two boards slightly together. Use the right size screw driver, one that fits the screw-slot snugly and, if necessary (especially in hardwoods), coat the threads with soap or wax so they'll drive easier.

If the screw is to be concealed, countersink deeper than necessary, or counterbore instead, and cover the screw with putty as you would a nail. Wooden plugs

SCREW SIZE REFERENCE CHART

Size	Body Dia.	¼	⅜	½	⅝	¾	⅞	1	1¼	1½	1¾	2	2¼	2½	2¾	3	3½	4
		SCREW LENGTHS AVAILABLE (IN INCHES)																
0	.060	x																
1	.073	x																
2	.086	x	x	x														
3	.099	x	x	x	x													
4	.112		x	x	x	x												
5	.125		x	x	x	x												
6	.138		x	x	x	x	x	x		x								
7	.151		x	x	x	x	x	x	x	x								
8	.164			x	x	x	x	x	x	x	x	x						
9	.177			x	x	x	x	x	x	x	x	x	x					
10	.190			x	x	x	x	x	x	x	x	x	x					
11	.203				x	x	x	x	x	x	x	x	x					
12	.216					x	x	x	x	x	x	x	x	x				
14	.242						x	x	x	x	x	x	x	x	x			
16	.268								x	x	x	x	x	x	x	x		
18	.294									x	x	x	x	x	x	x	x	x
20	.320										x	x	x	x	x	x	x	x
24	.372																x	x

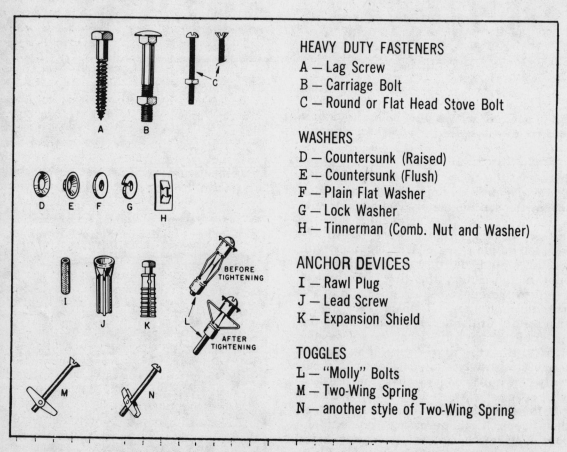

HEAVY DUTY FASTENERS
A — Lag Screw
B — Carriage Bolt
C — Round or Flat Head Stove Bolt

WASHERS
D — Countersunk (Raised)
E — Countersunk (Flush)
F — Plain Flat Washer
G — Lock Washer
H — Tinnerman (Comb. Nut and Washer)

ANCHOR DEVICES
I — Rawl Plug
J — Lead Screw
K — Expansion Shield

TOGGLES
L — "Molly" Bolts
M — Two-Wing Spring
N — another style of Two-Wing Spring

BEFORE TIGHTENING

AFTER TIGHTENING

There is a fastener for every occasion, and it will pay you to know them all.

DRILL SIZES FOR BODY & LEAD (PILOT) HOLES

SCREW SIZE	LEAD HOLE	BODY HOLE
0	—	53
1	—	49
2	56	44
3	52	40
4	51	33
5	49	1/8
6	47	28
7	46	24
8	42	19
9	41	15
10	38	10
11	37	5
12	36	7/32
14	31	D
16	28	I
18	23	19/64
20	11/64	21/64
24	3/16	3/8

NOTE:
Body hole is the same for soft and hard wood.

Lead hole may be slightly larger depending on wood density.

Counterbore hole, if screw is to be hidden with wood plug, should equal head diameter of screw.

Lead holes recommended for #2, 3, 4, and 5 screws are more necessary for hardwoods than softwoods

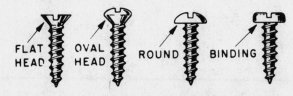

FLAT HEAD   OVAL HEAD   ROUND   BINDING

Sheet metal screws have the thread running up to the head. They can shake loose.

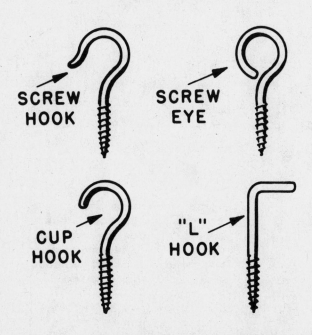

SCREW HOOK   SCREW EYE

CUP HOOK   "L" HOOK

Above are the most common special devices to be found about the house or workshop.

are often used. The screw hole is counterbored at least ¼" and the hole filled with a wooden plug. Special "plug cutters" are available which do a good job of cutting the plugs so that the grain runs crosswise to match the surface grain of the work. Dowels should not be used for this purpose where appearance is a very important factor.

If the screw hole is too large or has become enlarged through repeated removals, partially fill it with steel wool or wood splinters or plastic metal, then replace the screw.

Sheet metal screws are self-tapping and require a hole slightly smaller than the screw diameter. These are used to hold sheet metal together, or to attach something to a sheet metal surface, or sheet metal to another object or surface. For sheet metal joining, types "A" and "B" are available, the former for sheet metal gauges up to 18, the latter for use on sheet metal up to 6 gauge. Shank diameters run from No. 4 to No. 14 in lengths from ⅛" to 2".

Washers are used for appearance and to add strength. Plain flat washers are used under the heads of round head wood screws and lag screws and under both head and nut of bolts, especially in soft woods. The countersunk washers, either flush or raised, are used under the heads of flat head wood and sheet metal screws to keep the screw-head from digging into the material and to improve holding power and appearance.

A fastener does not have to be a nail, a screw, or a bolt. Items like corrugated "nails" are extremely useful to hold butted ends together or even miters where appearance doesn't count too much, or where the fastener can be placed on the back side. Too, there is a type of corrugated fastener for which a special set is sold so it can be set beneath the surface of the wood and puttied over like a nail.

"T" plates and angle plates are special shaped, drilled pieces of metal (usually brass) that can be overlaid to hold two or more parts together. When selected in wrought iron the plates add a decorative detail to a project, much like wrought iron hinges and latches. These can be obtained countersunk for the countersunk screws or with plain holes for round head screws. Sometimes they are supplied with special screws with square heads and cross slots for special appearance.

The most important thing to remember is that there is a right fastening for every job, and a right way to install it. •

Adhesives

Contact cement is ideal for edge veneering on plywood. Rolls of matching woods are available, and a neat job is hard to detect from solid wood. And you have the advantage of the warp-proof laminations. Take great care in placing the strip, for once in contact it cannot be removed.

The new adhesives go beyond the scope of former glues, and research has developed one for the exact job you want it to do.

THERE are test houses in existence today which have been completely assembled without the use of a single nail or other type fastener. This is indicative of the progress that has been made in adhesives. Progress which, as far as the home shop is concerned, not only means better and stronger projects, but easier projects as well. For the use of the right adhesive in the right place most times means a bond that is stronger than the materials being joined. This means that the complicated joinery, so necessary years ago because of the design of the joint itself had to carry much of the load due to inferior adhesives, is no longer necessary. Because of modern adhesives, a simple rabbet or dado will often do today where a dovetail might have been necessary yesterday.

In all cases the application of the adhesive itself is easy, but since no one product is adequate for every gluing job, the trick is in knowing what adhesive to use, and where. In addition to checking the information here, you should carefully read the instructions printed on the labels of the containers and follow them to the letter. This will assure maximum efficiency of the product, hence the most satisfactory job.

Many times the preparation of the wood itself causes a poor bond, if not an outright failure. A wood that contains oil or pitch (lemonwood, certain pine, teak) will have a surface film that will interfere with the glue bond. Casein glue is good for these situations but even beyond this be sure that the mating areas are thoroughly sanded. This will help the glue to grip. Don't sand a part and then put it aside for gluing later. Sand it fairly soon before you're actually going to glue. Any hard, dense surface, oily or not, will make a better bond if the surface is slightly roughened by cross-sanding.

Always apply glue carefully, using just enough to do the job with a minimum of squeeze-out. Always clean away the excess glue immediately. Sometimes a glue will stain so badly that the only solution is to bleach it out.

When gluing dowel, mortise-and-tenon and similar joints always be sure that excess glue can escape. If this isn't done, clamping could create enough pressure in the glue to split the wood. Often, it finds its way *through* the wood to appear as a stain on the surface. Dowels should be grooved, ends of tenons should be chamfered to provide room for, or allow excess glue to escape.

Glue-setting time can often be hastened, but never in a manner not recommended by the manufacturer. For example, the setting time of a urea-resin glue joint can be speeded up through the application of moderate heat to the joint. A heat-lamp is practical to use on small projects. Many types of adhesives should not be used if the shop temperature is below 70 degrees. The wood should be warm. Don't bring it in from an outside storage rack and glue it immediately. Wait for it to warm. •

Read the manufacturer's directions carefully, and follow them to the word. He has spent a lot of research to make the product do the job it's supposed to. Prepare the surfaces properly, and wait out the full drying time for both mating pieces, for a good job here can last the life of the piece.

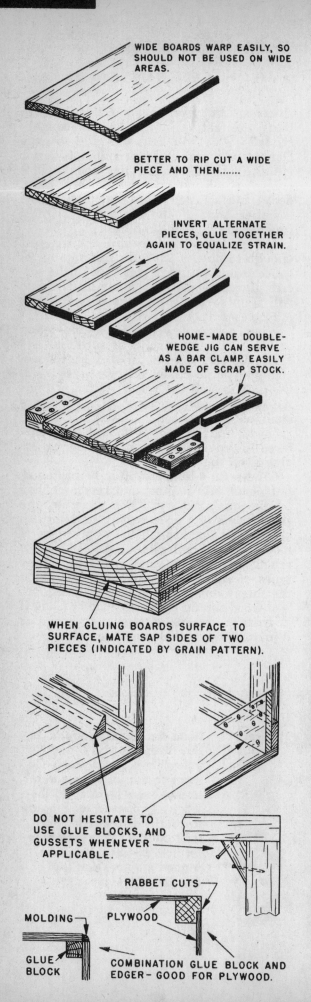

WIDE BOARDS WARP EASILY, SO SHOULD NOT BE USED ON WIDE AREAS.

BETTER TO RIP CUT A WIDE PIECE AND THEN.......

INVERT ALTERNATE PIECES, GLUE TOGETHER AGAIN TO EQUALIZE STRAIN.

HOME-MADE DOUBLE-WEDGE JIG CAN SERVE AS A BAR CLAMP. EASILY MADE OF SCRAP STOCK.

WHEN GLUING BOARDS SURFACE TO SURFACE, MATE SAP SIDES OF TWO PIECES (INDICATED BY GRAIN PATTERN).

DO NOT HESITATE TO USE GLUE BLOCKS, AND GUSSETS WHENEVER APPLICABLE.

RABBET CUTS

MOLDING

PLYWOOD

GLUE BLOCK

COMBINATION GLUE BLOCK AND EDGER- GOOD FOR PLYWOOD.

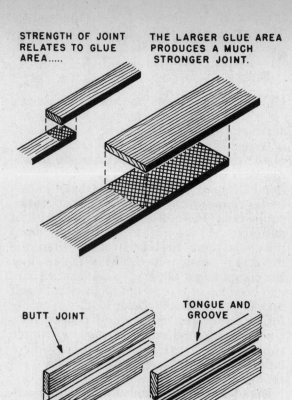

STRENGTH OF JOINT RELATES TO GLUE AREA......

THE LARGER GLUE AREA PRODUCES A MUCH STRONGER JOINT.

BUTT JOINT

TONGUE AND GROOVE

A TONGUE AND GROOVE JOINT IS STRONGER THAN A BUTT BECAUSE OF GREATER GLUE AREA.

Be sure to wipe off any excess cement immediately before it stains the wood.

ADHESIVE TERMINOLOGY YOU SHOULD KNOW

ADHESIVE—Means more than glue. A broader term indicates the material that causes mating of parts that are brought into contact. "Glue" does not include the modern resin adhesives.

ALBUMIN—Type of soluble, dried blood. Mixes cold but sets under heat. Chemical reagents sometimes used. Water resistant.

ANIMAL GLUE—Cooked from bone and hide waste. Does not stand up under moisture exposure. Should not be used hot in a warm room.

BINDER—The ingredient of an adhesive which provides most of the adhesive action which holds pieces together.

BLISTER—Usually associated with veneering. When anything interferes with any area of the veneer from making firm contact, it bulges, is called a blister.

BOND—The adhesive grip where parts come in contact.

CASEIN—Made from dried milk plus other ingredients.

CATALYST—A reagent designed to speed up a chemical reaction that hardens the resin adhesives.

CEMENT—Often used to indicate a kind of adhesive—Contact cement, model cement, etc.

DELAMINATION—Where the layers in a laminate pull apart because the adhesive fails.

DRIER—Industry uses a kiln to thoroughly dry materials to be glued (veneers).

GLUE JOINT—That area of a project where the glue comes in contact with matching parts.

MATCHING—The gluing down of veneers in such a manner as to afford the most attractive appearance; sometimes veneer grains form a design such as a diamond or a full burl.

RESIN—A manufactured material used in plastics. Resin adhesives are used for wood and are better and more durable than the older glues. PHENOLIC resin adhesives are chemically made and harden under heat. Available in liquid, and powder form. Some of them are made so a special accelerator permits them to harden at moderate temperatures. UREA resin adhesives harden under heat plus a catalyst.

SIZING—A diluted adhesive applied to a surface to prepare it for full glue application. Good to do when woods of different densities are glued together and on end-grain joints. Anyplace where porosity or grain character of the wood might absorb too much of the glue.

SOLVENT—Liquid in which dry glue is dissolved.

SQUEEZE-OUT—The glue which is squeezed out from between parts being joined when pressure is applied. (Should be cleaned away with a damp cloth before it has a chance to stain wood.)

THERMOPLASTIC—Descriptive of materials which soften under heat.

THERMOSETTING—Usually descriptive of adhesive which hardens under heat. •

Contact cement is a blessing for large panels that cannot be clamped easily.

It also makes strip and trim finishing easier by eliminating nails and putty.

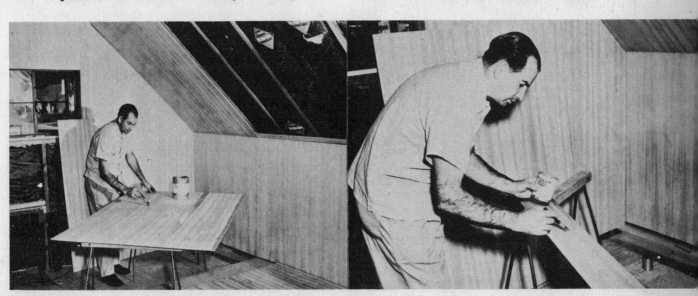

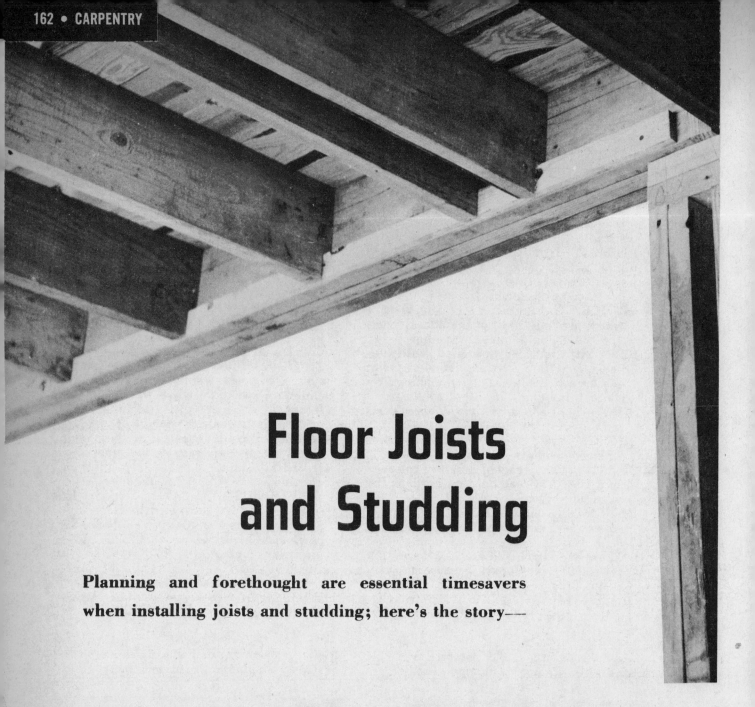

Floor Joists and Studding

Planning and forethought are essential timesavers when installing joists and studding; here's the story—

AFTER the foundation forms have been removed it's time to think about installing the joists and studding. The carpenter then places the 2x6 sills and the girder or sleeper in position. A 2x10 floor joist should not span over 16 feet, so that a house over this width will require two sections of floor joists to reach across the floor of the house. The central ends therefore must be supported by a girder running lengthways of the house and level with the top of the sills. The sills are carefully checked diagonally from opposite corners of the house to prove the sills are square. Ells, porches, or other projections from the main building are squared separately by diagonal measurements across their opposite corners. When the exact location of

the sills have been determined, two nails are driven into the masonry on each side of each corner to temporarily hold and mark the sills.

So far, there has been no provision to place the central girder but until the sills are leveled it is difficult to determine just how high this girder must be placed. Usually the girder, or sleeper as carpenters call it, is a 6x8, set on edge. The carpenters will stretch a line from the center of the recess on top of the sill to a similar point at the other end of the foundation to indicate both the top and the position of the girder. The carpenters measure down from this line to each pedestal, deduct the width of the girder, cut and erect the posts, normally 6x6's. The posts are set to a straight

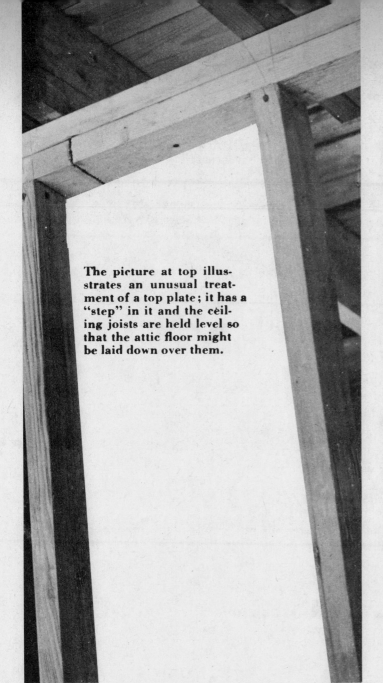

The picture at top illustrates an unusual treatment of a top plate; it has a "step" in it and the ceiling joists are held level so that the attic floor might be laid down over them.

Above, bottom view of floor joists and subflooring and 2x8 "cats" used for bracing between joists, toenailed in.

Above, another view of joists and subflooring from below; here, "X" 2x4 bracing is seen before nailing.

line with the recesses and are braced in position. Since the girders rest on 6x6 posts, the two ends near the center of the basement have only a 3-inch bearing. Most builders use a 6x6 block, about 18 inches long, for a cap and this thickness must be deducted from the length of this post. Frequently, two 2x8 scabs are also nailed across this joint. After the posts are up, the carpenters remove the chalk line, saw out that portion of the sill over the recesses and cut the girder to the required length. Generally these are in two pieces and are manhandled to the top of the posts and into the recesses in each end wall. Since these recesses with the sill are probably 8 or 8½ inches deep, both ends of the girder are shimmed up until the top is exactly level with those sills that are adjoining.

Next Come The Joists

Floor Joists: When the sills and girder are in place the house is ready for the floor joists. These are usually 2x10's—12 to 16 feet long, squared on the outside end and allowed to lap past each other on the girder. However, the first and last joists that are on each end must be flush on the outside with the end sills and are cut so they will meet square or butt over the girder. The distance between floor joists in residences is usually 16 inches, center to center, but with the joist *next* to the outside it is not possible for both pieces to be exactly 16 inches from the outside joist which is straight, while in this second set, one joist

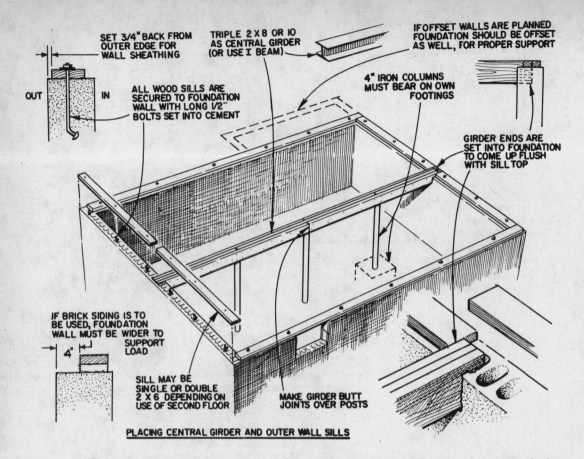

SET 3/4" BACK FROM OUTER EDGE FOR WALL SHEATHING

OUT   IN

ALL WOOD SILLS ARE SECURED TO FOUNDATION WALL WITH LONG 1/2" BOLTS SET INTO CEMENT

TRIPLE 2 X 8 OR 10 AS CENTRAL GIRDER (OR USE I BEAM)

IF OFFSET WALLS ARE PLANNED FOUNDATION SHOULD BE OFFSET AS WELL, FOR PROPER SUPPORT

4" IRON COLUMNS MUST BEAR ON OWN FOOTINGS

GIRDER ENDS ARE SET INTO FOUNDATION TO COME UP FLUSH WITH SILL TOP

IF BRICK SIDING IS TO BE USED, FOUNDATION WALL MUST BE WIDER TO SUPPORT LOAD

4"

SILL MAY BE SINGLE OR DOUBLE 2 X 6 DEPENDING ON USE OF SECOND FLOOR

MAKE GIRDER BUTT JOINTS OVER POSTS

PLACING CENTRAL GIRDER AND OUTER WALL SILLS

Details for laying down 2x6 sills after foundation is in are illustrated; note the methods for securing sills and central girder so maximum strength of structure will be inherent in home.

Further details of central girder construction are seen below; subflooring is cut flush with sill edge and not butted into it for strength.

Bay window can be supported without concrete foundation by means shown below; joists are extended beyond the foundation.

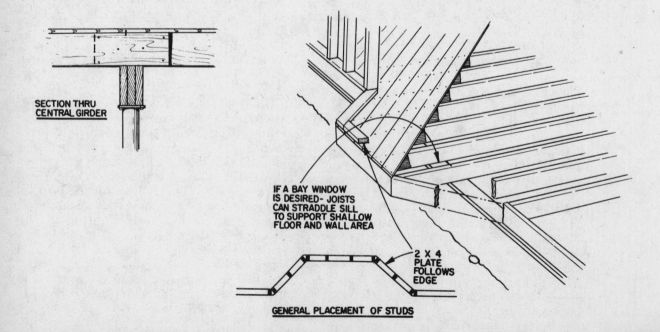

SECTION THRU CENTRAL GIRDER

IF A BAY WINDOW IS DESIRED- JOISTS CAN STRADDLE SILL TO SUPPORT SHALLOW FLOOR AND WALL AREA

2 X 4 PLATE FOLLOWS EDGE

GENERAL PLACEMENT OF STUDS

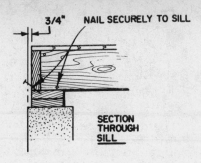

3/4"   NAIL SECURELY TO SILL

SECTION
THROUGH
SILL

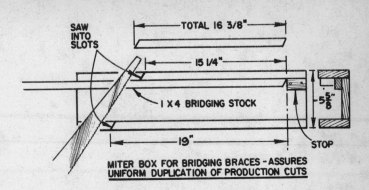

SAW
INTO
SLOTS

TOTAL 16 3/8"

15 1/4"

1 X 4 BRIDGING STOCK

19"

5 5/8"

STOP

MITER BOX FOR BRIDGING BRACES - ASSURES
UNIFORM DUPLICATION OF PRODUCTION CUTS

Note that double sill is placed ¾ inch
in from foundation edge; sill is anchor-bolted
to foundation, floor joists are toenailed in.

Drawing details construction of miter box
that is intended for use in cutting cross
bridging; it's necessary time and labor saver.

In addition to two methods of laying down subflooring detailed below, plywood can be used.

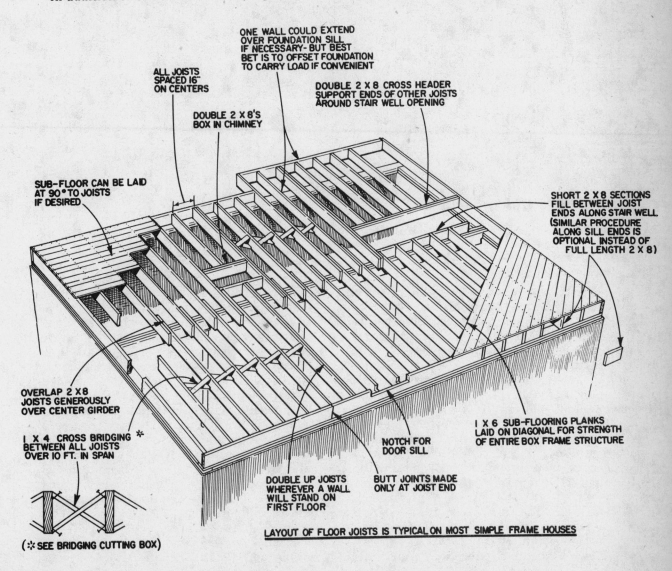

ONE WALL COULD EXTEND
OVER FOUNDATION SILL
IF NECESSARY- BUT BEST
BET IS TO OFFSET FOUNDATION
TO CARRY LOAD IF CONVENIENT

ALL JOISTS
SPACED 16"
ON CENTERS

DOUBLE 2 X 8 CROSS HEADER
SUPPORT ENDS OF OTHER JOISTS
AROUND STAIR WELL OPENING

DOUBLE 2 X 8'S
BOX IN CHIMNEY

SUB-FLOOR CAN BE LAID
AT 90° TO JOISTS
IF DESIRED

SHORT 2 X 8 SECTIONS
FILL BETWEEN JOIST
ENDS ALONG STAIR WELL
(SIMILAR PROCEDURE
ALONG SILL ENDS IS
OPTIONAL INSTEAD OF
FULL LENGTH 2 X 8)

OVERLAP 2 X 8
JOISTS GENEROUSLY
OVER CENTER GIRDER

1 X 4 CROSS BRIDGING *
BETWEEN ALL JOISTS
OVER 10 FT. IN SPAN

DOUBLE UP JOISTS
WHEREVER A WALL
WILL STAND ON
FIRST FLOOR

NOTCH FOR
DOOR SILL

BUTT JOINTS MADE
ONLY AT JOIST END

1 X 6 SUB-FLOORING PLANKS
LAID ON DIAGONAL FOR STRENGTH
OF ENTIRE BOX FRAME STRUCTURE

(* SEE BRIDGING CUTTING BOX)

LAYOUT OF FLOOR JOISTS IS TYPICAL ON MOST SIMPLE FRAME HOUSES

A table saw is one of the most useful labor-savers (see Tools and Materials); here, studs are cut.

overlaps the other, so carpenters set one joist on each side of the 16-inch mark. From here in the joists can be set exactly 16 inches from each other, except where a partition or stair well interferes.

Usually carpenters measure and mark on the sill the position of cross partitions, stair wells, fireplace, chimney or other openings that require a double joist or any that are out of position before they start on the erection. It will be obvious that partitions on each side of the girder will be different, and double floor joists will not always be opposite. In fact, the central joists may be so confused that carpenters will start the 16-inch rhythm from the other end and work out the central portion the best way they can.

Two carpenters, one standing on the sill

and the other on the girder, can erect all floor joists very quickly. Frequently the edges of the joists are not exactly straight, and carpenters place the curve or crown edge uppermost. After the joists have been placed, the carpenters use a straightedge 10 to 14 feet long and place it over the joists near the ends. Some joists will probably be low and will have to be shimmed up with shingles. Other joists may be exceptionally high and will have to be notched out on the bottom where they rest on the sills or the girder. The straightedge is passed over the joist at both ends, but unless the joists are exceptionally straight it will be difficult to get all the joists exactly level.

Usually one-eighth of an inch all around is considered close enough. After the joists are leveled, they are nailed permanently to the sills and the girder.

As soon as the joists are in place, carpenters usually place the bridging. This is an X row of double bracing, placed between each floor joist, midway between the girder and the side sills. Usually they consist of two 2x4's or 1x4's cut and fitted so each will run from the top of one joist to the bottom of the adjacent joist to form an "X." Most building codes specify that joists with over an 8-foot span must be bridged. These short braces are usually cut in a miter box.

Stair Well: Basement stairs require an opening in the floor joists that will allow at least 72 inches headroom from the header across the ends of the floor joists to the stair tread directly below. Most city codes require 76 inches for what is termed headroom. With 2x10 floor joists, the floor system to the top of the finished floor is 9½ inches plus 1½ inches, or 11 inches plus 76 inches for headroom for a total of 87 inches from the finished floor to the tread directly below the header at this end of the stair well. Stair steps, as cut on the stair stringer, should be about 8 inches for the riser and 10 inches for the tread. On top of the tread in the stringer is nailed a 11½-inch stair tread or, in the case of a basement stair, perhaps a 2x12, so that the tread has a nose which measures about 1½ inches past the riser. Since the risers are 8 inches, the stairs descend 8 inches at each step for 11 risers to allow for the required 87 inches for the headroom and the thickness of the floor system. Thus the headroom and the necessary length of the stair well is determined by the number of risers. Carpenters make the stair well just long enough to go past the last necessary riser. The stairs and the well begin with a riser at the floor and the well stops just as soon as the vertical measurement will reach the eleventh tread. The result is 11 risers and 10 treads. The stair stringer has dropped vertically 11x8 or 88 inches and has moved horizontally 10x10 or 100 inches; 100 inches only places the header directly over the eleventh riser and it lacks the 1½ inches of nosing, previously mentioned, on the tread to allow the vertical measurement to reach the eleventh tread. Therefore, the required length of the stair well is 10 treads times 10 inches plus 1½ inches of nosing or 102 inches for the assumed size of risers, tread, headroom and floor joists.

Stair wells that are parallel to the floor joists require double joists on each side and double headers.

If the stair well is across the joists, it is necessary to allow for double headers on each side or 6½ inches plus the net opening. In this case, carpenters usually place the floor joists complete and cut for the stair well later. This means that the floor joists against the well must be supported from below on each side of the opening before

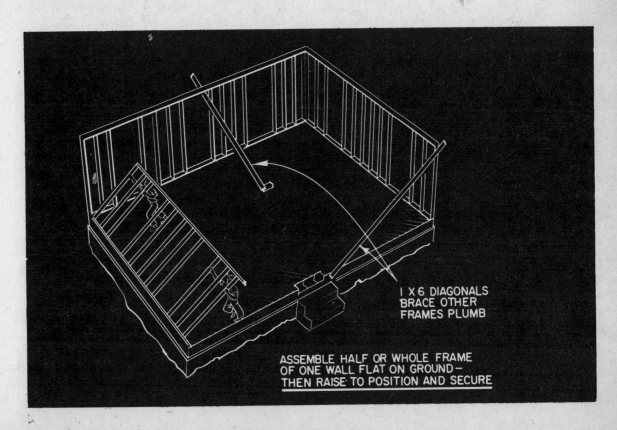

I X 6 DIAGONALS BRACE OTHER FRAMES PLUMB

ASSEMBLE HALF OR WHOLE FRAME OF ONE WALL FLAT ON GROUND — THEN RAISE TO POSITION AND SECURE

they can be cut. And after the long headers are in place and the basement poured, permanent posts or some method of support must be placed at each corner of the stair well.

Interior Brickwork

Fireplaces: These are frequently on the outside wall and require an opening in the foundation, floor joists, and the studding. This necessitates establishing the width of the fireplace. The plans should show the size of the opening in the front of the fireplace and the brick on each side of the opening but carpenters should check the figures. Occasionally dimensions on a fireplace will be found that the masons cannot lay. Dimensions should be close to the multiples of the size of the brick. This size varies but ordinarily they measure 2⅛x4x8 and a half-inch mortar joint makes the measure 2⅜x4¼x8¼ for each brick. The number of bricks on each side of the front opening, called the projection, must be 1, 1½ or 2 with measurements of 8 inches, 12½ inches, or 16½ inches and cannot be any other. Similarly the measurement over the opening should be close to a multiple of 4¼ inches. Thirty inches, which is a common width is 3½ bricks plus 2 inches for mortar joints. To allow for the different sizes of bricks and their mortar, carpenters usually allow 1½ inches over the net width on each side of the fireplace

for the opening in the foundation and the adjacent house studs.

To set the floor joists requires that the distance the fireplace projects into the room be known or can be determined, to which normally must be added 18 inches for the width of the hearth. Assuming an actual projection into the room of 10 inches, plus 18 inches for the hearth and 3½ inches for the studding, makes the inside of the floor joist or the header 31½ inches to the *outside* wall. Fireplaces require a double header on all three sides regardless of whether the floor joists butt against the hearth or are parallel to it. If the house has a full basement, the projection into the room also projects almost this much inside the outside wall and requires a foundation to the basement floor. As a rule this is made of brick and is part of the masonry. Another item that belongs to the masons is the form under the hearth. Ordinarily they nail a 2x4 header in the soft mortar of the brick work and another to the floor joist or the header. Short pieces of shiplap are cut to go between. This is covered with mortar and a final thickness of tile is level with the finish floor.

A double 2x6 header is placed in the wall studs over the brick work forming the mantel. Usually the bottom of this header is about an inch below the specified height of the mantel. That is, carpenters place across the brick work forming the mantel,

Below, a different treatment of flooring; main girders are 4x6 set on posts with 2x4 blocking at panel edges; building costs are cut and with plywood used, construction is speeded.

Thick fir plywood above, differs in construction from diagram below in that it is set flush with foundation edge. Technique saves labor, time, material. Plywood is "squeakless" subfloor.

Construction details of flooring method pictured at left and above; panels should be applied across main girders with staggered joints. Nail with 10d common or 8d common ring-shank nails, spaced 6 inches on all bearings. Under resilient flooring, set nails in floor 1/16th inch.

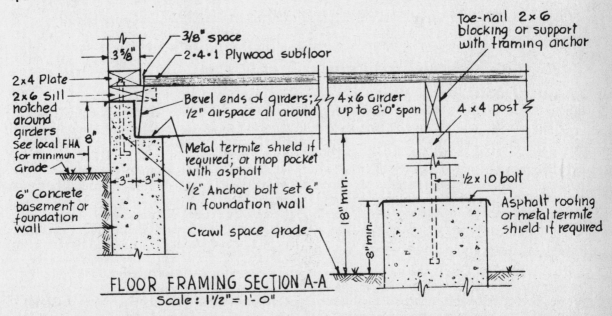

FLOOR FRAMING SECTION A-A
Scale: 1½" = 1'-0"

REAR ELEVATION

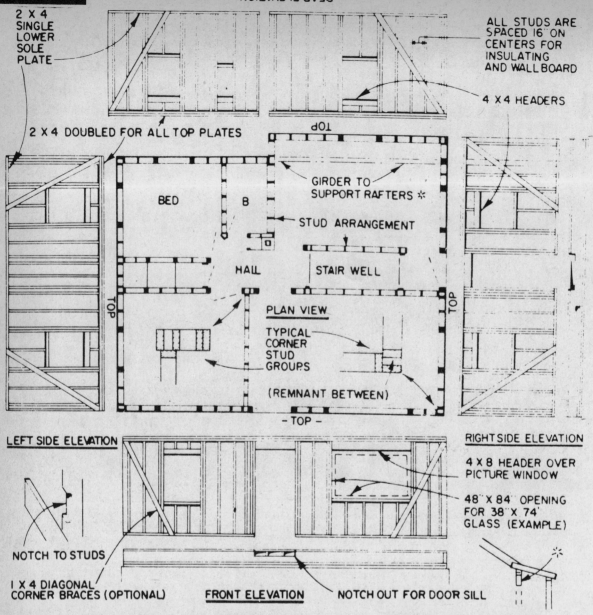

2 X 4 SINGLE LOWER SOLE PLATE

ALL STUDS ARE SPACED 16" ON CENTERS FOR INSULATING AND WALLBOARD

4 X 4 HEADERS

2 X 4 DOUBLED FOR ALL TOP PLATES

TOP

GIRDER TO SUPPORT RAFTERS ✲

STUD ARRANGEMENT

BED   B

HALL

STAIR WELL

TOP

PLAN VIEW

TYPICAL CORNER STUD GROUPS

(REMNANT BETWEEN)

- TOP -

LEFT SIDE ELEVATION

RIGHT SIDE ELEVATION

4 X 8 HEADER OVER PICTURE WINDOW

48" X 84" OPENING FOR 38" X 74" GLASS (EXAMPLE)

NOTCH TO STUDS

1 X 4 DIAGONAL CORNER BRACES (OPTIONAL)

FRONT ELEVATION   NOTCH OUT FOR DOOR SILL

DRAWING SHOWING PLAN OF SIMPLE FRAME HOUSE AND DETAIL STUDDING FOR EACH WALL

A typical plan for arrangement of studding is shown; construction is basic for homes.

short 2x4's to which is nailed ¾ inch of finished boards for a total of 2½ inches. This should be the specified height but to allow a little clearance above the brick work the bottom of the header should be placed about 1½ inches below this specified height. Actually, many carpenters place the adjoining wall studs and omit the rest of the framing, except the top plates, until the fireplace is in place.

Putting Down The Floor

Rough Floor: The house is now ready for the subfloor of inch sheeting. Normally these are 1x10 boards that have already been used in the forms and are more or less stained with concrete. In the past these boards were laid at right angles to the floor joist and had to be cut to butt at a joist. Today, most carpenters lay the flooring diagonally. A short piece of scrap is laid across at one corner of the floor joists system at about a 45-degree angle with the tongue against the joists. The boards are laid so each end projects beyond the sills. After several boards have been laid it will become necessary to use two boards to reach across the floor. In this case, the carpenters lay the first board with about half of one end covering a floor joist and the other end projects beyond the sill. The second board butts against the first. One end partly lies on the same joist and the other end projects beyond the opposite sill. Seldom are any of the boards cut or squared. If the raw ends do not fit by over

Above, a home with all wall frames up; headers are 4x4s; the top plates are doubled 2x4s.

half an inch a carpenter will trim the second board to fit the first or if a board is too long a carpenter will cut it so as to use the extra length somewhere else. When the flooring is complete the carpenters will nail a 2x4 temporarily even with the sills, as guides to trim off the floor sheeting. The projecting ends are then chopped off with a sharp hatchet or cut with a power saw. The flooring is also cut or chopped around the openings in the floor. Ordinarily all one-inch sheeting from 6 to 10 inches wide is nailed with two 8d nails at each intersection with a floor joist, rafter or stud.

The Walls

Studding, Top and Bottom Plates: The carpenters are now ready to erect the out-

side studs which establish the height of the rooms. If this height is not specifically stated custom sets it at 8 feet. The rough frame of the outside wall around the entire house consists of a 2x4 laid flat on the rough floor above the sill and is termed the bottom plate. From this the studding rise to make the height of the rooms and on top of these are a double row of 2x4's laid flat called the top plates that will support the rafters. This is simple but the openings required for the windows and doors are a little more difficult until an enormous number of figures are memorized. To begin with the outside wall starts from the rough floor and at the top ¾ of an inch of plaster will lap down below the top edge of the top plate. Therefore, instead of the outside wall being 8 feet high it must be 96 inches, plus ¾ inch for finish floor and another ¾ inch for the plaster and just to be certain there is enough height, carpenters usually add another ¼ inch making 96 inches for net height, ¾ inch for finish floor, ¾ inch for the plaster on the ceiling, ¼ inch for an extra allowance, equaling 97¾ inches as the total height required for the outside wall.

The first act of the carpenters is to cut the 2x4 studs that stand erect between the top and bottom plates. Since there are three 2x4's laid flat and if they are standard thickness they will probably measure $3x1\frac{9}{16}$ or 4¾ inches; 97¾ inches minus 4¾ inches is 93 inches as the length of the studs to be cut in between the plates.

While one carpenter is cutting the studding another is laying out the position of these studs on what will be the top and bottom plates.

Framing For Doors

Rough Frame for Windows and Doors:

Before it is possible to lay out the position of the studding, it is necessary to know the width and length required for the rough frame for the windows and doors. Generally the plans show the width of the doors. Normally this is 3 feet for the front door, 2 feet 6 inches for the back and inside doors and less for closet doors. On both sides and across the top of each door is a finished frame, with an inset ½x1⅜ inches or 1⅞ inches to receive the door. This frame is frequently spoken of as the jamb and measures, without the inset which does not have to be considered, one inch thick for the front door and ¾ inch for the back and inside doors. The jambs in turn are set inside of what is termed the rough frame. This consists of a 2x4 on each side that are called door studs and are nailed to the adjoining wall or house studs. On top of these door studs and across the top over the doorway is a double 2x4 spoken of as the header. Between this rough frame and the jambs or finish frame is ¼- to ½-inch space or clearance to allow

Helpful construction hints when erecting studding are detailed below; all are aimed at strength.

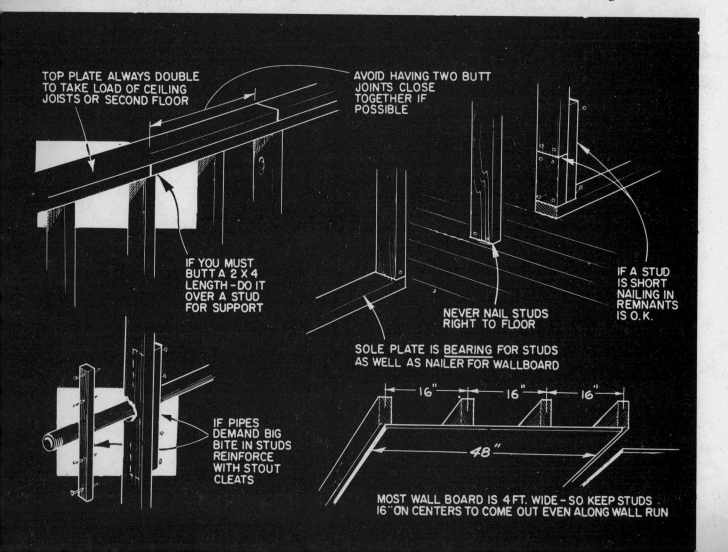

TOP PLATE ALWAYS DOUBLE TO TAKE LOAD OF CEILING JOISTS OR SECOND FLOOR

AVOID HAVING TWO BUTT JOINTS CLOSE TOGETHER IF POSSIBLE

IF YOU MUST BUTT A 2 X 4 LENGTH – DO IT OVER A STUD FOR SUPPORT

IF A STUD IS SHORT NAILING IN REMNANTS IS O.K.

NEVER NAIL STUDS RIGHT TO FLOOR

SOLE PLATE IS BEARING FOR STUDS AS WELL AS NAILER FOR WALLBOARD

IF PIPES DEMAND BIG BITE IN STUDS REINFORCE WITH STOUT CLEATS

16"   16"   16"

48"

MOST WALL BOARD IS 4 FT. WIDE – SO KEEP STUDS 16" ON CENTERS TO COME OUT EVEN ALONG WALL RUN

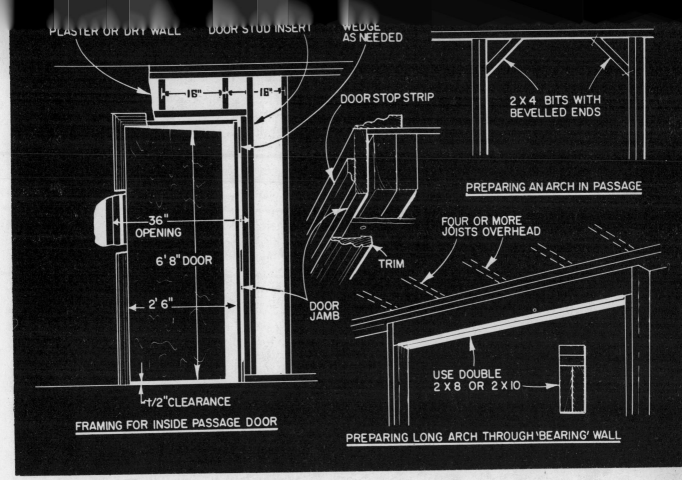

PLASTER OR DRY WALL   DOOR STUD INSERT   WEDGE AS NEEDED

16"   16"

DOOR STOP STRIP

2 X 4 BITS WITH BEVELLED ENDS

36" OPENING

6' 8" DOOR

PREPARING AN ARCH IN PASSAGE

FOUR OR MORE JOISTS OVERHEAD

2' 6"

TRIM

DOOR JAMB

t/2" CLEARANCE

FRAMING FOR INSIDE PASSAGE DOOR

USE DOUBLE 2 X 8 OR 2 X 10

PREPARING LONG ARCH THROUGH 'BEARING' WALL

Doors and archways require special framing; "bearing" archway uses double 2x8s, 2x10s.

the assembled jambs an easy entrance. On each side, in this space, wedges are driven to make and hold the jambs absolutely plumb and rigid for the door hinges.

As a rule carpenters place front and back door headers over the outside doors when the studs are raised and it is necessary to determine the height they shall be placed and the length of the door studs. The length of height of doors vary but normally in houses, they are 6 feet 8 inches. The 2x4 door studs rest on the bottom plate but the portion of the bottom plate in the doorway, when the jambs are placed, is cut away, so here is 1⅝ inches that must be deducted to obtain the length of the 2x4 door studs. The 4x4 header over the top door jamb is nailed to the top of the door studs. Therefore the length of the 2x4 door studs for the door is as follows: 6 feet 8 inches or 80 inches for the height of the door, assumed; 1 inch for the top jamb, for the front door; ½-inch clearance between the top jamb and the header; ¾ inch supposedly for the thickness of the finished floor; ½ inch as an allowance for the thickness of the threshold. (See *Windows and Doors*); equals 82¾ inches as the total distance from the rough floor to the bottom of the door

header. From this is deducted 1⅝ inches for the thickness of the bottom plate leaving 81⅛ inches as the actual length of the door stud as it rests on top of the bottom plate under the above conditions.

The allowance for the back door is very similar, except most back doors are only 2 feet 6 inches instead of 3 feet, and the jambs or finish frame may be only ¾ inch instead of an inch as for the front door.

Allowances for the height of inside doors are a trifle different but they add up the same: 6 feet 8 inches or 80 inches for the door; ¾ inch for the door jamb over the door; ½ inch for clearance between the jamb and the header; ¾ inch for the finish floor; ¾ inch over the floor for clearance for the rugs; equals 82¾ inches for the total height from rough floor to the header.

As ordinarily constructed the 2x4 bottom plate is uncut at this time and door studs rest on top of the plate. Therefore the actual length of this door stud is also 82¾ inches less 1⅝ or 81⅛ inches, the same as for the other doors. The allowance for the width of an inside door, or any door, is very similar to that described for the front door, except for variations in the thickness of the door jambs.

Above. a sectional view of the framing required for a house with bottom plate for top story studs laid on top of floor joists.

Above, partition studs with inside door frame; note the extra studding near the door frame that contributed extra strength to structure.

D H (Double Hung) is specification assurance that both sash shall be hung on weights or springs.

The general assembly of a window closely resembles a door, except the glass dimensions as written on the plans makes it necessary to add for the wood surrounding the glass. Fortunately with the exception of the central piece between the two panes, termed the meeting rail, this surrounding wood known as the sash is always 2 inches. Thus to obtain the width between the wall studs for the window opening it is necessary to allow for this sash, the finished window frame which is also called the window jambs, the clearance as with the door and the 2x4 window studs that are nailed flat to the wall studs.

Today most double sash windows use some form of spring balances set into the sash. The window jambs are nailed through the wedges in the clearance space to the 2x4 rough frame or window studs. For the height of the top headers, it is an unwritten law to place the top of all window sash even with the top of the outside doors which, as described, placed the header 82¾ inches above the rough floor.

Small house-size plate glass windows, cottage windows, single and multi-paned windows, in fact all other windows, including double metal sash windows, are measured over the sash and may have either the standard sill or the flat form. Otherwise the frames are usually standard except there is no slot for a parting strip or a meeting rail and the outside stop is similar to an inside stop. The allowance for height is usually 1½ inches for the top

Above, a laminated girder (for strength) is shown above a large door opening in the studded partition; girder's strength is great.

Framing is for an inside basement wall for a basement playroom, on concrete block supports; diagonal bracing is used temporarily.

jamb and clearance and about 1½ to 2¾ inches, depending on the shape of the sill for a total of 3 to 4½ inches over the size of the sash.

The depth of top headers varies with the length of the span. As a rule it is customary to use two 2x4's for a 36-inch span or less. From 36 inches to 54 inches, 4x6's are used and 4x8's to 72 inches.

In this connection it is interesting to note that in recent years, homeowners are demanding extra wide front windows that require double 2x12 headers. These are placed directly against the top plates of the outside wall. As mentioned before, a room 8 feet high requires the outside wall to be 97¾ inches from the rough floor to the top of the top plate. The bottom of the door header is set at 82¾ inches leaving 15 inches of the wall above the door. These large windows with a 11½-inch header and 3¼ inches for the top plate require 14¾ inches and automatically set the bottom of the 2x12 header within a quarter of an inch of being level with the bottom of the door header which is close enough.

There are other forms of windows, like metal sash or plate glass without sash, in which the carpenter must find out definitely their size before the adjacent studs can be placed. Some stucco houses are now being built with metal single *sash* without any finish frame. The plaster is rolled around on the inside for inside trim and stop and the same is done with the stucco on the outside. The stool is a special shaped tile.

The window frame must be set before the house can be plastered and if it should

Above, a fireplace partially constructed with mortar below the hearth, the clean-out and the brick work almost ready for tiling.

Framing, seen from basement, is for the fireplace shown at top; notice the double studding used for strength of support.

Here, steel post supporting steel girder is seen in basement with floor joist framed into the girder; note the shims at the girder bottom.

A steel girder is used to support floor joists in this home; steel pillars support girder, allow for more open space than use of wood.

Teco Triple-Grip metal joist hangers are used to brace 2x4 blocking against 4x6 girders as alternate to toenailing subfloor framework.

Bottom plates are here laid down over plywood subflooring; see page 44 for details of framework construction beneath subfloor.

happen that an opening is wrong, it is still possible to knock out the offending 2x4's and replace.

Erection of Studding: After the rough floor sheeting is finished, the floor is swept clean of blocks and chips and the house studding is ready to be erected. Two lines of 2x4's which are to form the top and bottom plates for one side of the building are first laid out on the floor. The different pieces forming each plate are nailed together with short 2x4 scabs on the side of the plates that will be inside the wall. Both plates must be exactly the same length as the side sills, so carpenters simply lay one at a time over the sill on the floor. The 2x4's lie on the floor side by side with one edge up, they are ready to be marked for the position of the studs. It is important to remember that lath or wallboard, which is four feet long, must be nailed to this studding at every corner. Studs must always be placed 12, 16 or 24 inches center to center.

Outside wall corners have two main forms that provide studs for lath or wallboard. The topmost is the easiest to build, and is the one laid off on the 2x4's in the illustration. Two of the 2x4's for the corner are erected with the studs on the side of the house. The third stud is erected with the studs on the end of the house. A drawing shows the arrangement of the corner studding where a partition joins the outside wall and also the arrangement of the studs where two partitions intersect. Also illustrated is the marking of the plates for one side of a house with windows for two bedrooms and a bath. The small letters are the letters carpenters usually use to mark on the position of each stud. Thus C on the plate means cripple or corner; S is a full length wall stud; P, the stud in the corner next to a partition; W, window stud next to the window frame; and D, is a door stud.

The carpenters first lay out the studs for both corners and the two studs forming the corner of each intersecting partition. The rooms are seldom the exact size indicated but usually include one partition and sometimes both the partition and the outside wall. When the position of the partition is marked, the carpenter marks the position of all the studs. Usually the last one next to a partition or the end of the house will be less than 16 inches but if it is only an inch it must go there. A four-foot wall board will not stretch. After the partition is past, the first stud is again 16 inches, much the same as the floor joists. The next step is to mark the position of the windows and doors.

Right, corner of bottom plate (2x4) laid plywood subflooring is butt-jointed; studs will be 16 inches on center on plate.

Left, outside studs, partition studs and ceiling joists are here temporarily braced and ready for rafter erection.

Right, two-story house uses double bottom plate for upper level; the diagonal bracing is only temporary.

Below, cripple studs (2x4) are toenailed below a picture window, are placed on 16-inch centers

Remember, there is no real substitute for careful workmanship

After the plates on the first side are marked and lettered, the plates are spread stud length apart on the floor with the marked edge up and the house studs, door and window studs and at least the top headers are nailed in position. The wall is then raised and braced in position. This side is followed by one end, the second side and the last end in that order, to avoid as much as possible, the interference from braces.

When the four outside walls are up and nailed together at the corners, the house is plumbed and braced across the studding, carpenters place their plumb levels on both sides of at least two corner studs and shift that whole side until it is plumb. A second carpenter then nails a diagonal brace to the studding on the inside to hold that side in place. If the frame is large, carpenters often plumb all four corners.

In this connection any box-like structure can be kept true if the bottom is started square and level by carefully holding like members exactly equal in length. Thus if the sills are level and the studs are equal in length, the top plate will be level. Similarly if the plates are of equal length and two corners are plumbed, the top plates will be square with the floor and each other.

The partitions are now laid out with openings for inside doors raised and nailed into position. Usually the carpenters raise the smaller rooms first, as sometimes the necessary room to assemble each wall becomes a problem. It will be noted that each partition left the outside wall with the studs in the 16-inch position and is called the first corner. At the other end of each partition the last regular stud is normally not spaced 16 inches and this is termed the second corner. As ordinarily laid out, each side of every room will thus have a first and second corner and every corner must provide two studs for the wallboard. Occasionally, for inside walls that do not have a door, studs can be set edgeways, so the framing for the wall is only 1½ inches thick. The plates also have to be set on edge and the correct length of these studs cannot be cut with accuracy until the width of these two plates has been determined.

The plumbing in the bathroom requires a pipe to go through the roof for ventilation. In some localities the building code specifies that 4-inch cast iron pipe shall be used. The rule on this pipe requires that the wall for this outlet be made of 6-inch studs and plates. Usually the carpenters check with the plumber to be sure the position on the plans is satisfactory. The plans may also show a small error that carpenters are supposed to correct. Frequently the tub is set between two partitions that are shown as five feet apart. A 5-foot (or 5′ 6″) tub measures exactly that. The inside plaster butts against the top edge of the tub to form a watertight joint and no allowance for this is necessary but carpenters stretch 5 feet on the plans to 5 feet ½ inch so the tub can be placed without difficulty.

After the house is plumbed and the partitions are in place, a carpenter will walk around the outside and carefully look through the framework for studs that are out of plumb or position or any other discrepancy. The top plate is now doubled with another 2x4, which laps the joints of the top plate below at the corners and intersections. The outside corner studs must also be braced on each side with short 2x4's cut in between the studding. Ordinarily the carpenters place a straightedge or a string from the top of the corner to the bottom plate at about a 45-degree angle and mark on the studding where the line for these pieces should be. The pieces may be cut from a pattern, scratched to fit or the miter box for the bridging may be re-cut for a 45 angle (12x12) with a stop for the proper length.

The Ceiling

Ceiling Joists: These are laid on the top plates of the partitions and the outside walls. Usually they are parallel to the floor joists and should be used, as much as possible, as part of a truss to keep the rafters from spreading the walls. If the house has only an attic they are called ceiling joists and where the span is less than 11 feet and on 16-inch centers they may be only 2x4's. If the house is one and a half or two story, they are considered floor joists and are usually 2x8's. On homes with a gable end, the first joist is laid just inside the top plates, so as to allow room for the gable studs a little later to set on the top plate. For hipped roofs the first joist must be set back far enough from the wall plate that is parallel to clear the hip rafters and be in the 16-inch position for the wallboards on the ceiling below. To support the wallboard in the corner under the hips, carpenters cut 2x4 inserts to fit between the rafters. The joists are now placed 16-inch centers up to the first partition either above or below. At this point carpenter procedure varies. If the parallel partition will be above for a room upstairs, some will put in two extra joists nailed together and will hold the 16-inch spacing for the other joists. Others will put in two joists 3½ inches apart and start the 16-inch spacing on the other side, which makes the sheet rock men cut the panels at this point. If the upstairs room size is close, many will change the size a little to avoid placing an extra joist. When the ceiling joist being laid approaches a partition *below,* one joist must be placed on the *far* side for the wall board panels and the 16-inch spacing starts again. To provide a bearing for the panels on the *first* side, carpenters nail a 1x6 flat on the top plate. Where partitions below are close together, like closets or bathrooms, the first partition may be disregarded and bearings for the wallboard panels are provided by

a flat 1x6 projecting on *each* side of the plate. It is not absolutely necessary that a ceiling joist be provided at every partition. In the above instance, it would have saved the sheet rock men, as they are called, very little cutting.

Due to the short span allowed for 2x4's, most ceiling joists, even in attics are 2x6's and these in turn are supported at the central ends by what is called bearing partitions running crossways of the joists the length of the house. On account of the 4-foot wallboard on the ceiling below, many of the joists will have to butt on top of a 3½-inch partition and should be scabed with a second short 2x4. Occasionally ceiling joists are extended past the outside plates to act as ceiling joist for a porch or patio. They are also extended over small insets in the outside wall, so the roof and the gutters will be in a straight line. Ceiling joists are seldom bridged and

Note alternate methods for grouping corner studs, technique for installing 1x4 bracing.

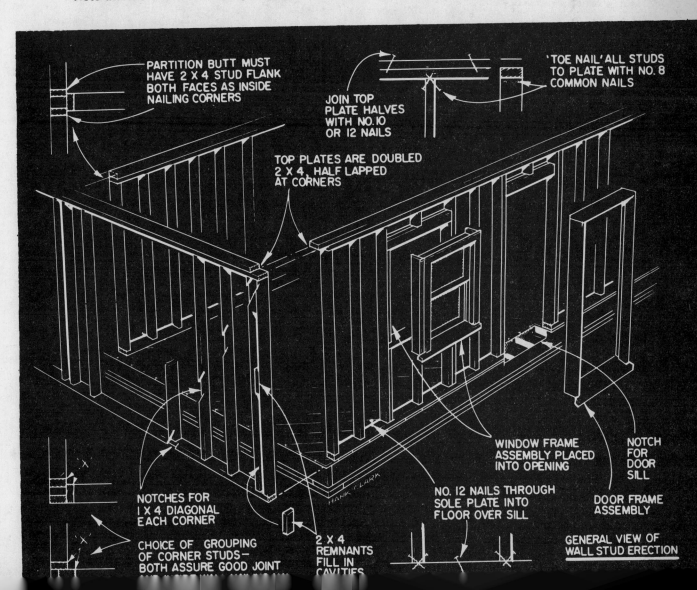

GENERAL VIEW OF WALL STUD ERECTION

Studding technique is same for all floors of home; studs are always supported by a base plate.

if they are, full size square pieces are used for fire prevention purposes. City codes frequently require such bridging over bearing partitions.

And Now The Gables

Gables: These are erected after the rafters are up and usually have studs spaced at 2-foot centers. Most carpenters figure the length, which is simple. If the rise is 6 inches per foot (¼ pitch), each succeeding gable stud is 12 inches longer than the shorter stud next to it and the first one may be set more than 2 feet from the corner. If the gable is parallel to the ceiling joists, and they usually are, the first ceiling joist, which has been placed even with the inside edge of the plate, allows room for the gable studs to rest on the top plate and they can be toenailed to the ceiling joist. If the ceiling joists, placed 16-inch centers, *butt* against the *gable,* carpenters may erect the gable studs with the *same spacing* so they can be nailed directly to the ceiling joists or they may use a bottom plate on top of the ceiling joist. Gable studs are erected one at a time and are cut to be below and flush with the rafter on the outside so the rough sheeting can be nailed to both members. If a partition from inside of the house intersects with the gable, partition studs must be provided in the same manner as in the walls below for the wallboard. •

Above, a corner of room with exterior siding up, subflooring down; diagonal subflooring makes for greater strength than straight.

Above right, upper corner of wall framing shows double top plate supporting ceiling joists; as a rule joists center over studding.

Basement stairway is braced by railing that butts onto triple 2x4 studding; note center 1x8 support, customary in wooden stairway.

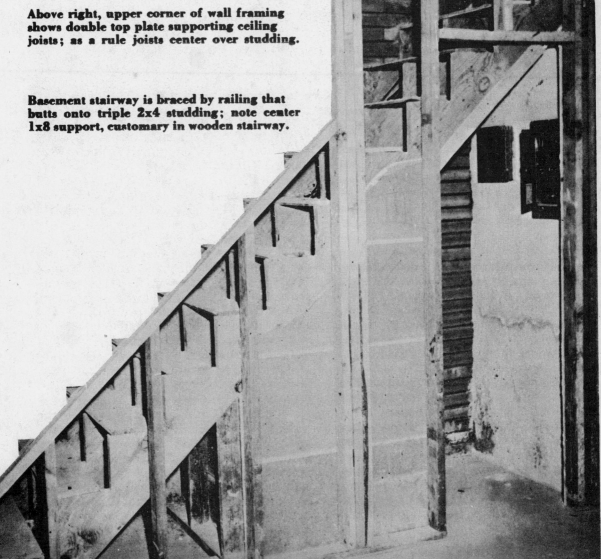

Roofs and Rafters

This section of a home might seem complicated to build, but here it's all simplified for you

Here solid sheeting is laid on the rafters as a base for shingles, which will be laid down next.

A GOOD HOUSE CARPENTER can cut jack rafters as fast as his partner can nail them in place. Rafters are not complicated. They are simply the hypotenuse of a right angle triangle, the same as any other brace. They are always marked (laid out in carpenter's language) with the aid of a square.

Common Rafters: Illustrated is an ordinary gable roof with the rafters in position. Generally, in ordinary residence construction, the plane or instructions call for the roof to have a certain pitch, like 1/6, ¼, ⅓ or ½. This means that the rise of the rafter is 1/6 to ½ the width of the house and is not 1/6 or ½ the run of the rafters which is natural to assume. The run of a single rafter is its horizontal span and is half the width of the house. The rise is the other leg of the triangle and the rafter is the hypotenuse. Thus, if 32 feet is the width of the house, 16 is the run of the rafter and 1/6 pitch allows 5 feet 4 inches as the rise for the rafters. One-quarter pitch would mean an 8-foot rise with the same run and ½ pitch would have a rise of 16 feet.

Length of Common Rafters: As men-

tioned in tools and materials, there is on one side of the carpenter's square a scale of inches with divisions in twelfths. This is considered as a 1/12 scale, in which one inch on the square represents one foot and 1/12 division stands for one inch. To determine the length of the rafter, simply measure with the 12th scale of a second square, or a rule, from the figure in inches on the blade of the first square that represents the run *to* the figure on the *tongue* that represents the rise. This indicates in inches 1/12 of the actual size.

Another method to determine the length of common rafters is from tables that show the required length of the rafter per foot of *run* for the various pitches. These are usually stamped on the blade of good squares.

Plumb and Horizontal Cuts: The run of a rafter is one side of a triangle and the rise as determined by the pitch is the second side. The plumb and plate cuts are exactly the same as if the rafter were a brace. In our illustration the rise is 10 feet and the run is 15 feet. The square is placed with the figures 10 and 15 on

SIMPLE METHOD OF FINDING THE TWO CUTS ON ALL COMMON RAFTERS

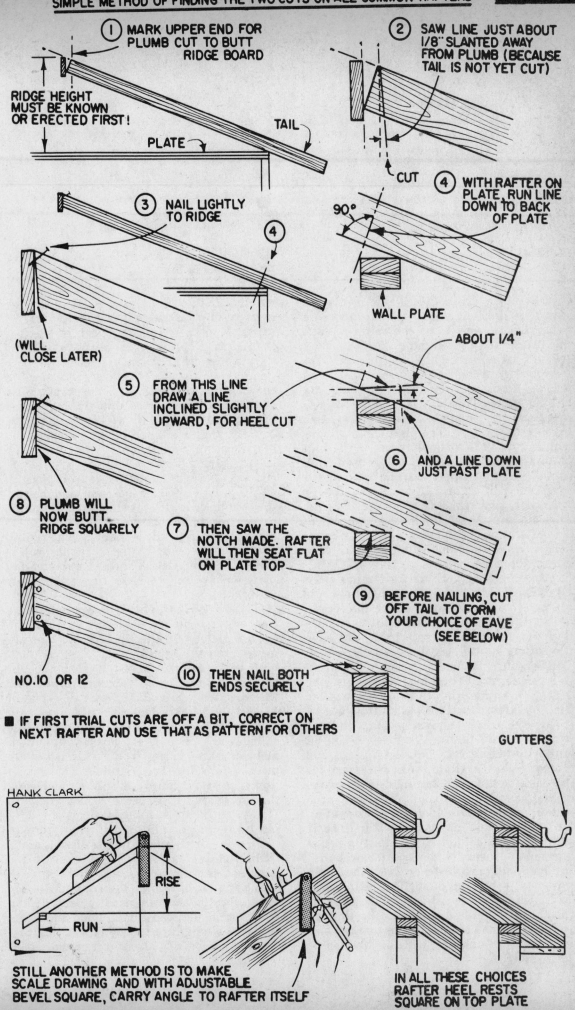

(1) MARK UPPER END FOR PLUMB CUT TO BUTT RIDGE BOARD

RIDGE HEIGHT MUST BE KNOWN OR ERECTED FIRST!

PLATE

TAIL

(2) SAW LINE JUST ABOUT 1/8" SLANTED AWAY FROM PLUMB (BECAUSE TAIL IS NOT YET CUT)

CUT

(3) NAIL LIGHTLY TO RIDGE

(4)

(WILL CLOSE LATER)

(4) WITH RAFTER ON PLATE, RUN LINE DOWN TO BACK OF PLATE

90°

CUT

WALL PLATE

ABOUT 1/4"

(5) FROM THIS LINE DRAW A LINE INCLINED SLIGHTLY UPWARD, FOR HEEL CUT

(6) AND A LINE DOWN JUST PAST PLATE

(8) PLUMB WILL NOW BUTT RIDGE SQUARELY

(7) THEN SAW THE NOTCH MADE. RAFTER WILL THEN SEAT FLAT ON PLATE TOP

(9) BEFORE NAILING, CUT OFF TAIL TO FORM YOUR CHOICE OF EAVE (SEE BELOW)

NO.10 OR 12

(10) THEN NAIL BOTH ENDS SECURELY

■ IF FIRST TRIAL CUTS ARE OFF A BIT, CORRECT ON NEXT RAFTER AND USE THAT AS PATTERN FOR OTHERS

GUTTERS

HANK CLARK

RISE

RUN

STILL ANOTHER METHOD IS TO MAKE SCALE DRAWING AND WITH ADJUSTABLE BEVEL SQUARE, CARRY ANGLE TO RAFTER ITSELF

IN ALL THESE CHOICES RAFTER HEEL RESTS SQUARE ON TOP PLATE

Sheeting need not be top grade of lumber; money is saved here without sacrifice.

Rafters must be cut with precision; see illustrations in this chapter for details.

one edge of a 2x6. The 10 side meets the mark for the length and the 15-inch side is parallel to the run on the rafter. Mark the 10 side for the plumb cut.

The final mark for the length is next on the top edge of the rafter and the heel cut is marked across the side of the rafter to the bottom edge. This cut is parallel to the plumb cut and marked with the same figures on the square. The plate cut is a horizontal cut so the rafter will rest on the wall plate and can be marked square with the above mentioned heel cut or in the above example with 10 and 15 with the 15 edge parallel to the run. Mark on the 15 side. This cut must also adjoin the heel cut to fit on two sides of the wall plate. Most carpenters usually limit the depth of the heel cut to about two inches.

After the length of the rafter has been established and the plate and plumb cuts marked, most carpenters check the length of the rafter *below* the plate cut to be certain there is enough rafter for the eave projection, or tail, as it is usually called. This length is normally given on the plans as a certain projection from the walls, like 2 feet, meaning the ends of the rafters shall be 2 feet from the walls of the house. If there is nothing shown or said, the carpenters should find out from some one in authority before rafter material is cut and erected. The length of rafter necessary for the eave or tail is determined in the same manner as the main roof. Two feet projection means a two-foot run. Two feet on 1/6 pitch is 12.64 inches times 2 or 26 or 27 inches. Very seldom is the length cut at this time. Normally the builder or someone has delivered 2x4's or 2x6's that they expected to be long enough, probably 20's or 22's and the carpenter, after he has laid out the plate cut, merely checks the required length on the first rafter marked and assumes the balance will be the same

length. If the length is not there, the job stops until a longer length is delivered.

Hip Roofs: Another form of roof is known as a hip or cottage roof and contains a hip rafter at each corner.

A hip rafter has the same rise as the common rafter. It is also the hypotenuse of the rise and the run, but the run is the diagonal of the run of two common rafters at right angles to each other. That is, the hip is over the diagonal of the run of one rafter from the *side* of the house and the run of another common rafter from the *end* of the house. When the rise and run of the hip is known, the hip has the same properties as a common rafter of this size except for a few adjustments. The plumb cut along the side of the hip at the top is 10 by 21½ inches. The heel cut and the plate cut are on the same figures like any rafter.

On the job carpenters simply measure the length required for each hip and the central jacks, and the cuts for the hips are made from the number 12. Thus ⅓ pitch with a 15-foot run and a 10-foot rise becomes 12x8 for the cuts for the rafter. For the hips, a square 12x12 has a diagonal of 17 and the plumb, heel and plate cuts are 17x8. There is one more cut on the hip, called the side cut. It is only about an inch long and varies from 17x17¾ for 1/6 pitch to 17x20¾ for ½ pitch. The variation is so small for a cut only an inch long that some times carpenters just guess it, 17x18 or 17x20. Actually the cut is run of hip by length of hip, mark on the length.

On some carpenter squares, there is a notation for *side cut of hips* and where there is no notation there is a table for *length of hips per foot of run* of the common rafter for each pitch that is normally used. Thus ⅓ pitch is marked 18.78, and since this side cut is length of hip by run of hip, this cut becomes 17x18.78. In other words, 17

Erecting the ridge pole is a three-man job; end gable rafters are put up to hold ridge.

Front view of home at later stage of erection; note frame construction for a dormer window.

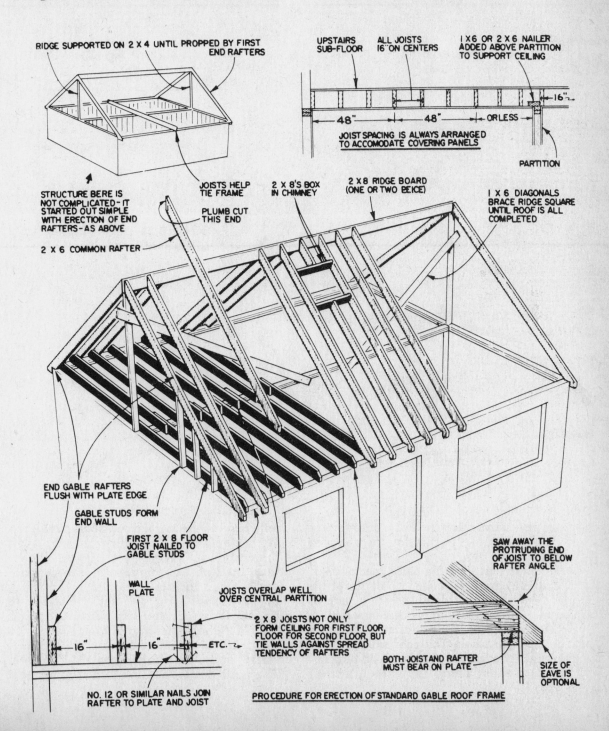

RIDGE SUPPORTED ON 2 X 4 UNTIL PROPPED BY FIRST END RAFTERS

STRUCTURE BERE IS NOT COMPLICATED—IT STARTED OUT SIMPLE WITH ERECTION OF END RAFTERS—AS ABOVE

JOISTS HELP TIE FRAME

PLUMB CUT THIS END

2 X 6 COMMON RAFTER

UPSTAIRS SUB-FLOOR

ALL JOISTS 16" ON CENTERS

1 X 6 OR 2 X 6 NAILER ADDED ABOVE PARTITION TO SUPPORT CEILING

16"

48"   48"   OR LESS

JOIST SPACING IS ALWAYS ARRANGED TO ACCOMODATE COVERING PANELS

PARTITION

2 X 8'S BOX IN CHIMNEY

2 X 8 RIDGE BOARD (ONE OR TWO PEICE)

1 X 6 DIAGONALS BRACE RIDGE SQUARE UNTIL ROOF IS ALL COMPLETED

END GABLE RAFTERS FLUSH WITH PLATE EDGE

GABLE STUDS FORM END WALL

FIRST 2 X 8 FLOOR JOIST NAILED TO GABLE STUDS

WALL PLATE

JOISTS OVERLAP WELL OVER CENTRAL PARTITION

SAW AWAY THE PROTRUDING END OF JOIST TO BELOW RAFTER ANGLE

16"   16"   ETC.

2 X 8 JOISTS NOT ONLY FORM CEILING FOR FIRST FLOOR, FLOOR FOR SECOND FLOOR, BUT TIE WALLS AGAINST SPREAD TENDENCY OF RAFTERS

BOTH JOIST AND RAFTER MUST BEAR ON PLATE

SIZE OF EAVE IS OPTIONAL

NO. 12 OR SIMILAR NAILS JOIN RAFTER TO PLATE AND JOIST

PROCEDURE FOR ERECTION OF STANDARD GABLE ROOF FRAME

Attic view from inside of a hip roof before flooring is put down; sheeting on roof is laid.

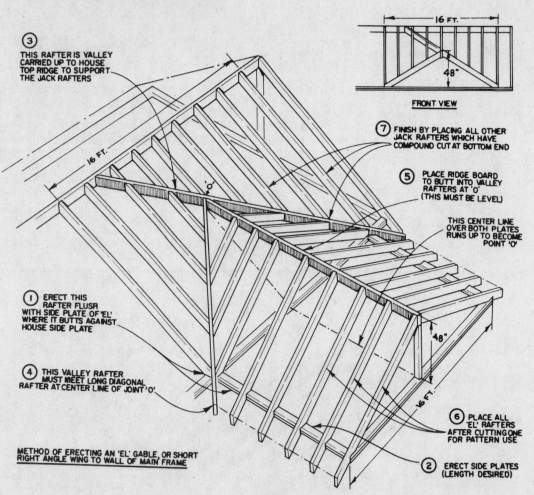

③ THIS RAFTER IS VALLEY CARRIED UP TO HOUSE TOP RIDGE TO SUPPORT THE JACK RAFTERS

16 FT.

16 FT.

FRONT VIEW

⑦ FINISH BY PLACING ALL OTHER JACK RAFTERS WHICH HAVE COMPOUND CUT AT BOTTOM END

⑤ PLACE RIDGE BOARD TO BUTT INTO VALLEY RAFTERS AT 'O' (THIS MUST BE LEVEL)

THIS CENTER LINE OVER BOTH PLATES RUNS UP TO BECOME POINT 'O'

48"

16 FT.

① ERECT THIS RAFTER FLUSH WITH SIDE PLATE OF 'EL' WHERE IT BUTTS AGAINST HOUSE SIDE PLATE

④ THIS VALLEY RAFTER MUST MEET LONG DIAGONAL RAFTER AT CENTER LINE OF JOINT 'O'

⑥ PLACE ALL 'EL' RAFTERS AFTER CUTTING ONE FOR PATTERN USE

② ERECT SIDE PLATES (LENGTH DESIRED)

METHOD OF ERECTING AN 'EL' GABLE, OR SHORT RIGHT ANGLE WING TO WALL OF MAIN FRAME

bears the same relation to the cuts for the hip as 12 has to the cuts for the common rafter.

The plate cut for a hip has a special trick. A common error is to cut the depth of the plate cut the same depth as for a jack or common rafter, so that, in the drawing the depth at O is the same as that of the jack. This is a mistake. The roof sheeting will lie parallel to the plate and instead of bearing on the hip along OC (see drawing)

will rest on the top corner of the hip at O. With standard widths like 2x4's or 2x6's the corner at O from ¼ to ½ inch higher than the line OC for the different pitches but ⅜ of an inch is so close for all pitches that the small error will not be noticed on the sheeting for the roof. Thus to lay off the plate cut on the hip, ⅜ inch is added to the depth of the plate cut for the common rafter, as in the drawing in this section. The plate cut is then marked through this

Attic louver is important for the ventilation of top floor; sheeting is laid over rafters.

Ceiling joists brace rafters in attic, are all cut same size; insulation for wall is in.

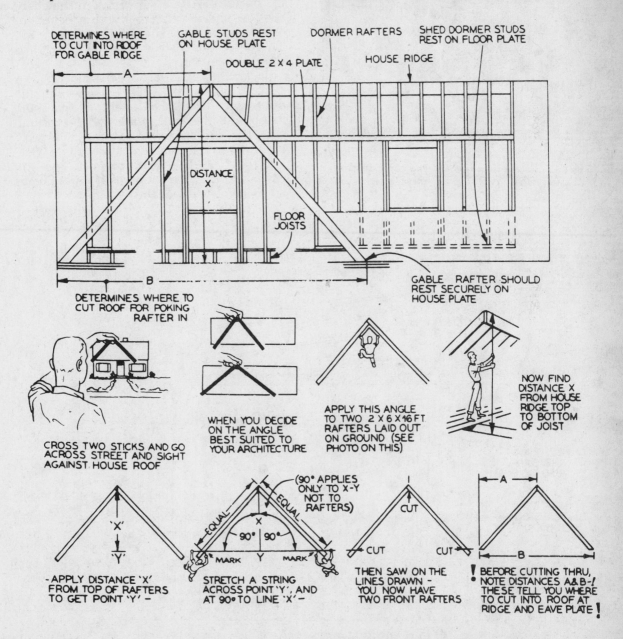

DETERMINES WHERE TO CUT INTO ROOF FOR GABLE RIDGE

GABLE STUDS REST ON HOUSE PLATE

DORMER RAFTERS

SHED DORMER STUDS REST ON FLOOR PLATE

DOUBLE 2 X 4 PLATE

HOUSE RIDGE

A

DISTANCE X

FLOOR JOISTS

B

DETERMINES WHERE TO CUT ROOF FOR POKING RAFTER IN

GABLE RAFTER SHOULD REST SECURELY ON HOUSE PLATE

CROSS TWO STICKS AND GO ACROSS STREET AND SIGHT AGAINST HOUSE ROOF

WHEN YOU DECIDE ON THE ANGLE BEST SUITED TO YOUR ARCHITECTURE

APPLY THIS ANGLE TO TWO 2 X 6 X 16 FT RAFTERS LAID OUT ON GROUND (SEE PHOTO ON THIS)

NOW FIND DISTANCE X FROM HOUSE RIDGE TOP TO BOTTOM OF JOIST

'X' 'Y'

-APPLY DISTANCE 'X' FROM TOP OF RAFTERS TO GET POINT 'Y' -

(90° APPLIES ONLY TO X-Y NOT TO RAFTERS)

EQUAL EQUAL

X 90° 90°

Y

MARK MARK

STRETCH A STRING ACROSS POINT 'Y', AND AT 90° TO LINE 'X' -

CUT

CUT CUT

THEN SAW ON THE LINES DRAWN - YOU NOW HAVE TWO FRONT RAFTERS

A

B

BEFORE CUTTING THRU, NOTE DISTANCES A & B - THESE TELL YOU WHERE TO CUT INTO ROOF AT RIDGE AND EAVE PLATE !

Illustration shows one very basic method of estimating angle of attic dormer; read carefully.

Here construction has started on a shed dormer which will be an extra attic room.

point and square away from the heel cut.

This deepening of the plate cut lowers the lower end of the hip so the corner edge is level with the other rafters but does not affect the top end where there is a similar trouble. To avoid this excess height at the top end the corners of the hip F and E (see drawing), are simply pushed down and out a small fraction until these corners are level with the adjoining jack rafters.

Valley Rafters: These are actually hip rafters that appear to be upside down. Their length, plumb, plate and side cuts are the same as for the hips, except it is not necessary to make any allowance for the backing. With a valley rafter, the edges are low and the sheeting with a bevel cut only bears in the center of the valley rafter. Therefore the plate cut has the depth as the common rafter.

Jack Rafters: These are the short rafters that fit against the hips, as shown in the drawings. They lie parallel to the common rafter and the heel, plate and the plumb cuts that fit against the hip are exactly the same as the common rafter for the various pitches. The crosscut of the plumb cut is the only exception as it must be cut on a bevel to fit against the hip. This is

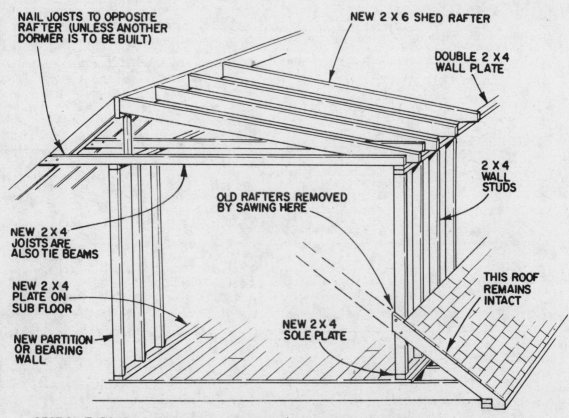

NAIL JOISTS TO OPPOSITE RAFTER (UNLESS ANOTHER DORMER IS TO BE BUILT)

NEW 2 X 6 SHED RAFTER

DOUBLE 2 X 4 WALL PLATE

2 X 4 WALL STUDS

OLD RAFTERS REMOVED BY SAWING HERE

NEW 2 X 4 JOISTS ARE ALSO TIE BEAMS

NEW 2 X 4 PLATE ON SUB FLOOR

NEW PARTITION OR BEARING WALL

NEW 2 X 4 SOLE PLATE

THIS ROOF REMAINS INTACT

SECTION THROUGH SHED DORMER BUILT INTO 'EXPANSION' ATTIC ROOF

Here is a long view of a hip roof that has sheeting laid down; angles add to final cost.

called the side cut and is across the top edge of the jack. It is similar to the side cut of the hip. That is, it is length of jack by the run of the jack, mark on the length. These figures, of course, change with each jack, so carpenters use length of common rafter by their run which also can be transposed to be length of common rafter per foot of run in inches by 12. Thus for ⅓ pitch, this means 14.42 inches by 12, mark on 14.42. Some squares carry the side cut for this pitch as 12 and 10.

Length of Jack Rafters: This determination is based on the fact that if the jacks are spaced an equal distance apart and have the same pitch each succeeding jack will be shortened an equal measurement. Further due to the method of construction, the two common rafters that meet at the top end of the hip, one from the end and one from the side of the house, have identical runs. This means that the bases of these two rafters are an equal distance from the corner of the house. Thus in the drawing SC is equal to SP. Therefore each jack rafter when spaced 2 feet on the plate shortens the run of the next shorter jack 2 feet. If the spacing is 16 inches the run is shortened 16 inches. There are various methods to determine the change in length.

For example a run of 15 feet and a rise of 10 feet is ⅓ pitch which is in the table as 14.42 inches of rafter per foot of run, so each jack with 2-foot spacing is shortened 28.84 inches, 16 inches times 1⅓ feet—19.23 inches.

Also the run is 15 feet and the length of the common rafter is 18 feet ⅜ inch. A division yields 1 foot 2⅖ inches as length of rafter per foot of run. A two-foot space is again 2 feet 4⅘ inches.

Or, since the length of the rafter is 18 feet ⅜ inch and the distance to the corner of the house is 15 feet, this means 7½ two-foot spaces. Therefore each jack is shortened 18 feet ⅜ inch divided by 7.5 or 2 feet 4.8 inches.

Erection of Rafters: Ordinarily, for the erection of common rafters, the carpenters will build a small movable scaffold of a height sufficient to reach the peak of the roof. It rests on loose boards across the ceiling joists. The rafters for a gable *end* are erected, carefully plumbed and braced. Most carpenters cut the first pair of rafters the best they can and mark a third piece. The first pair is used to erect the gable and the fit at the peak is noted. If the fit is not too good, and it frequently is not, the marked piece is adjusted accordingly and used for a pattern. Later the gable sheeting will thoroughly brace and cover the poor joint. The rafters are now cut and stood on end against the side of the house.

In the erection, the regular rafters are placed first, leaving gaps for the ells, then the hips, valley rafters, hips for the ells and finally the jack rafters and the valley jacks. Valley rafters require ridge boards in the main roof and most carpenters use ridge boards in the ells.

Ells: Today many homes require at least two ells, one over part of the house and one over an attached garage. Frequently, fine homes may have three or four. In fact carpenters often encounter floor plans that require considerable ingenuity to design a roof without breaking some of the horizontal lines that are necessary to make a nice looking home.

A drawing in this section shows the necessary framing for a simple ell. It requires one long valley rafter, which is placed in exactly the same manner as a hip rafter and its run is over the diagonal of a square formed by the run of the rafters for the main house. The side and plumb cuts and the length are determined the same as for a hip. The other valley rafter is shorter and butts against the long valley, but due to the fact that it has the same pitch, the plate, heel and plumb cuts can use the same figures. The length is the same multiple per foot of run for the com-

Roof sheeting can be trimmed swiftly with a power circular saw after it has been laid.

mon rafter for the ell as used for the hips. The side cut is different, valley against valley, and the cut is made square across the top.

After the main roof and the valley rafter are in position, carpenters erect the two hips for the ell. The jacks for the ell are erected and then the short valley jacks between the valley rafter and the hip of the ell. The cuts are the same as for any jack to a hip but it is easy to become tangled in the direction of the bevels. When one is right it will save time to keep the stub end that is cut off for a pattern. Normally carpenters measure for the length of these valley jacks.

Sheeting for Roofs: For regular gable roofs, the sheeting is simple. If the roof is to be covered with composition shingles, the boards are laid close together. For cedar shingles, 6-inch boards are placed about 4 inches apart. This allows a 16-inch shingle to have a 6-inch lap and the nails to be in rows 10 inches apart. If the gable eaves are not closed over, carpenters often stop the regular sheeting back one rafter from the end and cover the last space and the gable projection with a better grade of lumber, generally 4-inch tongue-and-groove ceiling laid close together. The

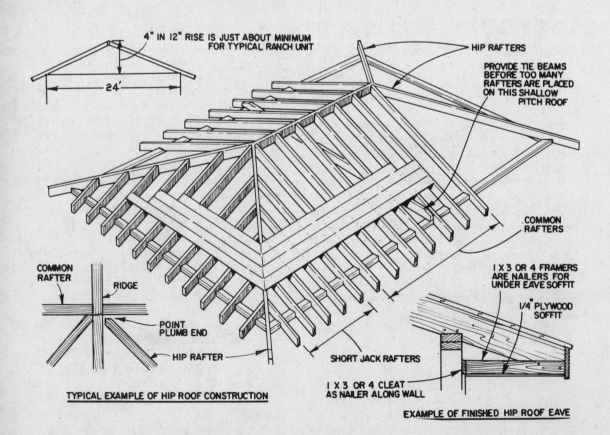

TYPICAL EXAMPLE OF HIP ROOF CONSTRUCTION

EXAMPLE OF FINISHED HIP ROOF EAVE

same method is used with an open cornice at the wall eaves. The regular sheeting is stopped at the plate and the eave projection is sheeted with ceiling lumber.

For hip roofs, the sheeting has a special cut across the width of the board over the hips and in the valleys. Actually most carpenters do not bother with either of these cuts. Usually they nail the boards in position on the sides of the roof and allow the ends to project past the hips and then saw the ends off close to the hip and parallel to the incoming sheeting around the corner from the end. This makes the cut so close that any nails that are used have to be toe-nailed to the hip. When the end sheeting is placed and cut it overlaps and then both pieces of sheeting can be nailed to each other and to the hip.

In the valley the procedure is slightly different. The boards on the main roof are allowed to project through into the ell and are sawed off flush with the valley rafter. The sheeting, however, coming in from the ell must butt against the side of this sheeting and must be cut with the square or the bevel square before it is nailed through the other sheeting and into the valley rafter. This cut is also length of rafter by the run. Mark on the run. •

Metal flashing is necessary for joints in roof; it drains off water, acts as insulator.

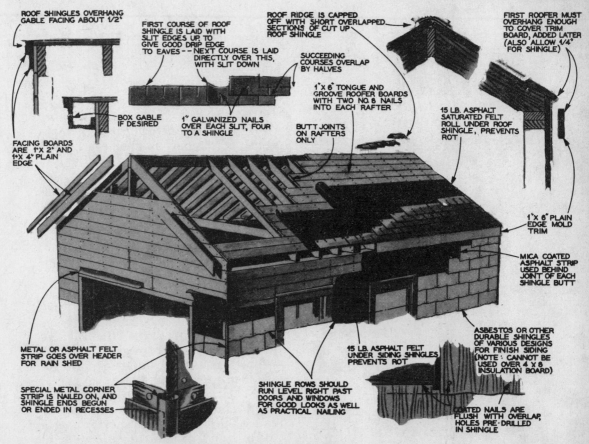

ROOF SHINGLES OVERHANG GABLE FACING ABOUT 1/2"

FIRST COURSE OF ROOF SHINGLE IS LAID WITH SLIT EDGES UP TO GIVE GOOD DRIP EDGE TO EAVES--NEXT COURSE IS LAID DIRECTLY OVER THIS, WITH SLIT DOWN

ROOF RIDGE IS CAPPED OFF WITH SHORT OVERLAPPED SECTIONS OF CUT UP ROOF SHINGLE

FIRST ROOFER MUST OVERHANG ENOUGH TO COVER TRIM BOARD, ADDED LATER (ALSO ALLOW 1/4" FOR SHINGLE)

SUCCEEDING COURSES OVERLAP BY HALVES

1"x 6" TONGUE AND GROOVE ROOFER BOARDS WITH TWO NO. 8 NAILS INTO EACH RAFTER

15 LB. ASPHALT SATURATED FELT ROLL UNDER ROOF SHINGLE, PREVENTS ROT

BOX GABLE IF DESIRED

1" GALVANIZED NAILS OVER EACH SLIT, FOUR TO A SHINGLE

BUTT JOINTS ON RAFTERS ONLY

FACING BOARDS ARE 1"x 2" AND 1"x 4" PLAIN EDGE

1"x 6" PLAIN EDGE MOLD TRIM

MICA COATED ASPHALT STRIP USED BEHIND JOINT OF EACH SHINGLE BUTT

METAL OR ASPHALT FELT STRIP GOES OVER HEADER FOR RAIN SHED

SPECIAL METAL CORNER STRIP IS NAILED ON, AND SHINGLE ENDS BEGUN OR ENDED IN RECESSES

15 LB. ASPHALT FELT UNDER SIDING SHINGLES PREVENTS ROT

SHINGLE ROWS SHOULD RUN LEVEL RIGHT PAST DOORS AND WINDOWS FOR GOOD LOOKS AS WELL AS PRACTICAL NAILING

ASBESTOS OR OTHER DURABLE SHINGLES OF VARIOUS DESIGNS FOR FINISH SIDING (NOTE: CANNOT BE USED OVER 4 x 8 INSULATION BOARD)

COATED NAILS ARE FLUSH WITH OVERLAP, HOLES PRE-DRILLED IN SHINGLE

ROOFER BOARDS, ASPHALT SHINGLES, AND ASBESTOS SIDING

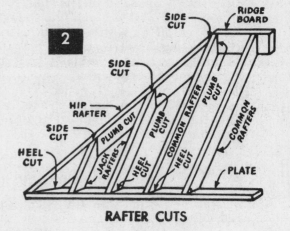

					18	17	16	15	14	13	
LENGTH	COMMON	RAFTERS	PER FOOT	RUN	21 63	20 81	20	19 21	18 44	17 69	16
"	HIP OR	VALLEY	"	"	24 74	24 02	23 32	22 65	22	21 38	20
DIFF	IN LENGTH OF JACKS	16 INCHES	CENTERS		28 7/8	27 3/4	26 11/16	25 5/8	24 9/16	23 9/16	22
"	"	2 FEET	"		43 1/4	41 5/8	40	38 7/16	36 7/8	35 3/8	33
SIDE	CUT	OF JACKS	USE		6 9/16	6 15/16	7 3/16	7 1/2	7 13/16	8 1/8	8
"	"	HIP OR VALLEY	"		8 1/4	8 1/2	8 3/4	9 1/16	9 3/8	9 5/8	9

How to Use the RAFTER and

Knowledge of this tool will simplify the job of cutting rafters to the proper angle and length

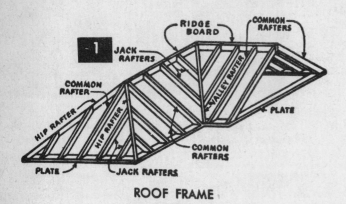

ROOF FRAME

RAFTER CUTS

Square serves as guide to make the plumb cut at the upper end of a common rafter.

THE modern rafter square may look complicated but a knowledge of higher mathematics isn't necessary to understand it. By following a few simple rules the carpenter will find it easy to determine the length of any common, hip, valley or jack rafter for any pitch of roof and to make the proper plumb, heel and side cuts.

These rafters and the cuts made on them are illustrated in figures 1 and 3 respectively. In case you're wondering, the jack rafter is distinguished from the common rafter because it doesn't extend the full distance from plate to ridge.

The face of the Stanley Square R-100 is printed across these two pages. The back is printed on the following page. The longer and wider part is called the body and the shorter part is the tongue. The point at which tongue and body meet is called the heel.

FRAMING SQUARE

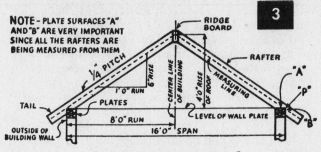

NOTE - PLATE SURFACES "A" AND "B" ARE VERY IMPORTANT SINCE ALL THE RAFTERS ARE BEING MEASURED FROM THEM

SPAN, RUN, RISE and PITCH

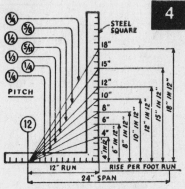

PRINCIPAL ROOF PITCHES

An understanding of the square is based on some simple relationships existing among the span, run, rise and pitch of a roof, as in figure 3. Here the span is 16 feet and the rise is 4 feet. The pitch is the rise divided by the span. Hence this roof has a ¼ pitch. Other relationships are easily worked out: Given the pitch and the span, you can multiply the two and get the rise (¼ × 16=4). Figure 4 will aid in visualizing pitch relationships.

Now for a simple problem: Find the length of a common rafter for a building 20 feet wide, where the rise of the roof is 6 feet 8 inches. Since this square is based on the "rise per foot run" principle, you convert 6 feet 8 inches to 80 inches. Divide this by the run (or half the span) and you learn that the rise is 8 inches per foot run. Reference to the tables on the square (figure 5) tells you that the length per foot of run is 14.42 inches. This multiplied by the 10-foot run gives you 144.2 inches. Divide by 12, it gives you 12.01 feet—or, for practical purposes, a strong 12 feet.

If you had been given the elements of this problem in different terms,

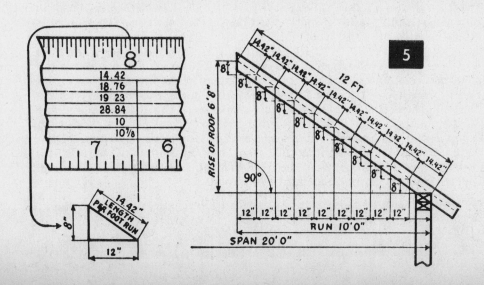

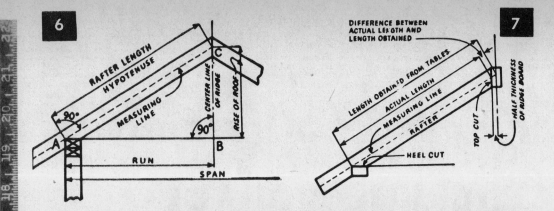

you would work as follows: Span is 20 feet, pitch is ⅓. Multiply to find the rise and you get 6 feet 8 inches or 80 inches. Divide by the run (10) and you find that the rise per foot run is 8 inches. Then you proceed as before.

However, lest you find all this too easy, you must remember that the length which the square gives you is the "measuring line," or the distance from the outer edge of the plate to the center of the ridge. This length is shown in figure 6. Thereafter you must make a correction to find the actual length of the rafter. This is done by deducting half the thickness of the ridge (figure 7). This thickness must be measured at right angles to the plumb line and marked parallel to that line. Of course the tail (figure 3) must also be considered in the final length.

Now to make the plumb and heel (or top and bottom) cuts for a common rafter 12 feet 6 inches long with a 9-inch rise per foot run: Here you get the top cut mark at B on the centerline of the rafter (figure 8) by laying the square with the 12-inch mark of the body and the 9-inch mark of the tongue at the upper edge of the rafter. Since half the thickness of the ridge is 1 inch, you measure that distance, C, at right angles to the cut mark and slide the blade accordingly. The dotted line of the tongue in the diagram shows where the top cut is made. Shifting the square to the other end of the rafter, you get the seat (heel) cut in a corresponding way.

With hip and valley rafters (figure 9) the procedure is basically the same. Suppose you want to find the length of a hip or valley rafter for a roof which has a 10-foot span and a rise of 8 inches per foot run. Referring to the table, you find 18.76 under the 8-inch mark (figure 10). Multiply this by the run, which is 5, and you get 93.8 inches or 7 feet 9¾ inches. To get the top and bottom cuts of hip or valley rafters you use 17 inches on the body of the square and the rise per foot run on the tongue (figure 11). The deduction for the ridge is measured the same as for the common rafter except that half the diagonal (45°) thickness of the ridge must be used.

By means of the square and some of its other tables you can also find the side cuts for hip, valley and jack rafters. Figure 12 represents the position of a hip rafter on the roof. If the rise of the roof is 8 inches to the foot, first locate the figure 8 on the outside edge of the body. Under this figure in the bottom line of the tables you will find "10⅞". This figure is taken on the body of the square and 12 inches is taken on the tongue. The square is applied to the edge of the back of the hip rafter and the side cut, CD, comes along the tongue. In making the heel cut for the hip rafter an allowance must be made for the top edges of the rafter which would project above the line of the common and jack rafters if the corners of the hip rafter were not removed or "backed." The hip rafter must be slightly lowered by cutting parallel to the heel cut a distance which varies with the thickness and the pitch of the roof.

The scales of the Stanley square are broken down into divisions of the inch—from eighths on the front to thirty-seconds on the back. There is also the hundredth scale on the back at the heel. With the aid of a pair of dividers, any decimal fraction of the inch can be obtained.

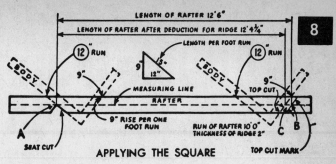

Before attempting use of the rafter and framing square, study the drawings carefully and read the text thoroughly.

APPLYING THE SQUARE

Besides the rafter tables, the square includes (1) an octagon square scale by means of which a square timber can be shaped into an eight-sided one; (2) a brace measure that gives exact lengths of common braces and (3) an Essex board measure which gives the contents in board measure of almost any size timber. The octagon square scale appears on the face of the tongue, the brace measure is found on the back of the tongue and the Essex board measure is on the back of the body. In using the Essex scale, figure 12 on the outer edge of the scale represents a 1-in. board, 12 in. wide. It is the starting point for all calculations. All inch graduations on either side of 12 represent the board width and all figures in the column under 12 represent the length. Thus, to find the board measure of a board 8 ft. long and 11 in. wide, locate the length in feet in the column under the 12 and then find the width in inches on the top edge of the square. Then follow the lines to where they meet and learn that the number of board feet is 7-4 or seven and four-twelfths. •

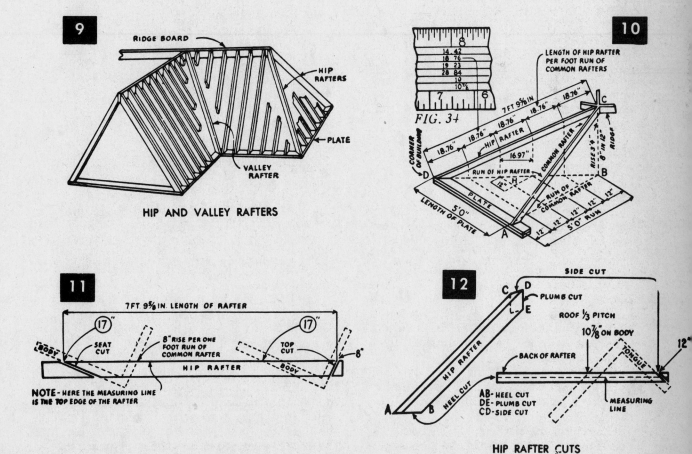

HIP AND VALLEY RAFTERS

FIG. 3+

HIP RAFTER CUTS

Outside Finish

WHEN the rafters are up carpenters mount in place the roof sheeting and finish the wall and gable sheeting, if this is not already in place. Between the walls and the sheeting on the roof an awkward corner is formed; the wall sheeting can be fitted between and around the rafters before the roof sheeting is placed much easier than if the roof is sheeted first. It is also easier to sheet the gables before the roof is covered.

After the house is sheeted carpenters build the cornices (see illustration) from a scaffolding.

Cornices

It will be noted that many of the boards and moldings in these cornices require special cuts at each end. Altogether there are three different cuts:

(1) Plumb cuts that are square across the top, like the gable molding meeting at the ridge.

(2) Plumb cuts with a 45-degree miter, such as would be necessary on the end of the frieze from the *gable* joining the frieze from under the eaves.

(3) Miter cuts across the edge but square with the side which would be required on the *eave frieze* to miter with the frieze from the gable.

These cuts are made in a miter box. The box is usually made of a 2x6 bottom—4 feet long with two 1x10's for sides on a type of box made to cut a cornice board square down the side and a 45-degree miter across the top. The square is first laid across the top with 12 and 12 on one edge and both top edges are marked on this angle. Each side is then squared and marked down the side from the end of the angle marks. Both side marks are then carefully sawed out with one cut of the saw across the box down to the 2x6. Now any irregular molding or board placed in the box can be sawed through these cuts and be square one way and have a 45 miter cut the other way.

For a 45-degree plumb cut to fit a certain required pitch of the roof, another cut is required in which the box is marked on a 45 across the box as before but the plumb cut is marked and sawed out down the side. However, with this kind of a cut, what carpenters call rights and lefts develop, and two different cuts must be made in the boxes as shown.

The confusing factor in these single and double bevel cuts is that out of the four possible positions for each cut, usually only one is right and there is no man, book or revelation that can help much. It is purely a matter for your own visualization faculties. The pieces fit in the corner of the miter box with the bottoms of the box often representing the roof of the building. On the most confusing cuts, it helps to mark the length first. Then place the molding parallel to its future position and roughly

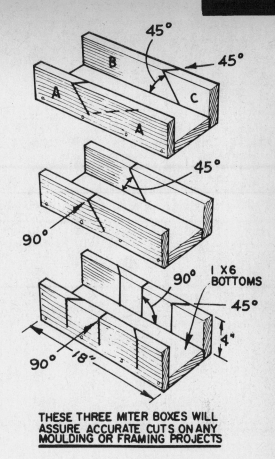

THESE THREE MITER BOXES WILL
ASSURE ACCURATE CUTS ON ANY
MOULDING OR FRAMING PROJECTS

Design of outside finish is overlapping type, is particularly suitable for all climes.

See text for details of uses to which miter boxes, easily constructed, are readily put.

scratch the direction of the different bevels on both ends.

These moldings are expensive. Hip roofs are easier, as all the cornices are cut square and on a 45. Professional carpenters put these up like siding but the inexperienced man can expect trouble. The difference between cuts is so subtle that it is difficult for an ordinary man to look at a piece and be positive the cut will fit, especially with the piece upside down in the box from the

way it is placed against the home's roof.

Erect the gable molding at one end, first. Measure the length carefully and add $\frac{1}{16}$ of an inch for fitting, nail it lightly, then place half the eave molding next to it at both ends. When these four pieces are fitted, they can be nailed solid. If one of the gable molding is too short cut out about a foot and insert a longer piece which can be scratched to fit. The molding on the other gable is then placed and the two

Below, plywood comes in a large variety of textures, and makes a particularly fine exterior.

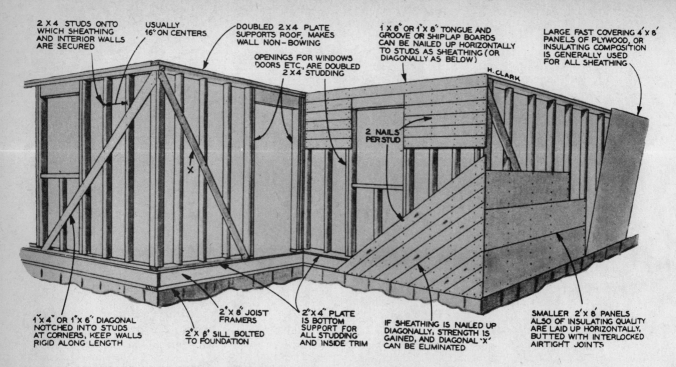

2 X 4 STUDS ONTO WHICH SHEATHING AND INTERIOR WALLS ARE SECURED

USUALLY 16" ON CENTERS

DOUBLED 2 X 4 PLATE SUPPORTS ROOF, MAKES WALL NON-BOWING

OPENINGS FOR WINDOWS DOORS ETC., ARE DOUBLED 2 X 4 STUDDING

1 X 6" OR 1 X 8" TONGUE AND GROOVE OR SHIPLAP BOARDS CAN BE NAILED UP HORIZONTALLY TO STUDS AS SHEATHING (OR DIAGONALLY AS BELOW)

LARGE FAST COVERING 4' X 8' PANELS OF PLYWOOD, OR INSULATING COMPOSITION IS GENERALLY USED FOR ALL SHEATHING

H. CLARK

2 NAILS PER STUD

X

1 X 4" OR 1 X 6" DIAGONAL NOTCHED INTO STUDS AT CORNERS, KEEP WALLS RIGID ALONG LENGTH

2 X 8" JOIST FRAMERS

2 X 8" SILL BOLTED TO FOUNDATION

2 X 4" PLATE IS BOTTOM SUPPORT FOR ALL STUDDING AND INSIDE TRIM

IF SHEATHING IS NAILED UP DIAGONALLY, STRENGTH IS GAINED, AND DIAGONAL 'X' CAN BE ELIMINATED

SMALLER 2 X 8' PANELS ALSO OF INSULATING QUALITY ARE LAID UP HORIZONTALLY, BUTTED WITH INTERLOCKED AIRTIGHT JOINTS

WALLS OF AVERAGE HOUSE TODAY IS WOOD FRAME CONSTRUCTION, SHEATHED WITH ANY OF SEVERAL MATERIALS

pieces to finish the eave molding can be scratched for length.

There are two forms of moldings. Unsymmetrical moldings always carry the same edge up and cuts must be made accordingly. The symmetrical molding, theoretically can have either edge up but actually the first cut establishes the top and unless the top is marked it is more confusing than the unsymmetrical form.

Siding

After the cornice has been erected, the carpenters place the window and door frames and the outside trim. The house is now ready for the outside covering. With normal lap siding, the outside trim for the openings is 2 to 4 inches of flat or molded finish lumber mitered at the corners. The side pieces rest on the sills and are set to expose about ½ an inch of the window or door frames and the cut on the bottom end is normally 2x8 to fit the sill. The outside trim varies with the class of outside covering. Stucco plaster is normally 1½ inches thick and a narrow, thick trim is nailed to

Flintkote insulation and other fiber insulation can be cut to size and to fit on power saw.

Plywood sheathing is fast, tough, within price range of most home builders; consider it.

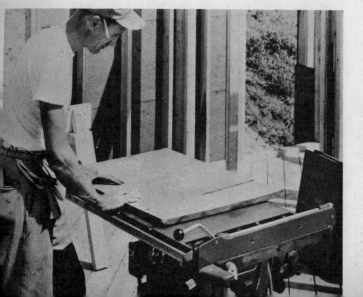

ASPHALT FELT USED
UNDER ALL SIDING

ASBESTOS CEMENT SHINGLE
IS LOW COST, PERMANENT,
NEEDS NO MAINTENANCE

VERTICAL TONGUE AND
GROOVE BOARD, BLIND
NAILED, AND PAINTED

WOOD BEVEL SHINGLE IS
PAINTED, STAINED OR SPECIALLY
TREATED TO WEATHER WELL

PLYWOOD PANELS WITH
BATTENS OVER JOINTS

STUCCO IS CEMENT COAT ON
METAL LATH, SECURED TO WOOD

WIDER
FOUNDATION
FOR BRICKS

BRICK OR STONE
VENEER SETS AWAY
FROM SHEATHING,
HELD WITH CLIPS

SOME OF MATERIALS USED OVER SHEATHING TO GIVE FINISH TO OUTSIDE WALLS

three edges of the frames. Brick veneer makes the walls of the house over 9 inches through but the normal 5¼-inch frames are usually used and the trim is a simple quarter round. The brick veneer stops a few inches short of where the cornice will be and a 2x4 cap is laid on top and toe-nailed to the wall sheeting. The cornice is started from there. The carpenters usually show the mason how high their walls should go.

Lap Siding: This is a clear grade of soft lumber. It is usually made 6 to 10 inches wide with one edge ⅛ of an inch thick and the other ½ an inch. The amount to be exposed should be adjusted so there will not be a narrow width at the top next to the frieze board. Carpenters measure the distance from the bottom of the sheeting that laps over the foundation to the bottom of the frieze board and divided by the desired exposure. Normally there is a fraction left and this fraction is redivided among the necessary courses of siding so all the course from top to bottom will have the same exposure. Thus, if the distance

Plywood exterior sheathing (textured) is put up over insulating paper; it goes up fast.

Here, sheathing is up on entire house, ready for exterior work; see drawings for details.

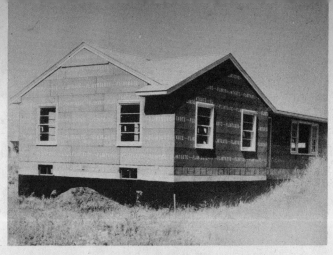

Scaffolding frames are still up on this home; roofing is completed at this point.

Now windows are in and roofing is completed; drawing below outlines roofing, siding details.

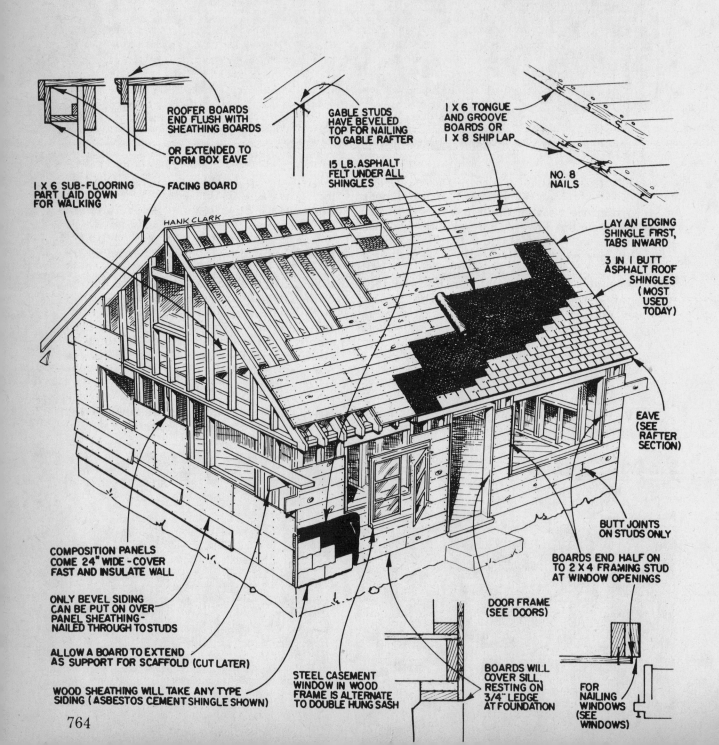

ROOFER BOARDS END FLUSH WITH SHEATHING BOARDS

OR EXTENDED TO FORM BOX EAVE

FACING BOARD

1 X 6 SUB-FLOORING PART LAID DOWN FOR WALKING

GABLE STUDS HAVE BEVELED TOP FOR NAILING TO GABLE RAFTER

15 LB. ASPHALT FELT UNDER ALL SHINGLES

1 X 6 TONGUE AND GROOVE BOARDS OR 1 X 8 SHIP LAP

NO. 8 NAILS

LAY AN EDGING SHINGLE FIRST, TABS INWARD

3 IN 1 BUTT ASPHALT ROOF SHINGLES (MOST USED TODAY)

HANK CLARK

EAVE (SEE RAFTER SECTION)

BUTT JOINTS ON STUDS ONLY

BOARDS END HALF ON TO 2 X 4 FRAMING STUD AT WINDOW OPENINGS

COMPOSITION PANELS COME 24" WIDE - COVER FAST AND INSULATE WALL

ONLY BEVEL SIDING CAN BE PUT ON OVER PANEL SHEATHING - NAILED THROUGH TO STUDS

ALLOW A BOARD TO EXTEND AS SUPPORT FOR SCAFFOLD (CUT LATER)

WOOD SHEATHING WILL TAKE ANY TYPE SIDING (ASBESTOS CEMENT SHINGLE SHOWN)

STEEL CASEMENT WINDOW IN WOOD FRAME IS ALTERNATE TO DOUBLE HUNG SASH

DOOR FRAME (SEE DOORS)

BOARDS WILL COVER SILL, RESTING ON 3/4" LEDGE AT FOUNDATION

FOR NAILING WINDOWS (SEE WINDOWS)

Siding is on and house is completed; use care, time and caution for a perfect finish.

Asbestos shingles have been applied over fir plywood sheathing; it's fireproof, insulates.

to be covered is 97 inches with a 4½-inch exposure, it means 21 courses and a space of 2½ inches left at the top, so the exposure is changed to practically 4⅝ inches. Carpenters generally lay the number of courses out on two measuring sticks, in this case 97 inches long with a mark, in this instance, every 4⅝ inches. The measuring sticks are then nailed temporarily just around the corner so the marks are in plain view as the siding for that wall is nailed on. Generally marks, corresponding to those on the measuring sticks are made on the outside trim of each opening, so that as the siding is built up from the bottom each course can be kept straight and parallel past the openings and around the corners for the entire building. Usually every course is checked with the eye.

Some carpenters, instead of marking on the outside trim use a template, and it is also used wherever a piece looks crooked. If the siding is warped or crooked, a carpenter may use the template at almost every nail to be sure the piece is in the right position. One finish nail is driven at each stud and is placed to catch the top edge of the lower piece and the bottom edge of the board on top. At the corners

most builders now prefer to make a 45-degree miter joint, either with the aid of a miter box or a special factory made saw in a rigid frame that holds it at any desired single angle but cannot cut a double bevel. The corners of the lap siding are covered later with special shaped metal shingles. On *inside* corners carpenters usually nail a square piece of finish ¾x¾, the full height of the wall; the lap siding is fitted to this piece with a square cut. Normally the miter cut is made first and then put in place. No effort is made to place the other end on a stud. Unless the piece must be scratched to fit against an outside trim, it is nailed as is with the square end nailed to the sheeting. The last piece in each course at the far corner is mitered first, scratched for length and cut square. Carpenters are very careful to keep each course of the siding absolutely straight as nothing exposes poor carpentry like crooked siding.

The Gables

At the gables the siding is put on much the same as the rough sheeting. Normally it butts against the gable frieze and it must fit close. It is rather inconvenient to use

Fifteen pound asphalt felt is used under all shingles, whether they're on roof or on siding.

Cupola is an attractive feature often added; they're easily constructed, also ventilate attic.

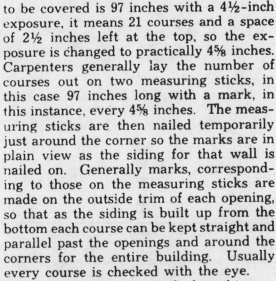

Here siding is fitted over asphalt felt which is laid over plywood sheathing; it's nailed on.

What amounts to a cutaway view shows details of sheathing, felt, and shingle installation.

Close-up shows workman installing shingles, which come in every color and texture.

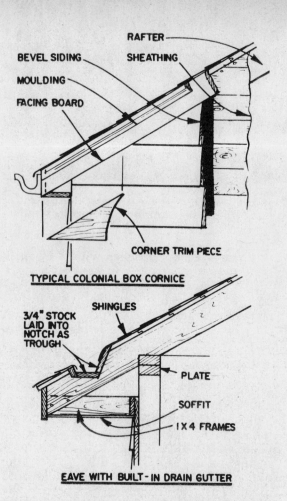

TYPICAL COLONIAL BOX CORNICE

RAFTER
BEVEL SIDING
SHEATHING
MOULDING
FACING BOARD
CORNER TRIM PIECE

EAVE WITH BUILT-IN DRAIN GUTTER

SHINGLES
3/4" STOCK LAID INTO NOTCH AS TROUGH
PLATE
SOFFIT
I X 4 FRAMES

Above, construction details of a drain gutter.

The how-to of exterior siding illustrated.

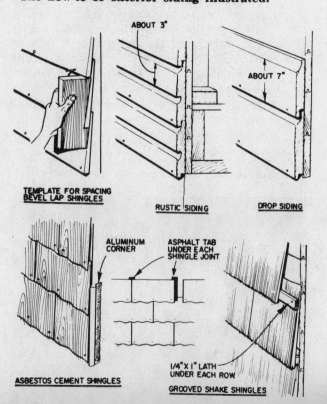

ABOUT 3"
ABOUT 7"

TEMPLATE FOR SPACING BEVEL LAP SHINGLES

RUSTIC SIDING

DROP SIDING

ALUMINUM CORNER
ASPHALT TAB UNDER EACH SHINGLE JOINT

ASBESTOS CEMENT SHINGLES

1/4" X I" LATH UNDER EACH ROW

GROOVED SHAKE SHINGLES

Unique eave in which rafter top edge is cut with downward curve so shingle meets gutter.

Hip proof with popular type cornice; plywood is used for bottom framework, adds strength.

the guide stick that was used on the walls for these courses below the window so the carpenters take a template and set two nails in the last board placed for the next board to rest against. Each piece is cut with the bevel first, either with a pattern or a bevel square and the other end of the second piece is usually scratched to fit.

Many gables have a window, sometimes two, and special care is required to keep the siding straight and at an equal distance from the top of the window on each side. If they get off, the first piece over the window will show a different exposure on the pieces below on each side. If the windows require 10 or 15 courses it is very likely to happen. Above the windows one piece will usually reach across the gable. The distance is then carefully measured for the long points and a carpenter on the ground may cut the bevels on both ends. He then lays a new piece on top with the correct exposure and marks this for the long points but he does not cut it until it is certain the first is the right length. It is almost impossible to cut all of these pieces exactly the right length but at this height, above the eye level, the siding can be lowered or raised at least a quarter of an inch to make it fit without being noticeable.

Plaster Grounds: As soon as the lap siding and the cornice are in place and all driving of nails and pounding on the house has ceased the plasterers are ready to start. Before, frequently only the day before they will arrive the carpenters stop all other work and place the plaster grounds. These are small strips, ¾x¾ normally specially ripped, that carpenters place in the corners between the wall and the rough floor. They are nailed to the bottom wall plates to serve as a gauge for the plasterers, so this corner will be straight and even for the baseboard. •

Cornice construction details are shown; note generous use of strong supporting members.

Below, note that roof rafters project through to give added support to cornice (see art).

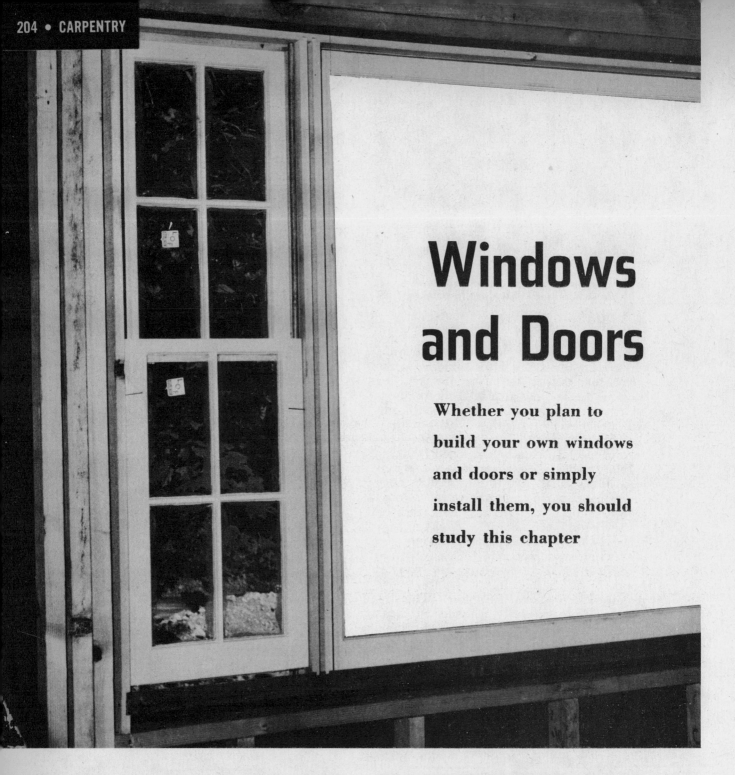

Windows and Doors

Whether you plan to build your own windows and doors or simply install them, you should study this chapter

BEFORE A READER can visualize the motions necessary to build a window or a door in a house, the names of the different pieces must be learned. A window with a one-piece trim has 18 different named pieces, counting the rough frame and the wedges, as shown in the illustration. Most of these have descriptive titles that are self-explanatory. The top inside and outside trim are not shown in the figures. The outside door has 14 different named pieces, counting the pieces in the rough frame. Carpenters can tell by the shape where each member belongs.

The order of erection of the window sash and the outside doors often depends on the climate. If the weather can be expected to be warm and without too much rain, the window sash and the outside doors are not erected until after the plasterers are through. If the weather is frosty or cold, both outside doors are hung, the window sash put in place and the heat turned on, as fresh plaster must not be allowed to freeze. Builders do not mind placing the sash first but the plasterers are almost certain to scar the front door. Some builders take a chance or tack on paper. Others may have

Inside view of window frame of a picture window, showing header against top plate.

Close-up of top of window with a filler under header to make the correct height.

Window jambs, double sash and inside stops in place, ready for the inside trim.

a temporary door made and hung or perhaps hang a curtain.

Windows: In this chapter, it can be inferred that each window and door is built complete at one time. This is never the case. Windows and doors have both been partly described in chapter on floor joists and studding, as the width of the frames must be estimated at the time the wall studding is placed. The frame and outside trim for both windows and doors must be assembled and installed before the lap siding is placed or the house is plastered. After the house is plastered, the sash, doors and

ORDER OF ERECTION OF WINDOW COMPONENTS

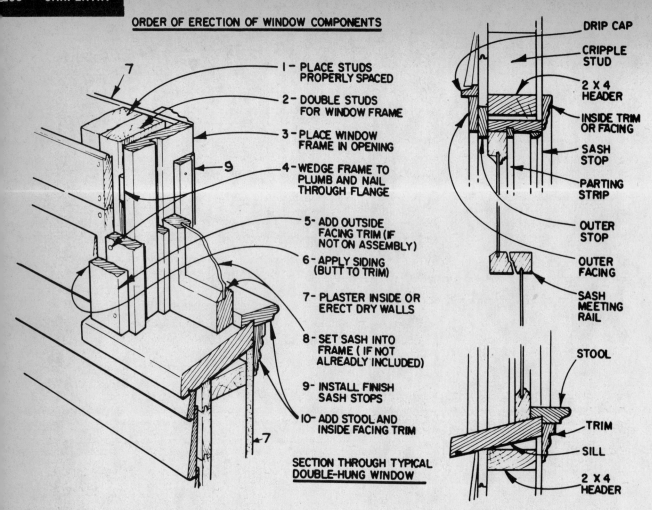

1 - PLACE STUDS PROPERLY SPACED

2 - DOUBLE STUDS FOR WINDOW FRAME

3 - PLACE WINDOW FRAME IN OPENING

4 - WEDGE FRAME TO PLUMB AND NAIL THROUGH FLANGE

5 - ADD OUTSIDE FACING TRIM (IF NOT ON ASSEMBLY)

6 - APPLY SIDING (BUTT TO TRIM)

7 - PLASTER INSIDE OR ERECT DRY WALLS

8 - SET SASH INTO FRAME (IF NOT ALREADY INCLUDED)

9 - INSTALL FINISH SASH STOPS

10 - ADD STOOL AND INSIDE FACING TRIM

SECTION THROUGH TYPICAL DOUBLE-HUNG WINDOW

DRIP CAP

CRIPPLE STUD

2 X 4 HEADER

INSIDE TRIM OR FACING

SASH STOP

PARTING STRIP

OUTER STOP

OUTER FACING

SASH MEETING RAIL

STOOL

TRIM

SILL

2 X 4 HEADER

inside trim are then placed in position.

Another item in the text subject to misinterpretation is the size of different pieces of rough and finish lumber. There are hundreds of different planing mills and it is obvious that all will not make exactly the same sizes. Thus 2x4's will vary in thickness from 1½ inches to 1¾ and the width from 3½ to 3¾. Larger 2x4's are subject to the same variations and where a close estimate of the size is required, it is a common sight to see carpenters measuring these pieces and the same for one-inch shiplap sheeting. Finish lumber has similar variations. Different mills have different fractional sizes although all will be sold and called, the full size. Window sash and doors are not only true to the sizes stated but are actually that size to a sixteenth, except the length of some doors are made to be trimmed on the bottom.

In the larger cities, the window and door frames have been cut, fitted and are delivered assembled, frequently even to the outside trim. All that is necessary is to set these in place from the outside and check the fit. The side jambs should be about half an inch or less on each side from the window studs. Since the window jambs with the outside stop are 5¼ inches wide, and the width of the wall is a 2x4 plus the rough sheeting or 4½ inches; thus ¾ of an inch should project into the room. This is called the room or plaster projection. Lath and plaster or rock lath and plaster also measures ¾ of an inch thick and when it is applied to the inside wall it must be flush with the inside edge of the jambs. The window sill is considerably longer than the opening is wide but a notch is cut in each end, as shown in the drawing, so the central portion of the sill lies between the two window studs and it also projects into the room ¾ of an inch so that the plaster will be flush with it. This plaster projection for the sill depends on the depth of the notch, so the first act of the carpenters, after setting the frame in position, is to draw the projecting horns of the sill close against the rough sheeting with a couple of partially driven nails in the outside trim and check to make sure the sill has the necessary ¾-inch projection. If it has not, the notch can be trimmed a little deeper, as it is essential that all three jambs and the sill have this projection into the room, and no more.

The frame is now in position but probably not plumb. This is done by driving

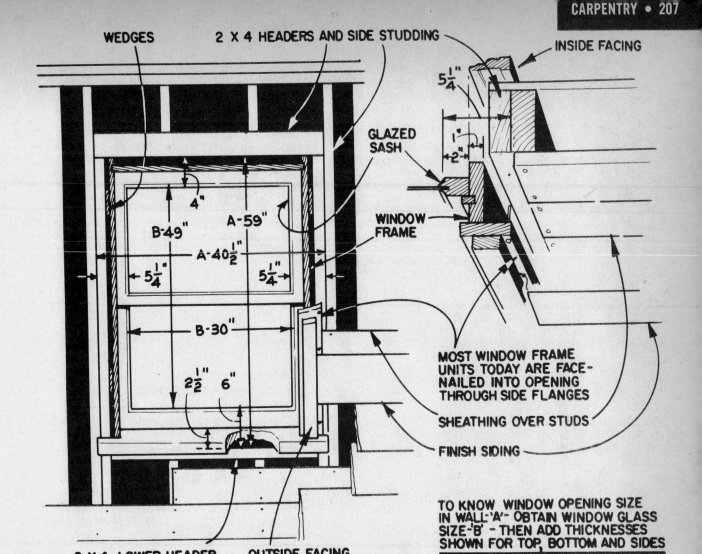

WEDGES

2 X 4 HEADERS AND SIDE STUDDING

INSIDE FACING

$5\frac{1}{4}$"

GLAZED SASH

4"

B-49"

A-59"

A-$40\frac{1}{2}$"

$5\frac{1}{4}$" $5\frac{1}{4}$"

1"

2"

WINDOW FRAME

B-30"

$2\frac{1}{2}$" 6"

MOST WINDOW FRAME UNITS TODAY ARE FACE-NAILED INTO OPENING THROUGH SIDE FLANGES

SHEATHING OVER STUDS

FINISH SIDING

2 X 4 LOWER HEADER   OUTSIDE FACING

TO KNOW WINDOW OPENING SIZE IN WALL 'A'- OBTAIN WINDOW GLASS SIZE 'B'- THEN ADD THICKNESSES SHOWN FOR TOP, BOTTOM AND SIDES

Right, a well-trimmed multiple window with sliding sash for basement; note top trim.

Window showing outside trim ready for siding; blocks give effect of a foundation.

Below, double-hung window in place; note that the insulation has been tacked into place.

wedges or shingles between the outside of the jambs and the window studs, which are about half an inch apart, and checking with the plumb level. The carpenters then nail the outside trim to the rough sheeting, put a nail or two through the wedges, and the frame is set. A little care must be used in placing these wedges. Carpenters usually place the top and bottom wedges close to the end of the frame and these can be fairly tight but the one in the center must not be driven enough to bulge the frame. Both sides of every frame should be checked with a straightedge for this error. Most carpenters try a square in each corner and a bulge in a window jamb will generally show.

In recent years many builders are using sheet rock or plasterboard, instead of plaster. Plasterboard only measures ⅜, ½ or ⅝ inch thick instead of the standard ¾ of an inch. Such walls require a special narrow jamb for this thinner wall instead of the standard 5½ inches and the room projection is correspondingly less. Standard jambs cannot be ripped in the field to fit these walls that are only 4⅞ to 5⅛ inches thick.

As a rule the sash and the glass are in separate bundles and to place the sash in the frames it is necessary to remove the parting strip, insert the top sash and attach the spring balance to the frame. The parting strip is replaced and the lower sash and spring balance are placed. There are a great variety of these spring balances and there will probably be more. Normally the method of attachment is explained in a booklet with each shipment. They are so simple that the correct installation is generally self-evident. Fitting the sashes in the jambs is very close work. They should be planed down to where they just barely can be moved up and down. As soon as it rains they will probably be stuck tightly but in a few years they will be too loose.

Close-up of completed cornice shows plancier
in place, and the finished window frame
for a single sash window, ready for finish.

A new approach to bay windows is shown;
window studs are hung down from ceiling
joist in the overhang. Generally, these studs
are hung from ends of rafters, which must
be placed to fit the window when it's placed.

Either before or after the sashes are
placed, the house is plastered; when the
carpenters return they finish the inside
trim. This consists of the stool in a number
of different shapes, the inside stops and the
window trim. The stool is placed first. In
the drawings the stool is shaped to fit the
sill with a notch and horns very much
like the sill and the window side trim and
inside stops butt against this stool. Many
modern builders have changed this stool
to what amounts to an inside stop. It is
shaped to fit the sill and the top surface
is level. The ends fit *inside* the window
jambs but its width is flush with the *edge*
of the sill. The original three pieces of
trim, a stool and an apron are changed to
four pieces of inside trim that go all around
the window and the apron is discarded.

In the assembling, the inside stops,
mitered at the top corners, are placed next.
Carpenters usually put the top piece up
first, mitered at the ends, close against the
sash and nailed to the top jamb. The two
side pieces of inside stops are then fitted
between the top stop and the stool or the
bottom stop whichever it may be and are
not mitered at the bottom corners.

Inside Trim

Inside trim has a number of variations.
The majority are probably a single piece of
soft finish lumber two or three inches wide,
but it may be the same shape in hardwood
or a molded shape or two pieces and occasionally three pieces. To obtain a professional looking job a carpenter requires
a special tool to cut these 45-degree miter
cuts.

In the erection, procedure varies but one
method is to set a bevel square to a perfect
45 and make 45-degree marks on the plaster
from each corner that requires such a cut.
Normally inside trim is set back from the
inside edge of the jambs ⅛ to ¼ to an inch
so this much of the jamb is exposed. With

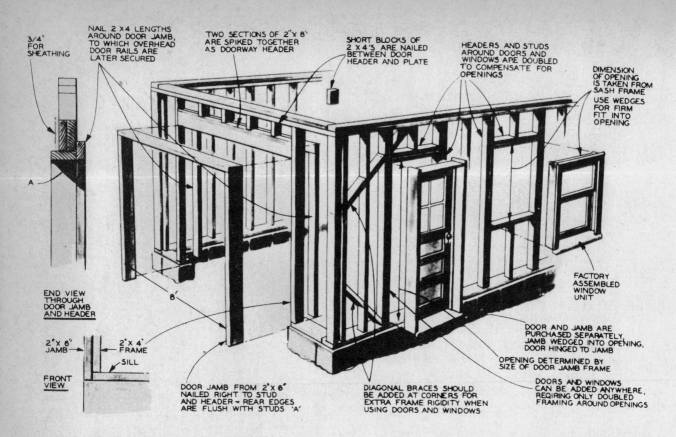

3/4" FOR SHEATHING

NAIL 2 x 4 LENGTHS AROUND DOOR JAMB, TO WHICH OVERHEAD DOOR RAILS ARE LATER SECURED

TWO SECTIONS OF 2" x 8" ARE SPIKED TOGETHER AS DOORWAY HEADER

SHORT BLOCKS OF 2 x 4'S ARE NAILED BETWEEN DOOR HEADER AND PLATE

HEADERS AND STUDS AROUND DOORS AND WINDOWS ARE DOUBLED TO COMPENSATE FOR OPENINGS

DIMENSION OF OPENING IS TAKEN FROM SASH FRAME

USE WEDGES FOR FIRM FIT INTO OPENING

A

END VIEW THROUGH DOOR JAMB AND HEADER

2" x 6" JAMB

2" x 4" FRAME

SILL

FRONT VIEW

8'

DOOR JAMB FROM 2" x 6" NAILED RIGHT TO STUD AND HEADER ~ REAR EDGES ARE FLUSH WITH STUDS 'A'

DIAGONAL BRACES SHOULD BE ADDED AT CORNERS FOR EXTRA FRAME RIGIDITY WHEN USING DOORS AND WINDOWS

OPENING DETERMINED BY SIZE OF DOOR JAMB FRAME

DOOR AND JAMB ARE PURCHASED SEPARATELY, JAMB WEDGED INTO OPENING, DOOR HINGED TO JAMB

DOORS AND WINDOWS CAN BE ADDED ANYWHERE, REQIRING ONLY DOUBLED FRAMING AROUND OPENINGS

FACTORY ASSEMBLED WINDOW UNIT

PLACING DOOR JAMBS AND WINDOWS

Although drawing illustrates garage structure, basic placement of doors and windows is correct.

Smooth putty with broad putty knife for best appearance; wipe away excess at once.

four-piece trim the bottom piece is set first, as close as possible to the marks with an exposure of say $\frac{3}{16}$ of an inch, but it is only nailed with two partially driven nails until the other four pieces are set. The two side pieces are then fitted to the two bottom corners, trimmed to fit the marks at the top corners and also have the $\frac{3}{16}$-inch exposure. These are nailed temporarily until it is found if the top trim will drop in between the two sides and have the required expcsure. This is slow, close work. A daylight fit is the limit. A $\frac{1}{16}$-inch crack is a blemish.

Three-piece trim is much easier. In this case, the top piece is fitted to the marks first, nailed temporarily and the side pieces are fitted in between the stool with a square cut and the top trim.

In some localities where the window and door *frames* have to be shipped in, the members are all cut to fit and a bundle made for each opening. The size of the glass it will fit is marked on each bundle for the windows. The *sashes* are usually all together and carefully boxed. The doors may not arrive until later. Since it is necessary for the carpenters to place the window and door frames and the outside trim before the house can be plastered or the lap siding put on, these bundles must be

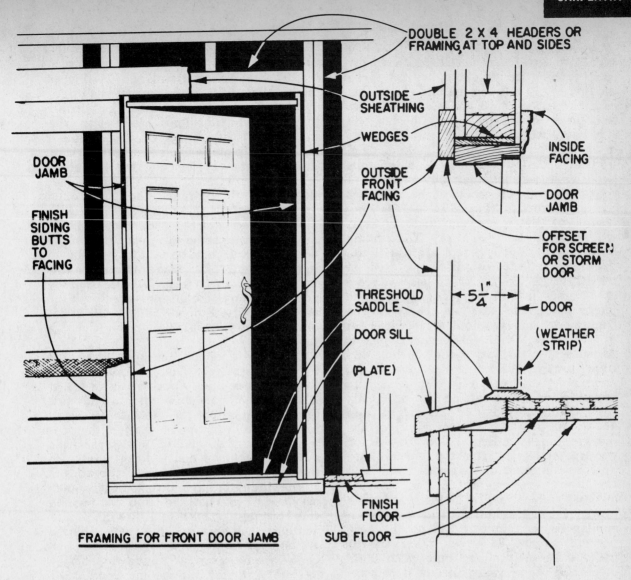

DOUBLE 2 X 4 HEADERS OR FRAMING AT TOP AND SIDES

OUTSIDE SHEATHING

WEDGES

OUTSIDE FRONT FACING

INSIDE FACING

DOOR JAMB

OFFSET FOR SCREEN OR STORM DOOR

5¼"

DOOR

(WEATHER STRIP)

DOOR JAMB

FINISH SIDING BUTTS TO FACING

THRESHOLD SADDLE

DOOR SILL

(PLATE)

FINISH FLOOR

SUB FLOOR

FRAMING FOR FRONT DOOR JAMB

Right, a window wall for porch of a house; it opens after fashion of venetian blinds.

Below, French doors are popular, give effect of a window wall; these lead to dining room.

opened, the required pieces abstracted for each opening and the bundles retied so the pieces will not become mixed. In this case, the carpenters have to assemble the four pieces of the frame. As a rule, the sills have two special slots rabbeted close to the ends about a quarter of an inch deep to receive the lower ends of the side jambs and this recess automatically establishes the width while the length of the jambs set the height for the desired sash. It is simple to nail the jambs into these recesses while they rest on the floor. The parting strips and the outside stops are usually on the jambs and they should fit close against the sill. The top jamb also has two slots or recesses for the top ends of the side jambs the correct distance apart. So the frames are made without a measurement or a thought. One light diagonal brace is nailed across the inside edge to hold the frame square. It is then turned over on the floor and the three pieces of outside trim are nailed on. This outside trim is set back from the *inside* edge of the *outside* stop about half an inch so this much of the outside stop is exposed to form a recess for window screens. The top corners are mitered the same as the inside trim. Note that the outside trim butts against the window sill which has a slight bevel. The lower end of the outside trim requires a similar bevel, generally 2x8 on the carpenter's square. However, there are so many different molding mills with their own ideas of improving the shape of window sills that this is a variable figure.

Plate glass windows, cottage windows, swinging windows with hinges and multipaned windows are spoken of and shown on the plans as sizes outside to outside of the *sash*. The jambs carry no parting strips and have both inside and outside stops nailed to the side of the jambs close against the sash. The jamb is a smooth board and since the outside stop is not on the edge as part of the jamb, like double sash, it measures 5¼ inches wide. The frames are placed, plumbed, squared and nailed the same as previously described. The outside trim is normally set back ¾ of an inch on the edge of the jambs—not for screens—but to match the outside trim on the other openings.

All About Doors

Doors: Most homes have two outside doors and before a house can be plastered these frames must be in place, as well as the frames for the inside doors. The frames and their trim will be delivered assembled or in bundles. Outside doors have a sill

very similar to a window sill, as shown in the drawing, which normally is 1½ inches thick. When it is in the correct position it must be flush with the finish floor inside the house which ordinarily is ¾ of an inch thick. At the time the walls were raised the bottom plate was across the doorway. This was cut away flush with the door studs but in order to make the inch and a half sill flush with the finish floor, the rough flooring must also be cut away even with the inside edge of the plastered wall. In the past and for some sills today, part of the floor joists must also be cut away, as shown in the drawing. With modern flat door sills this is not always necessary. Occasionally porch floors may be flush or even with the main floor of the house and no sill is required. The joint is simply covered with a threshold.

After the door sill has been fitted, the frame is assembled. Outside door jambs on the room side have a *recess*, ½ by 1¾ or 1⅜, that the door closes into on both side jambs and the top. Where it is necessary to assemble the frame on the job, the projecting part of the jamb has been rabbeted away at the lower end to form a notch so the cut portion rests on *top* of the sill and all the carpenter has to do is to fit this notch over the sill and nail the jamb into the end wood of the sill. This establishes the proper width for the door and the correct height of the door jamb. The ends of the top jamb have been similarly cut away and the top jamb is nailed into the end wood of the *side jambs*. After the frame is assembled, most carpenters will nail on the outside trim while the frame is on the floor. Usually outside door frames which ordinarily measure an inch and a half thick overall by 5¼ inches wide have a ⅜-inch dap rabbeted in the *outside* edge. The outside trim, ¾ inch thick, is then set exactly on the edge of this dap to make a recess for the screen door which is usually 1⅛ inches thick. Generally the placing of the outside trim is very similar to the outside trim for the windows and normally of the same pattern or shape. It usually consists of three pieces, mitered at the top corners and the trim rests on the sill with a bevel cut to fit.

When the outside trim and frame are assembled and the strips of paper around the rough opening are tacked to the rough sheeting, the frame is placed in position with the required plaster projection, wedged plumb, squared and the outside trim nailed to the rough sheeting, the same as for the windows.

As soon as the house is plastered, the carpenters return, put in the window sash

Above, a large wardrobe closet with sliding doors that require a top and bottom track for this purpose; note decorative trim.

Right, flush doors come in many varieties; this one has six-sided decorative window.

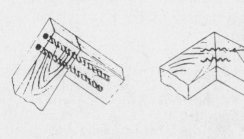

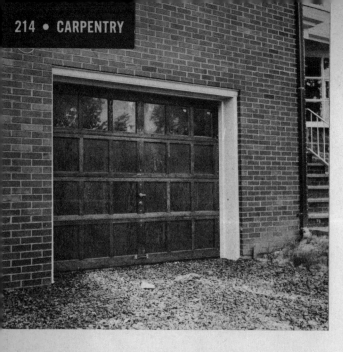

Overhead garage door with transom has standard frame and trim, comes assembled.

and hang the outside doors so the house can be locked up. The outside doors are placed between the side jambs and fitted except at the lower end. They are then wedged up against the top jamb and the position of the hinges are carefully marked square with the jambs on both the *doors* and the *edge* of the jamb that is exposed. The bottom edge of the lower hinge is usually set 11 or 12 inches from the bottom of the door. The top of the top hinge is 7 or 8 inches from the top of the door. The door is now taken down, the pins in the hinges are pulled and each half is laid in its proper position against the marks and the outline is scratched. A chisel cuts this out to the exact depth of the hinge. A little care is necessary on this dap. A common error is to make this dap too deep and the door closes against the jamb before it is closed. It would not be the first dap to be filled out with cardboard to make the hinge flush. The hinges, when they are screwed in place (usually driven three-quarters of the way with a hammer), must be absolutely parallel to the door and the jamb or square. Also the width of the uncut wood, as measured *across* the wall, on the door and the door jamb *behind* each hinge must have exactly the same width for all the four halves, usually about a quarter of an inch. If either half of the hinge on the door or the jamb is set deeper from the inside face than its mate, the door will either not swing into the groove or fit too loosely. Some carpenters dap out and place three halves of the hinges but the fourth dap at the bottom of the jamb is cut a little short in length and this half of the hinge is not screwed on. The door is then carefully blocked up to its position about half open and the four halves are pinned together. This leaves the half of the hinge

not yet screwed to the jamb flapping and it can be closed against the jamb and the exact position can be seen. The dap is enlarged to fit and this half of the hinge is screwed in place.

The door is now hung and ready for the lock. As a rule carpenters place the inside door knob 36 inches from the rough floor and the position is marked for several inches across the side of the door and is carried around the edge of the door. This does not mean that either the latch or the bolt will be on this line but after an examination of the lock it gives something to measure from. There are almost an infinite variety of different styles and types of door locks but they have one thing in common. A cavity must be made in the front edge of the door for the body of the lock and a hole must be bored in the side of the door for the spindle of the door knob which must hit exactly the aperture in the body of the lock designed for this spindle. The cavity in the edge of the door may be any size from $\frac{1}{2}$ by 4 and 4 inches deep to a $\frac{5}{8}$-inch hole, depending on the lock. The hole in the side may vary from about a half inch to $1\frac{1}{2}$ inches for a cylinder lock in the front door. Modern locks are more simple. The cavity for the body of the lock is about a $\frac{3}{4}$-inch hole and the hole for the spindle may be about the same. There are a few locks in which the latch and the door knob spindle are on the same level. The body of the lock carries a plate about 1x6 that sets into the edge of the door so it is flush with the wood, termed an escutcheon plate in the catalogues. When the hole is bored and the body of the lock is temporarily in position, this plate is placed. Its position is then marked and the recess chiseled out. Careful measurements are now made on the side of the door for the

This overhead garage door has a basic frame and no extraneous trim.

position of the spindle. Make the hole at least $\frac{1}{16}$ inch larger than required; if the spindle does not line up with the hole in the body of the lock, all you can do is to enlarge the hole with a knife, a round coarse rasp or a keyhole saw. When the lock in the door is in position, the two doorknob plates and the escutcheon plate have been screwed in place, the carpenters allow the latch to make a mark on the door jamb for the position of the striking plate which is dapped flush into the door jamb. A cavity must be chiseled out behind this plate so the latch and bolt can go through. The big trouble with this plate is how far from the edge of the jamb to set it. If it is too far in the latch will not catch when the door is closed and if it is not far enough the door is loose and rattles. The difference is less than a sixteenth of an inch.

As a rule to keep from scarring the inside trim, this is not placed until the lock and hinges have been installed. The two side pieces of inside trim are set on a ¾-inch block, so that later the finish floor can be pushed underneath. The trim is also set with the usual ⅛- to ¼-inch exposure on the jambs and nailed temporarily until the top trim has been fitted with mitered corners, the same as the inside window trim.

Ordinarily the back door is exactly the same as the front door, piece by piece, except the door and the lock are not as expensive.

So far there has been no allowance for the threshold to go under these two doors. The thresholds are not installed until the finish floor has been laid. They are first fitted for length between the door jambs and then the carpenters lay it on the finished floor close against the closed door and the required height is scratched on the door which is now taken down and cut a trifle

long, replaced, checked, taken down, planed to a close fit. The bottom of the door should touch the threshold. If it is a little tight, let it go. It will soon wear to a fit, besides doors shrink a little in time.

Inside Doors: The frame and trim for inside doors are normally delivered cut to fit but not assembled. There are three pieces of jamb generally 1¼ inches thick by 5¼ inches wide, rabbeted on both edges to receive the door on either side. There are four pieces of *side* trim and two pieces of *top* trim, mitered at the top corners and no sill. In fact, there is no support for the bottom ends of the jamb until it is in the wall. Carpenters assemble the three pieces of jamb on the floor and nail a piece across the bottom ends of the side jambs to hold these exactly at the same width as the top. The frame is then placed in the opening. The jambs, which are ⅝ inch longer than the door, are set temporarily on ¾-inch blocks for the benefit of the hardwood floor. The jambs are wedged plumb, squared in the corners and the plaster projection is checked for both edges on *each* side. The jambs are nailed through the wedges to the door studs. After the house is plastered, the side trim is also set on ¾-inch blocks and nailed to the jambs with ⅛- to ¼-inch exposure in the same manner as the inside trim for the windows and outside doors.

Normally the length of the inside doors are cut exactly to specified measurements, usually 6 feet 8 inches. The jambs, as purchased, are about ⅝ of an inch longer than the door so when the door is fitted and close against the top jamb the bottom edge of the door is ⅝ of an inch above the lower end of the jamb and also this much above the finished floor. This provides a clearance for the door to swing over the rugs. •

Inside Finish

Careful craftsmanship pays off in visible results on the inside work

AFTER THE HOUSE is plastered, the carpenters return. About all that can be seen is rough plaster and a rough floor. If they have not been forgotten the plaster in the bathroom will have a recess for one or two soap dishes and the necessary recesses in the studding for the other built-ins. The house is nearing completion. Normally the outside and inside doors would still have to be hung, the sash to be placed and the inside trim for both doors and windows to be fitted. This was described in previous chapters. The work to be done includes the baseboard, finish

for the fireplace and stairway. The kitchen cabinet must be placed, the shelving and the pole in the closets, medicine cabinet in the bathroom, the hardwood floor and the necessary hardware. The material should all be on hand.

Hardwood Floors: In the larger cities hardwood floors are a special trade and many builders will order this work to be done as soon as the plasterers are through. The finish carpenters usually lay the soft wood floors and in some localities they will also lay the hardwood floors.

Hardwood flooring as it is delivered to

Above, attention to details resulted in handsome fireplace, recreation area.

Above right, L-shaped kitchen work area is standard, also most convenient.

Right, inset in plaster wall is measured for maximum use of wall studs for support of the bathroom medicine cabinet.

Right, wrought iron rail can be bought commercially and installed in hallway to impart open look.

Staircase is seen from rear in basement; concrete blocks have been cut into and used for support.

the carpenters is often 2 inches wide and half an inch thick with a square edge. Normally it is 3⅛ inches wide, called 4 inch, with a thickness of ¾ inch but there are numerous variations. The wider boards are usually tongue and groove on both the edge and the end. The tongue and groove are slightly off center so the wearing surface is slightly thicker than the underside and it must be laid in that manner.

Hardwood floors may be placed either before or after the baseboard. If they are laid before the base, the builder will do the final sanding and waxing after the

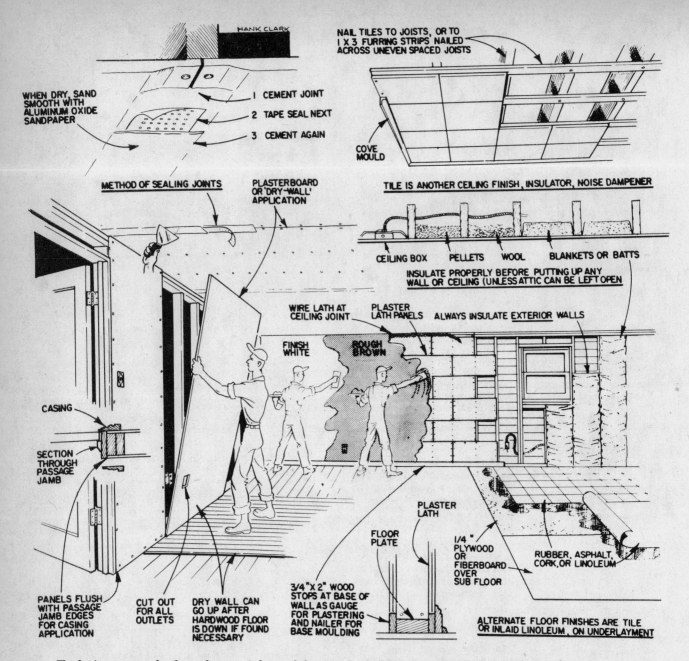

HANK CLARK

WHEN DRY, SAND
SMOOTH WITH
ALUMINUM OXIDE
SANDPAPER

1 CEMENT JOINT
2 TAPE SEAL NEXT
3 CEMENT AGAIN

METHOD OF SEALING JOINTS

PLASTERBOARD
OR 'DRY-WALL'
APPLICATION

NAIL TILES TO JOISTS, OR TO
1 X 3 FURRING STRIPS NAILED
ACROSS UNEVEN SPACED JOISTS

COVE
MOULD

TILE IS ANOTHER CEILING FINISH, INSULATOR, NOISE DAMPENER

CEILING BOX   PELLETS   WOOL   BLANKETS OR BATTS

INSULATE PROPERLY BEFORE PUTTING UP ANY
WALL OR CEILING (UNLESS ATTIC CAN BE LEFT OPEN

WIRE LATH AT
CEILING JOINT

PLASTER
LATH PANELS   ALWAYS INSULATE EXTERIOR WALLS

FINISH
WHITE

ROUGH
BROWN

CASING

SECTION
THROUGH
PASSAGE
JAMB

PANELS FLUSH
WITH PASSAGE
JAMB EDGES
FOR CASING
APPLICATION

CUT OUT
FOR ALL
OUTLETS

DRY WALL CAN
GO UP AFTER
HARDWOOD FLOOR
IS DOWN IF FOUND
NECESSARY

3/4" X 2" WOOD
STOPS AT BASE OF
WALL AS GAUGE
FOR PLASTERING
AND NAILER FOR
BASE MOULDING

FLOOR
PLATE

PLASTER
LATH

1/4"
PLYWOOD
OR
FIBERBOARD
OVER
SUB FLOOR

RUBBER, ASPHALT,
CORK, OR LINOLEUM

ALTERNATE FLOOR FINISHES ARE TILE
OR INLAID LINOLEUM, ON UNDERLAYMENT

Techniques, methods and materials used for inside finish are outlined in the illustrations above.

carpenters are through. If the floor is not laid until the carpenters are through, the baseboard is placed high enough so the flooring can be inserted underneath.

The first operation is to thoroughly clean the rough floor and cover it with tar paper, one room at a time. If the rough floor has been laid at right angles with the floor joists, the hardwood floor must be laid crossways even if it is the short way of the room. If the rough floor is laid on a diagonal the finish floor can be laid either way. Most carpenters usually start in the largest room. Since this flooring costs about 50 cents a square foot they are careful to combine lengths that have less than a foot cut off as waste. The first board is laid with the groove as close against the wall as is possible and be straight. When a doorway is reached at the *end* of the flooring, the hardwood men lay the flooring in the adjoining room until that room is even with the same door and the flooring is laid through the doorway for both rooms; 6d

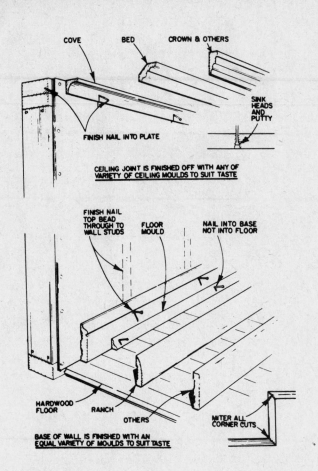

COVE   BED   CROWN & OTHERS

SINK HEADS AND PUTTY

FINISH NAIL INTO PLATE

CEILING JOINT IS FINISHED OFF WITH ANY OF VARIETY OF CEILING MOULDS TO SUIT TASTE

FINISH NAIL TOP BEAD THROUGH TO WALL STUDS

FLOOR MOULD

NAIL INTO BASE NOT INTO FLOOR

HARDWOOD FLOOR   RANCH   OTHERS

MITER ALL CORNER CUTS

BASE OF WALL IS FINISHED WITH AN EQUAL VARIETY OF MOULDS TO SUIT TASTE

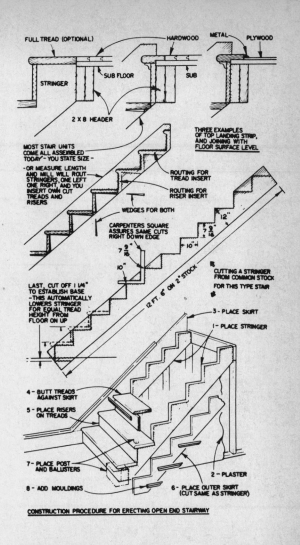

FULL TREAD (OPTIONAL)   HARDWOOD   METAL   PLYWOOD

STRINGER   SUB FLOOR   SUB

2 X 8 HEADER

THREE EXAMPLES OF TOP LANDING STRIP, AND JOINING WITH FLOOR SURFACE LEVEL

MOST STAIR UNITS COME ALL ASSEMBLED TODAY - YOU STATE SIZE -
- OR MEASURE LENGTH AND MILL WILL ROUT STRINGERS, ONE LEFT ONE RIGHT, AND YOU INSERT OWN CUT TREADS AND RISERS

ROUTING FOR TREAD INSERT

ROUTING FOR RISER INSERT

WEDGES FOR BOTH

CARPENTERS SQUARE ASSURES SAME CUTS RIGHT DOWN EDGE

12"
7 2/16
10"
7 9/16
10"

CUTTING A STRINGER FROM COMMON STOCK FOR THIS TYPE STAIR

12 FT. 6" ON 2" STOCK

LAST, CUT OFF 1 1/4" TO ESTABLISH BASE - THIS AUTOMATICALLY LOWERS STRINGER FOR EQUAL TREAD HEIGHT FROM FLOOR ON UP

3 - PLACE SKIRT
1 - PLACE STRINGER

4 - BUTT TREADS AGAINST SKIRT

5 - PLACE RISERS ON TREADS

7 - PLACE POST AND BALUSTERS

8 - ADD MOULDINGS

2 - PLASTER

6 - PLACE OUTER SKIRT (CUT SAME AS STRINGER)

CONSTRUCTION PROCEDURE FOR ERECTING OPEN END STAIRWAY

Stairways look complex; above, trade secrets.

Below, flooring tips; right, plaster wall details.

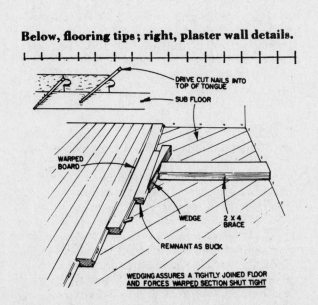

DRIVE CUT NAILS INTO TOP OF TONGUE

SUB FLOOR

WARPED BOARD

WEDGE   2 X 4 BRACE

REMNANT AS BUCK

WEDGING ASSURES A TIGHTLY JOINED FLOOR AND FORCES WARPED SECTION SHUT TIGHT

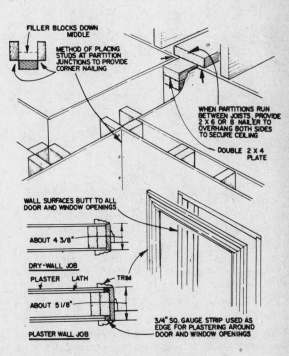

FILLER BLOCKS DOWN MIDDLE

METHOD OF PLACING STUDS AT PARTITION JUNCTIONS TO PROVIDE CORNER NAILING

WHEN PARTITIONS RUN BETWEEN JOISTS, PROVIDE 2 X 6 OR 8 NAILER TO OVERHANG BOTH SIDES TO SECURE CEILING

DOUBLE 2 X 4 PLATE

WALL SURFACES BUTT TO ALL DOOR AND WINDOW OPENINGS

ABOUT 4 3/8"

DRY-WALL JOB

PLASTER   LATH   TRIM

ABOUT 5 1/8"

PLASTER WALL JOB

3/4" SQ. GAUGE STRIP USED AS EDGE FOR PLASTERING AROUND DOOR AND WINDOW OPENINGS

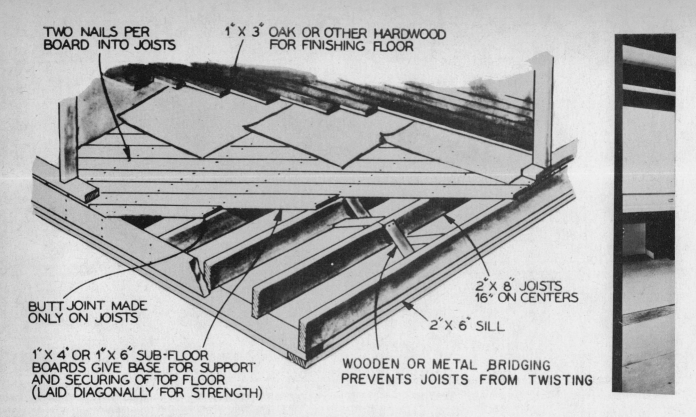

TWO NAILS PER BOARD INTO JOISTS

1" X 3" OAK OR OTHER HARDWOOD FOR FINISHING FLOOR

BUTT JOINT MADE ONLY ON JOISTS

1" X 4" OR 1" X 6" SUB-FLOOR BOARDS GIVE BASE FOR SUPPORT AND SECURING OF TOP FLOOR (LAID DIAGONALLY FOR STRENGTH)

2" X 8" JOISTS 16" ON CENTERS

2" X 6" SILL

WOODEN OR METAL BRIDGING PREVENTS JOISTS FROM TWISTING

FLOOR CONSTRUCTION IN AVERAGE WOOD FRAME DWELLING

Floor construction is detailed; plywood can also be used for subflooring—it's squeakless.

Hardwood flooring is usually put down by a professional, but skilled amateur can do it.

square nails are driven on slant above the tongue. Hardwood men have a special knack. They can drive these nails flush with the wood without a nail set and not scar either the top or the tongue. These floors must fit perfectly, a $\frac{1}{16}$-inch crack is large. The 2x4 is cut to fit each time it is required. Ordinarily carpenters can push the piece into place with a wood remnant and a large chisel or a wrecking bar driven into the rough floor. One of the worries in laying these floors is that they can be laid too tightly and will occasionally bulge several weeks after they are laid. Usually this is due to the fact that the flooring is delivered extra dry and later swells in the floor, especially in the fall of the year if the house is vacant, or for any reason the flooring absorbs moisture.

The Baseboard

Baseboard: This is often two pieces of similar molding that fit against the plaster next to the floor around each room. Cheaper houses may be limited to a single 1x4. The main member is usually a 1x6 cut on a 45-degree miter box at each end across the edge to meet the adjoining pieces. Since baseboards rest on top of the finished floor they are easier to place after the finish floor is laid. However, it frequently happens that the hardwood men

Floor tiles are manufactured by a number of firms; here they're put down over subfloor.

Wall-to-wall carpeting, usually laid by a professional, is put down with a stapling hammer.

are delayed and the finish carpenters will place the baseboard in position on ¾-inch blocks, which serve temporarily.

As a rule carpenters start in the largest room first on the longest side, and work toward the smaller rooms, doing the closets last. It saves lumber and avoids splices. Each side of each room should be of one board if possible. For measurement, most carpenters use a piece of quarter round for long lengths and add a measurement from a 6-foot rule. This measurement is then transferred to an uncut baseboard that will cut to advantage and both ends of each board are cut on a 45-degree angle across the edge so the long points represent the measurement. The next board should butt against one of these 45-degree cuts and fit.

The plastered corner usually has a rounded corner which requires that the back of the board be planed away to make a fit. Frequently one end of the baseboard will be against an inside door trim so that the 45 angle can be planed to fit and the square *end* against the trim can be scratched for length and cut square. Inequalities in the plastered wall often cause trouble. The lowest row of nails is driven low enough to hit the wall plate. The top row with two-piece trim is toe-nailed through the top corner to hit a stud

behind the plaster. These can be found by measurement from a first corner from which the studs have been placed 16 inches apart. Most carpenters can locate the studs by the difference in sound when they tap on the walls.

The second or top piece of baseboard may be only a quarter round or a 2-inch molded piece. It is placed and fitted the same as the wider section. It covers the nails toenailed in that section but its own nails are exposed. The floor molding is usually a small special shaped quarter round, ¾x½ that covers the joint between the baseboard and the finish floor and is nailed alternately to the floor and the baseboard. It should cover the lower row of nail heads in the baseboard. These pieces are dubbed off at a 45-degree angle at the end against the door trim.

The Fireplace

Fireplace: These can have almost any finish from raw brick, including the mantel, to finish paneling within 8 inches of the front opening. Normally the owner and his lady will have some ideas of their own. The wrong color can ruin a living room. The trim can be amplified to become a boxed mantel, a fancy trimmed panel above the opening, a fluted column of finish down the front on each side with more finish lumber

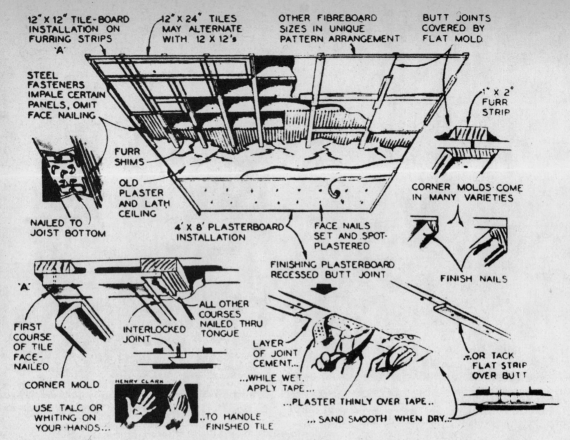

12" X 12" TILE-BOARD INSTALLATION ON FURRING STRIPS 'A'

12" X 24" TILES MAY ALTERNATE WITH 12 X 12's

OTHER FIBREBOARD SIZES IN UNIQUE PATTERN ARRANGEMENT

BUTT JOINTS COVERED BY FLAT MOLD

STEEL FASTENERS IMPALE CERTAIN PANELS, OMIT FACE NAILING

1" X 2" FURR STRIP

FURR SHIMS

OLD PLASTER AND LATH CEILING

CORNER MOLDS COME IN MANY VARIETIES

NAILED TO JOIST BOTTOM

4' X 8' PLASTERBOARD INSTALLATION

FACE NAILS SET AND SPOT-PLASTERED

FINISHING PLASTERBOARD RECESSED BUTT JOINT

FINISH NAILS

'A'

FIRST COURSE OF TILE FACE-NAILED

INTERLOCKED JOINT

ALL OTHER COURSES NAILED THRU TONGUE

LAYER OF JOINT CEMENT...

..OR TACK FLAT STRIP OVER BUTT

CORNER MOLD

HENRY CLARK

...WHILE WET, APPLY TAPE...

USE TALC OR WHITING ON YOUR HANDS...

..TO HANDLE FINISHED TILE

...PLASTER THINLY OVER TAPE..

... SAND SMOOTH WHEN DRY...

COMPOSITE VIEW SHOWING HOW ANY OF SEVERAL COVERINGS ARE QUICKLY APPLIED

over the ends to the wall. Such a fireplace will also have the baseboard around the columns and back to the face of the fireplace. Frequently on this class, the carpenters will have a rough plan and the material on hand but the rough backing of the finish lumber will be the carpenters design. Fortunately the mortar joint will take a nail with a little patience.

Stairs: There are an endless variety of stairs in both finish and form but after the principles are understood and the steps can be laid out they are not so difficult. The best step is 10 inches wide and 8 inches high on the rough stringer. However, steps will vary from 6 inches high to maybe 20 inches wide for front steps of public buildings to as steep as 9 by 9 for cellar stairs.

Cellar Stairs: These are usually the first stairs to be built. The first move of the carpenters is to determine the vertical height by measurement from where the foot of the stairs will be to the top of the finish floor. Assume this measurement is 98 inches. For an 8-inch riser this means 12 risers and 2 inches over, so that to come out even, 12 risers will have to be $8\frac{3}{16}$ inches high. Or if we use 13 risers each riser must be $7\frac{9}{16}$ inches high, which is probably a better height. Due to the floor which acts

as one tread there is always one less tread than risers so 13 risers means 12 treads. If each tread is 10 inches wide this makes 120 inches the length required for the steps.

The next operation is to lay out the risers and the treads on a 2x12 plank long enough for the stair stringer so each step is $7\frac{9}{16}$ inches high and 10 inches wide. The square is laid on the plank about 12 inches from the end so that $7\frac{9}{16}$ inches for the rise and 10 inches for the tread are on the edge of the plank and this position is marked entirely around the corner of the square which is then stepped along to the dotted positions and marked again until the positions for the 12 risers have been marked. The 13th riser is usually the header in the floor system and not a part of the stringer. It is now necessary to mark the stringer so it will fit against the basement floor and the header in the main floor of the house. Remember when the stringer is in position the risers are vertical and the treads are level. Therefore the cut to fit the header is parallel to the riser and at right angles to the last tread. The cut to fit the basement floor is parallel to a tread and back under the stringers at right angles to the bottom riser. So far no allowance has been made

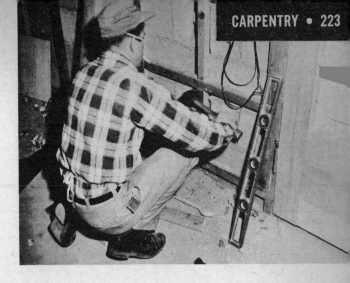

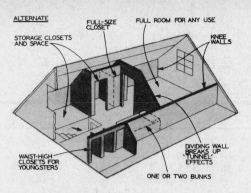

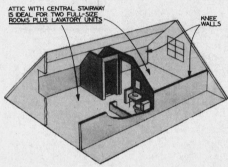

When planning to refinish your attic, be sure to make good use of the kneewall space.

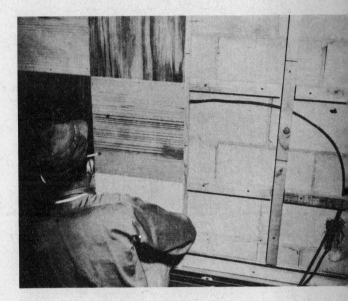

Here, plywood wall tiles are nailed to 1x2 furring strips in interesting pattern.

for the thickness of the treads which is usually 1¼ inches, unless a common 2x12 is used. The easiest way to make this allowance is to mark the stringer according to the figures calculated and cut the thickness of the tread off the bottom tread. This lowers the stringer and makes the top riser which is the header in the floor system $8\frac{13}{16}$ inches until the tread is placed when the riser is correct at $7\frac{9}{16}$ inches. It will be noted that the top step in our drawing is cut to 10 inches but when the top riser is placed against the header this distance is shortened to 9¼ inches, but when the second riser is placed the measurement is back to 10 inches.

After the stringers are cut they are set in place against the header of the stair well and tied to this header. Attic stairs or stairs for a second story can be nailed to the lower floor and the tie to the header is not important. Cellar stairs are different. Occasionally one stairs stringer can be tied to the studs of a wall or a basement post but frequently they are entirely open and the tie becomes of the utmost importance.

Plywood wall panels come in 4x8 size, are easily installed, come in a variety of textures.

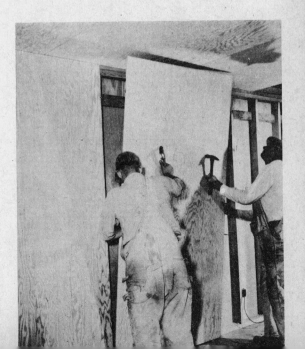

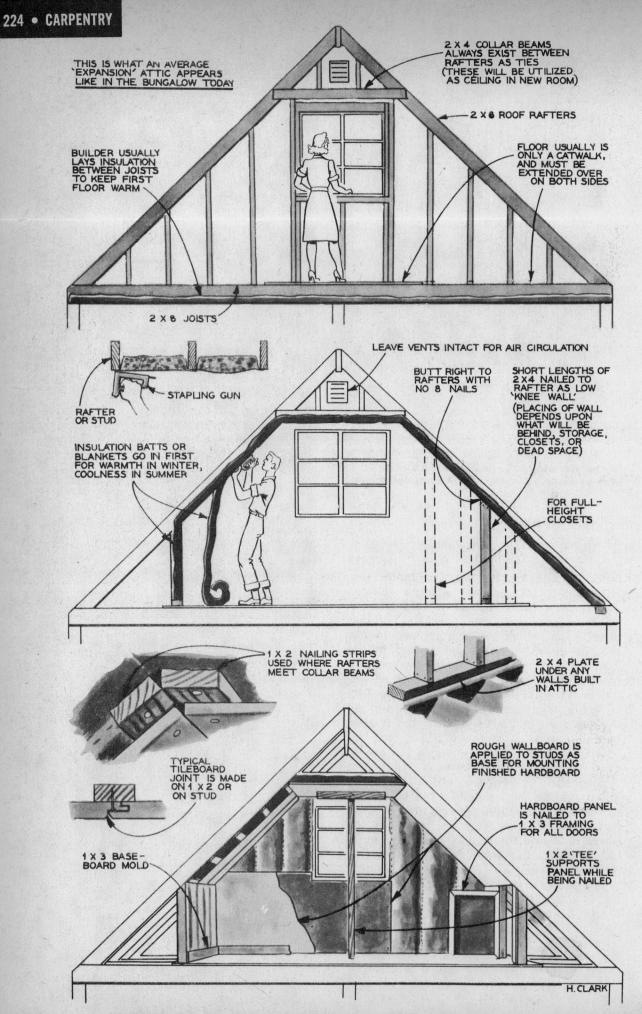

THIS IS WHAT AN AVERAGE 'EXPANSION' ATTIC APPEARS LIKE IN THE BUNGALOW TODAY

2 X 4 COLLAR BEAMS ALWAYS EXIST BETWEEN RAFTERS AS TIES (THESE WILL BE UTILIZED AS CEILING IN NEW ROOM)

2 X 6 ROOF RAFTERS

BUILDER USUALLY LAYS INSULATION BETWEEN JOISTS TO KEEP FIRST FLOOR WARM

FLOOR USUALLY IS ONLY A CATWALK, AND MUST BE EXTENDED OVER ON BOTH SIDES

2 X 8 JOISTS

LEAVE VENTS INTACT FOR AIR CIRCULATION

STAPLING GUN

RAFTER OR STUD

BUTT RIGHT TO RAFTERS WITH NO 8 NAILS

SHORT LENGTHS OF 2 X 4 NAILED TO RAFTER AS LOW 'KNEE WALL' (PLACING OF WALL DEPENDS UPON WHAT WILL BE BEHIND, STORAGE, CLOSETS, OR DEAD SPACE)

INSULATION BATTS OR BLANKETS GO IN FIRST FOR WARMTH IN WINTER, COOLNESS IN SUMMER

FOR FULL-HEIGHT CLOSETS

1 X 2 NAILING STRIPS USED WHERE RAFTERS MEET COLLAR BEAMS

2 X 4 PLATE UNDER ANY WALLS BUILT IN ATTIC

TYPICAL TILEBOARD JOINT IS MADE ON 1 X 2 OR ON STUD

ROUGH WALLBOARD IS APPLIED TO STUDS AS BASE FOR MOUNTING FINISHED HARDBOARD

HARDBOARD PANEL IS NAILED TO 1 X 3 FRAMING FOR ALL DOORS

1 X 3 BASE-BOARD MOLD

1 X 2 'TEE' SUPPORTS PANEL WHILE BEING NAILED

H. CLARK

DECORATIVE AND COLORFUL PANELS FINISH OFF ALL WALL SURFACES

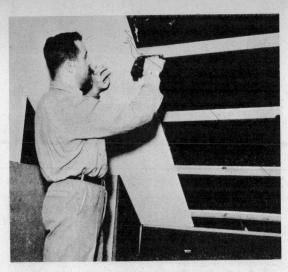

Insulation is stapled into attic roof, then furring strips nailed up to support panels.

Large closets in todays' homes are ready-made to receive easily built, space-conserving units.

The lower end rests loose on a concrete floor and the tie at the top end is all that keeps it from sliding down hill. There are several methods to make this tie. Our drawing shows one designed for a 2x10 floor joist. The trouble is that the floor is only 11 inches thick (9½ plus 1½). The step requires normally 8 inches and 1¼ inches for regular stepping and 1½ inches for 2x12 which is often used for cellar treads for a total of 9½ inches, leaving a bearing of only 1½ inches for the stringer against the header. To give more bearing another 2x4 can be nailed to the bottom edge of the header which will give 3 inches of bearing for the stair stringer plus the thickness of the tread when it is in place, as shown in the drawing. To keep the stringer from sliding forward on the concrete floor, a vertical 2x4 is nailed to the back of the header, or a floor joist if it is in line, and that portion of the stringer that is cut to go under the header can be nailed to this 2x4, as shown in the drawing. It will be noted that the floor joists are parallel to the stair stringers which makes the rough flooring parallel to the top riser and the finish floor to butt against the riser. Normally this joint is covered by a thin threshold.

Occasionally the stairs will run crossways of the floor joist instead of parallel and the stringers rest against a floor joist, or a parallel header between two cross headers.

Right, composition board and plywood are best materials to use in constructing built-ins.

To make best use of all space, consider installing built-in drawer units in walls.

Trim and molding around doors can be bought ready-made or be made by owner.

Valances add to attractiveness of a kitchen window; they're easy to build, install.

The Landings

Landings: Basement stairs often have landings which must be built first to replace a tread. That is, if risers are 8 inches, the landings must be some multiple of 8 inches from the top of the floor and likewise they will be a multiple of 8 inches from the basement floor. There are two sets of stair stringers. The top pair rest on the landing and the second set butt against the equivalent of a header underneath the floor of the landing. These landings are simply a table set on four legs with a top of finish flooring. Underneath the top, outside the legs, are four pieces to support the floor, the same as for any table, only in this case they are usually 2x6's with the side next to the lower stair set low enough to act as a support for these stringers. There is a little allowance to be made in the height due to the fact that the landing floor is usually ¾ inch thick and the regular treads will have a different thickness.

The position of the landing is determined by the 10-inch treads. If it is assumed the head of the stairs is 96 inches from the wall where the stairs must turn, this will allow 6 treads 10 inches wide or 60 inches and there is left 36 inches for the landing which is probably the width of the stairs. It is evident that the position of the stairs must be determined when the floor joists are placed.

The Attic Stairs

Attic Stairs: Normally the attic stairs and often the second story stairs are entirely enclosed. It frequently happens that the basement stairs will be below them. The rough stringers are generally placed before the house is plastered and are set 6 inches from the partition walls. These stringers can be nailed to the floor and made to hold firm against the top header. After the house is plastered, the first pieces the carpenters will place for these stairs for a two story home will be two skirt boards. These are ¾ inch x 11½ inches of finish lumber that are nailed through the plaster to the studs. The top end will probably fit against the upstairs baseboard and the lower end against an inside door trim. Both the risers and the treads butt against these skirt boards which should be placed as high as possible without showing any plaster in the corner between the tread and the riser.

In cheaper houses, the skirt boards may be omitted. In this case, carpenters usually line the corners between the treads and the plaster with a small molding for the benefit of the cleaning lady.

The Front Stairs

Front Stairs: These are usually exposed on one side with the other side against a partition. There is almost no limit to the inside finish of such a stair in a very fine home: Skirt boards underneath the treads on the exposed side, mitered to the risers, treads with mitered returns across the ends, fancy newel posts and balustrades, curved stair railing. Some of the fine old homes show an unbelievable perfection in workmanship. After 50 years, joints and holes above the nail heads vary from practically invisible to actually invisible.

Built-ins: Cupboards, dumb waiters, ironing boards, medicine cabinets and

Right, room shapes can be changed by use of built-in room dividers; plywood firms sell plans for these.

other special pieces have their top and bottom headers placed between the studs before the house is plastered.

Ironing boards are set in the wall between two 2x4 studs and against the back of the plaster on the other side of the wall. These are usually purchased and the size must be known and the headers placed before the house is plastered.

Medicine cabinets are always purchased all assembled with the door. They are usually made of metal, 14 inches wide and 4½ inches deep so they can be set between two studs, set 16 inch centers. They need two headers between the studs the required distance apart which also must be ascertained before the house is plastered. The cabinets carry holes for screws for attachment to the studs or the headers.

Cupboards and built-ins are normally made to order. They are set into inside walls against plaster on the other side the same as the above but they often project into the room several inches and will probably require headers anywhere from 14 inches to 46 inches long. It pays to check the size of the doors available before the headers are cut and placed.

These cupboards may extend through the walls and project into the rooms on each side as dumb waiters. The doors are omitted.

Here is a home-built kitchen unit ready for finish; Formica tops will be installed later.

Enamel is best over raw plywood to hide grain; other woods can be varnished.

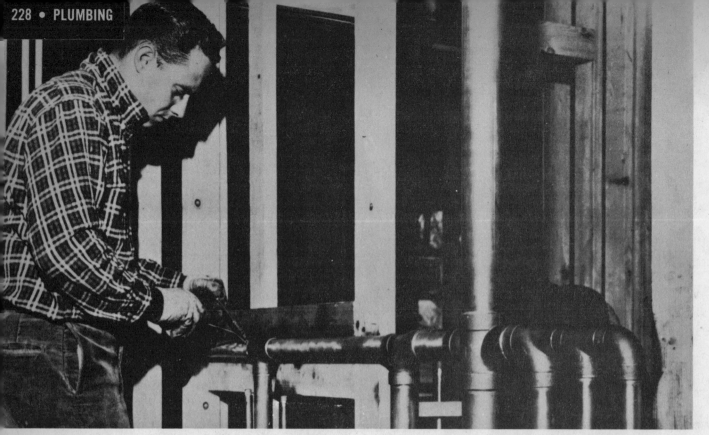

Chase Brass and Copper

Vents provide the air needed for free flow of sewage down the drains. Here several branch vent lines are connected to the stack. Stack is large, vertical drain and vent pipe extend up through the roof.

how plumbing works

... AND WHAT YOU SHOULD KNOW

A PLUMBING SYSTEM consists of two kinds of piping: one supplying water, the other carrying waste water and sewage away.

Water supply plumbing is very simple. It can be considered as an extended hose with many branches, leading the water wherever it is desired. Shutoffs and faucets control the water flow. Pipes can be small because the water is under pressure. Getting the pipes through walls, and wherever they are going, presents few problems because of this small size.

Water supply pipes which extend upward a story or more are known as risers. To prevent water-hammer, a banging in pipes caused when faucets are quickly turned off, vertical lengths of pipe are commonly installed near each faucet to serve as air-chamber shock absorbers.

Drainage pipes are large. They have to be because the relatively slow flow through them is by gravity. Because of the gravity flow, drainage pipes must have a continual pitch of at least ¼ inch per foot from the time they leave a fixture until they reach the sewer. Even the fittings used in assembling drainage pipe have a built-in pitch.

Large vertical drain pipes are known as stacks. Horizontal drains are usually called waste pipes, or soil pipes if they carry toilet sewage. A stack that carries toilet waste is known as a soil stack.

The main drainage line from the house is known as the house drain. It continues 5 to 10 feet out through the foundation and after that point is known as the house sewer. The house sewer connects either to a septic tank, or to a public sewer in the street.

Vents. It is difficult to pour liquid out of a can that has just one hole punched in its top. Punch another hole for air, and the liquid flows freely. For the same reason, drain lines need air, and it is supplied by vent pipes. There must be a vent pipe near each fixture. A vent may continue on up through the roof and be open to the air, or several vents may connect onto a single large vent, or stack, which extends up through the roof to the air.

Installation plans for plumbing are usually shown in a schematic drawing like this. You may find it helpful to use these symbols in planning your plumbing project.

Chase Brass and Copper

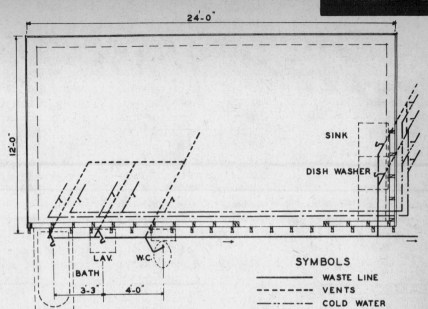

SINK

DISH WASHER

SYMBOLS

———————— WASTE LINE
– – – – – – – – VENTS
–·–·–·–·– COLD WATER
–··–··–··– HOT WATER

LAV.

W.C.

BATH

3'-3"   4'-0"

24'-0"

12'-0"

Vent pipes (below) extend through to the open air above the roof and, where there is any danger of frost, should be at least 3 inches in diameter. Flashing is used to seal up the vent-roof joint.

Roughing-in is the installation of all plumbing except for fixtures. Pipe ends are capped until the wall finish is complete. Shown are the stack, branch vents, wastes, and water lines.

Dow Saraloy Flashing

Trap is the U-shaped pipe which holds water and seals off sewer gases from the house. Vents prevent waste from siphoning traps dry. To check if a trap is properly filled, open as shown here.

Cleanouts must be provided wherever the drain line makes a turn, or where any stoppages might occur. Brass cleanout plug here is installed where house drain exists through the foundation.

In addition to supplying air to facilitate the free flowing of waste water and sewage, vents allow the escape of dangerous and unhealthful sewer gases from the system. So that these gases do not escape into the house, it is of vital importance that every joint in the venting system be airtight. Vents also prevent waste water from coming back up through traps at lower levels.

Traps are used to seal off the gases in the drainage lines. A trap usually consists of a curved piece of pipe which always remains filled with water. Waste passes freely through the trap, but the water level remains undisturbed as a seal. Here again, the vents play a part. If a fixture drain were not properly vented, the rush of waste water from the fixture would create a vacuum and suck the trap dry. Such siphonage is a hazard to health, for it opens the sewer to the house.

In older houses, if water goes down the drain with a great sucking sound, it usually indicates the trap is being siphoned. In such cases, and where the installation of a vent to correct the condition would be extremely difficult, many codes permit the installation of a special "anti-siphon trap." It does the job of a standard vented trap. •

House drain becomes the house sewer at a point 5 to 10 feet beyond foundation line. Cast-iron drain pipe is being connected here to a fiber pipe, acceptable in some areas for sewer lines.

All vent and drainage lines must be pitched at least ¼ inch per foot. Here the house sewer line, connecting to septic tank, is being tested for pitch. The opening in foreground is a cleanout.

Septic tank is a watertight receptacle, typically of 750 or 1000 gallon capacity, in which sewage, by bacterial action, is converted into liquid and absorbed by soil.

PLUMBING TERMS

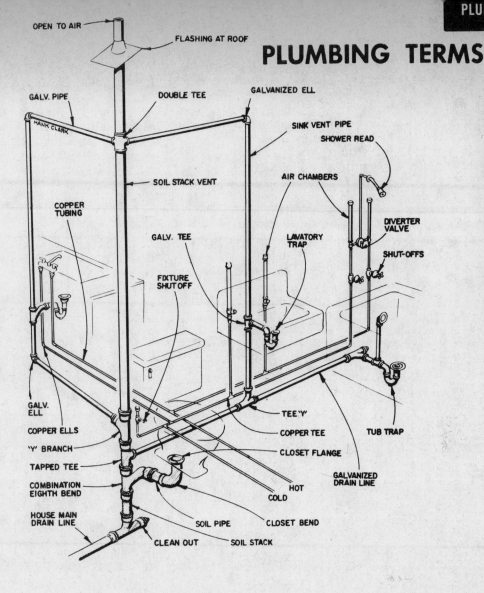

OPEN TO AIR
FLASHING AT ROOF
GALV. PIPE
DOUBLE TEE
GALVANIZED ELL
HANK CLARK
SINK VENT PIPE
SHOWER HEAD
SOIL STACK VENT
AIR CHAMBERS
COPPER TUBING
LAVATORY TRAP
DIVERTER VALVE
GALV. TEE
SHUT-OFFS
FIXTURE SHUT OFF
GALV. ELL
COPPER ELLS
'Y' BRANCH
TEE 'Y'
TAPPED TEE
COPPER TEE
TUB TRAP
COMBINATION EIGHTH BEND
CLOSET FLANGE
GALVANIZED DRAIN LINE
HOUSE MAIN DRAIN LINE
HOT
COLD
CLEAN OUT
SOIL PIPE
SOIL STACK
CLOSET BEND

Air chamber: A short length of vertical pipe, usually connected near a faucet, which serves to cushion the shock when water flow is abruptly stopped.

Branch: Any secondary water pipe or waste line which serves one fixture only.

Cleanout plug: An access opening for servicing clogged drain pipes.

Closet flange: A fitting for attaching a toilet to its drain pipe.

House drain: The main drainage pipe which conducts the discharge from all branch pipes to a point just outside the house foundation wall.

House sewer: The piping that continues from the end of the house drain and which connects to a septic tank or the public sewer in the street.

Main: A principal pipe to which branches are attached.

Plumbing: All pipes and fixtures for water supply and for both sanitary and storm drainage.

Riser: A water supply pipe which extends vertically at least one story.

Roughing in: Installation of the entire plumbing system except for fixtures. This includes installation of drainage, vents, water supply piping, and fixture supports.

Septic tank: A large water-tight receptacle which receives sewage from the drainage system and by bacterial action converts it to harmless liquid.

Soil pipe: A pipe carrying toilet sewage.

Stack: A main, vertical soil, waste, or vent pipe.

Trap: A curved pipe, holding water, which prevents the backpassage of gases from the drainage system, while allowing free flow of waste water or sewage through it.

Vent: A pipe supplying air to drainage lines.

Waste pipe: A pipe carrying other than toilet sewage.

Wet vent: A section of pipe serving for drainage as well as venting.

the right kind of pipe

... MAKES ALL THE DIFFERENCE

THERE ARE MANY kinds and qualities of pipe for water supply, drainage and vent lines. By understanding the strong and weak points of each type of piping, you'll be prepared to make the best selection for your own particular needs. An ideal pipe would cost less, be easier to install, and last longer than any other. Unfortunately, there is no one piping material which meets all these requirements. Local codes may also have some say about which varieties of pipe you can use.

Water Supply Pipes. Galvanized steel, copper, brass, plastic, and galvanized wrought iron pipe are commonly used for water supply systems. Black iron pipe is not used; it rusts too quickly. Lead pipe is not recommended, though it may be used for making a "gooseneck connection" between the water main in the street and the house service line.

● Galvanized steel pipe has the lowest initial cost of all types. Its usual life is from 15 to 30 years and in some areas gives what is considered satisfactory service. New York City code, for example, requires it. However, if it has to be replaced at any time, it's cost to you will be far higher than the most expensive kind of plumbing you can get.

Steel pipe is subject to deposits of salts and lime which gradually restrict water flow and which may eventually choke the flow off completely. It is corroded by both

GALVANIZED STEEL PIPE

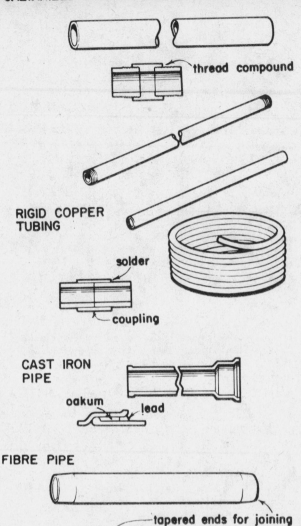

thread compound

RIGID COPPER TUBING

solder

coupling

CAST IRON PIPE

oakum   lead

FIBRE PIPE

tapered ends for joining

coupling

Tools required for roughing in copper plumbing in an entire house. For the large tank of gas, a small hand-torch can easily be substituted. Most are tools found in average home workshop.

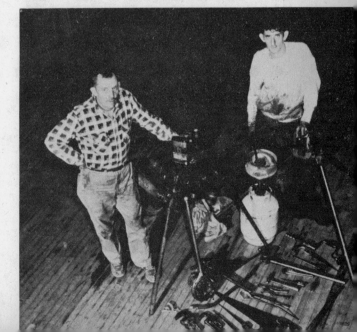

Cast iron is most durable material for drainage, waste and vent lines, but assembly is slower. Shown here are the tools used in roughing in a typical all-ferrous home plumbing installation.

alkaline and acid waters. Carbonic acid in water attacks the zinc coating of the pipe, then the steel itself. Hot water is more acid than cold, and so these lines usually give out first.

Steel pipe comes in standard 21-foot lengths threaded at each end. Usually a pipe of ¾ to 1-inch diameter is big enough to supply all the water needed for both hot and cold water systems in a house. The ¾-inch size is adequate for main hot water or cold water lines and ½-inch pipe for branch lines to fixtures. Sizes of pipe always refer to internal diameters.

● Copper is the easiest to install of all water-line types, and is the first choice for either the professional or the nonprofes-

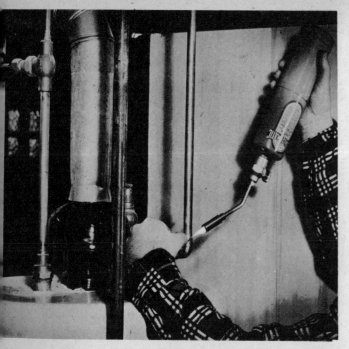

Copper tubing is unexcelled for both hot- and cold-water lines. It has such a smooth interior surface that it can be used one size smaller than galvanized steel pipe. Assembly is easy.

Because of its light weight, copper lends itself to "shop fabrication." Entire assemblies can be made wherever it is most convenient and then placed right into position in the house structure.

Copper & Brass Research Assoc.

sional installer. Copper will last as long as the house, and can meet the demands of areas where water is extremely corrosive. Its inside surface is much smoother than that of steel pipe, and one size smaller can be used without reduction of water flow. Where ¾-inch steel pipe is required, for example, ½-inch copper is more than satisfactory.

A ¾-inch copper line is usually enough to supply a house. A 1-inch size is used if there are flush valves on toilets, a lawn sprinkler system, a water-cooled air conditioner which discards water, or other heavy-demand equipment. For supply lines to toilet and basins, ⅜-inch tubing is commonly used, though some codes require ½, sometimes even ⅝-inch size. Supply to bathtubs is usually ½ inch.

Copper tubing costs a little more than steel pipe, but its fittings cost less and if you are paying for installation labor, your bill should be about 25 per cent less. Copper tubing is usually assembled by means of sweat (soldered) fittings, occasionally by flare or compression fittings. Sweat joints are easier to make than threaded joints, and they are stronger. Threading pipe thins it down, weakens it.

Copper tubing is made in three wall thicknesses: K, L, and M. Type K is the heaviest and is used underground. Type L is somewhat lighter and is used for in-

terior plumbing and for radiant heating installation. Type M is lightest and is designed especially for radiant heating.

Both Type K and Type L tubing are available either in rigid (hard temper), or flexible (soft temper) varieties. Rigid tubing is usually offered in 20-foot lengths, though Sears offers it in 10. Flexible K type is produced in 60 and 100-foot coils, but you may be able to buy part of a coil. Type L is also available in 30-foot coils.

Flexible tubing is best for running up through existing walls in remodeling jobs, or when replacing clogged or rusted out galvanized pipe. It's also better for ground burial, for it can be readily bent around rocks and other obstructions. It will take some freezing without being appreciably damaged and will give a little, rather than burst, as earth settles.

Because of its flexibility, soft temper tubing requires fewer fittings, and it is best for vertical lines where some bending is often necessary. However, hard temper tubing, with solder fittings, makes the neatest installations and is required for horizontal lines. Flexible tubing, used horizontally, is likely to sag, creating pockets which make drainage difficult. Solder fittings can be used with either flexible or rigid tubing, but flared or compression fittings are designed for flexible tubing only.

Cast-iron drainage is heavy, has many joints, and is so bulky that thicker walls are required to accommodate it. Cost of the material, however, is much less than the cost for copper tubing.

Because cast iron is so heavy, it often may require special, sturdy support. A completed installation is never so neat-looking or as compact as copper. But it's much more durable.

● Brass pipe is the most expensive of all types. Originally it was used as yellow brass, composed of 60 per cent copper and most of the rest zinc. Then it was found that red brass with an 80 per cent copper content was more durable. The feeling today is that for most water purposes straight copper is superior, and brass is now commonly used only for exposed water supply lines which are chrome plated.

Like copper, brass water pipe has very smooth inside surfaces and can be used one size smaller than steel or iron pipe. It is joined with threaded fittings. Brass has about the same wall thickness as steel pipe of comparable size, and threads are the same.

● Wrought iron. Cost is high, use limited. It's a durable pipe, resistant to certain corrosive waters. It is not to be confused with steel pipe.

● Plastic pipe is tough, lightweight, easy to cut, handle, join, and is inexpensive. It is unexcelled for cold water lines, but as yet cannot be recommended for general use with hot water for it won't take temperatures above 160 degrees.

Plastic is the number one choice for well pipes, water sprinkling systems, swimming pool plumbing, running a line for a hose cock, for connecting to a water softener, or any other cold water use, codes permitting. It is not harmed by occasional freezing,

Even though you make other drainage, waste and vent lines of copper, you will still have to switch to cast iron for any underground piping, and for section where main drain leaves house.

For vent section of stack, you can save money in material cost and in labor by switching from cast-iron pipe to Transite pipe. This cement-asbestos pipe is joined by standard caulking.

Copper is available in both hard temper and flexible varieties. The flexible kind is easily bent and shaped by the hands alone, but hard temper copper can be bent only by means of a special tool.

won't rust, corrode, or rot. The Orangeburg Company, one of the largest producers of plastic pipe, guarantees their product unconditionally for twenty years, and will even pay labor costs if replacement should be necessary during that period. Tests indicate plastic pipe will easily last in excess of thirty years.

Plastic pipe comes in several types. Polyethylene pipe is the lightest pipe of all, is joined by means of slip fittings and stainless steel clamps. A vinyl type (PVC, or polyvinyl chloride), is commonly joined by solvent cementing of slip fittings, may also be threaded or welded. Plastic pipe is readily available in sizes from ½ to 2 inches. One hundred feet of the ½-inch size weighs 7 pounds, costs $8, as compared with 30 pounds and $30 for copper, and 100 pounds and $15 for steel. It comes in long lengths (up to 3500 feet in some cases), requires fewer fittings.

Drainage and Venting Pipe. Types commonly used are cast iron, threaded steel, copper, plastic, lead, bituminized fiber, asbestos cement, and vitrified clay.

● Cast iron, almost without exception, is the choice for the underground, main

drainage line that extends from the base of the soil stack, through the house foundation wall and from 5 to 10 feet beyond. It has no superior for use as the line running from that point to the septic tank or public sewer in the street. Cast iron is also frequently used for the soil stack (the main vent and drainage line which extends up through the roof), and for branch drainage and vent lines connecting to it. Sometimes, however, for reasons of economy, these branches are made of steel.

Cast iron is very durable and long lasting. It is generally accepted that it will last the life of the house. It is also expensive, heavy, and time-consuming to assemble. Because of its weight, it needs strong support. Because of its bulk, it requires a 2x6 stud wall instead of a standard 2x4 one.

Cast-iron pipe comes in 5-foot lengths and commonly in 2-, 3-, and 4-inch (nominal) inside diameter for homes. One end of each pipe length terminates in a hub or bell, into which the straight spigot of the following section fits. This joint is sealed with a rope-like packing, called oakum, and lead. The lead is usually poured in when molten, but lead wool, which is

Cascade Pools

Plastic pipe is low in cost, light in weight, flexible, extremely durable, and easy to cut and assemble. It comes in coils and also in unbroken lengths of hundreds of feet. Plastic is not as yet suitable for hot water lines, but it has proven to be unexcelled for wells, sprinkling systems, swimming pools, and other cold-water uses.

pounded in cold, may be permitted in some cases.

Cast-iron pipe comes in service weight, and "standard" or "extra heavy weight." Save by using service weight when codes permit. Because of a new spin method of manufacture, service weight pipe is as durable as the standard pipe was formerly.

Lengths of cast-iron pipe are available with a hub at each end. These are handy for cutting short lengths of pipe, since two short sections can be made from one pipe, each piece having a hub end.

● Steel pipe can be used for the main stack and vent lines, but it cannot be used underground. It's far lighter than cast iron, an important consideration in remodeling jobs, particularly in an old house whose structure may not be able to take an excessive amount of added weight. For drainage and vent purposes, steel pipe comes in diameters from 1¼ to 4 inches. It is easily assembled with a chain wrench. Special threaded cast-iron drainage fittings are used with steel pipe. It is not the longest lasting pipe by far, but it is low cost and can offer adequate service particularly in remodeling an older house.

● Copper is made in type M for drainage and in a special economical DWV weight (drainage, waste, vent), permitted by codes in many areas for above ground use. Type M, being heavier, has generally satisfactory durability. It is, however, considerably more expensive than cast iron. Type DWV, thinner walled, is not so durable as type M, but under normal use can be expected to give many years of service.

Either type is light in weight (only about ¼ as much as cast iron), and certainly the easiest type of drainage system to install. A special fitting connects it to the cast-iron underground house drain. The 20-foot lengths in which the copper tubing comes means fewer joints. Assembly is quick and easy with solder-joint drainage fittings. These special fittings are made with a built-in pitch of ¼ inch per foot. The smooth interior of copper tubing and lack of shoulders at joints means faster drainage and less likelihood of clogging.

● Bituminous fiber pipe, such as Orangeburg, is used for house sewers and in septic tank installations. It is lowest in cost of all types, light in weight, comes in 5-foot lengths so that few joints are re-

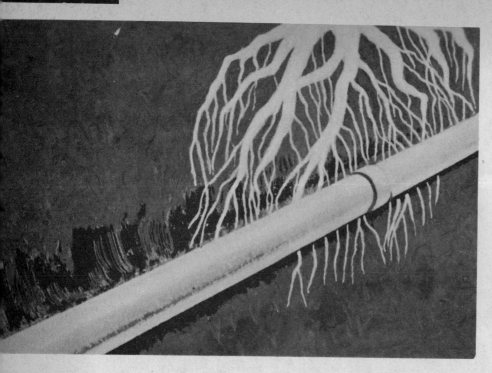

Roots can be destructive to house sewers. If joints aren't tight, roots may enter and clog the line. The fewer the joints, and the more permanent they are, the less trouble for you.

Johns-Manville

Bituminized fiber pipe is most economical kind for sewer and septic tank disposal lines. Assembly is simply made by snap couplings. At right—perforated type used in drain fields.

Orangeburg Mfg. Co.

quired as compared with clay pipe. Joints are made simply by tapping on fittings, are so tight root penetration is seldom a problem. Cutting can be done with an ordinary carpenter's handsaw.

The pipe, impregnated with coal tar pitch, is rotproof and noncorrosive, but excessively hot water and some chemicals may soften it. Because it is slightly flexible, it can take soil movement without cracking or pulling out at the joints. On the other hand, unless its bed is properly made, and backfilling done exactly as directed, it is subject to crushing or collapsing. Codes may require you to come at least ten feet out from your foundation with cast-iron pipe. After that, you can save by switching to a bituminous fiber pipe. An adapter connects it to the spigot end of cast-iron pipe.

● Vitrified clay pipe is often used for building drains which run underground. It doesn't corrode or wear, and if it isn't subject to stresses which crack or break it, it will last indefinitely. For home sewer lines, 4-foot sections are the popular choice, but other lengths are available. Each section has a bell at one end for joining to the plain end of the next pipe section. Joints are

made by packing in oakum to a depth of about ½ inch, then sealing with an asphalt joining compound. The oakum is necessary to keep the compound from getting inside the pipe.

Drawbacks are its many joints, and the possible invasion of them by tree roots if joints are defective, also the increased labor in laying it as compared with the longer-length lighter-weight piping. Most joint trouble with clay pipe in the past was because mortar was used for jointing it. Stick with asphalt, either hot or cold, and you aren't likely to encounter trouble.

● Other types. Asbestos-cement pipe is used for sewer and vent lines, comes in five and ten-foot lengths, can be cut with a carpenter's handsaw. It has the advantage of fewer joints and light weight.

Concrete pipe is similar to vitrified clay pipe in its use and assembly, but it is not as durable.

Plastic pipe promises to come into widespread use shortly for both drainage and vent lines. Plastic is light in weight, noncorroding, easily assembled. All that is holding it back at present is code acceptance and price. ●

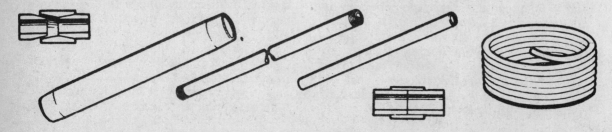

Brass has been largely displaced by copper for home plumbing systems. It's still used, however, for chrome-plated exposed piping, such as that found in water supply lines and lavatory traps.

Chase Brass & Copper Co.

Lead is not recommended for water lines, but has limited uses elsewhere. One of its few applications is for "closet bends," the section of pipe joining the toilet to the soil line. The right kind of pipe, you'll find, does make a difference.

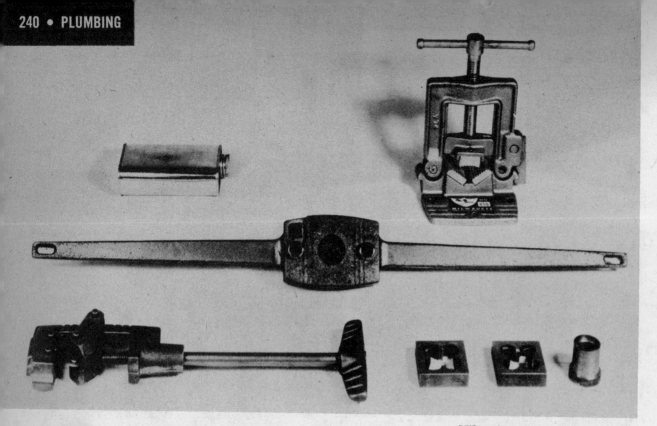

Milwaukee Tool & Equipment Co.

A kit of tools for cutting, threading and working steel pipe can be bought for about $30, and is a worthwhile addition to any workshop. It will cut pipe to 2 inches, thread ½- and ¾-inch pipe.

plumbing tools

... AND HOW TO USE THEM

OFTEN, HALF THE JOB is having the right tool for it. Watching a plumber at work, it's apparent how large a role his tools play in his work and how simple they make otherwise difficult jobs. It is wasteful of effort, and sometimes dangerous, to try to undertake a job with makeshift tools.

Many of the tools needed in plumbing are ones that can have continuing use around the house, and are worthwhile additions to any workshop collection. A good pair of pipe wrenches, such as those made by Ridgid, will be of regular use to you. You're also likely to find enough continuing use for pipe cutting and threading tools to justify acquiring a set. Most economically, they can be bought in kit form. One, manufactured by the Milwaukee Tool & Equipment Company of Milwaukee 46, Wisconsin, includes a pipe vise, a threader for ½- and ¾-inch pipe, a cutter for pipe up to 2 inches, plus a can of cutting oil. It sells for just over $30.

Other tools, which are specialized and rarely needed, can be borrowed or rented. Sears, Roebuck stores lend light or heavy tools free for installing plumbing when you buy your plumbing materials from them.

Pipe Vises. A vise with toothed jaws is needed for working with iron or brass pipe, but not for copper. You can't hold pipe steady enough for cutting or threading in a mechanic's vise. If you have a standard mechanic's vise, you may, however, be able to buy serrated pipe jaws to adapt it for plumbing use. If you plan to buy an all-purpose vise, get one that is a combination pipe and mechanic's vise, and it will serve for your occasional plumbing jobs.

For limited use, it is possible to improvise a pipe holding tool with a pipe wrench. The wrench is set between cleats and the pipe is slipped through a U-bolt or large staple. Or you can use a mechanic's vise, in combination with a pipe wrench, for the purpose. The vise is tightened just enough to hold the pipe firmly. The wrench takes the real grip which keeps the pipe from turning.

A good pipe vise, with up to 2-inch capacity, costs about $15, but you can buy a satisfactory vise with a capacity to 2½ inches for only $10. A small vise, with a capacity to 1¼ inches sells for $5 up. Some

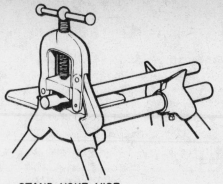

STAND YOKE VISE

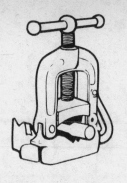

BENCH YOKE VISE

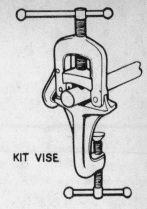

KIT VISE

POST CHAIN VISE

The most popular vise types include stand yoke, bench yoke, and post chain vises. Note the differences as is shown here. Also pipe jaws can often be added to ordinary mechanic's vise, adapting it for plumbing use, doubling the ordinary duty.

Milwaukee Tool & Equipment Co.

PIPE JAWS

Bench vise is bolted to workbench flush with the front edge. Position vise so even long lengths of pipe can be held in its jaws. Release on vise side permits rapid freeing of held pipe.

Pipe must be held firmly for cutting. Place a cutter wheel on line of desired cut, advance it by turning handle slightly each time the cutter is revolved. While working, use cutting oil.

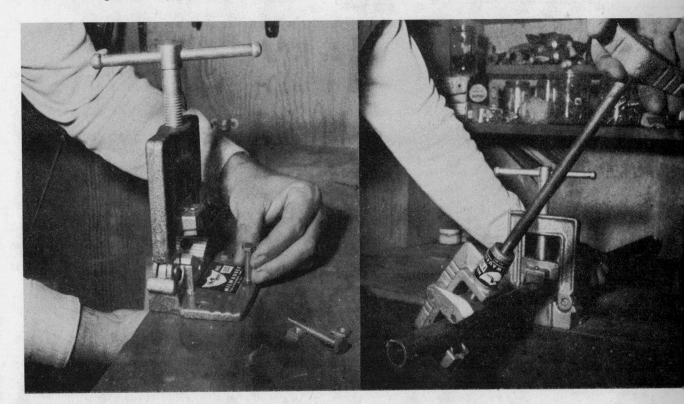

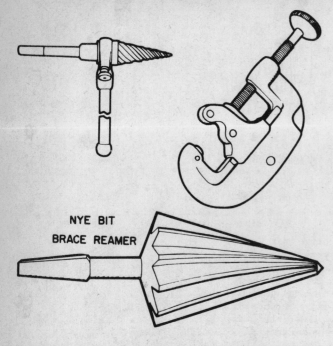

NYE BIT
BRACE REAMER

Simplest reamer has tapered shank to fit any standard brace-and-bit. Spiral ratchet reamer is used by professional plumbers. Tubing cutter has reamer which folds away, protects pockets.

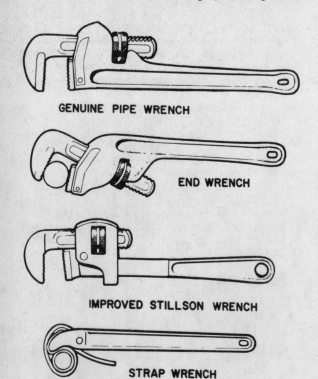

GENUINE PIPE WRENCH

END WRENCH

IMPROVED STILLSON WRENCH

STRAP WRENCH

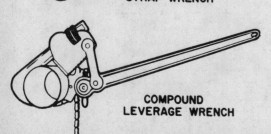

COMPOUND
LEVERAGE WRENCH

vises have pipe rests and benders on their base.

Vises are hinged, so that by releasing a catch, the pipe is easily removed sideways. Pipe jaws are replaceable; some are reversible. In large vises, rods and pipes under ⅜ inch are held securely at either side of the vise jaws. A long-jaw design, as in the Milwaukee vise, holds the pipe securely without damaging it, for the pressure is divided over the whole length of the holding jaws.

Some vises are designed to bolt to a bench, others clamp to it or are easily portable and attach to any bench or plank. A "post vise" can be attached by a chain to a lally column or other post.

Another type of pipe vise has a link chain, and is known as a chain vise. Pipe is held between a jaw and the chain. A chain vise usually has a down-under handle for tightening, but one new Ridgid model has a convenient top screw. The chain vise is a somewhat more compact tool than the standard pipe vise, and the price is likely to be lower. You can get one with up to 2-inch capacity for only $6. They are available with pipe rest and pipe benders.

Pipe and Tubing Cutters. These tools cut faster and better than a hack saw. It takes an expert to get a free-hand square cut with a hack saw, but a cutter gives a square cut every time, and a square cut is essential in getting a threading tool started right, and making flare joints.

Technique of use is simple. Loosen the cutting wheel by turning the handle until the tool can be slid on the pipe. Tighten the wheel on the cutting mark until it begins to bite into the pipe. The handle is turned a little every time the tool is revolved around pipe or tubing. This tightening of the

Wrenches for working with pipe and plumbing fittings include heavy-duty, end, Stillson, strap, compound leverage, chain, spud, and hex wrenches. The new hex wrench will give a four-sided grip.

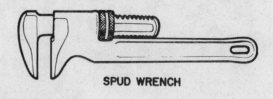

SPUD WRENCH

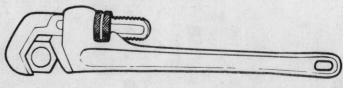

handle keeps advancing the cutter wheel, until it finally comes all the way through. In cutting pipe, apply thread-cutting oil to the cutter wheel and the pipe as you work.

You can buy a "Saunders-type" cutter with capacity to one inch for about $6, to two inch for $9, a better one for $13.50. Most have a minimum capacity of ⅛ inch. Cutting wheels are usually replaceable for a dollar or two.

A standard type cutter has two rollers and one cutter, but you can also get models that have several cutting wheels. A 4-wheel cutter is designed for work in close quarters where it isn't possible to turn the tool completely around the pipe.

Tubing cutters cut copper, brass, and aluminum. One with 1-inch capacity can be bought for about $2, 1½ for about $3.50.

Reamers. A reamer is needed to remove internal burrs in pipe or tubing after cutting. Burrs will slow the flow of water or waste, may eventually cause clogging. Tubing cutters often have fold-in or retractable reamers attached.

Pipe reamers for use in a bit brace, for pipe to 1¼ inches, can be bought for about $2.50. These have spiral flutes and a tapered square shank. For pipe to 2 inches, prices begin at about $4.50. Plumbers use reamers with a ratchet handle. They are very convenient, but cost from $15 up.

If you don't have a reamer, you can use a file instead.

Wrenches. It is important to use the right wrench for the job at hand. Otherwise you can damage the pipe or fitting, the tool itself, or bruise your knuckles.

Stillson, pipe, chain, or strap wrenches are used for turning pipe or other round

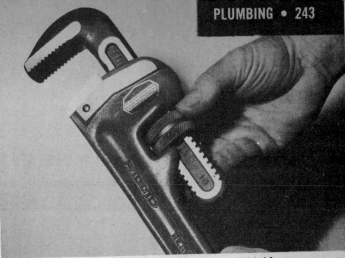

Ridgid

Heavy-duty pipe wrench is most important item in a plumbing kit. Two are needed: one to hold the pipe while other turns on fitting. The 18-inch model shown will handle pipes up to 2 inches.

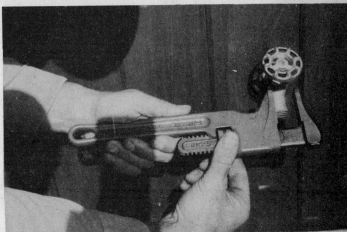

Ridgid

Spud wrench is handy utility monkey wrench, useful in gripping square or hexagon nuts and other flat-sided plumbing parts. Always adjust the wrench so its jaws fit snugly and fully on work.

Chain wrench is ideal for hard to get at spots. Needs less than ⅝-inch clearance to get at the work. Where handle swing is limited, the ratchet action allows new bite without removing the tool.

End pattern pipe wrench makes work easier when pipe is close to wall, or quarters are cramped. The offset is its only difference. Its operation is the same as any straight pipe wrench.

Ridgid

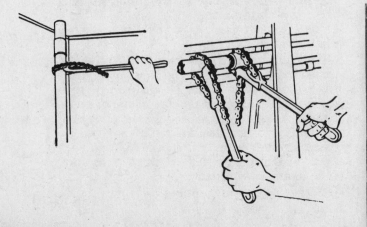

SQUEEZE
TO LOCK ONTO WORK

PRESS HERE
TO RELEASE!

Vise-Grip wrench can be used as an adjustable end wrench, pipe wrench, locking wrench, pliers, clamp, or portable vise. A squeeze wrench locks jaws on work, frees both hands to do many other things.

Self-gripping pliers have many plumbing uses. A toothed-jaw model serves as combination plier and wrench for places you can't reach with a pipe wrench. Smooth-jaw pliers are for plated fittings.

Channellock

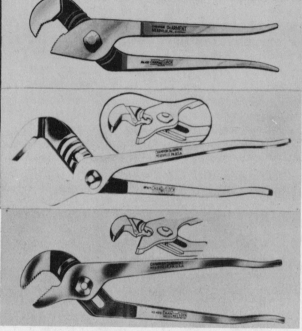

stock. They should not be used on nuts or other flat-sided parts, for they will chew off the corners and will make it so the part can no longer be turned easily. A large pipe wrench, however, can safely be used on nuts that are an inch or more across without danger of damaging them.

Stillson-pattern wrenches are normally considered as "normal duty" pipe wrenches as compared with heavy-duty pipe wrenches. Two pipe wrenches are usually required. One holds the pipe while the other turns on the fitting. A 10- and an 18-inch wrench are usually best for average jobs, but some prefer 10- and 14-inch sizes. Actually, 10-inch wrench is designed for pipe to 1-inch, and 18-inch for pipe to 2 inches. The 14-incher handles 1½-inch pipe nicely.

The size of a pipe wrench is figured by the total length of the tool, plus a nominal extension of the jaws. A 14-inch wrench is thus the tool with its jaws open 1½ inches, an 18-inch, with the jaws open 2 inches.

Always turn a pipe wrench handle in the direction of its open jaws. That makes the jaws tighter. Don't abuse a wrench by twisting it sideways. It may get the jaws out of alignment.

Don't use a pipe or other toothed wrench on chrome pipe, or pipe you don't want marred, without taping the pipe so the teeth can't bite through. The preferred tool to use in such cases is a strap wrench or girth wrench.

To avoid bruised knuckles, pull a wrench instead of pushing it. If you must push, use the palm of your hand. It will protect the knuckles. A length of pipe over the wrench handle will give you extra leverage, but the wrench was not designed for that much extra stress, and may not take it. Also remember that the wrench gets tighter as you turn it, and may crush a pipe.

A good tool to use instead of a pipe

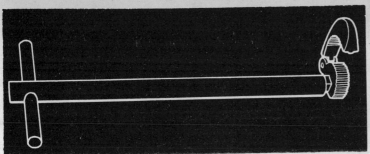

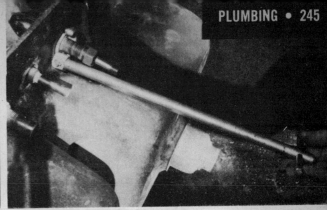

Basin wrench is designed for getting at nuts in close quarters and hard to reach spots, such as basin nuts, traps, flush valves, and ball cocks. Jaw is reversible, so that it can tighten or loosen.

Adjustable wrenches are versatile tools, but are only for light duty work. Always turn the wrench handle in the direction of its open jaws, never turn it the other way. Also don't twist sideways.

Sears, Roebuck

TURN WITH THE WRENCH

wrench on smaller sizes is a pair of locking pliers such as Vise-Grip. You can get a Vise-Grip into a corner where it is impossible to use a pipe wrench. For doing a job, like connecting a gas stove, a man with a Vise-Grip can beat one with a pipe wrench every time. You can buy a 10-inch Vise-Grip at your hardware store for under $3.

On faucets, valves, and other equipment, with flat-sided parts, use a spud (monkey) wrench, open end or adjustable wrench, or a pair of smooth-jawed Channel-lock pliers. For added protection of plated fittings and surfaces, tape them or use a strip of cardboard. On adjustable wrenches, put pressure on the stationary jaw only. Turn it only in the direction the wrench was designed to turn. The lower, adjustable jaw should always point in the direction of wrench movement, should never be pulling away from it. An adjustable wrench is not made for heavy use, and you are likely to break it if you exert heavy pressure, especially if its jaws are wide.

Open end or adjustable wrenches should fit snugly on the work. If they don't, they'll slip and round off the corners of the nut or fitting you're turning. Working in close corners, where you can't turn a nut or fitting far enough so that your open end wrench will fit on the next pair of flat sides, turn the wrench over and you'll find you can get a fit.

A ratcheting chain wrench is for use where a pipe wrench can't get. The chain needs only ½-inch clearance, and when you have parallel pipe lines which are very close together, or when a pipe is against a wall or in some other hard-to-get-at spot, it provides the answer. The ratcheting ac-

tion gives a new bite quickly, and without removing the wrench from the work. It is a time and effort saver where hand-swing is limited. The chain wrench will fit any shape bar, as well as to pipe and conduit.

A plier wrench, such as the Channel lock, gives strong gripping power in tight places that can't be reached by a pipe wrench. An interlocking principle prevents slipping under any load, since the heavier the job, the greater the interlocking action. Smooth-jawed Channel-lock pliers open to two inches for gripping sink trap nuts. The smooth jaws don't harm plated fittings.

A basin wrench is for tightening nuts in close and hard-to-reach places. These include basin nuts, traps, flush valves, etc.

End pipe wrenches are designed for use when pipe is close to a wall, or quarters are otherwise close. Aside from having the end pattern, it is like standard pipe wrenches.

You can usually get replacement parts for any pipe wrench made by a reputable manufacturer. Parts include handle, hook jaw, heel jaw, springs, nut and pin.

Threading Tools. A tool for threading pipe consists of a stock, which may be one- or two-handled, and a die and guide bushing or ring for each size pipe to be threaded. The die fits in the head of the stock along with a guide bushing. In some cases, the stock itself may be a guide for one pipe size. Some stocks have three die holders. These three-way threaders can thus thread three common sizes of pipe with no change-over required.

In setting up a threader, the guide bushing goes on the pipe first, serves to align the pipe and the die. The die fits in a receptacle on the other side of the stock. Each

3-WAY PIPE THREADER

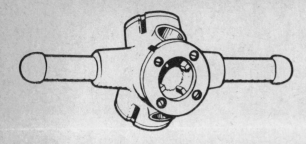

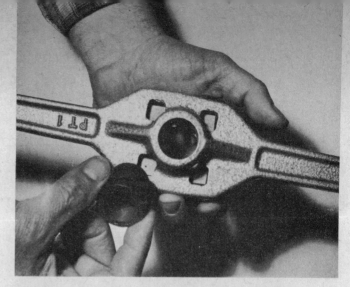

A three-way pipe threader has a stock accommodating three die-holders, and can thread three common sizes of pipe with no time or effort lost in making a changeover. It is a professional tool.

Threading tool has a guide bushing for each size of pipe to be threaded. The bushing fits into the stock. In the popular Milwaukee threader, the stock itself is a guide for one pipe size.

All threading photos courtesy of Milwaukee Tool & Equipment Co.

Die fits into receptacle on other side of stock from bushing. Face of the die is marked for the size of pipe for which it is to be used. Cover fits over die, is tightened by thumb screws.

In starting thread, stock is turned clockwise on pipe end until the die takes hold. The stock is then turned half a turn forward, back a quarter turn, until the cutting of thread is completed.

Before and during cutting of thread, cutting oil must be liberally applied to the die and the threads. The oil lubricates and cools the die, prolongs its life by preventing loss of temper.

Thread is cut until pipe's end projects half a turn beyond the end of the die. Threader is then removed by turning it counterclockwise. Wipe away surplus oil, chips, and job is done.

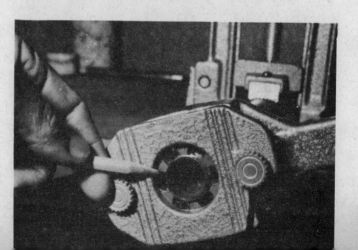

Round, file-type Surform is a handy tool for smoothing and enlarging pipe holes through floors, walls, and ceilings. It can cut through plaster, wood and masonry with almost the same easy facility.

Stanley Electric Tools

When roughing in pipes, saber saw is just the thing for cutting open floors and walls, notching studs and joists. Here saber saw is starting cut-out for countertop installation of the sink.

Plumb and slope of pipes are frequently important. Also a good, accurate level is an essential tool. A Magnetic torpedo level will cling tightly to ferrous pipe, leaving hands free for other tasks.

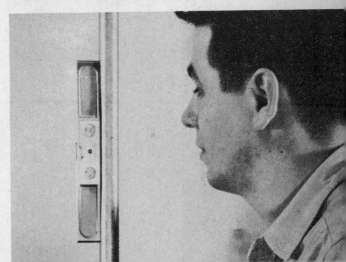

die is marked with the size of pipe for which it is used. Typically, the die is placed so that the lettering on it faces up toward the cover plate on the stock. The larger diameter of die threads are faced toward the guide bushing. The die cuts a tapered thread.

The threader should be oiled with cutting oil before starting the thread, and oiled liberally all during the threading process, usually every two or three turns. The oil lubricates and cools the die and prolongs its life by preventing loss of its temper. In starting the thread, turn the stock clockwise until the die takes hold. Turn the stock forward half a turn, then back a

quarter turn to break the chips. Continue until the pipe's end projects half a turn beyond the small end of the die. Remove the threader by turning it counterclockwise. Wipe away all surplus oil and chips, and the pipe is ready to use.

You can't cut good threads with a die that is worn, damaged, or clogged with chips, or if you skimp on oil while threading.

A threader with ratcheting action is especially helpful when working on pipe in close quarters.

Pipe taps are used for cutting internal threads. Some taps are offered in combination with drills which cut holes of exactly

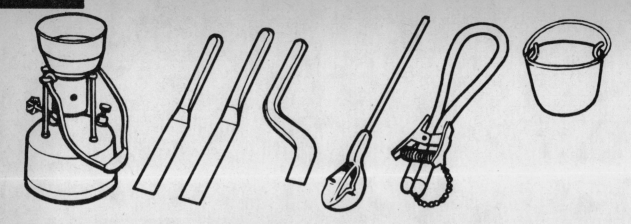

Tools used in working with cast-iron pipe include a gasoline furnace, offset yarning iron, caulking irons, cast-iron lead-melting pot with a pouring ladle, and an asbestos joint runner for protection.

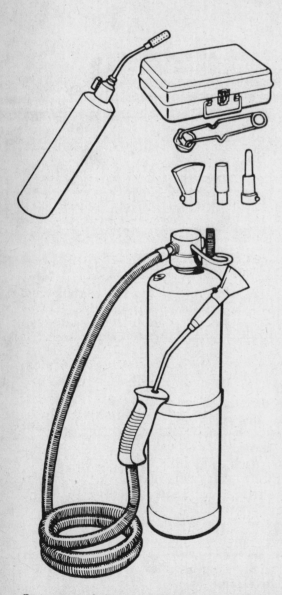

the right size for threading by the tap. Taps are marked with nominal pipe size and the number of threads per inch. The following table shows the drill size required for each size tap.

Tap	Drill	Threads per inch
1/8	21/64	27
1/4	29/64	18
3/8	19/32	18
1/2	21/32	14
3/4	15/16	14
1	1-3/16	11-1/2

Torches and Furnaces. A propane torch is far easier to use and much more convenient than a gasoline blow torch. The

Sears, Roebuck

Propane torches are available in inexpensive kits that come complete. New, handy type for plumbing has tank which clips on belt, and an extension hose. It is far less tiring and easier to handle.

Gasoline blow torches are more complicated to operate than propane ones. The better gasoline torches feature seamless, solid brass tanks, 2200° flame. Lower-priced models are of steel.

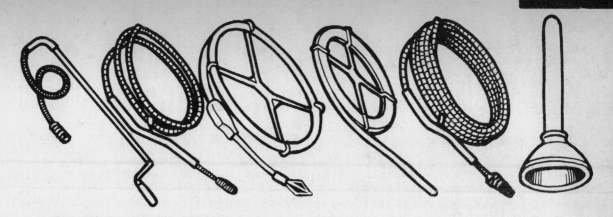

Tools for cleaning out clogged drain lines include closet auger, hood-end cleanout auger, flat sewer rod, flat, spring-steel auger, drain and trap auger, and a rubber force cup, sketched above.

handy disposable cylinders which contain its fuel are available everywhere, cost under $1.50. A torch is needed for making solder joints on copper tubing, for loosening frozen plugs, thawing pipes. It can also be used, if necessary, instead of a furnace for melting lead. Propane burns at 2300 degrees.

Torches are dangerous, especially when working in close quarters. Plumbers keep a water hose handy, just in case they start a fire. Use a piece of asbestos board or a doubled sheet of asbestos as a guard. Some wall insulation is inflammable, and if a wall has no fire-stop, a draft inside the wall may carry sparks upward and start a fire where you can't reach it unless you tear the wall open.

For a gasoline blowtorch, use only white unleaded gas. Fill the tank half-full, screw its plug tight. Pump the torch to build up air pressure. Then, holding one hand over the torch nozzle, open the needle valve, and let gas drip in the priming cup. When the cup is half full, turn off the valve, mop any spilled gas, and light the cup.

The flame serves to heat the vaporizing chamber. Just before the flame goes out, open the needle valve slowly to ignite the torch. If fire streams out, the vaporizing chamber isn't hot enough, and you'll have to start over.

When the torch is burning properly, pump occasionally to keep up air pressure. When shutting the torch off, avoid closing the valve too tightly. It will contract as it cools, and may freeze the needle in its seat.

A plumber's gasoline furnace is used for melting lead. Essentially, it works like a blowtorch. If the quantity of lead to be melted isn't large, you can apply a propane torch flame to a ladle to do the job. Further

details on melting lead, for caulking joints in cast-iron pipe, are given in another chapter.

Other tools used in caulking joints are a yarning iron for packing oakum in the joint, caulking irons for packing in lead, and an asbestos joint runner with spring clamp for pouring joints in horizontal pipe. Another type of joint runner employs rubber instead of asbestos.

Test Plugs. These are used to seal toilets and the open end of soil pipes when the stack and drainage system is being tested for leaks. In the test, the stack is filled from the roof with water. The plug itself may have a filler pipe or a cock. Turning a large wing nut expands the rubber plug, sealing the pipe or toilet opening.

Clogged-Drain Tools. A rubber force cup at the end of a stick, known popularly as "plumber's friend," dislodges obstructions in drains by means of air pressure. A force pump does a similar job, but develops more pressure. It has a plunger which is worked up and down.

A special auger, consisting of a flexible coil of spring steel with a crank at one end for rotating it, is used for cleaning toilets. Large augers or snakes, either worked by hand or power operated, may have special points, root cutter devices, or brushes to clean sewer and soil pipes. Sewer rods, with revolving spear points, come in lengths to 100 feet. When you call on professional help to do a job, this is the type of equipment they may have. One type may be powered by either a ¼-inch or a ½-inch electric drill.

Valve Seat Dresser. If replacement of a washer doesn't stop the drip, the seat is likely to be rough and require refinishing. The simple tool used costs under $1. •

copper tubing
... AND HOW TO WORK WITH IT

COPPER TUBING is the easiest kind of piping to install. You can use it for drains, vents, and water supply lines when adding an extra bath or powder room, for a new sink in the playroom or darkroom, or for adding sill cocks at convenient spots outdoors.

You can use it to replace rusted out or choked-up sections of galvanized piping. Special adapters make the connection from one kind of pipe to the other. You can use copper for extending heating lines, or replacing old-style standup radiators with space-saving, inconspicuous and more efficient baseboard units. It's just the thing for hooking up a new water heater or water softener. Almost no special tools are required in working with copper—no heavy wrenches or vises, no threading equipment.

In figuring the length of tubing needed for a connection, measure from the end of one fitting to the start of the next one; then add on the depth of the tubing which goes into each fitting.

Copper is quickly and easily assembled by "sweating" joints. The tubing in its fitting is heated until the solder touched to tubing melts. When the solder fills the joint, the job's done.

Chase Brass & Copper Co.

Types and Sizes. Copper tubing is available in heavy-duty type K and lighter type L. The latter is satisfactory for almost any above-ground home water line use, code permitting. Use type K underground. Either type can be had in flexible or rigid temper.

Use the flexible for vertical lines or for snaking through existing structures or close quarters. Use it underground. It will withstand some freezing, can be routed around obstructions, isn't bothered by minor earth movements. Flexible tubing is easily bent, making measurements for length less critical, and the necessity for joints fewer. It also comes in longer lengths. Rigid tubing comes in 20 footers,

maximum. Of course, in a single installation you may have to use both rigid and flexible types, employing each where it suits to best advantage.

You can use one size smaller copper tubing than galvanized pipe and get an equivalent water flow. Since a typical iron water pipe is ¾ inch, the typical copper one is ½. Fixture supply lines to toilet and lavatory may be only ⅜ inch. Sizes are ID (inside diameters). Small copper tubing, such as is used for oil lines, is usually sized OD (outside diameter). Main supply lines for the entire house are usually no more than ¾ inch. In sizing hot water lines, be especially careful not to oversize them. The smaller pipes have less heat loss, and

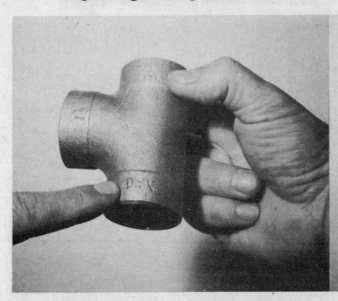

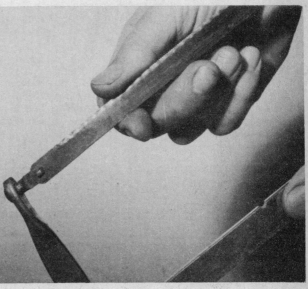

Special fittings are used for copper drainage lines. The lightest weight, lowest-cost fittings are Type DWV. Examine the fitting closely and you will be able to find identifying marking on it.

Tubing may be cut with a hack saw. Use a blade with 24 to 32 teeth per inch. Use the former for heavy and the latter for thinner tubing. Then set the blade so that the teeth point forward.

To assure square-cut ends, make simple wood fixture to hold the tubing along with a slot to guide the saw blade. The cutting is done on the forward stroke only. Use light, easy strokes.

Sears, Roebuck

You can buy a tubing cutter that will handle up to 1½-inch stock for a little more than $3. Cutting blade is advanced by simply turning screw, as the tool is revolved around the tubing.

Chase Brass & Copper Co.

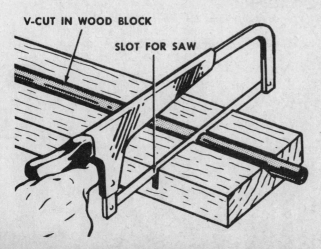

V-CUT IN WOOD BLOCK

SLOT FOR SAW

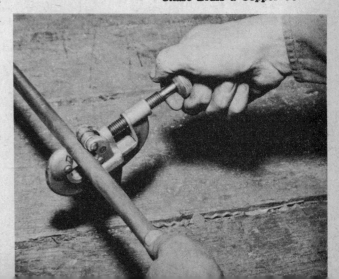

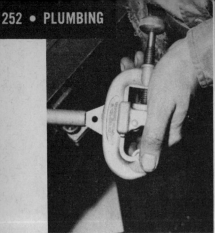

Cutting tube creates burr which must be removed, or the flow through pipe will be slowed and clogging will be encouraged. Almost all tubing cutters have built-in reamer for this purpose.

Chase Brass & Copper Co.

Tubing and fitting sockets must be cleaned before soldering. Clean them even if they appear to be bright and shiny. Use steel wool, fine emery or sand cloth, or special wire brush.

Some types of soldering flux must be stirred before using. Some contain a cleaner so that burnishing copper before soldering is unnecessary. Shown is a very popular soldering paste.

Apply the soldering flux to the cleaned tubing ends and then to the fittings. Put each piece of tubing into its fitting; then revolve the tubing so that flux is distributed evenly all over.

For average home plumbing use, solid wire 50/50 solder is the best. It is half tin, half lead. Approximate amount of solder needed for a joint is equal to the diameter of the tubing.

Apply heat to joint until the solder melts freely when touched to the metal. The solder will be drawn into the joint regardless of whether it is being fed down, up, or to the side.

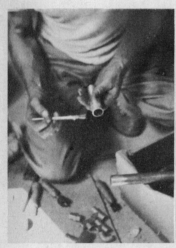
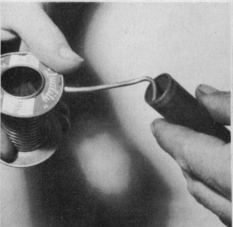
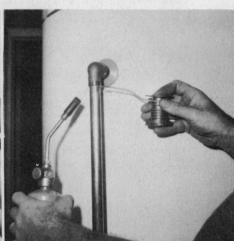

Once you have the knack of working with copper, you can use your skill for such things as extending your heating system. The radiant baseboard heater is merely finned copper tubing.

Here finned copper tube used in baseboard heating is soldered to return line to boiler. Low-cost Type M copper tubing is especially designed for use in home radiant heating systems.

Flexible copper tubing has a special advantage in remodeling home plumbing because it can be snaked through walls. By use of bending spring, it's readily bent, eliminates fittings.

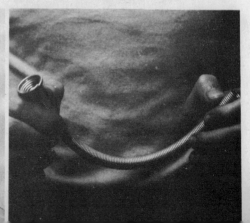

so you save on the cost of heating water

For drainage lines, type L, or lighter weight DWV tubing is used. The initials DWV stand for drainage, wastes, vents. Special drainage fittings are used for drainage and waste sections, but regular fittings may be used for the vent sections, which carry gases only. With the exception of shower and floor drains, which are usually 2 inches, and toilet drains which must be 3 to 4 inches, other drain and vent lines are usually 1½ inches. Main stacks are of 3-inch tubing, sometimes 4.

Measuring, Cutting, Bending. In measuring the length of pipe required in order to make a connection, measure the distance from the face of one fitting to the face of the other fitting. Then, add on the depth of the hub in each fitting.

Remember that if a piece of tubing is cut too long, you can always make another cut and shorten it to just the right length. If a piece is cut too short, however, and doesn't go all the way into the socket of the fitting, a perfect solder joint isn't possible. The moral: When in doubt, cut the tubing a little long, then refine your measure, perhaps by an actual test fitting.

Copper tubing may be cut either with a hack saw or with a tubing cutter. Since a cutter which will handle up to 1-inch tubing costs under $2, and one for up to 1½ inch costs only a little more than $3, it's a worthwhile tool to acquire if you have any considerable amount of plumbing to do. However, you can make good square cuts with a hack saw and a simple wood jig which you can knock together in just a few minutes. The slot in the jig will guide your saw blade, and the V-cut will steady the tubing. Some vises are equipped with guides for hack-saw blades and can be used for cutting tubing square.

Use a fine-toothed blade in the hack saw, one with 24 to 32 teeth per inch, the former for heavier tubing, the latter for thinner stuff. Set the blade so the teeth point forward. Cutting is done only on the forward stroke. Use light, easy strokes. After cutting tubing, remove burrs inside it with a file or with a reamer.

Rigid copper can be bent with a special tool. The tool is too expensive for the non-pro to buy, but you may find it useful if you can borrow one. Flexible tubing is easily bent by hand. Bend it slowly and in a wide radius to prevent kinking. To prevent kinking on sharp bends near the end of a section of tubing, you can insert a special spring steel bending tube to prevent wall collapse. A set of six bending tubes for bending tubing from ¼ to ⅝ inch diameter costs under $1.50 at Sears.

TYPICAL SOLDER-TYPE FITTINGS

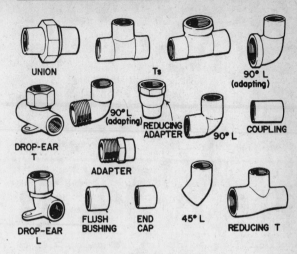

TYPICAL RIGID-COPPER-PIPE FITTINGS

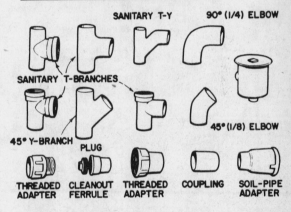

TYPICAL FLARE-TYPE FITTINGS

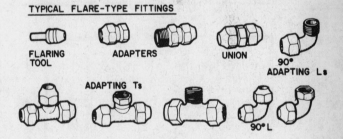

Soldering Joints. There are six simple steps in making a good solder joint.

1. Thoroughly clean and brighten the end of the tube and the socket of the fitting. Clean them even if they look clean and shiny. Use steel or fine emery or sand cloth or a special wire brush made for the purpose. Don't use a file. It's too coarse. The tube end must be round, in no way flattened or dented.

2. Apply a thin coat of flux or soldering paste to the cleaned end of the tube and to the fitting. Some flux must be stirred thoroughly before use. You can also get a preparation that combines flux and cleaner so that removal of oxidation from pipe and

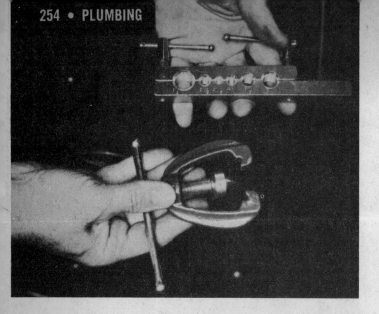

Flaring tool with screw yoke makes it possible to have perfect flared joints every time. The model shown here will handle six sizes of tubing, ranging from 3/16 to ⅝ inch, outside diameter.

General Hardware Mfg. Co.

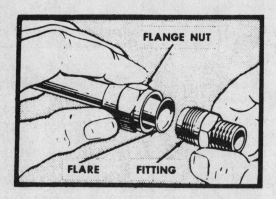

FLANGE NUT

FLARE   FITTING

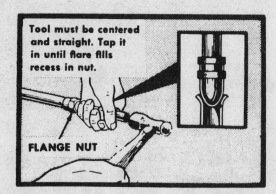

Tool must be centered and straight. Tap it in until flare fills recess in nut.

FLANGE NUT

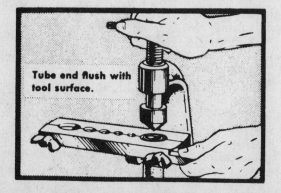

Tube end flush with tool surface.

fittings is unnecessary. Be sure the tubing fits all the way up against the stop in the socket.

3. Place the tube in the fitting. Revolve it once or twice to spread the flux. Several joints and fittings which all go together in one assembly can be prepared, then soldered in one operation. But never let fluxed joints stand more than 2 or 3 hours before soldering.

4. Apply heat to the fitting with torch, moving the flame so as to distribute the heat uniformly. On large fittings, such as on a soil stack, it is a good idea to apply two flames, one on each side to get uniform heating. Avoid overheating. It may burn the flux and destroy its effectiveness, making it necessary to reclean and reflux. Overheating cast fittings may cause them to crack.

5. When end of wire solder is touched to the joint, it should melt on contact, flow in and fill the fitting immediately, even if the solder has to travel sideways or straight up. Apply solder at one or two points only. Do not feed it around the full circumference of the tube.

When a line of solder shows completely around the joint, it's full up. Some plumbers like to add a fillet around the joint. Don't apply flame to the solder, and don't continue to heat the joint once you're applying solder. If you do, liquid solder is likely to keep running through the joint. With tubing longer than 1¼ inch, to assure equal distribution of solder, it is recommended that the fitting be moved, or the tube be tapped, while the solder is fed. While the joint is still hot, wipe away surplus solder with a rag or brush.

6. Allow joint to cool without disturbing it. Don't run water through the tubing until it has cooled. Cold water on a hot cast fitting may crack it. If, on testing, the joint leaks, the tube has to be completely drained before you can reheat the joint to solder-melting temperature. Any residual water will prevent it. When doing a solder joint near an already completed joint, it may be necessary to wrap the already finished joints with rags to keep their solder from melting.

Flare-Type Fittings. These are made with soft-temper tubing and are used where joints may occasionally have to be disconnected and remade, or where fire hazard makes soldering a joint impractical. Flare type fittings have threaded flange nuts which hold the fitting and pipe together.

Flaring can be done with either a flaring tool or a flanging tool. Before flaring the tubing remove the coupling nut from the

 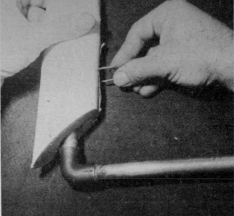 

Insulation of hot water lines will reduce your fuel bills. Used on the cold water lines, insulation will prevent any sweating. Fiberglas type shown costs about 75c for 3 ft.

Insulation can help prevent frozen pipes. Popular felt type of insulation is attached with clips, can be mitered, as shown, for trim fit at elbows. Other joints are neatly wrapped.

"No Drip" insulation is brushed on cold water lines to prevent sweating. It can be especially useful on pipes which are concealed in walls. Is also available in tape form.

J. W. Mortell Co.

Variety of hangers are available for use with copper tubes. Hangers should be placed no more than 6 feet apart for rigid ½-inch tubing. Soft tubing requires closer support.

Pipe strap can be bought in rolls 10-feet long for about 50 cents. It can be used to secure any size tubing. It is readily bendable, and closely spaced holes make attaching easy.

Water supply lines must be securely supported, but not so tightly as to prevent expansion and contraction. Wire hangers are especially good in meeting these requirements.

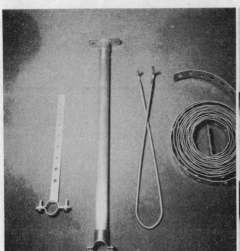  

fitting and slide the nut onto the tubing. Drop some oil on the tube end, insert the flaring tool straight and centered, and tap tool with a hammer until the flare fills the recess in the nut. The nut can now be screwed onto the fitting threads.

Use a pair of adjustable or open-end wrenches to do the tightening, placing one on the body of the fitting to hold it, while the other tightens the nut. Tightening the nut forces the flared end of the tubing up against the rounded end of the fitting, making a tight seal.

In using a flanging tool, the tube should be inserted so its end is flush with the tool.

Hangers. On rigid copper tubing, hangers should be placed no more than six feet apart for ½ inch, eight for ¾ and 1 inch, and ten feet for 2 inch. Soft copper tubing requires somewhat closer spacing to prevent sagging.

Supply lines must be securely supported or they may vibrate and create noise, but hangers or clamps should not fit so tightly that they prevent expansion and contraction. Install water lines with a slight pitch, when necessary, to allow complete draining.

WHAT YOU SHOULD KNOW ABOUT . . .

galvanized steel and cast iron pipe

Oakum, hemp treated with pitch to make it moisture-proof, is yarned into cast-iron joints to within about 1 inch from the top. Joints are then filled with molten lead brim to the top.

YOU CAN USE threaded galvanized steel pipe for both water supply and drainage lines. Though the labor involved in installing it is more than required for copper, the initial cost of steel for water-line piping is lower than any other. For drainage, only service-weight cast iron costs less than steel. A package steel drainage system for a one-story house with a basement costs around $60. A copper system costs $80. A cast-iron system with service-weight pipe costs approximately $50.

Steel is somewhat lighter than cast iron, and is usually easier to install in remodeling jobs. Sold by mail order houses, pipes in packaged systems are cut and threaded to your exact specifications, so all you have to do is to assemble. Steel water pipe is usually no different from drainage pipes, but fittings are of special design.

Measuring and Cutting Steel Pipe. In measuring the length of pipe required for a connection, allowance must be made for the distance its threads go into fittings. To get the correct length, measure from the face of one fitting to the face of the next, then add the amount of thread length needed as indicated by the accompanying table. In working with ¾-inch pipe, for example, an extra half inch is needed for screwing into a fitting. This amounts to a full extra inch of length, above the face-to-face measure, when the pipe is screwed into a fitting at each end.

In screwing a pipe into a fitting, not all the threads are used. To try to use them all may result in splitting the fitting.

All threaded-pipe connections are made up quite tight. Large wrenches make the job easier. Note here how the pipe itself is used as a brace to steady connection while fitting is turned on.

Pipe vise is best tool for holding pipe while turning on a fitting. It is important to screw the fitting on as far and as tightly as possible, but not so tight as to (very possible!) split the fitting.

TYPICAL CAST-IRON-PIPE FITTINGS

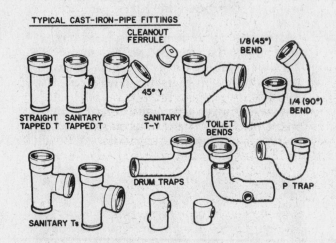

For tightening most pipe and fittings, two pipe wrenches are needed. One holds the pipe in a fixed position while the other wrench turns the fitting on. Foot can be used to pin one wrench.

TYPICAL GALVANIZED MALLEABLE FITTINGS

Pipe Size (inches)	Amount pipe is screwed into fitting (inches)	
	Standard fitting	Drainage fitting
½	½	—
¾	½	—
1	⅝	—
1¼	⅝	⅝
1½	⅝	⅝
2	¾	⅝
3	—	⅞
4	—	1

By careful planning, and making the most direct connections, you can reduce the number of fittings and the amount of pipe cutting and threading necessary. By use of nipples, short pieces of pipe already threaded and usually ranging in length from 1⅛ to 12 inches, you can further reduce the amount of cutting and threading.

If you are doubtful about pipe size, measure its circumference. If you don't have a tape measure, use a piece of string, then measure the string length with a ruler. The accompanying table gives pipe

Lighter than cast iron, steel is easier to use in remodeling jobs. If ordered from mail-order house, pipes can be cut and threaded to exact specifications. Note the variety of fittings shown above.

TYPICAL STEEL-PIPE FITTINGS

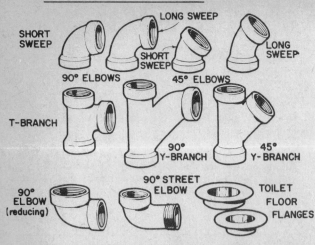

Steel water pipe is usually no different from drainage pipes, but the fittings are of a special design. Note better contours, smoother finish.

In calculating pipe length needed to complete a run, measure from the face of one fitting to the face of the next, then add or subtract thread needed for particular fitting.

Face-To-Face

Face-To-Face

Sears, Roebuck

Steel pipe can also be cut with a hack saw, but a portable saber saw with a metal-cutting blade is a great time-and-muscle saver. Ordinary vise and one hand are used to keep the pipe steady.

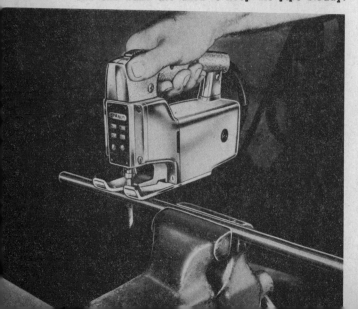

sizes based on string length. Use fittings the same size as the pipe.

String length (inches)	2⅛	2⅝	3¼	4½	5¼	6
Pipe size (inches)	⅜	½	¾	1	1¼	1½

Steel pipe must be held rigidly for cutting and threading operations. A pipe vise is best for this purpose. Use a 24-teeth-to-the-inch blade in your hack saw for cutting, with its teeth directed foreward. Cut on the forward stroke only, and at a rate of about one stroke per second. Faster cutting may overheat the blade and it will break.

After cutting, remove burrs from the inside edge of the pipe end with a round file or a pipe reamer. Unreamed pipe ends increase resistance to water flow from 6 to 10 times.

In cutting with a pipe cutter, cut is made by gradually tightening up on the cutting wheel, by screwing in the handle, with each

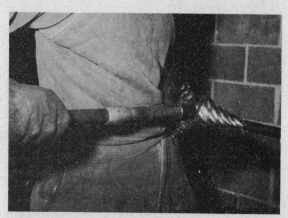

After cutting pipe, you'll find burrs along its inside edge. Get rid of them with a reamer. Burrs like these reduce the rate of flow through a pipe and make it very easy for clog-ups to develop.

Pipe vise on stand is convenient for working outdoors where length of piping poses no problems. The best way to cut steel pipe is with a wheeled cutter. The ends are then always exactly square.

revolution around the pipe. Apply cutting oil to the wheel as you work!

Threading and Joining. Full details on how to thread pipe are given in the chapter on "Plumbing Tools."

Never hold a threaded part with a wrench. It will damage the threads, and the resulting connection is likely to leak. If you must hold where the threads are, protect them by first putting two nuts on them, locked tight.

Always use pipe compound on threads in making connections. It helps insure against leak and will make the connection easier "to break" in the future if you want to take it apart. Cotton string is not usually used on threads, but if threads are imperfect, string may help make a tight connection. Put compound on male (external) threads only. If compound is put on the female (internal) threads, it is likely to get inside the pipe and start clogging. It may also work its way into valves and cause trouble.

Threads are tapered, so turning gets harder the farther you screw them in.

Larger wrenches make work easier. Note what large wrenches plumbers use.

A pipe vise can serve in place of a wrench for holding pipe firmly while a fitting is being turned on it. However, before making any assembly permanent, check to make sure you'll have necessary clearance for turning on other nearby fittings. You may have to revise the order in which you make connections.

Ordering Fittings. In asking for a fitting, always give the size first, then the name of the fitting. The size of a fitting and the size of the pipe used are always the same. Thus, a ¾-inch elbow is for ¾-inch pipe.

It is necessary to give the size of only one outlet on the fitting unless the outlets are of different sizes. In that case, give the larger first, the smaller second, and if there is an inlet or branch, name it third. If there are two branches, as in a cross fitting, the smaller of the two branches is named last.

Bushings are hexagonal fittings with both external and internal threads, and are used to connect a pipe or fitting of one size to a pipe or fitting of different size. In

You can have pipe threaded at a plumbing shop, but it's far more convenient to thread your own. You can do it with a tool borrowed from a mailorder house or rented from tool-rental agency.

Apply pipe joint compound to male (external) threads on pipe end, never to female (internal) threads. Compound helps make the joints tight against the leakage of either liquids or gases.

In ordering fittings, specify the same size as the pipe they are to fit. For reducing fittings, give larger or main outlet sizes first, then branch or smaller outlets—see sketch.

If pipe end isn't squarely cut, or if dies are worn or damaged, it may be difficult to cut good threads. Imperfect or damaged threads can often be salvaged with a little careful file work.

To assemble steel pipe over 2 inches in diameter use a chain wrench. Screw pipe as tightly as possible by hand. Place chain around pipe. Insert chain ends between tool prongs.

Sears, Roebuck

Nicholson Files

Sears, Roebuck

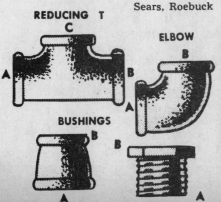

REDUCING T

ELBOW

BUSHINGS

Pipe for holding

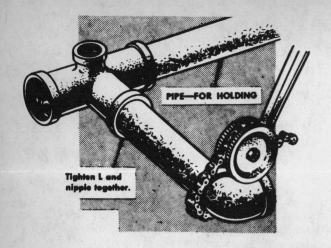

PIPE—FOR HOLDING

Tighten L and nipple together.

In making steel pipe assembly with chain wrench, make use of a pipe to hold your work against the thrust of the wrench. Here a toilet branch drain is being connected to a tee fitting in this fashion.

Sears, Roebuck

Even if you do use copper or steel pipe for your plumbing, you're almost certain to have to switch to cast iron where it goes underground. Look for C-I mark to be sure of industry's standard quality.

To cut service-weight cast-iron pipe, first mark line of cut all the way around pipe, using chalk or scratching pipe with a nail. With a hack saw, you can accurately score this line 1/16 inch deep.

To cut extra-heavy pipe, mark the line of cut by grooving with a triangular file. With pipe across a 2x4, use a hammer and chisel and continue cutting all around the pipe until it breaks evenly.

specifying a bushing, give its external size first, then the internal size.

External threads, as indicated previously, are known as male threads, internal as female. A street elbow is an elbow with male threads at one end, female at the other.

Unions are fittings designed so that a line can easily be disconnected. They are used near appliances, water heaters, water meters, and other equipment that may on occasion have to be pulled out. There are union tees and union elbows. Use these combination fittings and you can often save using two separate fittings.

A cap is used to close the end of a pipe. Plugs are used to close one end of a fitting.

Fittings used for drainage are different from those used for water pipes. They have no internal ledge or shoulder, and they have a pitch, corresponding to the pitch of the drainage or vent pipes with which they are used.

The name of a fitting sometimes changes. Fittings used on water pipes to change the direction of flow are called elbows. On drainage pipes they're called bends. A ¼ bend is the equivalent of a 90-degree elbow, a ⅙ bend is a 60-degree turn, and a ⅛ bend is a 45-degree turn. You can get bends with either short or long sweeps. The long sweep is a more gradual turn and reduces flow friction and resistance.

Cutting Cast-iron Pipe. Standard length is 5 feet. Use a double hub pipe when

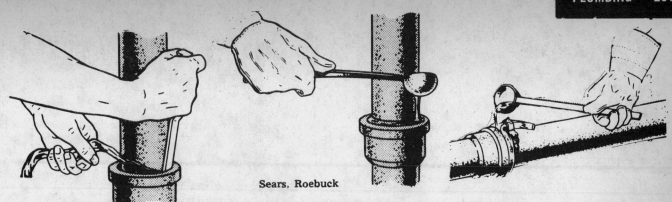

Sears, Roebuck

In joining cast iron, be sure both pipes are in perfect alignment and that joint is same size all around. With yarning tool, pack joint tightly with oakum to within 1 inch of the top. To avoid the danger of spattering lead, wear gloves, avert eyes and face, and extend ladle as far as possible from body. In one continuous pour, fill joint until the lead stands slightly above rim. See middle picture, above. Horizontal, even upside-down joints, can be poured by means of a joint runner (top right picture). Fit it tight against bell and, if necessary, use putty or clay around space to prevent leakage of lead from joint.

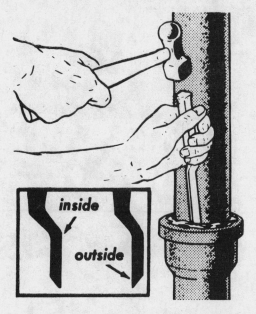

inside

outside

After the lead cools, inside and outside caulking irons pack it tightly back against the pipe and surrounding bell. Don't pound too hard or you may loosen the lead mass instead of tightening it.

pieces shorter than that are needed. When this pipe is cut, each piece will have a hub, and thus be usable. In measuring length of pipe needed, allow for pipe which goes into the hub of the pipe following it. This amounts to 2½ inches for 2-inch pipe, 2¾ inches for 3-inch pipe, 3 inches for 4-inch pipe.

To cut service-weight pipe, groove it $\frac{1}{16}$-inch deep with a hack saw, then tap with a heavy hammer on the part to be lopped off until the pipe breaks at the groove. The pipe should be supported on the side of the groove opposite to where you are doing the tapping. A 2x4, or a mound of dirt, does nicely. To cut extra-heavy pipe, keep tapping with hammer and chisel all around the pipe until it parts.

Caulking Joints. Cast iron is connected by caulking. Place the spigot end of one pipe into the bell end of the following pipe, using a level to be sure it is straight and true. Some codes require 1 inch of lead in a joint, others permit ¾ inch. For an inch of lead, use one pound of lead for each inch of pipe diameter, per joint. For ¾ inch of lead, allow 1½ pounds of lead for a 2-inch pipe, 2¼ pounds for a 3-inch pipe, and 3 pounds for a 4-incher.

The best way of melting lead is with a plumber's furnace. Put the lead in the pot, small end down. It melts quicker that way. Be sure all equipment is dry. Moisture causes lead to sputter and splash out. You can also melt lead by merely playing an ordinary propane torch on a lead pot, or even a properly supported ladle.

While lead is melting, use a yarning iron to pack the rope-like oakum into the bottom of the hub, exercising care to see that the joint space is equal all the way around. Oakum swells when wet, and helps make a tight seal. It also prevents lead from running into the pipe. You can get oakum in 27-inch lengths. One length is needed for 2-inch pipe, two lengths for 3-inch. After oakum is packed to within an inch (or ¾ inch) of the top, pour the lead on.

First heat the ladle by holding it alongside the melting pot for 5 or 10 seconds. Use of a cold or wet ladle can result in an explosion. So can pouring lead into a joint that is wet. When the ladle is warm, push the dross floating on top of the lead to one side, and dip the bright metal. Pour it, in a single, continuous operation, to the top of the hub, or better yet, so it stands slightly above the top rim.

For horizontal joints, use an asbestos or rubber joint-runner. This device keeps the lead from running out of the joint as it is poured.

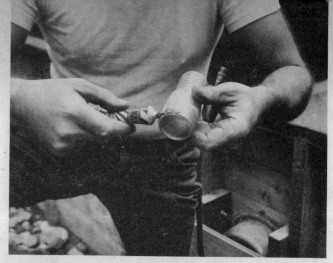

Before attaching pipe to a fitting, a stainless steel clamp is slipped over the pipe end. Clamp is tightened on the smooth shank of the fitting behind serrations. Large pipes take two clamps.

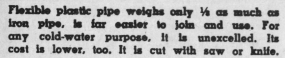

Flexible plastic pipe weighs only ⅛ as much as iron pipe, is far easier to join and use. For any cold-water purpose, it is unexcelled. Its cost is lower, too. It is cut with saw or knife.

Flexible plastic pipe is readily joined to any threaded fitting by means of an adapter. Joining compound is put on adapter threads and it is turned into fitting. Pipe then goes on adapter.

TIPS ON USING . . .

flexible plastic pipe

THE DAY when the entire house will have plastic plumbing is not far off. Plastic pipe has already proved itself superior in many ways for cold-water lines, and its use for drainage systems is at hand. Plastic pipe is gaining widespread use for sewer lines. What we shall probably see in the immediate future is use of plastic plumbing for everything except hot water lines.

Work is still being done on developing a plastic pipe which is suitable for hot water. The newest plastic being used for the purpose is polypropylene. It seems good, but whether it can withstand 180° temperatures and water pressure for years without breaking down is still to be proved.

But plastic has been perfected for many uses. Here's how you can use plastic, save work and money, and get better plumbing.

You can't beat plastic pipe for water service lines, swimming pool plumbing, lawn sprinkler systems, and jet well installations. Polyethylene plastic pipe weighs only ⅛ as much as steel pipe. One man can easily carry a 300-foot coil of the 1-inch size.

Plastic pipe requires fewer joints, is far easier to work. You don't need pipe cutters or threading tools. You can cut plastic with any saw, often with just a sharp knife. Flexible polyethylene plastic pipe, such as that made by Orangeburg and others, is one of the most popular varieties. It is assembled by means of hard plastic fittings, and you need only a screwdriver for the

Flexible polyethylene plastic pipe is ideally suited for swimming pool plumbing, jet well installations, and lawn sprinkler systems. Shown in photo is attachment to sprinkler head.

Plastic pipe will withstand severely corrosive soil chemicals, high pressure, and is resistant to freezing. When you use it for lawn sprinklers, you don't have to drain lines in winter.

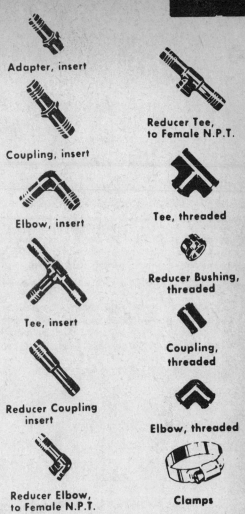

Adapter, insert

Coupling, insert

Elbow, insert

Tee, insert

Reducer Coupling insert

Reducer Elbow, to Female N.P.T.

Reducer Tee, to Female N.P.T.

Tee, threaded

Reducer Bushing, threaded

Coupling, threaded

Elbow, threaded

Clamps

A variety of valves and fittings are available for use with plastic pipe. Shown are fittings for polyethylene pipe. All fittings are made of polystyrene plastic. Clamps are stainless steel.

Orangeburg Mfg. Co.

job. The pipe is made of high molecular weight polyethylene, the fittings of molded polystyrene.

How to Use Flexible Plastic Pipe. When flexible plastic pipe is used in a well installation, because of its very light weight, no special rig is needed for lowering the pipe down the casing, or for pulling it up again should repairs be necessary. Well casings themselves are being made of hard plastic. Because of the flexibility of the polyethylene pipe, no clearance is needed above a well for pulling up pipes. This makes it possible to put the well directly under the house.

Plastic pipe is not subject to rust, scale, or corrosion. It never has any "pipe taste." Its smooth interior surface means no

turbulence and a minimum of resistance to water flow.

Polyethylene pipe is readily joined to threaded pipe or threaded fittings by means of adapters. When making a connection to a threaded fitting, the adapter is first screwed into the fitting. As a lubricant on the threaded end, Pipe-Tite Stik or Permatex No. 2 may be used. When the adapter has been turned in hand tight, it should be given one turn with an open-end wrench. Don't use a pipe wrench.

After putting a clamp loosely on the plastic pipe, push the fitting into the pipe up to its shoulder. Soaking the pipe-end in hot water for a minute will make it easier to insert the fitting. Screw the stainless steel clamp securely to the straight shank

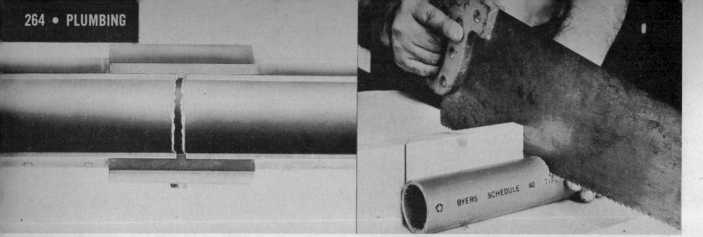

Cutaway view of a cemented joint on PVC pipe. Cemented joints are by far the speediest kind to make, and are the preferred type. Such joints are stronger than the pipe itself without joints.

To get a sound, leakproof joint, it is important to follow recommended procedures exactly. Use miter box to insure squarely-cut pipe ends. Ends must butt fully against fitting shoulder.

Sanding will eliminate burrs, assure tight fit. After sanding, clean pipe ends and fittings with rag dampened with a cleaner such as methyl ethyl ketone (MEK), acetone or similar ketone solvents.

With a clean brush, apply special PVC solvent cement liberally to fitting, including shoulder of fitting, and butt end of the pipe. Small can of cement is good for countless number of joints.

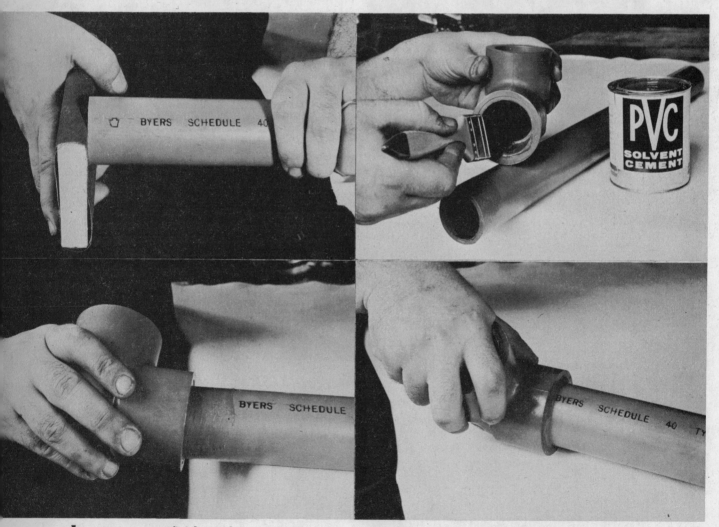

As soon as you finish applying cement, insert pipe into fitting and give it a ¼ (90°) turn. The time from start of cementing to completion of the ¼ turn must never exceed 1½ minutes.

Block the fitting tightly, or otherwise see that its position is held for several minutes, to insure a complete bond. Never disturb the bond by readjusting the pipe after the ¼ turn is made.

Though PVC pipe is rigid, it may readily be bent by application of heat. First pack the pipe with sand, or use a pipe-bending spring to support walls. Apply torch heat, but not right on pipe.

If pipe begins to scorch, you're holding it too close. Apply heat uniformly around pipe. When it begins to soften, bend it to desired angle, then hold it briefly while it cools and stiffens.

of the fitting *behind* the serrations. For pipe sizes over 1-inch, double clamping is recommended, with the second clamp placed *over* the serrations.

In placing flexible plastic pipe in a trench, be sure the trench bottom is free of sharp stones and other edged objects. Don't pull the pipe tight in the trench. Run it in a snake line, allowing at least one extra foot per 100 feet for thermal contraction. Don't make sharp bends with the pipe. If bends are necessary, use elbow fittings.

When the installation is complete, try it out under maximum pressure to see that all joints are secure and free of leaks, then backfill, using rock-free earth in the first six inches over the pipe. After that, backfilling can proceed as you please.

Installing PVC Pipe. For plumbing lines inside the house itself, one of the more popular varieties of plastic is PVC (polyvinyl chloride), such as that made by Byers, a company with a long-established reputation as a manufacturer of wrought-iron pipe. This rigid type of piping has been proven for cold-water systems, and is commercially available from coast to coast. PVC pipe was first developed in Germany in 1935, and has been widely used in Europe for more than twenty years.

PVC pipe can be joined by threading, or welding, but the simplest means of all is by cementing, sometimes called solvent welding. Solvent welding of PVC waste and vent lines takes only ¼ the time it takes to assemble bell-and-spigot pipe, and the pipe's weight is only ⅕ as much, making it far easier to handle and to support. Using this plastic pipe, a trained plumber can make every connection in a typical house in no more than ten minutes! Is it any wonder that the age of plastic plumbing is upon us?

In joining PVC pipe by cementing, be sure to cut pipe ends square, so they'll butt fully against the shoulder of the fitting. After cutting, sand the end of the pipe so it is smooth and will make full contact with the fitting shoulder.

Clean the pipe ends and fittings with a solvent, such as MEK (methyl ethyl ketone) or acetone. Using a clean brush, apply cement liberally to the fitting, its shoulder and to the butt end of the pipe. Insert the pipe into the fitting and give it a quarter turn. Important: No more than 1½ minutes must elapse from the time you start applying the cement until you complete the quarter turn. Don't disturb the pipe for several minutes after the quarter turn is made or you'll ruin the bond.

Drying of the cement is far enough advanced in from 16 to 24 hours to permit use of the line. The higher the air temperature, the quicker the drying time. Properly made, a cemented joint is stronger than the pipe itself.

PVC pipe may be readily bent. To do it, pack the pipe with sand, then heat it. You can use a torch for the purpose, but keep the pipe fairly far from the flame, so you don't overheat the material and scorch it. By exerting a little pressure, you can feel when the pipe has become soft enough for bending. Instead of sand, a metal spring, like that used in bending copper, may be used to support the pipe walls and prevent their flattening.

All plastic piping has a higher rate of thermal expansion than metal pipe, and the line must have enough freedom to move to accommodate changes in length. Expansion loops, or line offsets, can provide the necessary adaptability. Commercial expansion joints are also available for the purpose. •

HOW TO PUT IN ... drainage lines

Chase Brass & Copper Co.

The house drain is the large horizontal pipe that carries all plumbing wastes out beyond the house wall. Copper is the easiest kind of piping to use in making any good drainage connection.

IN NUMBER and size of pipes, the drainage system is by far the most important part of home plumbing, but the technique of installing, adding to, or remodeling it is not difficult.

In water pipes, the flow is under pressure. Drainage flows by gravity, and without pressure, so pipes must be large and have a steady downward slope toward point of disposal. Drainage lines must also be vented to the open air, for otherwise any movement of wastes through them would tend to create a vacuum which would slow down or stop the flow.

The large vertical drain lines which continue up through the roof as vents are called stacks, soil stacks if they receive any discharge from toilets, waste stacks if they do not. Similarly, horizontal drainage pipes are called soil lines or waste lines, depending on the source of the drainage they carry.

A Stack Is Needed. If you are adding a bathroom or a half bath, you will require a soil stack close at hand. In remodeling, it is to your advantage to connect up to an existing soil stack, if that is possible. If branch drain and vent lines are obsolete, or must be replaced, you can use DWV copper tubing for the purpose, and connect on to the existing cast iron stack by means of adapters. If you are adding only a sink or lavatory, you will need a waste stack for it. Since this is likely to be only 1½-inch pipe, it isn't a serious expense if you have to add a new one.

If you are installing a new soil stack, you can put it in a standard 2x4 partition, if you use copper. But if you are remodeling, it will probably be better to run your stack up outside a wall, instead of opening up a wall to do it, so the bulk of the piping material won't be so important. When you put a stack outside a wall, you can box it in. Covered with plasterboard and decorated like the rest of the room, the alteration will be scarcely noticeable, especially if it's in a corner. Stacks can also be run up through closets. In other cases, wall sections can be thickened inconspicuously, by setting new studs against existing wall studs.

In a new house, or new addition, of course, there is no problem of where to put a stack, or how to open up walls and floors so drainage lines can be run, but planning in any case can reduce the cutting of the

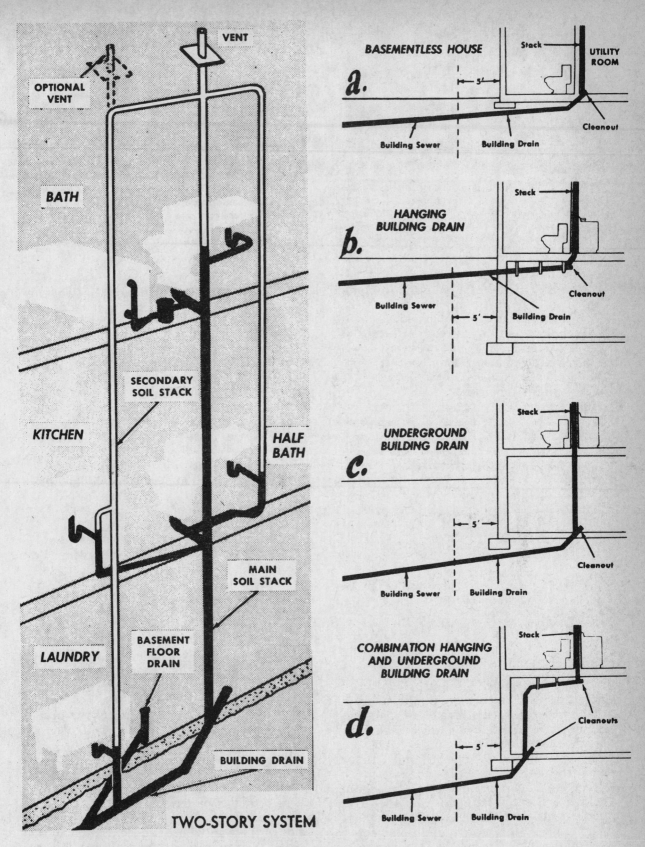

VENT

OPTIONAL VENT

BATH

SECONDARY SOIL STACK

KITCHEN

HALF BATH

MAIN SOIL STACK

LAUNDRY

BASEMENT FLOOR DRAIN

BUILDING DRAIN

TWO-STORY SYSTEM

a. **BASEMENTLESS HOUSE**

Stack — UTILITY ROOM

5'

Cleanout

Building Sewer — Building Drain

b. **HANGING BUILDING DRAIN**

Stack

Cleanout

Building Sewer — Building Drain

5'

c. **UNDERGROUND BUILDING DRAIN**

Stack

5'

Cleanout

Building Sewer — Building Drain

d. **COMBINATION HANGING AND UNDERGROUND BUILDING DRAIN**

Stack

Cleanouts

5'

Building Sewer — Building Drain

Sears, Roebuck

Study this layout and you will see how simple the drain-and-vent system for a two-story house can be, and the ease with which a first-floor half bath may be added to existing plumbing.

Here are four ways in which a drain and sewer line may be installed. And if you are adding a bathroom, you may find it simpler and better to add a second septic tank to handle its waste.

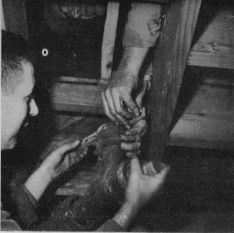

First step, left, when you install stack: Position closet bend attached to T plumb line. Then drop it through T and Y or a T-Y connected to house drain and center underneath it. Center photo, T-Y fitting includes cleanout ferrule. Top of T-Y fitting must be centered exactly under stack. Also align so it is exactly level. Right, T fitting, to which closet bend is attached, is caulked into T-Y of house drain. If there is a gap, insert pipe to bridge gap between the T-Y and the T. Study photos for installation details.

house structure to a minimum. Though cast-iron pipe diameter may be only 2, 3, or 4 inches, you have to consider that the bell end of each pipe section or fitting will be 4, 5¼ and 6¼ inches, respectively.

Steel pipe comes in long lengths, so it is sometimes possible to avoid fittings in the wall, and the pipe will then go into a minimum space. When planning fittings to go into a wall, don't overlook the clearance needed for turning the fitting within the space. Twice as much space is needed for turning a fitting as is required for the fitting alone. See the accompanying table for clearances required.

CLEARANCES NEEDED FOR STEEL PIPE
(inches)

Pipe Size	Pipe Alone	Pipe and Fittings	For Turning Fitting
1½	2	3	6
2	2½	3½	7
3	3½	5	10
4	4½	6	12

Toilet Drainage. Roughing-in dimensions for each fixture are supplied by the manufacturer. In the case of a toilet, these dimensions will tell you where the closet bend (the toilet drain) must go, and how far the center of its opening must be out from the wall.

On the first floor, if there is no ceiling below, a closet bend can be installed from underneath and there is need to cut only a hole where the branch drain connects to the toilet itself. If a new soil stack is being installed, a second hole will have to be cut for it.

If there is a ceiling on the room below, it is usually preferable to install the closet bend from above. Remove enough of the

flooring so that the drain, and the T of the stack to which it connects, can be set in place.

If installed from above, in this manner, don't permit the drain to rest on the ceiling. Rest the pipe on a cross brace, made either of a 2x4 or a metal strap. If installed from below, this drain also requires support. It can be a 1x4 or 2x4 nailed across the joints, or if the closet bend runs across the joists, a trapeze to support it can be made of 1x4's. In the latter case, an extension of the bend will also be needed to reach the floor above. The toilet floor flange, which is attached at the top of the bend, should rest on the finished floor.

If the bend is of cast iron, or is designed for fitting to cast iron, caulk it to the T before it is installed. In this way, the necessity for pouring a vertical lead joint is avoided.

The House Drain. If the stack is to connect to a new underground drain leading outside, drop a plumb bob through the center of the T, which has just been fixed in position, and locate the spot exactly under it. From this point a trench must be dug to the foundation wall where the drain will leave the house. You will probably have to break up a strip of the basement's concrete floor to do it. It can be patched up afterward.

The top of the drain pipe, when installed, should be approximately 1 foot below floor level at the stack, and slope 1 inch in each 5 feet to the basement wall. The house drain continues for 5 feet beyond the outside of the wall where it becomes the house sewer. To get through the wall, you'll have to break through it, or tunnel under it.

If there is to be a basement floor drain, it can connect to the house drain by means of a Y-fitting. If you have a septic tank, however, it is recommended than any base-

Ingersoll-Humphreys

Lead closet bends are better for they have certain amount of give. When testing completed drainage system for leaks, end of a lead bend is easily pinched together and sealed. Wall-hung toilets are popular and occupy no floor space. Center photo, hanger fitting of wall toilet is caulked into soil pipe fitting. Every part of house drain and sewer must be accessible to cleanout. Clean-out plug is needed at every change in direction. Cleanout here is in T-Y fitting. Note how Y fits closely, then into the wall.

When a house is built on a slab, all the major drain lines must be in place before concrete is poured. However, specially fitted toilets and baths can be installed with above-slab piping.

In remodeling, it's frequently best to make use of an existing soil stack, and attach new drain and vent lines to it. Shown are possible arrangements for one and 1½ bathroom installations.

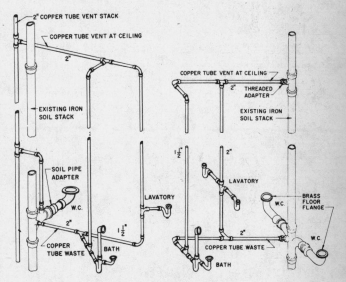

Copper and Brass Research Assoc.

ment floor drain empty into a separate dry well, or connect to the disposal field after the septic tank. It is inadvisable to flood a septic tank with too much waste water.

The base of the soil stack connects to the drain by means of a Y and a ⅛ bend. First, caulk the ⅛ bend to one section of cast iron pipe, then caulk the Y to it. Place this assembly so that the plumb bob from the T fitting above is centered directly over the middle of the Y opening. Check the top of the Y to see that it is exactly level. Concrete is now poured around the assembly to fix it in place.

After the concrete has set, the stack can be installed from the Y up to the T. Cut the last section of stack pipe, as required, so that the spigot end of the T will fit ex-

actly into the last section's hub. Raise the T just enough so that the fit can be made. A cleanout plug is caulked into the other branch of the Y.

If the house drain is suspended from the floor joists, the connection between the T at the closet bend and the drain can often be made with only a T-Y fitting. In other cases, you may have to insert a section of pipe between the T-Y and the T. In assembling the house drain, caulk two or three lengths of pipe together before hanging it and the job will be easier.

Completing the Stack. In completing the rest of the stack, insert sanitary T's at the proper height for branch drains to sink, lavatory, or tub, remembering that branch drains slope 1 inch in every 4 feet. Branch drains, using threaded steel pipe, are installed outward from the stack. A closet-bend-T assembly can be installed at the second floor for a toilet there.

Install standard T's for branch vent connections to suit your convenience. These don't require accurate positioning. Vent lines, using steel pipe, are assembled by starting one pipe upward from the branch drain being vented, and another pipe at the T in the stack. The two sections are joined by means of a long screw, or split coupling. One pipe end is threaded more than standard so that both parts of the split coupling can be turned onto it. The larger part of the split coupling is then turned back to join both pipes and wicking is used to seal between the two sections of the coupling.

If it is necessary to offset the stack in the drainage section, use ⅛ bends. Offsets in the vent section, perhaps needed to miss a roof rafter, can be made either with ⅛ or ¼ bends.

The stack should extend at least 6 inches above the roof, and the roof-pipe joint sealed with flashing. If the flashing is a prefab metal one, get one designed for the size pipe you are using and the pitch of your roof. New plastic flashing has many advantages. It is easier to use, and is likely to be longer lasting and less subject to leaking. Saraloy 400, a new plastic flashing material by Dow, is admirably suited for use on vents. Cut a hole ⅓ the size of the vent in a piece of the flashing. Coat the underside of the flashing and the roof surface with the special adhesive pro-

There is no limit to the ways in which drainage pipes can be arranged, provided pitch is maintained and sharp turns avoided. Left, a toilet is connected to a soil stack beyond stack base. In center photo, two toilets (left and right of pipe) are connected to one center stack by a 45° Double Y arrangement. A Long Turn 90° Double T-Y is frequently used in similar situations. Right, the 90° Double T-Y is used for joining two toilets to a single stack. Note how connections have been made below ceiling level, and how framing has been arranged to box all pipes in. Plan layouts carefully.

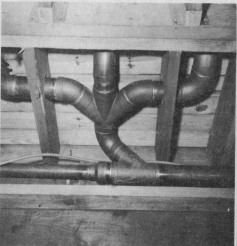

Because of copper's light weight, long sections of it can be assembled where it is convenient, then lifted into place. Below, fitting is a 3x3x1½-inch copper to copper to copper 90° T-Y. Perforated copper strap, ¾ inch wide, hangs this house drain to floor joists. Waste line, center photo, goes to kitchen sink. Note continuous pitch of the line, and how it is kept out of the way. By hanging house drain near ceiling and bringing it down only when it has to pass through house wall, maximum headroom is gained. At the wall, copper T-Y fitting is joined to cast iron, as shown in photo at far right, below.

Chase Brass & Copper Co. photos

vided, then stretch the flashing over the pipe and pull it down to make a bond with the roof. The bonded area should extend 6 inches out from the base of the vent stack. The flashing will fit the pipe very snugly and be absolutely weathertight.

Roofing should overlap vent flashing at the top and each side only. The lower side of the flashing overlaps the roofing. Where there is danger that frost might plug up a vent terminal, it must be not less than 3 inches in diameter. If you are using a secondary stack that is smaller than this size, use an increaser just below roof level so that it is at least 3 inches in diameter above the roof.

Drainage using copper tubing is simpler by far than that employing cast-iron pipe. Connections and fittings are essentially the same, but assembly is much easier. Joints are made by sweating, as described in the chapter on copper tubing, and take only a fraction of the time that is required for caulking cast iron joints. Weight of copper, too, is much less, so that bracing is less of a problem, and one man can handle long lengths or entire assemblies without difficulty.

Testing the Drainage System. When drainage lines are complete, they must be carefully tested to be sure all joints, both in the drain and vent sections, are absolutely tight. This must be done before walls or floors are enclosed. All pipe openings must be capped or plugged for the test.

Caps are used at the ends of most fixture drain lines. The toilet bend, if it is lead, can be sealed by pinching its top

Below left, 3-inch copper main vent stack fits in a standard 2x4 partition. Closet flange in foreground is soldered to a closet bend which in turn is joined by a T fitting to the stack. Sanitary tee fitting connects to kitchen sink trap, center. Fitting below is a cleanout. Vent line extends upward, connects to main stack. Branch vents often connect to inlet in stack increaser. New plastic flashing makes installation of shower pans easy for the nonprofessional plumber. Pans are quickly joined with a special solvent. Clamping ring connects it to shower drain.

Dow Chemical Co.

When all drainage and vent lines have been completed, they are filled with water brim to the top of roof vents. Then all joints are carefully checked, photo below, to see if there are any leaks. Twin lavatories are gaining favor because they greatly increase usefulness of a bathroom. Center, drain connections for the two basins are easily joined to single pipe with a Double T-Y fitting. Branch vent lines may be joined to main vent stack at almost any convenient height. To save on number of fittings needed, join two branch vent lines to stack with 3x3x1½x1½-inch 90° Double T-Y (center photo, below).

Possible basement plumbing installation for an automatic washing machine, above left. A trap is attached to a branch waste line with a 90° T-Y copper to compression joint with a metal ring. Toilet is attached to closet bend by means of a closet flange. Flange may be soldered to copper tube or to a 90° street elbow. Flange may be protected during construction by a wooden cover. In freezing weather, a vent terminal less than 3 inches in diameter is likely to be clogged by frost. To avoid that, use increaser fitting to enlarge small vent stacks to at least 3 inches, as shown at top right.

Where the house drain is below basement floor level, a floor drain may be connected to it. Where house drain is hanging one, best solution is to install a sump for basement drainage. Sump pit is a tile pipe sunk in floor. Float starts pump running whenever water level rises beyond certain point. Arrangement like this is first-rate insurance against flooded basement. In testing completed drainage system for leaks, house drain is usually sealed by means of a test plug. Rubber stopper on device is spread when it is compressed, fills end of pipe watertight, shown in photo at right, directly above.

House sewer line should connect to city sewer in street as directly as possible, and should preferably have pitch of two per cent, or about ¼ inch per foot, but ⅛-inch pitch is acceptable.

House sewer line can be made of cast iron, clay, cement, cement-asbestos, plastic, or bituminous fiber pipe. Below, a new cement-asbestos pipe is assembled by means of a special adhesive.

Johns-Manville

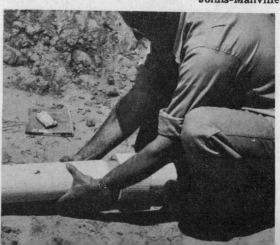

together and soldering it. Otherwise, a test plug can be borrowed from a plumbing shop for the purpose. The house drain, too, is similarly plugged. Plugs have a rubber spreader placed between two flanges. By turning a wing nut, the rubber is expanded to greater diameter, sealing the pipe.

The entire drainage and venting system is filled with water through the stacks on the roof. Water should be allowed to remain in the pipes at least 12 hours and all joints carefully inspected for leaks. The plumbing inspector will make his investigation while the system is filled, so call him when you are ready.

If any joints need remaking, the water first has to be drained out to below the level of the joint, for it is impossible to solder any pipe or remake any joint containing water. If you fill stacks brimful, leaks will quickly make themselves known by a sharp lowering of the water level.

The House Sewer. This is a continuation of the house drain from a point 5 feet outside the foundation wall. The house sewer continues either to the city sewer or past the septic tank to the beginning of the disposal field or leaching wells.

The house sewer line may be cast iron, clay, concrete, cement-asbestos, plastic, or bituminous fiber pipe, depending on local code requirements and your own preference. It is usually 4 inches in diameter, and never smaller than the house drain.

The trench in which it is laid is usually from 5 to 6 feet deep and 2 feet wide. It should be as straight as you can make it. If a bend is required, it should be a gradual one. For making a right-angle turn, use either a long-sweep ¼ bend, or two 45-degree L's, with a cleanout.

A cleanout is required for every 50 feet of sewer line, and for any change in pitch greater than 22½ degrees. Cleanouts are installed in T fittings inserted in the sewer line. A cleanout ferrule or plug is installed at ground level.

The sewer preferably should have a pitch of 2 per cent, approximately ¼ inch per foot, but a pitch of only 1 per cent, approximately ⅛ inch, is sometimes permissible. To get the correct pitch, stretch a line and level it, using a line level. Every ten feet, the ditch will be about 2½ inches deeper if the pitch is 2 per cent. Use a marked pole for ease in measuring the depth.

The depth of the connection to be made at the city sewer must, of course, be determined before you can decide on the grade required for the house sewer. Depth of the city sewer may be determined by removal of manhole covers on both sides of the proposed connection, and lowering a long stick. The depth of the sewer at your lot front can then be calculated.

If it is necessary to pitch a house sewer more than ¼ inch per foot, restrict the steeper part of the grade to the section between the house and the curb line, then reduce the grade to a ¼ inch between the curb and the city sewer.

Connection of the house sewer to the city sewer is usually made by a representative of the appropriate city department, or by a contractor under bond.

New plastic flashing is effective means of sealing stack-roof joint. Neoprene type is shown in left and center photos. At the right, completed installation is made with Saraloy 400, another plastic.

DuPont photos Dow

water pipes
. . . AND HOW TO INSTALL THEM

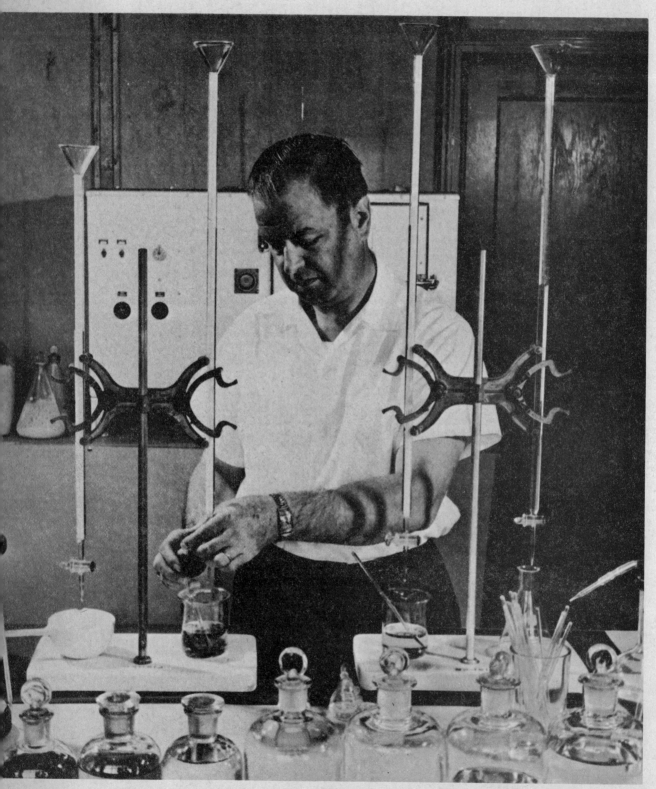

Chase Brass & Copper Co.

Consider the type of water in your area when deciding which kind of piping to use. Copper is best in most sections. Here a metallurgist studies effects of various waters on copper.

THE PIPE which brings water into the house, either from a private well or from city mains, is known as the water service line. The minimum size of this line is ¾ inch. It will deliver up to 10 gallons per minute, which is usually considered sufficient for from 1 to 10 fixtures. A 1-inch pipe will deliver up to 18 gallons per minute and is considered adequate for up to 20 fixtures.

A ¾-inch main will supply two ½-inch branches. A 1-inch main will supply two ¾-inch branches.

Running the Service Line. Tapping the city water main is usually done by the water company, and requires a special tool which plumbers do not have. The water service line to the house must be laid on undisturbed earth below the frost line. If it is laid on backfill, settlement can cause rupturing of the pipe.

If the pipe cannot be laid below the frost line, it sometimes can be adequately protected by insulation. Aside from safeguarding the pipe from freezing, having it 3 to 4 feet deep will protect it from damage should trucks or other heavy vehicles cross the area. It is best never to run a house service line under a driveway.

Type K flexible copper tubing is a good

Important things to watch in water-pipe installation: run pipe as directly as possible, use adequate size pipe, use minimum number of fittings.

By using flexible Type K copper tubing for house water-service line, excavation to avoid boulders, tree roots and other obstructions can be avoided.

Water meter, if required, may be placed in water-service line near curb, or right inside house. Curb stop (shut-off) is on street side of the meter.

LINE TO WATER MAIN

Mueller Brass Co.

Outdoor water meter is often installed in a protective box. In some cases, the curb stop may be reached by removing the cover, as shown here. It can then be turned on or off by special key.

Pressure reducing valve is important where water pressure is in excess of 80 pounds per square inch, or where it fluctuates widely. By adjustment, you can set this valve at any pressure.

Where water pressure is low, use pump and tank like those used in pumping well water. Usual range of pressure is from 20 to 40 pounds p.s.i.

One-inch main supplies hot and cold-water needs. Individual hot and cold line are ¾ inch, reduced to ½ inch for branch lines supplying fixture groups.

Plan water and drainage lines together. Risers carry water from floor to floor. They can be placed in same stud space used for drainage, stack lines.

choice for the water service line, for it comes in long lengths and usually can be laid without joints from city main to the house. Though it is advisable to run the line as straight and direct as possible, when necessary the flexible tubing can be readily curved around boulders or other obstructions. Galvanized wrought iron is also widely used in many areas for water service.

Where codes permit, plastic pipe performs excellently as a water service line. Cost of ¾-inch Type K copper is about 60 cents per foot. The same size in plastic pipe costs little more than 10 cents per foot, is available in rolls up to 2000 feet long.

The water service pipe may be placed in the same trench as the house sewer pipe if it's kept at least 12 inches above the sewer line. This is best done by placing the water pipe on a solid shelf at one side of the trench. It is important to keep joints in the water pipe to a minimum.

A corporation stop, for turning off the water, is screwed into the hole made in the water main by the tapping machine. A section of flexible pipe, commonly known as a gooseneck, connects it to a curb stop, another shutoff, which is placed between the street curb and the property line. This stop can be reached with a long key after removing the cover of the gate box placed above it. From here to the house, the water service pipe slopes upward. This permits draining it, when necessary.

The service line comes up through the basement floor or passes through the foundation wall. Use a masonry drill, or a star drill and hammer, for cutting a foundation opening. After the pipe has been passed

through, caulk around it with a bituminous caulking compound. Don't use mortar. Flexibility is important. In a basementless house, entry is commonly made into a utility room.

Inside the House. It is common practice to install a ground key valve, with a drain, on the service just inside the house. It functions as a handy shutoff when repairs are being made to the house plumbing.

If water pressure is over 80 lbs. psi (per square inch), installation of a pressure-reducing valve is recommended. Its cost: about $15. It will prevent pipe noises, water hammer, and save wear-and-tear on pipes and fittings. With the pressure-reducing valve, the water can be kept at a uniform 40 lbs. psi around the clock, or set at any other pressure desired.

Next in the line comes the meter, if one is required. It will be installed by a representative of the water company. Alternately, a meter may be installed at the corporation stop in the street.

Where water pressure is below requirements, a pump and pressure tank can be installed to bring the pressure up to the desired level. It is similar to equipment used in pumping water from a well.

On the house side of the water meter, a gate or ground-key valve is installed, followed by a globe valve which can be used for draining water from all pipes in the house if the house should ever be unheated during freezing weather. The valve is often installed on a short spur line so it in no way interferes with the flow of water through the main. All horizontal lines in the house system have a slight slope back to this point.

Split shingles are useful in aligning pipes in holes. Pipes should have room for expansion movement, but not enough leeway to rattle or vibrate.

Standard rough-in height for shower is 76 inches, with shower head at about 66 inches. Most women prefer shower head at about 60 inches. Suit yourself.

Shown: typical water pipe connections to bathtub are: hot water left, cold right, tub spout between. Plug at top is for shower, if one is used.

Planning Water Distribution. Plan your water lines in the house so that they travel the most direct route to fixtures. Directness is important, for each turn adds friction and loss of water pressure. Be sure the pipe is of adequate size. Adequate pipe size is important not only for a full flow at fixtures, but for proper operation of washing machines and dishwashers.

Piping that is too small is subject to water noises, vibration, and water hammer. If there isn't enough flow, water demand in one part of the house may cause an abrupt slackening of flow elsewhere. If anyone is in a shower when this happens, the results can be serious scalding. If you are using copper, in average circumstances plan on ¾-inch tubing for main hot and cold water lines, ½-inch for branch lines to all fixtures, with the exception of lavatories and toilets which are adequately served by ⅜-inch tubing.

Supply lines can be run across the bottom of floor joists, or parallel to joists and between them. Where lines run across joists, furring strips can be used to bring the ceiling level below the pipes. Lines can also be run across the top of joists by notching the joists.

Use a minimum number of joints and fittings. It will mean less work, less cost, less possibility of leakage, and reduction in resistance to water flow. You can eliminate some joints by use of flexible tubing for risers. Risers are vertical pipes which extend from one floor to the next. Use rigid tubing for horizontal lines. It's neater, and there's no danger of sags, which might trap water and prevent draining of the line, should that ever be necessary.

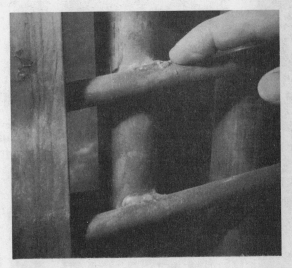

Where these water pipes cross drain lines they have been soldered together. This is to prevent pipe movement, which might be noisy, and which could eventually wear a hole and cause a leak.

A good antihammer air chamber is made of tubing one size larger than the line it serves. In this case, 1-inch tubing is used for the chamber on a ¾-inch line. Chamber is about 12 inches high.

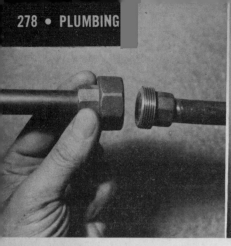

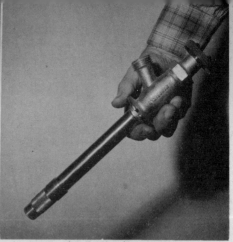

Mansfield Sanitary, Inc.

At water heaters, water softeners, dishwashers, filters, it is advisable to insert union in lines so pipes can be easily disconnected for any servicing. This will save headaches later.

On body of a stop-and-waste valve, arrow points in the direction water should flow through valve for correct installation. By opening knurled cap, water can then be drained.

Outside hose cocks subject to freezing require a shut-off valve inside the house. Frost-proof wall hydrants, however, like the one shown, can be safely left on in any season.

Latest push-button faucet control simplifies supply lines, as mixing of the hot and cold water is done at the heater and only one line need be run to each faucet. Flow is controlled.

In typical basement or crawl-space installation water lines are run across or between joists. Where to locate the hot water tank is an important part of your planning. It usually goes near kitchen.

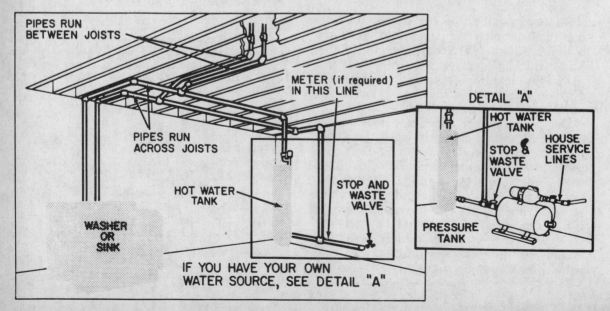

PIPES RUN BETWEEN JOISTS

PIPES RUN ACROSS JOISTS

METER (if required) IN THIS LINE

HOT WATER TANK

STOP AND WASTE VALVE

WASHER OR SINK

IF YOU HAVE YOUR OWN WATER SOURCE, SEE DETAIL "A"

DETAIL "A"

HOT WATER TANK

STOP & WASTE VALVE

HOUSE SERVICE LINES

PRESSURE TANK

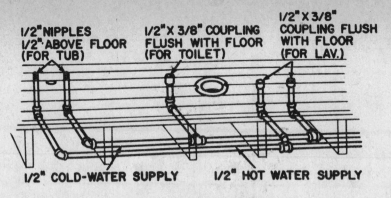

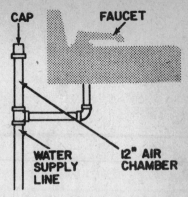

Water lines need not be run up through walls to serve first-floor fixtures. They can be brought up through floor, as shown. By use of a cabinet lavatory, the piping to it is easily concealed.

Sears, Roebuck & Co.

An air chamber is a dead-end section of pipe in which air is trapped. It absorbs the shock of water flow suddenly being stopped. A separate chamber is usually provided for every faucet.

Sears, Roebuck & Co.

You can also save on the number of fittings by using combination types. For example, you can use a union-tee or a union-ell instead of separate union and tee or ell fittings.

When installing both water pipes and drainage pipes, plan them together. Frequently water pipes can pass through the same openings provided for the larger drainage lines. Supply lines to a second-floor bathroom usually are run up next to the stack, the large vertical drain and vent pipe that extends up through the roof. Avoid contact between pipes and electrical cables. Such grounding may cause interference on radio and TV. When touching is unavoidable, wrap the point of contact with insulating tape. In walls, run branch lines through notches cut in partition studs.

Keep hot and cold water lines a minimum of 6 inches apart. If they are closer, the hot water line will lose heat to the cold one, and the cold one will sweat. If the pipes can't be separated, insulate them. Avoid running water pipes in exterior walls if there is any danger of their freezing there. If they are run there, always place wall insulation between the pipes and the exterior sheathing.

In areas where the summer climate is humid, always insulate cold water lines which run through walls or floors. It will prevent their sweating and discoloring paint or wallpaper on walls or ceiling, may even be necessary to safeguard the wall or ceiling structure itself. One of the easiest types of insulation to apply for this purpose is NoDrip Plastic Coating. It is brushed on. Further details on pipe insulation may be found in the chapter on plumbing noise.

Plan water lines with the location of your water heater in mind. If the heater is oil- or gas-fired it will have to be placed near a chimney or vent. Electric heaters, of course, do not need this provision. The heater, in any case, should be as close as possible to kitchen and bathrooms to minimize long runs of hot water pipes and attendant losses in heat. Where bathrooms are widely separated, two heaters may be both a convenience and an economy.

Hot water pipes are always connected to the left-hand faucet on sinks, lavatories, and other fixtures. Keep this in mind when bringing pipes up to the fixture. Where bathrooms are back-to-back, or where there are basins on two sides of a partition, pipes have to be crossed over if conventional, old-style faucets are used. However, with a Moen-style single-control faucet, no crossing is necessary. The faucet handle is merely taken off and reinstalled 180 degrees from its original position. That reverses its hot and cold inlets, but doesn't affect its operation otherwise.

Where water pipes attach to a hot water heater, pool filter, dishwasher, water softener, or other device that may on occasion have to be disconnected for servicing, put a union in each line. The connection can then easily be taken apart or made, whenever or as often as necessary, by merely turning the hex nut.

Adding New Branches. Do you want to install a basement shower, an automatic clothes washer or dishwasher, add an extra sprinkling outlet, a drinking fountain? The easy way to do it is with "Quick-Tee" connectors. The same connectors can also be used for making air, vacuum and gas connections. A neoprene gasket between the connector and the pipe makes the joint leakproof. Connectors are available for ½- and ¾-inch iron pipe and ⅝-inch OD

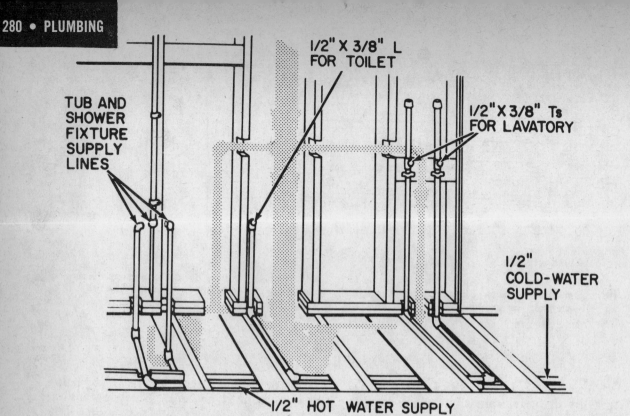

1/2" X 3/8" L
FOR TOILET

1/2" X 3/8" Ts
FOR LAVATORY

TUB AND
SHOWER
FIXTURE
SUPPLY
LINES

1/2"
COLD-WATER
SUPPLY

1/2" HOT WATER SUPPLY

Sears, Roebuck & Co.

A typical installation, where the supply pipes are brought up through the wall to the fixtures, looks like this. Note how the plate (the doubled member under the studs) is notched to accommodate pipes.

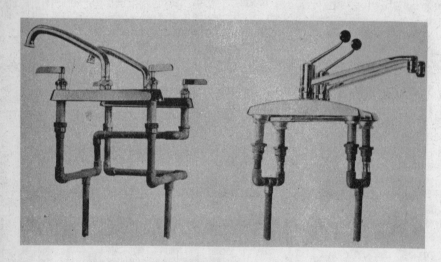

When two sinks are installed on opposite sides of a partition, piping has to be crossed over, as on left, if ordinary faucets are used. By use of Moen-style faucets, right, piping is simpler.

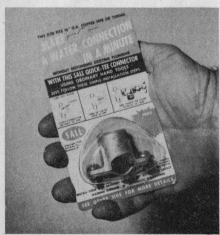

Adding a basement shower, a hose cock, or installing a clothes washer or a dishwasher is greatly simplified by the use of the new saddle-type tees. They may be used on either copper or iron pipe.

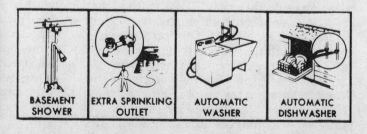

BASEMENT SHOWER   EXTRA SPRINKLING OUTLET   AUTOMATIC WASHER   AUTOMATIC DISHWASHER

In six easy steps, as shown in photos, the water is shut off, the tee is attached to the pipe, and a ¼- or ⅜-inch hole drilled. A threaded hosecock, or any other threaded connection may then be made.

(outside diameter) copper tubing (shown).

In industry these tee fittings are used for making quick connections for air-operated power tools; on the farm, for installation of milking machine stations. They have many non-plumbing applications, as well, such as use as brackets for iron pipe handrails, and hanging signs from pipe.

In making a water pipe connection with one of these tees, first turn off the water in the pipe. Sand or steel-wool the pipe to remove scale or dirt. Clamp the connector to the pipe and tighten its hex nuts. The connector used on copper tubing has screws.

Drill a ¼- or ⅜-inch hole in the pipe in the fitting's threaded opening. Blow out any metal chips. Now add a faucet, branch pipe, or any other threaded pipe fitting. Turn on the water, open the faucet to flush it out. That's all there is to it. •

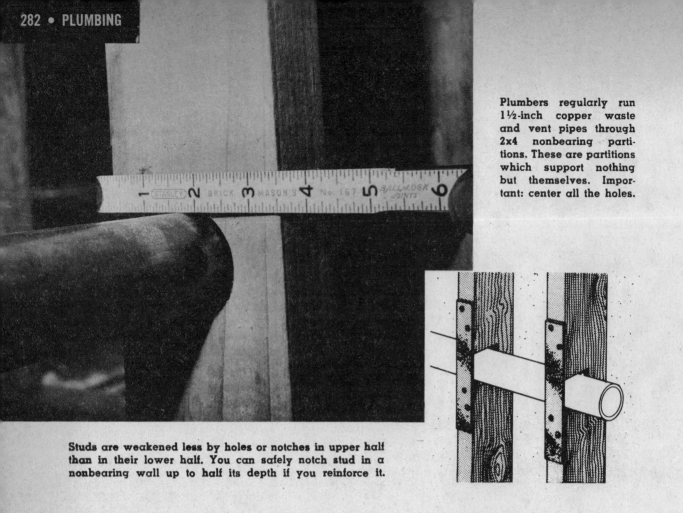

Plumbers regularly run 1½-inch copper waste and vent pipes through 2x4 nonbearing partitions. These are partitions which support nothing but themselves. Important: center all the holes.

Studs are weakened less by holes or notches in upper half than in their lower half. You can safely notch stud in a nonbearing wall up to half its depth if you reinforce it.

THINGS YOU SHOULD KNOW ABOUT . . .

cutting studs and joists

IF YOU PLAN to conceal plumbing pipes inside walls and floors, you'll have to cut studs and joists to do it. Joists are the horizontal members which support floors. Studs are the vertical framing members inside walls. Since any cutting of these members may weaken the house, it is important that such cutting be kept to a safe minimum.

How to Avoid Cutting. Water pipes are so small in size, they never present any problems in concealment. Big drainage pipes, however, do. In remodeling, when possible, instead of trying to conceal drainage pipes, run them up outside the walls and box them in.

A good method is to locate pipes in a corner. A jog in the wall, or closing in a small triangular space at a corner is scarcely noticeable, even if it includes a stack. The toilet itself may be set cater-corner against this new wall.

Where large drainage pipes run horizontally, if placed just outside the wall at ceiling level, they can be boxed in inconspicuously. Other horizontal drain pipes can be concealed by cabinet work, as in a vanity lavatory, or in a cabinet for linen and bath necessities.

If you are building an addition, by spacing joists to accommodate your plumbing, you can largely avoid cutting of these members. Never place a joist directly under a wet wall (a wall containing plumbing). Instead, place two spaced joists under it, just far enough apart to allow a 3- or 4-inch stack to be run up between them.

Avoid cutting joists by running pipes between them instead of across them. When possible, run pipes below joists in basement or crawl space, or above joists in an unfinished attic.

Often you can avoid cutting joists, or minimize the amount of cutting, by making use of the space occupied by flooring and subflooring, and laying a new floor over stripping, as shown.

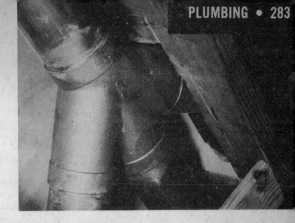

You can safely run a 1½-inch pipe through any 2x8 joist if you center the hole between top and bottom. You may have to use a bend fitting to bring branch waste line off at the right level.

A cut through joist weakens it far less at the top than at the bottom. When a severe cut, like that shown, is necessary, keep the cut as close as possible to the top and reinforce the joist.

Plan placement of cuts carefully before you make them. The hole cut for branch waste pipe had to be shifted twice because of miscalculations. A cross member to adjoining joist adds support.

When a pipe has to cross joists, try to locate required notching as close as you can to point at which joists are supported. The deep notching, photo above, hardly weakens the joists at all.

Cutting Through Joists. You can safely bore a hole anywhere in a joist if it is centered between top and bottom and is not over ¼ the height of the joist at the location of the hole.

You can safely notch joists at either top or bottom, but only in the end quarters. FHA regulations permit notching in the end thirds of joists.

Don't notch a joist more than ⅙ its depth, except that you can notch it ⅓ its depth at the top, if the notching is no farther from the face of support than the depth of the joist. For example, on a 2x8 joist, notching would have to be within 7½ inches of the face of the joist's support. You're safe if you don't notch a joist more than ¼ the depth of the joist at its point of bearing. The depth of the joist here is often less than its depth elsewhere.

Always remember that the depth to which a joist may be safely cut decreases very rapidly as you move away from its point of support. Excessive cutting of joists will result in sagging, shaky floors, cracking and falling of ceiling plaster, and, in extreme cases, collapse of the structure. When a floor sags, it may interfere with drainage, for it may rob a drain pipe of its pitch, or even make it pitch in the wrong direction.

The one thing for which a joist may be cut completely through is to accommodate a closet bend. No more than one joist should be cut, however, and the cut end should be braced substantially.

Cutting Studs. According to new FHA minimum standards, unless reinforced with steel plates or furring across the notch, wall studs should never be notched more than ¼ their depth, nor should a hole bigger than 1¼ inches be cut or drilled in a 2x4 stud, or bigger than 2 inches in a 2x6 stud.

These regulations are somewhat stiffer than the general practice among plumbers. Their standard practice has been to notch

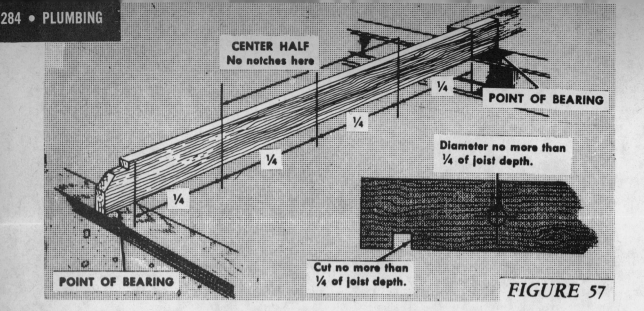

CENTER HALF
No notches here

POINT OF BEARING

¼

¼

¼

¼

¼

Diameter no more than
¼ of joist depth.

Cut no more than
¼ of joist depth.

POINT OF BEARING

FIGURE 57

Don't notch a joist at all in the center section. The closer you are to the point of bearing, the deeper you can safely notch a joist. Notches made in joist's bottom edge will weaken it the most.

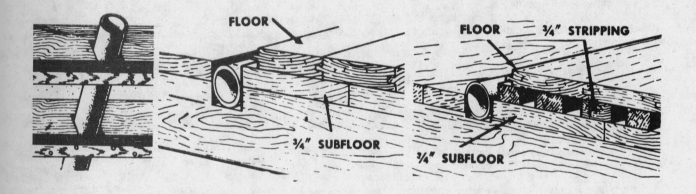

FLOOR

FLOOR

¾" STRIPPING

¾" SUBFLOOR

¾" SUBFLOOR

Sears, Roebuck

Reinforce joist, left sketch, over or under notch with a 2x2 or steel strap. Then reduce notching of joists, center and right, to minimum by using space where flooring and subflooring is, or by using stripping.

the lower half of a stud up to ⅓ its depth without reinforcing. This permits them to run 1½-inch branch drains through 2x4 nonbearing partition walls.

Plumbers will notch a stud up to half its depth in its upper half without reinforcing if the partition is nonbearing. But they won't cut two studs in succession in this manner, or leave less than two uncut studs in a partition unless the cut studs are reinforced.

In no case does a competent plumber notch a stud over ⅔ its depth, for such a stud is worthless. It's impossible to reinforce it adequately.

Plan Ahead. Don't permit yourself to make mistakes. They will result in your cutting studs or joists, and then cutting them again to correct the original placement of holes or notches. This is unnecessary weakening of the house structure. Carefully consider every cut before you make it to be sure it is absolutely necessary and that it will be exactly where you want it.

In arranging bathroom fixtures, plan their placement to minimize cutting. A lavatory placed on a wall opposite the toilet may require far more cutting of joists than one placed on the same wall as the toilet. Consider the direction in which joists run, and place fixtures so that pipes can run between joists rather than across them. If you do have to cut joists, always remember it is far better to do it near their ends. Never cut a joist in its center half.

Often, how much you can cut a member is just a matter of common sense. If its ob-

Running pipes through holes in center of joists is good system, but you may not have clearance for getting the pipes through the holes unless you plan ahead; install plumbing as you build.

This may look like severe cut, but actually the member cut isn't supporting anything at this particular point. On right and left, where it supports joists, member has adequate support underneath.

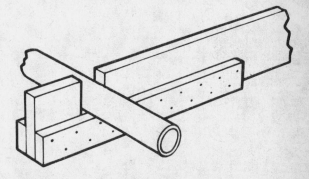

These two holes cut in floor are for the plumbing of two bathtubs placed back to back. Since the floor is a non-structural member, large cuts like this can be made wherever you require them.

It takes only a little time to nail a length of 2-inch lumber to each side of the joist under a notch. It gives the joist important reinforcement where it is most needed—along bottom edge.

vious that you are cutting away a main support, stop. The size of the member isn't always a sure indication of its importance. If you do have to cut away a main support, can you brace it as strongly as before by a reinforcing member placed close by? If so, put in the reinforcement before you make the cut.

Consider how substantially the house is built. If joists are on 12-inch centers where joists normally would be on 16-inch centers, you obviously can be a little more liberal in your notching. On the other hand, if the floor has 8-inch joists and really should have 10-inchers, go easy. If a floor already shakes when you walk across it, think what might happen if you weakened it. A cross beam, and a couple of lally columns to reduce span of joists will help.

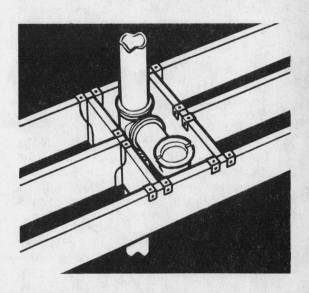

It is sometimes permissible to cut one joist to permit installation of a closet bend. When this is done, support the cut ends of joists securely. Use metal joist stirrups for maximum strength.

Glissade, Inc.

When you replace outmoded fixtures with attractive new ones beauty is added as well as value to your home. Lavatory vanity comes as a complete unit, with the basins and faucets already in proper place.

HOW TO INSTALL . . .

new fixtures

FIXTURES ARE INSTALLED after roughing-in of plumbing for them is complete. The roughed-in plumbing includes drainage and water-supply pipes.

Where an entire bathroom is being installed, the tub is the first fixture put in place. It is connected before the walls are finished. After finishing of the walls, toilet and lavatories are installed.

Care of Fixtures. Uncrate new fixtures carefully. Most damage to fixtures is done in unpacking them. Don't pry or hammer against a fixture in getting a crate off. Opened properly, crates usually unfold easily.

When you remove the crate, place the fixture on a blanket, or on excelsior pads and packing taken from the crate. If you have to slide a bathtub, place it on blocks of wood first. You can chip the edges on a fixture by sliding it on a rough floor or forcing it against a wall.

Once fixtures are damaged by scratching, or by being struck by tools, there is little that can be done about it. Cover fixtures to protect them. Cover bathtubs with a thick pad made of newspapers and wheat paste. It is a better covering than brush-on plastic types. Children can pick loose the plastic at a corner and rip the entire cover off.

Installing new fixtures is very simple. In addition, so many people are doing it that the necessary tubing and fittings for the job are now being sold in just about every well-stocked hardware, plumbing store.

The bathtub is the first fixture to be installed. The bathtub flange goes snugly against the wall studs. If you are remodeling, then it will be necessary to remove part of wall finish.

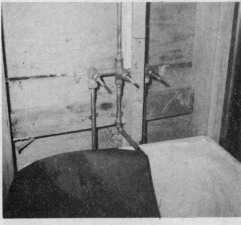

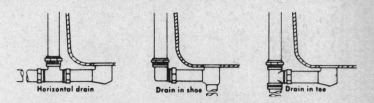

Diagrams above are of the tub's drain which can be hooked up to your plumbing in various ways. The bath drain can be ordered with the drain in a shoe, a drain in a tee, or it can be used as a horizontal drain (diagram at the left).

Protect tub against damage during installation. Cover it with newspaper applied with wheat paste.

Further, a plastic cover doesn't protect against the impact of dropped tools. You can buy paper covers, but what is the point of it when old newspapers make a superior cushion? Since wheat paste is soluble in water, soaking the paper makes it easy to remove after the job is complete.

Get the tub covering on right away. If the bathroom is to be tiled—and there is no better finish for bathroom walls than ceramic tile—the muriatic acid sometimes used in cleaning tile can mar the fixture's finish. Never stand in a bathtub, if you can avoid it, even when you do have it covered.

Wrap masking tape around the ends of roughed-in pipes. Plasterers will otherwise remove the caps on the pipe ends and plaster will get on the threads. Tape also protects fittings, specifically the spindles on which handles fit.

The end of a closet bend, after installation, should be closed to keep out debris during construction. An easy way to do it is to nail boards across the floor flange that's soldered to the bend. Another

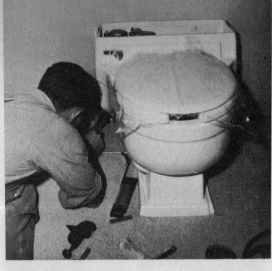

Most lavatories are supported by hangers attached to wall. For solid support, use a 1x4 board recessed in studs at the required height.

Caulk outer rim of toilet bowl to make watertight seal. Wax ring is used for seal at drain. Position bowl on flange, twist slightly to seat it.

method is to cut out a wooden plug of the appropriate size to fill the flange opening.

Installing a Tub. Most tubs are designed to fill completely a space between three walls. In remodeling, if a tub doesn't quite fill the existing space, build out one wall so it does. If the built-out space is large enough, you can use it for a built-in cabinet. When a tub is set against an outside wall, be certain the wall is insulated. Bathing comfort will suffer if it isn't.

Tub installation differs slightly according to the kind of tub and its manufacturer. Some tubs are installed on hangers nailed to studs. These metal devices help level the tub and also contribute toward eliminating the cracks and openings which frequently develop when such a support is not used. A mastic filler may be used between tub and hanger to make a waterproof seal.

In the installation of the typical steel tub, 1x4-inch boards are nailed to wall studs at

A counter style lavatory doesn't need hangers, special clamping ring is used. The trap is connected first (above) then the water supply tubes.

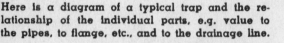

Here is a diagram of a typical trap and the relationship of the individual parts, e.g. value to the pipes, to flange, etc., and to the drainage line.

Below is detailed diagram for setting the hookup of supply piping from existing wall plumbing that is directly behind the wall onto the lavatory.

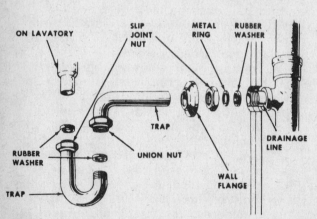

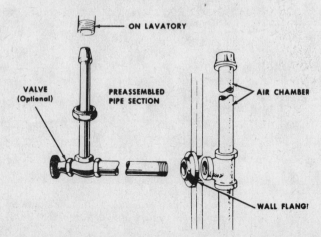

exactly the right height to support tub flanges when the tub is resting on the floor. The tub is anchored to the boards with screws through flange holes. Before this is done, a check is made to verify that the floor of the tub slopes toward the drain. Otherwise the tub won't empty properly. Some tubs employ a base strip as flashing to prevent water from infiltrating under the fixture.

It is necessary to have an access panel behind the tub, so that plumbing can be reached for servicing. The panel can be in an adjoining room or in an adjacent closet.

The tub branch drain and trap will already be in place. All that is necessary now is to connect the fixture's drain to the drain pipe end in the floor behind the tub. It is connected by means of a slip-joint nut, just like that on a lavatory. Supply line connections are also very similar to lavatory supply connections.

Grab bars are an absolute essential for safe use of tub or shower. Plan for them before applying finish to walls, so that you can add studs or cross-braces into which the grab bars can later be screwed. These bars may have to withstand a pull of 300 pounds or more so just fastening them into plaster isn't likely to be sufficient. Keep a record of where studs or reinforcements are. They may be difficult to locate exactly after the wall finish is on.

Place an "L" or vertical bar 24 inches from the shower end of the tub, with the bottom of the "L" 26 inches from the floor.

Installing a Toilet. A toilet should have a minimum clearance at its front of 18 inches. No wall or opposite fixture should be closer than this. No wall should be closer to the sides of the bowl than 15 inches, measuring from the bowl's center line.

Some toilets combine the tank and bowl in a single piece, others have a separate tank and bowl. Roughed-in plumbing will have provided a floor flange. Two bolts come up through this flange, and the toilet fastens to them. If the toilet requires 4 bolts, the 2 extra bolts go into the bowl's front holes and are screwed into the floor. Use special toilet-bowl bolts. These have wood threads at one end, machine threads at the other. If the floor is concrete, use regular machine bolts set head down into holes and fill around them with mortar.

With the bowl upside down on a protective pad or blanket, make a putty ring about 1 inch high around the outside rim of the bottom. Place a wax ring around the discharge opening. If the floor level is above the top of the flange you will have to double the ring. Now carefully set the toilet down on the flange bolts, twisting the bowl slightly to spread the putty and wax and make a tight seal.

If the toilet has a separate tank, you'll probably find that it is held by two bolts and that a "flush ell" is provided to make the connection between tank and bowl. If the tank rests on the bowl, a gasket will make a tight seal as the two units are bolted together. Water supply connections can be made with Plumb Shop tubes. Get the 12-inch size for connection to the wall, a 20-inch size for one to the floor.

A new type of toilet is wall-hung. These come in several different styles, but typically are supported by a heavy hanger bolted to the wall studs on the inside of the wall. The discharge end of the toilet fits into the soil pipe, which is part of the hanger assembly, and makes a watertight fit by means of a gasket.

Don't overlook the need for a tissue holder when planning your toilet installation. Standard placement for this is 6 inches in front of the toilet and 26 inches from the floor, measuring to the holder's center. •

One-piece toilets, like the one in the center drawing, have tank and bowl as a single unit, so that no assembly is required. A water supply connection is similar to that for basin, as sketched on left, but special toilet supply tubes are used. At right, is connection to floor employing straight and not angle valve.

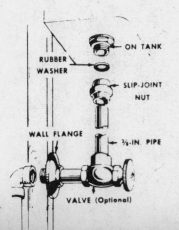
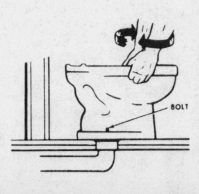
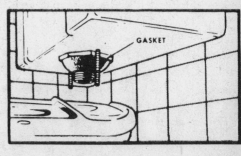

COMPLETE GUIDE TO REPAIRS . . .

faucets
sink sprays
toilets
clogged drains
pipes and tanks

There are many different faucet models, and a little study may be needed before deciding how to take yours apart. Some handle screws are concealed under screw-in or snap-in caps, below.

Constantly dripping faucet wears out fixtures and can waste $5 worth of water in a year. New snap-in washers and snap-in seats make job of repairing faucets much simpler than heretofore.

faucets

DRIPPING FAUCETS stain fixtures, and each faucet that drips can waste $5 per year in water. Frequently, all a drippy faucet requires is a new washer, and chances are you've replaced them many times. However, do you know about new snap-on washers, for which you don't need screws, and which last much longer? Do you know how to take apart and service the new, more complicated faucets? What about faucets that have no washers?

The fix-it facts are given here.

Why Faucets Leak. If a faucet leaks around the stem, it usually needs new bushing or packing in the bonnet-shaped nut that is just under the handle. If a faucet drips, it needs a new washer. If a new washer doesn't stop the drip, the seat against which the washer compresses is rough or water-cut and needs either re-

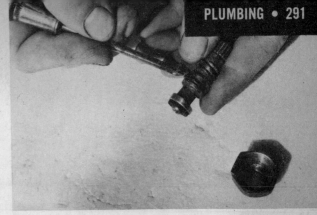

To replace a washer on some faucets, it isn't necessary to remove the handle. You merely unscrew the packing nut. In the model shown above the packing nut is hidden under the handle.

Most packing nuts have a graphite washer or other packing which serves to stop leaks around the faucet stem. This faucet uses a plastic O-ring for the purpose. It can be replaced easily (above).

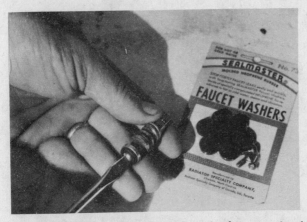

If the old screwhead breaks off when you try to unscrew it, pry washer away and use pliers to remove screw stem. Some prefer to use a short-bladed screwdriver when changing the washer.

New snap-in washers are on a swivel, so turn with the faucet spindle instead of grinding on seat. Hence, they last longer. Gauge comes with washers for measuring faucet seat size.

finishing or replacement. If a faucet requires frequent washer replacement, it's a good bet its seat is rough and needs refinishing.

The first step in most faucet repairs is to shut off the water. You may be able to do this under the fixture. In other cases you may have to shut off the branch line under the house, or perhaps even shut off the entire house supply. If you have everything you need for the rapair job, you aren't likely to have to keep the water off for long, possibly no more than a few minutes.

You'll need a smooth-jawed wrench and a screwdriver. An adjustable or Channellock-type wrench is ideal for faucet repairs. If your wrench has teeth, use tape or cloth to protect chrome from being marred by it. Before you begin work, lay a thick pad of newspapers in the fixture basin to protect it against the damage which might be caused by an accidentally dropped wrench. The newspapers will also prevent washers and screws falling down the drain.

Stem Leaks. If water oozes from around the stem whenever the water is turned on, try tightening the packing nut slightly. The packing nut is the flat-sided bonnet or cap which fits on top of the faucet body. If tightening the nut doesn't stop the leak, the packing inside it is defective. Remove the faucet handle and packing nut.

A screw holds the faucet handle on its shaft. Sometimes you have to unscrew a little knurled cap to get at the screw. In other cases, the screw is under a snap-on cover which can be pried off with a screwdriver. Tap the underside of the handle with the screwdriver handle, or rock it back and forth slightly to free it from the serrations on top of the shaft.

Dig the old packing out of the packing nut with the tip of your screwdriver. Press the new packing washer in place and carefully slip the packing nut back on the faucet stem. Don't twist the packing nut back on the stem. The stem's teeth might damage the washer. The packing nut should be tightened until the washer com-

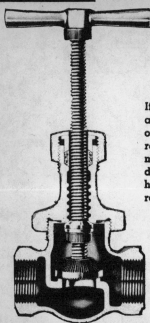

If you put in a new washer, and the faucet still leaks, or if the washer wears out rapidly, the faucet seat may need refacing. The drawing at the left shows how a very inexpensive refacing tool fits in easily.

O'Malley Valve Co.

presses snugly, efficiently against the stem.

Bonnet or packing washers come in a variety of sizes and shapes and the easiest way to get one that fits properly is to take the packing nut and faucet spindle to the store. Some faucet bonnets are packed with fine stranded graphite asbestos. A temporary repair of a stem leak can often be made by wrapping string around the stem handle just inside the packing nut. Wrap the string in the same direction that the handle turns when you are shutting it off.

A few newer faucets have a plastic sealing ring, or O-ring, instead of packing. This ring can be pried out of its groove, and replaced. Get a ring for your particular make of faucet, for these rings not only differ in diameter and thickness, but

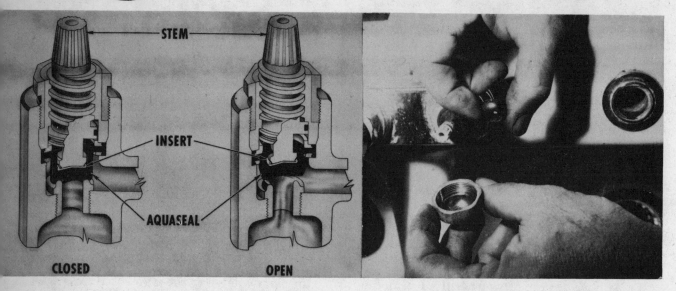

New dripless Aquaseal valve used in some new faucets has a diaphragm instead of a washer. A stainless steel insert acts as bearing plate. Water pressure raises the valve from the seat.

Graphited, gumdrop-shaped packing washers come in many different sizes and types. To get a replacement for one, take worn washer or faucet assembly along with you when you go to the store.

Moen faucets contain no washers, and are almost completely trouble-free. If any trouble should develop, you can remove holding clip at rear with nail and get all replacement works for about $2

Cutaway model of a Moen faucet shows revolving stainless steel slot which controls both mixing and the flow of water. Also seen here are two O-rings used as seals in the faucet assembly.

in the hardness of their material. Frequently, you need only turn a ring over and you can get more good use out of it.

Replacing Washers. It isn't necessary to remove the faucet handle to replace a washer. Unscrew the packing nut and the entire assembly will turn out if you turn it as if you were turning on the water. Individual hot and cold water faucets turn counterclockwise. Mixing faucet handles turn in opposite directions. The cold faucet usually turns on clockwise.

Just as you can reverse an O-ring, so you can turn a deteriorated washer over and make it do if you don't have a new one that fits. You can buy an assortment of faucet washers and screws for under 25 cents. Because of lack of standardization, you may not get what you want if you try

Older model Moen is serviced by removing its escutcheon. It may be taken apart in one or two sections. Handle is removed by driving out pin. Turn nut under basin to remove entire unit.

Below is a diagram of a typical faucet with all the parts. Note the positions of each unit of the faucet and the order in which they are put on the unit. Also see how packing is above washer.

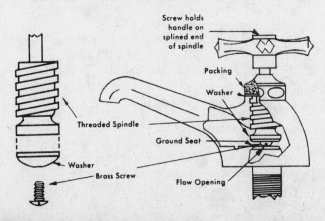

to buy washers by size. For example, there are four different sizes of ⅜-inch washers. You can get ⅜ small, ⅜ medium, ⅜ large, and simply ⅜.

It's a good idea to replace the screw holding the washer before the screw gets to the point where a screwdriver won't hold in its slot. Handle corroded screws carefully or their head may break off. In that case, cut away the washer and turn out the screw with pliers. Use only brass screws to hold a washer, never an iron screw. If the washer screw has fallen out of the spindle and is inside the faucet, you can flush it up after removing the stem by briefly turning on the water. A rag mounded around the faucet opening will keep water from spilling over the basin rim.

An improved type of washer requires no screw. It snaps into the spindle hole. Because the washer swivels, it can't grind on the seat, as ordinary washers do. Thus it lasts longer. To install this type of washer it is first necessary to remove the rim on the end of the faucet stem. Rip it off with pliers, then smooth up the metal with a file. After snapping in the washer, be sure it turns freely.

Replacing Seats. If the faucet continues to leak after the washer has been replaced, the seat is pitted, scored, or otherwise defective. It can be refaced with a seat dresser, a simple tool that can be had for less than a dollar. To use the tool, slip the faucet's packing nut over the tool's shaft, then replace the nut on the faucet body. Tighten it so that the tool's cutter is brought to bear on the faucet seat. Turning the tool's handle grinds the seat smooth.

In some faucets, the seat is part of a cylindrical sleeve which is easily replaceable. In other cases, if the threads on the spindle are worn, you can get an entire new valve insert assembly, including new spindle and seat. Browse through your hardware dealer's plumbing department and you are likely to find just the replacement parts you need to bring your faucets back into first-class operating condition.

You can get snap-in seats to match snap-in washers. A gauge supplied with snap-in washers is used in measuring the seat hole. The largest section of the gauge which can be inserted and turned in the hole tells you the seat size needed.

The new snap-in seat is positioned over the seat hole, using a pencil, wire, or small stick as guide. Tap the seat into the hole, using a hammer and a dowel or any other blunt-ended tool which can be pressed against the top of the seat. Spacer washers placed under the packing nut can give additional height if it is needed to allow for the extra thickness of the seat. •

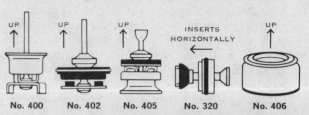

There are five different types of these diverter valves. By far, the majority of kitchen faucets contain the Model No. 405. The No. 406 is used in a few single-lever faucets, including Moen.

No. 400   No. 402   No. 405   No. 320   No. 406

The next best thing to an electric dishwasher is a thumb-controlled automatic faucet-spray. A special valve in the faucet spout diverts the water to the spray when the control is touched.

You can't attach an automatic sink spray to just any faucet. It has to be a faucet specifically designed for the purpose. When replacing faucets, be sure to get ones that will take a sink spray.

sink sprays

THERE ARE TWO TYPES of automatic sprays. The most common is a spray for rinsing only and is usually called Rinse-Quik. The deluxe type, usually known as Dish-Quik, contains a reservoir of concentrated detergent and sprays either clear water or suds. It is equipped with a nylon brush and is the preferred choice for rinsing, washing dishes, cleaning vegetables, etc.

All manufacturers of faucets with automatic sprays have joined together to market a single, standardized line or repair and replacement parts. These are obtainable, together with complete instructions, from The Automatic Spray Service Center, 1700 E. 58th Place, Los Angeles 1, Calif. Write to them for any information about automatic sprays.

Trouble with an automatic spray may stem from several different conditions. Improper original installation causes a great percentage of problems. The spray systems also wear out or become damaged in use. They don't last as long as the faucets, and if your spray was installed ten or twenty years ago, it isn't surprising that it may need service or replacement. The new Dish-Quik and new Rinse-Quik, as packaged for replacements, and the new hoses, are far superior to many earlier models.

If Water Doesn't Divert Satisfactorily. Unless accidentally damaged, the automatic diverter valve will usually last the life of the faucet. If all, or nearly all, of the water is diverted from the faucet spout to the spray when the thumb control is pressed, the diverter valve is satisfactory. If none or not enough of the water is diverted, the following steps may correct the condition:

1. If the faucet has an aerator, remove it for cleaning. A clogged aerator will alter water pressure inside the faucet fitting and prevent the diverter valve from operating.

The fact that bathroom lavatories don't have a hole to accommodate a spray needn't stop you. It's a simple matter to drill the extra hole that's required in the counter beside the basin, as in photo.

2. If the nozzle of the spray is clogged, unscrew and clean it. The single-hole type of nozzle almost never becomes clogged, but the multiple-hole rubber nozzle may under certain water conditions.

3. Be sure the hose is not kinked. Any stoppage of the hose, either by clogging or kinking, will prevent the diverter valve from operating.

4. If above steps do not correct the condition, check and clean the diverter valve:

a. Remove the faucet's swing spout by unscrewing the connecting ring or nut. Wrap it with damp cloth or tape to protect the chrome.

b. In nearly all faucets, the diverter valve will now be visible and can be plucked out by its stem.

c. In some makes of faucets, a bushing must be removed from the opening before the diverter valve can be plucked out.

d. Remove the spout's aerator, if it has one. Now replace the spout and turn on hot and cold water to wash out any foreign matter.

A kitchen sink is not the only place a spray is useful. Installed in the bathroom, a spray is ideal for both shampooing and giving the baby a bath. Installation here is with a Moen faucet.

e. Again remove swing spout. Rinse off diverter valve. When you are sure it is clean, replace valve. In most cases this will be with the pluck-out stem up.

f. The swing spout must now be replaced to its proper position. The diverter valve will not function properly if the spout rides too high. Here is the proper way to replace a swing spout: Grasp the base of the spout with one hand and press down as you rotate it back and forth with other hand. Continue to rotate back and forth as you tighten connecting ring or nut with your fingers. Do not tighten with a wrench until you are positive the spout is in the proper position.

In nearly all instances, these steps will correct the diversion, but, if not, it is advisable to obtain a replacement diverter valve. Most plumbers have a stock of replacement diverter valves or you can order one by writing direct to the Automatic Spray Service Center, enclosing $1 and specifying the model number that you require.

The steps listed above for cleaning and checking the diverter valve also apply to single-lever faucets, but for some of these faucets the steps required in removing the spout and the diverter valve are more complex. If you experience difficulty in these faucets, write direct to the manufacturer or to the Automatic Spray Service Center for assistance.

Hose Troubles. If a hose is broken, kinked, or otherwise damaged, it should be replaced with the correct official replacement hose. Do not attempt to take the brass connections off your old hose and put them on some similar type of hose. A hose with the wrong inside diameter will prevent the diverter valve from functioning.

In ledge-mount installations, if the hose is difficult to raise and lower, the problem is usually caused by drain pipes, disposers, wiring, etc., being in the way of the hose. If the hose is properly installed, it can be adjusted to miss most of these obstructions. Sometimes, installing a new hose guide helps. They cost 80 cents.

If the hose leaves black marks on the sink, get a new hose. Prior to 1958, hoses were of a synthetic rubber which tended to leave black marks after several years of use. New hoses are vinyl coated and do not "chalk off," or leave black marks.

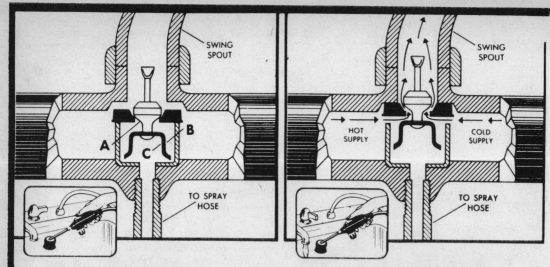

Figure 1: REST POSITION

Hot and cold taps are turned off: The valve rests in the cup like this. Note that the valve head, connecting rod and piston are joined together as one unit that is free to rise and fall independently of the washer. Three surfaces govern operation of the valve: (A) Face of the poppet-valve head. (B) Top surface of the piston. (C) Bottom surface of the piston.

Figure 2: WATER FLOWS TO SPOUT

Water supply is "turned on" and spray thumb lever is up, in "off" position: Water pressure lifts the washer. Then, because upward water pressure against C and A creates more force than the downward pressure against B, the valve head-piston unit is raised. Water then flows around spacers on top of the piston, through the washer and into the swing spout.

Portable dishwashers of the type recently developed that connect to the end of the swing spout cause back-pressure in the water supply lines. The pressure is great enough to burst hoses made prior to development of these dishwashers. The new type hoses are especially designed to meet any pressure requirements. A 30-inch replacement hose costs $1.60. A 4-foot hose is $2.10.

Defective Sprays. If the nozzle of a Rinse-Quik spray is clogged, it can be removed by unscrewing it for cleaning with a toothpick, pin, or any pointed instrument. Do not attempt to repair the thumb-control assembly. Special tools are needed. If the spray is worn, corroded, or damaged, it can be replaced with a new one for $2.40. Any Rinse-Quik can be replaced with a Dish-Quik, if you desire. These sell for $9.95, are the best type to have for dishwashing.

The rubber nozzle on Dish-Quik can be removed for cleaning out sediment, but it is recommended that no other repairs be attempted. Special tools are required to

If water doesn't divert the way it should, spray nozzle may be at fault. Remove the nozzle or rubber head and clean out the holes with a brush or toothpick, then flush it and reassemble. Most common cause of diverter failing to work is a clogged aerator. Remove the aerator and clean its many screens. A toothbrush is fine for the job. Flush the parts out well and reassemble. Four of the more common types of diverter valves are shown in photo, far right. Pencil points at the most common model, No. 405.

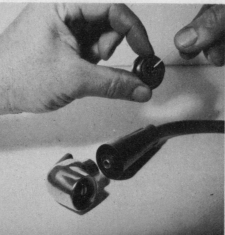

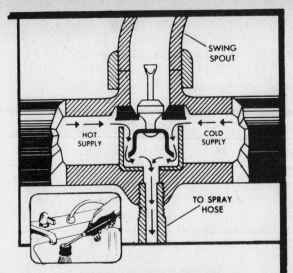

Figure 3: WATER FLOWS TO SPRAY
Spray thumb lever is pressed down to "on" position: Because spray and hose are now "open," water pressure against C "bleeds off" through the hose. This leaves pressure against surfaces B and A. Because B is larger than A, the downward force is greater. Thus the piston unit snaps down, closing the opening to the spout. Water then flows into the hose to the spray.

Automatic Spray Service Center

Leaks around spray guide sometimes happen with old-style flat guides. The new cup-shaped guide does a better job of keeping spray upright and prevents drips. They are sold for about 80 cents.

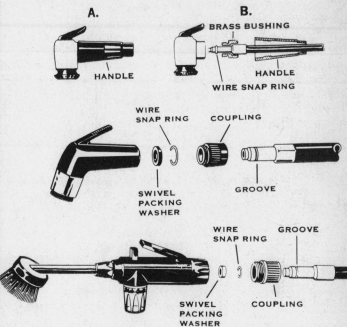

reassemble it. Any Dish-Quik can be mailed to the Automatic Spray Service Center for repair. Repair and replacement of all necessary parts, except brush and hose, is made for $2. A new brush is $1.

It is necessary to cap the hose when mailing Dish-Quik to the Center for repair, so that the faucet can be used. A cap-type pencil eraser, slipped over the spray-end of the hose and taped, is the easiest way. It is best not to kink the hose. This might cause a break which may mean replacing the entire hoseline.

Either a Dish-Quik or Rinse-Quik can be used as a replacement on any model spray. Sketches show how spray heads are attached to hoses. The wire snap ring is pried off to remove coupling.

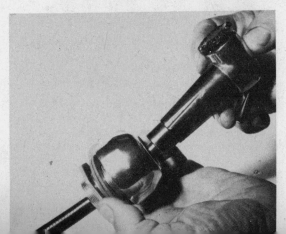

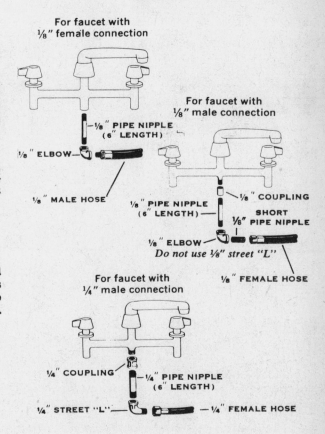

For best installation, never attach the hose directly to body of the faucet fitting. Hose is easier to raise and lower and avoids pipes better if you attach it is as shown in sketches.

toilets

THERE'S NO NEED to put up with toilets that won't stop running unless you jiggle the handle, or which stop flushing unless you keep the handle down constantly. These and other toilet repairs are easy to make. Replacement parts are available at hardware stores, dime stores, or by mail order.

Tank Fills, but Water Still Runs. Inside your toilet tank is a large, floating ball. This tank float controls an intake valve or ballcock. When the float rises, it shuts the valve off. When the toilet is flushed, it drops and turns the valve on. The valve, in its mechanics, is very much like an ordinary faucet. It even has a washer. If the water still runs after the tank fills, it is because the valve is not fully closed, or else leaks.

Raise the tank float gently by taking hold of its arm or rod. Does the water shut off? If it does, it indicates the float hasn't been riding high enough. Unscrew it from its rod and shake it. If you hear the slosh of water inside, get a new float. A leaky or waterlogged float doesn't have enough bouyancy to turn off the intake valve.

If a shutoff valve is handy, you can turn off the toilet water supply there. A quick and easy way to shut it off is by hooking the float in an up position. A clotheshanger does the job fine.

If the float ball has no leak, but still doesn't ride high enough on the water to shut off the inlet valve, adjust its float level by bending its rod. Bend float down for quicker shutoff.

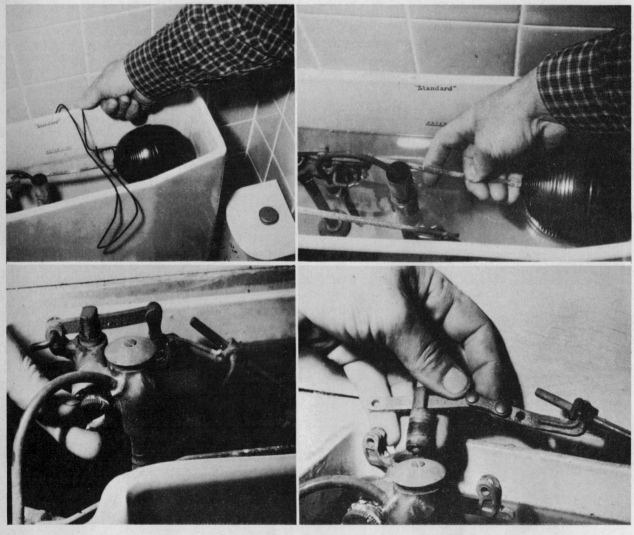

A slow-filling toilet is not only a nuisance, it is also likely to be very noisy, for small inlet opening usually means a whistling valve. Adjust valve for faster flow. Some have a setscrew.

If you raise the float rod all the way and the inlet valve doesn't shut off, it's defective. Take it apart for inspection by carefully removing the two screws that hold the assembly together.

Some of the new plastic floats are immune to leaks. If the float is good, but the tank fills too high, bend the float rod so that the float will be about ½ inch lower.

Don't bend the rod by grasping the ball. You may cause the ball to begin leaking. Bend the rod at its center, holding on to the rod only. If the rod is bent up, the level to which the tank fills will be higher. The tank should fill to about 1 inch from the top of the overflow pipe.

If raising the tank float doesn't shut off the water, the inlet valve needs attention. Shut off the toilet water supply, then flush its tank. Carefully remove the two thumb-

A flush ball that's not operating properly will cause toilet to run without the tank filling, or won't permit flushing unless you keep the handle down constantly. Inspect the ball and seat for wear.

A large size force cup will cure most toilet bowl stoppages. Fill bowl to brim, then work cup up and down forcibly. When water runs out, you know you have worked clogging matter free.

screws that join the float rod to the valve assembly. You can now lift out the valve stem. The valve's washer may be held on the end of the stem by a brass screw, a threaded brass ring cap, or it may merely snap in. Replace badly corroded screws or ring. Most better grade inlet valves have a lifetime nylon seat and so won't require any attention.

If the valve is badly deteriorated, you may want to replace it with a new one. You can get a replacement for as little as $3. A new type, for which many advantages are claimed, is the Hydo tank valve, made of nylon. It cuts refill time almost in half for it's constructed to open at full flow and continue full flow until shutoff, and it shuts off with the water pressure, not against it. The continuing rapid flow eliminates valve whine, which usually starts as the valve cuts down the water flow. The unit, made by Hydo Valve Corporation, Austin 5, Texas, is available to fit any tank.

Water Runs, but Tank Doesn't Fill. If you have to jiggle the handle a few times before the tank starts filling, the trouble is in the rod system which raises and lowers the flush ball.

Fasten the float in raised position by putting a stick under it, or supporting it with a bent clotheshanger, then flush the toilet. With the tank empty, study the action of the lift wire and flush ball as you trip the toilet handle. Is the guide adjusted so that it lowers the ball directly on its seat? You can loosen the setscrew on the guide and adjust it as required so that it will. Since you may not be able to get a screwdriver in position for turning the setscrew, use the edge of a table knife. If the lift wire is badly bent or corroded, unscrew it from the ball and replace it. Float rods and lift wires come in standard sizes. If you need a new guide, take it along to the store for matching.

If jiggling won't properly seat the ball and stop the running, inspect the ball and its seat. Clean the seat with steel wool or emery cloth. If the ball is in bad shape, replace it. For about $2.50 you can get a device which eliminates the problem of guides and improperly seating balls. It consists of a guide tube which makes it impossible for the ball not to seat properly. Sears sells them.

If Flush Handle Must be Held Down. If you have to hold the handle down to keep the toilet flushing, it's because the flush ball isn't being lifted high enough when you trip the handle. The water rushing through the flush ball's seat pulls the ball back on the seat too soon.

Most toilet bowl stoppages are right at the top bend of the trap and can be cleaned with an ordinary auger. In using auger, exercise extreme care not to scratch bowl or let tool strike it.

The sure cure for sweating toilet tanks is a tempering valve. Valve mixes a small amount of hot water with the cold water entering tank. It is very cold water in tank that causes sweating.

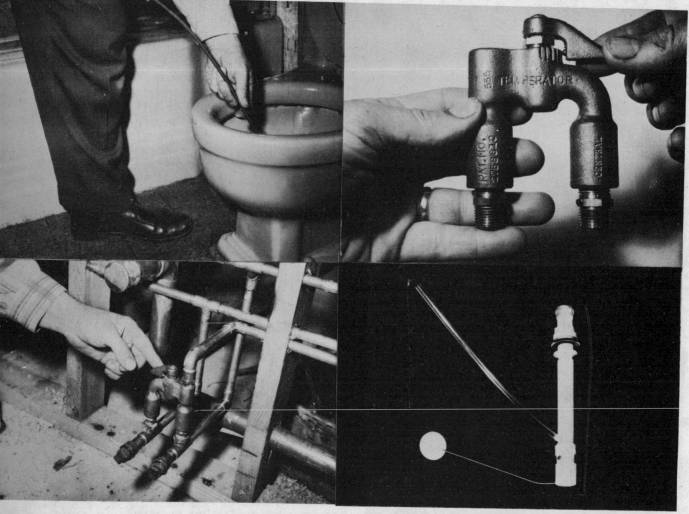

Two lower inlets of valve are attached to hot and cold water lines. Upper outlet line goes to toilet. Adjustment at top of valve regulates the amount of hot water. Very little is needed.

New Hydo ballcock valve can be used to replace defective inlet valve and float assembly. Valve is made of nylon, reduces average fill time almost in half. Note small diameter of the float.

Cure the trouble by shortening the linkage wire that raises the ball.

Overflow Tube Disorders. The overflow tube is for carrying away the water if the inlet valve should fail to shut off. Sometimes the overflow tube rots out at its base. This will allow a constant dribble of water down into the toilet bowl. Either replace the tube, or get an entire new assembly.

The slender curved tube that runs from the inlet valve to the overflow tube is known as the refill tube. Its purpose is to replenish the water in the toilet bowl and trap while the tank is refilling.

Slow, or Noisy Filling. There is an adjustment on the inlet valve to regulate the water flow into the tank. If it is turned down too far, the tank will fill slower than desired and is likely to gurgle and whistle. On some toilets you must first loosen a setscrew before you can change the flow adjustment.

The water entering the tank goes through a tube which empties near the bottom of the tank. It is known as the hush tube. If the hush tube breaks off, entering water will fall noisily into the tank. If the toilet filling sounds like Niagara, the hush tube is gone.

Cure: replace the tube.

Leaks Under the Toilet Tank. The two openings in the bottom of the toilet tank are for the water supply and for the toilet flush elbow. There are nuts and gaskets at these two points. Sometimes a leak at

If the works in your tank are in bad shape, you can get an entirely new tank trim. This new type, adaptable to most existing fixtures, was designed to eliminate all common tank problems.

You can get a special auger, designed for toilet traps, for under $2. The type shown has a wooden handle, rubber guard, and is 5½ feet long, ample for reaching all the way through toilet trap.

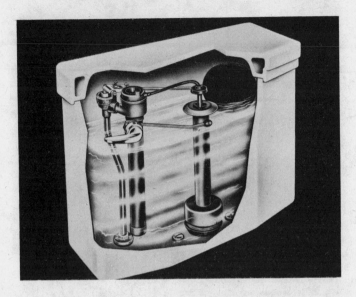

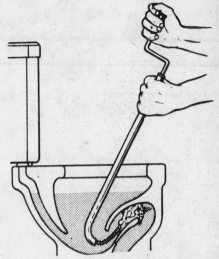

Sears, Roebuck & Co.

either of these places can be stopped by tightening the nut. At other times, the gasket must be replaced.

If there is a leak at the floor line, it may indicate an improper seal between the toilet bowl and the closet bend. This seal is usually made with one or two wax gaskets. Correcting the trouble involves taking up the toilet and putting in new gaskets.

Sweating Toilet Tank. The tank sweats because it has cold water in it. When hot, humid air strikes the tank, moisture condenses on it, just as it condenses on a cold glass of water.

There are several ways to go about curing a sweating toilet tank other than putting a tray under the tank with a tube leading to the bowl. One is to install an insulating liner in the toilet. It helps keep the cold water from chilling the tank. Another is to put an uninsulated tempering tank in the basement or other warm spot. This tank allows the water to warm up before it gets to the toilet.

The best way is to install a Temperator. This is a valve which adds a little warm water to the cold water entering the tank. By raising the temperature of the tank water, the tank itself is warmer and condensation is eliminated. You can regulate the amount of hot water mixing with the cold to just the necessary amount. Very little hot water is needed. Don't use too much. In winter, when condensation isn't likely to be a problem, you can shut off the Temperator altogether.

Clogged Toilet Bowl. If a toilet becomes clogged so that it drains very slowly or not at all, something has been thrown in it that doesn't belong there. Any paper, other than toilet tissue, is likely to clog the bowl.

First, try to remove any foreign material which is obviously the cause of the clogging. If flushing won't wash the obstruction through, wait a while. Paper, soap, or other clogging matter may soften enough in half an hour or so to permit washing down.

A large rubber force cup, or plumber's helper, will quickly clear most clog-ups. If the stoppage is more serious than this, you can try a toilet auger. This is not like ordinary snakes or augers. It is a stiff wire which slides in a steel tube, and is especially designed to go through toilet traps. It usually has a rubber guard and a crank.

Fill the bowl with water to the rim. Water helps clear out the trap and also will tell you when you have unplugged the stoppage, for it will run out. Draw the end of the snake up to the curved end of the auger and put the curved end in the curved trap of the bowl. Force the snake through by turning the steel crank. Always turn it in the same direction.

If water runs out of the bowl and the toilet flushes, it may still not be entirely clear. As a test, put several feet of toilet paper in the bowl and when it's wet, try to flush it down. The idea is, if a bottle or comb is caught in the trap it may let water through but won't permit solids to pass.

If the toilet doesn't flush the paper, use the auger again. Sometimes objects wedged in the trap can be freed only by removing the toilet and turning it upside down. •

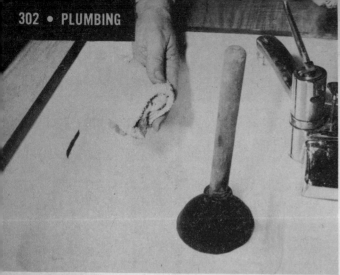

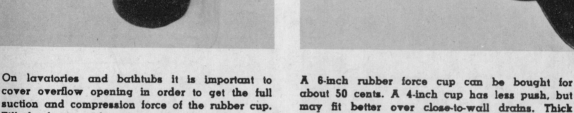

On lavatories and bathtubs it is important to cover overflow opening in order to get the full suction and compression force of the rubber cup. Fill the basin with water well above cup level.

A 6-inch rubber force cup can be bought for about 50 cents. A 4-inch cup has less push, but may fit better over close-to-wall drains. Thick coat of petroleum jelly is sometimes helpful.

Some pop-up bathroom drains can be removed by getting a hold around their rim and lifting up while jiggling the drain control handle. Matted hair is often the number one cause of clogging.

Plug type drain is removed for cleaning by a quarter turn and lifting out. Older plunger type requires loosening nut under bowl at back. Pull out rod attached to plunger and lift the stopper.

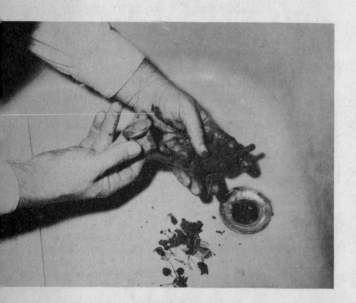

clogged drains

NOT ALL CLOGGING IS SIMPLE. An understanding of the right way to go about attacking a clog-up can save you time, effort, and sometimes considerable grief. The tools required, in any case, are few and inexpensive. For less than $5 you can get both a serviceable drain auger and a force cup, and they'll quickly pay for themselves.

If you are confronted with a stoppage and don't have an auger handy, you can often make a length of BX cable serve, or even a wire hook made from a clothes hanger.

First, Check Extent of Clogging. Most trouble in kitchen sink drains is caused by hardened grease and fat which catches coffee grounds and eventually builds up to a point where the drain is blocked. In lavatory basins, clogging is usually caused by entangled hair, lint, and sludge. Blocking is particularly likely if there is a 90-degree bend in the drain line.

When a fixture clogs, always check to see if any other fixtures are clogged or backing up. If the kitchen sink is the trouble spot, before taking action, run water in the bathtub and lavatory to see if they are clear.

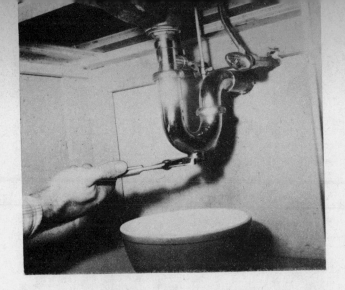

When use of a force cup doesn't clear the drain, open up its trap. Use smooth-jawed pliers, such as Channel-lock, to avoid damaging chrome finish. Provide basin under trap to catch waste water.

If trap has no cleanout plug, you can remove the entire trap by loosening the slip nuts on either end of it. If the clogging material is not in trap, use snake to get back into branch drain.

When pouring chemicals into a drain, do it through funnel to avoid possible damage to porcelain. In replacing a trap, make sure its rubber washers are still firm and tight.

Sears, Roebuck & Co.

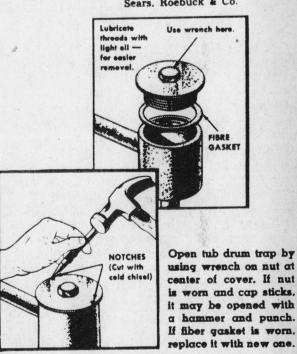

Open tub drum trap by using wrench on nut at center of cover. If nut is worn and cap sticks, it may be opened with a hammer and punch. If fiber gasket is worn. replace it with new one.

Check particularly on fixtures in the basement. Avoid flushing toilets. If the main drain is clogged, you don't want toilets overflowing on the floor.

If other fixtures are clear, you can assume that the stoppage is only local. In kitchen sink, remove the basket strainer. In lavatory, take out the pop-up drain. Most of these can be removed by simply turning counterclockwise and lifting. On a few, it is necessary to disconnect a ball joint and a lever. Removal of the matted debris from the pop-up stopper is often all that is needed to open a basin drain.

Next, Use the Rubber Force Cup. In lavatories and tubs, hold a wet rag over the overflow so you get full suction and com-

pression as you work the cup up and down. The cup works better, in some cases, with a thick coat of petroleum jelly on its bottom edge.

Be patient. It may take a hundred or more pumps to clear the drain. If you achieve sluggish drainage, you can often use a chemical cleaner to finish the job of completely clearing the drain. These cleaners are usually a mixture of lye and aluminum chips. The lye acts on grease and insoluble soap curds. When water meets the mixture there is a violent reaction, generating heat and gas. The churning and heat may loosen the clogging material.

Never use a plunger after you've used chemicals. If the chemicals aren't success-

When drain is frozen, thaw it by first removing all possible water, then pouring pound of salt into trap. Follow with boiling water. Pouring boiling water down drain also dissolves grease.

When all house drainage is blocked, the place to go to work is at cleanout plug where house drain exists through foundation wall. If exterior line is clear, then check cleanouts on interior drains.

ful in opening the drain and you call a plumber, be sure to tell him you've used chemicals so he can take necessary precautions.

Opening the Trap. It's usually wise to open the trap before resorting to chemicals. If you have to open the trap after using chemicals, wear rubber gloves and don't get anything on your skin or in your eyes.

Some traps have a cleanout plug at the bottom. Take it out. Have a pail or bowl handy to catch the waste water. If there is no plug, remove the trap by unscrewing the two slip joint nuts that hold it in place. You may now be able to clear the obstruction from the trap with a wire hook made from a clothes hanger. After you've done this, you can scour the trap clean with a bottle brush.

If the stoppage is not in the trap, but in the branch drain line beyond, you'll have to use an auger, often called a snake. The snake can be run through the trap cleanout plug and without removing the trap, but it's somewhat more difficult. Run a foot of the snake into the trap, slide the snake handle up to the trap, tighten it there and turn it. Keep advancing the snake as circumstances permit.

Always turn the snake in one direction. If it catches into an obstruction, you won't lose it by reversing. Once you've pierced the obstruction, replace the trap plug and pour boiling hot water down the drain. The hot water is to dissolve grease. If you have no luck, go back to reaming with the auger.

Second floor fixtures usually have short horizontal runs to the stack, and so are generally easier to clear than fixtures on the first floor. On the first floor, you may be able to go to the basement and remove a cleanout plug on the line and work from there. Bathtubs may have a drum trap with an access cover in the floor. Sometimes the drum's cap is covered by a metal plate which must be removed. In other cases, a drum trap may have access from underneath, in the basement.

On floor and storm drains, scoop out accumulated dirt with an old spoon taped to a stick. Where stoppages are caused by the accumulation of sand, stick a hose in the drain and flush the sand out. You can pack rags around the hose where it enters the drain to keep water going where it should.

The chapter on toilet repairs deals with stoppages of that fixture.

Drains That Back Up. If you have a gurgle on first floor fixtures and water backs up from the second floor, the cause may be a clogged vent. Often wasps build their nests in a vent, restricting its opening, or waste material is forced up into a vent by use of rubber plungers and it hardens there, blocking the opening. Spray wasps to kill them, then clear the vent by putting a snake down it from the roof.

Excess suds can clog drains and bubble out in fixtures far from their point of origin. Wash water containing high-sudsing detergents or soaps flow down drains with a spiral motion which helps further to whip

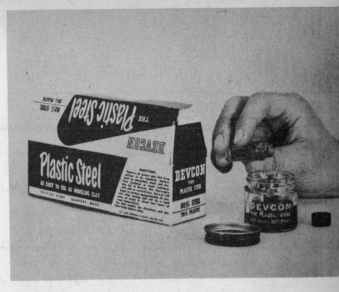

Cleanout by cleanout, work backward on house drain line. Where you discover blockage, use a snake. If plug is frozen fast, difficult to loosen, applying torch flame directly may help free it.

A frozen drain pipe may have split in places. It isn't necessary, in most cases, to replace the pipe. It can be patched effectively with plastic steel. Use according to the directions.

up suds. So much suds can be formed, they'll be forced out of all open drains along the way. Suds can climb several stories above their point of origin. This is often the case in apartment buildings and multifamily houses.

Always choose low-sudsing or controlled suds detergents for your wash. Suds in synthetic detergents are no indication whatever of their cleaning power. You are better off without suds.

Frozen Drains. If water backs up into a sink or washbasin because of a frozen drain, remove the trap to get out as much water as you can. Replace the trap, pour a pound of salt down the drain, followed by boiling water. Give it a half hour to thaw.

Drainpipe cleaner poured down the drain also generates considerable heat and is frequently effective in thawing the line.

When thawing drain pipes by the direct application of heat, start at the lower end of the pipe so the water can run off as the ice melts.

In any case of freezing, always be prepared for the possibility that a pipe may have been ruptured and that it will begin to leak upon thawing. Inspect lines for such leaks.

Clogged Main Drain. If all fixture drains are clogged, the trouble lies in the main house drain. First, check the drain where it leads through the foundation wall to the outside. You will find a removable plug at this point. Open it and check if the line beyond is clear. If it is, the trouble may be in

the house trap, if there is one. Look for it.

The trap will be in the soil line near where it leaves the house. Open the trap and poke around in it with a stick. If you find an obstruction, put on a rubber glove, reach in and take it out. At other cleanout plugs along the drain, you will find good places for inserting a flexible snake.

If a plug on the drain won't come loose, even after playing a torch on it, it may be necessary to chisel it out. If it has a thin brass shell, you can chisel a hole in the middle and pry off the top, then fold the rest of the threaded ring inward. When you replace it with a new brass plug, coat the threads with vaseline for a good seal.

If there is blocking between the house and the street sewer, or septic tank, it is usually because of roots. You'll need a plumber who has the special tools needed for the job of rodding them out. If you empty into a city sewer, you can discourage roots by occasionally flushing a pound of blue vitriol (copper sulfate) down the toilet. Other commercial chemicals are packaged for the purpose. Some are designed to kill roots in sewers and are said to be harmless to trees and shrubs. Don't use them if you have a septic tank.

The other possible reason for failure of a sewer is that it has collapsed. It doesn't always take a heavy truck riding across the line to achieve this dire result. Weight of soil alone may do it to some pipes.

Replace the line with cast iron. It won't be subject to this failing. •

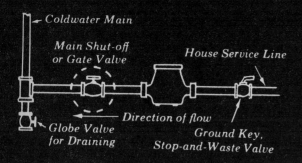

Coldwater Main

Main Shut-off
or Gate Valve

House Service Line

Direction of flow

Globe Valve
for Draining

Ground Key,
Stop-and-Waste Valve

If there is an emergency requiring that water be shut off in a hurry, it is often quicker to shut off the entire house than to search for a branch valve. Main shutoff may look like this diagram.

pipes and tanks

A BURST PIPE OR TANK is an emergency calling for quick action. Sweating, leaky, noisy, half-clogged pipes and tanks, on the other hand, are nuisances that we are likely to put up with because we don't know exactly what's best to do about them. Knowing what to do is half the battle in correcting their faults.

Pipe Leaks and Breaks. Shutting off the water at the nearest valve will stop the flow, but, of course, you don't want to leave the water off for long. Even if the leak seems like a big one, you may be able to stop it by merely wrapping it with tape. It may still leak slightly, but you can often hold it that way until more permanent repairs can be arranged. Wrap larger sections with rubber or plastic sheeting held with hose clamps. It's a good idea to have a few such clamps on hand for emergencies.

One-inch automobile hose fits ¾-inch pipe. Three-quarter inch garden hose usually fits ½-inch pipe. You can use either of these for effective temporary repairs. At the hardware store you can buy inexpensive metal sections to screw over pipe ruptures and which can serve indefinitely. Similarly, you can stop a leak in a small pipe by using a section cut from a scrap of larger pipe. Use a piece of inner tubing or other rubber as a gasket under the larger pipe section and fasten the device in place with hose clamps.

If a burst pipe is inside a wall or under a floor, trace it to its nearest accessible fitting on either side. It may be necessary or advisable to open a section of the wall or floor. To make a permanent repair, cut the pipe off near the fittings. If it's a cold water line, you can use plastic pipe to make the new connections. Otherwise, use a new length of flexible copper tubing, bypassing the leaking section. The old section can be left in place.

If a copper pipe springs a leak at a joint,

you can't resolder the joint as long as there's water in the pipe. The water forms steam and you can't get the pipe temperature up high enough to make the solder stick. However, you may be able to tap the existing solder around the joint back into the crack with a hammer and small chisel and stop the leak. It's an old plumber's trick.

To stop leaks in compression type fittings, or in traps, take a few turns of string around the tubing and tighten the nut on it. The string will expand when it gets wet and seal the leak.

Where a pipe section has been severely damaged or is in an advanced stage of deterioration, the only thing to do is replace it, as detailed later in this section.

Tank Leaks. Once a tank springs a leak, it almost always means it's badly corroded inside, that its metal is worn thin, and that a new tank is needed. However, temporary repairs can often extend its life by many months.

To repair a hot water tank, you may have to remove its insulation. If a very small hole is causing the trouble, you may be able to plug it with a round toothpick, or an ordinary sheet-metal screw and rubber washer.

To repair more sizable leaks, it is necessary to drain the tank to below the level of the leak. First, shut off the heat. A hot water tank can be drained by opening the cock at its bottom. You can attach a rubber hose to the cock for leading the water away, but don't run very hot water through plastic garden hose or you'll ruin it. If your hose is of plastic, let the tank stand until it cools a little. Opening hot water faucets on your lowest fixtures may also help drain the tank.

A variety of plug screws are available to stop leaks. You can also use an ordinary tapered lead expansion plug for the purpose if you enlarge the leak enough to ac-

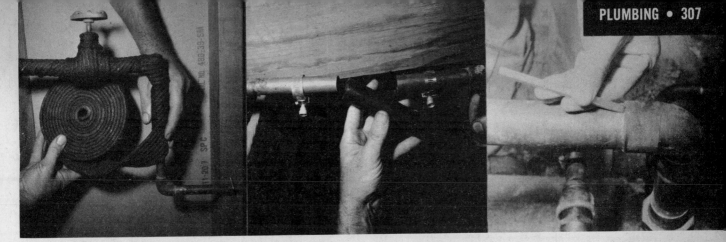

New insulating tape for stopping drip from cold water pipes comes in rolls, is wound spirally. The tape sticks of itself and short pieces of it are easily formed around valves and fittings. You can buy inexpensive pipe sleeves for clamping onto pipe ruptures and stopping leaks. Often you can make a semipermanent repair with a short section of automobile, or other hose, and clamps. If a pipe leaks at a joint, you can sometimes stop it by tightening the fitting slightly. Leaky solder joints can often be mended by pounding the solder back into the joint crack. Heating joint slightly will help this procedure.

If a length of cold water pipe must be removed, you can replace it with plastic pipe. Attach plastic pipe with adapters to the nearest fittings. Plastic pipe is conveniently flexible. Flexible copper tubing makes an easy replacement for a ruptured, leaky, clogged, or otherwise deteriorated steel pipe. Screw an adapter into the nearest fitting, solder the tubing to it. A leak in a boiler usually means it is worn out, but you can often extend its life by many months with a boiler plug, or a self-tapping screw (below).

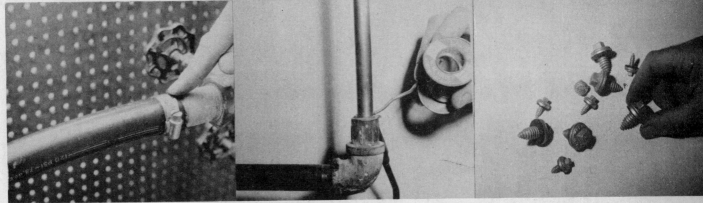

Orangeburg Mfg. Co.   Parker-Kalon

commodate the plug. Putting a screw into the plug expands it to a tight, sealing fit. Boiler plugs usually consist of a square-headed sheet metal screw and washers and are turned in with a wrench.

Another type of tank-leak plug uses a toggle or wing bolt with rubber and metal washers. It is tightened with a screw-driver, grips the inside of the tank with its spread wings.

Clogged and Corroded Pipes. A temporary drop in water pressure is usually due to overtaxing of water supply facilities by heavy usage close to your home. If low pressure is chronic, the most common cause is clogging of supply pipes by scale and corrosion. If the hot water pressure is lower than cold water pressure, you can be almost sure pipe clogging is responsible, for the warmer the water, the more rapidly scale and corrosion form. A rise of 40 de-

grees in water temperature doubles the rate of clogging.

Scale is predominantly a problem in galvanized iron pipe, seldom causes any trouble in brass or copper, and, of course, the latter materials never rust. Scale is caused by hard water, can largely be prevented by use of a home water softener. Scale forms faster whenever there is resistance to flow, as at fittings. Sometimes by replacing only the fittings, the flow can be improved considerably.

In cases where low water pressure is not caused by clogged pipes, but by lack of pressure in the city mains, you can get relief by installing a pump and pressure tank to boost your pressure to the desired level. This equipment is the same as that used in pumping water from a shallow well.

In heating coils, scale acts as insulation.

There are many kinds of materials available for stopping cracks and leaks. A blowtorch is a fast way of thawing a frozen pipe, but it is hazardous. Take every necessary precaution for fire safety. You can avoid freezeups by using frostproof hosecocks like these (top right), available in stores in many sizes.

Plastic coating, below, left, insulates pipes and tanks and stops them from sweating. It is best to use nonrigid pipe fasteners or cushion rigid fasteners with rubber padding as shown in center photo, below. Antihammer chambers for water pipes are usually concealed inside the walls, but you can buy commercial devices to serve the purpose which can be installed outside walls, like one shown directly below.

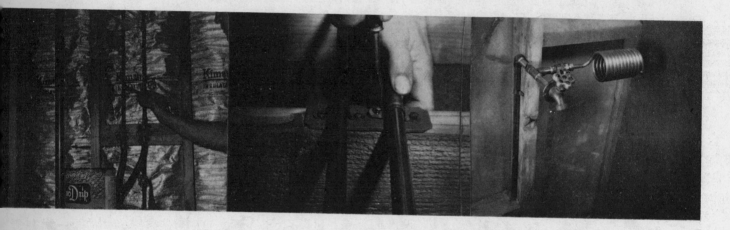

Scale in limestone-caked coils or pipe can be softened and removed with a solution of 1 part muriatic acid in 4 parts water. Let it stand in the coil 4 to 6 hours, then flush thoroughly. Repeat the treatment if necessary.

Frozen Water Pipes. Start thawing at an open faucet so that steam which is generated can escape. It is safer to use low heat, such as supplied by a hair dryer or heat lamp than a propane torch. A heat lamp can be used to warm a pipe concealed inside a wall. Keep it far enough back from the wall so it won't scorch it. Use an aluminum reflector to concentrate the heat.

You can wire an electric soldering iron to a frozen pipe, moving it along to a new point as the pipe thaws. The heat will travel a considerable distance along the pipe. An electric iron can be used in similar fashion. Or you can buy an inexpensive electric heating cable, wrap it around the pipe, to do the job. Don't ex-

pect immediate results. If the entire area through which the pipe passes can be heated, results may be rapid. Otherwise it may take hours to melt the ice. Be prepared for leaks when it does.

If convenient, wrap bath towels around the frozen pipe and pour boiling water on them. Continue the water in a dribble so as to sustain the temperature.

Thawing of frozen pipes can be done electrically with a welding generator or an appropriate type of step-down transformer. The electrical leads are connected at two places on the pipe with the frozen section between. The resistance of the pipe to the current heats the pipe and melts the ice. Call a welding shop, or a plumber with electrical thawing equipment, to have it done.

Sweating Pipes and Tanks. Water pipes and tanks sweat because they contain water that's much colder than the surrounding air temperatures. Stop sweating by insulating. The best time to apply pipe

NOISES

Block fastened between elbow and wall prevents "water hammer"

Shelf bracket makes effective pipe support.

Use of pipe straps to support pipe at bend.

Arrows indicate direction of flow.

Another type of water-hammer silencer looks like this (above, left). It can be installed up, down, or sideways. One advantage of commercial-type silencers is that they never become waterlogged. Various ways to support the pipes and prevent water hammer are shown in detail in the photo above, right.

Gerber Plumbing Fixtures Corp.

Always work from a fitting when replacing a defective pipe section. If the fitting is a union, so much the better, for otherwise you'd need to supply a union in making the assembly, see photo.

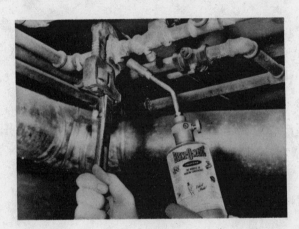

insulation is when humidity is low and pipes are dry, as in winter. One of the best insulators for cold water pipes is a tape. It comes in rolls and is of a material containing ground-up cork particles. Known as NoDrip Tape, it can be wound spirally around pipes, is easily formed to go around valves and various pipe fittings. It sticks by itself easily and requires no adhesive.

The same product is also available as a thick, plastic coating, also containing cork granules. This liquid NoDrip can be brushed or troweled on pipes or water tanks, and by several applications be built up into a thick, protective layer.

You can also cover cold water pipes with asbestos stripping, available in rolls. It is applied with special paste, but you can also use ordinary wallpaper paste for the purpose. Asbestos, too, is usually applied spirally, though you can tear off short lengths and apply it lengthwise. By soaking strips with paste, you can mold the material to conform to elbows, tees, and other fittings. The material shrinks as it dries, makes a tight fit.

Pipe Noises. When pipes clog up, restricting the size of their opening, the speed of the water going through them is increased. Water passing through the narrow openings whistles and hums. The only cure is to replace the pipe.

New pipe can be noisy, too, especially if it is of smaller size than needed to handle the flow of water demanded of it. The moral: In new construction, don't use ½-inch pipe when ¾-inch is required. If you are stuck with pipes that are too small you can muffle their sound by wrapping them in several layers of hair felt, or equivalent sound-absorbing insulation.

Use strap-type pipe hangers for fastening pipes to joists. They allow pipe movement, and don't conduct vibration as readily as straps. On concrete walls, attach pipes to wood blocks.

The most common type of pipe noise is caused by water hammer. If there are no air chambers on the lines, you can get manufactured devices which don't require opening up walls for installation. If you have air chambers and are afflicted with water hammer, the chambers are probably waterlogged and require draining.

Waterlogging isn't unusual. Water under pressure gradually absorbs the air in the chambers. If the chamber is above faucet level, shut off the water supply and open the faucets. This will usually drain out the chambers, but sometimes it is necessary to take the caps off the top of the chamber pipes to insure draining, especially if the pipes are ½ inch or less in diameter. For that reason, in new plumbing, it's always wise to make the chamber one size larger than your original supply pipe. •

American Standard

Twin Ledgelyn lavatories in a custom countertop doubles convenience in this modern bath with contour tub and shower head. Off-the-floor Glenwall toilet permits wall-to-wall carpeting, easy cleaning.

Planning the Bathroom

Careful and thoughtful design will help ease bathroom traffic congestion.

A BATHROOM can be many things to many people. This depends on: just what you want the bathroom to be able to do; how many people it should accommodate during the morning rush-hour; how elegant you want it to be; how basically utilitarian during the evening constant-use hours; how easy and helpful for visitors; how easy to keep clean and sparkling.

Some people tend to look on the bathroom as simply an outhouse with plumbing and a shower added. To our way of think-ing, this approach should have gone out with the Dark Ages. Others feel the bathroom should be strictly utilitarian and austere. That's fine if you like a spartan existence, but it does seem a little foolish to spend a lot of time, money and effort to modernize a bathroom and then to leave it as a cold, barren room simply for the want of a few choice finishing touches. Then there's the ultra-elegant school of thought that considers the bathroom as a logical outgrowth of the sumptuous baths of ancient Rome. To them we doff our hats in admiration, for providing the elegant movie sets for those much-publicized bubble-bath scenes featuring voluptuous cinematic sex-goddesses.

The ultimate choice for the middle-of-the-road homeowner has to be somewhere between this last extreme and the strictly utilitarian approach. The bathroom should be a pleasant, possibly beautiful room, but not necessarily over-elegant. It should be a joy and a pleasure to use. It should not be beset with such problems as lack of storage space, poor lighting and ventilation, and fixtures that are inconvenient to use. It should be "human-engineered" as much as feasible—electric outlets should be convenient to shaving mirrors and should be "live" all the time, whether the lights are on or not; there should be grab bars for getting into and out of the bathtub; people should not have to be contortionists to reach the toilet tissue.

The strictly utilitarian bathroom has its place, too. This could be a second, half-size bath with a stall shower instead of a tub; it could be the toilet and tiny wash basin squeezed into that converted closet under the first-floor stairs or behind the kitchen. Both the opulent and the utilitarian baths have their place in today's home, but that doesn't mean you have to ignore pleasant decorative touches in the smaller ones.

One of the first things to consider in planning this all-important room, is how many people will be using it and when. Obviously, if a single bathroom is to service three people rushing to get ready for work or school all at the same time, the layout and design will need special treatment. Such a situation may also call for a second small unit in the bedroom area.

There is certainly no reason why at least the main bathroom can not have a luxurious appearance, as long as it provides all the basic functions that one normally expects of a bathroom. The degree of luxury depends on several things: first, the amount of space available; next, the amount of money you are willing to spend on decorating; and most important of all, your own ingenuity and decorating ability.

If we start with a large-size room and a medium-size family (two children or more), one thing becomes apparent immediately—a single washbasin will not be enough. It's fairly common practice today, space permitting, to build two lavatory basins into a single countertop or king-size vanity, with plenty of elbow room separating the two. This can be done in a spartan modern fashion, or it can use the elegance of specially styled vanity enclosures either connected or separated.

Next, consider the location for the other major fixtures in the bathroom; the bathtub-shower combination and the toilet. In the truly busy bathroom, these three major functional items should be completely separated into self-contained rooms, each

Safety is an important built-in design feature here, with several grab bars in the bathtub area, and a low-silhouette sunken tub to make stepping in and out of the tub as easy and as safe as possible.
American Standard

with their own door. This way the room can function as three separate bathrooms in one without anyone getting in anyone else's way and without offending anyone's modesty or need for privacy.

If you have the space for a second bathroom in the main bedroom area, by all means add one. This will give you much more latitude to work with the main one. Depending on the style that you ultimately select, a bathroom can look like an elegant lady-in-waiting's boudoir, or again like a relatively bare, purely functional room. It's the highly decorated bathroom that's especially intriguing and it can offer an excellent workout for milady's imagination.

Let's start with the bathtub, since this is the largest single item to be installed. We immediately have a problem—should the shower enclosure be made with hanging curtains, or with sliding doors? Both methods have a great deal to commend them. The curtains provide an opportunity to change color schemes or patterns within the bathroom periodically, or to reflect seasonal changes. They also can be re-

moved very easily for washing and provide maximum accessibility to the tub for routine cleaning.

The sliding doors are more practical from a safety standpoint, and insure that no water will leak out of the tub onto the floor during the shower. Glass doors are easier to clean in some respects, and more difficult in others. They are definitely of high nuisance value when cleaning the bathtub unless they are entirely removed each time—something we can hardly expect the lady of the house to do. It's not too difficult to guess which method the missus will ultimately favor, since after all she is the one who has to keep the place clean. It does seem to be a truism that men favor the glass door stall-type shower in a tub. Whichever one you choose, it must be coordinated with the rest of the bathroom layout and motif.

The second item is the washbasin, or more properly the lavatory. Whether you install a single or a dual basin, it's a good idea to enclose it with some kind of a cabinet or vanity. A bare minimum type

American Cyanamid Co.

Acrylite sheet plastic is used for skylight as well as for decorative motif on the sliding tub-shower door and room divider. A space-saving idea here, since second half of the sliding doors on tub is stationary, is the placement of the custom-built twin lavatory counter.

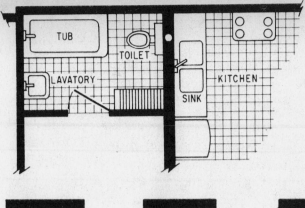

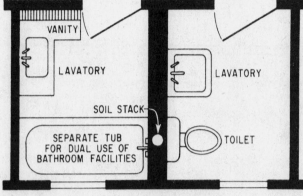

cabinet can be constructed of plywood and aluminum corner channels and covered over with a suitable veneer. More elaborate cabinets can be purchased ready-made along with a marble surface and an elegantly designed sink. These are available from Sears, Roebuck, American Standard, and other plumbing supply houses in a variety of patterns, colors and sizes.

Bear in mind that there are two distinct classes of basins: one is specifically designed for building into a countertop type vanity; the other is designed for an open bottom with a supporting pedestal or just plain, ugly, exposed plumbing. This latter type of basin cannot be built into a countertop vanity later on. It's just not made that way.

The third major item is the toilet. Unhappily, there is not too much latitude for choice here. A toilet is a toilet, and there's nothing you can do to make it look like anything else. The only real choice is whether to use a tank or a pressure-operated type. This selection is dictated by: available water pressure; type of plumb-

Cannon Mills

Scalloped woodwork sets off this unusual vanity in a bathroom setting that's strictly feminine.

American Standard

Note the separate closed-off room here for the toilet, suiting bath for double duty when needed.

ing; and whether you use city water, or draw water from your own well. Pressure toilets tend to use more water than a tank type, but don't require the sometimes aggravating waiting time between flushes that water closets do. This last feature is especially appreciated when you're getting rid of some messy disposable baby diapers.

The wall space above a toilet is usually wasted, and a little advance planning, such as moving the toilet 9 or 10 inches farther away from the wall, gives you just the right clearance for a floor-to-ceiling built-in wall cabinet. This cabinet can contain several open shelves for towels, soap and knick-knacks and can even sport a few doors with paneling to match the vanity. A side-access door to the cabinet at the toilet level provides space for short-handled brooms, toilet bowl brush, and other necessary items that you'd just as soon keep out of sight.

The ever-present shaving mirror and medicine cabinet have given way in some

Bleak, old-fashioned bathroom cries out for complete overhaul. It has one big factor in its favor—its huge size. New installations will not require any major plumbing changes.

New design uses the same locations for major fixtures, with addition of vanity, recessed medicine chest, storage shelves, a stall shower with overhang to "build in" tub area.

Finished bathroom shows how imaginative planning can reduce plumbing costs while modernizing room.

cases to elaborately designed hanging wall mirrors which can enhance the decorator touch. Naturally, a mirror that does not hide medicine chest storage space must be augmented by adequate cabinet space somewhere else in the bathroom. An ever-present aggravation is the lack of adequate storage space of any kind in most bathrooms, and certainly this is something that should be designed into the overall plan from the very outset.

Be sure to consider adequate lighting for the bath. All too often, antique bathrooms have only a single naked light bulb in a rather dilapidated-looking fixture above the mirror. A pair of parallel fluorescent lights on both sides of the mirror provide plenty of the ideal kind of light for shaving, but may not blend too well with the decorative theme, nor do they give good overall room illumination. Standard fluorescent fixtures in the bathroom have an austere, spartan appearance that is best suited only to the unadorned, ultra-streamlined (and barren) bathroom. The well decorated bathroom will call for some in-

Ideal layout uses interior doors for multi-use.

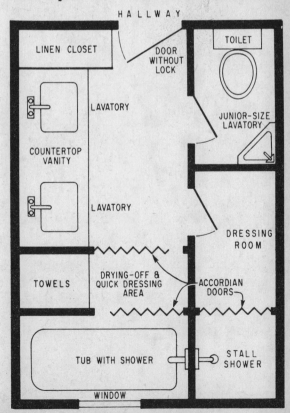

genuity in disguising the fixtures—perhaps recessing them in the wall next to the mirror, or using a mirror/medicine cabinet combination that has the fluorescents built in. If you see no clear-cut way of using fluorescents in your period bathroom design, the answer is a simple, but uneconomical one—incandescent lamps.

Incandescent lamps in appropriate fixtures on both sides of the mirror certainly will provide enough light for shaving and other cosmetic activities. There are many variations on the incandescent theme, including the popular actors' dressing-room type strings of flesh-tinted lamps. This treatment is growing in popularity, and there are many fixtures available for this kind of lighting arrangement. A separate ceiling light of some kind should also be provided, along with two or three wall outlets that remain live even when the lights are turned off. These outlets are important for operating the inevitable bathroom accessories, such as radios, razors and the many rechargeable battery convenience appliances that are so important today. The wall outlet is also a good place to mount a nightlight to guide sleepy-eyed young-

Marlite Div., Masonite

Marble-top vanity and oval-shaped lavatory provide focus for bathroom styling, carried through to classical fixtures and general elegance.

American Standard

Handsome dark panels are dramatically set off by the top-lighted waterproof mural over tub. The well-lighted vanity area boasts large mirror.

sters to the right room during the darkest parts of the evening.

There are accessories of many kinds, styles, shapes and purposes available. If you're planning a period bathroom, then you might well consider some of the gold-plated plumbing fixtures for the bathtub and vanity. Of course, such elegance must be followed through with appropriate lighting fixtures, mirrors, towel racks, soap dishes and other important basic accessories.

There will come the day in your bathroom remodeling when the little woman decides that she wants a wall-to-wall carpet, even though you've spent many tedious hours laying down a very attractive floor tile. Just be sure that the rug fits properly when you cut it, and that it will be easy to remove for machine washing. If you want to dissuade the wife on this carpeting bit, you can always point out that they have a tendency to shrink when they've been washed several times (or let her put it down herself a couple of times).

Also, after a while, corners of the rug will tend to bunch up, especially in the high-traffic area near the door. Soon after, the rug edge will start catching under the door when it's opened, causing wrinkles and bunching in the rug and all sorts of other associated evils. The rubber backing on the rug will start to tear in small spots. The tears will get bigger, and will need resewing each time the rug is laundered. After you've finished with all these arguments, make sure you have a hefty pair of scissors to cut the new rug to proper fit when you install it. •

Howard Miller Clock Co.

Bathroom Remodeling Tips

These short cuts can rejuvenate a bathroom without a major overhaul.

FOR A BATHROOM that's not quite ready for the full treatment, but cries out for certain kinds of improvements, a guiding principle to follow could well be, "it's the little things that count." There are certainly many small improvements that can be made on the surface in an existing bathroom without putting in major new fixtures, new walls, floors and ceilings. This is especially true if the bathroom is not quite ancient enough to require major overhaul, but does need something—perhaps you're not quite sure what.

One surface improvement that has become very popular in recent years is the addition of sliding stall doors to existing bathtubs, converting them into stall-type showers. These doors can be added to just about any bathtub that has a flat rim. Of course you wouldn't want to add it to curved-rim, clawed-foot bathtubs of the kind that date back to the turn of the century, since obviously this is a bathroom that can benefit only from a complete overhaul. But in today's bathrooms, or even those of a decade or so ago, adding the sliding doors both modernizes and makes life a little easier. Installing sliding glass stall doors immediately will eliminate the possibility of the lady of the house decorating with a touch of color in the shower curtains. The best known type doors are made of translucent glass; they provide a sturdy stall wall and have grab and towel bars inside. The one big difficulty with the sliding glass door is that it makes bathtub cleaning at least twice as difficult as it already is, since only a little less than half the bathtub is accessible for cleaning at a time.

Built-in Service Module System can also be wall-mounted. Contains clock, radio, many other items.

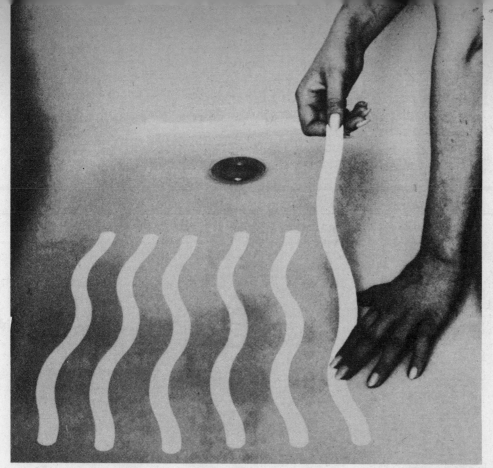

Bath Mate tub and shower strips are nonskid and are applied like tape as shown. Both wavy lines and straight lines are available in four colors.

3M Co. photo

This problem is nicely solved by the use of plastic folding shower doors such as those made by Showerfold Door Corp. These doors require about the same kind of installation as glass doors do, with metal framing on the bathtub rim and opposing walls. But since the folding doors are of much lighter weight than the glass, the hardware is not quite so heavy-duty, and is easier to install. Of course, the doors are also available in a variety of decorator colors, once again giving the lady of the house a chance to exercise her decorative bent. These doors are also made in sizes for stall showers. The top of the door glides in a track on the bottom of a solid plastic extension that can run right up to the ceiling for a completely enclosed compartment—great for steam baths if you like them.

While we are in the bathtub area, one constant source of difficulty, especially in older bathrooms, is the loosening and chipping of the waterproof caulking at the joint between the bathtub and the wall tiles. There are several ways to repair these seams, including the conventional caulking compound in a caulking gun, which unless properly applied and allowed to dry a considerable length of time, will only flake and chip off all over again. One easy method is to use a simple silicone rubber-like caulking compound that comes in an ordinary toothpaste-like tube, made by Gen-

eral Electric. This material never quite dries completely, but always maintains a certain amount of rubbery consistency.

Probably one of the easiest, cheapest and handiest ways of putting on caulking compound is with the Thermogrip glue gun made by the United Shoe Machinery Corp. Plug the gun into a wall outlet, and it will melt and dispense special caulking compound purchased in short, hard sticks. The caulking is quite inexpensive, and it flows freely once the gun has heated up. As soon as it leaves the gun, it starts to cool and harden along the bathtub seams or wherever else it is applied. This is an excellent and easy method of handling perennial caulking problems. While you're at it, the glue gun can be used to mend furniture and just about anything else around the house that can benefit from thermo-setting adhesive.

A safety item for the bathroom made by 3M (the "Scotch" tape people) is a series of adhesive-backed strips of non-skid material for bathtub bottoms. These strips can be laid down very easily by the missus and are definitely a plus safety feature in these slippery and potentially dangerous areas. The little woman can lay down these strips in the bathtub bottom in the space of a couple of minutes, and they'll stay there regardless of cleaning, scrubbing, etc., until you lift them off with a razor blade.

While you're on the safety first aspect of the bathroom, you might want to consider installing one or more grab bars in the bathtub area. These bars can make life a little bit easier and safer for everyone in the family during showers and plain old-fashioned tub baths. The bars can be installed in a variety of ways depending on your bathtub arrangement and the degree of permanence you want.

To install a vertical bar, anchor a shower-curtain rod to the ceiling joist with long wood screws. The other end can press against the edge of the bathtub on a rubber pad. Be sure there's plenty of tension to hold the foot of the bar in place against the rubber pad on the bathtub rim. Use some liquid solder or other metal-to-metal sealing compound at the overlap joint on the bar. If possible, braze or solder the joint in the bar. Once installed, it will provide an excellent handhold for all members of the family regardless of their size.

A horizontal grab bar can be installed somewhat the same way, parallel to the tile wall that runs the length of the bathtub. This bar can be anchored to the tiles with adhesive at both ends of the tub, or the tile can be removed. Then the grab bar can be fastened to the wall and new tiles cut to fit around the bar's ends.

Another area that is certainly a fertile field for surface decorative treatment is plumbing fixtures. New fixtures can replace troublesome old faucets with a degree of elegance that normally is restricted only to new installations. Faucets by Moen for example, can be installed on existing

Caulking the tub, sealing cracks around the window frames, or almost any gluing job, is easy with the new Thermogrip electric glue gun. Refills for gun are available, inexpensive.

The function of a bathroom can be expanded with items like this Porta-Dryer 115V by the Maytag Co. It can be set on a counter, hung on a wall, rolled around room on casters.

United Shoe Machinery photo

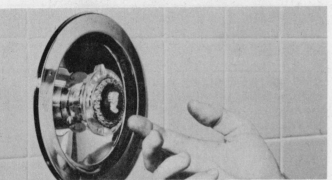

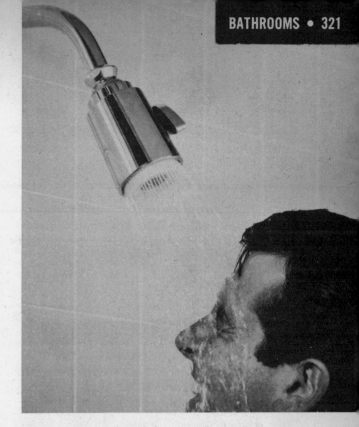

Lavatory faucet or shower valve, Moen's new jewel trim easily and gracefully improves the bath.

Moen's adjustable shower head is a real luxury item, simple to install, an instant improvement.

basins very easily with a minimum of plumbing know-how and rearrangement.

The old problem of proper temperature control in the shower can be solved once and for all with a Moen single-knob shower control installed over existing shower fixtures. Simply remove the old knobs and the new Moen control fits over the double valve arrangement covering both. It provides a single-knob control without calling for any tile tearout and replacement, or any new plumbing arrangements.

A new shower head is another benefit that you'll enjoy immediately and with very little expense and effort. Shower heads are mounted with standard screw threads and can be replaced quickly and easily with any of a wide variety of fixtures on the market.

If you have a conventional open-bottom lavatory and would like to have a little cabinet storage space under it, you can build a simple, custom vanity that fits exactly flush with the bottom of the basin's overhang. It's not possible to build a countertop vanity around an existing sink of this kind, since there would always be the problem of leakage around the seam. But using aluminum corner brackets and some ¾-inch plywood faced with your favorite color and pattern of Formica, you can build a sink-size cabinet with an access door for under-the-sink storage space—an excellent modernizing and utilitarian

touch that can be added to existing bathroom setups.

The old-fashioned lighting fixture above the shaving mirror and medicine chest should be replaced with a modern straight-line fluorescent, both for better illumination and for some savings in operating cost. Fluorescents are a lot cheaper to run than incandescent fixtures, since they use much less electricity for the same amount of light, and bulb replacement cost is something that you don't have to think about for two or three years at a time. If you happen to have one of the old-fashioned round wall fixtures, you'll have to do a little plastering and filling so the edges of the round hole won't show beyond the edge of the slim-line fluorescent channel.

This is pretty easy to do and won't take more than a few minutes.

The list goes on. There are many little things you can do in the way of adding extra space and useful accessories to the bathroom. There are shower nozzles with flexible hoses and hand showers attached, surface-mounted towel racks, towel rings, and paper cup dispensers that will certainly come in handy.

A trip to even such a commonplace store as your neighborhood supermarket will provide you with still more ideas, since small bathroom accessories are a standard stock item today just about everywhere you go. •

Ceramic Tiles

They're prettier, more durable and easier to install than ever before.

Different treatment uses hexagonal tiles on the vanity, accent colored tiles placed randomly on floor.

ASIDE FROM WATER, the ceramic tile is probably the oldest ingredient that's traditionally found in the bathroom today. The trouble is that many of the tiled bathrooms that we see are rather ancient; the tiles are old and yellowed, have cracked or crazed surfaces, and have a definite antique quality about them.

Modern ceramic tiles come in a wide variety of colors and sizes and lend themselves to the esthetic redesign of virtually any kind of modern bathroom. Now, it's even possible to apply tiles right over the surface of old tiles, without removing them. This certainly can take a lot of the effort out of modernizing bathrooms.

This technique for applying tile uses a new rubber-based adhesive that makes it possible to modernize old tile installations quickly without a lot of inconvenience and at a very modest cost. In fact, according to the Tile Council of America, Inc., tiling over tile is even quicker and easier than conventional tile setting on smooth walls. A standard toothed trowel is used to apply

and spread the adhesive over the old tile. The new tile and matching accessories such as grab bars, soap and tumbler holders and towel racks, can be set in place in the usual manner right over the old tile surface. The adhesive stays plastic and workable for about two hours, giving you plenty of time to set and align the new tiles.

The big advantage here is the saving in both back-breaking work and time. Ordinarily, modernizing would require ripping out all of the old tile, resurfacing the wall to provide a new tile base, and then a brand-new installation from top to bottom. All this takes time—lots of it, and a certain amount of expertness in working with ceramic tiles.

If you are working with a new tile installation in a really old bathroom, then chances are that you don't have to worry about ripping out the old tiles. Many of the older bathrooms will have wooden wainscoting with wallpaper above it, all of which should be removed before preparing the walls. In any ceramic tile installation,

U.S. Ceramic Tile Co. photos

Vertical stripes of three differently colored tiles add an unusual decorative touch to these walls. The light color duplicates the tone of the floor and bath units, other colors picked to blend or complement.

always do the walls before the floors, although the wall and floor surfaces should both be prepared in advance.

Preparing the floors for tile depends on the type of underfloor that is already in place. Where the subfloor is concrete, a bed of tile mortar ¾ inch to ¼ inch thick should be laid down—provided the floor is not subject to any external moisture or dampness. Expansion joints will be needed in the bed and in the tiles themselves—a gap filled with a strip of neoprene rubber held in place by mortar on both sides. The expansion joint should be directly over any joints in the structural floor itself, and wherever the tile work is going to butt up against perimeter walls, curves, columns, pipes and so on.

Subfloors that may contain some dampness should first be covered with a 15-pound felt paper or a 4-mil thick polyethylene film. Then comes a thin layer of mortar, then a reinforcing layer of lath and more mortar. The ceramic tile will be laid on top of the mortar bed with adhesive. When preparing the subfloor, be sure that the mortar bed surface is absolutely smooth, since any irregularities will show up in the tile and cause premature wear, breakage, cracking and other problems.

The wooden subfloor permits a variety of possible treatments including the same kind of subfacing as the concrete floor, if maximum protection is wanted. On a substantial wooden floor where there is only

going to be moderate traffic, it's possible to use just a layer of primer and the adhesive over the wood subfloor, although this method really isn't recommended in most cases. If it's not possible to provide the mortar protection for a wooden subfloor that's going to be subjected to a lot of heavy use, then a layer of ⅝-inch plywood sheets should be laid down first, with a ¼-inch gap between sheets. Nail the plywood in place, and then cover over with epoxy mortar $\frac{1}{16}$ to ⅛ inch thick.

Preparing wall surfaces depends on the area of the bathroom that is going to be tiled. Naturally, the wall area around bathtubs and showers will have to be prepared for much heavier duty than ordinary wainscoting tile in the rest of the bathroom. It's possible to set tile directly on dry walls with a single layer of primer and adhesive, although it may be preferable to use a multilayer base the same as used on concrete floors. The felt paper, mortar and lath should be used in all shower and bathtub areas. The tiles can then be set into place with neat cement or dry-set mortar.

The rest of the installation will be a lot easier. All that will be needed for the wainscoting will be a layer of primer on the wall surfaces, and then the adhesive spread over several square feet of wall at a time. Use a standard toothed trowel for this, and make sure that the spread is not too thick, since any extra adhesive will squeeze out between the tiles. At the same

Do walls first. Use toothed trowel to apply the adhesive sparingly. Tiles self-space for grout.

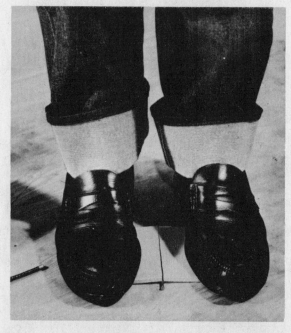

Mark tile to be cut parallel to ridges on back. Scratch front with glass cutter, break over nail.

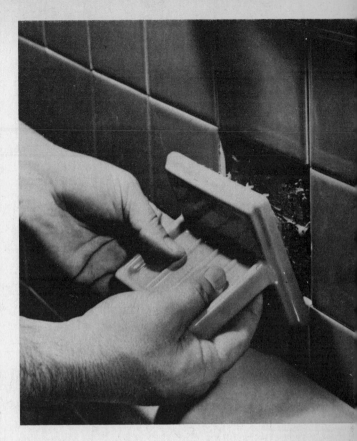

Soap dish is installed last. Note row above the dish is a "trim" row, top edge is rounded off.

To fit glazed tiles around plumbing, simply nip off corner bits until area is made large enough.

Let adhesive set for 24 hours before applying the grout. Mix grout, water, thick as heavy cream.

Mounted tiles are treated like a large single as they are set in adhesive over exterior plywood.

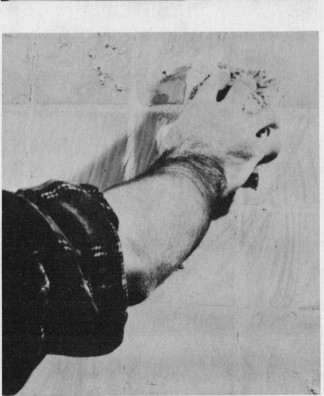

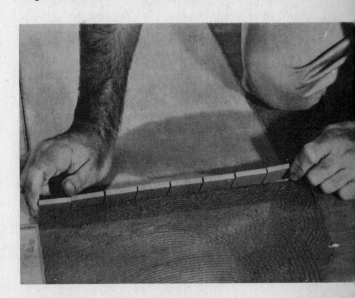

time, be very careful to avoid bare spots. Start with the bottom course and work up. When you run into any protrusions, such as plumbing for faucets and fixtures, you'll have to nibble away at tile corners with a pair of nippers or pliers to make them fit. Break off a tiny piece at a time, and enlarge the hole slowly until it's just the right size. Any unevenness in the hole that you make will be covered later by the plumbing trim plates.

When you reach corners and the top of the tile, you may have to cut the last course of flat tiles to a smaller size. To do this, scratch the glazed surface with an ordinary glass-cutting tool, cutting against a metal straightedge. Then place the tile on the floor, glazed side up, with a large finishing nail under the scratch. Step on the tile with both feet, one foot placed on each side of the scratch in the surface, and the tile will break cleanly along the scribed line.

Once the tiles have been set in place, allow the adhesive to dry at least 24 hours. Remember that the adhesive remains plastic for several hours, and the tiles can be adjusted and realigned during this time.

Special accessories designed for tile walls, such as soap dishes, tumbler dishes, toothbrush holders, towel racks and so on, should be set in place while the adhesive under the wall tile is still plastic. Generally, these accessories are designed to occupy a single square tile space, and you should leave spaces open for them when applying the tile. You can purchase the accessories in colors to match the tiles that you use on the walls. Be sure to buy these items at the same time you buy the tiles, so color matching won't be a problem later on.

Once the adhesive has fully dried behind the tiles, the next step is to apply grout. Mix the grout with water until it's about the consistency of heavy cream. You don't

Decorative effects must be carefully planned as to color, pattern and general interior decor. Mix tiles of various sizes, shapes; use with rugs, wallpaper, etc.

American Standard

U.S. Ceramic Tile Co.

Second bathroom's small size calls for small-size tiles on floor, shelves and vanity tops as shown.

have to wear rubber gloves when applying grout, but they will make cleanup a lot easier. Apply the grout with a sponge or a squeegee, and spread it evenly over the tiled surface making sure that it fills all of the cracks between the tiles. After the grout has hardened, clean off the tile faces with a damp cloth or sponge, and the job is done.

Laying ceramic tile floors requires the same basic steps as the tile walls. If you are upset by the idea of piecing together all of those tiny squares, don't let it worry you. These tiny tiles are already laid out in large groupings glued to paper backing sheets that cover a large area at a time—this includes ordinary squares as well as intricately patterned tiles. Just lay the sheet of tiles down on the adhesive with the paper backing side facing up. Let the tiles set in the adhesive for at least a day and then remove the paper very carefully, wetting it with a sponge and warm water. Once the paper is off, spread grout over the floor tiles the same way as you did on the wall.

Specialized types of tile that you will

need are the odd trim pieces with one edge beveled. These are the tiles that will form the uppermost course of the wainscoting. The beveled edge brings the tile smoothly to the plaster or plasterboard wall surface itself. Other special tiles are the curved corner pieces for intersections of wall and floor tiles, and special curved finishing pieces where a beveled tile will not reach all the way to the existing wall at the top of the wainscoting.

Other areas that can benefit from ceramic tiles include countertops and bathroom vanities. This type of treatment requires special planning and color coordination, since the countertop patterns and colors will dictate the kind of decorating treatment that your wife can use when she applies the finishing touches. The vanity countertop is certainly a worthwhile place to experiment with unusual tile design and to let your artistic bent have a certain amount of free reign. The area to be covered here is small enough so that you can expect to change the surface treatment after only four or five years, if you decide that the change is necessary. •

INSIDE STORY ON HEATING

Year-round comfort is the purpose of the modern home heating system

Home heating is a correct combination of many components. These consist of a heating plant, a distribution system, controls, safety devices and accessories. The heating plant—a furnace or boiler, usually—provides the energy to warm a house. The distribution system divides and circulates the heat. Controls regulate heat just as the residents want it. Safety devices prevent overheating and guard against other dangers. Accessories cool, control humidity, clean the air and do other interesting things.

The whole thing adds up to total comfort. That's what good heating is all about. If your present heating system doesn't measure up to total comfort, it may need modernizing.

Solar house makes use of low-angled rays of the sun that come through large double-glazed windows on the south wall of a house. Sunshine blankets the floors with warmth.

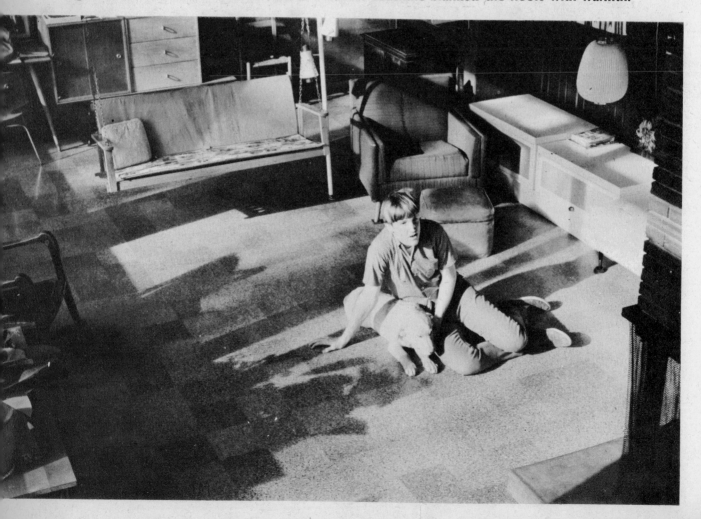

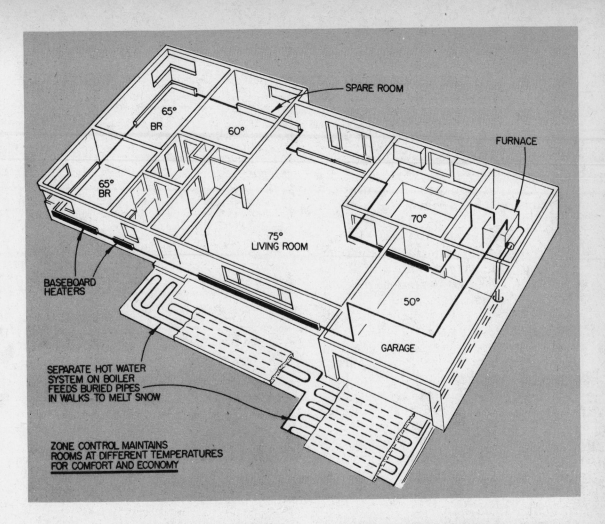

SPARE ROOM

FURNACE

65°
BR

60°

65°
BR

70°

75°
LIVING ROOM

50°

GARAGE

BASEBOARD
HEATERS

SEPARATE HOT WATER
SYSTEM ON BOILER
FEEDS BURIED PIPES
IN WALKS TO MELT SNOW

ZONE CONTROL MAINTAINS
ROOMS AT DIFFERENT TEMPERATURES
FOR COMFORT AND ECONOMY

Heat is one form of energy. Energy is the power to do work; heat energy added to ice melts it. Its power to do work changes the ice from a solid to a liquid. Heat energy added to air doesn't change the physical form of the air at all. Instead it raises the air's temperature. For home heating purposes, heat is measured in two ways: temperature and quantity. The Fahrenheit degree is the unit of temperature measurement; the British thermal unit (BTU) is the unit of heat quantity.

To picture the difference between temperature and quantity of heat, visualize water in a pan on the stove. If its temperature is 68 degrees and you turn on the stove and heat it up to 78 degrees, all this tells you is how hot, not how much heat. To know how much heat was required to raise the temperature of that water 10 degrees, you need to know how much water there was. If there was 1

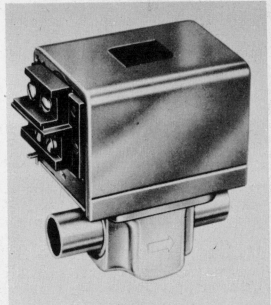

Compact zone-control valve for hydronic and steam heating lines closes off flow of heat when the thermostat is satisfied.

quart (2 lbs.) of water, then you can figure the quantity of heat in BTU's. A BTU is the amount of heat needed to raise the temperature of one pound of water one degree Fahrenheit. It's about the same heat as you get from burning a wooden kitchen match. In the example, two pounds of water had its temperature raised 10 degrees. This took 2 times 10, or 20 BTU's of heat.

In a heating system the burning of fuel releases BTU's which are used to heat the air in your home. The most popular fuel is gas. There are nearly 30 million customers for gas heat. Next in line is oil heat with some 10 million customers. Electric heating is coming on fast. Past the 3 million mark, electric heat is expected to have 19 million users by 1980. With electric heat, BTU's are given off as the electricity is converted to heat through tiny resistance wires. Homes beyond gas mains can still heat with gas—liquefied petroleum gas. Called L-P gas for short, it is delivered by truck. Coal as a home heating fuel gets a cool reception by most homeowners.

HEAT LOSS

In practical heating work the amount of heat that escapes from a house through its walls, floors, and ceilings is figured in BTU's per hour. Called *heat loss*, this can be calculated for any indoor-outdoor temperature difference. The coldest temperature it's likely to get during a severe winter is chosen as a *design temperature*. Design temperature varies from area to area. Heat loss is figured at design temperature outdoors and 75 degrees indoors.

Since the BTU is such a small amount of heat, it takes many thousands of BTU's per hour to heat a home on a cold day.

Heat is like a liquid, it flows. Heat always flows from the warmer temperature to the colder one. Heat flows out of a house in cold weather, into it in hot weather. The greater the temperature difference, the greater the heat flow.

Heat flow can take place in three

HEAT IS DRAWN FROM BODY TO COLD WALL | WITH HEAT ON WALL NO BODY HEAT IS LOST

Your body radiates heat to a cold wall. When walls are properly warmed, body heat can be kept at a pleasant, proper level.

Radiated heat reaches and warms all surfaces and objects in room. Convected heat circulates through a room as warmed air.

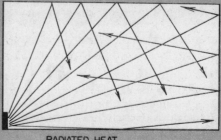

RADIATED HEAT

CONVECTED HEAT

ways: conduction, convection and radiation. Conducted heat travels through a substance, for example, through the wall of a house. Convected heat moves in a fluid. Air is a fluid. So is water. Both are used to move heat around in a heating system. Radiated heat travels through space. The sun's heat reaches us by radiation. Radiated heat doesn't warm the air it travels through, only the object it lights on. All objects radiate heat. The higher their temperature the more heat they radiate.

A heating system isn't supposed to be something to warm people occupying a building in cold weather. People generate their own heat. What a heating system must do is help the body regulate the rate at which it gets rid of its excess heat.

The principal things that affect comfort are air temperature, movement, humidity and radiation of heat from the body. Since comfort depends partly on heat radiated from the body, a room with a large expanse of windows seems cooler than a small-windowed room at the same temperature. Heat radiates from your body into and through the cold window panes. Less heat is radiated to a *warmer* wall. A room without drafts seems warmer, too, than one in which icy air brushes against you.

A heating system that can do the following is sure to make a comfortable home: maintain a 75-degree temperature in every room with no more than 3 degrees variation room-to-room; keep a relative humidity of up to 30 percent; prevent cold drafts from large windows; and hold the floor-to-ceiling temperature differential to a minimum.

Five kinds of heat can be used in the house heating system: warm air, hot water, steam, radiant electric and unit heaters. Though steam heating was once popular, it's rarely used in houses today. Hot water heat has replaced it.

WARM AIR HEAT

With warm air heating, the heating plant is called a furnace. A plenum chamber, usually on top of the furnace, collects heat. On modern forced-air systems a blower forces heated air out of the furnace plenum. Old-style systems work by gravity. Forced-air furnaces may be up-flow, down-flow or horizontal-flow, depending which best suits the house. Ducts, 4-inches in diameter and larger, connect to the plenum and channel warm air around to the rooms. In the rooms, wall diffusers or floor registers direct the warm air into the room to best counteract cold drafts. Return air is picked up at one or more central locations and ducted back to the furnace, runs through a filter and is then reheated and recirculated.

Warm-air heating systems are designed and installed according to the manuals of instruction issued by the National Warm Air Heating & Air Conditioning Association. The systems are classified by arrangement of ductwork and heating outlets. The simplest uses pipes running from the hot-air plenum directly to the room outlets. There may be more than one outlet per room arranged around the perimeter of the house. This simple pipe system is especially suited to square or rectangular floor plan homes with basements.

Another type that's popular for a slab-on-ground basementless house is the perimeter loop system. A looping duct embedded in the concrete slab is fed by radial ducts, also embedded in the slab. A down-flow furnace is used with this system. Cold air enters at the top of the furnace and heated air is blown out the bottom. Return air ducts in the perimeter loop system are usually run above the ceiling.

A crawlspace plenum system can be used on one-story houses built over a crawlspace. The furnace and registers have no ducts connecting them. Warm air is blown directly into the crawlspace through short ducts that aim it toward the outside walls. Registers placed around the perimeter of the house open into the crawlspace and let heated air up into the rooms. Warm crawlspace air also warms the floors by conduction. Such a crawlspace should be well insulated and the ground covered with a vapor barrier.

Still another type of warm-air heating is called the extended plenum system. A

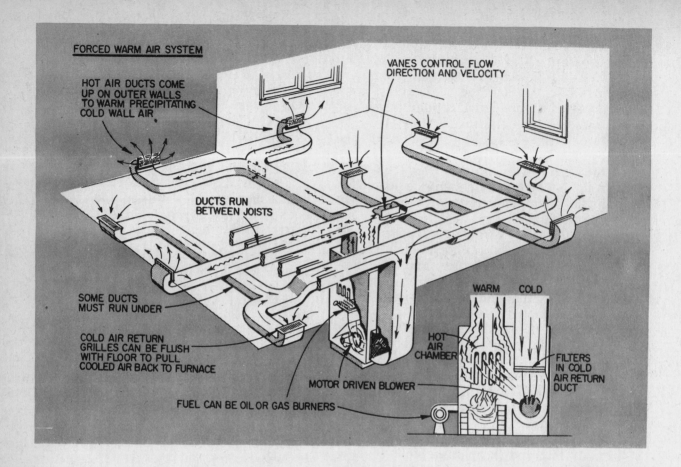

FORCED WARM AIR SYSTEM

VANES CONTROL FLOW
DIRECTION AND VELOCITY

HOT AIR DUCTS COME
UP ON OUTER WALLS
TO WARM PRECIPITATING
COLD WALL AIR

DUCTS RUN
BETWEEN JOISTS

SOME DUCTS
MUST RUN UNDER

COLD AIR RETURN
GRILLES CAN BE FLUSH
WITH FLOOR TO PULL
COOLED AIR BACK TO FURNACE

MOTOR DRIVEN BLOWER

FUEL CAN BE OIL OR GAS BURNERS

WARM   COLD

HOT
AIR
CHAMBER

FILTERS
IN COLD
AIR RETURN
DUCT

large duct, or ducts, take off from the hot-air plenum and run for most of the length of the house. Smaller ducts take off from these to serve room outlets. The extended-plenum system is adaptable to long, rambling houses with basement or attic furnaces.

Advantages claimed for warm-air heat are filtration, humidification and easy adaptability to air conditioning. By adding an outdoor air intake, a forced-air heating system will deliver freshened air to all rooms. Constant mixing of the air is said to minimize temperature differences from room to room and between floor and ceiling.

HOT-WATER HEATING

Hot-water heat, also called hydronic heat, uses a boiler to heat water that's circulated through finger-size pipes to all rooms of the house. A pump provides the push. In each room a radiator releases heat from the water into the room by both radiation and convection. Radiators are usually installed in baseboard units or convectors that prevent anyone from coming in contact with a hot radiator surface. Yet they allow air to circulate over them. Forced-hot-water systems are designed and installed according to criteria of the Institute of Boiler and Radiator Manufacturers.

Hot-water heating has three variations, each named for the way the distribution pipes are arranged. The *series loop* system is the least expensive. In it, hot water travels through the first radiator, then the second, then the third and so on until it gets back to the boiler for reheating. No radiator valves can be used. Shutting one radiator off would stop all circulation. There is little control of temperatures, room to room, unless more than one series loop is used.

The one-pipe hydronic system is better than the series loop. It will take care

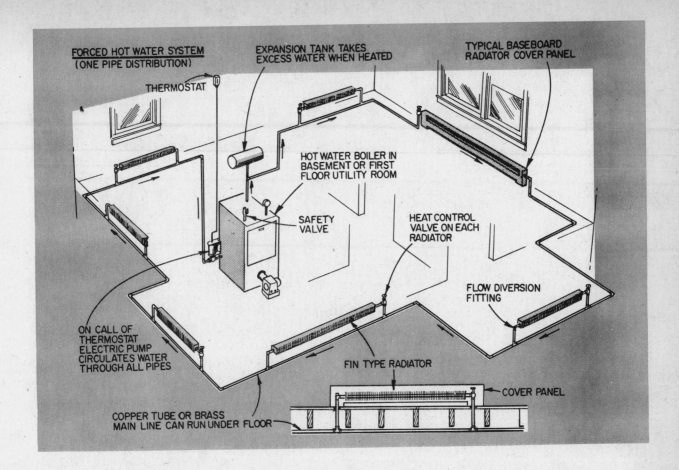

FORCED HOT WATER SYSTEM
(ONE PIPE DISTRIBUTION)

THERMOSTAT

EXPANSION TANK TAKES
EXCESS WATER WHEN HEATED

TYPICAL BASEBOARD
RADIATOR COVER PANEL

HOT WATER BOILER IN
BASEMENT OR FIRST
FLOOR UTILITY ROOM

SAFETY
VALVE

HEAT CONTROL
VALVE ON EACH
RADIATOR

FLOW DIVERSION
FITTING

ON CALL OF
THERMOSTAT
ELECTRIC PUMP
CIRCULATES WATER
THROUGH ALL PIPES

FIN TYPE RADIATOR

COVER PANEL

COPPER TUBE OR BRASS
MAIN LINE CAN RUN UNDER FLOOR

of any but the largest houses. A single supply pipe loops around to all radiators and returns to the boiler. Each end of every radiator is connected to the supply loop by a *flow-diversion fitting*. These fittings are like pickpockets. Each one grabs off a little of the circulating hot water, runs it through the radiator and back to the supply loop again. The rest of the water flows past that radiator. Adjustment is provided for controlling the amount of hot water each radiator receives.

The two-pipe hydronic system is used in large, expensive houses. It's like the one-pipe system but provides separate supply and return piping systems.

Forced-hot-water heating advocates say it achieves a balance between radiated and convected heat, making you feel comfortably surrounded by a "ring of radiant warmth." Sounds nice. Hot-water heat is claimed to be better, since dust, odors and germs are not circulated. Hydronic heating is simple to install. Zone control is easy with it too, by supplying different amounts of heat to different parts of the house.

Steam heat's one-pipe and two-pipe systems are similar to hot-water systems except steam circulates itself through the system. No pump is used. The return trip to the boiler is by gravity with steam in its liquid state.

RADIANT HEATING

Radiant heating, whether electric or hot-water, is said to be the ultimate in comfort, like being in the sun on a pleasant spring day. Moreover, there's nothing of the heating system to be seen—no radiators, no registers. Just pipes hidden in the walls, floors and ceilings.

The warmed surfaces give a combination of conducted and radiated heat to the room. Rugs and other insulating floor coverings over a radiant-heated floor

HOT WATER RADIANT HEAT IN FLOOR CONCRETE SLAB

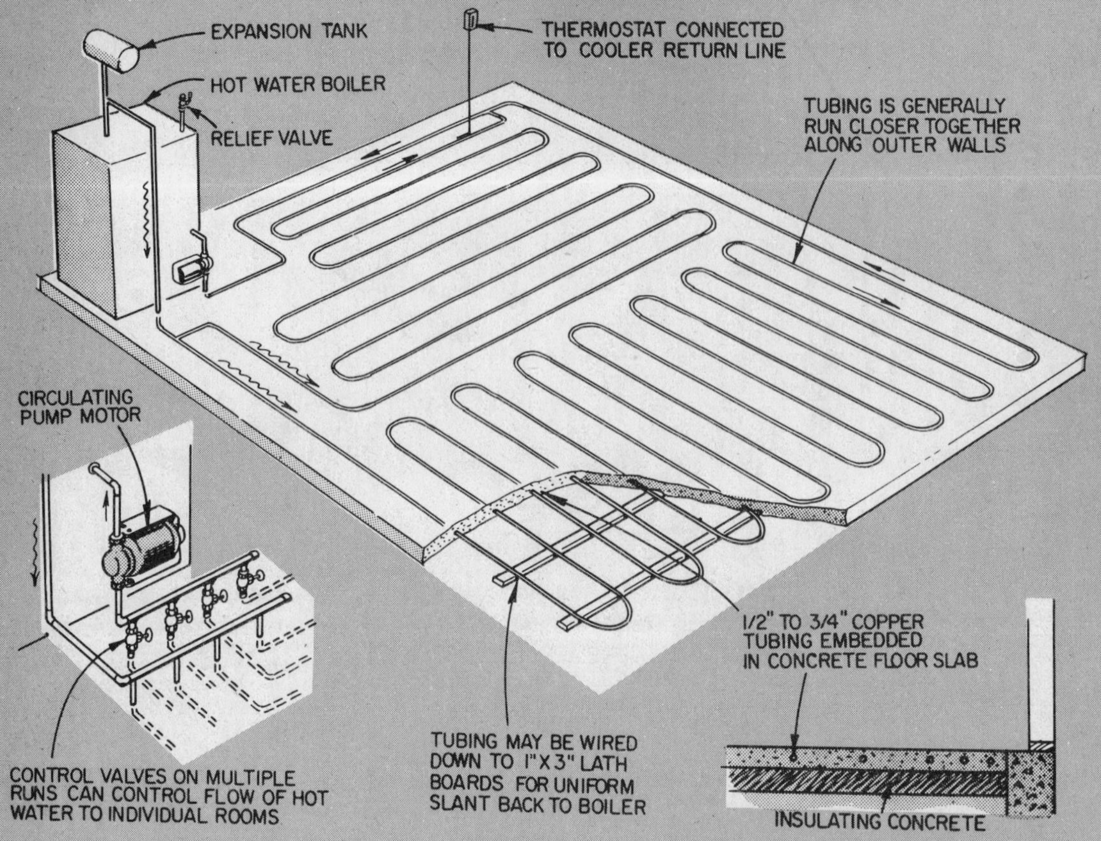

EXPANSION TANK

THERMOSTAT CONNECTED TO COOLER RETURN LINE

HOT WATER BOILER

RELIEF VALVE

TUBING IS GENERALLY RUN CLOSER TOGETHER ALONG OUTER WALLS

CIRCULATING PUMP MOTOR

CONTROL VALVES ON MULTIPLE RUNS CAN CONTROL FLOW OF HOT WATER TO INDIVIDUAL ROOMS

TUBING MAY BE WIRED DOWN TO 1"X 3" LATH BOARDS FOR UNIFORM SLANT BACK TO BOILER

1/2" TO 3/4" COPPER TUBING EMBEDDED IN CONCRETE FLOOR SLAB

INSULATING CONCRETE

RADIANT ELECTRIC CEILING

ELECTRIC RESISTANCE CABLE IN CEILING PLASTER

EMBED IN WET PLASTER APPLICATION

HEAT WAVES RADIATE DOWNWARD

TEMPERATURE CONTROL ON WALL

FUSE BOX

create balancing problems by getting in the way of heat transmission. Floor surfaces in a radiant system are usually at less than 80 degrees. Ceilings normally don't get hotter than 120 degrees.

Temperature regulation can be tricky because radiant hot-water heating is slow to respond to changes in heating needs. It takes time to heat up and cool off.

ELECTRIC HEATING

Electricity can be used as the "fuel" in hot-water or forced-air heating systems. But it can also be routed to resistance wires or panels in rooms, and be used directly as a type of heating system.

Electric utilities are competing hard for the home heating market. Because of the high fuel cost, electrically heated homes are usually insulated and weatherstripped to the hilt. The idea is to keep heat loss to a minimum. This adds to the initial cost of electric heating.

Electric heating is great. But it tends to be doggone expensive, at present, anyway. Those living in TVA areas and the Pacific Northwest have an advantage. Rates there are already low.

With an electric rate of 1½ cents per kilowatt hour or less this type of heat may be worth thinking of. You'll usually need a 200-ampere electrical service entrance and 220-volt service. Insulation will be needed on the order of 6 inches in the ceiling, 4 inches in the walls and 2 inches in the floors. Many electric utilities offer all kinds of inducements to get you started heating electrically. Check with your utility. What's more, look into things such as cost of adding insulation to an existing house, costs of installing the various systems and cost of maintenance (some types of electric heat have no moving parts). Also, if you'll want air conditioning, you may need a system of ducts anyway. Don't count on saving the expense of installing them.

Ceiling Cable—One popular method of electric heating is with resistance cables embedded in the ceiling to furnish radiant electric heat. These are used with plastered or plasterboard ceilings. The

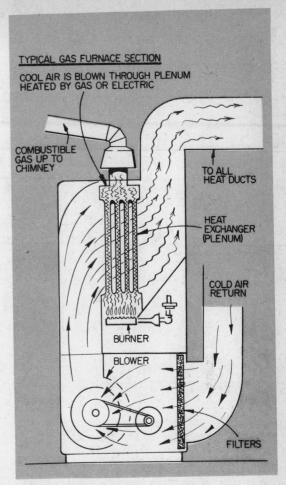

TYPICAL GAS FURNACE SECTION
COOL AIR IS BLOWN THROUGH PLENUM HEATED BY GAS OR ELECTRIC
COMBUSTIBLE GAS UP TO CHIMNEY
TO ALL HEAT DUCTS
HEAT EXCHANGER (PLENUM)
COLD AIR RETURN
BURNER
BLOWER
FILTERS

Above, components of furnace that create heat, transfer it to air, circulate it to rooms. Combustion products go up chimney.

Electric boiler is so compact it fits on wall. Piping is same as with any boiler.

The heater's resistance wires fit into heating duct. Wiring connects to house system.

wires are fastened to the ceiling before installing the finished wall surfacing.

Special plasterboard panels containing a conductive film are installed with the dry-wall radiant heating method. It's really catching on. U.S. Gypsum makes a panel called "Thermalux Electric Heating Panel." The initial cost for heating

with this system is said to be between that of hot-water and forced-air. You can probably install the panels yourself if you get full directions on how to do it.

In another system a vinyl sheet containing copper mesh conductor in nylon netting is adhered to the ceiling as in wallpapering and wired into the system.

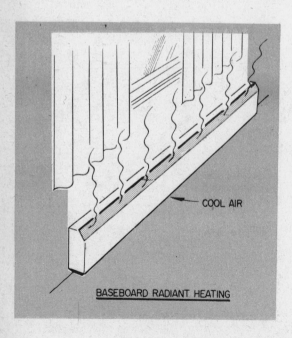

COOL AIR

BASEBOARD RADIANT HEATING

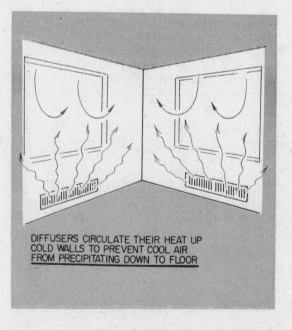

DIFFUSERS CIRCULATE THEIR HEAT UP COLD WALLS TO PREVENT COOL AIR FROM PRECIPITATING DOWN TO FLOOR

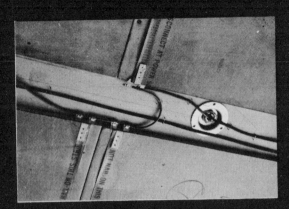

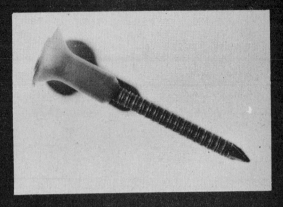

Plasterboard heating panel is the newest thing in electrical heating. Panels are cut to fit, nailed to ceiling and wired.

Use nails insulated with plastic shoulders to keep metal from coming in contact with the resistance-heating layer in each panel.

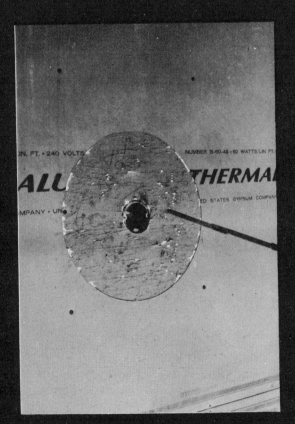

Resistance layer in panel's surface is cut back around fixture boxes and other metal projecting through it to prevent burn-out.

You need insulation above every ceiling with this type of heat to make heat travel down into room, not up to floor above.

Apply adhesive to back of ½-inch plasterboard to ready it for stick-on insulation.

quired between all floors and on all walls and ceilings.

Heating Units—Next most popular are electric baseboard heating units. These are mounted near the floor, usually along outside walls of rooms and especially under windows. Air flows through them and up the wall, keeping cold drafts from settling to the floor. They're controlled by a thermostat, one per room, if desired. Air circulation is by convection. The benefits of perimeter heating can be had in this way. You can gang up as many baseboard units as the house electrical system will stand. A whole house can be heated this way if its electrical system has enough zap. You can also get radiant heated panels that mount below a window or in a too-cool room to provide supplementary heat.

Electric Central Heating—An electric furnace is much like a gas or oil furnace with a blower and ducts to distribute the heat provided by resistance wires in the furnace. Duct heaters are mini-furnaces that fit right in a large duct. Electric boilers for hydronic heating use electricity instead of gas or oil to heat water in the boiler. From there, the system is the same as any other hot-water heating system.

Heat Pump—The heat pump can heat or cool a house, depending on which direction it moves the heat. During the heating season, it wrings heat out of the

It can be painted over. With thermostat control, an electrically wired-up room becomes a giant-sized radiant heater. No duct-work is needed. Comfort is supposed to be outstanding. Insulation is re-

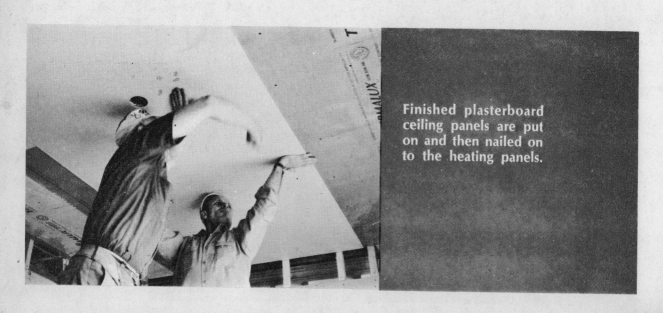

Finished plasterboard ceiling panels are put on and then nailed on to the heating panels.

Heating a home addition is easy if you use electric valance heaters on outside walls.

air outside your home, raises its temperature by concentrating it and brings the heat inside. During the cooling season the heat pump squeezes heat out of room air, concentrates it and pumps it outside. Heat pumps are most common in milder climates where there is enough heat in the winter air. Manufacturers claim that refinements make heat pumps practical even in colder climates. Some pumps use water instead of outdoor air as the medium.

HEAT FROM THE SUN

Solar heating has been around for some time, but isn't yet practical for most heating needs. However, since the sun's heat is free, this method has appeal. The simplest kind of solar heat makes use of large double-glazed windows on the south wall of a house. With these the sun

can shine into the house, blanketing its floor with warmth. In a house with floor-to-ceiling windows on most south rooms, the heating plant may shut off in mid-morning and stay off until after dark even on the coldest sunny days. Some solar heat is available on cloudy days. Since this heat is not stored, a full-fledged heating system is required to heat the house at night.

A drawback, the large windows that let heat in during the day, let heat out at night. They should be provided with insulating draw-draperies.

A generous roof overhang is needed in a solar house to provide shade for eliminating the sun's rays altogether in summer months when the sun is high in the sky.

Another type of solar heat uses heat-collecting panels on the roof to heat water, which is then stored in a large insu-

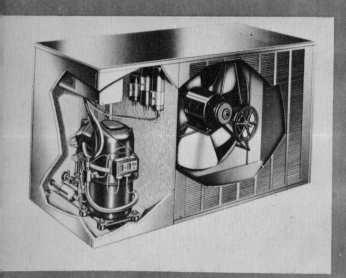

Wrap-around filter media placed in furnace removes large dust particles from air.

Heat pump's mechanism is reversible to let heat be taken from or put into the house.

The heated air is circulated through furnace and ductwork by squirrel-cage blower.

Electric resistance furnace works like a hair dryer with the air being blown over glowing wires of heating elements, right.

Photos from Lennox Industries

lated tank. The hot water is circulated as needed to radiators around the house, the same as in any hydronic heating system. A small standby heating unit provides heat when solar energy won't do the job by itself. The cost of heat-collecting panels currently limits this type of solar heating to warm, sunny climates. You can't get a straight answer out of anyone as to which kind of heating is best. Each one warms up to his own type of system and runs cool on the others. The truth is that any of the modern heating systems can be fully comfortable,

clean, quiet and completely satisfactory if properly designed, installed and adjusted. Get good advice on design from experts. The installation and adjustment you can do yourself.

UNIT HEATERS

Add-on heating for supplying additional heat to hard-to-warm rooms or house additions may be done with unit heaters. These can be gas, oil or electric. Don't expect them to heat a whole house uniformly. And don't look for the heating comfort you'd get from a well de-

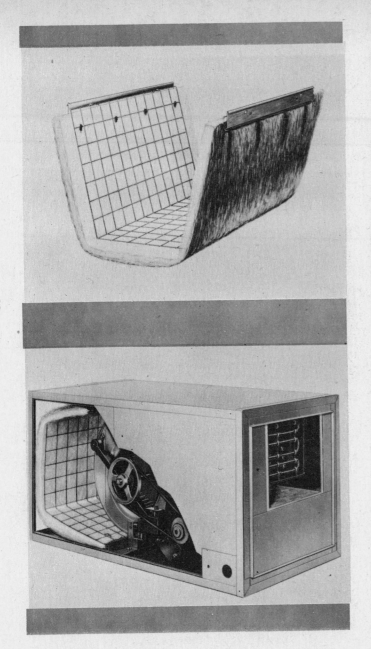

Floor furnace — This fits into a hole cut in the floor with a grating over it. Heat comes up through the grating and warms the room. Cold air settles back through the outside of the same grating. Thermostat control is available. Floor furnaces are made in oil or gas. An outside vent or chimney connection is necessary. A floor furnace is capable of heating more than one room.

In-the-wall heater — Oil, gas or electric, the wall heater is normally installed between studs in an outside wall. Air comes in at the bottom, is heated and blown out at the top. Venting with gas is through the wall to a combination intake-exhaust fitting. This does away with the need for a vent stack to the roof. Most wall heaters have circulating fans and thermostats. They'll heat more than one room. Both convection and radiant heat are produced.

Fireplace — A fireplace is a born loser's method of heating a house. Most of the heat goes up the chimney. The newer circulating fireplaces built around metal units reclaim more of the heat. Even they won't supply more than emergency heat in cold weather. Enjoy a fireplace, but don't look to it for a fulltime heat source.

Portable heaters — These electric jobs come with or without blowers to help circulate heat. They're plugged into a 110-volt outlet and operated as needed to warm a small room, such as a bathroom, or to take the chill off a cool room while it is being used.

Gee whiz stuff — Such dreamy additions to a heating system such as air-ionizing and ultraviolet air treatment may someday be commonplace. Lennox Industries now offers an activated charcoal purifier to remove chemical and gaseous contaminants from circulated air.

Put it all together and you have modern climate control, summer and winter, day and night. Today's heating system has come a long way from the old potbelly. Who knows what the future will bring, perhaps a personal heating unit that blankets you with sunny warmth wherever you are. Then home heating would be less important. Until then, modernize your heating system and keep it working at top efficiency.

signed central heating system. The unit must match the fuel.

Unit heaters heat by both convection and radiation. The different types are: room heaters, in-the-wall heaters, fireplaces, and portable heaters.

Room Heater — Available in gas, oil or electric, some models of room heaters are equipped with thermostats. They're the modern version of the coal- or wood-burning stove. You can't cook on 'em. Gas and oil types require a flue. Some come with blowers for circulating heat across the floor and around the room.

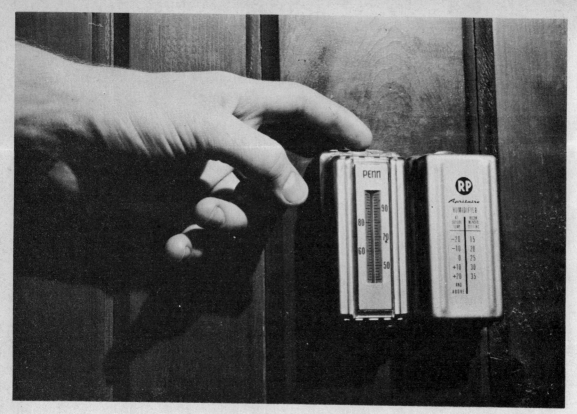

Don't touch that dial or you'll be a thermostat-jiggler. Set the thermostat where you and your family are most comfortable and leave it. That's the modern way.

MEET YOUR HEATING CONTROLS

Controls function automatically to give you service and safety.

The modern heating system has many controls. They are of two kinds: operating controls and safety controls. Operating controls regulate the flow of fuel to the heating plant and turn it on and off. The thermostat is the most obvious one. There are others. Safety controls protect you and your family from unsafe conditions connected with the fuel or the heat. One of these is the flame-sensing device that shuts off the fuel supply if a burner doesn't light.

Your thermostat is the heating system's envoy to your house. It tells the heating system what temperature you want the house to be kept. The thermostat can only ask for heat. It's up to the heating system to deliver. A good thermostat can control temperatures so closely no one will ever notice any variation. Sometimes more than one thermostat is used for zone-controlled heating. A thermostat is placed in each zone.

Thermostats are merely electric switches. Most of them work on 24 volts of current. In many, a temperature-sensitive bimetallic spring inside reacts to temperature changes. As it does, it opens and closes a set of electrical contacts. The contacts say "go" or "stop" to the burner or, in electric heating, the resistance elements.

A thermostat is affected only by the air that comes in contact with it. Therefore, it should be located in the most lived-in room, usually the living room. Don't put a thermostat in interior passages such as hallways. These are slowest to take notice of house temperature changes. The thermostat shouldn't be placed in rooms directly above the heating plant. These rooms aren't typical of the rest of the house. Keep a thermostat off a warm wall, behind a refrigerator or stove and away from radiators or registers. Don't locate it on an outside wall either. Heating experts recommend putting the thermostat on an inside partition about 18 inches from an outside wall, not near doors to the outside. The wall shouldn't be in the sunlight at any time during the day. Keep radio, television and lamps away from your thermostat. Their heat tends to mislead it. Air circulation around the thermostat should be good, but don't place it in a draft.

The height of the thermostat is important too. Ideally it should be 2½ to 3 feet from the floor. But if small children roam the house, locate it four feet high, out of their reach.

MODERN SYSTEMS

The most modern heating systems have both indoor and outdoor thermostats. The outdoor ones sense outside temperature changes and adjust the temperature of the heating medium—water or air—for comfort. Homes that have radiant heating especially need this dynamic thermostatic duo to give the heating system advance notice of temperature changes. This keeps the system in tune with the weather. Some stats are so sensitive that a 1/10th degree change in temperature will adjust the burner flame.

Most thermostats have small resistance heating coils below the temperature-sensing device. When the thermostat is calling for heat, its coil gives the sensing element a hotfoot, making it cycle off sooner than it otherwise would. Residual heat in the furnace or boiler brings up the room temperature to the desired point. As soon as the thermostat switches off, the heating element cuts off too, letting the temperature sensor cool

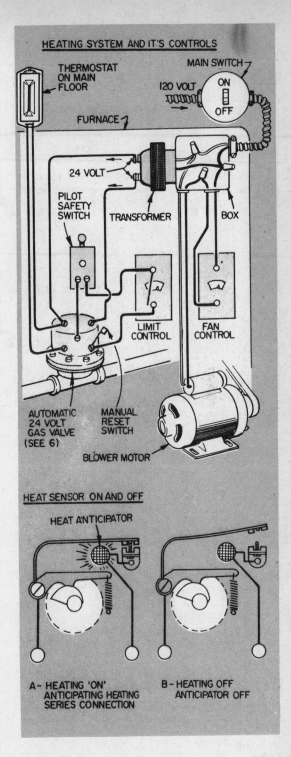

HEATING SYSTEM AND IT'S CONTROLS

THERMOSTAT ON MAIN FLOOR

MAIN SWITCH

120 VOLT ON OFF

FURNACE

24 VOLT

PILOT SAFETY SWITCH

TRANSFORMER

BOX

LIMIT CONTROL

FAN CONTROL

AUTOMATIC 24 VOLT GAS VALVE (SEE 6)

MANUAL RESET SWITCH

BLOWER MOTOR

HEAT SENSOR ON AND OFF

HEAT ANTICIPATOR

A- HEATING 'ON' ANTICIPATING HEATING SERIES CONNECTION

B - HEATING OFF ANTICIPATOR OFF

again. The effect is to make the thermostat extremely sensitive to temperature variations.

An air conditioning thermostat is like this, but it works in reverse. It has a heater that operates while the thermostat is switched *off*, rather than on.

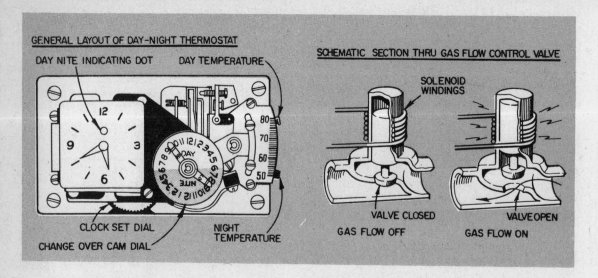

GENERAL LAYOUT OF DAY-NIGHT THERMOSTAT

DAY NITE INDICATING DOT   DAY TEMPERATURE

CLOCK SET DIAL

CHANGE OVER CAM DIAL

NIGHT TEMPERATURE

SCHEMATIC SECTION THRU GAS FLOW CONTROL VALVE

SOLENOID WINDINGS

VALVE CLOSED

GAS FLOW OFF

VALVE OPEN

GAS FLOW ON

Many types of thermostats are available. Some are combinations that will serve both heating and cooling.

Should you set your thermostat back at night, as many people do? There is a theoretical 6 percent saving to be had. The hangup is that you may not realize any saving at all by night setback. It depends on how much of a setback you give, how long the setback is in effect and how the heating system responds to it.

Experts offer these rules for night setback: Set back for sleeping comfort, not for economy. Don't set back more than 6 degrees. Any saving may be wasted in reheating your house in the morning. Skip your setback when the outdoor temperature gets really low, and on windy nights.

If you dig night setback, look into replacing your present thermostat with a day-night clock-thermostat that does the setting for you automatically. Then you won't have to get up to a cold house. Today's trend is to set the thermostat and forget it. Modern indoor climate control makes a year-round setting of 75 degrees practical.

Face it. Even if you could save 6 percent of your heating bill, would it be worth the discomfort of getting up to a cold house?

CIRCULATION CONTROLS

A blower or pump control is usually located on the furnace plenum or on the boiler water jacket. This controls circulation of heated air or water. When the burner warms the heating medium sufficiently, the control switches on the blower or pump motor. Even after the burner stopped, the motor keeps running until the temperature of the heating medium has fallen to a predetermined level. Then the control switches off its motor.

For safety, a limit control is needed on burner operation. If the temperature in the furnace or boiler should get too high, as from a clogged air filter or airlocked water pipes, the limit control will shut off the burner. The burner will stay off until all excess heat has been dissipated. Then it may come on again. The limiting operation is fully automatic. There's nothing to reset. The temperature in forced-air furnaces and open hydronic systems shouldn't exceed 200 degrees. On many systems both circulation control and limit control are in one unit.

On boilers there's also a pressure switch to cut off burner operation when the boiler reaches operating pressure. And there's a low-water cutoff float in the boiler to stop the burner if the water level drops dangerously low. An additional safety blowoff valve opens mechanically to relieve excess boiler pressure.

A solenoid control for opening the fuel valve when the thermostat signals "on" is used in gas heating. They function on

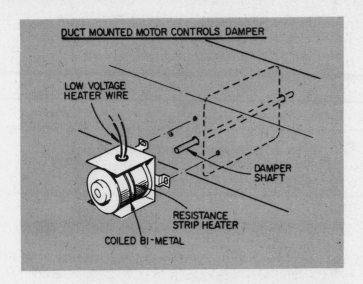

DUCT MOUNTED MOTOR CONTROLS DAMPER

LOW VOLTAGE
HEATER WIRE

DAMPER
SHAFT

RESISTANCE
STRIP HEATER

COILED BI-METAL

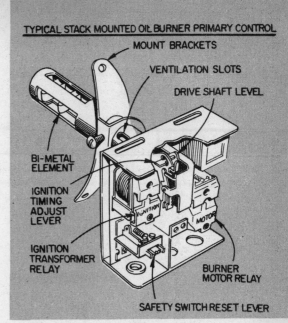

TYPICAL STACK MOUNTED OIL BURNER PRIMARY CONTROL

MOUNT BRACKETS

VENTILATION SLOTS

DRIVE SHAFT LEVEL

BI-METAL
ELEMENT

IGNITION
TIMING
ADJUST
LEVER

IGNITION
TRANSFORMER
RELAY

BURNER
MOTOR RELAY

SAFETY SWITCH RESET LEVER

low voltage supplied directly through the thermostat. Thermostat resistance and solenoid valve resistance should be compatible.

Automatic pilot controls on a gas burner are provided to shut off the burner's gas supply should the pilot flame snuff out. Often a thermocouple heated by the pilot flame does the trick. Some systems shut off only the main burner gas. Because L-P gas is heavier than air, its safety control must shut off both the burner and the pilot gas. Such a unit is called a 100-percent-shutoff pilot. One is required with each L-P gas appliance to prevent gas from collecting in a basement or crawlspace when the pilot goes out.

Electric heating systems are switched on with relays that isolate the low thermostat draw from the high heating element draw. Time-delay controls often are used to cycle one set of elements, then another and then another, to prevent overloading the house power lines unnecessarily.

PRIMARY CONTROL

Most oil burners have what is called a *primary control*. It's loaded with relays and other complicated devices. The primary control stays ready at all times to switch the oil burner on or off, depending on what message it receives from the thermostat. The primary control always remains subordinate to the limit controls,

however. If they say "no," the primary control can't start up the burner.

The primary control supervises starting, running and stopping of the burner. Its most important job is to tell whether there's a flame in the firebox during the initial start as well as during the running period. All burner primary controls begin a "safety" program at the start of each cycle. This shuts off the burner if a flame doesn't catch.

Primary controls can be stack-mounted; burner-mounted with a stack-mounted sensor; burner-mounted with a heat-sensitive sensor in the firebox or air tube; or burner-mounted with a light-sensitive flame detector. The light-sensitive ones are the quickest-operating.

Mechanical draft controls on all burners eliminate downdrafts that might blow out a gas pilot and prevent excessive chimney drafts from affecting the fire in an oil burner.

Controls are designed to be mostly trouble-free, and good ones are. Once in a while they need service. Call a serviceman unless you know what you're doing.

High quality forced air furnaces have Palm Beach blower controls to run blower faster or slower, depending on bonnet temperature.

HELPFUL HEATING ACCESSORIES

One unit will eventually take care

of heating and cooling the home

The goal of heating experts today is building total comfort into a home heating system. A heating plant and distribution system alone won't do it. You need some heating (and cooling) accessories.

Air conditioning is bigger than heating. The day is coming when your heating system won't be up-to-date unless it cools too. A cooling system may actually be separate from the heating system with a single central refrigeration unit outdoors, and cooling coils inside ducts to create and distribute cool air. The size of the cooling unit must be based on the cooling load of your house, just as the heating system is based on its heating load. Proper design will enable the cooling system to keep the house at 75 degrees and 50 percent relative humidity all summer long. Other temperature-humidity combinations are possible if preferred.

The size or capacity of cooling equipment is figured in "tons" or BTU's of heat-removing capacity per hour. One ton of cooling is the amount that would be done by a ton of ice melting in 24 hours. It figures out to about 12,000 BTU's each hour.

Don't get an air conditioning unit that's too far oversized for the load, or it won't run enough to control house humidity. And don't get a unit too far un-

Automatic snow-melting can be added to a hydronically heated house by simply burying pipes in the concrete and then hooking the buried pipes into the home heating system.

Better Heati-Cooling Council

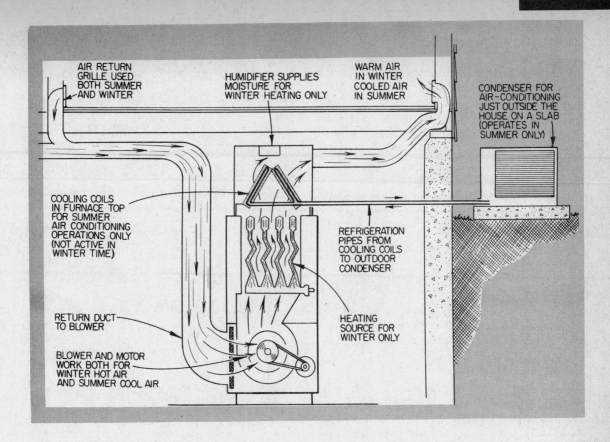

AIR RETURN
GRILLE USED
BOTH SUMMER
AND WINTER

HUMIDIFIER SUPPLIES
MOISTURE FOR
WINTER HEATING ONLY

WARM AIR
IN WINTER
COOLED AIR
IN SUMMER

CONDENSER FOR
AIR-CONDITIONING
JUST OUTSIDE THE
HOUSE ON A SLAB
(OPERATES IN
SUMMER ONLY)

COOLING COILS
IN FURNACE TOP
FOR SUMMER
AIR CONDITIONING
OPERATIONS ONLY
(NOT ACTIVE IN
WINTER TIME)

REFRIGERATION
PIPES FROM
COOLING COILS
TO OUTDOOR
CONDENSER

RETURN DUCT
TO BLOWER

HEATING
SOURCE FOR
WINTER ONLY

BLOWER AND MOTOR
WORK BOTH FOR
WINTER HOT AIR
AND SUMMER COOL AIR

dersized or it won't handle the load on really hot days. An average U.S. home needs from two to four tons of cooling, depending on its size and location. Cooling capacity figures are listed on the nameplates of modern cooling units.

Air-conditioning systems can be either the through-the-window or through-the-wall kind or centrally ducted. Fuels are usually electricity, but can be gas, too.

Sometimes cooling can be added to a forced-air heating system. Other times ideal cooling requires larger ducts, a more powerful blower and cool air outlets that are placed high on the wall rather than on the floor. Don't sacrifice good cooling by shackling the air conditioner to a heat-distribution system that's not designed for cooling as well as for heating.

DEHUMIDIFICATION

Sometimes removal of moisture from the air makes life more comfortable, even without cooling. Basement rooms in most climates nearly always need dehumidification in summer. If the house isn't air conditioned, moisture-removal is accomplished with a separate unit, usually one on casters that can be rolled

where it is needed. If placed over a basement drain, the unit never needs emptying. Otherwise, collected water must be dumped regularly to avoid overflowing.

With a gauge called a *humidistat* that controls operation of the dehumidifier, you can keep your home's relative humidity at reasonable levels to prevent mildew. Most units have a humidistat built in. If not, a plug-in type can be used. The rooms being dehumidified must be kept closed. No machine can dehumidify the outdoors. One unit, if it has the capacity, will dry all the rooms open to it.

HUMIDIFICATION

The opposite of removing moisture from the air, humidification, puts water into the air. It's almost always needed during the heating season when heated air tends to be dry.

Humidity—water vapor in the air—is so important in imparting the feeling of warmth that with ample relative humidity, the temperature can be lower and still be comfortable. Tests have shown that most people are comfortable at a combination of 30 percent relative humidity and 75 degrees. For a drop of 30 percent in relative humidity, the room temperature must be raised five degrees to maintain the same body comfort. Such an increase in indoor temperature would show a 10 to 15 percent increase in your fuel bill.

Outside winter air at 20 degrees and 40 percent relative humidity, when heated to 72 degrees inside your house, dries out to only 6 percent relative humidity. This is drier than the Sahara Desert. Humidity should stand at 30 percent, except in very cold weather. There aren't many houses where the relative humidity in winter can be above 30 percent without condensation problems on walls and windows. At this humidity, a temperature of 75 degrees is comfortable to most people (98 per cent of those tested). This corresponds to the temperature at which most people keep their thermostats.

Some of the needed moisture in a house is put back into the air by breathing, washing, cooking, showering, etc. But this is often only enough to keep the humidity level at 10 to 15 percent during cold weather. The rest of the moisture must be supplied artificially by a humidifier.

The small plate-type humidifiers that come with many furnaces and mount to the hot air plenum won't add enough water to be worthwhile. They lack evaporative power. You need one of the big, powerful units that literally throw water into the air. As much as 8 to 16 gallons of water a day may be needed. A good unit that can handle this job costs upward of $50. You may save that in doctor bills the first year. Colds and other respiratory infections are greatly reduced by having proper home humidity. I've personally experienced this. Didn't believe it when my doctor told me. Static shocks are done away with too.

Minerals in the water are a problem with humidifiers. They build up and eventually affect performance. The best ones are self-cleaning. Lennox makes one that flushes away mineral deposits automatically.

A humidifier is best when controlled by a humidistat. The humidifier can operate long enough to reach the desired humidity, then shut off.

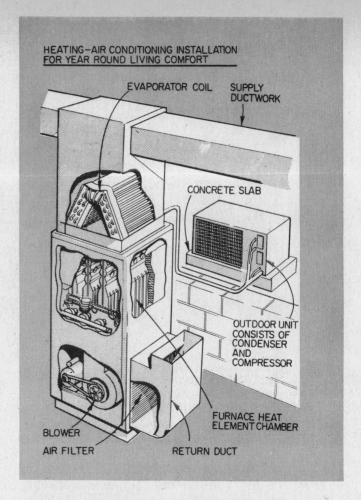

HEATING–AIR CONDITIONING INSTALLATION FOR YEAR ROUND LIVING COMFORT

EVAPORATOR COIL
SUPPLY DUCTWORK
CONCRETE SLAB
OUTDOOR UNIT CONSISTS OF CONDENSER AND COMPRESSOR
FURNACE HEAT ELEMENT CHAMBER
BLOWER
AIR FILTER
RETURN DUCT

Relative humidity to strive for is: 15 percent at 20 degrees below zero; 20 percent at 10 below; 25 percent at 0; and 30 percent at 10 above and higher.

To help the humidifier, your home should be tightly calked, weatherstripped and have a continuous vapor barrier around the walls and ceilings. If there isn't a vapor barrier, you can paint one on with an oil-base paint. Once that's on you can paint over it with any kind of paint.

ELECTRONIC AIR-CLEANING

Dust settling on furniture is like an iceberg. It warns of a huge unseen dirty air problem. A cubic foot of city air may contain more than 400 million unseen dirt particles floating around. Pollen, tobacco smoke and other irritants are there, too. Modern electronic air-cleaning can eliminate 95 percent of the air-

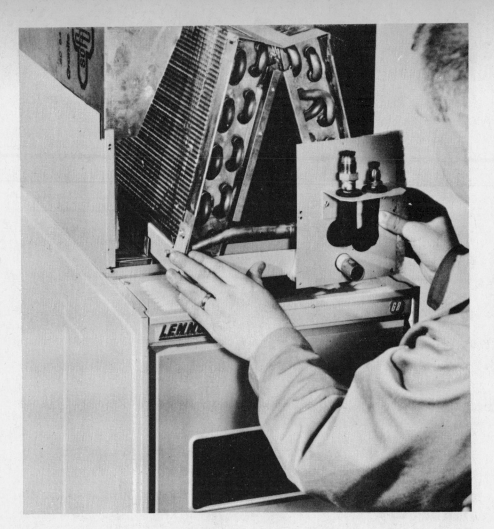

Air-conditioning cooling coils are placed in furnace airstream and then are piped to an outdoor condenser.

Lennox Industries

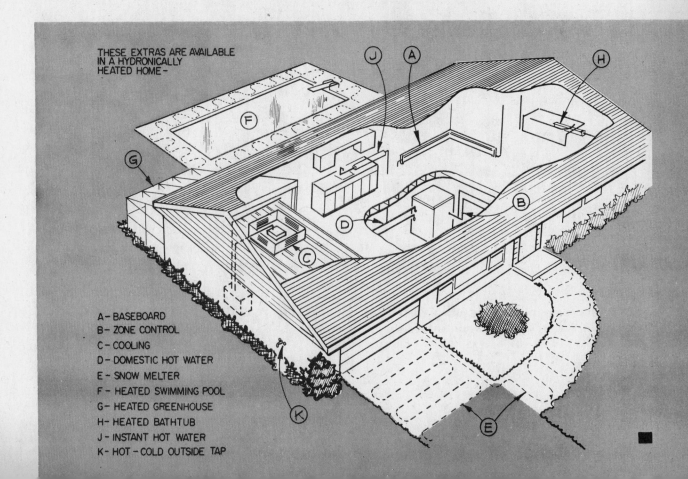

THESE EXTRAS ARE AVAILABLE IN A HYDRONICALLY HEATED HOME—

A— BASEBOARD

B— ZONE CONTROL

C— COOLING

D— DOMESTIC HOT WATER

E— SNOW MELTER

F— HEATED SWIMMING POOL

G— HEATED GREENHOUSE

H— HEATED BATHTUB

J— INSTANT HOT WATER

K— HOT-COLD OUTSIDE TAP

Before you fasten it tightly with sheet metal screws, level furnace humidifier on the metal hot-air plenum.

Lennox Industries

An outdoor air intake pipe on a forced-air system can freshen up your home. The pipe leads to the furnace cold-air return.

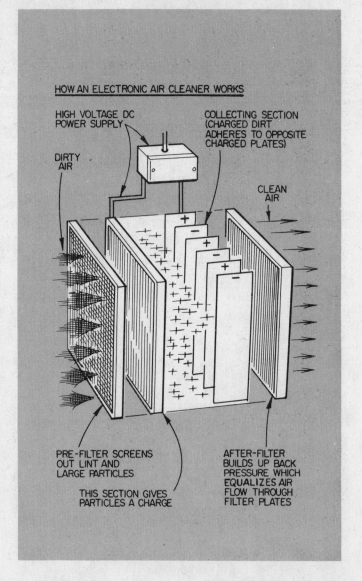

HOW AN ELECTRONIC AIR CLEANER WORKS

HIGH VOLTAGE DC POWER SUPPLY

COLLECTING SECTION (CHARGED DIRT ADHERES TO OPPOSITE CHARGED PLATES)

DIRTY AIR

CLEAN AIR

PRE-FILTER SCREENS OUT LINT AND LARGE PARTICLES

THIS SECTION GIVES PARTICLES A CHARGE

AFTER-FILTER BUILDS UP BACK PRESSURE WHICH EQUALIZES AIR FLOW THROUGH FILTER PLATES

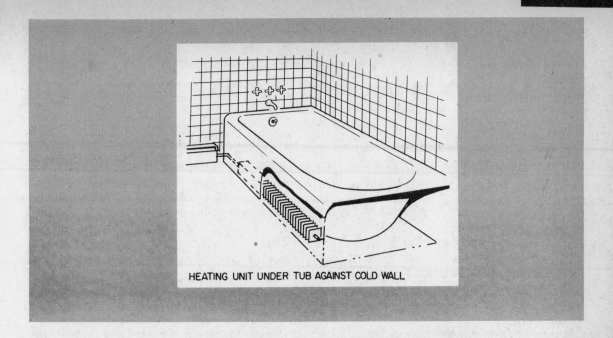

HEATING UNIT UNDER TUB AGAINST COLD WALL

borne dust and 99 percent of the pollen passing through the system. Most of these impurities in the air bypass a furnace air filter only to be recirculated.

Most electronic air cleaning units have screens to filter out the large particles of dirt. One has two treatment sections to trap tiny particles electronically. The first stage or ionizing section electrically charges the particles passing through it. The second stage or collecting section uses electrically charged metal plates that work like magnets to attract charged particles entering from the first stage. Material collected by an electronic air filter must be cleaned out every so often. Some units do this automatically. Others are manually cleaned.

An electronic air cleaner is usually installed in the return-air duct of a furnace. For houses without forced-air heating, individual room units are available.

OTHER ACCESSORIES

Outside air vent—A small outside air duct piped into the return-air side of a forced-air furnace makes a tremendous difference in the air freshness inside a house. A damper controls the flow of fresh air. A grille keeps out water and vermin. The slight positive air pressure it produces counteracts infiltration of cold air from outside.

Instant hot water—Hot faucet water at the turn of a tap can be supplied by water heating coils built right into the boiler in a hydronically heated house. This eliminates the cost of a separate water heater and saves floorspace.

Automatic snow-melting—A system of tubing embedded in driveway and sidewalk concrete circulates heated water and antifreeze. The heat melts ice and snow accumulations. Heat is supplied by the boiler in a hydronically heated house. A swimming pool can be heated this way, too.

Heavy additional heating loads, such as snow-melting, must be figured when boiler size is calculated. Swimming pool heating, since it's off-season, need not be taken into account.

Heated bathtub—Whether you have dry or wet heat, as they term warm air and hot water heat, you can supply a little extra heat underneath the bathtub to warm it. It will seem more friendly when you shower or bathe. With dry heat a heating duct is run to the under-tub area and a vent cut in the subfloor to permit full air circulation. With hot water heat a small radiator is installed under the tub.

MAINTAINING YOUR HEATING

A small improvement in the efficiency of a heating plant can bring big savings in fuel bills over a year's time. This is true whether the heating plant is steam, water or air; gas, oil or electric. For this reason—for safety too—most heating experts recommend an annual inspection of the whole heating system. A good time to do it is well before the heating season

is on. Then if any repairs or adjustments are needed, you have time.

Your central heating system consists of five separate systems: (1) Fuel burner. (2) Furnace or boiler. (3) Heat distribution system (ducts, pipes). (4) Room heating units (radiators, registers, convectors, etc.). (5) Controls (thermostat, dampers, pump, blower, etc.). All must

Replace dirty air filters at least twice a year to ensure proper furnace operation.
Lennox Industries

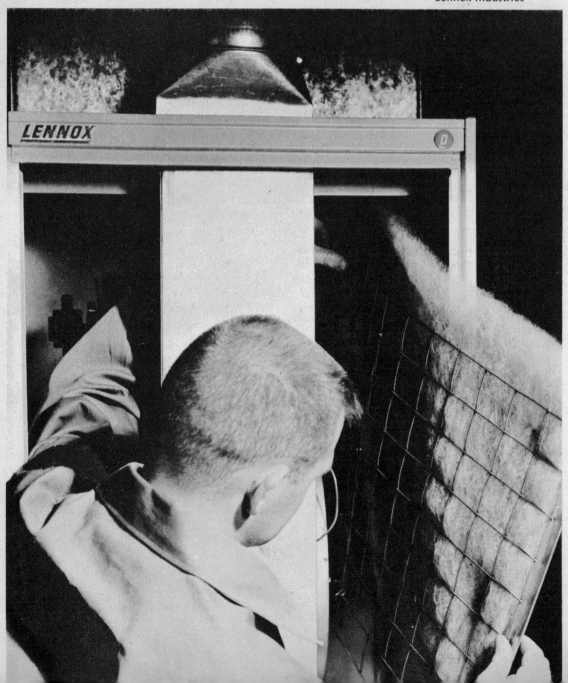

SYSTEM

A periodic check-up will keep your heating system operating at its best

be in good order if you're to get efficient heat.

An obvious starting point is the heating plant. While you are working around the heating plant, clean it inside with a vacuum cleaner. Soot and scale are insulators that can keep combustion heat from getting through to the house. This wastes fuel up the chimney. Remove the access hatch. Use the brush attachment of your vacuum to clean soot deposits from the inside of the combustion chamber. Boiler scale can be attacked with a stiff-bristle wire brush. The longer the handle the better.

CHECKLIST

Lubrication—Motor, fan or water pump bearings may need lubrication. Those that aren't self-lubing should have their cups or filling tubes oiled at least twice a year with the lubricant recommended by the manufacturer. Usually this is a good grade of 30-weight motor oil. Make sure the furnace switch is turned off when you oil.

Belt adjustment—When you lubricate is the best time to check and adjust tension of the fan belt on a forced-air furnace. Turn off the switch and tighten a loose belt by turning the cradle bolt beneath the blower motor. The belt should have 3/4 to 1 inch of play midway between pulleys. A belt that's too loose may slip and wear out quickly. At the same time it may not drive the blower as fast as it should. A belt that's too tight wears out belt, motor and fan bearings faster than a properly adjusted belt does.

A belt can cause creaking or squealing noises in the heating system when it reaches the worn out stage. Any belt that is noisy or is cracked or frayed should be replaced.

While you're in this section, vacuum the blower's squirrel cage to remove accumulated dust.

Clean the filter—Nearly all forced-air heating systems use filters to trap dust in the moving air. Most of these are of the

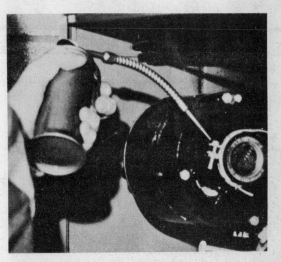

Unless self-lubrication, fill oil cups on blower and oil pumps with oil twice a year.

Give blower belt ¾-inch of play between pulleys. A too-tight belt wears out fast.

Lennox Industries

Make sure collars on blower assembly are tight. Turn set screw with allen wrench.

Vacuum fins of blower cage to restore efficiency and eliminate circulating dust.

Leave burner service to a technician. Do-it-yourself here can be dangerous to you.
Lennox Industries

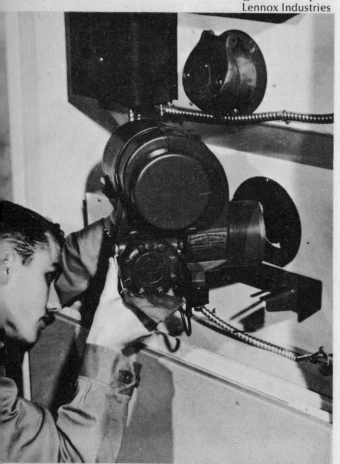

replaceable glassfiber type in which the fibers are coated with an oil that grabs and holds tiny bits of dust. However, after the fibers have trapped all the dust they can hold, the rest of the dust can go right on by. An air filter in this condition can only trap large lint particles. What's more, air movement is restricted, cutting down on the amount of air circulation your heating plant can provide.

Unless you have a means of re-oiling a glassfiber filter, don't try to clean one. Consider it used up and get a new filter element.

You should change filters every month during the heating season in cold climates. Install them with the arrows on the frames pointing in the direction of air flow. Neglected filters cause more complaints of poor heating than any other single factor.

Check breathing—Your furnace or boiler must have air, just like you need air to breathe. The biggest danger is that in a tightly sealed home your burner may become oxygen-starved. This can result in lethal gases being released into the house. Whether the heating plant is located in a closet, basement, attic or crawlspace, provide some ventilation. Have a screened vent, a door with grille in it or, in the basement, leave a window open about an inch. The storm sash could be left off a loose basement window to provide combustion air to a basement burner.

If you smell burning fuel and can't get rid of it by providing ventilation, call your serviceman fast.

Air that gets pushed out by a kitchen or bath vent fan or outside-vented clothes drier must be replaced. The same is true of fireplace draft air. Keep adequate breathing air for your heating plant by having a window open several inches while these are operating.

Pilot light—In spite of what you've heard about turning off a gas heating plant's pilot light during the off-season, you won't save money by it. Heat from the tiny pilot keeps your furnace dry inside, helping to prevent corrosion.

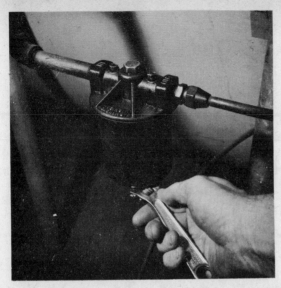

Take apart and clean fuel filter once a year for free flow of fuel during winter.

Find unwanted leaks in firebox of burner with a candle. The flame follows drafts.

OIL BURNERS

Most old oil burners have fireboxes too large for the capacity of their burners. You can check yours by measuring the area of the firebox in square inches. If the area is more than 75 square inches for each gallon-per-hour capacity of the burner nozzle, you should have a smaller box. Your present firing box is easily made smaller by installing a liner kit. Johns-Manville makes one called *Cerra Form* out of ceramic-fiber panels. These assemble into a smaller firebox inside your present one.

As part of your annual inspection of an oil burner, have a combustion efficiency check made by your serviceman. The efficiency should read 75 percent or more. Have him check the baffles in the firebox. Are they in place and are there enough of them? Air leaks into the firebox should be sealed off with calking.

You can inspect the burner nozzle to see that it's the right size for the diameter of your firebox. Check it against these ideal chamber diameter-nozzle gallons per hour combinations:

```
10-inch —  .50 to  .85 gph.
11-inch — 1.00 to 1.25 gph.
12-inch — 1.35 to 1.50 gph.
13-inch — 1.65 to 1.75 gph.
```

Flush out the fuel oil strainer to get rid of dirt collected by it. If there isn't one, you'd do well to install one between the fuel tank and burner.

If your oil burner has no draft stabilizer, you are likely losing too much heat up the chimney. Install one.

With any burner, a good chimney should be clean and free of obstructions. Knock soot accumulations from the chimney's inside walls by lowering a brick tied to a string. Afterward debris should be removed from the clean-out opening at the bottom of the chimney. Lacking a clean-out opening, you'll have to pull off the vent pipe from your heating unit and remove the soot there.

Some things should be left to the pro's. Don't fool with the pilot flame and safety controls on a gas burner. Never mess with the ignition parts on an oil burner. Leave the oil pump alone too. Your serviceman should do the checking of the safety valve on a steam boiler and the pressure relief valve on a hydronic system. Your family's safety is at stake.

HEAT DISTRIBUTION SYSTEM

What you can do to your heating distribution system for increased efficiency depends on what type of system it is—

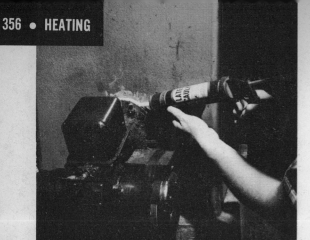

Calk crack around oil burner to seal off efficiency-spoiling air leaks in the firebox.

Knock off soot collecting on chimney wall by scuffing it with brick tied to a cord.

With inlet valve on, to admit fresh water to system, flush dirty water from boiler.

Drain expansion tank to replace its air-charge during heating system inspection.

air, water, steam or electric. Radiant electric heating components require little maintenance. Electric furnace types, in which air heated by electricity circulates through ducts, need the same attention any forced-air distribution system needs.

Ducts — Ducts and pipes running through unheated spaces should be insulated. Heat loss into such areas, ups your fuel bill. In basements where the heat is utilized, you needn't insulate. Return runs may not need insulation in milder climates.

Ducts should be calked at joints where escaping heat would be wasted. Use calk that sticks tightly to metal and can take heat. Both silicone calks and the new acrylic calks work well.

Drain expansion tank — Every modern hydronic heating system makes use of an expansion tank partly filled with water. As the water in a closed system is heated, it expands against a cushion of air. Some of the air becomes dissolved in water, and the tank gets waterlogged. Its air cushion is depleted. For that reason an expansion tank should be drained every year to restore the full air cushion.

Flush your system at the same time. Open the drain valve at the bottom of the boiler and flush until clear water comes

Vacuum air registers to remove accumulated dirt and dust, using special attachment.

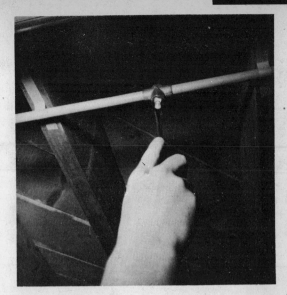

Flow valves balance hydronic heating systems. Screw slot shows angle of the valve.

out. Then refill to the proper point on the gauge.

Vent radiators — Air collects at the tops of radiators in a hydronic system and should be bled off every year. A radiator that's half filled with air is only half a radiator. Open the vent on each unit until all the air escapes. Then close it firmly.

Radiators, convectors, registers — Heating is efficient only when air can freely circulate around and through a radiator or convector. Radiator covers and marble or wood shelves on top of radiators, block air circulation. If you must use a radiator cover, be sure the design is correct. Ample space should be provided at the bottom for cool air to enter and at the top for hot air to get out.

Also be sure that draperies, rugs and furniture don't restrict heat from around registers and radiators. Dust or dirt on registers and convectors prevents free movement of heated air. Keep them clean. Most vacuum cleaners have an attachment for this purpose.

One trick to help a convector pour out heat is to paint the back of its cover flat black. This will make it transmit heat like a radiator. You can do this easily while you have the cover off. Vacuum the fins too.

COMFORT ADJUSTMENTS

Whether you have forced-air or hydronic heating, your heating system should be adjusted to provide constant circulation of the heating medium. This is done for comfort. The blower or pump is adjusted to run all the while the outdoor temperature is below 45 degrees. This gives you tablespoon quantities of heat continuously, not bucketsful every hour, as other adjustments give.

Constant circulation is accomplished by adjusting the blower or pump limit control settings and sometimes the flow of air/water. Your heating serviceman can make the adjustments for you.

BALANCED HEATING

Chances are three out of four that your heating system is out of balance. Many are. Unbalance leaves some rooms too warm, others too cool. This is true even of new houses. Whether your system is hydronic or forced-air, balancing is done in much the same manner. Balancing the system yourself in not complicated, in fact you can probably do as good a job as a professional. You can spend the necessary time, without call-backs or wasting of time waiting for the system to normalize after each adjustment.

All you can do to service an electronic air cleaner is to see if the fuse has blown.

Make a balance adjustment during cold weather when the sun is not shining so that the heating system has a good load on it. Balance is achieved by restricting the flow of heat to rooms that need more. Of course, the room where the thermostat is located should stay at proper temperature all the time.

Before making a heat balance adjustment, storm windows should be installed, filters should be cleaned, expansion tank drained, air bled from radiators and the blower or water pump operating properly. All windows and doors that would normally be closed when maximum comfort is required should be closed.

Begin balancing by opening all the restrictions in ducts or pipes. In ducts these are in form of dampers. There is normally a damper in each individual duct run. Sometimes control of heat is at the registers. Check these too. Usually each control has a screw slot or other indicator showing the damper- or valve-position. Full flow is when the screw slot is parallel with the flow. In hydronic systems the restrictors are valves located in supply pipe runs where they tee off to a radiator.

Carry an accurate thermometer around to each room. Check the temperature about four feet from the floor. Record the readings. Then you'll see which rooms are too warm and which are too cool. They should all be within 2 degrees of the thermostat setting.

Close the dampers or valves slightly in runs leading to rooms that are too warm. Changing the flow to one room will usually affect the flow to all rooms, so don't over-adjust on the first try. Reducing the flow of heat to warm rooms should provide adequate heat to cool rooms. If they're still too cool, further reduce heat flow to the other rooms or restrict the input of heat to the room containing the thermostat.

Be sure to allow ample time after a change in adjustment for the rooms to reflect it fully in a temperature change. Forced-air systems react faster to a change than hydronic systems do. Radiant systems are slowest to react. In a radiant system make your next check the following day.

Mark the damper positions for future reference.

Your thermostat may need adjusting of its heater scale to give proper burner cycling. Have a serviceman do it.

Fiber glass on top of boiler or furnace plenum chamber saves heat by insulation.

You can make obvious repair to air conditioning system, like tightening fittings.

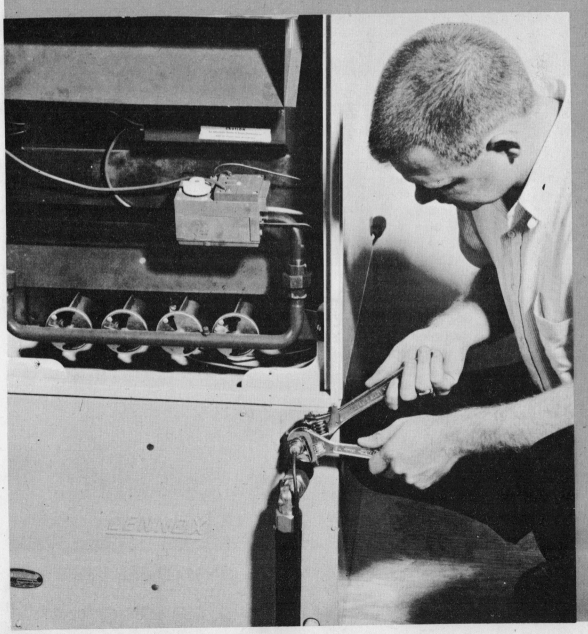

HEATING A HOME ADDITION

Plan your heating carefully for maximum economy and efficiency

For radiant-hot-water-heating home, nail additional copper pipes to plaster back-up material spaced according to heating plans.

Heating and plumbing for a home addition is a big job. But if you know what you're doing, you can handle it all right. Tackle the jobs in this order: (1) heating, (2) rough plumbing (piping) and (3) finish plumbing. The heating is installed first because it's the least flexible. Even more flexible than plumbing is electrical wiring. Do that only after the rough plumbing is in.

You may either extend pipes or ducts from your present heating system into the addition or heat it with a separate system. The separate system can be as simple as wall or floor furnaces or, for tops in comfort, a complete central heating system. With a separate system you'll need to allow space in the addition for the heating plant and any chimney or venting required.

If you try to tap heat from the existing house system, be sure it's big enough to handle the load. Not many are. Actually they shouldn't be.

To know how much heat you need, you'll have to calculate the heat loss of your addition. There are several methods of figuring heat loss, some more detailed than others. The Montgomery Ward general catalog has a section telling simply and clearly how to make the calculations. Your heating equipment dealer will be glad to figure it for you if you take him a set of plans. Any heat loss calculation is based on design temperature. This varies across the nation.

CHIMNEY

A new heating plant usually means a new chimney. Instead of building one all the way up from the basement, use a prepackaged chimney. It comes in sections that are screwed together. Such a chimney is fully insulated and is supported by the house framing. Only a small space is needed for it. Roof flashing and chimney cap are a part of the package. Your heating plant is vented into the lower end of the chimney once it's installed.

Fuel lines to the heating plant should

be run much like plumbing. Copper tube with flare fittings is suitable either for oil or gas.

The biggest job in installing the heating system is making the duct or pipe runs around to the rooms. You may have to cut holes here and there. Less cutting is involved with forced-hot-water heat than with forced-air. This is because water pipes are much smaller than air ducts.

You'll need some authorative advice on number and size of ducts to serve each room. The same with water pipes and radiators. Your heating equipment dealer is the best source. Have him help you plan the entire distribution system in return for your parts order.

In general, make your duct runs between joists when you can. Don't avoid across-joist runs like the plague, though. There's nothing wrong with them. Rectangular ducts are made in short sections to fit between wall studs. Round pipes come in longer lengths and are easier to work with. Fewer fittings are needed. Special fittings will get you from round pipe to duct for an up-the-wall run. Every duct run starts with a take-off at the furnace plenum. Then comes the duct itself, then elbow to bend it where you want it to go. Boots are made for connecting ducts to registers. A diffuser is installed in the end of each boot to beautify it and to spread out the warm air.

Hot water heating pipes are so small they can be run across or between ducts, little matter. They slip through holes bored up into the wall above. There they are connected to radiators.

Whether you use air or water heat, be sure to include some means of flow-adjustment in every run. This will permit balancing the system when it's finished.

The heating plant should come with instructions on hooking up its controls. Usually it is merely a matter of running wires between the different controls and wiring them up as shown. If you run into anything that's not clear, ask your dealer.

You should provide an electrical switch for shutting off power to the heating plant for use when you work on it, and turn-off during the summer.

Why build a masonry chimney for your addition when you can assemble a pre-packaged chimney, supporting it on the house framing.

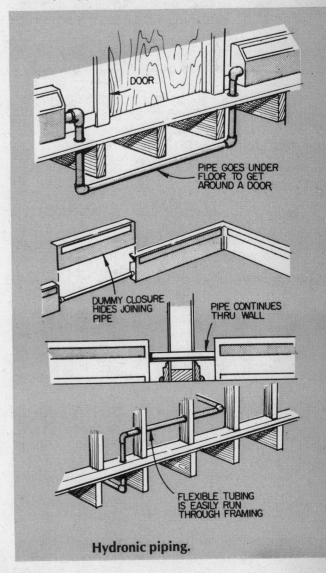

Hydronic piping.

PLUMBING

The big item in plumbing is the 3- or 4-inch soil stack. It's expensive. The soil stack reaches from the house drain all the way up through the roof. Try to place all your fixtures as close to the stack as possible, within reason, or course.

Once your addition's plans are made, shop around among plumbing supply dealers to find one who's helpful. You'll need more information than we can give you here. The most help is someone who can answer your questions. Many dealers will also help you figure the materials needed to do a job. Others are plumber-oriented. They discourage do-it-yourself business. Try to find one that doesn't. Some dealers even offer discounts to home handymen who are doing major remodeling work. That's the kind to have.

Drain-waste-vent pipes must be large enough to handle the flow without restricting it. The sizes given in the chapter on DWV pipes and fittings are normally adequate. For complicated plumbing layouts, values are assigned to each fixture and their pipe sizes computed from these. (See tables in chapter "Tips on Running Pipes.")

To use the tables, add up the fixture units for all fixtures that will use a main soil stack. Size the stack accordingly. Size the waste pipes and vents for their individual fixtures. See what size horizontal run is needed to handle them. All pipes serving toilets should be at least 3-inch. Add up the total of all fixtures in the house addition and size the main house drain line accordingly.

Always increase roof vents to at least 3 inches at a point 12 inches below the roof line and carry them 12 inches above the roof line. This is to prevent closure by ice.

If there are no code provisions to the contrary, you can take advantage of wet-venting. Here are maximum distances from a fixture trap to the stack without reventing. They apply to any wet-vented fixture:

> 1¼-inch pipe — 2½ feet
> 1½-inch pipe — 3½ feet
> 2-inch pipe — 5 feet

If any of your runs will be longer, you'll have to make revents for these fixtures. Remember, too, that wet-vents must not enter the soil stack below any toilet. Fixture drains that do, must be revented.

To make a 1½-inch revent, put a 1½-inch sanitary tee at the fixture stub-out behind the wall and continue the drain line as a vent run up above the fixture. Elbow it back and into the main stack above the point where the highest drain line is connected into the main stack.

While revent runs chop your stud walls full of notches, they sure beat drilling up through the roof. If long revent runs would be necessary, then go the secondary stack route. Usually this is a 1½- or 2-inch pipe leading up to the roof. A vent increaser below the roof line is required.

ASSEMBLING DWV

You'll nearly always find it easier to install a new main stack to serve the addition rather than to try tapping into an existing one in the old part of the house.

Start assembling a DWV system at the toilet drain. Cut all parts as necessary to fit. Sanitary tees may be ordered with 1½-inch side tappings for lavatory, shower or bathtub waste pipes. If you don't need one of the tappings, plug it.

Suspend the toilet drain parts from the joists or from nailed-on braces. Then work backward to them from the building's drain line in the wall or floor.

If the building drain and soil stack are different sizes or materials, you'll need an adapter or reducer between them.

Some provision should be made for rodding out every horizontal run of pipe, whether it's a 4-inch, 3-inch or a smaller waste pipe. This applies as well to a suspended horizontal drain, if one is necessary, between the soil stack and building drain. The usual method is through a clean-out opening at the far end of the pipe.

With the piping completed up to the toilet, build the soil stack up and out through the roof. Put in any branch tees for drains and revents as needed. Locate them so that all drains slope down ¼ inch per foot into the stack and all revents slope away from the stack. With cast iron you can use sanitary tees and invert them to get the proper slope as vent connections.

If the drainage portion of the soil stack has to be offset to clear a framing member, use ⅛-bends to do it. A ¼-bend may be used in the vent portion.

If a second floor toilet is to be plumbed in, build its drains first, then run the soil stack up to them from the first floor. This makes fitting easier.

Work out from the stack, building your branch waste and revent lines. If you use a secondary stack, build it up using the same procedure as for the main stack.

Stub out all drains so they can be fitted with fixture traps after the wall material has been installed. With steel pipe use a threaded nipple of any length loosely screwed in and capped until the fixture is installed. Then it can be replaced with what is needed for the fixtures. With plastic or copper, stub out at least an inch beyond the finished wall. You can saw the stub off the length later.

Framing that must be remodeled to accommodate drain pipes and fittings should be beefed up with cleats or headers. When a closet bend must cross a joist—never more than one—the joist can be cut short and its ends supported by headers as shown in the drawing in chapter "How to Modernize Your Plumbing."

WATER SUPPLY SYSTEM

Last of the rough plumbing is the water distribution hookup. Work from connections to the existing hot and cold water mains. If they're already overloaded, install new mains from the water heater to serve the addition.

Make your main line runs, then your branch runs. Stub out all pipes for fixtures in the wall if possible. Otherwise in the floor. Follow the rough-in dimensions illustrated.

Branch runs to fixtures should be carried to the point where they come through the wall to serve the fixture. At that point install tees. Going up from

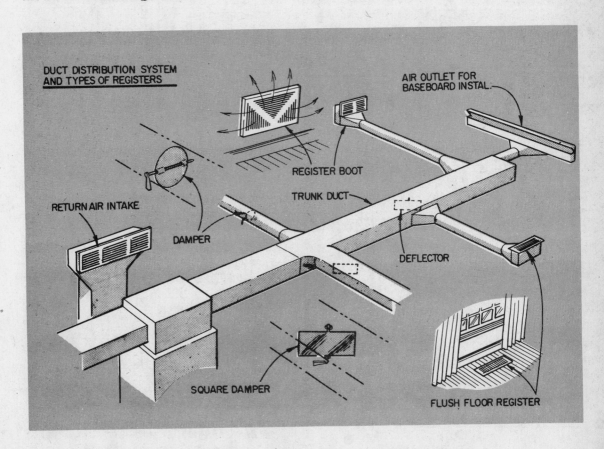

DUCT DISTRIBUTION SYSTEM AND TYPES OF REGISTERS

AIR OUTLET FOR BASEBOARD INSTAL.

REGISTER BOOT

RETURN AIR INTAKE

TRUNK DUCT

DAMPER

DEFLECTOR

SQUARE DAMPER

FLUSH FLOOR REGISTER

TWO WAYS TO SUSPEND DRAINS FROM FLOOR

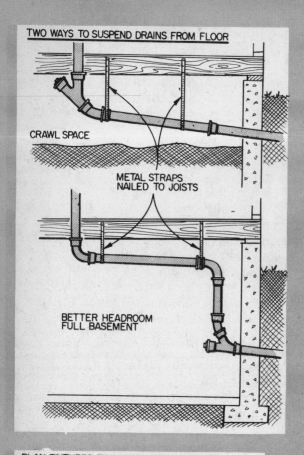

CRAWL SPACE

METAL STRAPS
NAILED TO JOISTS

BETTER HEADROOM
FULL BASEMENT

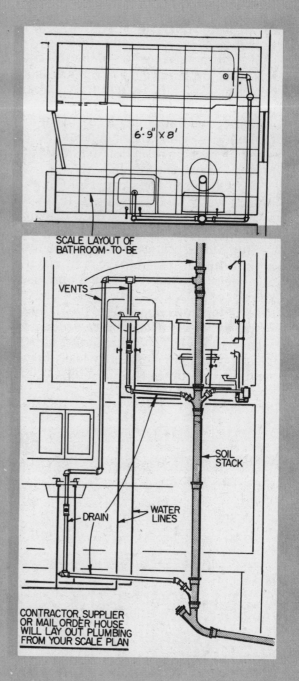

SCALE LAYOUT OF
BATHROOM-TO-BE

6'-9" X 8'

VENTS

SOIL
STACK

DRAIN

WATER
LINES

CONTRACTOR, SUPPLIER
OR MAIL ORDER HOUSE
WILL LAY OUT PLUMBING
FROM YOUR SCALE PLAN

PLAN FIXTURES TO AVOID CUTTING AWAY
TOO MUCH WOOD AND WEAKENING FLOOR

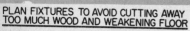

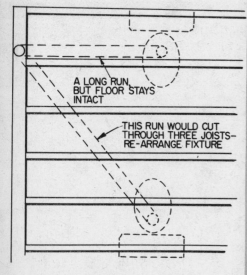

A LONG RUN
BUT FLOOR STAYS
INTACT

THIS RUN WOULD CUT
THROUGH THREE JOISTS—
RE-ARRANGE FIXTURE

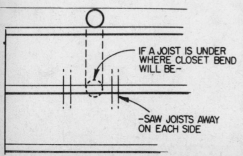

IF A JOIST IS UNDER
WHERE CLOSET BEND
WILL BE—

—SAW JOISTS AWAY
ON EACH SIDE

AND ADD 2" X 8" HEADERS

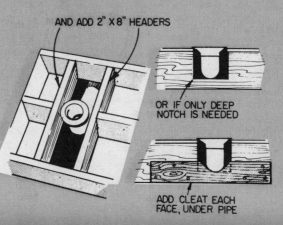

OR IF ONLY DEEP
NOTCH IS NEEDED

ADD CLEAT EACH
FACE, UNDER PIPE

FIXTURE UNITS

Fixture	Unit Values	Pipe Size	Horizontal Pipe (¼" per ft. slope)	Vertical Pipe
3-piece bathroom group— toilet, tub, lavatory	6	1½"	3	8
Toilet	4			
Bathtub	2	2"	6*	16
Shower	2			
Lavatory	1	3"	20**	30
Sink	2			
Laundry tub	2	4"	160	240
Floor drain	1			

* Waste only
** Not more than 2 tailets on horizontal line

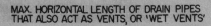

MAX. HORIZONTAL LENGTH OF DRAIN PIPES
THAT ALSO ACT AS VENTS, OR 'WET VENTS'

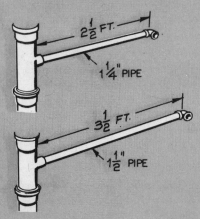

2½ FT.

1¼" PIPE

3½ FT.

1½" PIPE

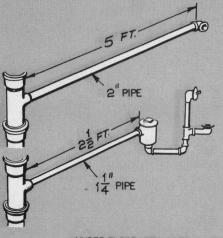

5 FT.

2" PIPE

2½ FT.

1¼" PIPE

LOCATING SOIL STACK BASE POSITION

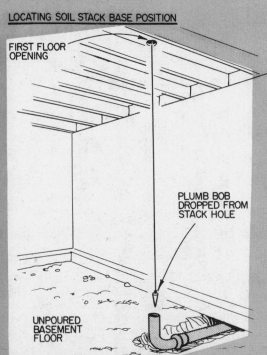

FIRST FLOOR OPENING

PLUMB BOB DROPPED FROM STACK HOLE

UNPOURED BASEMENT FLOOR

UNDER FLOOR VIEW OF TWO WAYS
TO CONNECT TOILET BEND

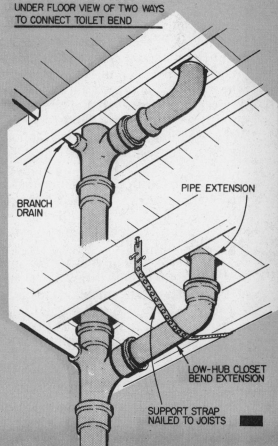

BRANCH DRAIN

PIPE EXTENSION

LOW-HUB CLOSET BEND EXTENSION

SUPPORT STRAP NAILED TO JOISTS

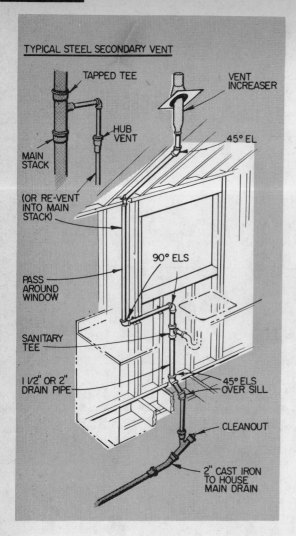

TYPICAL STEEL SECONDARY VENT

TAPPED TEE
VENT INCREASER
HUB VENT
MAIN STACK
45° EL
(OR RE-VENT INTO MAIN STACK)
90° ELS
PASS AROUND WINDOW
SANITARY TEE
1 1/2" OR 2" DRAIN PIPE
45° ELS OVER SILL
CLEANOUT
2" CAST IRON TO HOUSE MAIN DRAIN

ROUGH-IN DIMENSIONS

EYE LEVEL SHOWER
SINK HANGER
MIXER FAUCETS
TANK FILLER
SPOUT
10"
4"
4"
18"
16"
12"
8"
8"
14"
TUB DRAIN
8"
12"
VERTICALLY WITHIN 2 3/4" RIGHT OR LEFT OF DRAIN IN SINK

FIXTURE SUPPORTS MUST BE NAILED IN WALL BEFORE CLOSING WITH PLASTER

SHOWER HEAD BLOCK
2" X 6" LAVATORY SUPPORT
1" X 6" TUB RIM BACK UP BOARD
2" X 4" ON WALL BLOCK SUPPORTS MIXING FAUCETS

each tee, put in a 12-inch-long length of capped pipe for an air cushion chamber. The branch of the tee gets a short length of pipe that should reach out an inch beyong the finished wall surface. On copper or plastic, come out farther. Cut off the excess later. Cap the nipple until you're ready to install the fixture. This will keep things clean inside. Capping is necessary for testing too.

As you install branch water supply runs to the fixtures, remember that the cold water is always the one on the right side as you face the wall. The hot water should be on the left. Even pros sometimes go wrong here.

Selective control of your water supply system is a good thing to have. One valve at the meter shuts off all water in the house. A valve at the hot water heater shuts off hot water only. Even further control is desirable. Ideally there should be hot and cold water stop valve immediately beneath every fixture, or one in every fixture branch. Then you can re-pair a leaky faucet without shutting off water to any other faucet.

When every fixture has been plumbed in, the long-awaited day comes when you can turn on the water. You'll get a thrill out of watching it flow from the faucet and disappear down the drain. Your plumbing system will be working.

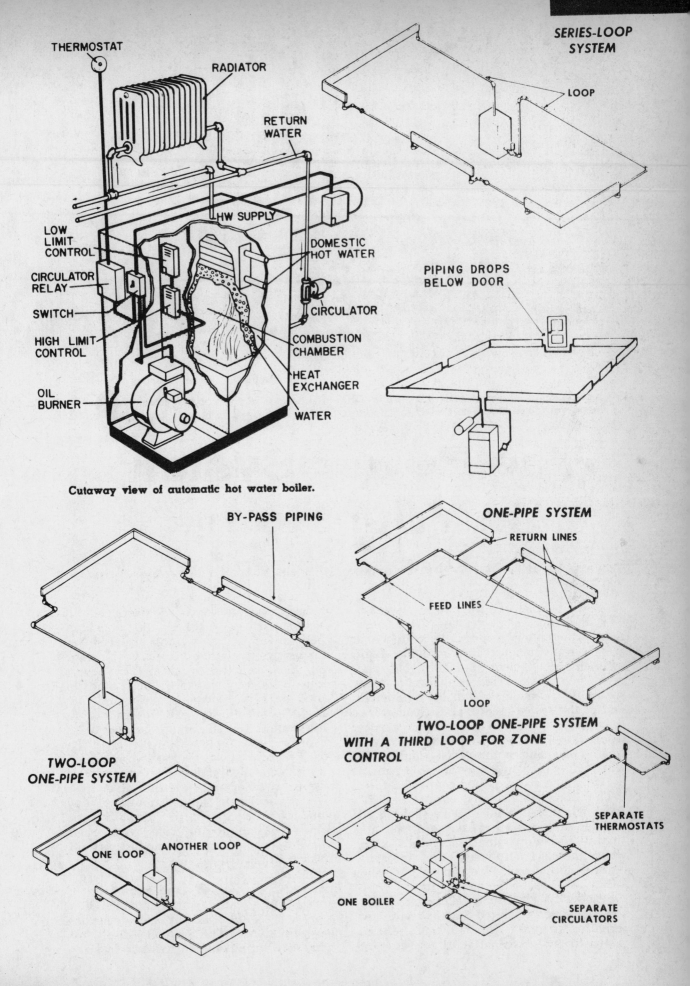

SERIES-LOOP SYSTEM

LOOP

THERMOSTAT

RADIATOR

RETURN WATER

HW SUPPLY

LOW LIMIT CONTROL

DOMESTIC HOT WATER

CIRCULATOR RELAY

SWITCH

CIRCULATOR

HIGH LIMIT CONTROL

COMBUSTION CHAMBER

HEAT EXCHANGER

OIL BURNER

WATER

Cutaway view of automatic hot water boiler.

PIPING DROPS BELOW DOOR

BY-PASS PIPING

ONE-PIPE SYSTEM

RETURN LINES

FEED LINES

LOOP

TWO-LOOP ONE-PIPE SYSTEM

ONE LOOP

ANOTHER LOOP

TWO-LOOP ONE-PIPE SYSTEM WITH A THIRD LOOP FOR ZONE CONTROL

SEPARATE THERMOSTATS

ONE BOILER

SEPARATE CIRCULATORS

Consolidated Edison Company of New York

The tall chimneys of power generating stations are a prominent sight in many cities. They carry off the waste gases resulting from the burning of coal, used to heat water to make steam to turn turbines.

The Power System in Your Home

You can identify its type by the number of wires entering the main switch box

MOST people take the power system of their homes for granted. They know that all they have to do is flip a switch, and a mysterious, magical force provides light when it's dark, heat when it's cold, and cold when it's hot. This speaks well for the reliability of modern electrical appliances and of the "juice" that makes them work. Inevitably, however, there comes a time when flipping a switch produces only a small noise and nothing else, and that's when you wish you knew something about the wiring and everything connected to it.

That knowledge is fairly easy to acquire. Although there's a lot of wire snaking all through a house, the basic systems are simple and understandable. Let's start where the electricity starts . . . at the generating station or "power house" . . . and follow through to the attic light.

Practically all commercially produced electricity in the United States is now "alternating current." This is usually abbreviated to AC as a matter of convenience

in both oral and written references. The early electric generating stations made direct current, or DC, but this suffered from the disadvantage that it could not be transmitted satisfactorily more than several miles from the point of origin. Lamps located near the power house would burn brightly, but those near the end of the line would be much dimmer because of loss of pressure or "voltage" in the wires. The great feature of AC is that it can be converted with high efficiency from any voltage to any other voltage, either up or down, over an enormous range of ratios. This is done by devices called "transformers," which have no moving parts, require only very minor maintenance, and last virtually forever in normal service.

Direct current is so called because it flows smoothly, evenly and without interruption, like water from a faucet. DC is what you get out of all batteries, regardless of size or type. The original Edison "dynamos," rotating machines driven by steam

A never-ending job at a power generating station—the taking on of coal. Here a tug nudges a loaded barge toward a waiting scoop at one of the Brooklyn (New York) stations of the Consolidated Edison Company. Many large power stations are located on waterways because coal can be transported more cheaply on the latter.

engines, delivered DC. Their modern counterparts, identical in electrical design but smaller in construction, are the charging generators in automobiles.

AC power is produced by rotating machines called "alternators," to distinguish them from DC "generators." In most large generating stations the actual turning power is provided by high-pressure, high-speed steam turbines. Steam is the vapor of boiling water, and requires a lot of heat. The usual fuels such as coal, oil and gas are used to keep huge boilers cooking round the clock.

The water wheel, a power device dating back to Biblical times, turns the alternators of the biggest generating stations in the world. The water comes from natural configurations in Nature, like Niagara Falls in New York, or from man-made dams which control vast rivers in various parts of the country.

In relatively smaller power houses alternators are driven directly by Diesel engines. In still smaller installations, found on isolated farms or in military service, they are driven by conventional gasoline engines.

The AC "Wave Form"

Figure 1 is the nearest possible graphic representation of the AC "wave form," or the way the current flows in a circuit. Let's follow the action of an alternator in terms

Below, one of the largest power generating plants in the world—the Astoria (Queens) plant of the Consolidated Edison Company of New York. The two large machines are steam-turbine driven alternators.

of time and generated voltage. For measuring time we'll use an imaginary stop watch that reads 1/60 of a second from start to stop; for showing voltage, a zero center meter whose needle moves to the right when current flows in one direction and to the left when it flows in the opposite direction.

With the alternator at rest, nothing, of course, happens. Let's click the stop watch the instant the machine starts to turn, and watch the voltmeter. With the first slight movement of the alternator, electrons in its wires are agitated and the meter needle starts to move, let us say to the right. As the rotation continues, the voltage builds up proportionately. At 1/240 of a second after the starting time the voltage reaches its peak value, and then starts to drop. It falls back to zero after another 1/240 of a second, or a total elapsed time of 1/120 second.

As the machine turns, another section of wires comes into play, and a new voltage is created just as the first one dies to nothing. It builds up in value exactly as its predecessor did, but it flows in the *opposite* direction, as a left-hand deflection of the voltmeter indicates. At 1/80 second after the starting time this second voltage reaches its peak value, which is identical with that of the first voltage, and then it, too, starts to decay. It drops to its zero 1/60 second after the starting time.

If we let the alternator run, the process keeps repeating itself. One complete variation of current from zero through peak to zero, and again from zero to peak to zero the other way, is called a "cycle;" each half is called an "alternation." The number of cycles per second (c.p.s.) is called the "frequency;" in this case 60, which is universally supplied to homes in the United States.

There is nothing magical about 60 c.p.s. It was probably adopted because there are 60 seconds to a minute and 60 minutes to an hour and the number suggested itself to the early American electrical engineers. For certain industrial and railroad purposes 25 cycles is used (why 25 and not 30, no one knows!) and in some factories 400 cycles is found. This is called "high-cycle" current and is advantageous for special applications calling for small but high-speed motors. In most of the rest of the world the standard is 50 cycles.

Because of an ability of the human eye known as "retention of vision," electric lights operated on 60-cycle AC appear to burn steadily. Although the voltage drops to zero three times in every cycle, it does this too quickly for the lamp filaments to cool off.

One alternation of the AC cycle is sometimes referred to as "positive" and the other as "negative." These are purely mathematical terms and are somewhat

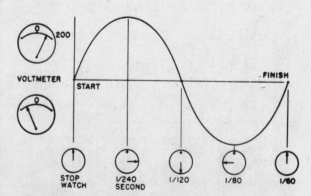

Figure 1: AC in action is shown in diagram form; fluctuations produce magnetic effects by means of which voltages can be stepped up or down.

Power companies are kept busy installing new distribution cables, with the increased demand for electric power; photo shows Con-Edison workmen greasing the path of four-inch electric cable.

misleading because "negative" conveys the meaning of uselessness or nonexistence. The two alternations are absolutely identical in their ability to do work.

The Distribution Network

Power is generated in modern stations at voltages between 11,000 and 14,000. By means of transformers, this is boosted to values ranging from 23,000 to as high as 275,000 volts, the higher voltages being used for the longest lines. The higher the voltage, the lower the current in amperes for any particular power load, and the smaller the wire required to handle the latter. This is an important consideration, as large diameter wire is heavy, is difficult to handle, accumulates dangerous quantities of ice and is buffeted around by strong winds; all these effects are reduced with thin wire.

As power is needed in various areas, the high voltages are brought to much lower levels by step-down transformers. A primary distribution point or "substation" changes them to between 2500 and 15,000 volts. A secondary distribution point, which may be merely a transformer on a pole or concealed in a vault below street level, brings the power down to the eventual consumer level. In residential areas this is usually either 115 or 230 volts, or both on the same circuit. See Figure 2.

The figure "115" is a flexible one. De-

This pole represents the last step in the power distribution network; high-voltage wires on the top of the pole are connected to a step-down transformer (in the large cylindrical case). From this the lower wires run through to home outlets.

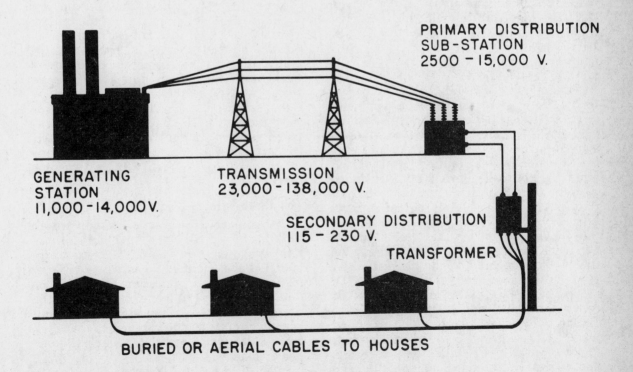

GENERATING STATION
11,000 - 14,000 V.

TRANSMISSION
23,000 - 138,000 V.

PRIMARY DISTRIBUTION SUB-STATION
2500 - 15,000 V.

SECONDARY DISTRIBUTION
115 - 230 V.

TRANSFORMER

BURIED OR AERIAL CABLES TO HOUSES

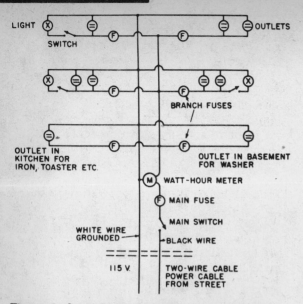

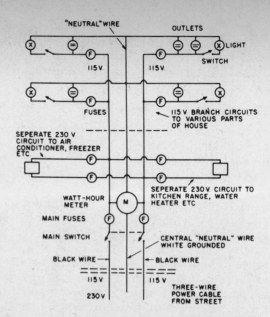

Figure 3 shows basic hook-up of two-wire power distribution generally found in older residences.

Figure 4 shows basic three-wire system, which makes both 115 and 230 volts available in house.

pending on the age of the power system, the number of houses fed by one transformer, the time of the day, the size of the actual wiring in the individual home, and the number and type of appliances in use at one time, the voltage may vary from 110 to 125. In older residential districts it will run to the low side; in newer ones steady readings of 120, 121 and 122 volts are normal. For purposes of discussion let's use 115 volts to represent all values between 110 and 125, and 230 volts for voltages from about 220 to 240. The figure of 208 volts appears in some cases, but this is a special value, not evenly related to either 115 or 230. It is taken up later in this section in the discussion of four-wire systems of distribution.

The Two-Wire House System

The majority of small houses built prior to the television and electric appliance boom of the post-World War II period are fed with a simple, basic two-wire power system. Two wires, running from the nearest secondary distribution transformer, enter the house. They might be suspended aerially from a pole on the curb line, or they might be completely out of sight in buried pipe. With such a two-wire service, the voltage is always "115." See Figure 3. One wire has white or gray colored insulation. It is connected to the nearest water pipe and is called the "ground" wire. The second wire has black insulation and is called the "hot" side of the line only to distinguish it from the other. The grounded wire is by no means "cold" by implication; the two wires can function only together, not separately. Standard practice is to keep

the grounded wire a continuous circuit throughout the house, and to insert fuses and switches only in the hot wire.

The main switch and the main fuse are usually in a single steel box. The cover of the latter is linked to the switch handle in such a manner that the fuse is accessible inside only when the switch is thrown to "off." With the switch open or the fuse burned out, the entire electrical system of the house is dead.

The watt-hour meter registers the power consumed in the house. Following it, there are usually several individual "branch" circuits, each with a fuse. These feed power to various parts of the house. If the builder was conscientious, he arranged the branch circuits so that the ceiling lights and the wall outlets in the rooms are on different branches. Thus, if an appliance plugged into a wall outlet blows a fuse, the room lights still work. It is also sensible to provide individual lines for outlets that require a lot of current: one in the kitchen, for instance, for an iron or toaster, and another in the basement for a washing machine.

The Three-Wire System

In many areas power is brought into a building by a three-wire, dual-voltage system, as shown in Figure 4. The center wire is called the "neutral," has white or gray insulation, and is grounded. Between this neutral and either outside black wire is the normal 115 volts. The various 115-volt branch circuits are distributed so that each half of the system carries about the same power load.

In most cases the three-wire system is

wired only to feed standard 115-volt lamps and appliances. It is a simple matter, however, to obtain a circuit from the two outside black wires alone to give 230 volts, for the operation of an air conditioner, a large freezer, etc. The advantage of using the higher voltage is that the current in amperes is reduced, and this minimizes heat losses in the line wires and the possibility of overloading the main fuses. A specific example is a standard ⅓ horsepower motor that works equally well on either 115 or 230 volts through a slight shifting of its internal connections. It develops the same ⅓ h.p. in either case and registers the same power on the watt-hour meter. However, while it draws 6 amperes on 115 volts, it takes only 3 on 230 volts.

The importance of minimizing line current is taken up in detail in the chapter entitled "Is Your Wiring Adequate?"

The presence of both 115 and 230 volts in the same house means that special precautions must be taken to prevent 115-volt appliances from being plugged into 230-volt outlets. There is no harm in making the opposite mistake; for instance, a 230-volt air conditioner just wouldn't start on the lower voltage.

The usual safety measure takes the form of power receptacles and matching plugs having oddly spaced connectors, quite different from the ones used with ordinary 115-volt lamps, irons, vacuum cleaners, etc. These fittings are generally of the "crow-foot" or "tandem-blade" type, and are treated in detail in the section of this book entitled "The Third Wire Is a Lifesaver."

To distinguish further between 115- and 230-volt outlets, it is the practice in some areas to paint the latter bright red.

Three-wire installations are standard in homes having all-electric kitchens. There is usually a separate heavy-duty 230-volt line from the meter directly to the range, which can easily take as much as 50 or 60 amperes even at this higher voltage. The range alone thus represents three or four times as much power as required for the entire rest of the house.

The Four-Wire System

The wave form shown in Figure 1 is a picture of AC as it would be generated in a simple, basic alternator. This is called "single phase" power because only one build up of voltage in each direction takes place during the 1/60 second of a complete cycle. In actual practice the large stations do not generate single phase power, but what is called "polyphase" or "three-phase" power. From it single phase circuits are derived as needed.

Until recently polyphase power was used exclusively for industrial purposes where motors of one horsepower or more constituted the major part of the load. With the increasing use of central air conditioning in the home, the power companies are putting

The voltage step-down transformers required in new residential areas are too heavy to be hung on poles. Instead, it is generally found necessary to place these bulky elements in nearby underground vaults.

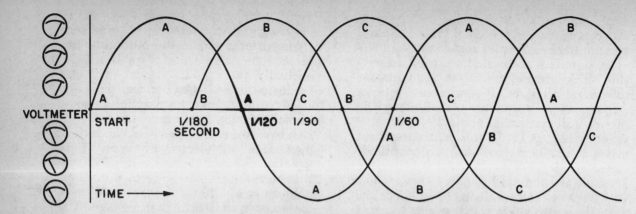

VOLTMETER

START   1/180   1/120   1/90   1/60
         SECOND

TIME

Figure 5: Three-phase power generated by most large generating stations. Curves A, B, C are of three separate voltages which flow in same circuit 1/180-second apart. This type is for large motor operation.

polyphase circuits into many new residential districts. These conditioners run to 2, 3, 5 and even more horsepower, and represent little "industrial" installations all by themselves.

If you have a somewhat older house and are considering the idea of modernizing its wiring, installing a big air conditioner to work through existing heat ducts, etc., by all means consult your local utility. The company's engineers know exactly what kind and size of power lines are available in the neighborhood, and will tell you whether a three-wire or a four-wire system will best serve your needs. This advice is free, as the company is glad to have you increase your use of electricity!

Look at Figure 5. The wave form or curve marked A is the same as that of Figure 1. It represents the voltage developed by one set of windings on the rotating alternator. As before, the first alternation is completed in 1/120 second, the complete cycle in 1/60 second. In an actual machine, there is not one but three sets of identical windings, separated 120 degrees or ⅓ of a revolution. As the alternator starts to turn from its theoretical dead starting point, the first winding starts to generate the voltage A and continues to do so as the motion continues. A scant 1/180 second after the starting time, the second winding comes into play and generates the voltage B, which is exactly like A. While voltage A is building up the second alternation of its first cycle, the third winding comes into play at the 1/90 second point, and generates the voltage C. This is a replica of its predecessors A and B. With the alternator turning over steadily, power is delivered THREE times during each cycle of 1/60 second duration, instead of only once. For motor operation, three-phase supply has the same advantage over single-phase supply that multiple-cylinder gasoline engines

have over single-cylinder jobs. The torque is smoother, and the motors themselves are simpler in construction and more efficient in operation.

The three windings on the alternator are in effect three separate generators, and can be connected in a number of very complex ways. Of course, the voltages can be stepped up or down in any desired fashion.

As it reaches the home, three-phase power takes the form of a *four*-wire cable from the street. People with some practical knowledge of electricity and radio are invariably confused by this wiring the first time they see it. They usually know about three-wire, 230-volt service, but they can't figure the four. The arrangement is really quite simple. See Figure 6. One of the wires

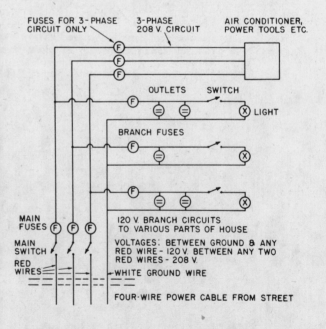

Figure 6: Basic four-wire, three-phase power system, with the watt-hour meter omitted for the sake of simplicity. The 115-volt circuits displayed here are distributed between ground and red wires.

again has white insulation, and as you might expect by now, is the grounded neutral. All the other three wires have red covering. Between the ground wire and *each* of the red wires you pick off 120-volt *single*-phase power for the usual 115-volt household machines and appliances. Each branch circuit has its own fuse. The big air-conditioner motor, a three-phase unit, is connected by three leads to the three *red* wires only, through its own set of three fuses. Because of the tricky interweaving of the three phase voltages, a separate return or neutral wire is not needed with a motor load. The voltage between any two red wires of the three-phase circuit is 208 volts when the voltage between ground and any one red wire is adjusted to 120 volts; repeat: 208 volts, NOT 230 or 240.

Both the starting and running current of a three-phase motor are relatively low. In an actual installation represented by Figure 6, the air conditioner goes on and off without having the slightest effect on the house lights or anything else connected to the single-phase branch circuits.

Three-Wire, 208-Volt System

In some residential districts of some of the major cities of the United States, the *only* power distribution system is of the four-wire, three-phase type previously described. The conventional 115/230-volt, three-wire system might not be available at all. A builder of medium-priced homes, which do not have central air-conditioning as original equipment, might not elect to bring the full four-wire service into them. Instead, he will ask for basic "115-volt" service, and let the buyers of the houses worry about the operation of air conditioners, driers, etc., that they might buy later.

Actually, what the power companies then install is *three*-wire service from the *four*-wire facilities on their street poles. One wire is the usual common ground; the other two are random pairs of the outside "phase legs." Neighboring houses are on staggered legs, so that the load is distributed over the wires and not concentrated on any one pair. See Figure 7.

Between the ground and *either* phase leg the voltage is a full 120, and this is led through the house to operate the usual "115-volt" lamps and appliances. Again, the lines are staggered between the common ground and the two phase wires, to distribute the load.

Now comes the joker: *The voltage across the two outside wires is not 240 volts, as it would be in an ordinary three-wire system if each half measured 120 volts;* IT IS 208 VOLTS, just as it was in the full four-wire system as detailed on the opposite page. Even some professional electricians are fooled; they see three wires and immediately say, "That's 115/230." It takes a voltmeter test and a call to the utility company to convince them that the voltages are 120 and 208.

Are there 208-volt appliances? Certainly. All you have to do is go and ask for them. •

Triple fuse block feeds three-phase power to large air conditioner in house having full four-wire service. Three wires on left go only to conditioner. White wire and dark wires on right go to house circuits, as shown in Figure 6 on opposite page.

Figure 7:
In this three-wire system, derived from four-wire, three-phase supply, single-phase power at 120 and 208 volts is available in an average house.

Power Is What You Buy

Volts, watts, amps and ohms are Man's method of measuring quantities of electrical power; to work with wiring, you should understand these terms.

VOLTS, amperes, ohms and watts are technical terms that add up to one important thing: your monthly electric bill from the local utility company. This is reason enough why you should know what they mean! Their relationship is very simple, and if you know any two of the values in a circuit you can easily figure the others

Volts, or "voltage," is a measure of the push or pressure of electrical energy. Ohms, or "ohmage," is a measure of the resistance of the wires, wiring and other electrical conductors through which electricity flows. Amperes, or "amperage," is a measure of the electricity that flows as a result of the push of the voltage against the resistance of the conductors. As appears logical, the higher the voltage and the lower the resistance, the higher the current. These three factors are expressed in "Ohm's Law," the simplest and most useful formula in all of

the complicated science of electronics. *amperes equal volts divided by ohms.*

Suppose an electric iron designed for service on 120 volts has a resistance of 10 ohms. How many amperes will it draw? That's easy: 120 divided by 10, or 12 amperes.

By simple transposition:

Volts equal amperes times ohms.

Ohms equal volts divided by amperes.

Like all standards, these electrical units are purely arbitrary. By international agreement, a conductor has a resistance of one ohm if it lets one volt push a current of one ampere through it in one second.

"Power" is the *rate* of doing work. The electrical unit is the "watt," and is merely volts times amperes. Strictly speaking, this should be expressed as the "watt-second," because by its own definition an ampere doesn't become an ampere until the current

The amount of electrical energy used in your home registers on a watt-hour-meter, which is usually located at the power-wire entrance to the building. The difference in readings from month to month, recorded by the utility company's meter reader, is multiplied by the rate per kilowatt-hour to give your bill in dollars and cents.

Consolidated Edison
Company of New York

has circulated for a short period of time.

(All four basic terms are named for pioneer physicists of the previous century. Ohm was a German, Volta an Italian, Ampere a Frenchman, and Watt a Scot.)

Since *watts equal volts times amperes* a simple transposition gives us *amperes equal watts divided by volts*. This is a very useful formula in practical work, because with it you can calculate the line currents of many appliances from the wattage figures on the name plates. Another useful one is obtained with a little mathematical juggling. You remember that *volts equal amperes times ohms*. Substituting *amperes times ohms for volts* in the power formula, we get *watts equal amperes times ohms times amperes* or *watts equal amperes squared times ohms*.

Impedance Versus Resistance

The foregoing formulas apply to all DC appliances and circuits, and to "heat" appliances used on AC circuits. In the latter category are ordinary screw-in and tubular incandescent lamps (but not fluorescents), laundry irons, toasters, broilers, room heaters, curling irons, immersion and bottle warmers, electric blankets, etc.

In all motor-operated appliances, television and radio sets and other devices using transformers or coils of wire on iron cores of one shape or another, the opposition to the flow of current through the wire is increased and complicated by certain magnetic effects. In addition to the straight resistance of the wire, the latter effects introduce a second factor called "reactance," and the total effect of the two is called "impedance." This is also expressed in ohms. "Resist" and "impede" have the same general meaning, but "impedance" signifies AC operation. Ohm's Law works just as well with impedance figures substituted for resistance. However, impedance values are of limited significance to practical workers; watts and amperes are more important and are readily calculated from simple formulas.

Although the impedance of a "reactive" AC appliance determines the current in amperes pushed through it by the line voltage, amperes times volts does NOT give its true power rating; the product is called the "apparent power." This is where people with a rudimentary knowledge of electricity often go haywire on their calculations. In many AC devices, the current and the voltage do not always act together, odd as this may sound. Sometimes the current doesn't flow until *after* the voltage has passed; sometimes it flows *before*. The true

power is indicated by a wattmeter, which is constructed to take these complex actions into account. The wattage figures on appliance nameplates are the true power.

The ratio of the true power to the apparent power is called the "power factor" of the device, and is expressed as a percentage. In pure heating appliances it is 100%, but in some broilers, hair dryers, etc., it may be less because of the motors in them. Motors for household machines and power tools run to as low as 40% and up to 75%; television and radio sets are somewhat higher.

Incandescent lights have 100%. power factor so a little straight arithmetic gives their current load. Add up the wattages of the individual bulbs on a circuit, divide by the assumed line voltage of 115 or 117, and the result in amperes is accurate enough for all practical purposes.

Many fluorescent lamps, on the other hand, particularly in older models and in sizes under double-48 inches, have very poor power factor, between about 45% and 60%. This is due to the presence in the circuit of lamp "ballasts," which consist of multiple turns of wire on iron cores. If only one or two such lamps are used in a house or apartment (usually in the kitchen), the extra line current is negligible.

In most newer types of fluorescents, the power factor is brought up to 90% and even 95% by the use of small capacitors (or "condensers"), whose purpose is to cancel or counterbalance the effect of the ballast winding. The extra cost is slight, and the reduction in line current becomes appreciable if, for example, several large lights are used in a workshop.

Regardless of the power factor, you pay only for the true watts. Your bills depend on the power of your appliances, the time they are kept on, and the utility's charge per kilowatt-hour of service. A kilowatt-hour means 1000 watts for a whole hour. Thus, a 500-watt laundry iron used for half an hour registers one-quarter kilowatt-hour on your electric meter. Read that again, and don't be confused by the fractions. If your power rate is say 3 cents per kilowatt-hour, the half hour's ironing cost only ¾ of a cent.

Figuring a Bill

Many people hesitate about buying air conditioners because they think they are "expensive" to run. The starting current of many conditioners is high for about three seconds, but after that they take less energy than many table-top broilers. For example, a typical room conditioner of standard make is rated at 1005 watts. Suppose you leave it running steadily during a very hot spell. For one full day the consumption is then 1005 times 24 hours, or 24,120 watt-hours or 24.12 kilowatt-hours. If the rate is 4 cents per K.W.H., the cost of running the machine is 96.48 cents, less than one dollar!

The wattage ratings found on appliances are figured on a basis of an "average" line voltage of 115 or 117.

Motor name plates bear the nominal horsepower rating and the line voltage and line current. The conversion factor is 746; that is, *horsepower equals watts divided by 746* or *watts equals horsepower times 746.*

On a typical ⅓ hp motor in my shop, the name plate reads "115 volts, 6 amperes." Volts times amperes gives the apparent power of 690 watts, but ⅓ of 746 makes the true power closer to 250 watts. Dividing 250 by 690 gives a power factor of about 40%.

Since the customer pays only for the true power he uses, why should he concern himself about power factor at all? If the wiring in his house is new and very heavy, he needn't. If it isn't, he finds that power factor rises to haunt him as he adds new machines such as clothes washers and dishwashers, garbage disposals, freezers, air conditioners, attic fans, etc., all of which have relatively low power factor. Low P.F. means high line current for the work done. The heating effect on the power wires of let us say 10 amperes is the same whether this current goes to a 1150-watt bowl heater of 100% P.F. or a 575-watt ventilator of 50% P.F.

I used the setup shown in the photo and diagram on page 21 to obtain a quick idea of the current drains of typical appliances:

Coffeepot, rated at 400 watts: 3½ amperes, 100% power factor.

Hot plate, rated at 700 watts: 6 amperes, 100% power factor.

Vacuum cleaner, rated at 550 watts: 6 amperes, 76% power factor.

High-fidelity amplifier, rated at 140 watts: 1.4 amperes, 83% power factor.

The higher the line current under any circumstances, the greater the power loss in the wires. The latter have appreciable resistance, and some work is done in overcoming it. The big joker here is that the heat loss does not go up gently with increased line current, but with the *square* of the current, as given in the formula *watts equals amperes squared times ohms.*

With current values on the order of 10, 15 and 20 amperes *squared*, or 100, 225 and 400, you can see that it doesn't take much

resistance in the lines or in connecting devices to cause trouble. A slightly dirty contact in a plug, having a resistance let us say of one tenth of an ohm, wastes 22.5 watts when the current is 15 amperes. This is juice you pay for but does nothing for you. Poor quality attachment plugs found with some table-top broilers and room heaters, which usually draw the 15-ampere legal maximum from one branch circuit, often becomes so hot that you can blister your fingers if you touch them.

High line current, regardless of whether the amperes are honest ones from high P.F. appliances or sneaky ones from low P.F.-ers, introduces a second joker: reduced line voltage at the appliances themselves. This angle is discussed in detail in the section entitled "Is Your Wiring Adequate?" which follows this chapter.

Knowing the power rating of an appliance and the approximate line voltage, you can work backward and make a pretty fair guess at the line current. It is important to know this so that you can add up the total current in any branch circuit and determine if the wire itself and the fuse or circuit breaker are of suitable size.

The formula was given previously as *amperes equals watts divided by volts* but this does not, of course, take power factor into consideration. Add about 50% more in the case of "reactive" AC appliances and you have a workable result. For example, take an air conditioner marked 900 watts, 115 volts. Dividing the first figure by the second, we get 7.8; call it 8, add 50% for power factor and the result is 12 amperes.

With a device like a coffee pot or an iron, having virtually 100% P.F., the simple division gives an accurate figure. For example, an iron marked 660 watts takes 5.7 amperes at 115 volts.

Low Versus High Voltage

From the formula *watts equals volts times amperes* you might get the glittering of an idea. Ignoring power factor for the moment, consider an appliance that takes 10 amperes at 120 volts, or 1200 watts. Would it do exactly the same job if it were designed to work on 60 volts and 20 amperes, again 1200 watts, or on 240 volts and 5 amperes, still 1200 watts? The answer is a strong, "Yes!" And since the power is the same in all three cases, so is your electric bill.

There is no advantage in going to lower voltage, but there is a tremendous advantage in going to the *higher* voltage: the line current is reduced by half, and with this lowered current heat losses and voltage drops in connecting wires come down, too. Remember that square-law business. With a plug resistance of .1 ohm, just for an example, the heat loss at 10 amperes is 10 times 10 times .1, or 10 watts, but at 5 amperes it is 5 times 5 times .1, or only 2½ watts! Some difference!

The starting current as well as the running current of motors is naturally lower on the higher voltage.

Cutting the current in half by going to 240 volts is the big reason why appliance dealers and utility companies urge customers to buy 240-volt air conditioners and to have an electrician run a separate line from the meter *if the house already has three-wire, 120/240 volt service.* A 240-volt motor doesn't cost any more than a 120-volt one; in fact, many of fractional horsepower motors used in home machines are readily convertible to either voltage through a quick switching of leads.

Practically all electric ranges are 240-volt operated. The wire required for 120-volt operation is prohibitively heavy and expensive to install.

Insulation No Problem

"What about the problem of insulation at the higher voltage?" No problem at all. If you'll examine sockets, outlets and other connectors closely, you'll see that they bear two current ratings, one in the 110-120 volt range and the other for 220-240. In other words, they're specifically designed for both voltages. Any standard power wires are more than adequately protected for 240 as well as 120 volts. Copper wire is expensive, but insulation is cheap.

In England, which must import every inch of copper it uses, the standard power line voltage for *all* house purposes has been 240 volts for as long as anyone can remember. Power cords there really look and feel like "cords," they are that thin.

So greatly does higher voltage alleviate the line overloading problem, and also make initial installation costs lower, that the power companies are going up the scale further than the 220-230-240 volt limit that has been standard in the United States for many years. In New York, for example, where huge new buildings with central air conditioning and whole ceilings of fluorescent lights are going up by the score, the Consolidated Edison Company is making 265/460 volt service available. This is a combination of single-phase power at 265 volts and three-phase power at 460 volts, exactly like the 120/208 volt service described in the section entitled "The Power System in Your Home."

Automobile manufacturers have shifted from six volts to twelve volts for precisely the same reasons of copper saving. The current needed at six volts to operate ignition, lights, radio, heater, cigarette lighter, convertible top, power doors and seats, etc., requires wire so heavy that installation is almost a plumbing job. With the current cut exactly in half at twelve volts, the wiring harness lends itself better to mass production methods.

Ignore any claims that the higher battery voltage is needed to give "increased power" for starting and other purposes in big present-day cars. This is pure advertising hog wash. Power in DC circuits, and there is no purer DC than comes from a storage battery, is just volts times amperes. •

Left, apparatus setup used to measure line current of appliances; AC ammeter is on left, plug-in box is at center and iron under test is at right. Below, right, here is the setup in diagram form. See text.

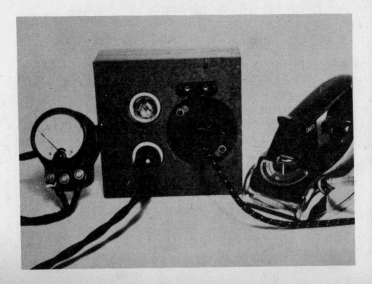

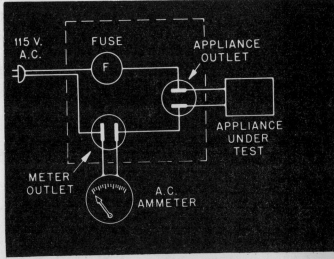

Is Your Wiring Adequate?

Ask your utility company to inspect it. Insufficient wiring causes faulty operation of appliances, reduced voltage and wasted power

THOUSANDS of new homes and apartments built each year are found to be electrically obsolete after only a couple of years of occupancy. When new appliances are acquired, the owners must spend large sums on additional wiring, and in some cases they are forced virtually to rip the old wiring out and to replace it with adequate lines.

"Inadequate" wiring creates a double problem: 1) It reduces the normal line voltage, often to the point where appliances cease to work satisfactorily; 2) It becomes overheated, and can readily start a fire in the home. Lights go dim, TV pictures shrink, a broiler doesn't cook the food in it, an air conditioner can't be used at all . . . all because of inadequate wiring. According to the Joint Industry Board of the Electrical Industry, four out of five homes and apartments in the great City of New York are insufficiently wired for appliances now found in them. The situation in other places is so bad that municipal ordinances are being drawn up which force the users of heavy-current machines to protect themselves. For instance, in Memphis, Tenn., appliance dealers are required to report to the city the sale of any device rated at 1,000 watts or more. The city then inspects the home of the purchaser to see that it is wired properly. Louisville, Ky., under an existing electrical code, can require property owners to install proper wiring or lose electrical service. In addition, the city is considering a new law patterned after the one in effect in Memphis, which would require buyers of appliances to prove they have the necessary circuits to carry the additional load. Affected would be air conditioners, room heaters, kitchen ranges, roasters, friers, broilers, garbage disposal units, large ironing machines, clothes driers and dishwashers.

The National Electrical Code, which forms the basis for practically all local electrical codes and ordinances, is a standard of safety. It deals primarily with the materials and methods of installation of wiring systems. However, these various codes cannot provide against the possibility of the wiring system becoming overloaded because of major additions to the home's electrical equipment. Code authorities recognize this limitation, and call attention to it in the introduction to the National Electrical Code, which states: ". . . an installation reasonably free from hazard, but not necessarily efficient or convenient. Good service and satisfactory results will often require larger sizes of wire, more branch circuits and better types of equipment than the minimum which is specified here."

Many people ask, "Why doesn't the local power company make sure the wiring in a house is sufficient? After all, the company is in the business of selling electricity and it's to their advantage to have a lot of appliances running properly."

The answer briefly is that your home is your castle, and what you do in it is your responsibility. If you chose to set it on fire by disregarding the limitations of its electrical system, the loss is yours. It may be yours alone, insurance notwithstanding, if subsequent investigation proves that your wiring was illegal and improper. Naturally, the utility companies don't like to lose customers, so many of them offer free wiring advisory service. Call the office of your local utility and find out. Note that this service is only *advisory*. The utility's actual responsibility ends with the power wires where they fasten to your house. The service entrance wires and everything else then depend on you. (The electric meter is the property of the utility but in

Fig. 2. Compare your main fuse box or circuit breaker box with the diagrams below. If it is the type shown at left, it is inadequate for present-day electrical loads. Consult your power company engineer.

BASIC CAPACITY:
Probably 3,600 watts

Typical 30 Amp.
Fuse Type
Main Switch

Typical 30 Amp.
Combination
Main Breaker and
Branch Circuit Panel

30 AMPERES
May be only 120 Volt
OBSOLETE

This will supply:

Lighting and a Few Plug-in Appliances.

BASIC CAPACITY:
14,500 watts

Typical 60 Amp.
Fuse Type Combination
Main Switch and
Branch Circuit Panel

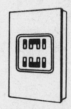

Typical 60 Amp.
Combination
Main Breaker and
Branch Circuit Panel

60 AMPERES
240 Volt
MINIMUM

This will supply:

Lighting and Plug-in Appliances—Electric Range—Water Heater.

BASIC CAPACITY:
24,000 watts

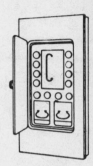

Typical 100 Amp.
Fuse Type Combination
Main Switch and
Branch Circuit Panel

Typical 100 Amp.
Main Breaker

100 AMPERES
240 Volt
ADEQUATE

This will supply:

Lighting and Plug-in Appliances—Electric Range—Water Heater PLUS any Major Appliances*

*With possible exception of Central Air Conditioning or Electric House Heating.

Typical Wattages of Some Lights and Appliances Normally Connected to General Purpose or Plug-in Appliance Circuits

LIGHTING watts

Ceiling or Wall (each bulb)...............40-150
Floor Lamps (each)...................150-300
Fluorescent Lights (each tube)............15-40
Pin-to-Wall Lamps...................50-150
Table Lamps (each)...................50-150
Ultra Violet Lamp.......................385

APPLIANCES watts

Baker (portable)...................800-1000
Bottle Warmer.......................95
Broiler-Rotisserie...................1320-1650
Casserole.......................1350
Clock.......................2
Coffee Maker or Percolator...........440-1000
Coffee Grinder.......................150
Corn Popper.......................1350
Deep Fat Fryer.......................1350
Egg Cooker.......................500
Electric Bed Cover.......................200
Electric Fan (portable).......................100
Electric Roaster.......................1650
Food Blender.......................230-250
Hair Dryer.......................235
Hand Iron (steam or dry).......................1000
Heating Pad.......................60
Heated Tray.......................500
Ice Cream Freezer.......................115
Ironer.......................1650
Knife Sharpener.......................103
Lawn Mower.......................250
Mixer.......................100
Portable Heater.......................1000
Radio (each).......................100
Record-Changer.......................75
Refrigerator**.......................150
Sandwich Grill.......................660-800
Saucepan.......................1000
Sewing Machine.......................75
Shaver.......................12
Skillet.......................1100
Television.......................300
Toaster (modern automatic)..........up to 1150
Vacuum Cleaner.......................125
Ventilating Fan (built-in).......................140
Waffle Iron.......................up to 1100
Warmer (Rolls, etc.).......................100
Waxer-Polisher.......................350

**Each time the refrigerator starts it takes several times this wattage for an instant.

One each (230 or 240 volt) for:
watts

Electric Clothes Drier...................4500
Electric Range...................8000-16,000
Electric Water Heater...............2000-4000
Room Air Conditioner* (½ or ¾ ton)...1200-1600
Water Pump*...................700-1500

One each (115 or 120 volt) for:
watts

Automatic Washer*.......................700
Built-in Bathroom Heater...........1000-1500
Dishwasher-Waste-Disposer...................1500
Electrostatic Air Cleaner.......................60
Home Freezer*.......................350
Mechanism for Fuel-fired Heating Equipment*..800
Room Air Conditioner* (1/3 ton)...........750
Summer Cooling Fan*.......................250-750
Waste-Disposer alone* (without Dishwasher)...500
Water Pump*.......................700
Workshop or Bench* (Total wattage will vary)

*The wattage of motor-operated equipment will vary, depending on the size of the motor. Individual circuits are necessary, however, in order to avoid frequent "blackouts," poor TV and radio reception. constant dimming or flickering of lights when the equipment is operating; to assure continuity of service from such devices as the home freezer and the heating plant, and to permit the use of plug-in and major appliances at the same time.

GENERAL PURPOSE CIRCUITS	For Protection They Need		You Can Connect All at Once
	Fuse or	Circuit Breaker	

For lighting and general use in living and bedrooms; lighting only, in kitchen, laundry, dining area.

Most homes built before 1940 still rely on one or two 15 ampere General Purpose Circuits for *all* lighting and appliance use. In many instances, even certain major appliances have been plugged in on these poor, overworked wires.

One 15 amp. plug fuse per circuit

(Ratings imprinted on handle.)

One 15 amp. breaker per circuit

1610-1800 watts

(20 ampere fuse or breaker permitted only when No. 12 wire is used.

PLUG-IN APPLIANCE CIRCUITS

To convenience outlets only (no lights), in kitchen, laundry, dining area — seldom found in homes built before 1940.

Most homes built since 1940 have one or more Plug-in Appliance Circuits, but some do not. And, often, the one Plug-in Appliance Circuit has since been forced to substitute as a Major Appliance Circuit, to serve some new appliance, like automatic washer, dishwasher, or home freezer. Then, it becomes overloaded each time it is shared with any of the plug-in appliances shown on the list at left.

One 20 amp. plug fuse per circuit

One 20 amp. breaker per circuit

2300-2400 watts on 2-wire circuits

(Only No. 12 wire is permitted for 20-amp. plug-in appliance circuits.) Modern practice is to use 3-wire circuits. These are each protected by two plug fuses, like those shown above at left—or by a double-handled breaker:

3-wire circuits are rarely found in older homes.

INDIVIDUAL EQUIPMENT CIRCUITS

Each of the major appliances and other equipment listed at left should have its own, individual branch circuit, in order to do its best work. If you have an electric range, water heater or clothes drier, you are sure to have a separate circuit for each one. They could not have been installed otherwise. However, in many homes, other major appliances have been connected to General Purpose or Plug-in Appliance Circuits which were already carrying more than their share of lighting and plug-in equipment.

2 Cartridge Fuses or

2 Plug-Fuses per circuit

One Plug-Fuse per circuit

1 Double-Handled Fuse per circuit

One Breaker per circuit

Nothing more than the appliance or equipment served by each circuit

Ratings of fuses and circuit breakers serving individual equipment circuits will vary—depending on what piece of equipment is to be served. Most of the 115 or 120 volt major appliances shown here are served by 20 ampere circuits

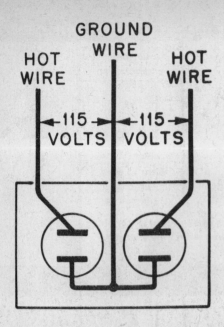

HOT
WIRE

GROUND
WIRE

HOT
WIRE

←115→ ←115→
VOLTS VOLTS

Fig. 3. As shown in diagram above, split outlet wiring permits use of two heavy-current appliances.

effect it becomes part of the permanent wiring installation in the home.)

In most older homes, the electric service entrance was planned to accommodate only lights and a few plug-in appliances, such as a toaster or an iron in the kitchen, radio sets in various rooms, and a portable vacuum cleaner. In such homes, certain newer machines cannot be used at all unless the entire service entrance is replaced by a larger one. Installing larger fuses than the present ones is no solution to the problem, and is an extremely dangerous and foolish practice.

A common mistake made by many people is to assume that the service entrance is "adequate" merely because it is "three-wire." Most homes built since about 1940 have three-wire service, which can accommodate an electric range and a water heater. However, few of them have three wires that are big enough to bring in sufficient electricity for today's needs. Wire of the No. 2 size is recommended as a minimum. Remember that you pay only for the electricity you use, no matter how large the service entrance may be. There-

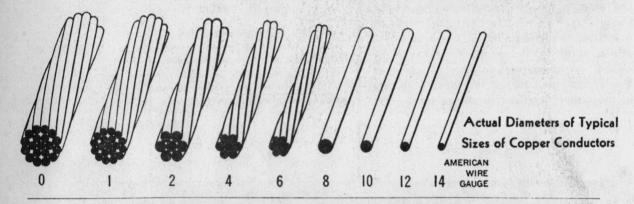

Actual Diameters of Typical
Sizes of Copper Conductors

0   1   2   4   6   8   10   12   14

AMERICAN
WIRE
GAUGE

PROPERTIES OF COPPER CONDUCTORS*

Size of Conductor AWG	Circular Mils	Ohms Per 1000 Feet 25°C—77°F Bare Conductor	Bare Conductor Diameter— Inches	Concentric Lay Stranded Conductors No. of Wires
14	4,107	2.575	.064	Solid
12	6,530	1.619	.081	Solid
10	10,380	1.018	.102	Solid
8	16,510	.641	.129	Solid
6	26,250	.410	.184	7
4	41,740	.259	.232	7
2	66,370	.162	.292	7
1	83,690	.129	.332	19
0	105,500	.102	.373	19
00	133,100	.081	.418	19

*From National Electric Code—1953.

fore, it pays in the long run to have it made big enough to permit future expansion. It can easily be too small, but it can never be too big.

It is difficult and risky for a layman to determine the actual size of the service entrance wires, as this usually means poking around the circuits while they are alive. Really the safest and cheapest thing to do is have the job done by a representative of the power company or by a local electrical contractor.

As a minimum, examine the main fuse box or circuit breaker box and look for an Underwriters' Label. If it is marked "Form 30," the service entrance is definitely obsolete. See Fig. 1. If the label has disappeared or if it has a different form number, compare your main panel with Fig. 2, and you'll get a fair idea of what you have.

According to modern standards, the service entrance in a 1000 square foot home should provide at least 4,500 watts for lighting and plug-in appliances (more in larger homes), *plus* any of the following permanently connected major appliances which are already in or are likely to be installed in the near future:

Automatic Washer	700 watts
Built-in Bathroom Heater (how many?) each	1000-1500 watts
Dishwasher	1500 watts
Clothes Drier	4500 watts
Electric Range	8000-16,000 watts
Water Heater	2000-4000 watts
Electrostatic Air Cleaner	60 watts
Home Freezer	350 watts
Mechanism for Fuel-Fired Heating Plant	800 watts
Room Air Conditioner, 1/3 ton	750 watts
Room Air Conditioner, 3/4 ton	1200 watts
Water Pump	700 watts
Waste Disposer	500 watts

What can be done about inadequate entrance service and equipment? The power company engineer or electrical contractor will probably recommend one or more of the following:

ALLOWABLE CURRENT-CARRYING CAPACITY, IN AMPERES, OF COPPER CONDUCTORS*

Based on room temperature of 30°C (86°F)

Size of Conductor AWG	In Raceway or Cable Not more than three conductors in raceway or cable; if the number of conductors is four, the allowable carrying capacity is 80 per cent of the values given.		In Free Air This generally covers open wiring on insulators, and knob and tube work.		
	Rubber Types R, RW, RU, RUW / Thermoplastic Types T, TW	Rubber Type RH	Rubber Types R, RW, RU, RUW / Thermoplastic Types T, TW	Rubber Type RH	Weatherproof Type WP
14	15	15	20	20	30
12	20	20	25	25	40
10	30	30	40	40	55
8	40	45	55	65	70
6	55	65	80	95	100
4	70	85	105	125	130
2	95	115	140	170	175
1	110	130	165	195	205
0	125	150	195	230	235

*From National Electric Code—1951.

INSULATION TABLE*

Insulation	Type Letter	Maximum Operating Temperature	Suitable For
Code Rubber	R	60°C (140°F)	General Use
Moisture-Resistant Rubber	RW	60°C (140°F)	General Use and Wet Locations
Latex Rubber	RU	60°C (140°F)	General Use
Moisture-Resistant Latex Rubber	RUW	60°C (140°F)	General Use and Wet Locations
Heat-Resistant Rubber	RH	75°C (167°F)	General Use
Thermoplastic	T	60°C (140°F)	General Use
Moisture-Resistant Thermoplastic	TW	60°C (140°F)	General Use and Wet Locations
Weatherproof	WP	80°C (176°F)	Open Wiring by Special Permission

*From National Electric Code—1953.

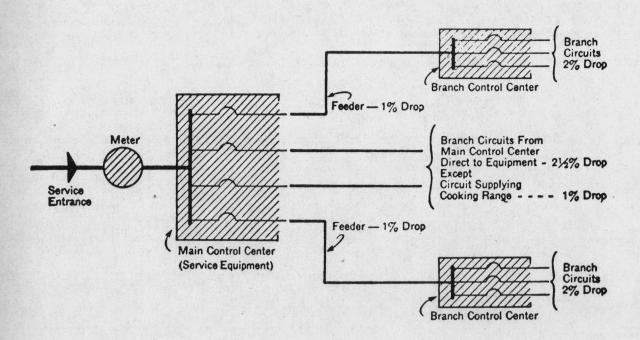

Fig. 8. This illustrates recommended allowable maximum voltage drops in a typical house wiring system.

1) Replace present service entrance wires with larger ones.

2) Replace outmoded fuse or circuit breaker box with one of larger capacity, probably a minimum of 100 amperes.

3) Retain present main panel as part of the service equipment and install a second main panel to increase the total capacity.

4) Replace old meter with a newer one.

This is only the beginning, of course. You have to work out from the fuse boxes into the branch circuits feeding the various parts of the house.

In some homes, a bad case of overloaded circuits can be relieved by having the automatic washer, dishwasher, freezer and other major appliances put on individual circuits. This may require some chopping of walls for the new wires and outlets, but it's worth the trouble. By the time a house needs new wiring it probably can also use a new paint job, and the two operations can be combined.

A modern and efficient method of increasing circuit capacity is to have one or more three-wire circuits installed, to serve convenience outlets into which you want to plug more than one high-wattage appliance at a time; for instance, a toaster and a coffee pot, at breakfast time, or a broiler and an iron, to permit a woman to press clothes while food is cooking. As shown in Fig. 3, this arrangement divides the openings of each convenience outlet between two different circuits,

greatly reducing the chance of overloading. The wires should be No. 12 in size.

Three-wire circuits also permit you to control one section of an outlet from a wall switch, while leaving the other section permanently alive for any plug-in purpose.

Wires and Voltage Drop*

The "circular mil" is the unit of measurement of the cross-section of wire used in electrical practice. One circular mil, abbreviated cir mil or cm, is the area of a circle 1/1000 of an inch in diameter. If the diameter of the wire in mils is known, the figure is simply squared and the result is circular mils. Because electrical workers rarely if ever have occasion to put a micrometer on copper wires, and because the cm numbers are very large and unwieldy even for small wires, this method of designation is rapidly falling out of favor. Instead, much more convenient one- and two-digit numbers, forming the "American Wire Gauge," or "AWG," are used in practical work. The accompanying table, Fig. 5, gives the relationships between gauge numbers, circular mils, actual wire diameters, etc. The AWG is the same as the "Brown and Sharpe Gauge," or

*Part of the material in this section has been abstracted from the "Westinghouse Home Wiring Handbook," Westinghouse Electric Corp., Pittsburgh, Pa.

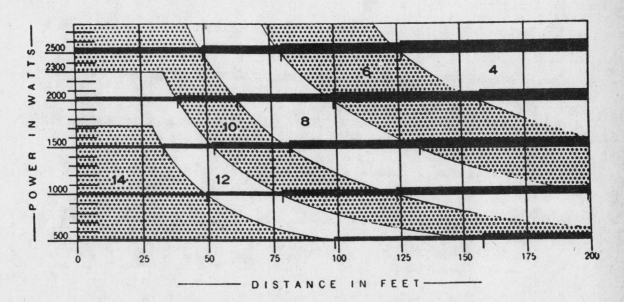

Conductor Size Based on Voltage Drop (115 Volt—2% Drop)

Fig. 9. With the aid of this chart you can determine what size wire you need.

"B & S." Fig. 4, shows the actual full size diameters of typical power wires from No. 14 through No. 0.

The conductor sizes given in Fig. 6, are based on current-carrying capacity of wire having type "R" insulation, which is a rubber compound, and the wires are assumed to be in raceways or cables. There are many varieties of insulation, but the ones listed in Fig. 7, are the ones in common commercial use.

Each type of conductor insulation affords a given maximum safe-operating temperature. If this "safe" value is exceeded for

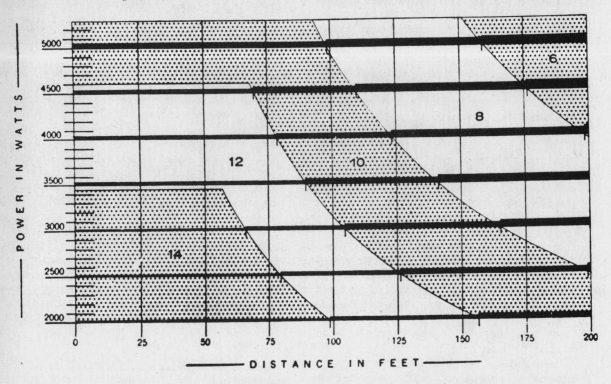

Fig. 10. **Conductor Size Based on Voltage Drop (230 Volt—2% Drop)**

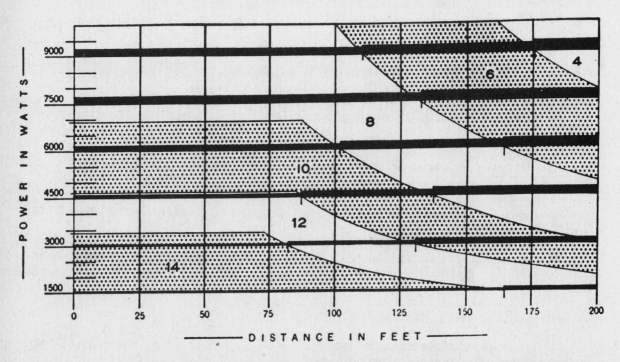

Fig. 11 **Conductor Size Based on Voltage Drop (230 Volt—2½% Drop)**

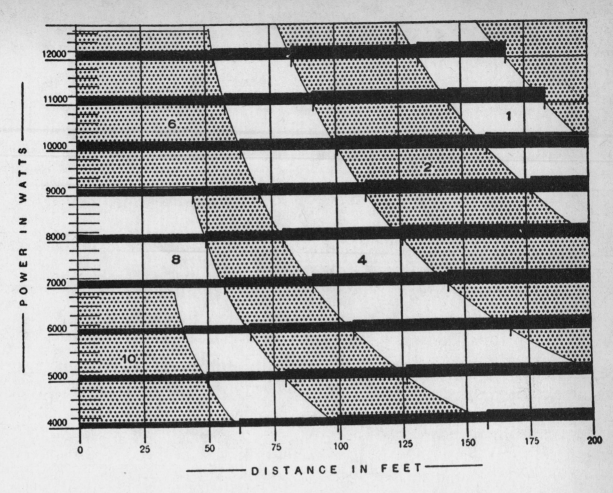

Conductor Size Based on Voltage Drop (230 Volt—1% Drop)

any considerable length of time, the insulation will deteriorate rapidly; under heavy overload conditions it can readily melt or burn off, permitting the copper wires to touch each other or the grounded cable in which they might be encased. If the fuses or circuit breakers are functioning normally, they will open and cut off further current.

The conductors of a wiring system should be of sufficient size not only as a safeguard against overheating, but also to restrict voltage drop. It is impractical to avoid *all* drop, but it can and should be held to reasonable proportions.

The recommended allowable maximum voltage drops in the various portions of a typical house electrical system are shown in Fig. 8. It is good practice to have the conductors of such a size as to keep the drops within the percentage limits indicated. The heavier the wire chosen for a circuit, the lower the voltage loss in it and the higher the voltage delivered to the appliance.

To determine if a conductor sized correctly for current-carrying capacity will also keep the voltage within allowable bounds, check against Figs. 9, 10, 11. Each covers a specific type of feeder or circuit. Based on economical voltage drop, load in watts and length of the circuit in feet, the proper size of conductor can be selected readily. Here's a practical example of the use of the charts:

Situation: A 115-volt branch circuit carries 1500 watts (13 amperes) a distance of 75 feet. It is desired to keep within 2% voltage drop, or 2.3 volts. Will No. 12 wire, having a carrying capacity of 20 amperes, do the trick?

Answer: No. Fig. 9 shows that No. 12 will carry 1500 watts about 53 feet with a 2% drop. To find the right size, start at the 1500-watt line at the left, and run your finger to the right until you meet the vertical line coming up from the 75-foot mark at the bottom of the chart. The point of intersection is clearly on the heavy line marked 10, which is the number of the needed wire. •

Testers and Tools

The Clicktester, Handitester and Lightester are simple projects to make; you'll find them invaluable for trouble-shooting appliances

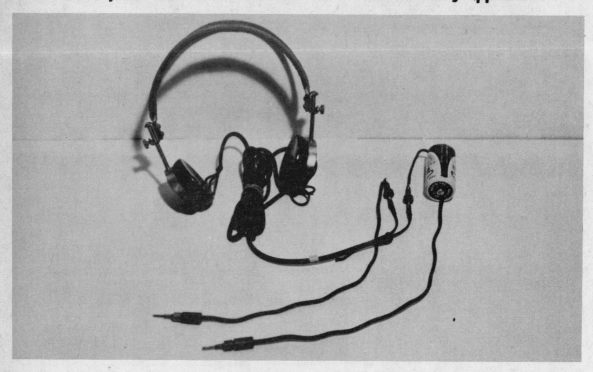

Here is the "Clicktester" wired but not assembled; the parts have been separated to show connections. The earphones, the single flashlight cell and the flexible test prods are connected in simple series.

ALL electrical appliances contain wire of one sort or another, through which current flows to perform a variety of tasks. In the case of heating devices, such as ordinary lamps, irons, grills, coffee makers, etc., the wire is purposely designed to resist or impede the movement of electrons. The latter, in pushing their way through this resistance, develop considerable friction, the outward effect of which is the desired heat. The most commonly employed resistance wires are alloys: nickel chromium, nickel copper, nickel chromium iron, nickel iron, and manganese nickel, which are sold under dozens of different trade names.

For most other purposes it is desirable to have wire of low resistance. Soft copper is universally used because it is cheap and workable. Only silver has a lower resistance value, and for this reason the contacts and sometimes even the wire of certain high-grade instruments are silver-plated.

In low-resistance wire, electron movement is converted into useful mechanical movement through magnetic effects, as in the case of motors, bells and buzzers, and other items.

Obviously, the wire path must be continuous, or no current can flow. Because wires do burn out in normal service or from accidental short circuits, or break from physical abuse, the basic test to be made on an appliance suspected of being defective is a "continuity" check. Fortunately, this can be done easily and quickly with some very simple and inexpensive testers, which you can make yourself either from "junk box" parts or a prepared kit.

The "Clicktester"

Consisting merely of an earphone, a single flashlight battery and a couple of pieces of wire, the "Clicktester" is entirely adequate for about 90% of all the trouble-

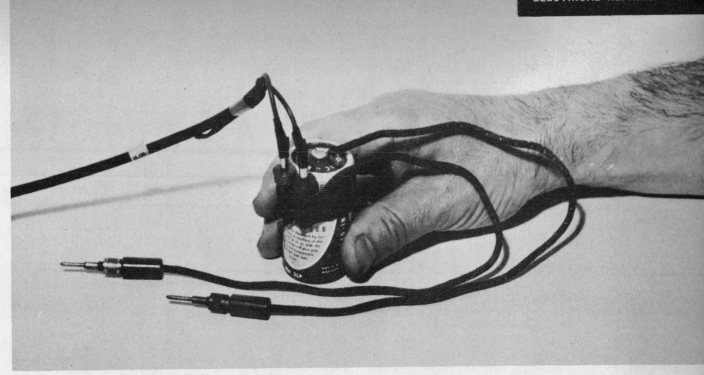

The two tip jacks for the earphone terminals are taped securely to the body of the flashlight cell. The length of the leads with the test prods is not critical; lamp cord between 12 and 18" is OK.

Check the condition of switches with Clicktester by tapping the probes against terminal screws.

Is wiring in fan OK? A test with Clicktester will give answer; no sound reveals an open circuit.

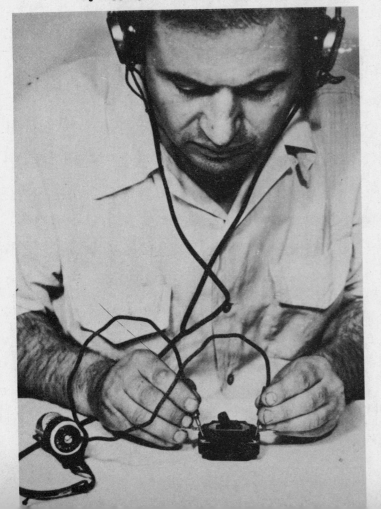

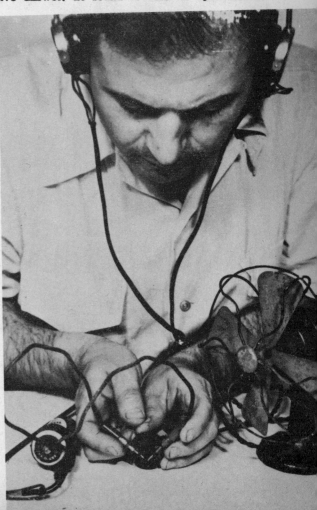

shooting you are likely to do on household electrical devices. *Any* single or double earphone intended for telephone or radio work will serve the purpose. Astronomical quantities of very sensitive military phones are kicking around the surplus stores, at a fraction of their real value. The radio mail order firms sell a perfectly suitable single phone for only 96 cents!

To facilitate connection to the end pins of the phone cord, you need two pin jacks, which cost 9 cents each; also two tip plugs, at 14 cents each, for use on the ends of two test wires or "probes." The latter can be any flexible insulated wire . . . a section of lamp cord is fine . . . about a foot long. The battery can be of either the "C" or "D" size. One that is too run down for a flashlight might have enough juice left in it for a year of tester service.

Cut a piece of insulated wire about 3 inches long; solder one end to the bottom of the battery and the other to a tip jack. Solder one end of a probe wire to the top (center) connection of the battery. Solder one end of the second probe wire to the second tip jack. Tighten the free ends of the probes to the tip plugs. The latter do not require soldering. Push the bared end of the wire through a hole in the body of the plug and catch it under the threaded head nut. Tape the tip jacks individually with friction or Scotch electrical tape, and then tape the pair to the body of the battery. Push the tips of the phone cord into the jacks, and you're in business. It will probably take you longer to read this description of the Clicktester than to make the item.

With the phones resting on the table, touch the free probe ends together. You will hear a loud click when you make contact and again when you break it. With the probes pressed firmly together, you will hear nothing. Don't be afraid of the metal ends of the probes. You can touch them freely, as the 1½ volts of the battery isn't enough to shock a gnat.

Using the Clicktester

In using the Clicktester, it is usually convenient to wear the phones, just to get them out of the way. Don't put them directly over your ears, but push them forward slightly. The clicks can be strong enough to be uncomfortable when they are sounding.

To illustrate a basic application of the Clicktester, let's try it on an ordinary switch. In the latter's off position, touching the probes to the connecting screws should produce no sound. Snap the arm to the on position and try again. This time you'll hear loud clicks as you tap the probes on the screws. These are the results you will obtain from a switch in normally good condition, but don't think that all switches respond that way. Because of failure of the internal spring or fusing of the contacts, a switch is likely to test either open (no clicks) or closed (clicks) with the arm in either the on or off setting.

The more wire in an appliance, the higher its resistance, relatively. You might therefore expect that the clicks will be weaker with a device like a fan or clock, for instance, than with a switch, which has practically no resistance. Actually, the difference is not very great, as you can readily tell by trying the Clicktester successively on an electric bulb, a fuse, a fan, an iron, a mixer, etc.

The Clicktester must not be used on parts or appliances connected to live circuits. The devices to be tested must be disconnected entirely. Observe the usual safety precaution of unscrewing the line fuse before touching the wires or terminals of any outlet. In the case of common appliances such as fans, mixers, air conditioners, irons, etc., it is, of course, only necessary to pull the line plug from the wall receptacle.

A device as simple as the Clicktester can be expected to have some limitations. The clicks indicate that the device under test has a continuous or closed circuit; however, the tester cannot distinguish between a normal low-resistance circuit and an extremely low resistance such as created by an internal short circuit or other abnormal condition. To do everything the Clicktester can do, and its missing 10% also, you need a *measuring* rather than an indicating instrument.

The "Handitester"

The Heathkit "Handitester," made especially for electrical trouble shooting, is such an instrument. A complete kit costs less than $15 and makes up into a professional-looking meter that will prove extremely useful not only for household appliances but also for the electrical system of a car and for the simpler elements of radio and even television receivers. Assembly and wiring are an evening's work. In a shiny black molded case, the completed tester stands only 6 by 3 by 2½ inches overall.

The Handitester is a combined voltmeter, ohmmeter and ammeter, all in one. The various functions are brought into play by means of a 12-position switch on the front panel. Connection between the tester and the circuit or device to be tested is made by flexible plug-in wires. One wire terminates in a spring clip, which is hooked to one

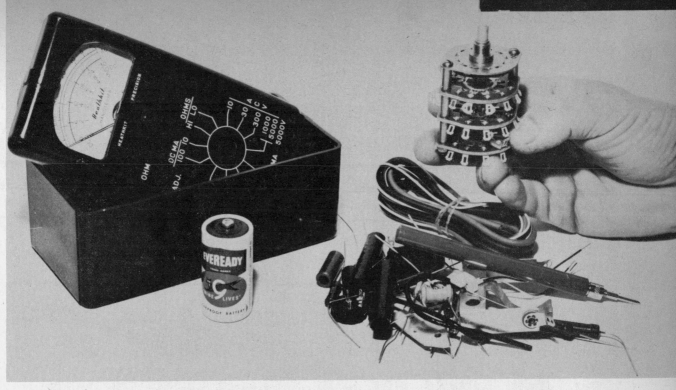

These are parts for Handitester as furnished in complete kit form. Meter unit is part of front panel. Hand holds three-deck "function switch." represented on front panel by control knob with pointer.

Inside view of completed Handitester. Battery on back of meter provides current for all resistance measurements. Wiring as seen here is compact.

terminal of the appliance; the other wire ends in a long insulated probe which is touched to the other terminal of the appliance.

Instruments of the Handitester type are known generally as "VOM's," for "Volt-Ohm-Meter." They are available in a large variety of both kit and factory-assembled models, from mail-order firms and from electronic supply stores everywhere.

As a voltmeter, the Handitester has 10 ranges, five each on DC and AC. Some of their possibilities for checking and trouble-shooting are listed on this and the following page for your information:

DC:

0 to 10 volt scale: flashlight, lantern, radio "A," and doorbell batteries; one-, two- and three-cell storage batteries.

0 to 30 volt scale: hearing aid and radio "B" batteries; six-cell storage batteries.

0 to 300 volt scale: larger radio "B" batteries; radio set "B" voltages.

0 to 1000 volt scale: electronic photoflash batteries; radio "B" voltages.

0 to 5000 volt scale: same as 1000 volt scale.

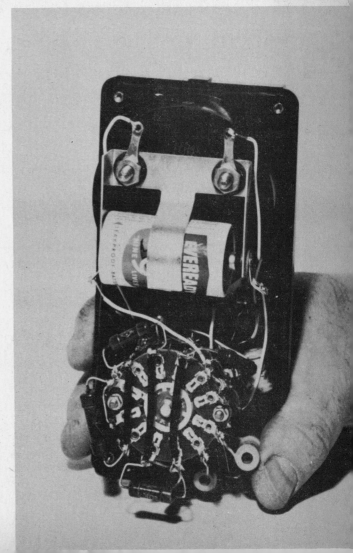

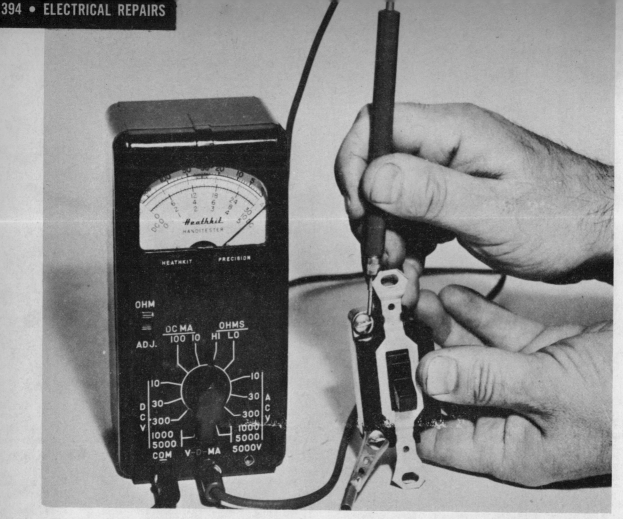

The value of a meter shows up in checking a switch for poor contacts. If they are poor, the meter reads an appreciable fraction of an ohm; if they are good, the needle bangs over to zero.

AC:

0 to 10 volt scale: some bell transformers.

0 to 30 volt scale: bell, toy train and house thermostat transformers.

0 to 300 volt scale: all two-wire, three-wire and four-wire power circuits.

0 to 1000 and 5000 volt scales: not much application.

As an ohmmeter, the Handitester is used like the Clicktester for continuity checking, except that it actually measures the resistance of the appliance in ohms instead of only showing a closed or open circuit. The meter has two resistance ranges: "LO," with easily read figures between 0 and about 500 ohms; and "HI," 0 to 50,000 ohms. Most appliances have normal resistance values well below 500 ohms. About the only ones running higher are small electric clocks, which measure between about 700 and 1000 ohms.

Zeroing the Meter

If the Handitester is set for LO ohms and applied to the same switch used experimentally with the Clicktester, the two extreme ends of the scale will come into play. First touch the probes together and turn the "OHM ADJ." knob on the front panel until the needle swings all the way over to the right or O position; this step is called "zeroing the meter." Separate the probes and the needle will fall back to the left end of the scale. Now touch the probes to the switch terminals. With the arm "off," the Handitester needle will not move, showing the switch to be completely open. With the switch "on," the needle will bang over to O ohms, or the equivalent of a dead short circuit. This is normal, as a closed switch should offer no appreciable resistance to the flow of electrons through it. If its contacts become loose or dirty, a condition that shows up on the meter as a slight value of resistance definitely above the O line, it can become quite hot and waste a lot of energy.

Ohmmeter readings have some significance in trouble-shooting only if you know the *normal* resistance values of appliances and machines. In this connection it is extremely interesting and instructive to make quick VOM checks on the usual devices found in the home or shop. Here are some actual readings:

Radio	5 ohms
Mixer	7 ohms
Toaster	11 ohms
Laundry iron	14 ohms
10-inch fan	22 ohms
1/3 hp drill-press motor	1½ ohms
7½-watt lamp	400 ohms
60-watt lamp	5 ohms
15-watt fluorescent heater	5 ohms
Small soldering iron	700 ohms
Large soldering iron	85 ohms
Gun-type soldering iron	7 ohms

As with the Clicktester, a VOM in its resistance-measuring function must not be used on live circuits. The current that makes the meter operate comes from a self-contained flashlight battery.

The "Lightester"

To determine if exposed wires and terminals in house power circuits are alive or not, it is very useful to have a simple "Lightester." This is nothing more than a lamp socket with a short length of flexible wire, the ends of which are fitted with insulated test prods.

The socket should preferably be of the "keyless" type, without a built-in switch. If only a common socket is on hand, tape or otherwise fasten the switch in its "on" position. The lamp can be of any size whatsoever. Because the tester is carried about, and because glass bulbs are fragile, it is a good idea to protect the lamp with a simple wire guard that clamps around the neck of the socket.

The test prods can be merely six-inch lengths of ¼-inch dowel. Solder the wires to headless nails about 1½ inches long, and tape them securely to the ends of the sticks. Touching the nails to a suspected power line tells you instantly if it is alive

With a switch in its off position, the ohmmeter needle should remain absolutely stationary when the test prods are applied to the terminals. A high resistance indication means internal leakage.

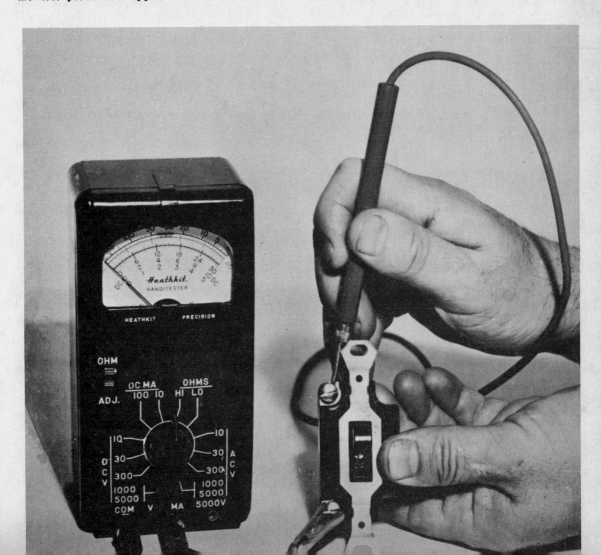

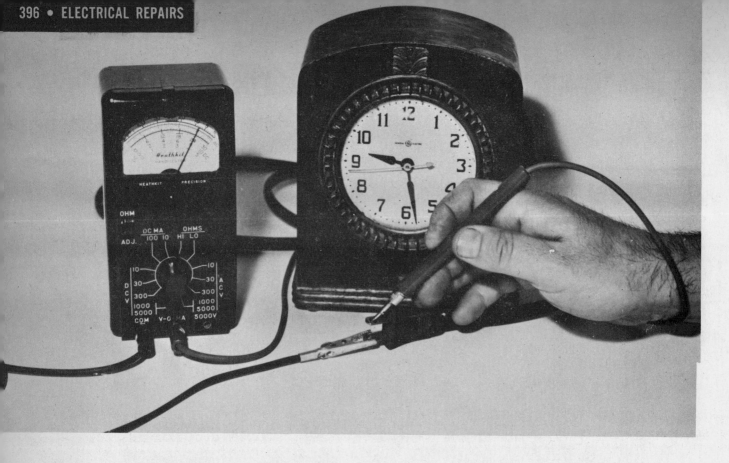

Above: With the Handitester set for ohms and connected to the prongs of a clock cord, the usual indication is several hundred ohms. No reading at all means that clock motor winding is open, or much less likely, that the power cord is open.

Below: The instrument shown in the photo is a VOM of a more advanced type (Precision Model 120), favored by electronic technicians and experimenters. Here it is being used to check the continuity and resistance of another clock motor.

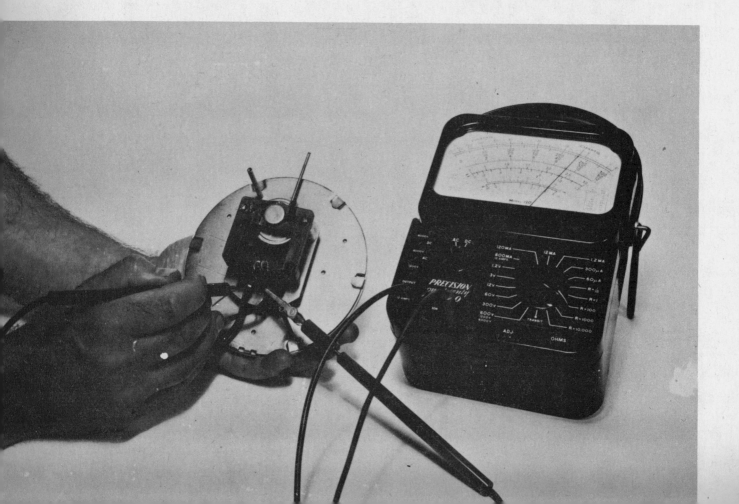

The "Lightester" consists merely of lamp and socket fitted with two test prods. The latter are dowel sticks with nails taped to their ends. Lamp can be any size. Protective cage is insurance against accidental breakage of bulb. This tester is very useful for quick check on 115-volt lines.

or dead. The wooden handles provide more than adequate protection against shock danger.

With a 115-volt lamp in its socket, the Lightester is, of course, limited to the checking of regular 115-volt circuits. If you're tempted to try it on 208- or 230-volt lines, you'll get a bright flash for half a second, and then you throw away the bulb. It is rather difficult to buy 230-volt lamps (impossible, in fact, in most parts of the country), so for checking these higher voltages it is better to use the 300-volt AC scale of a VOM.

Tools for Electrical Work

Any electrical repairs you can't make with the ordinary hand tools found in the basement or garage shop you probably can't make at all. Look at the picture of some basic tools and compare it with what you have in your own tool box: soldering iron or soldering gun: rosin-core wire solder; side-cutting, long-nose and diagonal-jaw pliers; assorted screwdrivers; knife for trimming insulation and cleaning wires; tape for covering joints in wire; hacksaw for cutting BX; and extension cord for bringing juice from a distant outlet when the circuit in a room is purposely opened to permit repairs.

Of obvious value are also such standard tools as wrenches, hammers, nut drivers, files, etc.

Tools for soldering take two different forms, the soldering "iron" and the soldering "gun." In spite of its name, the "iron" uses a tip of copper. This is heated by a coil of resistance wire inside the body of the tool. Depending on its size, an iron takes from two to five minutes to reach operating temperature. It is ready for use when solder touched to the tip melts instantly.

The "gun," so called because of its resemblance to a pistol, is actually a step-down transformer. The primary winding consists of many turns of fine wire, and is connected to the house power line through a trigger switch. The secondary is a single loop of metal tubing or rod between about ⅜ and ½ inch in diameter, its exposed ends being terminated by a relatively thinner V-shaped loop of copper wire. Because of the large step-down ratio of the primary-to-secondary turns, the voltage across the loop is very low, in the order of two to three volts, and the current is very high, as much as 100 amperes. This heavy current causes the copper end loop to heat up. There is no danger of shock from the exposed secondary rods, because the voltage here is low and also because they are not connected directly to the house power line.

The big advantage of the soldering gun is that it comes up to operating temperature in about three seconds. It is especially handy for making just one or a few joints in a hurry. You can be all finished with most jobs in the time it would take a straight iron to warm up.

There are some soldering tools *shaped* like guns that are actually of the resistance-heating type.

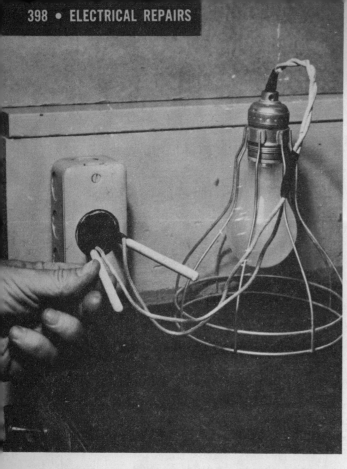

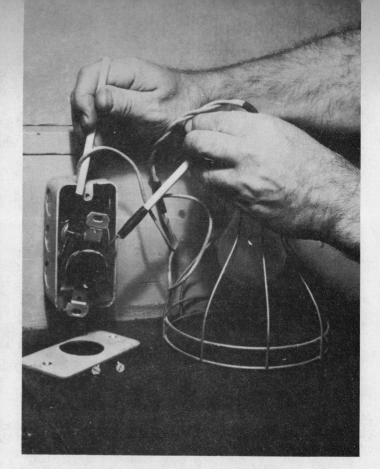

Is juice reaching prongs of wall outlet? Insert prods of Lightester. If no light, line is dead.

Is juice reaching terminals? If lamp goes on, one of contact springs in outlet itself is broken.

Lightester is especially valuable for determining whether power lines and fuses at cutout box are OK. Touch one prod to common ground (white) wire, other to house side of each fuse connection. Center fuse, lower row, leaves lamp dark, meaning it is blown out. Note method of holding prods by ends.

With test prod touched to terminal of lower right fuse, lamp lights up, showing that fuse and circuit are intact. Flickering of lamp often shows up loose or partially corroded fuses. Wire guard of Lightester provides convenient means of hanging the unit from any nearby edge that is available.

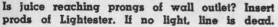

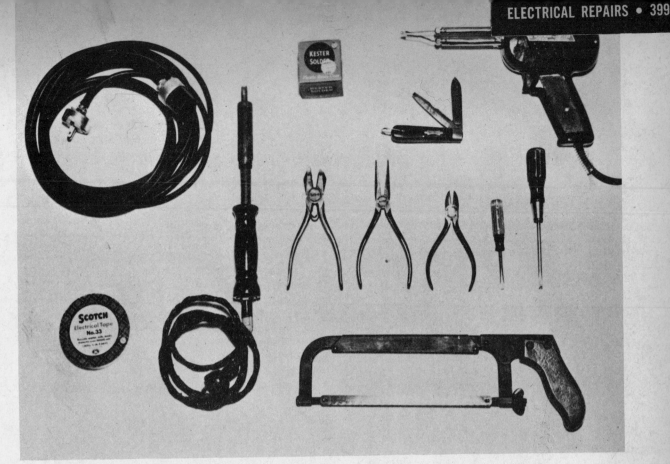

Basic tools needed for home electrical repairs are an extension cord, straight soldering iron, rosin core solder, knife, gun type soldering tool, a set of pliers, screwdrivers, plastic tape and a hacksaw.

Which type of soldering tool to choose? The answer is easy: *both*. For some operations one is preferable to the other. For instance, suppose you are working on a change in a power line, and want to solder a joint in it. Obviously, you can't use a gun if you kill the line first to make the latter safe to handle. The trick is to heat up a regular resistance-type iron, kill the circuit, and make the joint while it's still hot. A medium-size iron will hold its heat for about 30 seconds, which is more than long enough for several joints. A gun-type iron goes dead almost instantly when it loses its AC power.

Rosin-core solder is universally used for electrical connections of all kinds. The rosin is known as "flux," and its purpose is to prevent the formation of a layer of corrosion on the surfaces to be soldered when the hot iron is applied. Rosin, a derivative of turpentine, has no corrosive after effects.

Diagonal pliers are intend only for snipping wire, not for holding, squeezing or bending. Their jaws form a sharp V, and they can therefore be used in close quarters for trimming short pieces of wire.

Side-cutters combine cutting edges and flat, fairly heavy jaws. The latter are suitable for a wide variety of holding, turning and forming jobs. In the six-inch size, this is probably the most frequently used tool in all electrical work.

Long-nose pliers usually do not include cutting edges. They are intended for making loops in ends of wires and for light holding purposes. Do not use them for twisting nuts on bolts or similar heavy work. Once the slender jaws become distorted through this misuse, the tool becomes useless.

No one ever has enough screwdrivers. You need small, medium and large ones, because electrical appliances contain screws of widely varying dimensions. Fortunately, screwdrivers are cheap and last practically forever. If the ends become worn, they can be restored in a minute with a file or a grinder.

You will also need two or three sizes of Phillips-head (cross-point) screwdrivers. Handle these carefully and be sure to use the right size for the screw. When they wear out or are damaged they must be discarded, as it is virtually impossible to reshape them.

An excellent knife for electrical work is the Army tool known as the TL-29. This consists of a sturdy knife blade and a locking screwdriver blade in common handle. •

Wire Joints

Splicing wires is a simple chore

HAVE you observed that the cords furnished with many appliances seem to be just a trifle too short to reach the nearest outlet? An extension cord is a help, but the real cure is to add a permanent length of wire to the existing one.

Electrical and hardware stores carry a variety of cords and wires, and you can match the old and the new without much trouble. Joining them is a simple hand operation, and requires the use of only pliers, knife and soldering iron. If you are new at the game, it is a good idea, of course, to make a few practice joints with scrap pieces of wire.

Cords of all appliances contain flexible wire, which actually consists of a bunch of very fine wires held together by the covering of insulation. Solid wire is found in power conduits, bell circuits, intercom hook-ups and other fixed applications.

The secret of good electrical joints is merely cleanliness. The quickest and easiest way to brighten up wire is to scrape it very lightly with the *back* edge of a knife.

The wire inside most cords is bare copper. Depending on the age of the cord and the type of insulation, the metal might be of any shade from shiny bright to corroded black. In the better grades of cords, the wire is "tinned"; that is, covered in manufacture with a very thin layer of solder. This usually remains quite clean, and takes solder instantly.

Illustrations show typical splicing jobs. •

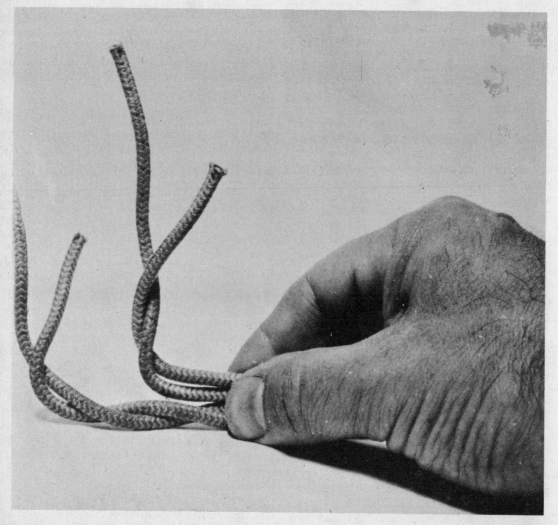

Spliced wire will show minimum thickness at points of joining if ends of the new and old wires are stagger-cut to length of about two inches. This is first step in splicing common twisted lamp cord.

Outer layer of insulation is best removed with sharp knife, in same manner as sharpening pencil. Make three or four short incisions, blade held at flat angle, then twist off insulation with the fingers. Be careful with depth of cut, to avoid nipping off outer strands of wire. Twist wires and scrape lightly with back of knife if dirty.

With practice, you can remove insulation quickly with side-cutting pliers. Sever insulation by making a carefully controlled cut, and with jaws still partially closed, pull the covering off. The trick is to cut the insulation without nicking the wire. Some types of insulation do lend themselves well to this method, while other types do not.

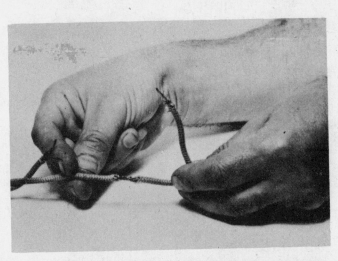

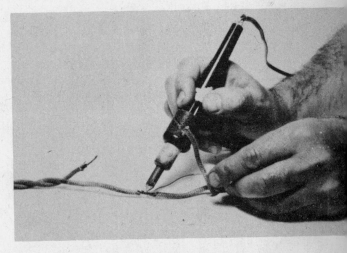

Twist together the long wire of one cord with the short wire of the other. Leave the other pair apart. The idea is to complete only one joint at a time. The job comes out neater in this manner.

Using rosin-core solder, make first joint solid. Then leave the iron in contact with the connection until all of the rosin has boiled out and you have only a shiny coat of solder remaining.

The next step is to finish the first joint by taping it tightly. A good sticky tape for this purpose is sold as "friction tape," is obtainable in a width of about ¾ inch and color is black.

Staggering preserves general lines of the cord. If it is not convenient to solder the joints, make them about two inches long and tie them up with three or four strands from the cut-off ends.

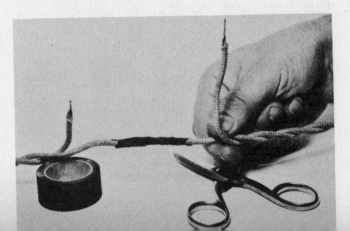

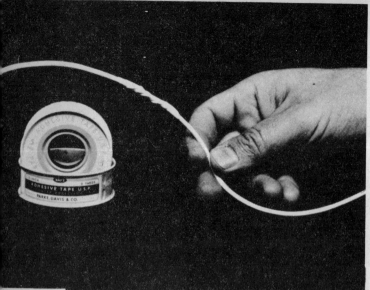

Light colored cords don't look attractive when spliced with black friction tape, so why not use white tape? Borrow some adhesive tape from the medicine chest. You'll find it sticks tightly and insulates well.

For splices that need protection against water, oils, acids, etc., an excellent tape is Scotch No. 33. It can be pressed with fingers to shape, and proves to be virtually air and liquid tight.

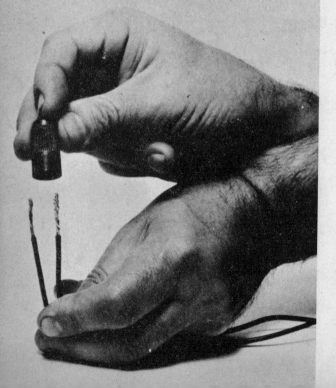

"Wire nuts" are widely used in both new and revamped electrical wiring because they offer quick and easy means of joining wires without soldering. This is an advantage when no current is available for a soldering iron (power circuit having been deactivated to permit work to be done on it) and when use of a blowtorch or other open flame is too hazardous (which is often the case). The wire nut comprises an insulated body with threaded metal insert. The wires to be joined are pushed into the latter and the nut turned in either direction two or three times; the threads bite into the wires and twist them together. Nuts are identified according to the wire sizes they fit.

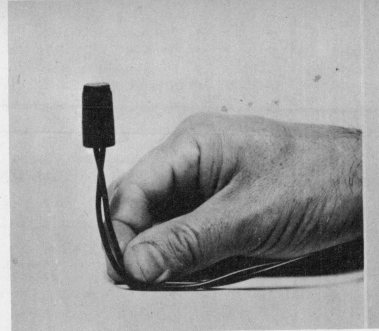

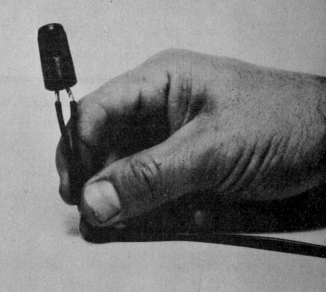

If the wires are bared to the proper length, a wire nut will be found to insulate your splice properly, and it is obvious that no additional covering in the form of tape is then necessary.

In this case, the wire ends have been bared too much and the unprotected sections remain exposed after the nut has been tightened. The joint can be easily opened and the wire then recut to fit.

Quick-heating soldering "gun" makes a fast job on wire splicing. Here, it is being used on single-conductor solid wire which is usually found in power conduits. See position of gun point and solder in relation to the joint. As the solder melts, the molten metal runs into the joint and forms a firm bond over the termini of the wires.

Solid wire in the No. 18 size, and smaller, is used for bell, buzzer, intercom and like low voltage applications. Easiest way to splice wire of this type is to twist the ends together with a pair of pliers. Soldering is advisable but not as important as in power circuits. Taping is necessary, of course, for prevention of short circuits.

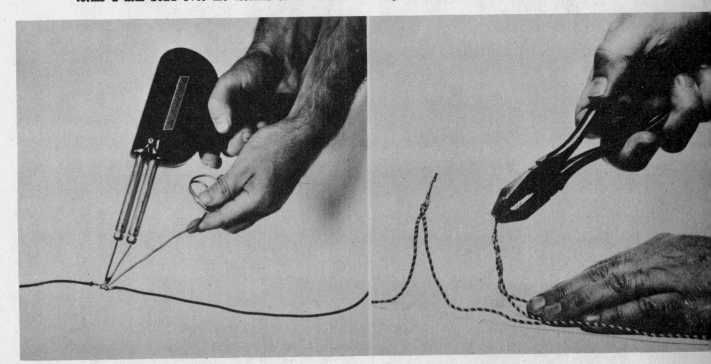

Cable and Conduit

Loom, BX and thin-wall are the most popular types for home power circuits

Some representative conductors of electricity: 1—Two-wire armored cable, or "BX," with extra grounding wire in the center. 2—Three-wire BX. 3—A two-wire nonmetallic sheath cable, with bare ground wire. 4—Three-wire, nonmetallic sheath. 5—Single insulated wires, colored black, white or red. These are used in thin-wall conduit.

Typical utility "knock-out" box for switches, outlets, etc., so called because cable openings in back, sides or ends are made in a few seconds by hammering through partially cut holes. Boxes are rectangular, square or round; varied sizes.

Utility box at left has fitting at top for thin-wall conduit; the one at right, for BX or loom. The mounting lips on all boxes are spaced uniformly to take all outlets and other varieties of fixtures.

IF YOU expect to install new power lines or renovate old ones, you should know something about cable and conduit.

The most widely used type, because it is inexpensive, flexible, easy to handle, and permitted by many local building codes, is nonmetallic sheathed cable. This is also known as "loom," because of the woven appearance of its outer covering. It consists of two or three insulated wires, with or without a bare ground wire, laid parallel to each other in a common outer jacket. For indoor applications, a combination of thermoplastic and paper insulation is employed. For tougher service, both indoors and outdoors, a combination of thermoplastic, fiberglass and polyvinyl insulation is better.

Loom can be cut with pliers and trimmed with a knife. It can be mounted quickly by means of U-shaped nail straps, driven in with a hammer.

Some municipalities do not permit the use of loom, and require instead metal-clad wiring of some sort. The most popular is steel-armored cable, universally known as "BX" for no reason that makes sense. It contains two or three wires, and usually also has a bare bonding or ground wire running between them and the outer cable. The latter is spiral-made of thin steel, and the whole cable is flexible enough to be pushed around corners.

BX is tough stuff. Cutting the steel jacket without nicking the wires inside is very tricky and takes quite a bit of practice.

Both loom and BX are available in rolls from 25 to 250 feet.

Thin-wall conduit is merely galvanized steel pipe in various diameters and in standard 10-foot length. It is readily assembled to standard outlet boxes and other fixtures by means of threadless, clamp-type fittings. It can be bent at a rather wide right angle with a special tool. It makes an extremely neat and fireproof job. Some local building codes specify this type of wiring.

Thin-wall is distinctly different from both loom and BX in that it does not contain its own wires. These are pulled through during or after the assembly of a whole system, usually with the assistance of a flexible steel tape called a "snake."

An advantage of conduit for many purposes is that it can be shortened, lengthened, taken apart and put together both easily and rapidly. The wires themselves, being loose inside the smooth piping, can be pulled out undamaged and reused. •

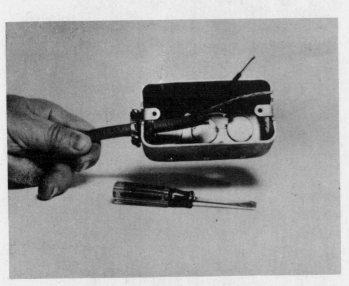

This is the method of bringing two-wire non-metallic sheath cable into an outlet box. Clamp at left end of the latter holds the wire securely.

U-shaped straps, equipped with built-in nails, offer an easy means of fastening a nonmetallic cable to wooden walls. Fasteners of a similar nature are available for use on masonry walls.

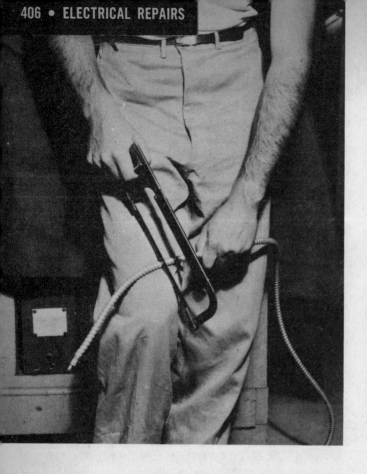

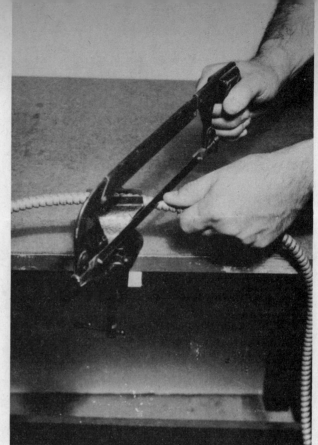

The BX cable is wiggly and difficult to hold by hand. Don't attempt to cut it this way; hacksaw is almost certain to slip or the cable to twist.

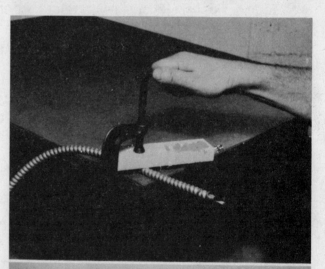

Best way to cut through the outer steel jacket of BX is with aid of vise. Hold the cable close to jaws; cut lightly at angle to the spiraling. Stop when inner paper insulation appears; twist off the cut section. This leaves wire ends free.

In the absence of a vise, a C-clamp and a block of wood will serve well to hold BX for cutting.

In a pinch, a large pair of pliers or a locking jaw wrench, when pressed hard against the workbench, will serve to keep the BX under control. Practice on scraps to acquire the knack of cutting a cable without touching the wires inside.

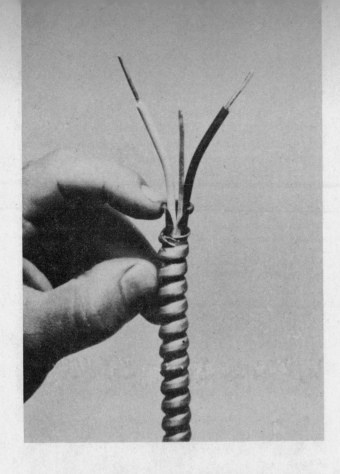

A special right-angle connector permits the BX to make a sharp entrance into the utility box. There are a great number of different fittings designed to ease assembly and wiring operations.

To protect wires of BX against possible chafing, push fiber bushing into cable. In photo at left, center wire is ground lead and rests against the cable. White wire in cable is always uninterrupted ground return; the white wire the "hot" side.

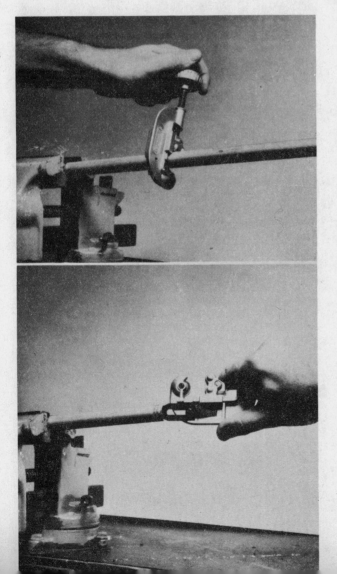

Thin-wall conduit is a seamless steel pipe of light weight. It can easily be cut with a hacksaw, but a much quicker and neater job is possible when done with a tubing cutter, as shown. Handwheel is turned as the tool is pulled around tubing and cutting wheel bites into the latter.

After only three or four revolutions of cutter, the sections of a conduit are easily separated.

Burr on inside of conduit must be removed to allow free passage of wires that will be inserted later. Simple reamer is part of tubing cutter.

"Persuader" puts round, even bend into thin-wall conduit. Tremendous leverage is applied through long handle of bender tool, a useful accessory.

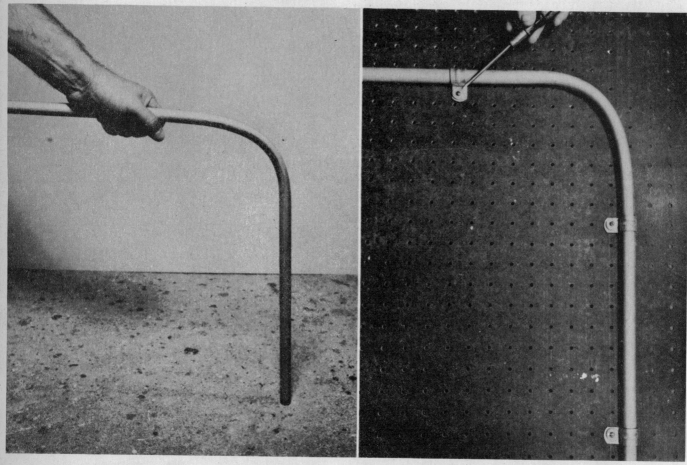

An uncramped bend in the thin-wall conduit is very essential to the passage of the wires. The smooth job results from the use of lever tool.

There is no difficulty when it comes to fastening a thin-wall conduit to a flat surface. This is solved by use of simple single-ended clamps.

The threadless ends of the thin-wall are readily fastened by a clamping-type connector, shown in the photo, right, attached to a utility box.

Right-angle fitting brings thin-wall close to outlet box. Hex nut on threaded shoulder tightens the internal split clamp against the conduit's end.

This double-ended connector, handled with use of two wrenches, makes a quick task of joining any two sections of the thin-wall conduit pipe.

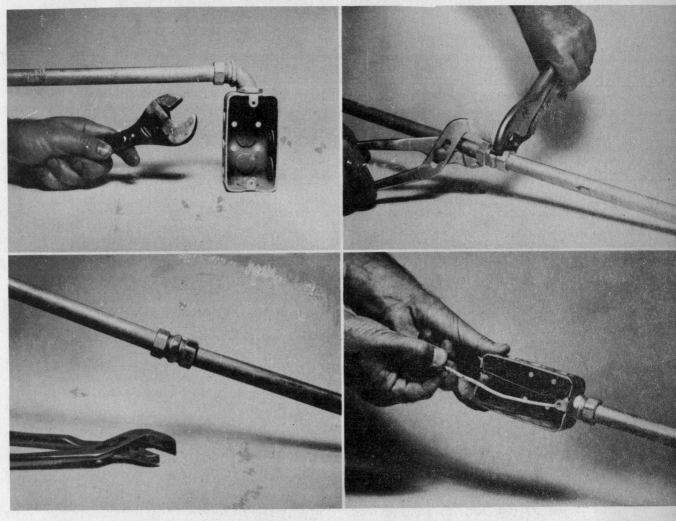

The desired result: This finished joint of two separate pieces of conduit is now neat and tight and allows free travel of wire through passage.

At this point, the actual wires are both pushed and pulled through the thin-wall conduit. This is usually the last part of assembly operation.

Neat, rugged and foolproof is this short installation of two duplex receptacles and thin-wall conduit on the back edge of a radio table. Outlet boxes are screwed down through their bottoms, so conduit does not require mounting straps.

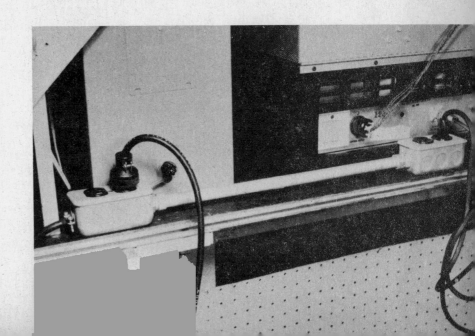

Play It Safe

Caution, common sense and proper grounding technique will prevent needless accidents

Opening the main switch kills current in all of the house wiring; however, this also means it will affect the refrigerator, furnace, etc. In many cases opening only a branch circuit is sufficient. A posted warning sign on an open circuit is helpful.

THE following item appeared recently in a New York newspaper. (Only the names of people and places have been changed.)

BUSINESS MAN KILLED WIRING FAN IN ATTIC

Townville, L. I.—John J. Doakes, 44-year-old business executive, was killed by electricity today while installing an exhaust fan in the attic of his new $40,000 home at 999 Shore Drive.

Members of the Townville Fire Department had to tear out part of the ceiling in an attic room to remove the body, which was crumpled in the space between the ceiling and the roof. An electric wire, which he was connecting to the fan, was clutched in one hand.

The accident occurred about 2 P.M. while his wife and their three children, two boys 19 and 15 and a girl 12, were on a shopping trip. His body was found about 3 P.M. by a neighbor, Joe Jones, who had been called by Mrs. Doakes after she was unable to find her husband when she returned.

Mr. Doakes was sales manager

for a printing firm. He had moved into the house just a week ago.

This tragic accident was obviously the result of simple, unadulterated carelessness. The victim had forgotten or neglected to kill the branch circuit on which he was working, and he himself was killed instead.

There is a difference between "forgetting" and "neglecting" in cases of this kind. A man can be fully aware of the joltage behind power line voltage, and he can fully understand the importance of removing fuses or snapping circuit breakers open. However, while he may intend to open the circuit, he may simply forget to do so before he climbs into the attic with his hands full of tools.

There is the strong possibility that the victim of the fan accident left the power on deliberately, so that he could have light while working in the cramped attic space. He may have figured that there was no danger as long as he handled only one live wire at a time. This was sheer neglect. Maybe he did handle a single wire at a time, but maybe, when he held the "hot" line, he brushed against the grounded sheath of BX as he groped on the floor for a roll of tape.

Clearly, the moral to all this is: PLAY IT SAFE. It's easy to do so by following

DON'T! Some housewives put mixers and blenders in the sink, while they are connected and running, to catch possible spillover. This is a dangerous practice, because the sink and the pipes near it are well grounded electrically, and there is always the possibility of a live circuit forming between them, the body, and one wire of connected appliance.

a few, common sense simple rules.

It would appear at first sight that the easiest way to avoid shock, when making repairs or installing new equipment, is merely to yank open the main switch. This deactivates all the wiring in the house and therefore you can touch *anything* with complete safety. This move is practicable if the work will take only a few minutes; say up to about 15 or 20. You must remember that pulling the main switch removes power from the kitchen refrigerator (and food freezer), which might be undesirable in warm weather; and also shuts down any modern heating plant, which might be undesirable in cold weather. With the main switch off you have no electric light, so you can work only in daylight in an area near a window.

Although an open main switch gives 200% safety, you can still have 100% safety, and the convenience of power for light, tools, etc., by removing the branch fuse only for the circuit that you want to touch. Presumably you have identified all the fuse or circuit breaker positions (see the chapter entitled "When Your Lights Go Out"), so this should take only a moment. Don't merely loosen the fuse in its socket; unscrew it completely and place it on the fuse box. Inform the other members of the family present in the house as to just what you are doing, and what outlets, lights, etc., will be inoperative while you are doing it.

With the line presumably opened by the fuse or breaker, give it a double check with the Lightester. If the bulb of the latter doesn't light, you can proceed.

Protect the Kiddies

An insurance company recently reported that about 40,000 electrical accidents in the home occur yearly in the United States. Considering the total population of about 170 million and the astronomical number of electric circuits and appliances in daily use, the figure is not a very large one. The sad part is that many of the victims who are seriously injured or killed are children. The fault is not theirs, but the parents'. Better protection in most cases calls only for a little common sense; in others for very inexpensive expedients.

The report listed these "bad actors": 1) open-type baseboard outlets; 2) lamp and other loose cords on the floors; 3) toasters and other appliances left connected after use.

Growing children are naturally inquisitive. They'll pick up hair pins, nail files, knives, forks, spoons, etc., and start investigating outlets and appliances. The metallic objects being perfect conductors of electricity, trouble is inevitable. Children have been known to pull out the two attachment plugs connected to a duplex wall outlet and to stuff the latter full of pins. Some of them stopped growing right then; others were more fortunate and escaped with nothing more than a strong jolt that threw them clear.

When the young son of Frank Bellek of Chicago had a narrow escape of this kind, papa decided to make a recurrence impossible. He designed a duplex outlet with a revolving cap over each section that turns automatically when the plug is removed

Want to save the life of someone in your family . . maybe yourself? Then do this every time before you allow anyone to put his fingers or a metal utensil of any kind into a toaster or other heat-type appliance with exposed elements. Also, store the toaster, when not in use, in a closet or on a shelf, out of the reach of children.

and completely covers the live contact springs. To reinsert a plug, you merely place the prongs in the slots in the cap, twist a quarter turn to the right, and press in. Bearing the appropriate name "No-Shok," this self-thinking outlet is truly an inspired contribution to life and safety. It is simple, inexpensive, easy to install. Millions have been sold and it has proved foolproof.

No different in size or appearance from a regular duplex outlet, a No-Shok can replace the latter in any box. It shouldn't take more than five minutes per outlet. Follow exactly the procedure given for the installation of a mercury switch.

Open toasters, broilers, etc., are another story entirely. You just have to get into the habit of removing the wall plug and tieing the cord around the appliance when a meal is finished. If possible, put the toaster in a kitchen cabinet, and close the door or cover of the broiler, to discourage

tampering by children who may be about.

Junior isn't the only one who needs to be indoctrinated with good electrical safety habits. With appalling carelessness, many an adult sticks a knife into a "live" toaster to free a piece of bread. The toast pops loose, and the adult usually pops up about three feet himself. This practice is dangerous even if the appliance is "off," because it really isn't completely off at all. The internal switch opens one side of the line and this cuts off the current. However, and this is a very big "however", the *other* side of the line is still connected to one end of the heating wires. If you poke a knife into the toaster you can very easily touch the latter and when you do you'll know it

Loose cords on the floor are a menace mainly to toddlers who are teething. Children at this stage bite anything they can reach. Witness the edges of a crib or play pen, which looks as if they have been attached by hungry beavers. An infant

DON'T! Of all crazy ways of getting electrocuted quickly, this one is probably the best . . or the worst. The hand holding a metal knife, which is poked into the toaster to loosen a piece of bread, is resting on the metal frame of the appliance, which in turn is resting on a grounded metal stove. Keep toaster on wood table, and keep knives, and such, out of it.

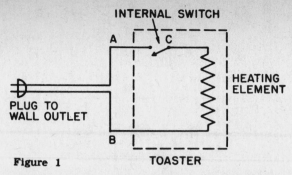

Figure 1

INTERNAL SWITCH

A   C

HEATING
ELEMENT

PLUG TO
WALL OUTLET

B

TOASTER

With the internal switch of a toaster "off," the line between the plug and point A is reasonably safe because it is isolated from the accessible heating element. However, any point in the toaster between C and B can readily become "hot" in relation to a ground if the plug should be in the wall outlet the wrong way. Moral: Don't poke any metal utensils or hardware of any sort into your toaster!

crawling on the floor is sure to discover all the flexible wires for lamps, radio and television sets, fans, air conditioners, etc., and to try them for taste. If the insulation is thin to begin with, or has worn through in spots vigorous chewing by baby may quickly bare the wires inside. Add a little salty saliva to make the connection more conducting . . . the result is horrible to contemplate. Nowhere else does preventive maintenance pay off in better terms.

In any household having a toddling child, it is usually necessary to clear all small objects off tables during baby's waking hours. If you don't do the job, he or she will. At night you can restore the room to its natural state. At the same time you remove the ash trays, flower pots, etc., also unplug the loose electrical cords and curl them out of sight. All you'll have to be concerned about then is baby cracking his head against a table, falling off a chair, getting wedged under the sofa, pulling the

curtains down on himself, and similar minor events.

Protection By and Against Grounding

Fixed wiring. and appliances, once installed properly, continue to work for years without developing or causing the slightest trouble. The same cannot be said of portable or semi-portable appliances and tools which contain motors and which therefore are subject to vibration and movement effects. In clothes washing machines these are further aggravated by the presence of soapy water, an excellent conductor of electricity.

To make use of the protective feature of grounding, you must know how circuits are grounded. Figure 2 shows a fundamental branch circuit such as might be found in any home. The white colored wire is uninterrupted throughout its length. At the meter, where the power lines enter the house from the street, this wire is thoroughly "grounded" by means of a connection to the nearest cold water pipe, which is a good "ground" because it is actually in contact with the earth for a considerable length. The primary purpose of this grounding is to provide a direct return path to the earth of accumulations of static electricity in the sky before and during a thunderstorm. Picked up by the long, exposed wires from the generating station, this static can and often does burn out power distribution systems. A *heavy* burst of static electricity takes the spectacular form of a bolt of lightning. Good grounding saves countless homes from serious damage. All overhead telephone wires are similarly protected, by "lightning arrestors" with a ground connection; and all outside radio and television aerials are supposed to be fitted with equivalent devices.

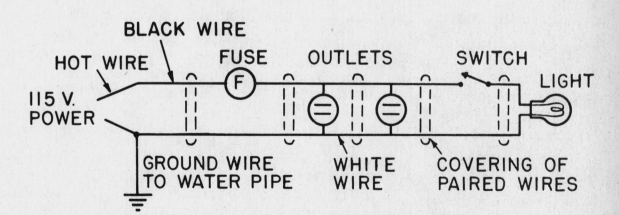

BLACK WIRE

HOT WIRE

FUSE

OUTLETS

SWITCH

LIGHT

115 V.
POWER

F

GROUND WIRE
TO WATER PIPE

WHITE
WIRE

COVERING OF
PAIRED WIRES

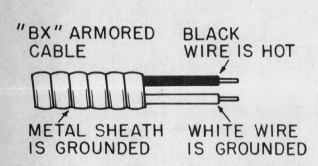

"BX" ARMORED CABLE   BLACK WIRE IS HOT

METAL SHEATH IS GROUNDED   WHITE WIRE IS GROUNDED

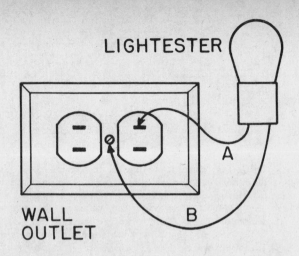

LIGHTESTER

WALL OUTLET   A   B

Figure 3

When power wires are encased in BX or other types of metal cable, the metal sheath is also grounded and becomes a parallel conductor to white wire.

Figure 4

A Lightester (see chapter on Testers And Tools) will demonstrate that a circuit can be completed through grounded frame of an electrical outlet box.

If the house is wired with metallic sheathed cable of one sort or another, this sheathing is likewise grounded. When wires are cut, the outer sheathing is clamped into holes in metal boxes containing switches, lamps, outlets, etc., and the continuity of the grounding circuit is thereby maintained. The white wire inside "BX" and other armored cable (see Figure 3) is thus actually part of the same common circuit as the outer armor. This is a very important but often overlooked fact, which some people find difficult to believe. If you want to be convinced, or need to convince others, a quick demonstration with the Lightester will do the

trick conveniently and to your satisfaction.

As shown in Figure 4, place one lead A in the shorter slot of a wall outlet. If the fixtures have been wired correctly, this is the "hot" or ungrounded side of the 115-volt power line. First touch the lead B to longer contact of the outlet, which is the grounded side of the line. The bulb will light, showing that the outlet and the bulb are both OK. Now, leaving A in the short slot, touch B to the center screw of the outlet's cover plate. If it is reasonably clean of paint, the bulb will light again, showing that the lamp circuit has been completed to the grounded side of the line. It will also light if lead B is touched to any other

DON'T! Bringing any connected appliance to the sink can mean danger. Never fill steam iron this way.

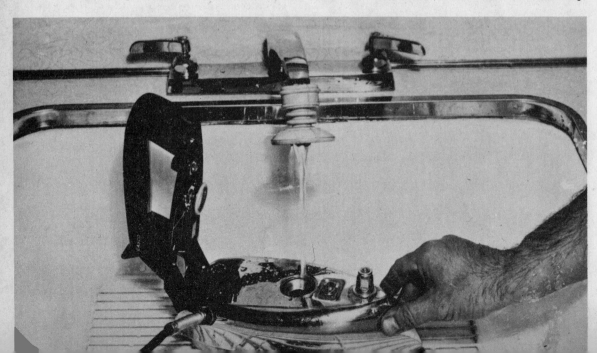

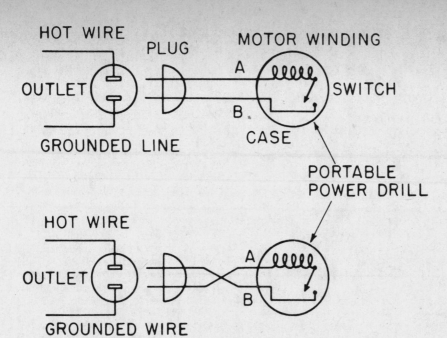

HOT WIRE

PLUG

MOTOR WINDING

A

OUTLET

SWITCH

B

GROUNDED LINE

CASE

PORTABLE
POWER DRILL

HOT WIRE

OUTLET

A

B

GROUNDED WIRE

Figures 5 and 6

The two diagrams illustrate the wiring arrangement of a typical portable drill. The case of the usual drill is completely insulated from the wiring. Note that the drill works equally well with either position of plug.

grounded object, such as a water or gas pipe, a radiator or a heating register. Every metallic part of the water or heating system of a house is bound to be a good ground because of the interconnection of their various pipes and ducts.

Now let's consider a typical portable device and see how it behaves under normal and abnormal circumstances. The ¼-inch electric drill is a fine example because it is so widely used in the home, the shop and the garage for a variety of purposes. Figures 5 and 6 show it in simplified diagrammatic form. The motor itself is represented by a coil of wire, the switch by an interrupted line, and the metal frame or body by a heavy circle. The switch and the motor are connected in simple series and two wires A and B pass through the case and terminate in an attachment plug. The drill works equally well with the plug inserted in the wall outlet either way, as indicated in Figures 5 and 6. If the motor winding, the switch and the line cord are all normally well insulated from the case, the latter is "cold" from the electrical standpoint. Thus, if a person is using the drill in a garage, and is standing on the cement floor as shown in Figure 7, no part of the current in the drill passes to him, although his feet are in firm contact with the ground to which wire B is connected.

It is well known that motor-operated tools, especially portable ones that are knocked around a great deal, often suffer internal injuries. The insulation on some motor windings is rather thin, and can readily wear through if the tool is used frequently. Suppose that any worn part of the winding makes contact with the iron

core on which it is wound. The core is part of the case, so a new connection C is established as shown in Figure 8. If the user plugs in the attachment plug and reaches for the drill, he will receive a surprise. Trace out the simple circuit and you'll see why. Current enters the drill from the hot side of the line through wire A, flows through the motor wire until it reaches the worn spot, bypasses from here to the metal case, through the arms and body of the user, through his feet and shoes in contact with the ground, and through the ground to make a complete path back to the grounded side of the power line. *The switch on the drill doesn't even have to be on.*

The severity of the shock depends on two main factors: 1) The condition of the skin. Clean, dry hands have a relatively high resistance and allow little current to pass through. Wet, dirty hands are much more conductive. 2) The effectiveness of the underfoot ground contact. Cement has a surprisingly low electrical resistance. The garage is almost sure to be close to a water pipe, so it is pretty well grounded. Cotton and woolen socks and ordinary shoes are good insulators if dry, and these items of clothing are what usually reduce the "shock" to a mere sting, which should be taken as a warning that the drill needs looking into.

Water Increases the Danger

Water on the floor enormously increases the danger, because it reduces the resistance of the floor itself, and, worse, that of the usually protective foot gear, if any is worn in the first place. Ignorance of this

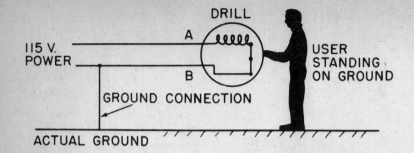

DRILL

115 V. POWER

A

B

GROUND CONNECTION

USER STANDING ON GROUND

ACTUAL GROUND

Figure 7

A portable drill in normal operation has switch closed; insulation protects user.

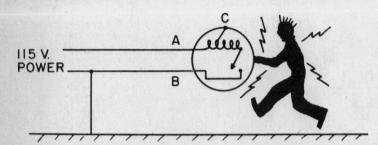

C

115 V. POWER

A

B

Figure 8

If motor winding should ground to case at point C, portable drill user is usually shocked because current will follow path through drill casing and through user's body to the ground and then back to the grounded power lead B as shown here.

fact was responsible for a particularly nasty fatality that occurred recently. A father and a young son washed the family car in the driveway of their home, in advance of shining it up. The boy, sloshing around in the water as all boys love to, reached for a power drill, which had been fitted with the usual polishing felt. The drill may not have even been defective. Water from the child's hands might easily have dripped into the case, making excellent contact with a hot connection inside. Brr . . cases like this give me the shakes.

Suppose that the partial grounding of the motor winding to point C occurred with the line plug reversed; that is, with A now grounded and B the "hot" side, as in Figure 9. What would happen to the user? As long as the switch is open, nothing. But the instant he closes the switch he establishes a good circuit from wire B, through the switch, through the section of winding between the switch and point C, and from there again through his body to ground.

Millions of small portable drills were bought by "do-it-yourself" enthusiasts, and numerous accidents occurred with them, before tool manufacturers got around to providing protection for them. This takes the form of a third wire in the flexible coil, with one end connected merely to the case and the other to any ground. In some drills the end of the ground wire is fitted with a threaded stud which is supposed to replace the cover plate screw of a duplex outlet; in others, it has a big spring clip, to clamp around BX or other metallic sheathing, or a nearby pipe. Newer tools now appearing on the market have their cords fitted with a *three*-prong plug which fits a new type of duplex outlet having three slots in a T-

shaped formation. The two parallel prongs on the plug are the normal current-carrying connections; the offset third prong is for the grounding wire only. According to the National Electrical Code, all new power tools, workshop and laundry machines are supposed to have this three-wire system.

(For detailed instructions on installing new three-wire safety cords in older drills and similar tools, see the next section of this book, entitled "The Third Wire Is a Lifesaver.")

Figure 10 shows how a grounded case protects the user of any appliance. The ground wire, in effect hooked back directly to the grounded line B, has extremely low resistance, so much lower than that of the human body that it short-circuits the latter out of any circuit combination.

Protection Is Complete

Consider several very real accidental possibilities in Figure 10. Suppose wire A wears through at point 1, where it enters the case. It touches the latter. There is now a very low resistance path for the current to flow from wire A to point 1, to the case, all around the case, and out through the ground wire back to the grounded side of the line. This is a thorough short circuit on the power line, and will kick out the line fuse or circuit breaker almost instantly.

Suppose wire B touches against the case at point 3. If it touches without breaking off, the normal, safe operation of the tool is not affected, because this connection is grounded anyway! If it breaks off, and either touches or doesn't touch the grounded case, the circuit to the motor is

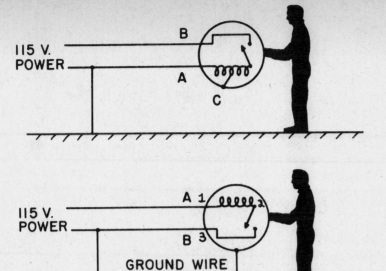

Figure 9

If grounded motor of the drill should have its line plug reversed, user will be safe—until he turns on the switch. He will then, of course, be shocked.

Figure 10

If metal case of the tool is well grounded with low-resistance wire, current flow under any accidental circumstances is confined between case and ground, and user does not suffer. If point 1 is grounded, line is short-circuited and fuse blows. If 2 is grounded, motor runs with switch open. If 3 is grounded, nothing will happen at all.

merely opened and the tool won't run when the switch is closed.

Suppose the junction point 2 of the motor winding and the switch becomes grounded to the case. When the tool is plugged in it will start immediately, even though the switch is still off. The power circuit from A is completed from 2 through the grounded case back to the grounded side of the line. The user still feels nothing because no current passes through his body; it's all going through the low resistance grounded case and ground wire.

More About Grounding

A separate grounding wire can easily be added to any tool or appliance not so factory-equipped. Fasten one end under any convenient screw on the case, tape the new wire along the present flexible cord, and attach a clip on the other end. It doesn't do any harm to remind you that this end must be grounded somewhere to do any good. The extra wire should not be any smaller than the wire in the present cord.

A separate grounding wire, with a screw-on clamp to fit on a water pipe, has been provided with most washing machines of recent manufacture. This wire should be placed so that it cannot be damaged or torn loose by clothes baskets, jars of laundry bleach, or other heavy objects. Loss of this grounding connection is invariably the reason some machines become "hot" and bounce their users across the room. (See section following.)

With some washers, the flexible rubber hose that goes to the cold water tap has a grounding wire woven into it. The machine thus is grounded automatically when it is hooked up.

Because water, gas and steam pipes are such good grounds, avoid contact with them when using *any* portable appliances. Certainly the worst place in this respect is the bathroom. With sickening regularity the newspapers report fatalities due to wet contact with exposed bowl heaters. A summer camper, a girl of 17, was killed recently when she tried to dry her hair with an electric dryer in a shower room. Radio and TV receivers of the AC-DC "hot chassis" type have shocked numerous occupants of bathtubs and have killed several children; all made the mistakes of twiddling the tuning or volume knobs with wet, soapy hands. Under more fortunate circumstances, the sets merely blew the fuses and plunged the bathrooms into darkness when the chassis made accidental contact with an exposed pipe or other fixture.

If electronic entertainment in the bathroom is important, at least make certain that the equipment is of the full transformer type. Better still for the purpose is a *battery-operated* transistor portable.

In the kitchen, get the family into the habit of keeping *connected* appliances away from the sink. One woman learned what happens when an electric frying pan is immersed in sudsy water for cleaning, with the plug still in the socket! She recoiled suddenly and gave herself a pretty thorough bath. Less funny was the experience of a mother who tried to give a six-month-old infant a quick cleaning off in the sink. Flailing its arms, the child pulled in a nearby toaster. Still connected, its exposed heating wires made a perfect return path to ground through the water. The baby was killed. •

The Third Wire Is a Lifesaver

Install grounding cords on motor-operated and "wet" appliances for safety

TO take the shock hazard out of any metal-body electrical appliance, you have to do only two simple revamping jobs: 1) Add a grounding wire to the present cord and replace the present two-prong non-polarized plug by a three-prong polarized plug; 2) Replace existing two-prong outlets by three-prong receptacles to take the new plug, or use polarized adapters.

Actually, the easiest way to add the life-saving third wire is to use a length of new three-wire cord. In this the ground lead is colored green, and the current-carrying wires are black and white. Electrical and hardware stores now carry such cords in various lengths, with a polarized plug already molded permanently to one end. If you prefer, you can buy the cord and the plug separately.

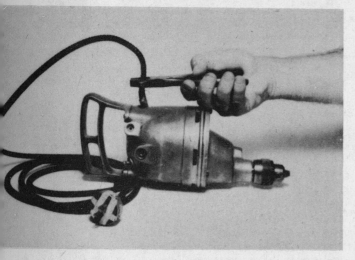

Portable drills, saws and other motor-operated tools are prime customers for three-wire safety cords. Old cord is probably torn, so cut it off.

With handle removed or case opened, two leads from motor are located, pulled out carefully and cleaned off. Colors are usually black and white.

Grounding prong on a polarized plug is the long round one, represented at other end by a green wire. Run a continuity check with volt-ohmmeter.

Pull end of new three-wire cord through hole in body of tool and solder black to black, white to white. To green wire solder lug that fits screw.

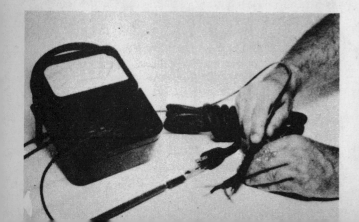

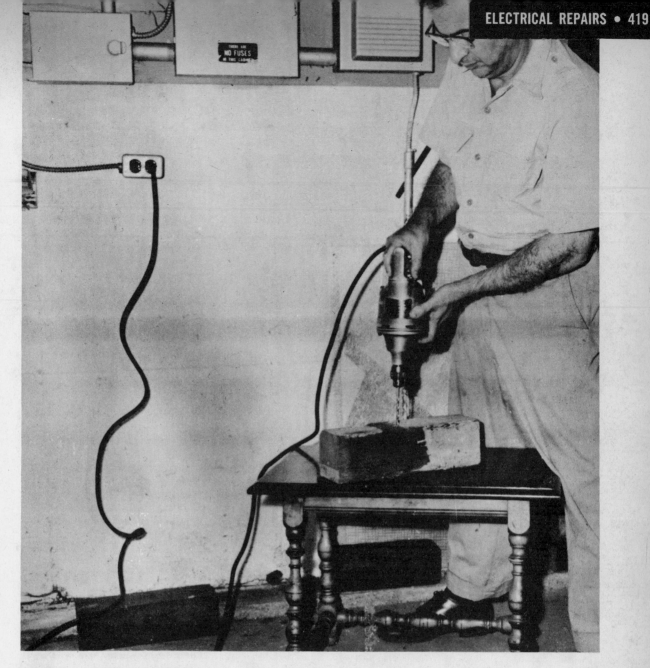

With your portable drill fitted with a three-wire cord, you can work in perfect safety even on a damp garage or cellar floor without danger of shock. In case of internal short-circuit, you only blow fuse.

After you tape the black and white splices, it is time to reassemble handle. Slip the ground lug over one screw and be sure to tighten well.

In order to take possible strain off your cord, as well as to increase its life, tape and then tie it securely to the under side of hand grip.

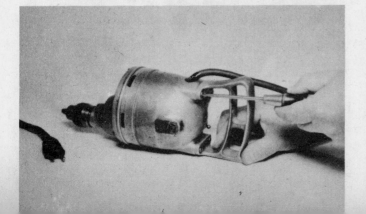

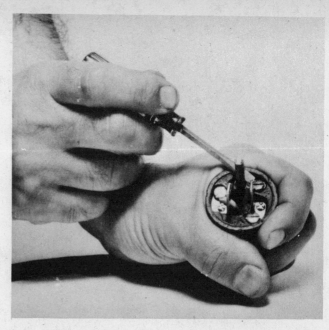

Make your own safety cord: Pull wire through polarized plug, trim off covering and insulation; clean and tin lightly to keep from coming apart.

Screwdriver points to green-colored terminal of ground prong of polarized plug. White lead must go to light prong and black lead to brass prong.

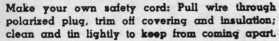

Old outlets in house or shop should be replaced by new polarized type to accommodate safety plug (left). However, satisfactory expedient, 75% safe, is in form of adapter.

For semipermanent use with a particular outlet, ground wire of polarized adapter can be fastened under mounting screw of receptacle cover plate, provided the box is grounded.

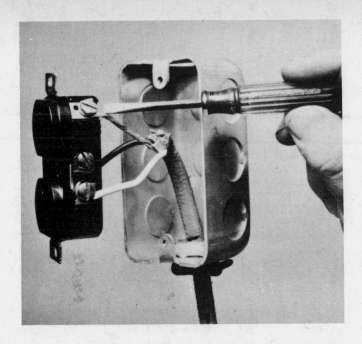

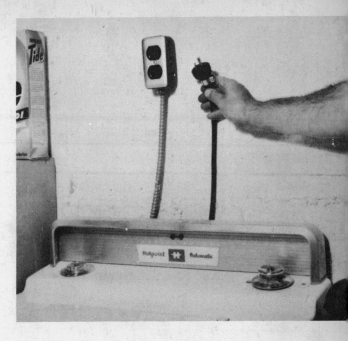

Screwdriver points to the green-colored ground screw of polarized outlet. Bare ground lead of non-metallic sheathed cable is shown connected.

Polarized receptacle and a polarized plug with three-wire cord mean complete assurance against power-line leakage when wet appliances are used.

The new polarized outlets look very much like the old ones except that they have three openings and three terminal screws. The one painted green is the ground connection. If metal outlet boxes are used with flexible armored cable ("BX") or rigid conduit, the ground connection to the green terminal is made automatically when an outlet is mounted, as this terminal is phyically part of the mounting ears of the outlet. If non-metallic cable is used, the bare ground wire woven between the insulated wires must be connected to the green screw. Replacing an old outlet is a screwdriver operation that takes a few minutes. Remember, of course, to pull the fuses first!

Study the accompanying pictures for practical how-to-do-it information on this important application of electricity. •

Pencil points to special tandem-blade polarized plug for 208/230-volt machines. Blades are in line but standard polarized plug's are parallel.

This is a "crowfoot" plug with matching outlet, also used for voltages higher than 115. Bottom (vertical) prong is used as ground connection.

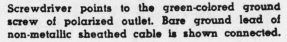

When the Lights Go Out—

—the fuses or circuit breakers have been overloaded. The only cure is to lighten the load, not to invest in larger protective devices

IF YOU have a headache, sometimes you can get temporary relief by swallowing a couple of aspirins. After the effect of the pills wears off, the headache may still be with you. If you feel so badly that you go to a doctor, he'll probably tell you that a headache is not an ailment by itself, but the symptoms of one.

To a large extent, the same goes for fuses. If fuses keep blowing out, merely replacing them with new ones is no cure for the overload somewhere in the house that is causing them to go "pfft." And replacing the original fuses with others of higher amperage rating is about as sensible as looking for a gas leak with a candle.

In some homes, in which no new heavy-current appliances have been added recently and everything is working satisfactorily, a fuse may go dead without apparent reason, and putting in a new one of the same rating restores operation to normal. In cases of this kind the original fuse itself was probably faulty. It may not have burned out at all, but merely devel-

Standard "plug" fuses have bases like lamps, and screw into receptacles in "cut-out" box. Keep a record on cover of latter of house circuits controlled by particular fuses to ease replacement.

"Cartridge" type fuses have exposed metal end caps, which fit tightly in spring clips in cutout box. Keep spares in latter. CAUTION: Even if fuse is blown out, end cap on side to meter is still "hot."

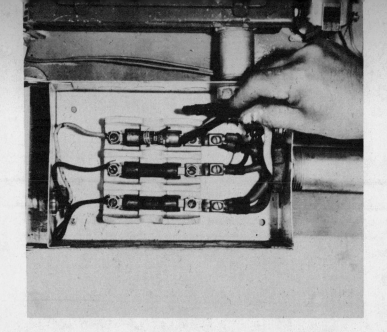

To remove a suspected cartridge fuse, first kill power by turning off main switch (have a flashlight handy if room is dark), then pry out with wooden stick. Turn on switch if light is needed during testing operation. Be sure to turn it off again before attempting to insert the new fuse.

oped an internal open circuit. The fuse wire may have become brittle and then broken under the influence of vibration from a passing truck, a slamming door, etc. I have examined many fuses that looked perfectly good yet showed positively and unquestionably as complete "opens" when given a continuity check.

Sometimes a fuse definitely blows out, and replacing it restores normal conditions. The burn-out may well have been due to a momentary short circuit which cleared itself, at least for the time being. For instance, a few strands of the flexible wire inside a cord for a floor lamp, a TV set, a fan, etc., might have worked against themselves because the cord has been stepped on a lot or otherwise abused. Enough current may have flown across these wires, during a second or so, to heat them and the fuse in the same circuit to the melting point. A new fuse holds, although the cord remains potentially dangerous.

Sometimes the touching wires, instead of flaring open, weld themselves together. New fuses then burn out as quickly as you put them in. Actually, it is better for this to happen, as then you know something is definitely haywire someplace and you are forced to go looking for it.

As a general practice, when troubleshooting the house power circuits, allow yourself *one* new fuse as a replacement for a blown unit. If this pops off, start shooting!

Heavy Starting Loads vs. Fuses

Blown fuses did not become a problem in most households until two highly desirable machines appeared on the market: first the clothes washer, which eliminates the most onerous of family chores; and then the air conditioner, which enables the family to sleep at night. The thing that puzzles owners of these machines is that they take less power than many other appliances that have been used for years without trouble. For example, a clothes washer takes only about 375 watts in normal operation and perhaps 800 or 1000 during a fast spinning cycle; a typical room air conditioner takes 800 to 1000 watts steadily. Compare these figures with the power consumption of a hand iron, 1000 watts; a bathroom heater, 1130 watts; a toaster, 1010 watts; a coffee maker, 830 watts; a frying pan, 1160 watts. If plugging in a 1000-watt iron doesn't bother the fuses, why does a 1000-watt air conditioner make them jump out of their skins?

The answer lies in the nature of both the fuses and the power load. An ordinary fuse, the kind you screw into a socket in a box in the basement, consists merely of a piece of wire of rather low melting point. As you probably know, electric current flowing in any wire must push its way through, and in so doing generates some heat. The higher the current, the higher the heat. For fuse purposes, an alloy wire is used that melts quickly if the current exceeds a certain value; the fuse wire is thin for low values of current and thick for high values. There isn't, and indeed there shouldn't be under ordinary circumstances, much leeway in fuse ratings. A fuse marked 15 amperes should not burn out with 14 amperes going through it, but it should be noticeably warm at 15 amps, pretty hot at 16 and just about melting at 17.

An 830-watt coffee maker plugged into a kitchen outlet takes about 7 amperes of current. For a fraction of a second after the appliance is turned on it takes more, but the interval is such a short one that the effect can be ignored for all practical purposes. A load of 7 amperes obviously places little strain on a 15-ampere fuse, which is

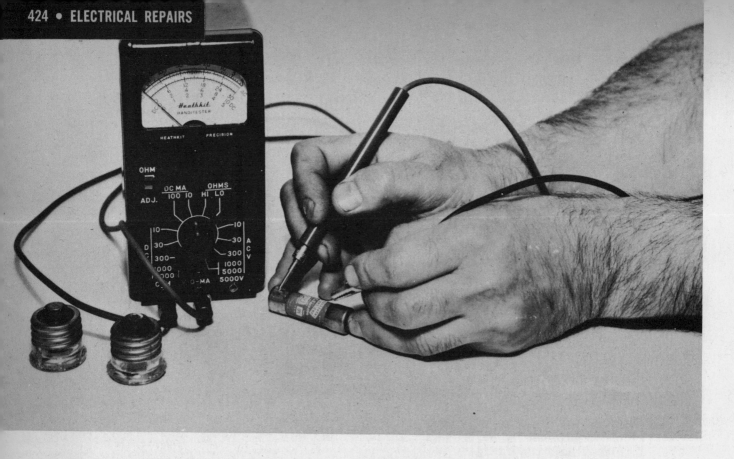

Quick test with Handitester shows condition of fuses. A good fuse registers 0 resistance, a blown one shows infinite resistance or open circuit. Check your fuses regularly and discard all defective ones.

the normal size for "branch circuits" in a home.

A standard size clothes washer is rated at 375 watts. While running it takes between 6 and 7 amperes of current.

A 15-amp fuse should therefore afford plenty of latitude. It would, except for an important physical consideration.

Into a large steel tub you dump eight or nine pounds of clothes and then add water almost to the top. If this loaded tub were out of the washer, I doubt if you'd be able to carry it more than a few feet without straining a muscle or two. This is the stationary, dead weight the motor in the machine must get into motion. When you turn the dial to "wash," the power circuit to the motor closes. During an appreciable part of the first second following, the motor struggles to develop the necessary torque, and in so doing *draws 25, 30 or 35 amperes of current from the line.* If the line is protected by an ordinary 15-ampere fuse, the motor usually doesn't even have a chance to turn over once; the fuse merely goes "pfft," as it should with an overload of 100% or more, and you're stuck with a washer full of dirty clothes.

Appliance dealers and customers alike developed high blood pressure before they discovered a vital bit of information in the instruction sheets that came with washers. This stated quite clearly that ordinary fuses cannot be used, but must be replaced with special ones of the "slow-blow" type, which cost only a few cents more. These fuses are designed specifically to handle motor loads. They get a bit warm during the starting period, but they hold up long enough to permit the motor to overcome the inertia of the tub and to get it rolling. The motor current then drops quickly to its normal running value 6 or 7 amperes. A slow-blow fuse rated at 15 amperes does the job.

The time delay in slow-blow fuses is pretty delicately adjusted to give a safe balance between convenience and protection. If the tub is overloaded with a few extra towels and a bedsheet, and is just so heavy that it locks the motor, the continuing flow of 30 or 35 amperes kicks out the fuse in a second or so. If it didn't, the motor and the wiring to it would start to smolder. Similar stalling sometimes occurs in slightly overloaded machines that have a fast spin cycle for drying the clothes. If slow-blow fuses of the recommended size for a particular washer blow out, you can be pretty sure that the tub merely is being piled too high.

Slow-blow fuses are so important to the satisfactory operation of washers that some manufacturers tape an actual fuse to the prongs of the attachment plug of the machine, as an inescapable means of calling the buyer's attention to it.

Exactly the same problem presents itself with air conditioners, except that it is more acute because these machines usually contain two motors: a pretty big one for operating a stiff compressor, through which the refrigerating liquid flows; and a smaller one, for a fan that pushes the cold air out. The starting current of a medium size cooler working on 115 volts can be as much as 50 amperes. A slow-blow fuse, of a size depending on the running rather than the starting current, is again the answer.

Actually, fusing is a relatively minor problem with air conditioners. Much more serious trouble is caused by the steady hour-after-hour flow of the running current through house wiring that is too thin to handle it without heating up. (See the section entitled "Is Your Wiring Adequate for Your Load?").

The motors used with home workshop power tools range between ¼ and 1 horsepower and they, too, have fairly high starting currents. However, except in the case of lathes (and then not always), the load is not applied until the tool reaches full operating speed, so blown fuses are not too frequent. A slow-blow fuse in the shop line is the cure if one is needed.

Types of Fuses

Most of the fuses found in homes are of the "plug" type. This term is somewhat misleading, as plug fuses have threaded bases exactly like those of lamps, and they screw into threaded sockets. Fuses that really plug in are called "cartridge" fuses. These have a fiber body and metal end caps, and fit into spring clips. Slow-blow fuses, which are sold under a variety of trade names, have screw bases like ordinary plug fuses and can be distinguished from the latter by their more complicated internal spring mechanism.

Plug fuses can be removed and replaced with little danger of shock, because the ends are completely insulated and are not part of the circuit. Cartridge fuses, how-

Cutaway view shows internal construction of Westinghouse thermal type circuit breaker, a fine safety device. Contacts are open. When handle is pushed to right, circuit is restored and handle is latched.

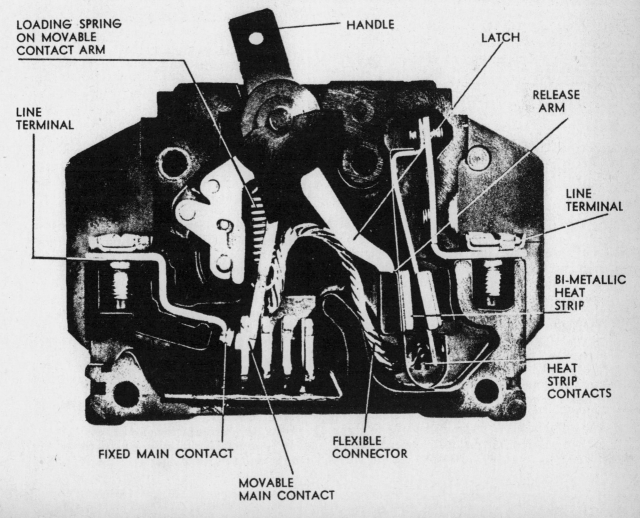

LOADING SPRING ON MOVABLE CONTACT ARM — HANDLE — LATCH — RELEASE ARM — LINE TERMINAL — LINE TERMINAL — BI-METALLIC HEAT STRIP — HEAT STRIP CONTACTS — FIXED MAIN CONTACT — MOVABLE MAIN CONTACT — FLEXIBLE CONNECTOR

Even a child can operate the circuit breakers used to protect electrical circuits. Double bank of 14 breakers (Westinghouse) is completely safe because all "hot" connections are inside wall box.

This heavy-duty two-pole circuit breaker is intended for use on 3-wire, 115/230 volt circuits. A Westinghouse "De-Ion" type, it is rated at 50 amperes. Breakers are more convenient than fuses.

ever, must be treated with great respect because of the exposed end caps. Even if such a fuse is blown out, the end on the power line side is still plenty "hot."

Testing fuses for condition is very simple. They are either open or closed. With the Clicktester, you will hear a loud click if the fuse wire is OK, or nothing if it is gone. With the Handitester, a good fuse shows as zero resistance; a dead one doesn't even move the needle of the meter. If intermittent contact inside a fuse is shown by an irregular clicking or a fluctuating meter needle, chuck it out. Fuses are so cheap that it doesn't pay to retain questionable ones.

Chart of Fuse Positions

The "cut out" box in most homes contains six fuses; more in many newer houses. It is highly advisable to know which fuses control which outlets and lights all through the dwelling. Have an assistant turn on all the lights in one room at a time, and also activate the wall outlets with portable lamps, a radio set, etc. Start removing fuses and let the assistant shout down or stamp on the floor when the juice goes off. Make up the data in chart form and cement or tape it to the cover of the fuse box. Also, keep a handful of spare fuses, of the right sizes for your power installation, within easy reach of the fuse box. You'll con-

gratulate yourself on your foresight in this regard the very first time a circuit goes dead unexpectedly, as it always does.

Circuit Breakers

In all but the lowest price brackets, the tendency in new home construction is now definitely toward the use of circuit breakers rather than fuses for protection against excessive current surges. A circuit breaker has a handle like a switch and looks very much like one; it is in fact a self-tripping switch that goes open when the current passing through it exceeds its rated value.

The breakers now coming into home use work on either a thermal or a magnetic effect, or a combination of the two. The thermal type employs a bi-metallic strip which flexes and trips one or more sets of spring-loaded contact points when the rated current value is passed. The magnetic type contains an electromagnet which does the same job. Most breakers incorporate a time delay feature like that of slow-blow fuses, and for exactly the same reason.

When a circuit breaker trips open on an overload, it can be reset in an instant; you merely push the handle back up. If the overload is still on, it will trip again. Like a good switch, a breaker will last a long time and rarely if ever will require replacement.

Because circuit breakers cost from 4 to about 25 times more than fuses, many people have gotten the impres-

New circuit breaker has screw base and can replace conventional fuses in regular cutout box without requiring changes in wiring. When current overload exceeds rating of breaker, center button pops up and circuit is opened. To reset breaker after overload is cleared, it is only necessary to press button down. This type of protective device is especially useful in homes and shops where occasional motor overloads at times occur.

sion that circuit breakers in general have magical properties and offer more protection than fuses do. This is not so. An overload that trips a $2.50 breaker will also burn out a five-cent fuse, and just as quickly and thoroughly. The most obvious advantage of breakers is convenience. A far more important feature, which is not as widely appreciated as it should be, is that in many cases they prevent a thoughtless homeowner from deliberately overloading his power lines.

Consider a "standard" house having branch circuits protected by regular 15-ampere plug fuses. A new table-top broiler arrives one day and all the members of the family gather round while it is unpacked, admired, and then, of course, plugged in to see how it works. Many such broilers take pretty close to 15 amps all by themselves. If current is being carried on the same line for lights or other purposes, there is a very good chance that the 15-amp fuse will evaporate. Great disappointment registers on the faces of mother and the kids. So what does pop do? Nine times out of ten, he will not resist the temptation to replace the 15-amp safety valve with a 20-amp plug. Result: the broiler goes on and his reputation as Mr. Fix-It is saved. What happens to the power line is another story. Sooner or later this practice leads to disaster.

If the house is equipped with 15-ampere circuit breakers, the breaker feeding the broiler line will flip open on the overload just as the fuse did. But this breaker is permanently bolted into the distribution box, with its connections out of sight. There's *nothing* you can do to it except push the handle back to "on." Every time it trips open it is warning you that the broiler is just too much for that line. You might swear at it a little, but the sooner you realize the significance of the tripping of a circuit breaker, the longer will your house last.

I have heard people say they don't like circuit breakers because "they don't allow any flexibility in operating certain lines in the house." This is cockeyed reasoning of the worst sort: The fact that breakers do not permit any such "flexibility" is the greatest argument in their favor. Probably 90% of all actual cases of fires, charred wiring, sluggish air conditioners and freezers, etc., would not have occurred at all if uncorruptible breakers had been used instead of easily "fixed" fuses, which are a danger in ignorant hands.

In this section the value of 15 amperes has been used in describing fuse and breaker protection for branch circuits in a house. This is the safe allowable carrying capacity of No. 14 wire, the size most commonly used in homes. However, much greater values are permissible with heavier wires, as explained in the section "Is Your Wiring Adequate for Your Load?" An overload is an overload, regardless. •

When the Bell Doesn't Ring--

—corroded button contacts or loose connections are usually at fault

YOU'RE finishing your morning coffee, and are disturbed by a loud pounding noise from the vicinity of the front door. You rush to open it and find the postman with a package in his hand.

"Whassamatter, Bill?" you ask. "Why didn't you ring the bell?"

"I pushed the button about a dozen times, but nothing happened. Saw your car in the garage, so knew you were still in. Here, sign for this, will you?"

"Bell doesn't work?" you mutter.

"Lemme try it." You do, and it doesn't. That evening you have a small repair job to perform. That is, it'll be small if you know your bell wiring arrangement.

In many older houses the general scheme of Fig. 1 prevails. The source of power is a bank of No. 6 size dry batteries, usually three or four of them connected in simple series. The front door "button" is merely a momentary contact switch which, when pressed, closes the circuit to a bell. If a side or rear door is customarily used for

Bell-ringing transformer invariably is located close to the fuse box; to make a quick check on it, set Handi-test (see Testers And Tools) to 30-volt AC range and connect test leads to binding posts. This one reads OK.

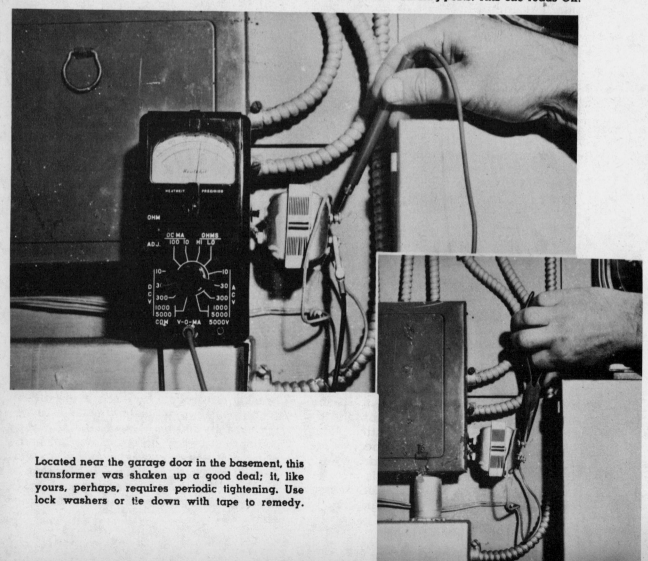

Located near the garage door in the basement, this transformer was shaken up a good deal; it, like yours, perhaps, requires periodic tightening. Use lock washers or tie down with tape to remedy.

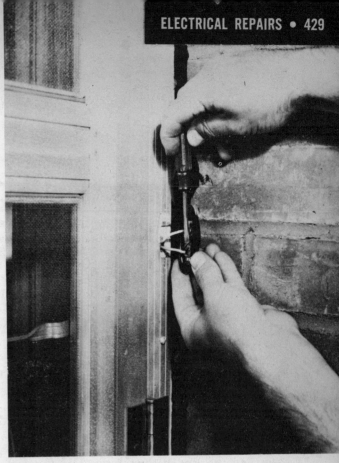

Exposed bell buttons are usual cause of failure of the signalling system. Inspect frequently; to get at connections, remove two mounting screws.

If short-circuiting button terminals with screwdriver makes bell ring, internal contacts are defective; new button is the simplest way of restoring service.

deliveries, access to a yard or driveway, etc., another button is located here and it operates a buzzer. Any number of bells or buzzers can be hooked in to work off a single bank of batteries.

In most houses built during the last couple of decades the batteries are replaced by a small step-down transformer. The primary side, identified by its heavy black and white covered wires, is connected *permanently* to any of the branch circuits supplying power to the house. The secondary side, identified by its two knurled head binding posts, is connected to the bell, buzzer, or chimes through door buttons, exactly as in the battery arrangement. See Fig. 2.

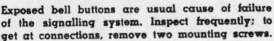

The transformer reduces the 115-volt line voltage to values ranging between 6 and 16. These have absolutely no shock danger, so it is not necessary to "kill" the transformer circuit, by opening the branch fuse to which it is connected, when you shoot trouble in the bell and button wiring.

"If the transformer is connected permanently to the line, doesn't it draw power all the time?" This question is probably framing in your mind. Yes, it does, but the amount is so small that it hardly over-

comes the friction of the bearings in the watt-hour meter. When a door button is pressed, a bell or a chime takes a few watts, but for such a short time that they add virtually nothing to the monthly electric bill.

The case of the transformer may feel very slightly warm to the touch. This is normal. It does not indicate overloading, but only the internal molecular friction of the iron core of the transformer as the alternating current goes through its periodic reversals. (See "The Power System in Your Home.")

Because they are activated for only a total of perhaps minutes over the course of a whole year, the bells, buzzers and chimes themselves rarely give trouble. If one fails to work, check these points:

1) The source of power. Dry cells last a long time, but they do dry out eventually. The usual sign of impending failure is an outcropping of a white chemical around the case. A dry cell in good condition measures 1½ volts. Three in series should check to 4½ volts, four in series to 6 volts. The Handitester, set for DC measurement, is fine for the job. If the batteries are more than a year old they should be suspected

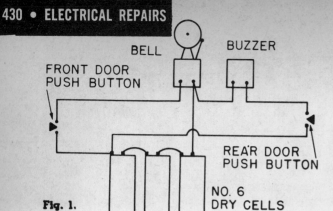

BELL   **BUZZER**

FRONT DOOR
PUSH BUTTON

REAR DOOR
PUSH BUTTON

NO. 6
DRY CELLS

Fig. 1.

Above, a common arrangement of bell and buzzer in older houses using dry cells as source of power.

of weakness and then checked for voltage.

The rated secondary voltage of the step-down transformer is usually marked on the case. Set the Handitester for AC on the 30 volt scale, connect the test leads to the brass binding posts, and you'll know in an instant if the transformer is putting out juice. It isn't necessary to disconnect the existing wires to the posts for this test.

If the meter shows no voltage, disconnect either of the wires to the binding posts, open the primary power line circuit by removing the line fuse, set the Handitester for LO ohms, and try a continuity check on the secondary winding. If it's OK, it will show either zero ohms or a barely perceptible fraction of an ohm. If the needle doesn't move, the secondary winding is either burned out (an unlikely prospect), or one of its connections inside has corroded loose. A replacement transformer is then the obvious answer.

If the secondary is OK, you can run a similar test on the primary. To do this, leave the line fuse out, open the cutout box and find the primary wires, and then

remove either one from its present connection. With the Handitester still set for LO ohms, again make a resistance measurement. If the primary winding is intact, it will register perhaps 25 ohms or so; if it is open, the meter needle won't move. Now you know positively if the transformer needs to be replaced or not. If it checks OK, reconnect the primary wire, close the cut out box, and replace the fuse.

Of course, it is assumed that the fuse in the transformer circuit is a good one, not that this is always the case! I once spent a frantic and thoroughly frustrating hour checking every inch of a simple bell circuit, until I had the inspiration to test the fuse. There was no reason for it to be open, but it was.

2) Loose connections. The nuts on many bell-ringing transformers do not hold very well, and are known to loosen if the unit is near a much-used door. Reinforce them with lock washers, or tie them down with strips of tape of any sort. Also inspect the screw terminals on the bells and buzzers.

The wire universally used for bell connections is No. 18 solid, with cotton or plastic insulation. Handle it carefully, as it has a tendency to break off if nicked or bent too sharply.

3) Push buttons. If the contacts are made of iron, as they are in many cheap buttons, they are bound to rust; if they're of brass they can still corrode and get dirty. If the batteries or transformer tested OK, unscrew a suspected button from the door frame and carefully pull it away so that you can get at the terminals. If they're rusty and pitted, don't be surprised. Scrape them off a bit, and short circuit them with the blade of a screwdriver. If the bell comes to life, you know what's at fault. •

In newer homes, a step-down transformer is permanently connected to the 115-volt line and supplies voltages between 6 and 16 for signalling devices. The transformer itself draws little current from the line.

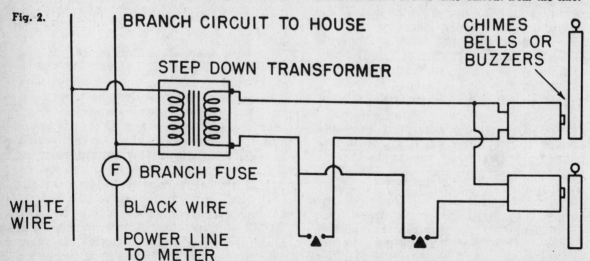

Fig. 2.

BRANCH CIRCUIT TO HOUSE

**CHIMES
BELLS OR
BUZZERS**

STEP DOWN TRANSFORMER

(F) **BRANCH FUSE**

**WHITE
WIRE**

BLACK WIRE

**POWER LINE
TO METER**

Coffee Maker

A COFFEE maker, like a toaster, is used only intermittently, and therefore enjoys long life. What usually requires replacement, during normal kitchen service, is the little light that comes on when the brewing process is completed. In most pots this is single-contact, miniature base lamp of the kind widely used as pilots in radio and television equipment. The method of getting at this light in a typical coffee maker is illustrated herewith.

Eventually, the main heating element might burn out. Putting in a new one is not always feasible, because of the sealed construction of the water chamber. In fact, it is often cheaper to buy a brand-new maker than to attempt to pry open the old one. •

Top right, turn pot over and remove knob of brew strength adjustment; tiny screw is on underside.

Above, remove any screws on the bottom plate and put these in a safe place, free from a loss hazard.

Center right, with cover removed carefully, thermostat mechanism, pilot light assembly are in view.

Right, fold bottom over. If bulb is faulty, replace with No. 47 lamp. Check connections for tightness, but don't bend or disturb the thermostat arms.

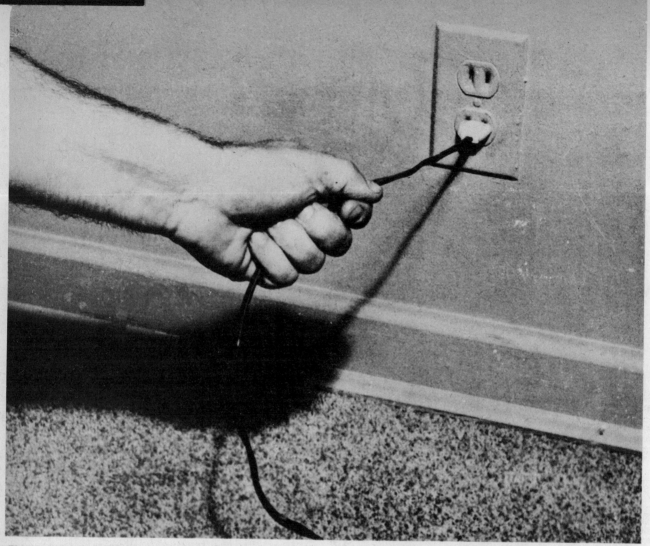

This practice more than any other puts an appliance out of commission. Neither the No. 18 stranded wire nor the molded attachment plug has the strength to withstand repeated yanking. Grasp the plug itself.

Don't Let a Cord Tie You into Knots

A mistreated connecting cord is often the cause of an appliance's breakdown. See that wires are well-insulated and don't abuse them

MANY common household appliances stop working unexpectedly not because of any internal breakdown but only because their connecting cords are stepped on, crushed, broken, cut, chewed by animals or otherwise mistreated. It seems rather obvious to say so, but an appliance can't operate if it doesn't receive power from the wall outlet.

Safety is strongly stressed by all elements of the electrical industry, but equipment manufacturers apparently have a blind spot when it comes to connecting cords. They produce appliances with strong, well-engineered bodies, and then, to save a few cents, they hook on flimsy cords with insulation so thin you can puncture it with a fingernail. Once installed, most appliances are not subject to physical abuse, but their loose cords often take a beating. Pay some attention to them and their life span will increase. And if you have to replace one, use heavily protected wire. •

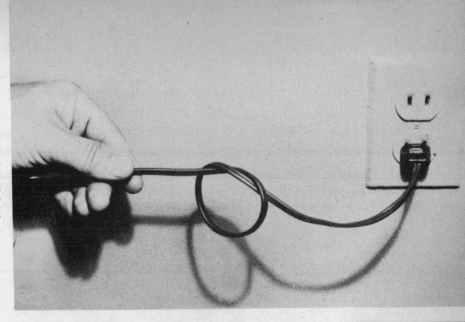

When a plug is removed from its outlet, a knot often forms in the cord because of the curl in the wire. Open it before re-inserting the plug. If knotted cord is yanked, it can sever the wire within the cord.

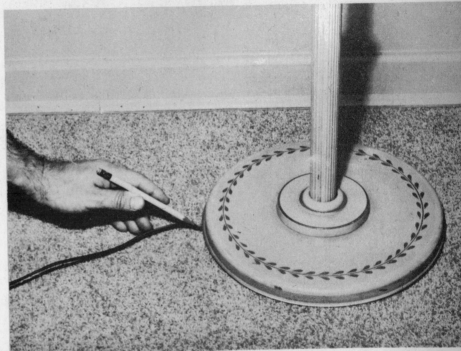

Some floor lamps provide no protection for the wire at point of emergence. Moving the lamp just a few times when cleaning the room will cause a short circuit. A layer of tape is an effective preventive measure.

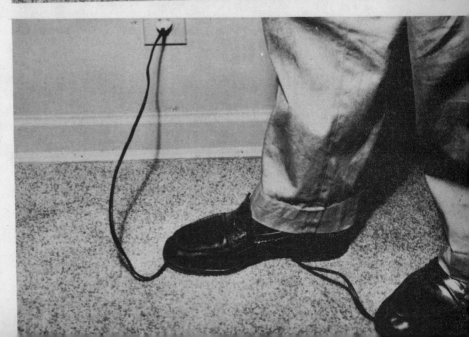

You can walk on a flexible cord only so many times before the insulation gives way. The bare wire is then both a shock and fire hazard, especially to the children. Place loose wires as near as possible to the wall.

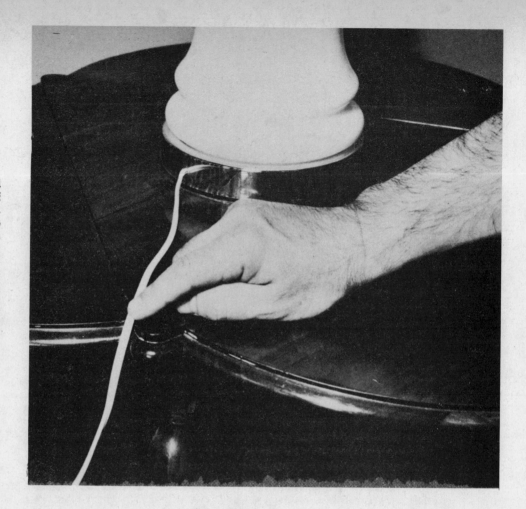

Don't let a cord get pinched in a section of a dropleaf table; if the wire is crushed, remove wall plug before touching it because strands sticking through insulation might well be "hot." Reinforce damaged section with layer of tape of nearest matching color. For white cord, white adhesive tape from the family medicine chest is ideal. Colored "Scotch" tape is also OK.

Vacuum cleaner cords take a particular beating because the appliance has to be moved around a lot. Try to keep the wire from under the wheels.

The sharp edge of a heavy pressing iron can do a lot of damage to the flexible cord. Keep the wire clear by hanging it over the back of ironing board.

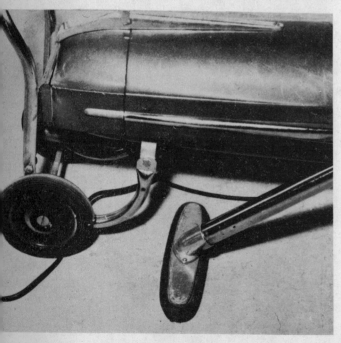

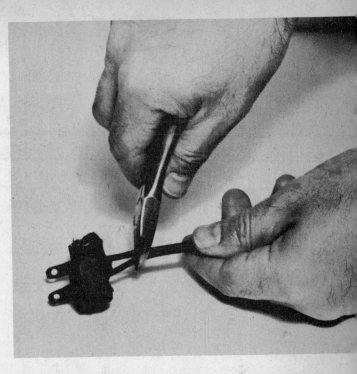

Many attachment plugs are made very cheaply of fragile compositions known in the trade as "molded mud." It is little wonder that they break up when stepped on or burn up when subjected to heavy current overloads. When buying replacement plugs, look for smooth, well-formed bodies, securely fastened prongs, terminal screws with broad heads, and fiber protection washers to fit over prongs and terminals, for your protection.

Never attempt to salvage a damaged plug by fastening the pieces together with tape or string. If the connecting cord is still in good condition, cut it off close to the plug, and discard the pieces of the latter. Use diagonal cutters, as above, or heavier "electrician's pliers." Examine wire carefully and trim off any sections near the end that show signs of crushing or bruising; these can be dangerous when you use the plug in the future.

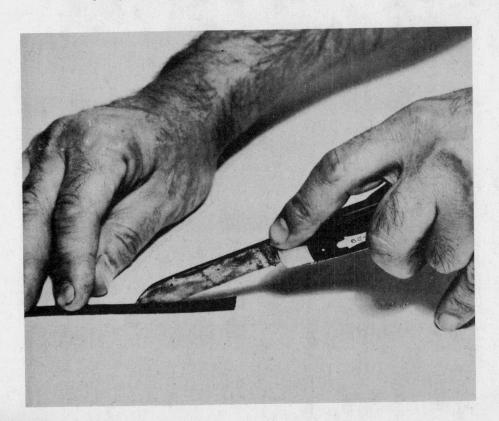

In preparing old cord for new attachment plug, first separate the ends a distance of about an inch and a half. Some cords require a sharp knife for this job; others in common use can be "zipped" apart without tools. Be especially careful not to damage insulation covering on each one of the individual wires.

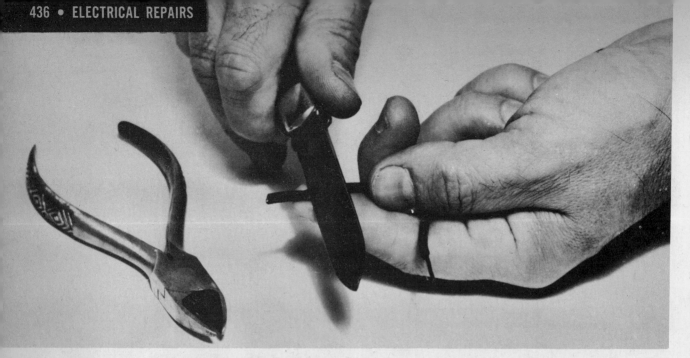

Using the sharp edge of knife, pare off insulation on each end of wire a distance of about a half inch.

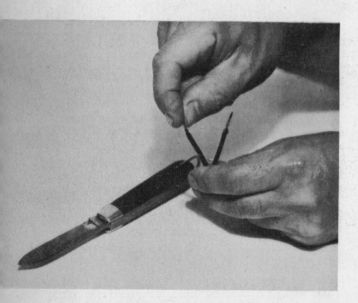

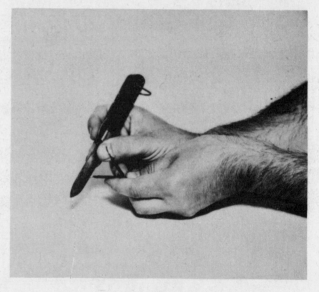

The next step in attaching a new plug is to twist together the loose strands at end of wires.

With back edge of knife, scrape end of wires clean and bright. Don't touch with fingers after this.

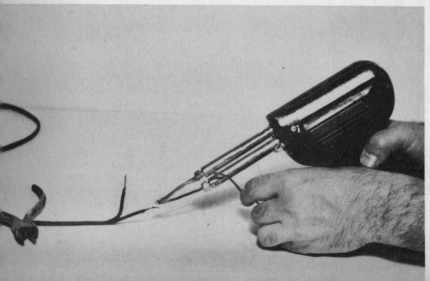

Apply thin coat of solder to each wire. This stiffens wires and makes them easier to fasten under the plug.

Immediately after soldering the loose end strands of the wire, poke the cord through the attachment plug. The one shown in the photo has a long neck or handle, which is very convenient for removing purposes.

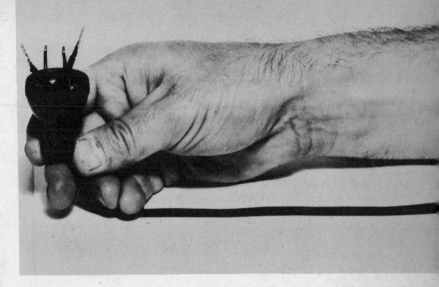

Starting from the pared ends of the wires, apply a layer of strong electrical tape back along the cord a distance equal to the length of the plug plus about a half inch. This tape will reinforce the insulation.

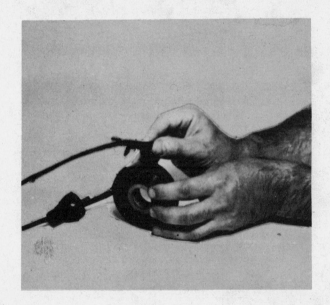

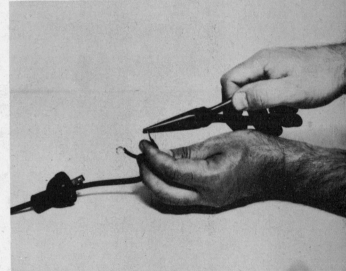

The wires are much easier to connect under the terminal screws of the attachment plug if they are first formed into U-shaped loops. Use long-nosed pliers to close the loops under screws and tighten.

When securing the wires under the terminal screws, make certain that no loose strands stick out. These are often the cause of overheating at the plug or of blown-out fuses. If appliance is of portable type and plug is inserted and removed frequently, make periodic examination of terminals and tighten again if necessary.

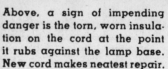

Above, a sign of impending danger is the torn, worn insulation on the cord at the point it rubs against the lamp base. New cord makes neatest repair.

An old unused lamp may be restored to service by following simple directions in replacing the cord. Often, that's all there is wrong with lamp.

Re-cording a Lamp

The extent of the damage to your present cord will determine whether or not it needs replacement; with luck all you may need to repair it is a piece of electrician's tape

THE flexible cords of table and floor lamps usually show the first signs of wear at the point where they emerge from the base. If there is any leeway in the wire, sometimes it can be pushed into or pulled out of its hole, taped over, and then put back into place. If the rest of the cord is also damaged in any way, it's better sense in most cases to take out the old cord and put in a completely new one. A typical job on a table lamp is shown in detail in the photo sequence. •

Remove the shade for safekeeping; it's usually held in place with a decorative nut or stud, which unscrews readily. Following this, obviously, the bulb is removed and then actual repair work begins.

Next, snip off the old wire at the base of the lamp. Save good sections for other uses. Below right, to disassemble socket look for word "press" on shell near switch. Insert blade of small screwdriver, twist slightly, then press end of socket downward. This opens the toothed joint between the halves of lamp socket.

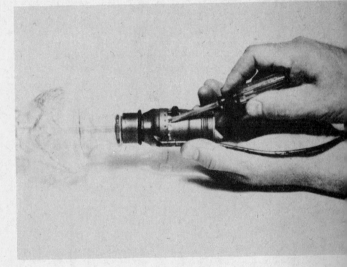

Next, remove old section of wire, inspect and clean socket, and tighten small screws inside shell as needed.

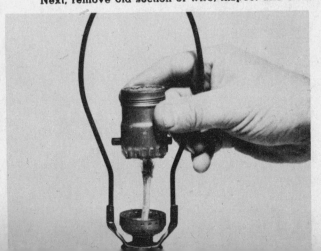
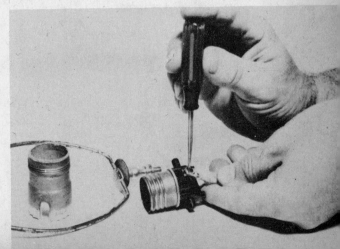

Next, check fit of socket and shade holder on neck of lamp; twist to right to tighten. Then, below right, feed the length of the new wire through the fixed part of the socket, down through base of the lamp.

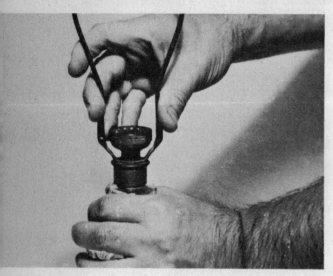
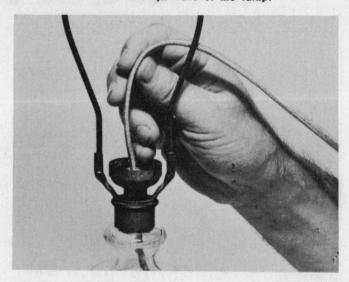

Separate ends of new wire, remove insulation, scrape clean and tighten wires under two screws of the socket shell. Then (below right) from the bottom pull wire down carefully till socket is in position.

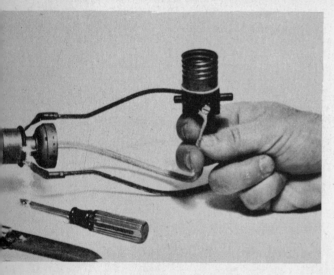

Now snap other section of socket back into position; start it at a slight angle and then squeeze along the bottom. Finally, protect new wire where it passes through base with ordinary white adhesive tape.

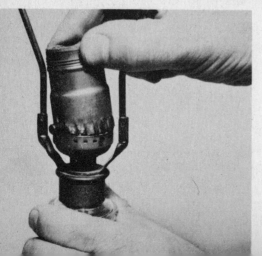

Bowl Heaters

Make a habit of testing your heater often to prevent accidents

Check for "grounding" by connecting Handitester to frame, each attachment plug in turn.

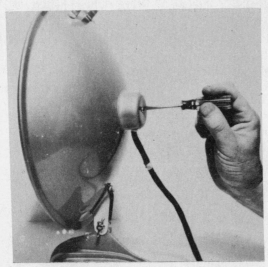

To get at connections to heating element, remove screw through the cap on back of heater's frame.

Check connections for tightness, insulation for breaks. Repair wire by twisting ends together.

A PORTABLE electric heater is often used in a bathroom or bedroom. Because people are likely to brush against it with bare limbs, it should be checked carefully and frequently for a "hot" frame, a condition resulting from accidental contact between the metal body and any part of the power circuit. This can be very dangerous, as explained in the section entitled "Play It Safe!"

For picture purposes, I bought a brand new heater. When I set up the Handitester for a simulated grounding test, I was astonished to see and hear the meter needle bang over to low ohms, indicating an actual ground! When I took off the end cap and examined the wiring, I discovered that the single screw holding the resistance wire element was rubbing through the insulation of one wire of the flexible cord. I fixed that in a hurry with a bit of tape. •

Effectiveness of heater depends greatly on shininess of reflector. Remove the line plug to clean.

Don't be fooled . . . not all tubular lamps are fluorescents. Here are two of identical size and appearance, but only the top one is a fluorescent, the tip-off being the double pin connectors at each end. The lower lamp is an incandescent, and has only one metal connector at each end, as shown in picture above.

Let There Be Light!

Here is a brief description of the operation and care of the two types of lamps used today—incandescent and fluorescent

THE electric lights commonly used in homes and offices are of two general types: incandescent and fluorescent. The incandescent lamp, invented by Thomas A. Edison in 1879, is a very simple thing. It consists of a wire sealed in a glass lamp, from which the air has been removed or replaced by a mixture of certain inert gases. The wire offers resistance to the flow of electricity. The friction of the electrons in pushing their way through raises the temperature of the wire to the point where it glows or "incandesces." The higher the temperature, the whiter the light.

Tungsten is the metal now universally used for incandescent lamp filaments. It burns at about 5000 degrees Fahrenheit, a fantastic temperature higher than that of any other artificial heat ordinarily encountered by man. At this temperature, asbestos or fire brick would melt like candle wax under a match. Why doesn't the tungsten wire consume itself? Because there is no air . . . that is, oxygen . . . in the bulb to support combustion, or burning.

In lamps smaller than about the 50-watt size, the air in the glass envelope or bulb is merely pumped out, leaving a vacuum or "nothing" inside. In most larger lamps, a mixture of nitrogen and argon is pumped in following the evacuation of the air. The purpose of these gases is to introduce some slight pressure on the filament and to retard evaporation of the tungsten. The filament not only lasts longer than it would in a plain vacuum, but during its useful life it can be burned at a higher temperature. This means better, brighter light.

In manufacture, the gas mixture is introduced at slightly under normal atmospheric pressure. The internal pressure tends to rise when the lamp is on, and in the case of lamps burning very brightly it goes a little *above* atmospheric pressure. This explains why the very brilliant lamps used in movie and still projectors, and in spotlights, often develop blisters and bulges. The intense heat of the filament softens the glass, and the rising gas pressure inside forces it outward. A projection

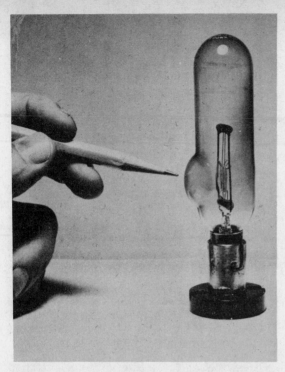

Will it pop out? Probably not for quite a while. Bulge in side of 300-watt projector lamp is due to combination of high filament temperature and inside gas pressure. Blackening is also natural.

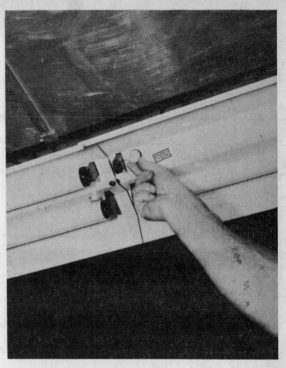

In most straight fluorescent fixtures, the starter is accessible only after the lamp is removed. It is not screwed in, but is held by contact springs. A quarter turn will serve to loosen or lighten it.

bulb that has been used a long time takes on a really grotesque appearance.

Eventually, the filament of an incandescent lamp consumes itself. The metal evaporates to the point of such thinness that it simply burns open. Any lamp burns up almost instantly if the glass envelope is broken. The super-heated tungsten combines with the oxygen of the air and goes pfft!

If heat rather than light is wanted from an incandescent lamp, it is operated at a lower than normal temperature. In this class is the "infrared" lamp, which is widely used for the treatment of muscular pains and aches.

If a great deal of light is wanted, a tungsten lamp is operated at higher than normal temperature. Of course, its life is thereby shortened, and this is the price paid for the increased brilliance. The popular "Photoflood" lamps used in picture-making are actually 64-volt bulbs operated on 115 volts. Their rated life is about six hours, compared with about 750 hours for a regular 115-volt bulb.

When a lamp fails to light, and another lamp tried in the same socket does light, it obviously has expired. Every home should have a supply of spares. It's possible to double-check a lamp by running a continuity test on it, but this is rather pointless. It takes less time to screw in a new lamp.

There are only a few simple precautions to observe in using incandescent lamps, and these relate mainly to their high operating temperature. Don't let paper, parchment, silk or other cloth shades come in direct contact with the glass. The material can readily char, and under some circumstances will actually burst into flames. Don't touch a hot bulb with your bare hands. If you don't want to wait until it cools off, grasp it with a handkerchief or a pot holder. Avoid splashing water on a bare bulb; the glass might implode (get that, *im*plode) and scatter fragments all over the room.

DO keep lamps clean and dust-free by wiping them occasionally, when cool, with a very slightly dampened cloth. Bulbs inside decorative globes or fixtures are often neglected in this respect and gradually become dim. *Internal* blackening is another matter, and cannot be avoided. It is the natural result of gradual evaporation of the tungsten filament. Sometimes the blackening reduces the light output to the point where it is more economical to replace the bulb, even though it still lights, than to continue to use it.

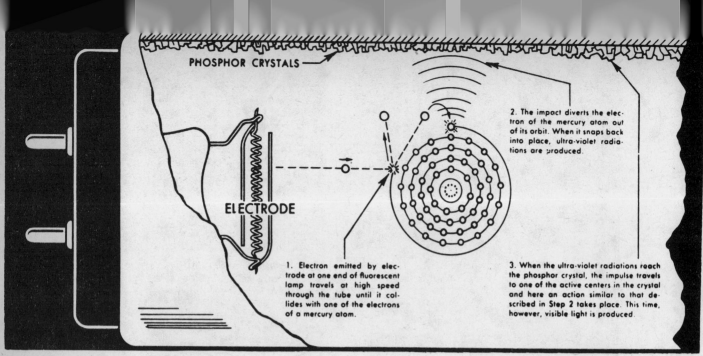

PHOSPHOR CRYSTALS

ELECTRODE

1. Electron emitted by electrode at one end of fluorescent lamp travels at high speed through the tube until it collides with one of the electrons of a mercury atom.

2. The impact diverts the electron of the mercury atom out of its orbit. When it snaps back into place, ultra-violet radiations are produced.

3. When the ultra-violet radiations reach the phosphor crystal, the impulse travels to one of the active centers in the crystal and here an action similar to that described in Step 2 takes place. This time, however, visible light is produced.

Westinghouse Electric Corporation

According to scientists, electrons inside fluorescent lamp release ultraviolet radiation from mercury.

Fluorescents Are Different

In a filament lamp, electric current flows through a solid tungsten wire and heats it to incandescence. In a fluorescent lamp, the two electrodes which are connected to the power line are completely separated inside a long glass tube. The latter contains a small drop of mercury, and its inner surface is coated with a chemical that has the property of glowing or "fluorescing" when struck by ultraviolet light, which itself is not visible to the human eye. Under the proper conditions, electrons flow back and forth between the end electrodes under the impetus of the line voltage. The theory is that they strike atoms of the mercury and release the ultraviolet radiation, which in turn impinges on the chemical coating and causes it to fluoresce.

The color of the light produced by flourescents depends on the chemicals or "phosphors" used as the coating. While white is the most usual color (actually, white is not a color, but a combination of all colors), it is also just as easy to obtain blue, orange, green, blue-white, yellow-pink, deep red and ultra-blue.

The electron-emitting electrode in each end of the tube is called a "cathode." In the

When removing or inserting lamp, make sure pins at both ends drop straight into slots in sockets; then twist quarter turn. Don't force into place.

If you suspect that the cathode wire is burned out, a continuity check with Handitester will give the answer. However, filament wires rarely burn out.

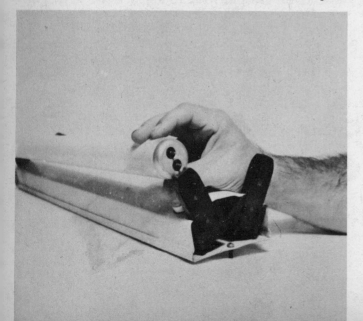

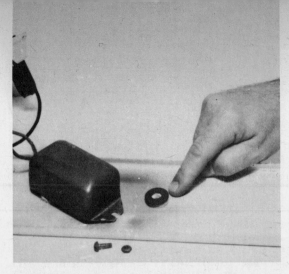

Annoying humming sound heard from fluorescent lamps is from vibration of core of ballasts. Remount the ballasts on large fiber or leather washers.

After installing fiber washers, tighten screws of ballasts only enough to assure grip. If you compress them too much, they won't silence ballasts.

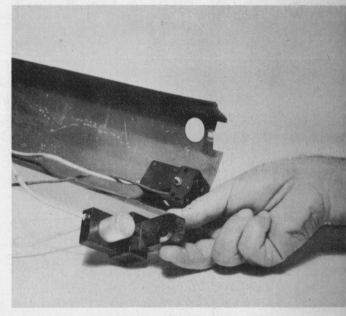

If new starter and new lamp don't produce light, check the ballast with your Handitester for continuity. The normal reading is around 30 ohms.

Receptacle for starter and socket for end of lamp are often combined. If they break from being forced, it's a simple matter to replace them.

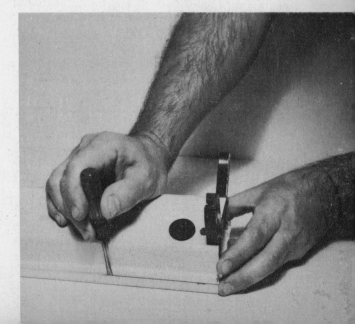

Pencil points to one of two ballasts concealed inside body of fluorescent fixture. When the latter is opened, it is easy to trace wiring.

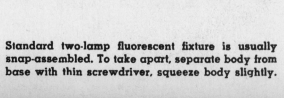

Standard two-lamp fluorescent fixture is usually snap-assembled. To take apart, separate body from base with thin screwdriver, squeeze body slightly.

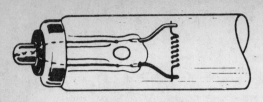

**INSTANT START
SLIMLINE TYPE**

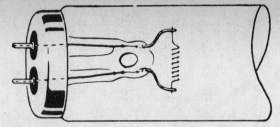

PREHEAT TYPE

HOT CATHODES

General Electric Company

These are common types of hot cathodes used in fluorescents. In preheat cathode, current flows first through filament, just as in incandescent lamp, and then is cut off. In instant-start cathode, the electrons are pulled off the surface by high operating voltage. While the instant-start type has a filament, its ends are short circuited in the stem and only one external connection is needed for it.

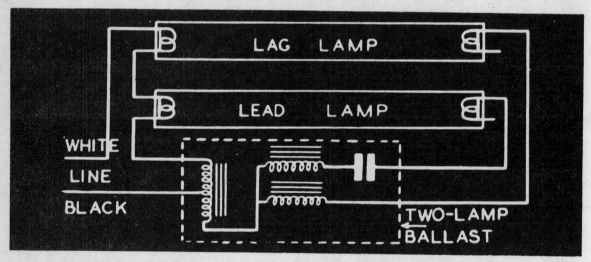

Westinghouse Electric Corporation

Above is a diagram of a typical two-lamp instant-start fluorescent. The ballast in this type of lamp contains a step-up transformer for boosting line voltage plus a capacitor for improving power factor.

fluorescents in most common use, this is a coiled tungsten wire filament, coated with a chemical that gives off electrons freely when heated. The tungsten filament does not contribute any illumination directly. Two auxiliary devices are needed to make the lamp work: a "starter" and a "ballast." In a basic lamp, the filaments, the ballast and the starter are connected in simple series. When the lamp switch is turned on, current flows through all the elements. The filaments can be seen to glow slowly. After a second or two, the contacts inside the starter snap open. This cuts off the current to the filaments, and at the same time causes the ballast to develop a momentarily high-voltage "kick." Surging through the lamp, this voltage starts acting on the electrons already loosened from the hot cathodes, and the double cycle previously described gets under way. One side of the AC power line remains connected to one terminal only of one cathode; the other

side of the power line goes to the ballast, which in turn connects to one terminal only of the second cathode. The filaments themselves are no longer incandescent. The electrons are pulled off their surfaces by the mere attraction of the voltage between the cathodes.

The ballast is a coil of fine wire on an iron core. It looks exactly like the "choke" coils found in radio and television sets. Once the arc inside the lamp is struck, the ballast acts to limit the current flow between the cathodes within prescribed values for each particular size and type of lamp. Ballasts generally have long life, but they carry current and are therefore susceptible to eventual failure.

Some lamps have "instant" cathodes which do not require pre-heating. They do require much higher starting voltages to jar the electrons loose. No starter is needed, as the first pulse of voltage is enough to start the electrons on their way.

GLOW-SWITCH STARTER

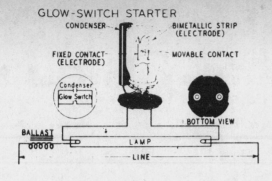

WATCH DOG STARTER

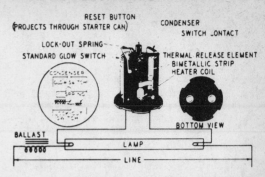

In the glow-switch starter pictured above, glass bulb is filled with neon or argon, depending on lamp voltage. On starting, voltage at starter is sufficient to produce a glow discharge between U-shaped bimetallic strip and fixed contact or center electrode (a). Heat from glow actuates bimetallic strip, contacts close and cathode preheating begins (b). This shorts out glow discharge, bimetal cools and shortly the contacts open (c).

At right is a diagram of a thermal-switch starter. On starting, the ballast, starter heating element and lamp cathodes are all in a series across the line since contacts of thermal-switch starters are normally closed. Cathode preheating current thus also heats the bimetallic strip in the starter and the contacts open. The inductive kick then starts the lamp itself with the normal operating current thereafter holding thermal switch (inset) open.

General Electric Watch Dog Manual Reset Starters use glow switch principle. During normal starting switch functions as described under illustration at left. This starter has an added feature which consists of a wire-coil heater element actuating a bimetallic arm which serves as a latch to hold a second switch in a normal closed position. When a lamp is deactivated or will not start after blinking on and off, enough heat is developed by intermittent flow of cathode preheating current so that latch pulls away and releases second switch.

THERMAL-SWITCH STARTER

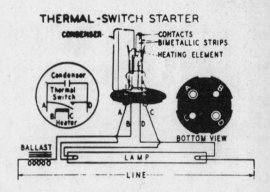

Unlike incandescent lamps, which will light under almost any conditions of line voltage, temperature and humidity, fluorescents are known to be somewhat sensitive in these respects. Their susceptibility to cold, especially, is not too generally appreciated, and is the reason for many mysterious cases of irregular or unsatisfactory operation. In an unheated garage or a partially heated basement, lamps sometimes don't strike at all in winter weather, but keep blinking on and off.

If a flourescent fixture has been working properly over a period of time, and then either refuses to start or works fitfully, either the starter or the lamp itself might be at the end of its useful life. Always try a new starter first, as it's much cheaper than a new lamp. If the trouble continues, you have no choice but to try a new lamp.

If the ends of a lamp remain lighted

steadily, with no sign of the tube striking for its full length, the strong likelihood is that the starter contacts have welded shut, or possibly a short circuit has developed in the little capacitor which is included in some starters to eliminate radio interference.

The filament wires of cathodes rarely burn out because they are heated to full incandescence for only a few seconds during the starting period. However, it is easy to test them with any continuity checker.

A new lamp may show swirling, spiraling, snaking or fluttering effects when first turned on, but usually clears up after it is well warmed up or has been turned on and off a few times. An old lamp sometimes starts swirling violently, and then resumes clear operation without warning. This is probably due to shifting distribution of the phosphors on the inside of the glass. •

Silent Switch Lets Baby Sleep

A mercury-type light switch is easily installed as a replacement for noisy controls—it's perfect for bedroom or bath

THE baby has finally fallen asleep, and with an inward sigh of relief you tiptoe out of the nursery. You go into your own bedroom, which is probably adjacent, and turn on the light so that you won't trip over the furniture. That does it.

"Yahhhh!" The click of the switch, sounding like the report of a .22 in the quiet of the house, has awakened the little darling, and you have to spend another five minutes quieting him/her down again.

There's really no need at all to suffer this sort of thing. For less than a dollar apiece you can buy absolutely silent toggle switches of the mercury type. These are regarded by some parents as the greatest boon since disposable diapers. Removing an old switch and installing a silent one is a simple screwdriver operation. It will take you about ten minutes to do the first switch and probably five for the second. The accompanying series of pictures shows how.

The utility of mercury switches is not restricted to households with children, of course. Plenty of adults of all ages are light sleepers and are disturbed by the short but sharp snap of ordinary switches. An especially important location for a silent switch is the bathroom. It enables a person to make a nocturnal visit to the latter without awakening another occupant of the same bedroom.

1: Wait! Before you reach for that screwdriver to open up the old switch, remember to pull the fuse that controls the circuit. If this darkens the room, have a flashlight handy, or do the job during daylight when you can see well.

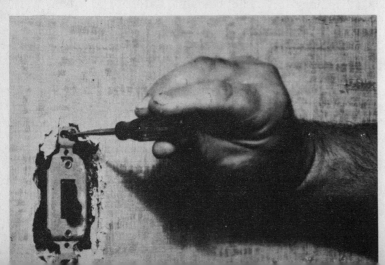

2: With the switch cover plate off, two more screws come into sight. These hold the "plaster ears" of the switch body to the wall box. They are often corroded, and may require a drop of penetrating oil before they come out.

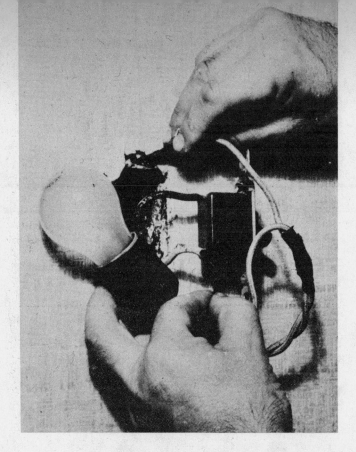

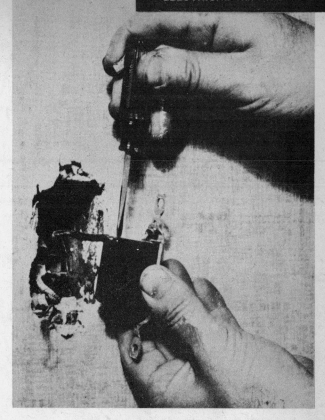

3: To make sure wires are dead after removing fuse, apply leads of a Lightester (see pg. 390) to switch terminals, and from the metal wall box to each of the terminals in turn. Safety first will pay off.

4: Pull switch out slowly (connecting wires are usually fairly stiff) and remove leads from under terminal screws; save switch for possible future use as a replacement in the basement or kitchen.

5: The wall box invariably has lots of dirt and bits of plaster in it. Clean this out with a brush while you're at it. By the way, an old paint brush will come in handy as a useful odd-job cleaning tool.

6: Clean the bared ends of the wires with the back edge of a pocket knife or use a small piece of emery cloth. A clean and bare wire is easiest to work with and assures you proper contact.

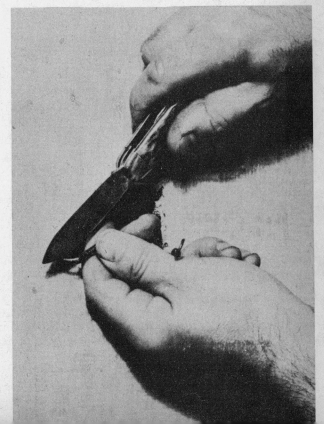

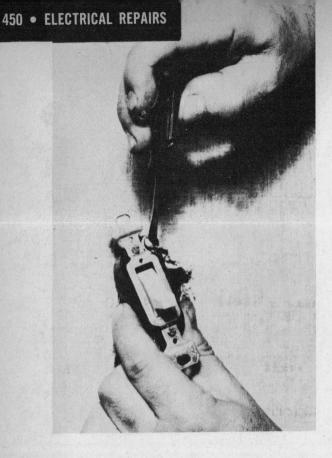

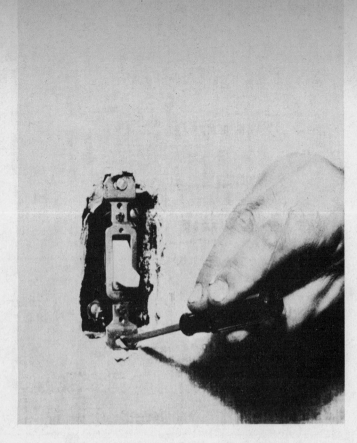

7: The next step is to fasten the cleaned ends of the wires to the terminals of the mercury switch; at this point be sure the end marked TOP is positioned that way before attaching the switch.

8: With wires attached to the mercury switch, push wires carefully back into box and press new switch gently into position. Then pass screws through "ears" of switch, center vertically, and tighten.

9: Using the plate from the previous switch, reassemble with the original screws; a plastic shield overlapping the plate helps keep fingerprints off the wall; it's a good investment.

10: Easy does it. The light goes on and off almost magically as mercury switch is flipped up or down. With no springs to wear out, this type of switch will last indefinitely; they're tops for bedrooms, bath.

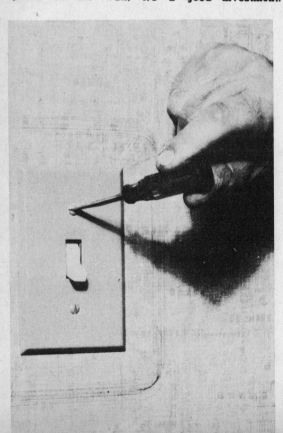

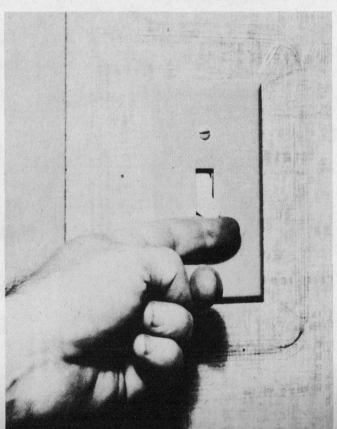

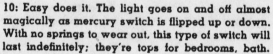

Another type of light control that is enjoying new favor among homeowners is the "tap switch." It has a single large center button, which responds to only very light pressure. Tap it once, and the light goes on; merely brush a finger against it, and the light goes off. Wallpaper behind transparent plastic shield makes the tap switch nice addition to any room.

Right: Provided with the tap switch is a cardboard template that can be painted to match the wall or used as a cutting guide for a scrap piece of wallpaper if the room is papered. Position the paper over the old switch plate so that the pattern matches the area around the switch as closely as possible. Then use a sharp knife to carefully cut out hole in the center.

Below: Tap switch, at right, fits standard wall boxes. Slots in ears permit accurate vertical positioning. At the left is the transparent plastic cover plate, with a piece of wall paper inserted on the inside. After the switch itself is wired and mounted in its box, the cover plate is merely pressed into position over the center button and you'll have task all done.

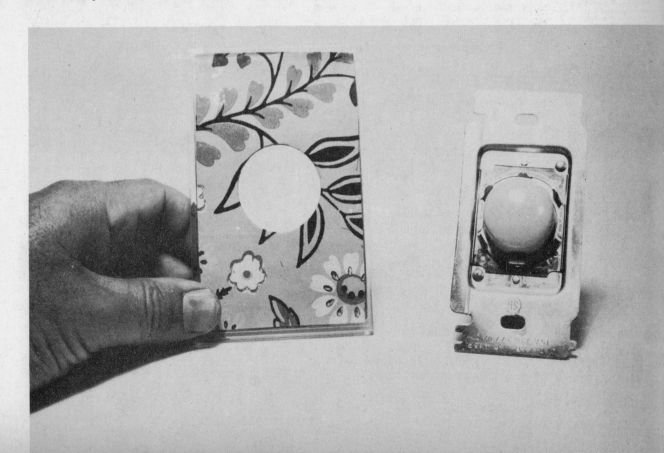

Outlet in garage was on loose flexible cord coming out of switch box. Insulation soon wore away. Owner decided to install a sturdy duplex receptacle on the wall, connected by BX cable.

After main switch was turned off, switch plate was loosened and flexible wires removed. New wire in BX will connect to exactly same points.

Extending an Outlet

EXTENDING a power outlet or replacing an unsatisfactory one is a common electrical job in homes, garages and shops. The accompanying picture sequence shows a typical Sunday-morning operation of this kind on a garage receptacle that was becoming dangerous. Flexible armored cable ("BX") is illustrated, but exactly the same technique is used for thin-wall conduit or non-metallic cable.

Caution: Kill the circuit first by opening the main switch or the circuit fuse. •

BX clamp was placed in knock-out hole in box through which flexible wire passed previously.

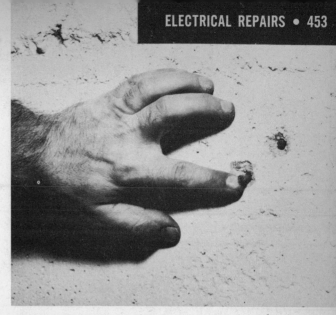

Holes for fastening screws of box were made in cement wall with 3/16" star drill and hammer.

Fiber-and-lead screw anchors were pushed into holes; these give a solid foundation for box.

Box for receptacle was mounted with two No. 10 wood screws, securely anchored in lead plugs.

Short length of BX between switch and new box is connected to duplex receptacle as shown.

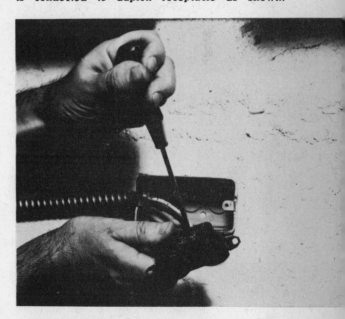

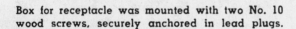

At switch box, ends of BX are connected where flexible leads were connected before. Match wires.

Finished installation offers two outlets instead of one, is completely protected, will last a long time.

Some Like It Hot

Your winter comfort depends on your furnace; learn what makes it work and keep it in repair

An actual cause of oil-burner "failure"—the AC power switch was turned off. In a house with small children, tape the switch in "up" position.

IT WAS after six o'clock in the evening, and Joe noticed that snowflakes were blowing against the small window of his washroom as he scrubbed his hands with a stiff brush.

"Good night to be home," he thought to himself, just as the office phone started to ring.

"Oh, no, not at this hour," he groaned. He let it ring a dozen times, then could resist no further. "A-One Heating Service, Joe Oily speaking."

The woman's excited voice meant only one thing, *trouble*. "Mr. Oily, you must come right over. The house is getting colder every minute and the furnace doesn't come on. I've set the thermostat to 80 and we have plenty of oil in the tank. By the way, this is Mrs. Smith."

Remembering that Mrs. Smith was a steady oil customer and also a subscriber to his annual service plan, Joe did not mention that his own wife had supper waiting for him, but instead he said, "I'll be over in ten minutes."

Joe started his "service" routine without even thinking. First he checked the oil level in the 275-gallon tank and saw that it read about ¾ full. With a lamp (the "Lightester") he checked the furnace line in the meter room and noted that it was alive. He went up the cellar stairs to examine the thermostat in the living room. He moved the adjusting arm back and forth and heard the contacts click softly as they opened and closed.

"Well, there goes my supper," he said to himself as he started back down the cellar stairs to get his tool box out of the car. When he reached the bottom he stopped suddenly, a puzzled expression frozen on his face. Then he laughed quietly, did a quick about face, bounded back up the stairs to the top landing and looked closely at the wall switch with the bright red cover and the white lettering: "Oil Burner Emergency Switch." It was the delayed mental picture of this switch that had stopped him a minute earlier. He looked at the switch in disbelief, but his eyesight was good and there was no question about it: THE HANDLE WAS DOWN, IN THE OFF POSITION.

This is a completely true incident from the records of a heating contractor in a typical residential community. It is by no means an unusual one. In any house with children between the ages of about fifteen weeks and fifteen years, unusual incidents are usual. A bright red oil burner switch, so markedly different from all the other switches in the house, is bound to attract the eyes of inquisitive youngsters, but it's not the only source of trouble. In most oil-burner installations, there is a cut-off valve in the pipe directly off the tank, and another just before the oil pump at the furnace.

Because the heating system of your house is by far the largest, most complicated, most expensive and most important single element in it, you should become thoroughly familiar with it. Your "bible" is the manufacturer's instructions. These were packed with the original equipment and should have been left for you by the builder. If the installer threw them out with the crating materials, as often happens, obtain another set from the manufacturer. Copy off all the identifying model and serial numbers you can find on the equipment and the name and address of the maker, and write directly to the latter. Be sure to mention that you would like to have a complete wiring diagram of your system, among other things. Most furnace manufacturers realize that homeowners don't monkey with heating plants just for the sake of playing around, but only to keep them in good operating order. Some of the literature they send back is very elaborate. The "dope" on the combination warm-air furnace and air-conditioning unit in my own home consisted of 48 letter-size sheets.

Heating Systems by Type

Home heating systems are classified according to the fuel they burn and the method of converting the heat of combus-

tion to room warmth. A generation ago coal was king because it had only to be chipped out of the ground and shipped off to distribution centers. However, all members of a household so thoroughly disliked the heavy, dirty work of shoveling in coal and taking out ashes that "automatic" systems using oil or gas as fuel became popular as soon as they were introduced. Hundreds of thousands of old coal burners have been converted to oil or gas, and virtually without exception new houses built since the end of World War II use these clean, convenient fuels.

In the "steam heat" system, probably the one in commonest use, a quantity of static water in a boiler is heated by an oil or gas flame to the boiling point. Steam is generated, and this pushes its way through connecting pipes to radiators, which become hot as the steam whirls around inside. The outer surfaces of the radiators warm the air in the room. As the steam gives up its heat this way to the radiators and the room, it condenses back to water, which dribbles back to the furnace to be reheated into steam.

In the "hot water heat" system, water is again heated in a boiler, but not to the point where it turns to steam. The hot water itself is circulated through connecting pipes to the room radiators, usually with the assistance of a motor driven pump, and returns to the boiler for reheating.

In the "hot air" system, the oil or gas flame heats up the air in the belly of a furnace. This warmed air rises by itself, or more usually is pushed along by a blower fan, through large sheet metal ducts or pipes which merely open out into the rooms of the house; the openings are called "registers." In older houses the warmed air gradually leaks out through windows and

The screwdriver points to heating resistor that accelerates the action of the contacts of a typical thermostat.

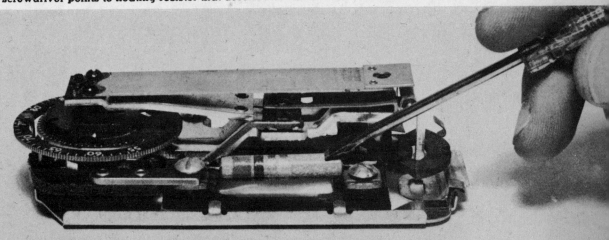

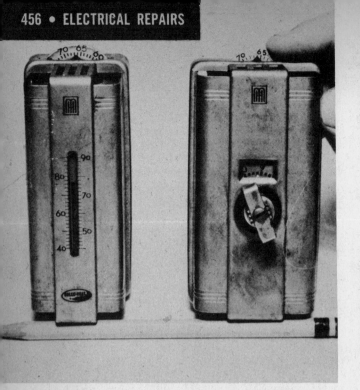

Left, a standard-type thermostat with wheel adjustment at top; right, a matching "night shut-off" with a mechanical wind-up and controlling clock.

doors and only fresh air enters the furnace (from a partially opened window or unsealed door) to be warmed and pushed up. In newer houses, especially those designed for central air cooling as well as heating, return ducts as well as entrance registers are built into the rooms. Most of the air is circulated back to the furnace and reused after being mixed with a little fresh air to keep it from going stale.

The methods have their advantages and disadvantages, What they have in common is a sensitive electrical control system, upon which the entire operation depends.

Although at first glance the wiring diagram of your particular installation may look like that of a television receiver, a little study of it and of the actual wiring will make it understandable.

The mechanism for turning the heat on or off is relatively simple. What makes a complete system a bit complicated is the presence of interlocking safety devices designed to prevent one thing: accidental fire or explosion.

Figure 1 is a simplified version of an oil burner system. The basic parts consist of the room thermostat TH; the transformer T1, which steps down the 115 volt A.C. line to about 24 volts; the relay R, which is an electrically controlled switch; the motor M, which turns the pump that brings oil from the storage tank and forces it through an atomizer nozzle in the furnace; the ignition transformer T2, which steps up the A.C. line to about 10,000 or 12,000 volts; and the spark gap SG, across which the high voltage jumps to form an intense electrical flame.

The thermostat TH is a temperature-sensitive switch, which can be set to close and open within narrow limits. A normal winter setting would be 70 degrees. Suppose the air in the vicinity of the thermostat cools just below this value. The two contacts of the thermostat close, and the device is said to be "calling for heat." The 'stat is directly in series with the 24-volt secondary of T1 and the winding of the relay R. The contacts R1 and R2 of the relay are normally open. When current from the 24-volt transformer flows through the contacts of the thermostat and the relay winding, the action of the relay is to pull the contacts R1 and R2 closed. These are in the 115-volt circuit to the pump motor M and the ignition transformer T. Oil is vaporized into the furnace and this vapor is ignited

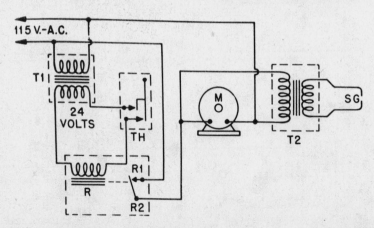

115 V.-A.C.

T1

24 VOLTS

TH

R

R1

R2

M O

T2

SG

Figure 1: This is a simplified diagram of an oil-burner electrical system as controlled by a thermostat, marked by the symbol TH. Full details of the current cut-off and supply are given in the accompanying text.

by the sparking across the gap SG. The action is very much like that of an automobile engine. Actually, ignition is needed only for a few seconds, after which the oil flame maintains iself.

The flame heats or boils the water in the boiler, or the air in a hot-air furnace, and the room warms up. When the air in the vicinity of the thermostat reaches 70, the stat contacts open, breaking the relay circuit and causing the relay contacts to open; this in turn cuts off the motor and the oil supply, and the flame dies out.

A complete diagram of an actual oil burner installation is shown in Figure 2. Let's follow this through and you'll get a pretty good general idea of how systems of this class operate.

A separate branch fuse F usually feeds the furnace line. S1 is the red-plated line switch previously mentioned. Normally it is kept on. Ignore S7 for the moment, except to assume that it is on. The step-down transformer T1 and one side each of the motor M and the ignition transformer T2 connect to the 115-volt line, as before. The thermostat TH now has three terminals, marked R, B and W, for red, black and white, respectively, the colors of the three-wire cable that connects the unit to the furnace. HR2 is a resistor, which provides a small amount of heat inside the thermostat case for a purpose to be described. S2 is a thermal safety switch. Its contacts normally are closed and furnish a path between the left end of the 24-volt winding of T1 and the winding of the relay R. HR1 is a thermal element that causes the contacts of S2 to open if current passes through it for more than a predetermined time. The relay now has three switch units, S2, S3 and S4, which operate together and are normally open. The switches S5 and S6 are part of a mechanism that is rotated by a heat-sensitive arm stuck into the exhaust stack of the furnace. With the latter cold, the central arm of S5 rests against the C or cold contact, and the H or hot contact is open. Switch S6 is a tiny glass tube containing two contacts and a few drops of mercury. It is so angled that the contacts are immersed in the mercury, or closed, when the furnace is cold.

The primary of T1 is connected permanently to the 115-volt line, just as in the case of a bell-ringing transformer. If the room is warm and the setting of the thermostat is satisfied, the B and W contacts are open. Since W goes to the right end of the T1 secondary and nowhere else, the entire 24-volt circuit is dead. This means that S2, S3 and S4 are open, and since S4 controls both the motor and the ignition the whole furnace is at rest. When the room cools down, the B and W contacts of TH close. This establishes the 24-volt circuit as follows: right end of transformer, W contact, metal arm of thermostat, B contact, lower contact of S3, center arm of S5, C contact of S5, heater resistor HR1, relay R, switch S2 and back to left end of transformer T1. Current passing through R causes its magnet to pull S2, S3 and S4 closed. For the moment, the closing of S2 has no effect, because the arm of this switch goes only to contact H of S5, which is still open. The closing of S3 establishes an auxiliary circuit to the heating resistor HR2, which at the moment is unimportant. The closing of S4, however, is most important. It turns on the motor and the ignition through the closed contacts of S6.

The Stack Control

If everything is normal, the oil flames, and hot exhaust gases start going up the stack to the chimney. In flowing over the heat-sensitive arm to which switches S5 and S6 are mounted, they cause this arm to twist. After several seconds, the movement is enough to move the arm of S5 from contact C to contact H; this opens the circuit to HR1 of the safety switch and keeps the relay circuit closed through switch S2. The same movement tilts S6 so that the internal wires are freed from the pool of mercury, and the circuit to T2 then opens, cutting off the ignition. The furnace is now running full blast.

When the room warms up, the B contact of the thermostat opens first. This does not open the 'stat circuit, as you might think. It is still intact, but this time from the W

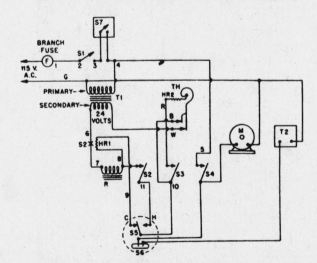

Figure 2: Detailed schematic diagram of an actual oil-burner installation as found in many homes.

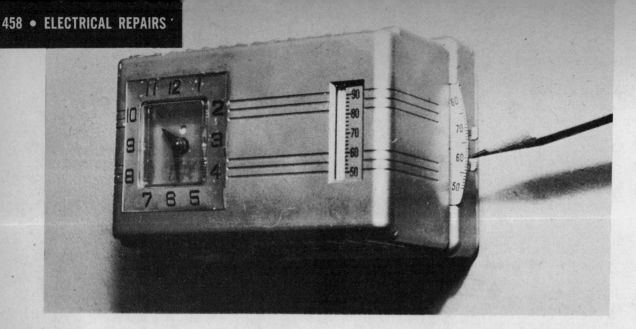

Modern thermostat with electric clock timer that runs on 24 volts has two temperature adjustments on right side of the case. The upper one is for the daytime, and the lower one is set for night-time lower temperatures.

contact, through the metal arm and the heating resistor HR2, through the closed contacts of S3, S5's contact H, switch S2, relay R, safety switch S2 and back to the transformer. Current flowing through HR2 heats it up, and some of the heat passes to the bi-metallic strip of the thermostat. This artificial heat accelerates the action of the latter and causes the contact W to open sooner than it would without it. With R and W both open, the 24 volt circuit is broken, the relay is deactivated, S2, S3 and S4 open, and the motor stops. As the furnace cools down a little, the heat-sensitive arm of S5-S6 twists back to starting position; S5 moves to the C contact and S6 tilts to close.

Heat acceleration is now more or less standard with room thermostats because it eliminates a lag that seems to be characteristic of unheated 'stats.

Preventing Oil Flood

Suppose now that for some reason the ignition system is faulty: S6 might be bad, T2 open or short circuited, the spark gap fouled. When the thermostat calls for heat the circuit includes S5 and HR1. The motor starts pumping oil, but it doesn't ignite. The chimney stack remains cold. This means that switch S5 doesn't twist, but remains against contact C. Current flows through the heating element HR1 of the safety switch S2. After a predetermined time, usually a maximum of 120 seconds, HR1 causes the contacts of S2 to pop open, as they do in a thermal circuit breaker. With S2 open, R is de-energized, S2, S3 and S4 open, and the opening of S4 particularly

shuts down the motor. If S2 did not open, the motor would continue to pump oil into the furnace, and it would quickly overflow onto the cellar floor and cause one grand mess. S2 *stays* open until someone resets it by hand.

When the Flame Fails

If the flame should fail after the burner has gone on properly, the quick drop in stack temperature causes S5 to untwist. The instant the arm leaves contact H, the relay circuit opens and again shuts down the burner. S2 is not affected. A momentary loss of power will also shut down the system. However, as the stack unit cools down further, S5 closes against contact C, and if the thermostat is still calling for heat the burner will start itself again, or "recycle," after a cooling off period of one to two minutes.

Initial failure of the burner to ignite, causing the safety switch S2 to lock open, might be due to air in the oil line, a bit of dirt lodged in the pump or something else that can readily clear itself in time. If you find this switch open when you are checking a cold furnace, always reset it for another trial before going further. When the motor starts this time it might blow the obstruction clear.

Now suppose a burner *keeps* running. If you leave it alone long enough, in the case of steam and hot water systems, it can build up a lot of steam pressure and eventually blow itself up. Most such furnaces have mechanical safety valves, but long before one of these starts whistling a pressure switch in the water chamber

Here is the inside view of the combination thermostat shown at the left; small pointers on round center dial are set for desired periods. To clean thermostat contacts pass a piece of white paper lightly between them.

should open. Connected into the power line as switch S7, this merely cuts off all power and the system shuts down.

In most oil burner installations the furnace also is the domestic hot water heater. A coil of heavy copper pipe carrying cold water is immersed in the water jacket of the boiler. The cold water is heated by contact with the boiler water, and passes on to a storage tank. In "tankless" systems the copper pipe is big enough to act as its own reservoir. In winter, when the furnace is on a great deal, hot water is plentiful. In summer, an independent thermostat in the water jacket turns the burner on for short periods to bring the water up to 140 or 150 degrees, as desired, but not high enough to bring on heat. This thermostat merely parallels the room thermostat's connections.

Gas-Fired Systems

Gas-fired steam and hot-water systems are somewhat simpler than oil systems because they do not require a pump motor or an ignition system. Instead of the pump motor, there is a magnetically operated gas valve, and for ignition there is a small, permanently lighted pilot flame in the fire box.

Any failure of the gas supply causes a thermal safety valve to cool down and lock

the main gas line shut. It cannot come on again by itself until the pilot is relighted and allowed to reheat the safety. This is a primary requirement in any gas system. The bi-metallic shut-off devices found in gas furnaces are extremely rugged and reliable and should be left strictly alone. Cases of failure are virtually unknown.

Forced warm air furnaces, particularly gas-fired jobs, are becoming increasingly popular because they are clean, easy to maintain, and fast in action, in addition to lending themselves to combination with a cold air unit. The wiring is easy to follow once you know the functions of the parts.

Inside views of standard (right) and night shut-off thermostats show (pencil) locked contacts of shut-off. Controls enable user to time the furnace turn-off.

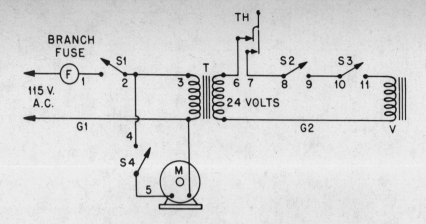

Figure 3: Schematic diagram of typical gas-fired furnace system.

See Figure 3, which shows the actual connections of a typical furnace. Simple, isn't it?

The branch fuse F and the main line switch S1 are familiar. T is again a 24-volt step-down transformer. There are three switches between the 24-volt winding and the electromagnetic valve V, which regulates the gas to the burners. TH is the usual room thermostat, which might or might not have heat acceleration. When the room is cool and the 'stat calls for heat, its contacts close. Before it can actuate the valve V and turn on the gas, two other switches must be closed. The first is S2. This is controlled by a pushrod which is part of a thermostatic element exposed to the pilot light in the gas chamber. If the pilot is properly lighted, the switch is closed. If the gas should fail at any time, the element cools off and quickly locks the switch open. When the gas comes on again, it cannot do any damage, as the valve V remains closed as long as S2 is open. If the pilot is relighted, S2 snaps closed after a minute or so.

The second safety switch is S3. This is normally on, and is called the limit switch. It is usually built in combination with S4, the blower motor switch. With S2 and S3 normally closed and S4 open, let's pick up from the room thermostat. This called for heat, so current from the 24-volt transformer flows through TH, S2, S3, V and back to the transformer. Energized by this current, the valve V clicks wide open, and immediately the gas is ignited by the pilot light. However, the motor M does not start at the same time, a fact that puzzles new owners of warm air systems. If it did, it would send cold air up through the ducts and that would make everyone unhappy. Instead, a thermostatic element in S3-S4 keeps S4 open for a period of three to five

minutes, while the air in the furnace chamber gets good and warm. Then S4 closes, and a blast of warm air is pushed through the system. When the room thermostat is satisfied it opens the circuit to V and cuts off the burners. However, the fan switch remains closed for another few minutes while it empties remaining warm air out of the furnace, and then the thermostatic element flips it open.

If the room thermostat is turned up rather high and keeps the furnace on for a long time, the furnace and the air it sends out can get too hot for comfort and safety. Here's where the limit switch S3 goes to work. It merely opens when a predetermined temperature is reached, thus opening the circuit to V and de-energizing the gas valve. The fan continues to clear the hot air into the ducts until its control switch S4 is thermostatically opened.

Night Shut-Offs

Under most circumstances it is advantageous to lower the house temperature during sleeping hours and to bring the thermostat up to a higher value about an hour before the family arises, so that the house is warm when they get out of bed. This is done by means of a double thermostat in one case, with a small electric clock timer as part of the integrated mechanism; or by a "night shut-off" with the night thermostat and the timer in a case separate from that of the main thermostat.

The controls, which can be set for any desired "night" and "day" periods, are arranged so that the two thermostats are connected in simple series. The day unit is always in the circuit, but the night 'stat, during the day hours, is merely short circuited. The timer opens this short circuit, and puts the night 'stat into action at night

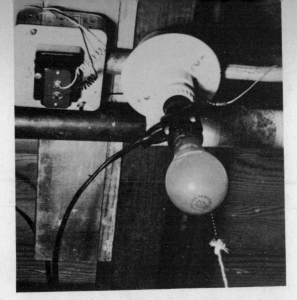

Ceiling view of separate transformer to run the clock of combination thermostat; it carries only 24V.

In typical gas-fired hot-air installation, step-down transformer is accessible with furnace front off.

and takes it out again in the morning. During the night, the burner is controlled by the lower setting. For example, suppose the normal day setting is 70 degrees and the night adjustment 65 (those five degrees make a big difference), and the room temperature falls to 68. The day 'stat calls for heat but it doesn't turn on the burner because the night 'stat is still satisfied. When the room drops to 65, the heat will come on.

Accidental misadjustment of the night shut-off is responsible for as many cold houses as is an open main switch. It's one of the last things a frantic homeowner usually looks into, but it should be among the first. Push up both day and night controls to 80; if that doesn't energize the heater, look elsewhere.

Troubleshooting

Before any trouble develops, familiarize yourself with the voltage distribution in the electrical system, with the aid of the Handi-tester or any similar voltmeter. In most installations, the step-down transformer, relay and stack control are combined in a single box, fitted with a cover that comes off easily. Leave the line power on, and don't touch any bare metal with your fingers; use the test probes of the tester. Study the technical literature from the manufacturer, identify each part and check the wires from point to point by their color.

Remembering Joe Oily's experience with the main switch, start at the fuse box and work on. With the tester set for A.C. volts on the 300 scale, you should read the full line voltage of 115 or thereabouts between the grounded side of the line, marked G in Figure 2, and the following points in the typical oil burner system illustrated: 1, fuse; 2 and 3, main switch; 4, transformer primary and pressure switch; 5, motor switch contact of relay. These readings will be the same whether the burner is on or off.

The R, B and W leads from the room thermostat usually terminate at binding posts with the same letter markings, somewhere in the furnace control box. With the meter on the 30-volt A.C. scale, use W as the common test point, and touch the probe to other points to obtain 24 volts with the burner off: 6, transformer secondary and one contact of safety switch; 7, other safety contact and one end of relay; 8, other end of relay, one end of heating element HR1, and fixed contact of S2; 9, other end of HR1, contact C of S5; 10, S5, S3 and B.

Absence of a reading between W and 7 is a sure sign that the safety switch contacts are open, a common but not often suspected cause of trouble. No reading at 8, after a normal reading at 7, means only one thing: an open relay winding. With the burner running, the only change is that point 11, S2 and H of S5, previously dead, now also read the 24 volts.

To make continuity and grounding tests on individual parts, set the meter for LO OHMS and proceed exactly as indicated elsewhere in this book in the safety, tools, and motor sections.

With a gas-fired air system, the checks are kindergarten stuff. See Figure 3. With the furnace in full operation, get 115 volts between G1 and points 1, 2, 3, 4 and 5; get 24 volts between G2 and 6, 7, 8, 9, 10 and 11. If the thermostat is not calling for heat, only G2-6 is alive with 24 volts, and points 7 through 11 read nothing.

Many cases of jittery furnace operation are due merely to loose connections, rather than to defective parts. Pump and blower motors sometimes run for hours in cold weather. Go over all leads with a socket wrench or pair of pliers. •

Some Like It Cool

Maintenance of your air conditioner is simple but important—if neglected, it will cost you comfort. Here, also, are tips to increase cooling efficiency

AN AIR CONDITIONER is an overgrown refrigerator, designed to cool a big box containing people instead of a small box containing food. Except for size, the mechanisms are pretty much identical, and both have achieved an extraordinarily high degree of reliability. Because an air conditioner is used only a few months out of the year, and then only intermittently rather than steadily, it can be expected to last a long time. It needs only minor maintenance attention.

About the only thing an owner of a conditioner can do for it is inspect the air filter

Stagnant pockets of air can be prevented by directing a stream of air ceilingward with an oscillating fan. This device will help circulate cooler air.

Here the ventilating louver on the underside of the roof overhang is covered with screening to keep out insects. Air flowing through here ventilates attic.

An attic fan keeps a constant flow of air moving; this acts as an invisible blanket of moving insulation in cooling downstairs. Note that it's belt-driven.

This is the most important operation in air-conditioner maintenance—keeping the air filter clean. The filter shown comes from a central-type unit.

frequently during the cooling season, clean it if it is of the renewable type, or replace it if it is of the disposable type. Practically all conditioners contain a filter of some kind to remove dust and dirt from the air before the machine cools and dehumidifies it and then pushes it into the room. As it gradually becomes blocked with the dust it entraps, the filter reduces the cooling ability of the machine. After a month or so of hot weather, during which the conditioner has been pumping away at a good rate, you're likely to find yourself saying, "Funny, the room doesn't seem to be as comfortable as it was." In central air-conditioning installations, which have the job of moving the air in an entire house, a filter can sometimes become blocked almost solid after a few weeks.

It takes only a few minutes to remove, clean and replace a filter. Some filters of the so-called lifetime type are washed under running water. Because the entrapped dirt is usually fluffy, a vacuum cleaner does a quick job on most other varieties. Frequent vacuuming keeps filters of the glass-wool type at top operating effectiveness and eliminates the need for replacement altogether. First take off all the surface dirt. Then slap the filter flat against the floor several times, and vacuum up the dust that shakes out.

With the vacuum cleaner set up, poke its nozzle carefully into the body of the conditioner, wherever you can reach easily without jogging anything. Of course, the control switch should be "off," or, better, the line plug should be pulled out of its receptacle. This internal cleaning is especially important in the early summer, after the machine has been idle for some months. At the same time, inspect the outside end of the machine, and don't be surprised if you find a family of sparrows well bedded down under it. The space between the window sill and the overhanging cabinet of the cooler is evidently ideal for nesting purposes, being sheltered from rain and snow and of just the right size for small birds.

Most of the "trouble" reported by purchasers of room conditioners is not really in the machines themselves, but is due to the inability of the power wiring and/or the fuses to handle the starting load, the running load, or a combination of these loads and other loads on the same line.

If slow-blow fuses or delayed action circuit breakers don't help, the purchaser is just out of luck, unless he has a firm understanding with the dealer covering just such a situation. Some short-sighted dealers will sell a customer any size machine he asks for, with the attitude that it's the customer's responsibility to know the capabilities of the power circuits in his house or apartment. Other dealers, interested in staying in business in their communities, practically make the customer prove his power lines are suitable before they'll take his money. This is a smart policy, because it protects both seller and buyer.

Improving Conditioner Performance

Because of the sealed construction universally used in refrigeration units, there is nothing you can do about changing the operating characteristics of a cooler. However, you can do a great deal to *help* it make the room comfortable and livable.

A conditioner draws air from the room over a series of cold pipes, which reduce its temperature and at the same time cause the moisture in it to condense out. The cooled and dried air is then pushed back into the room. A little fresh air from the outside is mixed with the room air to replenish the supply of oxygen. Without this mixing the recirculated air soon becomes stale, and occupants of the room start feeling woozy.

Even with the best of conditioners, however, the blowers are not always equal to the job of circulating *all* the air in a room. Warm air tends to rise, and cold air, being heavier, tends to sink toward the floor. If people in the room are smoking, inadequate circulation shows up quickly; the room takes on a bluish haze, and non-smokers who are allergic to nicotine display the initial signs of nausea.

The cure for this condition is so simple that it is overlooked by many sufferers. Set up a small electric fan as near the ceiling as possible, aim at the ceiling in the direction of the air conditioner, and run it at low speed. A fan doesn't cool, but it does move air. With a little experimenting as to position, you'll find that it does wonders in breaking up stagnant pockets of warm air near the ceiling and making the whole room feel cleaner.

In a living room or dining room, a good spot for the fan is the top of a breakfront, a book case, a china closet, etc. In a bedroom, a convenient location is the top of a high dresser.

If the fan is of the oscillating type, so much the better. In any case, keep the speed down, to prevent people from getting stiff necks. After all, the prime object of a fan is to achieve the maximum of comfort.

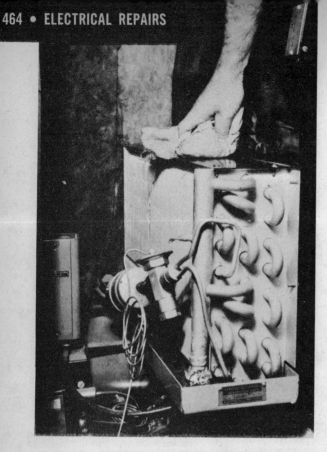

Occasional wiping and cleaning of refrigerating coil of central air conditioner is helpful in maintaining efficiency; this coil is typical of two-ton unit.

Keeping the Emerson Electric air conditioner in top working order is simple; the lifetime air filter slides out in an instant and can be cleaned in a minute.

Sun Protection Important

The effectiveness of an air conditioner in reducing air temperature depends to a large extent on that temperature at the start. No machine made by man can possibly overcome the full heating effect of the summer sun, but you can give a conditioner a fighting chance by keeping, *direct* sunshine away from the room you want to "condition." As a minimum, draw the blinds or pull down the shades on exposed windows. Outside awnings that keep the sun from striking the window area are very desirable. A darkened room *feels* cooler than a bright one. A few electric lights

generate less heat than a few shafts of sunshine, so the overall result is a gain in the direction of comfort.

It follows naturally that rooms facing north or east are easier to cool than those facing long hours of sunshine to the south or west.

In private houses, the most critical area is the roof, with the attic below it. If the house is in the open and is not completely shaded by large, leafy trees, the attic is a veritable oven after an afternoon of summer sunshine. Temperatures in it can reach incredible values; 115 to 140 degrees!

Trying to "air condition" the rooms under these ovens was a waste of electricity. Oh, yes, the attic floors might have deep blankets of insulation in them. Insulation is no cure-all; it *delays* the penetration of heat from the attic downward but it doesn't *prevent* it. The insulation itself soaks up heat, the way stones do in a slow fire; then, hours after sunset, it is still giving off some of that heat. This explains why room temperature can be in the 80's at ten p.m. when the outside air has already dropped to the 70's.

Since it is next to impossible in most locations to keep all sunshine off a roof, the only alternative is to get rid of the hot air under the roof as quickly as it forms. A powerful attic fan does the trick. The bigger the better! The standard sizes for homes are 24, 30 and 36 inches, these figures representing the diameter of the blower blades. The overall dimensions of the complete unit are greater. The controlling factor in some houses is the size of the trap door or other means of access to the attic. One chap I know installed *two* 20-inch fans because he couldn't get anything larger through the opening in the ceiling of a closet.

If the attic fan is big enough and the house is of the right shape, it can replace air conditioning altogether! A friend of mine installed a 36-inch blower in the ceiling at the head of the upper landing of a conventional two-story house. When he turns this monster on, newspapers and playing cards on the dining room table start floating upward like the props in a magician's levitation act. His attic temperature on a July day dropped from 121 to 96 degrees fifteen minutes after the fan was put into action. I took the readings, so I know.

In my house the attic is accessible but shallow, and I had to settle for a single 20-inch fan. Although this is small compared with the more desirable 24- and 30-inch sizes, it brings the attic temperature down as much as 20 degrees. In the rooms below the air temperature a foot below the ceiling used to be about 90; with the fan going, it falls to 82 or 83. Now the air conditioner works to the extent of keeping a party of eleven people comfortable throughout the house on a broiler of a day when the temperature is 93 and the humidity 76%.

When the air in the attic is pumped out through an opening in a side wall, other air must come in to replace it. The source of this air is important. If an individual air conditioner is used in only one room (the master bedroom in most cases), that room should be kept closed, and air from the rest of the house is allowed to be sucked upward through a grille of some sort in a hallway ceiling or through an open trap door in a room other than the air-conditioned one. If the house has a basement, doors leading to it should be kept open, as cellar air is often noticeably cooler than that in upper rooms.

If there is a unit in a room that cannot be closed off, or if the house is centrally cooled, the attic fan must not be allowed to draw air from the living area, because the conditioner can't possibly cool it at the same rate at which it is expelled through the attic louvers. You have to study the construction of the house and determine if suitable air passages can be cut in the ceilings and floors of closets or through hallways. I know of a 50-year old house in which an ideal "duct" was provided by the shaft of a dumbwaiter that formerly connected the kitchen, in the basement, with the dining room and the bedrooms, upstairs.

If the roof of the house has overhanging eaves that are safely accessible by ladder, by all means cut openings in them about a foot square; two or three on each side, depending on the size of the house. This is a relatively easy job. Bore one-inch holes in the corners, and use a keyhole saw for the rest. Cover the openings with screening, stapled or tacked in place. In the winter cover over with pieces of plywood or hardboard, held with wood screws. These openings have a chimney effect in combination with the roof rafters, and afford very good ventilation in moderate weather even with the attic fan off. Being on the underside of the eaves, they have the further advantage that they do not readily admit rain or snow.

Houses with flat roofs present a special cooling problem. Forced air evacuation obviously is out. Some "breathing" space undoubtedly is provided between the insulation and the roof surface proper, but this usually is not adequate when the weather gets sticky. If the edges or eaves of this roof overhang the walls of the house and are accessible, a series of underside louvers may be a big help. These should be placed at opposite ends of the rafters, so that air can blow through.

"Flat" roofs are never really flat, but are pitched slightly to shed rain. In areas in which water is plentiful, an owner might install a perforated pipe along the high end of the roof, and let water trickle over the entire roof surface to the gutter at the low end. The cooling effect is considerable, and the temperature in the rooms beneath drops to the point where air conditioning becomes successful.

If water is not so cheap that it can be wasted this way, the next best bet is a number of good-sized trees, placed so that they shade the roof, either completely or at least partially. The transplanting of trees is an organized business. You can have a small forest set up around your house in only a day. The trees are trucked in, their roots neatly bundled in burlap. A crew of men dig out holes of just the right size and shape. They drop in the trees, burlap and all, shovel back the earth, and are gone as quickly as you pay the bill.

Central Air Conditioners

There is every indication that the next big "gimmick" in the sale of private houses will be central air conditioning. All other major electrical appliances and gadgets are so commonplace that people take them for granted: refrigerators, freezers, dish and clothes washers, ironers, garbage disposals, broilers, mixers, etc.

Many "better" houses already include full air conditioning. Even some very moderately priced ones have provision for later installation of a unit or for immediate installation as an "extra." Mechanically, the job is less complicated than it appears at first sight. The basic heating system is of the hot air type. (Whether the fuel is oil or gas is immaterial). A system of ducts circulates the warmed air under the push of a turbine-like blower. For central cooling, the same ducts and blower are used, except that now they carry air cooled by a refrigerator unit set directly next to the furnace. In some installations the change-over from heating to cooling, or the other way, is controlled on a completely automatic basis by the relative settings of the hot and cold thermostats in the living area.

If an air conditioner stops working altogether, and you're sure that all fuses, breakers or overload devices are intact and power on, you must call a serviceman. •

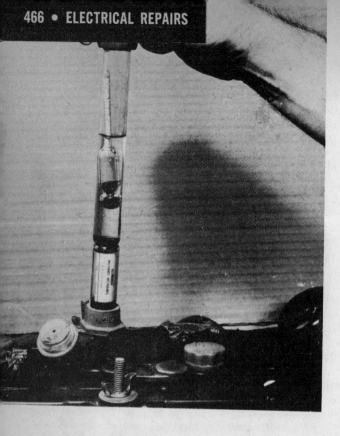

Here a hydrometer is measuring the specific gravity of the battery acid; the higher the float rides, the better the condition of the charge. This battery is pretty well up to full. Return acid to each cell after taking reading, and rinse hydrometer in clear water before storing.

When using an external charger, it is not necessary to disconnect the present wires to the terminals of the battery. Merely connect the charger leads, by their spring clips, directly to the battery posts. Charger plus goes to battery plus, minus to minus.

Batteries and Chargers

You'll not get caught with your charge down if you give your car battery reasonable care

YOU slide under the wheel of the car one frosty winter morning, turn the key in the lock, and start to push down the accelerator to race the engine a little. Only the engine doesn't race; in fact it doesn't even walk.

"Oh, no, stuck with a dead battery!" you groan.

This *won't* happen to you if you consider the car's electrical system merely an extension of the house's power system, and give it the same type of attention and preventive maintenance.

Why does a car battery hold up perfectly well during the summer and poop out in the winter, just when you need it most?

For two reasons: 1) the oil in the crank case is stiffer in cold weather than in warm, and the starting motor has a harder job ploughing through it; 2) The output or effectiveness of a storage battery falls off markedly as the temperature drops. In other words, when the engine needs the most starting energy, the battery is least capable of providing it!

There *is* a simple solution to this nuisance: check the battery frequently with the arrival of cold weather, and give it an overnight charge with a charger occasionally to keep it to full strength. The more frequently you stop and start the engine, and the less you use the car in the winter, the less chance does the battery have to accumulate a good charge from the charging generator, which works only when the engine runs.

A test on a storage battery with a voltmeter doesn't mean very much. A three-cell battery can read pretty close to its maximum of 6.6 volts, and a six-cell battery to 13.2 volts, and still make very little impression on a current-hungry starting motor. Did you know that a three-cell battery has to deliver between 200 and 300 amperes to kick over a modern high-compression engine?

The only reliable test is made with a hydrometer. This is a syringe-like glass gadget with a squeeze bulb at one end; inside the glass is a shot-weighted float. To use it, you merely unscrew each cap of the battery in turn and suck up about half a syringeful of acid. The weight of the acid compared to that of water (its "specific gravity") is a direct indication of the state of charge. The float is calibrated to show this specific gravity. Theoretical full charge is 1.3, or "1300," although with anything but a brand new battery a reading between 1200 and 1250 or 1275 is very good. When the reading falls below 1200 the battery needs a little shot in the arm.

A battery charger is a source of low-voltage direct current. It consists usually of a step-down transformer that reduces the 115-volt AC line to about 7 or 15 volts (for three- and six-cell batteries, respectively) after passing it through a rectifier that changes the AC to DC. Dual-voltage chargers are now common, to accommodate both types of batteries. To do an overnight boosting job, a charger for three-cell automobile batteries should produce not less than about 5 amperes, although 10 is even better; for six-cell batteries, ratings of about 3 to 6 amperes are adequate. Always disconnect a charger before starting the engine. •

Car vibration can loosen battery leads and sometimes make them jump off; inspect, clean, tighten.

Several times a year, remove the connector lugs from battery and clean terminals with sandpaper.

Wipe battery often with cloth dampened with water; check center caps of the battery for fit.

To minimize corrosion around terminals, caused by sulphuric acid vapor from cells, coat with Vaseline.

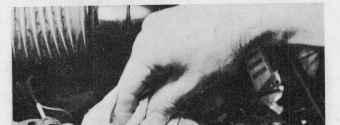

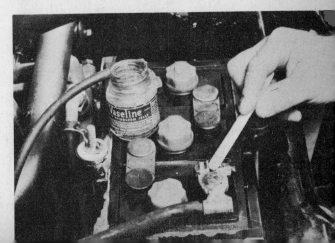

Electricity Outdoors

**The current interest in outdoor living brings up the matter of
extension of lines from the nearest source, with correct wiring**

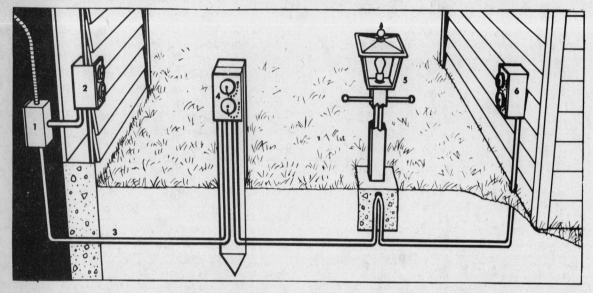

Typical outdoor wiring installation: 1—Junction box, with upper cable picking up power from basement
meter. 2—Waterproof duplex outlet on outside of house. 3—Underground cable through hole in foundation. 4—Utility outlet on post set into ground. 5—Pathway lantern. 6—Utility outlet on garage.

MOST small houses are built without
any provision for the use *outdoors*
of many useful electrical appliances and
devices. With the current trend toward
outdoor activities, power might be wanted
for such things as mowers, hedge cutters,
bug traps, barbecues, radio and television
sets, phonographs, movie projectors and
even commonplace lighting.

From the electrical standpoint, extending a line from the house or possibly a
garage is relatively simple. From the
physical standpoint it often is difficult because holes must be cut in exterior walls
to pass the extra wiring, and trenches
might have to be dug to carry the latter
to various points in the garden.

A quick and easy solution, if only a temporary one, is to make up a long extension
cord of good heavy wire, say three-con-
ductor No. 14 with polarized safety fittings
(see "The Third Wire Is a Lifesaver"),
and to string this from a heavy-duty
outlet in the kitchen, through a window,
and out to the patio or yard. Because
the normally-damp ground of a well-kept
garden is a perfect electrical ground, it goes
without saying that any appliance used

outdoors should have its frame grounded
through the green wire of the three-wire
safety cord. Without this, the user of a
motor-operated barbecue spit or a power
mower stands a good chance of being
flipped over on his ear the first time he
touches it.

Local building codes can be very tough
on the subject of underground wiring, so
check on them first before you buy outdoor outlets, lights and other fittings,
which tend to be somewhat costly because
of their weatherproof construction. In
some areas you can get by with plastic-
covered nonmetallic sheathed cable,
which is very easy to handle. In others
the law may call for lead-covered cable,
which costs about 50% more, and it might
even require the lead-covered cable to run
in conduit for extra protection.

In most houses the new line is most conveniently drawn from the basement
through a foundation wall. Take it off the
meter through its own fuse, and make it
at least No. 12 so that it will be able to
handle the heavy current load of a rotis-
serie. A buried line can be too small, but
never too big. •

Right:
Clean transformer contacts with a piece of fine sandpaper every two weeks.

Below:
Tape worn spots on the line cord, especially at point of entrance into the case.

Below, right:
Here is an electric clock turned upside down to redistribute the lubricant.

Clocks and Transformers

Keep them running indefinitely by following these simple instructions

THE operation of toy electric trains depends primarily on a transformer that steps down the 115-volt AC line to voltages not exceeding about 15. These are perfectly harmless. The transformer voltage is usually adjustable by means of a lever that moves against a series of contacts. It is important to keep the latter clean. Occasionally rub the contact surfaces lightly with a piece of fine sandpaper, tighten all connections, and inspect the flexible cord that goes from transformer to wall outlet.

Electric clocks rarely stop because they burn out. In most cases the trouble is due to settling or lumping of the lubricant inside. Before throwing a stopped clock away, turn it upside down and leave it in that position for several days. In all likelihood the lubricant will re-distribute itself, and the clock will run for ten years. •

THE REPAIR PROBLEM

It's not really a problem if you can obtain those vital replacement parts.

Housewife Liz Gardner, below, shows off the new line of Proctor-Silex "Lifelong" appliances, which are easily disassembled and assembled without tools. Part go bad? Snap it out, snap in a replacement!

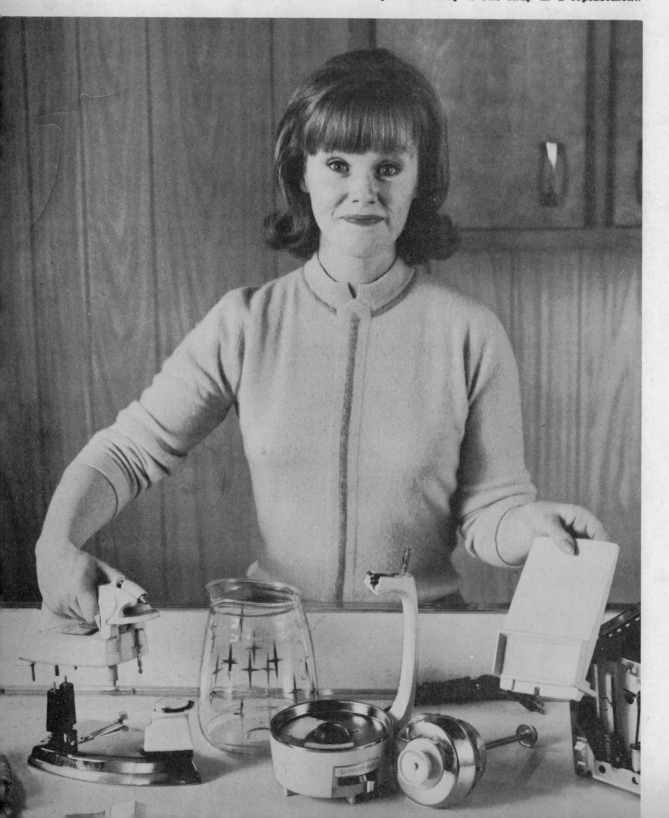

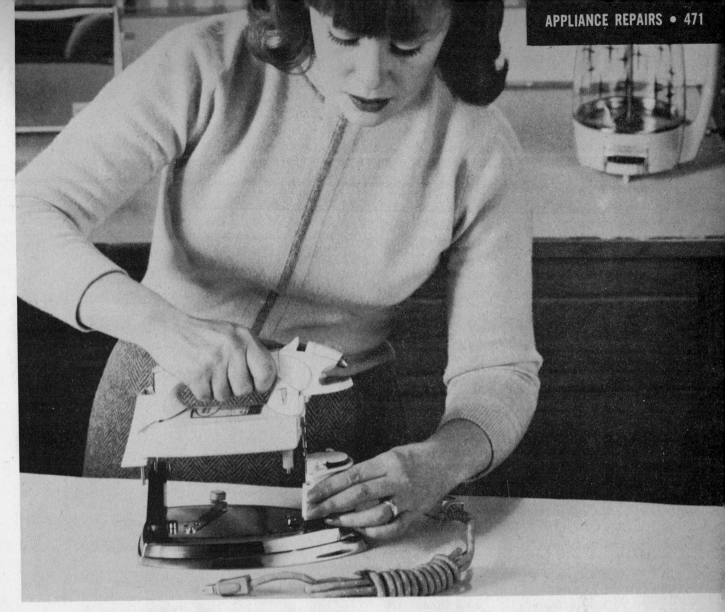

A WOMAN enters a housewares store with a small package under her arm and opens it after being greeted by a clerk.

"I bought this toaster here a couple of years ago," she says. "It seems to have stopped working. Can you fix it?"

The clerk looks into the appliance, jiggles the levers a couple of times, and then assumes a slightly pained expression. "It's burned out all right. This is a discontinued model and we don't have parts for it. However, we can send it to the factory for repair."

"How long will that take?" says the woman.

"Oh, usually about five or six weeks," he replies. "At this time of the year it might be a little longer."

"Five or six weeks! That's terrible!"

"Well, madame, we really can't help it. May I suggest that you consider a new toaster instead? It won't cost much more than the repairs and there's no waiting."

This condensed little story is representative of numerous similar episodes that

occur annually in the United States. Consumers have long had the impression that obsolescence is built into many appliances at the factory and that some manufacturers deliberately discourage repair by making replacement parts difficult to obtain. Some firms go even further; by riveting or welding some assemblies they make it virtually impossible just to open an appliance without, in effect, destroying it.

This attitude is particularly puzzling in view of the completely opposite policies of the radio-TV and automobile industries, to take just two examples. There are thousands of full-time and spare-time electronic service technicians scattered around the country who can make repairs either directly in the home or in their own nearby shops. People who have learned the do-it-yourself routine can find self-service tube testers in drug stores, supermarkets and other disparate places and can buy replacement tubes, batteries and some other components in them. There are countless radio dealers, and there is even a large

chain whose name, "Parts, Unlimited," describes its business accurately.

There are gas stations and garages at every crossroads, of course, and even more auto parts stores than radio dealers. The national mail-order firms supply everything from valve caps to complete engines, for cars first produced 40 years ago as well as for more recent ones!

There are encouraging signs that the electrical industry is reforming. Just as this book was being prepared, "Lifelong" household appliances that feature an original and exclusive concept in self-serviceability—a spray/steam/dry iron, a toaster, and an automatic glass percolator —were introduced by Proctor-Silex. Long favorably known for the quality of its products, this firm is a subsidiary of SCM Corporation.

The "Lifelong" line eliminates the problem of having urgently needed household electric equipment out of use while undergoing lengthy repair shop service, when that service is available at all.

The new development reflects adaptation of the modular concept to small electric housewares. Each appliance is made of basic components that can be readily disassembled and re-assembled *in the home without tools*. Get that, *without tools!* Should trouble develop, even a housewife can locate it by following the simplified instruction manual that comes with the device, and she can obtain the needed replacement part immediately from the same dealer who sold her the appliance. This plan supplements but does not replace the company's standard one-year guarantee against mechanical or electrical defects in its brand-name products.

The "Lifelong" appliances are well designed and the cost of the parts is reasonable. For instance, the iron is priced at $16.95 and breaks down to five modular components with tags from $1.50 for the fabric-plate selector to $6.95 for the Teflon coated soleplate. The toaster costs $12.95 and has six elements from 50 cents for the crumb tray to $4.95 for the chassis. The percolator retails for $17.95 and has seven components from $1.00 for the detachable cord to $4.95 for the base with the built-in heating unit. Since the latter is the part most likely to give out after extended use, a repair for less than one-third of the new cost is well worth a trip to the dealer.

When you go shopping for appliances it

A sign of welcome for people whose Sears appliances need fixing. The Center will do the work, or it will gladly provide all the replacement parts needed for the job, and helpful hints too.

is just as important to pick the right dealer as the best product. If you're interested in an iron, ask him pointedly. "Do you keep replacement heating elements in stock?" This is a fair question because these elements do burn out. If he says, "No, but I can get them," he might mean well, but it might take a month for a new one to reach him. That leaves you with the choice of being without an iron for that period or buying, or possibly borrowing, another one.

Then there's the often overlooked matter of the guarantee. Usually this is printed in tiny type on the packing box or the label of an appliance, and few people bother to read it until something goes wrong. Then they might discover that it is the manufacturer who makes the guarantee, not the dealer, and they might have to go to the nuisance and expense of sending the product to some distant service shop or to the factory itself.

Some of the big merchandising organizations such as Sears, Roebuck & Company, with stores everywhere as well as mail facilities, have met the appliance repair problem to the satisfaction of their customers not only with meaningful guarantees but also with full cooperation in furnishing parts. The Sears motto is "We service what we sell," but in addition to its numerous service centers it also encourages people to buy parts and to make all possible repairs themselves. Of course, this is very smart business, because the firm has the customer coming in not only for the original appliance and parts for it, but also for tools with which to do the work. And it makes a friend of the customer, who returns again and again for other kinds of merchandise.

Some practical suggestions on taking care of and repairing common small household appliances are given in this book. Proper maintenance on a regular basis will in many cases make repairs unnecessary or as a minimum it will greatly prolong the life of a device. You wouldn't dream of letting the oil in the crankcase of your car go down to the empty mark; you undoubtedly check the dip stick once a week or so, and add some oil when needed. With an appliance like a vacuum cleaner, for instance, you can do a similar job by emptying the dirt bag regularly, checking the motor brushes, tightening connections, etc.

Many of the small parts you might need for appliance repair are simple hardware items that you either already have in your basement or garage shop or that you can buy readily at local stores: such things as nuts, bolts and washers; insulating tape; line cords and plugs; solder and soldering connectors; pilot lights; bulbs of various shapes and sizes; coils of heating wire; etc.

If you need a particular component for a particular appliance, you should start by inquiring at nearby hardware or electrical supply stores. If a "Yellow Pages" classified directory is published for your area, look under both these categories and do some telephoning. First inquire about the part, and if the answer is negative ask the salesman if he can refer you either to another store or to the nearest factory authorized service station for your make of appliance.

If you didn't save the box in which the device was packed, examine its body closely. Usually the name and address of the manufacturer, the electrical characteristics, the patent numbers, and similar data are stamped on the bottom. Write a letter to the service department of the firm, explain your problem, and ask if they can help. You can expect one of the following things to happen:

1. Nothing. Just plain nothing. That is, the manufacturer, if he's still in business and your letter isn't returned by the post office, will simply ignore you.

2. The letter will be returned by the post office, marked "Unknown at this address" or "Moved. Left no forwarding address."

3. The manufacturer will send back a form letter advising you that your particular appliance is no longer in production and that no replacement parts for it are available. The gadget might be only two years old, but remember, the obsolescence rate of appliances is very high.

4. The manufacturer will send you a list of his authorized service stations and tell you to contact the nearest one.

5. The manufacturer will send you a price list and an order blank and will tell you cheerfully that he'll be glad to send you anything you want.

If your answer is No. 5 you're really in luck. If it's No. 4 you have a fighting chance to get your appliance fixed, even if this takes a couple of months. If the answer is No. 1, No. 2 or No. 3, salvage everything that's removable from the device, throw the rest of it away and go out and buy a new one from a firm that values your good will and wants to keep you as a customer who will pass the good word around to his friends. •

TOOLS FOR THE JOB

You need a lot of small ones, but they don't cost much and last a long time.

Even if you start fresh and have to buy all your tools new, you will find that they aren't expensive. Get the very top grade; they are definitely cheaper in the long run than imported "bargains."

THE maintenance and repair of household electrical appliances can be done readily with the aid of common hand tools such as those used for other house chores, for car work, for adjustment of lawn mowers and snow blowers, etc. In fact, anything that cannot be done with hand tools usually cannot be done at all at home, or for that matter even in so-called professional shops.

Consider the jobs that need doing: nuts and bolts to be removed or installed; wood and self-tapping screws to be taken out and put in; wires to be cut, cleaned, soldered and taped; plugs to be repaired or replaced; open and short-circuits to be identified, isolated and rectified; burned out fuses and heating elements to be replaced; noisy motors to be silenced, etc.

Sometimes a three-second application of a soldering gun to a broken connection restores a previously dead appliance to full working condition; or tightening a few screws on a grill puts the heating wires back into proper position and eliminates dangerous sparking; or a half-turn with a wrench cures a leak in a blender or coffee pot. Sometimes you can even affect a "repair" without any tools; for example, a noisy electric clock can usually be silenced if you merely turn it upside down and then

let it run that way for a couple of hours!

If you're new at the game of doing things around the house yourself—a role forced on virtually all men because of the cost and incompetence of "professionals" —you will learn by visiting any hardware store that tools are plentiful and inexpensive. Used properly, they will last a very long time and are therefore good investments.

Avoid cheap tools made in the Orient. They are cheap in quality as well as cost, and do not compare with American-made products in either finish or durability.

Pliers for Cutting and Holding

As a minimum, there should be three pairs of pliers in every tool box. The first is a 5-inch pair of side-cutters. The only function of this tool is to snip copper wire up to and including No. 18, the size commonly used as lamp cord. It has two ground edges about ⅞ inch long, very accurately fitted so that they cut well right up to their tips. This enables you to trim thin individual strands of flexible wire from under terminal screws and soldered joints, where they might otherwise cause trouble by touching other live contact surfaces. An easy way to ruin a good pair of side-cutters is to use them for slitting sheet metal or for loosening or tightening nuts and bolts. Reserve them strictly for wire cutting and they'll last practically forever.

The second tool is a 6-inch pair of what is called "electrician's pliers." Of much heavier construction than side-cutters, these have square jaws about ⅜ inch wide, with serrated inner surfaces for gripping bolt heads, nuts, bars, rods, wire and anything else up to about ¾ inch wide or in diameter. Except for the fact that the jaws

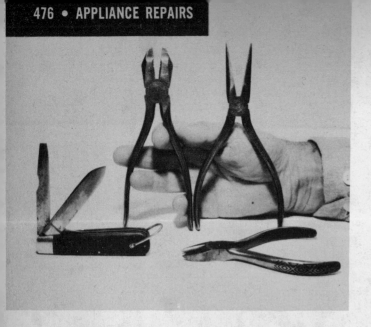

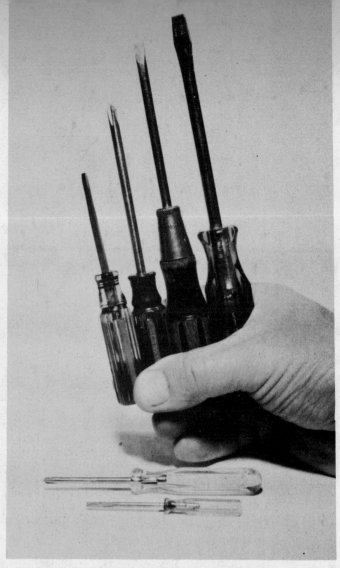

Standing, left to right: Army surplus screwdriver/knife combination; electrician's pliers; longnose pliers. Front: side-cutters, intended only for wire. These tools are handy for many purposes.

No one ever has enough screwdrivers, but this typical assortment takes care of most small electrical appliances. It includes drivers for Phillips head screws and conventional straight-slot types.

Box, left, holds small sockets and several handles for them. The nut drivers, right, are built like screwdrivers and do same job. The adjustable jaw wrench, center, is fine for occasional large nuts.

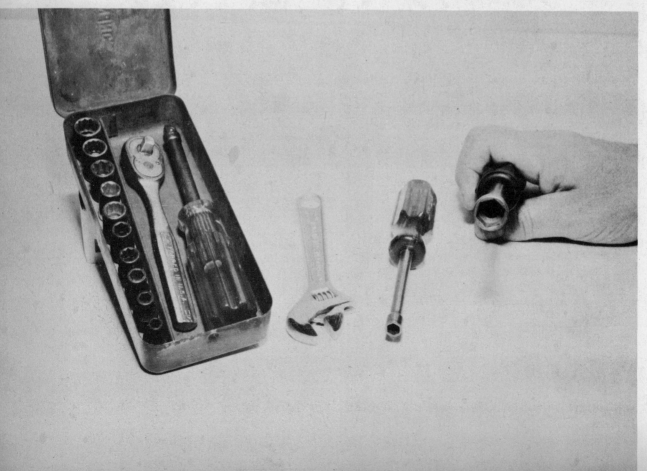

don't lock, this tool is virtually a small hand vise.

Between the jaws and the center hinge of the electrician's pliers is a pair of ground edges suitable for cutting wire of any size likely to be found in a home electric system. Formed into these edges are two pairs of half holes, which are very useful for trimming off the insulation on wires without nipping into the wire itself. After some experimenting on scrap pieces of wire you will know just how much squeezing pressure to put on the handles to sever different thicknesses of insulation on different diameters of wire.

The third pair of pliers is called "long-nose" because that's just what they look like. A handy size is 6½ inches long. The nose, which consists actually of two matching sections, tapers down almost but not quite to a point. The inside surfaces are flat, without cutting edges. The long-nose is intended strictly for light work, such as twisting wires around terminals, holding nuts while screws are being started into them, holding wires that are being soldered, etc. The flat inner surfaces can also be used for bending or forming *thin* sheet metal. Do *not* use the tool for loosening

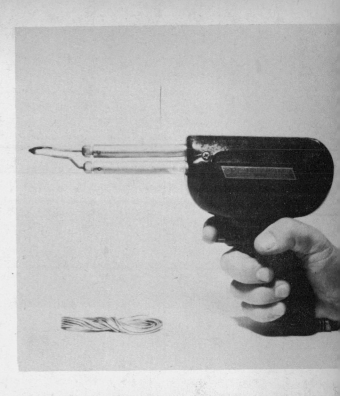

It looks like a pistol and it even has a trigger, but this is only a soldering "gun," probably the most important single tool in electrical repairs. The replaceable wire tip, left, is what gets hot.

You may have to cut or drill your way into some appliances, so the hack saw and drill (top) are necessary tools. Scissors for cutting tape and insulation and the arc-joint pliers are also of value.

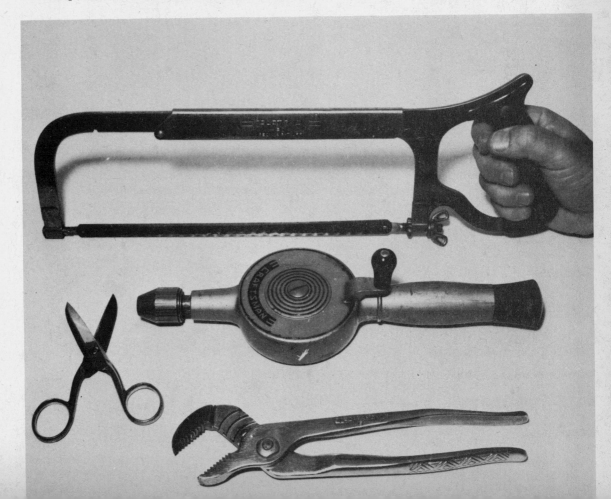

Socket wrenches such as those used in automobile work are indispensable for reaching some large nuts in recessed spaces, as in this drink blender. Arc-joint pliers are sometimes suitable too.

Locking type tweezers save much time and temper in retrieving small parts and in helping to put them back into position. They can securely hold even the thinnest screws, nuts, washers, lugs, etc.

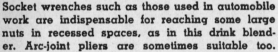

It is often helpful to supplement the soldering gun (center) with a small soldering iron of the pencil type (bottom), for which variety of screw-in tips is available. Hammer and file are other good tools.

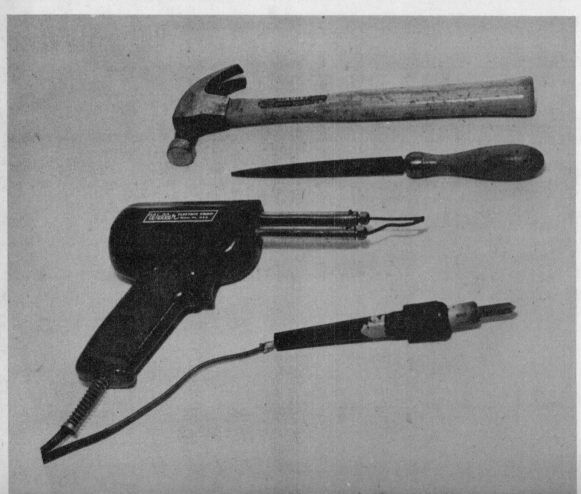

tight nuts or tightening loose ones; these are jobs for the electrician's pliers or a wrench.

Screwdrivers, Plain and Fancy

Conventional screws have straight slots in their heads, and screwdrivers to fit them therefore have blades with flat ends. However, manufacturers of appliances tend to favor the Phillips type of screw. In this, the heads are formed with two slots at right angles to each other and with slightly rounded bottoms, and they therefore require special screwdrivers with tips of mating shape. Why do manufacturers prefer this type over the simpler straight-slot kind? Because it lends itself better to fast assembly with air or motor driven tools. A Phillips bit centers itself almost automatically in the opening in the screw head and once in does not slip out.

Screwdrivers are cheap because they are simple tools. For the small screws found in most appliances you need at least three of both the flat and Phillips types, but you'll undoubtedly acquire more. There is considerable latitude in fitting flat blades to ordinary screws, but for Phillips screws you must have the exact size or you will mash the openings. In a pinch, if a Phillips isn't too tight, you can loosen it with a flat blade that enters one slot, but this takes careful twisting.

Nut Drivers and Wrenches

Another very useful small tool looks like a screwdriver but is actually in the wrench family. Called a "nut driver," it has the handle and the shaft of a screwdriver and the end of a socket wrench. The shaft is hollow for about half its length, so it can be slipped over the end of a long screw to reach a nut on it. Of course, you need a size for every nut. For electrical work the ¼-inch and 5/16-inch models are usually enough.

For larger nuts and bolts you have a wide choice of adjustable jaw wrenches or socket wrenches. A boxed assortment of sockets from 3/16 to ¾ inch, with ratchet, straight and angled handles, is very popular.

Two tools that look like pliers also are in the wrench family. One is called "arc-joint pliers" and has jaws that stay more or less parallel as their spacing is adjusted in five or six steps. The other is called "slip-joint pliers" and has slightly concave jaws that are adjustable to two positions. In some parts of the country this type is called "gas pliers" because at one time they were used extensively for tightening gas pipes and other round fittings.

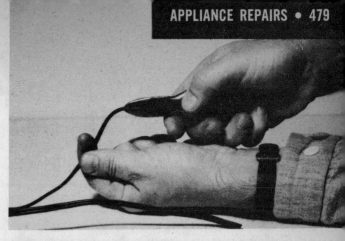

This picture and the nine following show steps in common job of extending a line cord and soldering the joints in it. First operation is to use side-cutters and to open all ends of wire about an inch.

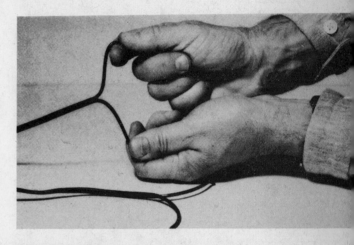

Now grasp the ends and pull them apart for length of about six inches. This works fine with "zip" cords, but with other types of wire you may have to ease the insulation apart with a sharp knife.

With side-cutters cut one wire in each pair back about four inches. Using a sharp knife, pare off about two inches of insulation on each. Mate the shorts with longs for joints that do not overlap.

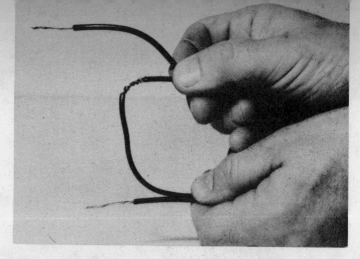

If wires are not already "tinned" (coating during manufacture with thin coating of solder) scrape them bright and clean with back edge of a knife. Keep fingers off wires, to maintain cleanliness.

Take the long wire of one cord and the short one of the other, cross the bared ends and twist together, using pliers as much as possible instead of fingers. Renew surface by more light scraping.

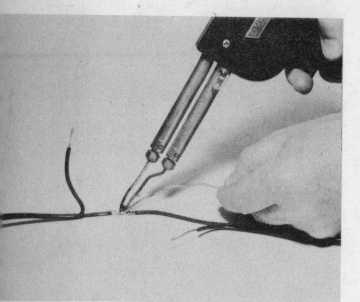

Hold down trigger switch of gun, wait about five seconds for tip to heat up, then apply solder and tip. Allow solder to run in well and flux to cook out. Remove tip, don't move wire until solder sets.

Snip off any loose strands of wire remaining after soldering and cover joint with a tight layer of electrical tape, which is black. If the color is objectionable, use common white adhesive tape.

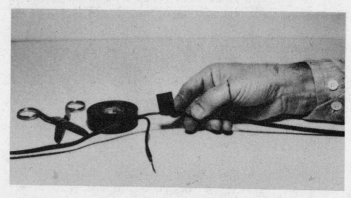

Make another twisted joint of the remaining two wires of the extended cord. Separate them slightly so that the hot tip of the gun does not burn adjacent tape. Snip off any loose strands of wire.

Put a layer of tape over the second joint, press the two wires together, and put a final second layer over them. Run this tape about an inch beyond the first layers and press it down firmly.

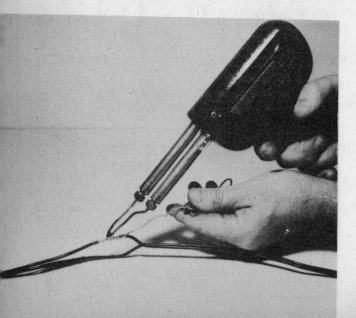

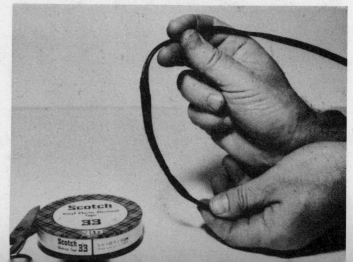

Miscellaneous Tools

A common hack saw is always useful for cutting bolts, metal bars and rods. A small hand or power drill is a necessity for making holes. A pair of scissors is for cutting tape and trimming insulation. A husky pocketknife of the Boy Scout type is for paring off insulation and scraping wires.

A pair of tweezers can't be beat for picking up, holding or retrieving small screws, nuts, washers, etc. A simple one of the kind used for cosmetic purposes, holding stamps, etc., will serve the purpose, but a better one, sold by radio supply houses, has a locking feature. This is of great help when you have to position a small part accurately.

One flat and one round file, of medium grade, are invaluable for removing burrs and similar rough edges from the metal cases or bodies of some appliances. A small round file, usually called a "rattail," will enlarge screw holes, a necessary job sometimes when a disassembled appliance twists out of shape slightly and the original holes don't match.

The Soldering Operation

Soldering is a very important process in all electrical and radio work, because loose or broken wires in appliances of all kinds are very common. Lots of people have trouble with it, only for a single, simple reason: the metal surfaces they try to join are not clean and bright. Sometimes they do scrape wires and terminal lugs until they shine, but then they pick them up with their fingers and deposit a thin film of body oil on them. Molten solder is almost like water in that it will not stick to a dirty surface, especially a greasy one.

The most popular soldering tool these days is not an "iron" but a "gun." The older iron type, still indispensable for many purposes, is not an iron at all. Its tip, which does the work, is made of copper, and it is heated by a coil of resistance wire in its base. The gun type, so called because of its obvious resemblance to an auto-loading pistol, works differently. Its tip is actually a U-shaped loop of thick copper wire, usually of square cross-section, which forms part of a single-turn secondary of a transformer. The primary coil of this transformer, consisting of about 150 turns of fine wire, is in the body of the gun. It is connected to the AC house line through a trigger switch.

In a transformer, the voltage developed in the secondary is directly proportional to the turns ratio of the primary and secondary windings. In the case of a soldering gun plugged into a 115-volt line, the voltage across the one-turn secondary is thus only a fraction of one volt. Because the wire tip has a low resistance, even this low voltage pushes a lot of amperes through it, and it gets hot enough to melt solder.

Although most guns are top-heavy and at first a bit awkward to handle, they have these important features: they come up to melting temperature in several seconds; they cool off quickly; the tips last a long time and are cheap and easy to replace; the tips can be bent to reach into very tight wiring that would surely be damaged by an iron with its bigger end.

The solder universally used for electrical work is a 50/50 mixture of lead and tin, formed as soft tubing filled with resin. The latter is called "flux." Its job is to absorb the slight products of oxidation resulting from the application of the hot tip of the soldering tool to the joint being soldered. Without flux, hot solder simply rolls away.

The technique in soldering wire joints and other connections is to hold the solder over the joint and the tip over the solder, and to let the latter melt its way into the joint while the resin cooks and smokes. The flux has an odor faintly reminiscent of turpentine, of which it is a derivative. Keep the iron in position for several seconds, or until the resin stops smoking. Then remove it *without disturbing the joint*. Watch the latter closely and you will see that it takes another few seconds to change color and finally harden.

Many people tend to remove the heat too soon. The usual result is that the flux rehardens on the joint, and instead of helping the solder to mate with the wires it actually prevents it from doing so. Under close inspection a joint can appear to be perfectly normal, yet even with testers as simple as the Clicktester and the VOM (see pages 390 and 399) it will prove, unbelievably, to be absolutely open.

Fortunately, copper takes to solder very well; soldered copper wire joints are strong both physically and electrically. Brass, which is an alloy of copper and zinc, also reacts very favorably. Iron is more stubborn. It needs not only a very hot iron but also a more virulent flux, usually acid in nature. Aluminum is almost hopeless. The easy way to make an electrical connection to iron or aluminum is to solder the copper wire to a copper lug of some sort and to bolt the lug securely to the metal. •

FILM SLIDE PROJECTORS

Keep them dust-free and pictures on the screen will be spotless.

THE WORD "projector" to most people used to mean "movie projector," but nowadays it is more likely to represent "slide projector." This is because of the popularity of Kodak's Instamatic cameras, which use an absolutely foolproof drop-in film cartridge and a four-sided flash cube. The combination produces color slides (and also color prints) of remarkable quality.

Slides require a projector, but this is not expensive and is a very good investment

Two popular types of film slide projectors using rotary magazines. The one at top is of flat design, and magazine sits horizontally. In the other, magazine slides vertically into one side of the case.

In flat-style projector, a coin-opening compartment is provided for storage of line cord, other accessories. In this view the machine is upside down. Grill, right, is exhaust area for cooling fan.

Always check the spare projection lamp immediately after buying it and before putting it away. Glass envelope diameters might vary a little, but base pins and heights of filaments must be exact.

A great gadget for blowing dust out of projector (or any similar machine that must be kept clean) is a plastic squeeze bottle with a small hole in its cap. First wash out interior and dry thoroughly.

Top section of case appears to be solid, but it snaps open easily. The slot in the center, above the round opening for the rotary magazine, is intended for single slides. Lens is at right end.

With top cover removed, below, left, entire system is exposed and can be dusted or blown out without disturbing anything. Bulb is in left compartment, condensing lenses and projection lens at right.

Top of lamp is covered by metal strip to protect eyes of user if he checks the operation of projector with current on. It is held in place by friction and snaps loose readily without using any tools.

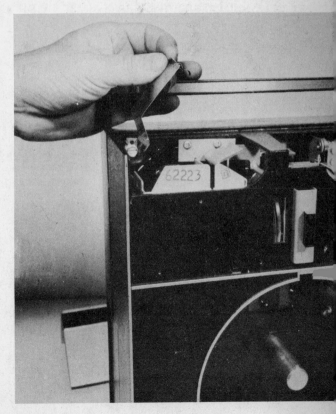

Lifting of shield leaves lamp accessible. Trick in removing it is to grasp firmly with the fingers and to PULL straight up without twisting. It has a keyed base, not usual bayonet or screw type. Projection lamp looks like radio tube, with pins in base. Top is painted to minimize upward glare. Filament is extremely bright and can cause temporary eye discomfort if it is viewed too closely.

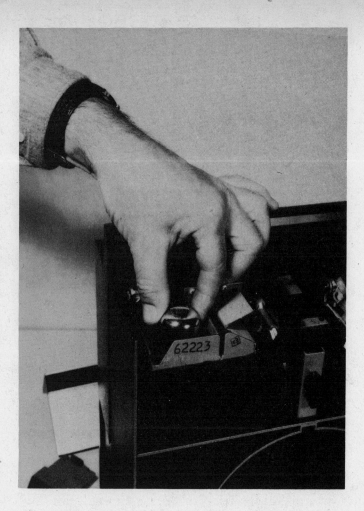

because slides are much cheaper than color prints on paper and their projected images can be blown up on a screen to spectacular dimensions.

Slide projectors are rather simple and require very little maintenance. The major repair, when a machine stops working, is usually nothing more than the replacement of a burned out lamp. All projection lamps run very hot, some so hot, in fact, that the glass envelopes (as the bulbs are called) often develop bulges. However, they rarely burst because all but the smallest projectors have cooling fans that come on when the lamps are turned on.

In addition to a fan, most projectors have additional protection for the slides in the form of a disc of special heat-absorbent glass positioned between the lamp and the condensing lenses. This glass puzzles many people because it is perfectly flat and obviously cannot help to concentrate the light on the film, as the condensers do.

Lamps have a nasty habit of burning out just as people start to show their slides of Europe or of their children. A spare should always be on hand, and the best place to keep it is right in the case of the projector.

The base of most lamps is similar to that of radio tubes. It is keyed in such a manner that it can be inserted in its socket in only one direction, and then its pre-focused filament is positioned correctly in relation to the projector's optical system.

Dust Is The Problem

Like other electrical appliances that operate in a hot, dry condition, slide projectors attract a lot of dust out of the air of seemingly clean rooms. It does no harm, but if it is allowed to accumulate on the condensing lenses between the lamp and the film and on the projection lens itself it can give the images on the screen a slightly fuzzy appearance. For this reason frequent cleaning is advisable. Some photographers make a habit of blowing out their projectors every time they set them up, and even of removing the lenses and

wiping them lightly with soft facial tissues.

The usual precautions about protecting line cords and other wires should of course be observed. The cables used with some remote control devices are rather thin and merit special attention.

The commonest operating fault with projectors is mechanical rather than electrical. This is jamming of the slides in the feed mechanism. Often it is due to bent or twisted slides, which simply cannot be accommodated in the narrow space of its carrier. If the trouble persists even with flat, undamaged slides, the machine itself is basically bad.

Jamming can be so annoying that no one should buy any projector without an iron-bound guarantee from the dealer (NOT the manufacturer) that he will take it back if it is not satisfactory. One way to get this protection automatically is to take the machine on a charge account. Run a couple of magazines of good slides and if even one sticks repack the whole thing and bounce it back to the seller. If it jams once you can be pretty certain that it will jam again. •

AMPERAGE REQUIREMENTS FOR A MODERN HOME

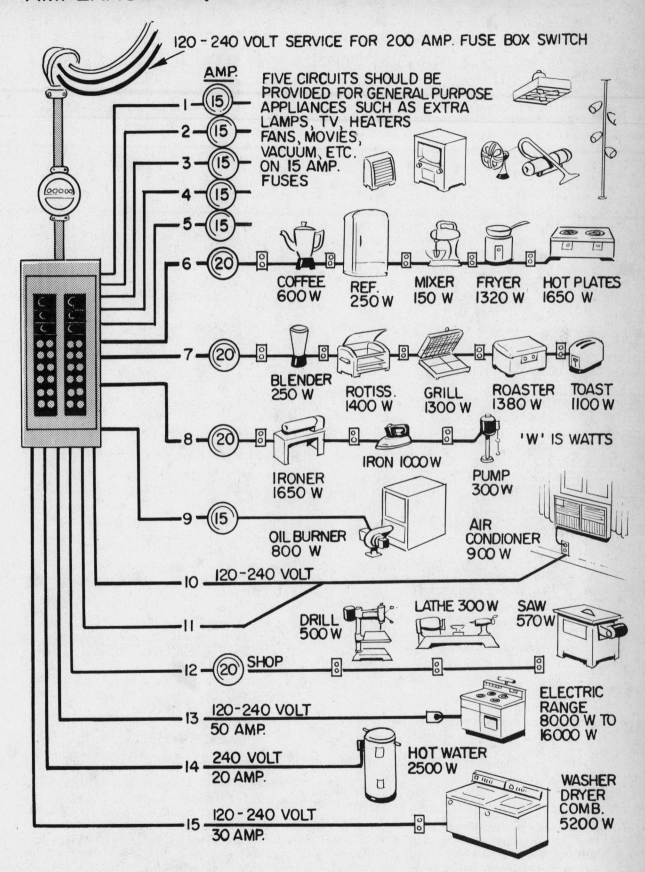

120 - 240 VOLT SERVICE FOR 200 AMP. FUSE BOX SWITCH

AMP.

FIVE CIRCUITS SHOULD BE PROVIDED FOR GENERAL PURPOSE APPLIANCES SUCH AS EXTRA LAMPS, TV, HEATERS FANS, MOVIES, VACUUM, ETC. ON 15 AMP. FUSES

1 — 15
2 — 15
3 — 15
4 — 15
5 — 15

6 — 20

COFFEE 600 W • REF. 250 W • MIXER 150 W • FRYER 1320 W • HOT PLATES 1650 W

7 — 20

BLENDER 250 W • ROTISS. 1400 W • GRILL 1300 W • ROASTER 1380 W • TOAST 1100 W

8 — 20

IRONER 1650 W • IRON 1000 W • PUMP 300 W • 'W' IS WATTS

9 — 15

OIL BURNER 800 W • AIR CONDIONER 900 W

10 — 120-240 VOLT

11 — DRILL 500 W • LATHE 300 W • SAW 570 W

12 — 20 SHOP

13 — 120-240 VOLT 50 AMP. • ELECTRIC RANGE 8000 W TO 16000 W

14 — 240 VOLT 20 AMP. • HOT WATER 2500 W

15 — 120-240 VOLT 30 AMP. • WASHER DRYER COMB. 5200 W

ELECTRIC IRONS

You have to take them apart completely to get at the heating element.

These two lightweight travel irons are typical. The one on the left is of the dry type and has a detachable cord. The other has a screw-on water reservoir for steam ironing and a permanent cord.

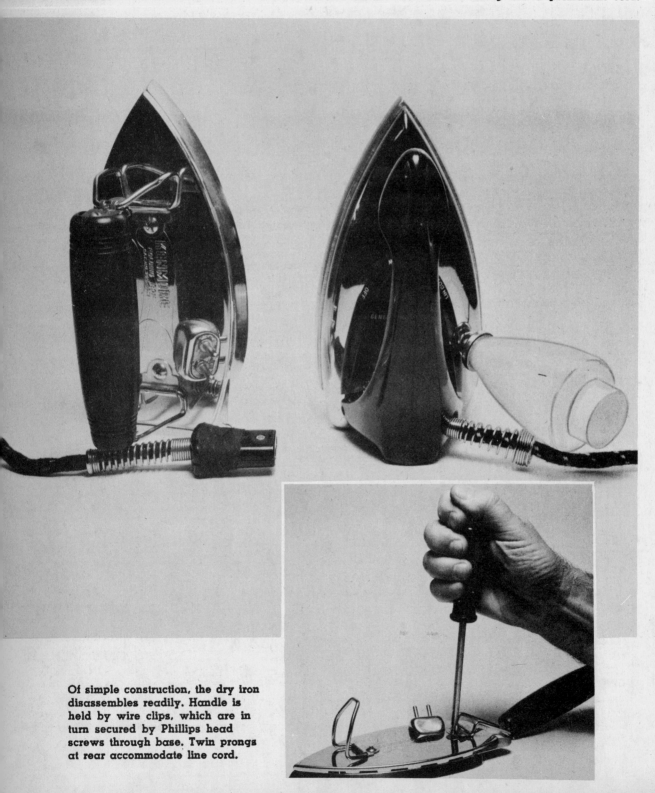

Of simple construction, the dry iron disassembles readily. Handle is held by wire clips, which are in turn secured by Phillips head screws through base. Twin prongs at rear accommodate line cord.

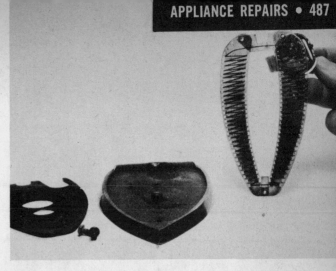

Polished top cover and handle, when removed, reveal a cast iron base. An additional plate here protects the heating element and is held by two more screws. There is no thermostat in this iron.

Heating element consists of flat resistance wire between thin protective sheets of mica. Any possible breaks can be spotted quickly. If element is burned out, a complete replacement is needed.

OF ALL small household appliances, the clothes pressing iron probably sees more service in terms of actual hours than any of the others. It uses a lot of current, runs very hot, is often pushed accidentally off the ironing board and is subject to other forms of mistreatment, so it is bound to need technical attention early in its life.

The line cord particularly takes a beating. Women tend to disconnect it from the wall outlet by jerking at it sharply, a practice that obviously doesn't help it any. In most cases they do this because the plug gets so hot that they are afraid to touch it, and you can't blame 'em. It often pays to install a better outlet, with husky springs to make tight contact with the prongs of the plug. Also, the latter should be bright and shiny.

Almost without exception, the cords supplied with irons, toasters, grills and other heavy current appliances are a special flexible wire, so soft it feels almost like string. The insulation is asbestos, for maximum heat protection. One end of the cord terminates in the line plug and is molded into it in such fashion that it cannot be separated from it. The other end might disappear into the iron and be anchored to screw terminals; or it might be fitted with a detachable flat two-prong plug that fits in a mating outlet on the back or on one side of the appliance.

The latter arrangement offers the advantage of quick and easy replacement if the original cord becomes hopelessly mashed. Replacement cords with fitted plugs are common items in hardware and electrical stores, are inexpensive, and are much less trouble than repairs. As a matter of fact, these special heat-proof cords are a confounded nuisance from the repair stand-

point. Once you slice them apart the asbestos tends to fall away, leaving the wires unprotected. The cords achieve their flexibility through the use of many strands of very fine, almost hair-like wire, and it is very difficult to clean them without inadvertently severing bunches of them.

It is easy to check a detachable cord for opens and shorts, as described under the Clicktester, page 18. If the cord is of the permanent type and the iron refuses to heat up, you have no choice but to open the appliance and to look inside for the trouble.

Some irons open readily, others defy all attempts. What often makes the job difficult or downright impossible is the unexpected complication of internal corrosion in steam irons. You remove the handle and the thermostat knob and uncover a big nut or a screw head. These, obviously, call for a wrench or a screwdriver, respectively. You apply the tool and find that it doesn't budge. You lean on it some more; still no action. You squirt a drop or two of penetrating oil to the head and try again, without success.

"It's only a threaded fitting, its gotta give," you mumble. So you take a breath and lean on the wrench or screwdriver with extra oomph. The fitting gives this time . . . maybe. More than likely you find yourself with the head of the bolt or screw in your hand, while the body remains frozen tight. About all you can do now is gather up the pieces of the iron and go out and buy a new one.

Corrosion is especially bad in areas having water unduly rich in minerals. Some appliance manufacturers recommend the use of distilled water to reduce the problem. Study the additional photo sequences through page 493

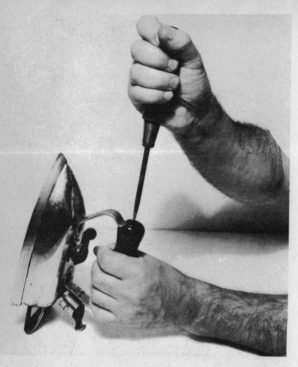

This is representative full-size iron of detachable cord type, with thermostat knob under handle. The first screws in sight are through the handle, so the first disassembly step is to remove them.

Handle "screws" turn out to be one long bolt. The upright brackets are riveted and immovable. Next step is to remove small center screw through the thermostat knob; latter can then be pulled off.

Details of thermostat mounting may not be clear from an examination. With a pair of electrician's pliers pull gingerly on the central shaft, but if it doesn't give right away don't try to force it.

A better approach seems to be at the large hex nut surrounding the thermostat shaft. Use an adjustable jaw wrench, socket wrench or arc-joint pliers, with possible assist from a drop of oil.

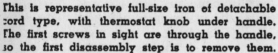

The "nut" turns out to be a deep, hollow threaded stud, whose function is to secure the entire top cover of the iron to the heavy base. Clean the threads with a wire brush or sharpened nail.

The cover now lifts off completely, and two large nuts come into view. The connector for the line cord remains in place, as does the shaft of the thermostat. Nuts appear to hold subbase to base.

Nuts appear to be corroded in place, but a bit of penetrating oil plus lots of leverage on the socket wrench breaks them loose. The iron must be braced to keep from turning as push is applied.

Cast iron subbase now picks off. The threaded studs obviously are anchored in the "sole" of the iron. The line connector and the thermostat shaft are still in place, on another subplate.

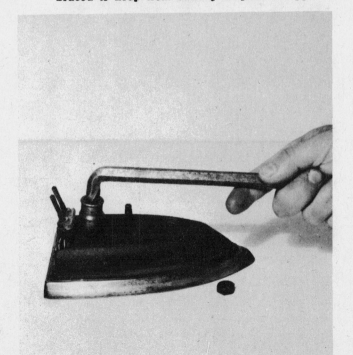

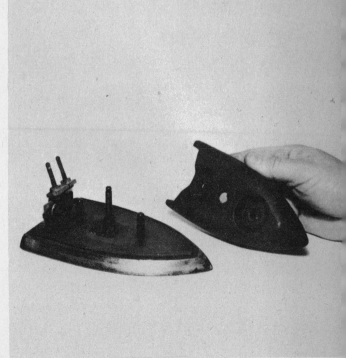

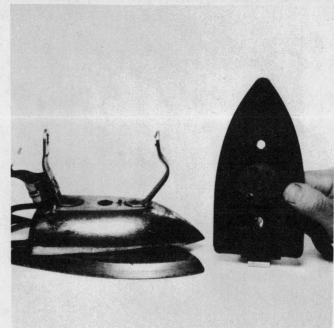

Tugging at the thermostat shaft shows the assembly to be loose of the base. It comes up very easily in one piece. Base is now bare, so heating element must be part of unit just removed.

About the size of half-dollar, the actual thermostat is a black disc set flush in the bottom of the heating assembly. Its purpose is to maintain a uniform heat, to prevent scorching of clothes.

The thermostat is held by two short connecting wires, part of the heat element, secured under screws. Loosen latter and entire thermostat, with control shaft, drops out through a center hole.

With thermostat out, the continuity of the heating element can be checked easily with Click-tester or VOM connected to twin prongs and with the two short tabs temporarily connected together.

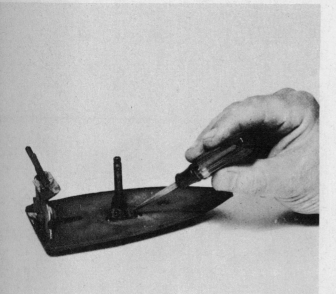

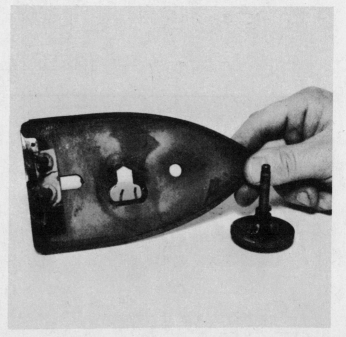

Before halves of heating form can be separated, it is necessary to dismount end prongs. This is a simple nut and bolt job. Observe placement of insulating washers and terminals of heating wires.

With connector prongs removed, top half of heating element can now be pushed to left, exposing wires inside. Some pieces of mica will come loose. The element consists of flat wire ribbon on mica form.

If wire is burned out, install a replacement element. Arrange mica above and below wires to prevent grounding and test with Clicktester to make sure ribbon is not in contact with metal sandwich.

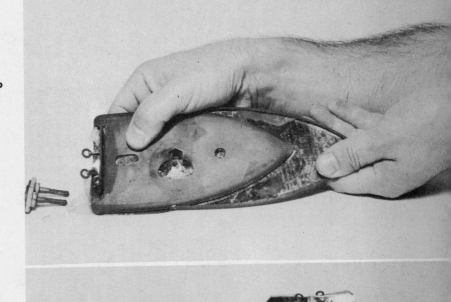

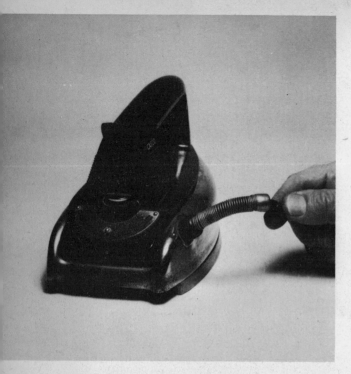

In this iron the cord is attached permanently. It is protected by a spring collar where it enters the body. The thermostat control is a small dial under the back end of the iron's hinged handle.

When the handle is raised a large hexangular nut comes into sight near the front of the iron. This apparently anchors the top cover to the base. The center hole is for water; iron is of steam type.

Well-fitting socket wrench is needed to dislodge the hex fitting. This was badly corroded, and it actually broke off at the last moment. This can be expected to happen with some very old irons.

Even with hex fitting off, cover of iron still was not loose. The only other fastener in sight was the setscrew of the thermostat knob, so this was loosened with aid of small hex setscrew wrench.

When the thermostat knob was pulled off, another body screw could be seen between the shaft and the handle. This came out readily. Round button next to screwdriver is water compartment seal.

Iron's cover was now loose but not yet removable. Last hitch turned out to be the flexible spring protector of the cord, which unscrewed quickly. Screwdriver points to "snubber" holding the wire.

The cover of the iron now slides off along line cord, and the terminal block for latter becomes accessible. Reason for iron failure is all too simple: one wire had broken away from its screw.

Toaster refuses to get hot, or stays hot, doesn't pop up the way it did before? A quick internal examination may show the fault to be only an open connection, or a large accumulation of baked raisins.

ELECTRIC TOASTERS

Collection of crumbs is usual cause of trouble. A good cleaning helps.

UNLIKE irons, broilers, and similar heat-appliances found in the kitchen, a bread toaster is used only for short periods perhaps once a day. Its wire heating element therefore enjoys a long life and rarely needs to be replaced. "Rarely" does not mean "never." With millions of toasters in active service, hardware and electrical shops find it profitable to stock replacement elements.

Most of the troubles that develop with toasters are mechanical rather than elec-

trical. Crumbs accumulating inside can readily jam up the release mechanism, the control switch, the wire guides that hold the bread in place, etc. If the family is fond of raisin bread, the toaster needs frequent cleaning. Raisins that fall out of the bread are baked by the heat to the hardness of pebbles, and may have to be pried out.

Some toasters have clean-out traps in the bottom. These should be opened once every couple of weeks. Toasters without such traps can merely be turned upside

Old style single-slice toaster has the virtues of simplicity and accessibility. If it stops working every couple of years it can be opened readily for inspection. Four small screws secure the top plate.

Side panels of toaster have small feet which go through slots in base and are twisted here about a quarter turn. Straighten them carefully with electrician's pliers and the panels will come off.

Sides and back of toaster peel off like an orange skin. It isn't necessary to remove front because mechanism connected to push levers is now in sight. The line cord (rear) is permanently attached.

Aluminum pan on bottom of toaster catches crumbs. Remove it frequently and clean it thoroughly with steel wool or abrasive nylon pad. An accumulation here of burned crumbs may give toaster bad odor.

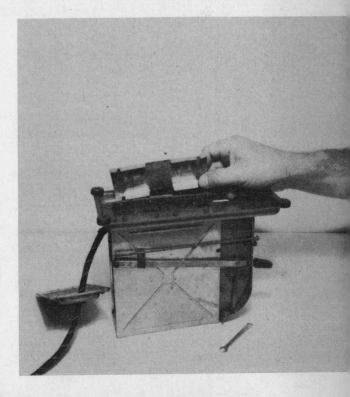

The wire guides that position the bread between the heating elements should fit loosely and come out easily. If they don't, pick them out carefully and scrape them clean with back edge of a knife.

In this toaster two parallel heating elements are held in spring clips in bottom of the base. To remove them, grab top edge with long-nose pliers; give a slight upward jerk to free them from clips.

Breaks in flat ribbon wire of heating element can sometimes be repaired with a patent resistance-wire cement. Joint does not usually last long, so the best bet is to have replacement unit on hand.

It is possible that element doesn't heat up in the toaster but looks good when removed. If continuity checks out with Clicktester or small VOM (below) fault must be in connections to the spring clips.

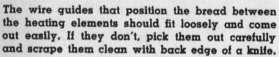

In 'this toaster, popping action depends on tension of coiled spring in the bottom plate. This can be adjusted with aid of long-nose pliers. Grab the end of the spring and try it on different notches.

In this more modern toaster, the clean-out plate at the bottom is hinged, and pops open when a button is pressed. Most crumbs can be shaken out, but the stubborn, burned-in ones may need stiff brush.

In a two-slice toaster there are two sets of wire guides to examine and clean. They are easily accessible when clean-out plate is opened. Do not use oil here. Scrape wires, and clean holes with a pin.

Use of screws rather than rivets facilitates opening of this toaster. Here a very small screwdriver takes out a long screw holding color-control knob. Note position of latter's pointer; replace same way.

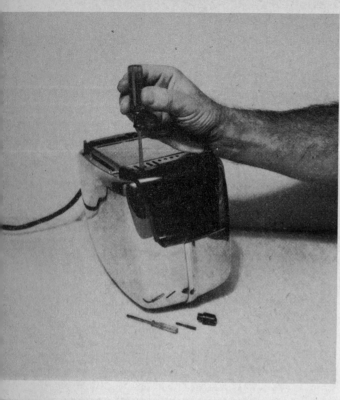

The molded front piece of the toaster, which includes the lever for lowering the bread into the heating chamber, is held by screws at the bottom. Remove slowly; they might be of self-tapping type.

Front of the toaster (below, left) with the molded end piece removed. The small lever that moves the bread holder down is now in view. If it doesn't work freely, it probably should be scraped lightly.

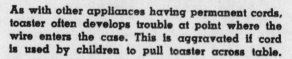

As with other appliances having permanent cords, toaster often develops trouble at point where the wire enters the case. This is aggravated if cord is used by children to pull toaster across table.

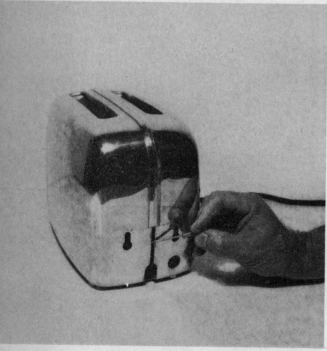

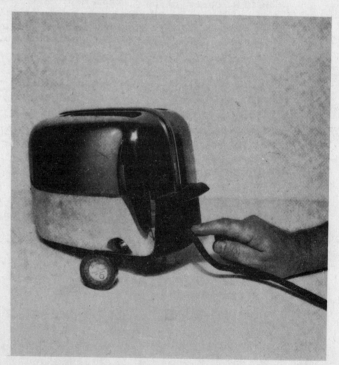

down and shaken vigorously to clean out.

A word of caution here that shouldn't be necessary but usually is: If a piece of bread gets stuck inside a toaster, resist the impulse to reach for a knife or fork and to dig it out. At least, resist for the half-second it takes for you to remove the line plug from the wall outlet. This simple, easy, sensible, obvious precaution can readily save your life. Warn the kids about this.

It just doesn't occur to many people that the red-hot wires in a toaster are very much alive electrically and that silver-plated cutlery is one of the best known conductors of electricity. Because the bread holders of all toasters are quite narrow, it is almost impossible to put a knife or fork into them without making contact with the wires, and then the fireworks begin.

Finally, do not keep a plugged-in toaster on a sink drain or adjacent counter that can become flooded. The water can cause the

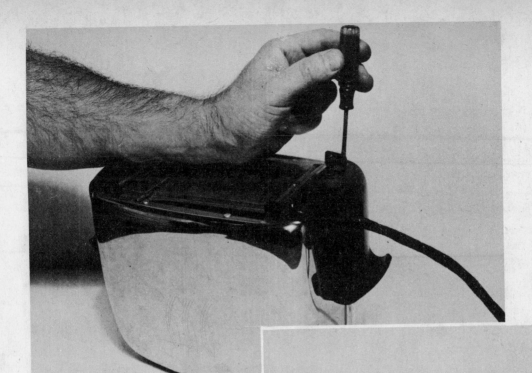

Breaks in insulation close to case cannot be mended unless molded end piece of toaster is removed. Almost identical in shape with front piece, it is held by two screws and can be dismantled in a jiffy.

With end piece slipped out over line cord, insulation and connections are accessible. Cut off loose insulation, then reinforce with a layer or two of tape, pulled tight about an inch each side of hole.

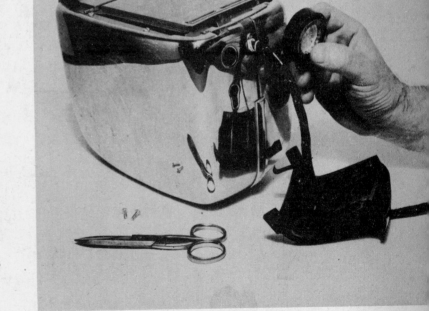

wires to make contact with a resultant surge of power. This is particularly dangerous if you like to bathe the baby in the sink, a common practice. Move the toaster or unplug it.

Sooner or later, it may be necessary to take a toaster apart, at least partially, to release a jammed mechanism, repair the connecting cord, replace the element, etc. Construction varies with make and price, but generally is rather simple. A screw-driver and a pair of pliers are usually the only tools needed for the job.

The accompanying photos show disassembly operations for two toasters: a new two-slicer and a single-slicer 25 years old. The latter is cleaned frequently, has needed only one of its two heating elements replaced in all that time, and continues to make perfectly good toast. The general procedures illustrated in the pictures can be applied to practically all toasters. •

Large ten- and eight-cup percolators (left and in center, above) have "strength" controls and pilot lights. Six-cupper (right) has neither and is therefore of simpler construction internally. All make good coffee!

COFFEE makers, like toasters, are used only intermittently, and therefore usually enjoy long life. The way for *you* to enjoy the coffee they produce is to observe a few simple precautions:

1) To assure proper action of the thermostat that controls the heating action, start with cold water.

2) Disconnect the line cord when the pot is empty. Letting it run dry or nearly so can put a strain on the heating element. With liquid to absorb heat from the latter, and with the protection of the thermostat, there is little likelihood of burn-out in normal usage.

3) Don't immerse the entire pot in water to clean it. A few rather expensive makers are so well sealed that they can be immersed, and the manufacturers make a point of this in their advertising. However, by far the majority of pots are not built to take this treatment. As it is, some water is bound to leak into the heating chamber at the bottom. This can cause corrosion in time. It is advisable to open the chamber once in a while and to check for signs of this condition.

4) Don't fuss with the thermostat. This usually consists of a bi-metallic strip that opens or closes as the surrounding temperature changes, and in so doing it opens or closes the power circuit to the heating coil. Because the range of movement is small, thermostats by nature are critical in adjustment. About all you can do with them is make sure that their connections are secure.

5) Most makers have detachable cords.

Six-cup pot looks sealed up tight, but actually only a single large machine screw holds the entire molded plastic bottom to the main body. This makes regular inspection and cleaning quite easy.

Large coiled heating element, center, starts the water gurgling within few seconds after the pot is plugged in. Irregular operation was cured by tightening prongs of receptacle with nut driver.

Bottom of this six-cupper is polished dish, like rest of body. When two screws through it were removed it felt loose, but small knob of thermostat control had to be removed to free it completely.

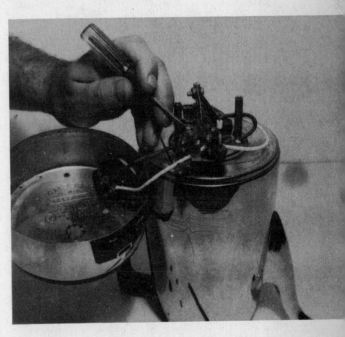

Bottom dish remains tethered by two heavy wires connecting to receptacle for line cord. Screwdriver points to pilot light, common No. 47 radio item. Flat thermostat assembly is to the right.

The bottom dish can now be picked off to reveal a cluster of small components between two vertical studs. The latter are threaded to take the screws that hold the dish tight against the body.

In this coffee maker the heating coil is entirely enclosed in a solid container, pointed out by finger. The screw that holds bottom dish goes into threaded stud. Parts and wires now accessible.

Large 30-cup party percolator, top, left, has molded plastic bottom, held by one large center screw and four twisted lugs. Note the overhanging spigot. This is vulnerable to damage; treat with care.

After center screw is removed, lugs are twisted straight with flat nose of electrician's pliers. This must be done very slowly to prevent them from cracking off; once gone, they cannot be replaced.

Inspect these in the usual manner for abraded insulation, bent prongs, etc. Incidentally, the same flat two-prong connector that goes into the receptacle on the pot is pretty much standard for irons and grills, too, so in a pinch, you can borrow the cord from one of these appliances.

Some makers include a little red pilot light to tell you that the brewing is finished and that the coffee is ready. This is usually a single-contact, miniature bayonet-base, low-voltage radio pilot, mounted behind a red jewel in the bottom of the pot. Look for a type number on its base, so that you can buy a replacement when needed. The No. 47 is widely used.

Many pots do not have "ready" indicators of any kind. The manufacturers evidently figure that an effective signal, even though it is sort of negative, is the end of the gurgling sound in the glass top.

If a coffee maker really does burn out—it *can* happen—in nine cases out of ten you had better figure on buying an entirely new one. Repair is virtually impossible, or at least both impractical and expensive, because most heating elements are in coiled tubes welded to the inside bottom of the pot. Instead of throwing the appliance away, consider the idea of using it as a flower vase; it might be a conversation piece, if not a particularly noteworthy piece of "pop" decoration.

Some suggestions for getting into several sizes of makers are contained in the accompanying series of illustrations. •

ELECTRIC CLOCKS

They last almost forever, but might sometime need minor attention.

ELECTRIC clocks rarely stop running because they burn out. In most cases the trouble is due to settling or lumping of the lubricant inside. This is bound to happen with a clock that is left fixed in one position for years. A sign of impending difficulty of this kind is a whining noise, like the stripping of gears. This is exactly what it is—the stripping of gears.

As a simple preliminary check, unplug an ailing clock and test it for continuity with the Clicktester or a VOM. The reading on the ohms scale will be several hundred ohms. If there is no reading, check directly at the motor terminals inside.

Some clock motors are not lubricated at all. Once one of these gets noisy or loses time because of gear slippage, the best thing to do is to chuck it away and get a new one. •

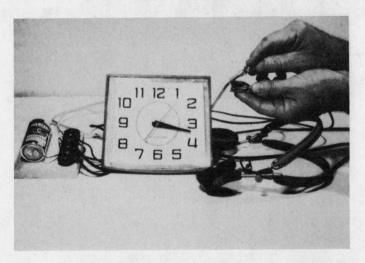

First step in checking an electric clock that has stopped is to make sure the cord and the motor are OK. Simply touch the test leads of the Clicktester to the prongs and listen for cracklings.

Similar test can be made with any small VOM. Set it to the X100 resistance range, clip one probe to one prong of line plug, and touch other probe to other prong. Clock should read 300 to 500 ohms.

If VOM gives no reading, indicating open circuit, don't quit. Now remove clock from its case, find the junction of the line cord and the motor terminals, and apply test probes for direct motor check.

No, the picture isn't upside down—the clock is. In nine cases out of ten of motor noise or loss of time, settling of internal lubricant is cause of trouble. Running clock this way resettles it.

ELECTRIC GRILLS

Inspect and check them frequently for "grounding," which can be dangerous.

This is an improved type of grill, with a hinged glass door to confine any spattering. Five-position thermostat is at the left. Permanently attached line cord is out of sight at rear. Sides are plastic.

THE table-top electric "hot plate" was for a long time a popular kitchen appliance with people who either did not have other means of cooking or just wanted to keep their cooking work to a minimum. It consisted essentially of a flat grid of resistance wire in coiled form, about ⅛ inch in diameter, on a ceramic form. Electricity passing through the wire heated it to redness. Pots or pans placed directly over the grid also heated up; not as thoroughly as they would over gas flames, but enough to cook food in them.

The "hot plate" was compact, clean, convenient. There was ("is" is correct for plates still in existence) only one trouble with it; it was frightfully dangerous from the shock standpoint, since the electrically "live" heating coil was in open sight.

Thousands of these plates are still around, many in working order or requir-

ing only minor repairs. Repair may involve only the replacement of the heating coil, a very simple job, but DON'T DO IT. The life you save may very well be your own.

If you find that a hot plate is just what you need for odd jobs around your shop or darkroom, such as melting glue or warming up cold developer, at least take the sting out of it by adding a cover of some kind over the resistance wire. A scrap piece of coarse screening or perforated "hardware cloth" is fine for the purpose. Prop it over the wire about ¼ inch by means of small stacks of washers or a couple of nuts and secure it with machine screws or self-tapping screws.

The basic hot plate, which generally didn't even have a line switch, has given way to much more elaborate grills having motor-driven spits, thermostatic controls, glass doors, etc. In one style some measure

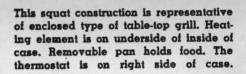

This squat construction is representative of enclosed type of table-top grill. Heating element is on underside of inside of case. Removable pan holds food. The thermostat is on right side of case.

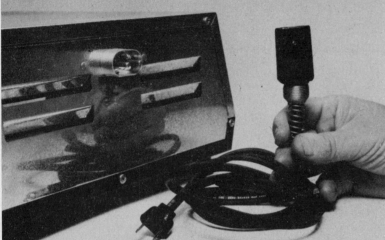

The line cord is detachable and fits into a receptacle on the back of the case. The flat plug is standard for heat appliances such as toasters, irons. The slots in the case are provided for needed ventilation.

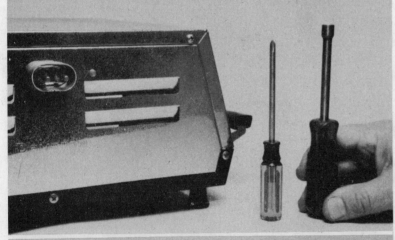

Two necessary tools for disassembly and repair are Phillips screwdriver (left) and a nut driver. With line cord removed, it is safe to put hands and tools inside the grill to loosen fastenings.

Knob of this thermostat has no set screw, but it comes off with a strong pull. On some appliances there may be a set screw through the front of the knob or on side; it might need a tiny hex wrench.

Screws come out readily, but the case of this grill was found to be locked together by four rivets through the support brackets of the handles. The heads had to first be ground off, then pushed through.

The manufacturer of this grill obviously didn't want it opened, but with the handle rivets removed it split apart easily. Reassembly later was not a problem, as self-tapping screws did the job of rivets.

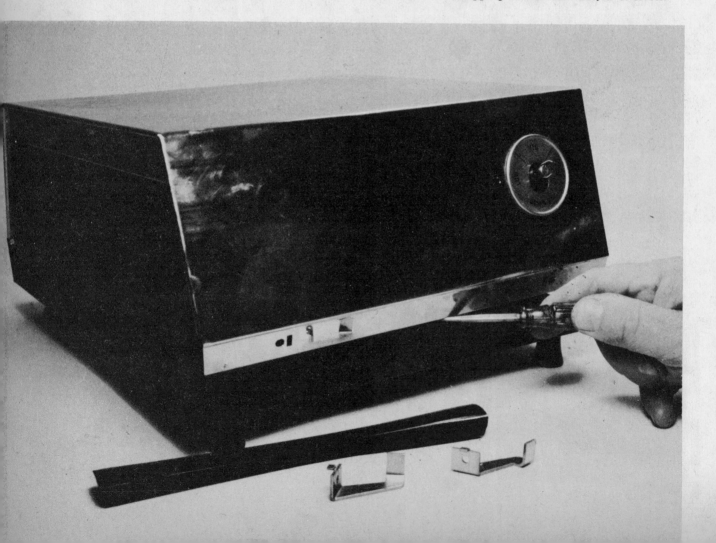

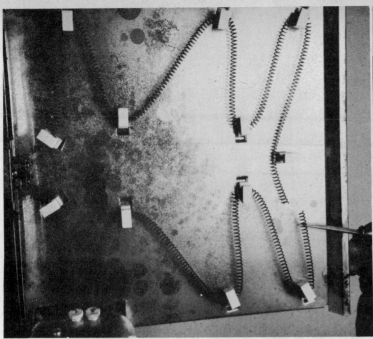

This is what usually puts a grill out of action: the coiled resistance wire has burned or broken open. This can be dangerous to user if the wire touches the frame; it becomes hot electrically.

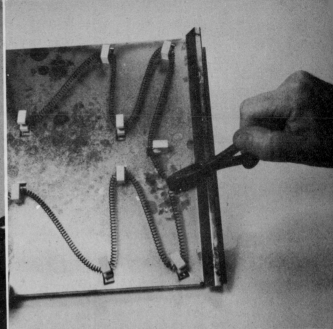

A temporary repair can be made by twisting the broken ends of the resistance wire together. This might or might not be practical, depending on how brittle wire has become, but it's worth trying.

of protection is afforded by the placement of the open resistance wire *inside* the body of the appliance, at the top or the bottom or both. An oversize pot or pan might still touch the wire, as might a knife pushed in to loosen a burned hamburger, so extreme care is still in order.

The overhead position of the heating element is common because fat dripping from food drops harmlessly to a bottom pan, rather than into the wire itself. However, if the wire should develop a break while the switch is on, and if it drops and touches an aluminum or stainless steel pot, and if the line plug is in the wall outlet the wrong way (wrong from the safety standpoint), and if the cook tries to remove the pot when she realizes the grill is cold—all these if's can add up to one nasty shock.

Under other possible circumstances, a droopy resistance wire touching the pot might put the equivalent of a short-circuit on the line, causing the fuse or circuit breaker on it to open and the whole line to go dead. This is good, if you can call trouble good, because then the entire grill is safe to touch even if the cook forgets to yank the line cord.

All adult members of a family should be instructed to PULL THE LINE PLUG FIRST AND IMMEDIATELY if a loaded grill, or for that matter any electrical appliance, shows signs of malfunctioning. Most people think first of saving the food, but this takes care of itself once the juice is cut off. If the resistance wire should burn out half way through the preparation (as it usually does!) the grill merely goes cold, so there's no real damage. If the thermostat sticks and the grill gets too hot, someone will smell it and rush in, and perhaps save the roast.

Thermostat Control

Grills with thermostat control generally have a single resistance element, distributed inside the case on small ceramic studs. The thermostat does not regulate the strength of the current, as many people seem to think. It keeps it on full until the temperature inside the case approximates its setting; then it shuts it off entirely. The wires cool off gradually, and when the case temperature drops below the setting the 'stat turns the current back on. At the highest setting the 'stat usually keeps the current on steadily.

Simpler grills might have a single three-position switch, reading OFF, MEDIUM, HIGH, or two separate switches marked

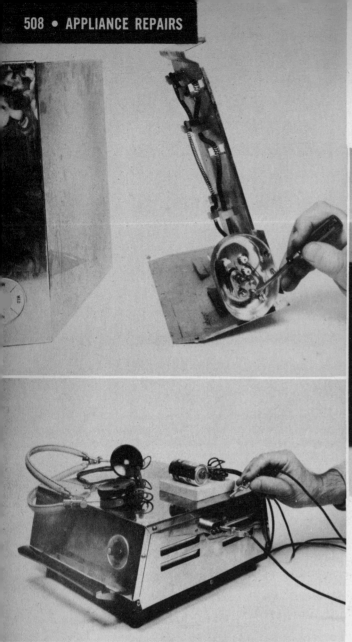

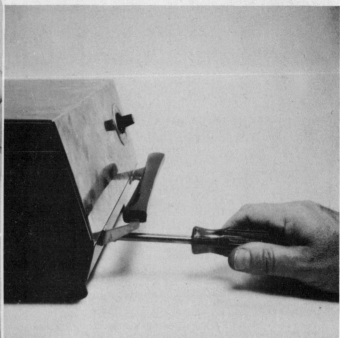

Single L-shaped member of grill case holds heating wire, thermostat (with screwdriver pointing to connecting wires) and the power line receptacle (out of sight). The unit is easy to inspect.

Either self-tapping sheet metal screws or screws with nuts can be used in refastening handles and sides of grill's case. They can then be removed easily if appliance needs service another time.

Something that should be done regularly: testing the grill for possible grounding of the internal resistance wire to the case. Turn thermostat to HI´ to make certain that the circuit is completed.

MEDIUM and HIGH. There are two separate resistance coils in these appliances; one is brought into play at MEDIUM and both at HIGH. It is entirely possible for a grill to operate at one heat but not the other, since the coils can burn out independently. In a thermostat-controlled unit an open element means no heat regardless of the setting of the control.

One thing can be said for the open-wire type of cooker: the resistance element can be replaced easily, and replacements are available. In fact, it is a good idea to obtain one the next time you're in a supply store and to stash it away with your tools, fuses, spare bulbs, etc., so that you'll be able to make a really quick repair when the original wire gives way.

After installing a new element, check the entire grill for possible "grounds" to the case. The Clicktester or any VOM will tell you positively if the wiring is safe or not. Remember, there should not be any electrical connection between any part of the resistance wire and any part of the case. If the Clicktester makes a noise or the VOM reads on the ohms scale when you touch the test probes to the wire and the body, look very carefully for looseness in the wire.

Protected Heating Elements

The naked resistance element in grills is bound to disappear eventually with the growing use of the slightly more expensive but certainly safer enclosed type. This is made like an immersion heater; that is, a rigid outer metal casing entirely encloses the actual heating wire, without making electrical contact with it. The heat from the

Glass door opens to reveal presence of two heat units of rigid tubing between which food is put for broiling. Both sides are done at once, without need for turning. This saves trouble.

To get at heat units, for inspection and cleaning, it is necessary to unhook front glass door and to pull them a little to the right. They snap out; interior is accessible.

Safety and convenience! The duplicate heat elements are rigid and rugged, are shockproof, can be cleaned with a knife or steel wool, are interchangeable and easily replaced.

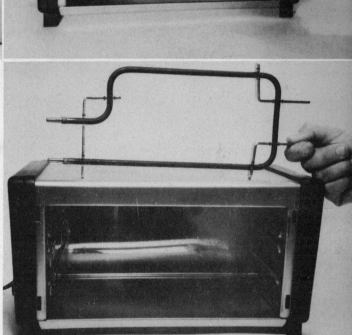

wire is transferred to the casing and the latter gets red hot, but hot or cold there is no danger of shock from it. Food can drip onto the element, but it does no harm and it can be scraped off readily, even with the current on.

A representative grill of modern design uses two such heating elements formed as rigid rectangles partially open at one short side. The ends of the elements are fitted with plugs which fit neatly and quickly into tight jacks inside the body of the appliance. Pull them out, and the smooth, unbroken surface of the grill can be cleaned in a minute. A burned-out unit can be removed and replaced by a new one in less time than it takes to read this sentence, and without tools of any kind!

Grills are in the same heavy-current category as irons, toasters, space heaters, etc. Their line plugs must be clean and fit tightly in the wall outlets. The cords must be protected from abrasion; and if they are of the detachable type, from getting lost.

General Maintenance

Examine the insides frequently, taking particular note of the condition and position of the heating wires if they are of the exposed variety. Try not to drop or jar the appliance, as this can cause the ceramic insulators holding the wires to crack or break off. When replacing plug-in heating elements, brighten the end connectors with fine sandpaper, emery cloth or steel wool and push them back firmly.

After cleaning the whole grill dry it well and make sure it is still dry when it is used the next time. •

SPACE HEATERS

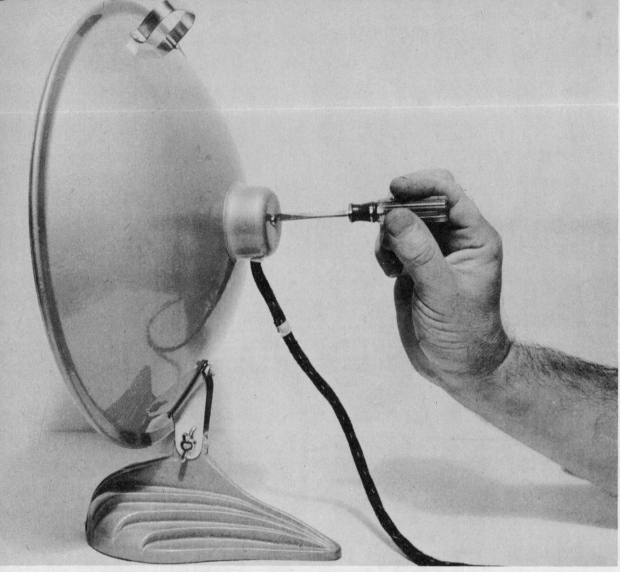

Representative bowl heater is hinged to a heavy base. Heater unit is in cup at back of reflector; removal of screw makes it accessible. There is no switch. Heater is controlled by the line plug only.

GREAT for taking the chill out of a room at the end of the line of a house heating system, portable space heaters are also great consumers of electricity. The bowl type takes 500 or 600 watts; larger models with self-contained circulating fans up to 1650 watts, the safe (and legal) limit on 110-120 volt circuits. In areas where electric energy is cheap and 220-240 wiring is available throughout a house, heaters taking 3000, 4000 and 5600 watts are common.

Small heaters consist usually of a coil of heating wire at the focal point of a polished metal shell. You simply plug 'em into an outlet and they're on. Larger ones have switch-selected degrees of heat intensity or fully automatic thermostat control; also, cutoff devices that turn off the current if a heater is upset accidentally.

Some inexpensive bowl-type heaters are potentially rather dangerous because their removable protective grills are of coarse mesh through which fingers, knifes, sticks and other objects can be poked quite easily. The possibility of burn or shock can be reduced if an additional covering of ½-inch

Heating element consists of coil of coiled wire on ceramic form. Line cord connects directly to screw terminals at base. Replacement coils are readily available. Simply wind in place, connect.

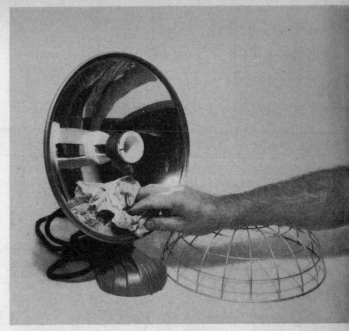

Heater effectiveness depends mostly on a shiny reflector. Unplug line cord, remove protective grill and clean frequently with soft cloth. The open grill should have a closer mesh for safety.

Spring-loaded plunger on bottom of the fan-operated heavy-duty heater mystifies many owners. It is an "upset" safety switch. If the heater is pushed over it cuts off current regardless of main switch.

square "wire cloth" is fastened over the factory-installed grill. This material is open enough to pass the radiated heat.

Ordinary window screening, which has spacing of only about $\frac{1}{16}$ inch, is a bit fine for the purpose, although it will serve in an emergency until the ½-inch mesh can be obtained. Some types of sheet grillwork is also suitable. This is thin aluminum, punched out in a variety of designs and patterns. It is often used as a decorative cover for room radiators.

Still on the subject of safety: The bathroom has long been known as the most dangerous part of the house, because of falls in the tub or shower. Don't make its record worse by putting an open space heater near either of the latter. It is all too easy for a person with a dripping hand or foot to establish a circuit between the room's plumbing, which is very thoroughly "grounded," and an electrically "hot" part of the heating element. It's better to chatter a little while getting dry than to risk electrocution.

Tight connections and clean plugs are essential to safe heater operation. The heating effect at points where there is appreciable resistance is aggravated by the fact that the power loss here is a function

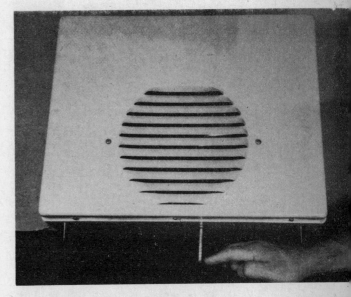

of the *square* of the current. To take some round figures as an easy example, suppose a dirty plug has a resistance of one ohm and the appliance takes four amperes. The simple formula for electrical power in watts is the current squared times the resistance. In this case the answer is merely four squared, or 16, times one, or 16 watts. Suppose a larger appliance requiring eight amperes is used. The heat loss is now eight

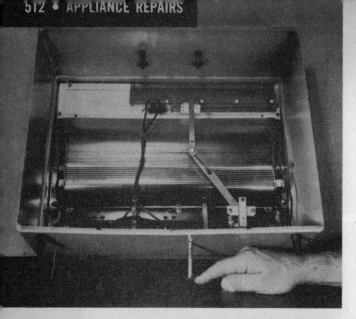

This is same view as in previous photo, but with the back of the heater body removed to show the back of the straight reflector and the internal wiring. Arm near center is control of thermostat.

squared, or 64, times one, or 64 watts!

Because plugs depend on mere sliding friction to make electrical contact with the brass fingers inside wall outlets, some slight resistance here and hence some heating effect must be expected. If you put your hand on a plug and feel only mild warmth, the contact is adequate. If it it too hot to hold, you need an outlet with tighter springs to bite into the prongs of the plug. It's easy enough to clean the latter, but there's no way of getting into the outlet.

The efficiency of electric heaters depends largely on the cleanliness of the reflecting surfaces, whether they are bowl-shaped or flat. The heat attracts dust, so frequent dusting is important. A very slightly dampened rag does the trick.

The elements of all electric heaters turn red and can quickly ignite paper and cloth. The appliances should therefore be used with great caution if small children are likely to be within reach of them. Kids are naturally inquisitive and find the warm glow irresistible.

If the cord furnished with a heater is too short to reach the nearest available outlet, use as least No. 16 or preferably No. 14 asbestos insulated flexible wire for the extension. Also, cut off or unscrew the present line plug and make soldered joints where the old and the new cords meet; then add the plug to the end of the extension. Most factory-installed cords have molded plugs that cannot be opened or used a second time. Discard them after they have been removed.

When buying a new plug look for one with a heavy base, preferably reinforced by a metal ring, and with husky screw terminals that can take No. 16 or No. 14 wire. Avoid the dime-store plugs of "molded mud." They just aren't made to carry 15 amperes for any length of time without starting to melt. •

Blower fan is on inside of back cover of heater. It is being checked here for continuity after it stopped working. Nothing was really wrong; one of its wires had merely shaken loose from terminal.

A smart safety check: with switch on, heater is being tested for possible "grounds" between the line cord and the body. "Grounding" does not affect heat, but makes body potentially dangerous.

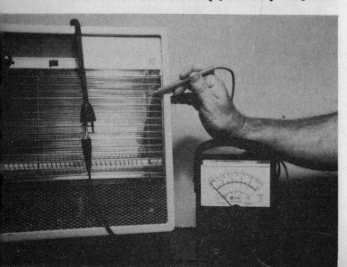

To repeat, space heaters can be warm friends, but they can also be hot-headed enemies if you are not careful with them. Generally, keep them out of the bathroom—and away from small children.

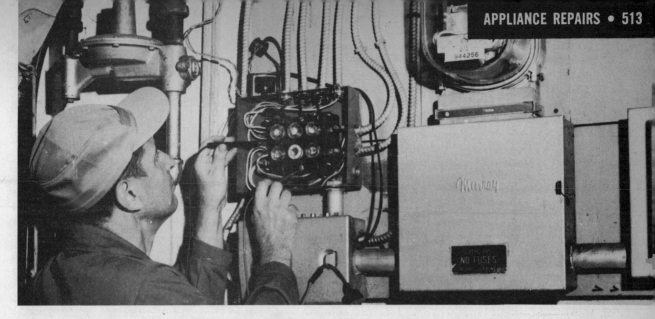

The time to become acquainted with your fuse box is when the electrical system of the house is in normal order. Make a record of which fuses control which circuits and keep the spares near the box.

FUSES ARE FOR SAFETY

Keep assortment of spares on hand for those emergencies.

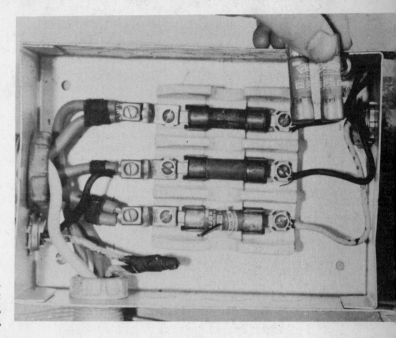

Cartridge type fuses are generally used on heavy current circuits such as those feeding electric ranges, central air conditioners, etc. Contacts exposed; use wooden stick to pry.

FUSES and circuit breakers are the safety valves of the house electrical system. A fuse burns out or a breaker snaps open, like a switch, when the current rating of the device is exceeded by an accidental short-circuit on the line or when too many heavy-current appliances are plugged into it at the same time.

In most homes the individual branch circuits from the meter use No. 14 wire and are intended to carry 15 amperes *safely*. If a fuse or breaker of this size opens frequently, there simply are too many appliances in use; they should be distributed among two or more branch circuits. Putting in larger fuses is sheer insanity. This can only lead to wiring fires.

More and more builders are putting circuit breakers rather than fuses into new homes because these devices cannot be corrupted. Fuses can be screwed in and out in a moment, but breakers are installed on a permanent basis. If one snaps open, you can reset it by pushing handle back, but you can't change its current rating.

Clothes washers take a rather heavy current for a few seconds on starting, and then a much lighter current for running. Circuits feeding them should be fitted with special fuses called "slow-blow," which are designed for this tricky operating action.

Fuses are cheap. Keep a handful in a handy place, *along with a flashlight*. Trouble is much more likely to happen at night than during the day, because that's when everybody is home and using lamps, TV, radio, etc. •

REFRIGERATOR

Though infrequently used, these can break

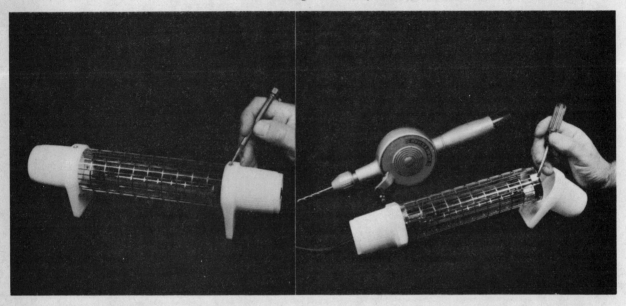

This type of defroster has a metal cage for its body and plastic end feet. The latter are fastened by blind rivets, put in with a special tool. Cord emerges from one foot. There is no switch.

If defroster appears to be defective and element needs to be tested, the only way to get into the cage is to drill out the rivets. They are generally hollow and collapse completely when drilled.

BECAUSE of the normal moisture in the meats and fruits kept in a refrigerator, ice is bound to form in the freezer compartment. Over a period of several months the accumulation can be large enough to crowd out packages of frozen food that should fit comfortably. "Defrosting" then is imperative.

To many housewives this is a nuisance job because they must first empty the compartment, wrap the food to delay softening, and then fill the space with successive pots of hot water. The pot routine is quite ridiculous, because for a few dollars you can buy a "defroster" that does the melting quickly and painlessly. This is nothing more than a small electric heater, very much like a section of a toaster or grill. The heating element is enclosed, so it is not affected by melting ice dripping onto it. The food still has to be removed, but the rest of the work is done by the defroster.

The system is to place the device inside the freezer compartment, to close the latter's door carefully over the line cord without bruising it, and to do the same with the refrigerator's main door. Leave the defroster on for about fifteen minutes

Of all metal construction, this style of defroster resembles a small griddle. An insulated handle makes it easy to hold when it heats up. Melting ice falls safely through top and bottom openings.

and then examine the ice for signs of softening. Usually you can hasten the defrosting by poking gently into the ice with a stiff knife; it will fall off in chunks, which can be swept out readily.

Since it is needed only a few times a year, a defroster should last almost in-

DEFROSTERS

from handling and storing. Here's how to make them right.

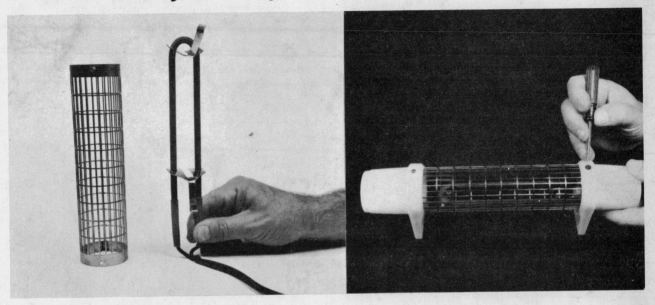

Disassembly effort may not be worth while, since actual heater wire may be enclosed in metal tubing and not accessible. However, faulty operation may be due only to loose conections at end.

If repair consists only of tightening loose connection, reassemble the cage and feet with small self-tapping screws or even short 4/36 or 6/32 machine screws. These will bite into the plastic.

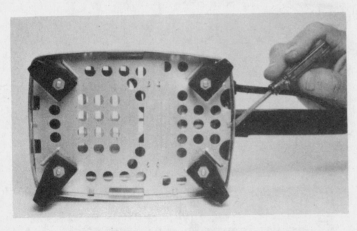

The bottom plate is held to body of defroster by twisted tabs. To remove plate for internal inspection, straighten the tabs slowly with flat-nose pliers so that they line up with slots in body.

definitely. It should, but it doesn't always. It usually suffers damage from being kicked around from one storage spot to another. In many households the cry is, "Where did we put the darn thing?"

Pay particular attention to the line cord, and especially don't slam the refrigerator doors hard against it. The wires inside the insulation can sometimes break even though the insulation doesn't. An indication of this trouble is an intermittent sound when the Clicktester is used or a jumpy meter needle when a resistance check is made with a VOM.

If a defroster fails to heat up, the heating element possibly is burned out or more probably there is something wrong only with the line cord. The only way to get at the truth of the matter is to open the device, if it can be opened at all without wrecking it. Screws yield to screwdrivers, but blind rivets usually have to be drilled out and then replaced by hardened self-tapping screws. If the heating element really checks out as open, it is usually cheaper to buy a whole new defroster than to waste time looking for a replacement element. If the line cord is OK, remove it and save it in your junk box. It's bound to be useful for future repair purposes.

In buying another defroster, look for one with a metal rather than a plastic case. Some of the imported plastics, known as "molded mud" in the trade, don't hold up very well to the extremes of heat and cold to which they are subjected. •

More modern style of sewing machine, with motor concealed in base, above. Electric light in reflector over work surface may require replacement often because of vibration. Cover screws remove easily.

ELECTRIC SEWING MACHINES

A small variable-speed motor makes needlework an easy job.

PROBABLY the first important power operated device in American homes was the sewing machine. Only a small motor was needed to replace the foot treadle, and it made the machine infinitely easier and more pleasurable to use. Nowadays treadle models are considered antiques, and often bring higher prices than they did when they were new.

There are two general types of electric sewers. In one, the motor is out in the open behind the hand wheel that sets the starting position of the needle. A small rubber disc on the end of the motor shaft bears against the rim of the wheel and drives it by simple friction.

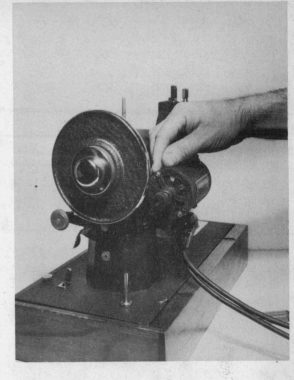

Mounted behind the main head, the motor of older sewing machine is out of the way of the user but is completely accessible. Finger points to one of two brushes, easy to get at in insulated sleeves.

Mounted on a spring-loaded bracket which pushes it against the large hand wheel, the motor turns the latter by means of a small rubber roller on its shaft. Keep these surfaces clean, free of oil.

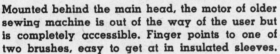

Inspect motor drive frequently, check for tightness of pulley, and oil motor bearings sparingly. Good idea to have spare pulley on hand. Clean the contacts of large plug, check cords for abrasion.

Speed control of machine in previous pictures is of stepped type. Screwdriver points to strips of resistance wire stretched between eyelets in insulated base. These warm up in normal operation.

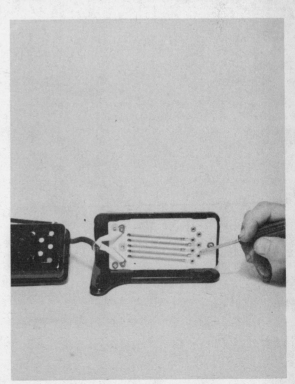

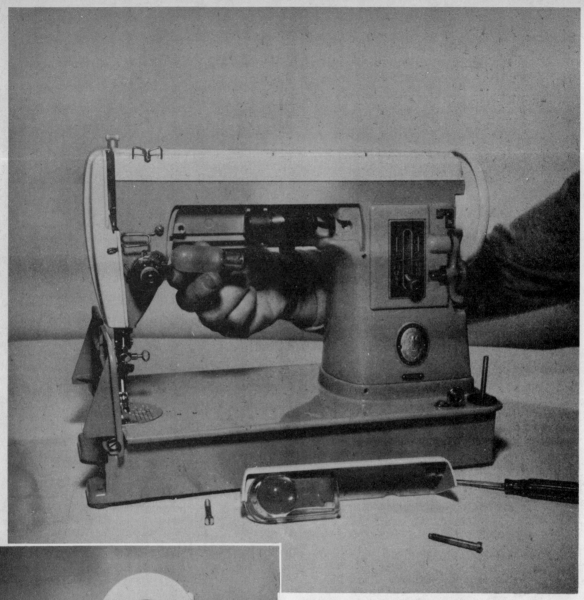

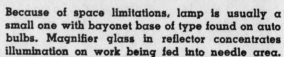

Because of space limitations, lamp is usually a small one with bayonet base of type found on auto bulbs. Magnifier glass in reflector concentrates illumination on work being fed into needle area.

There are two power cords for this machine. The one from speed treadle (left) plugs into receptacle at bottom; the line cord plugs in under the wheel. Plugs are different designs, can't be interchanged.

Foot Speed Control

The motor speed and hence the sewing rate are controlled by a small foot treadle. This actually is a "rheostat," the common electrical term applied to a variable resistor. With no pressure on its foot plate the power circuit to the motor is open. As the treadle is depressed the internal mov-

Interior of speed control (top, left) is rather simple. Main item to inspect is the spring that actuates the foot pedal. This is likely to move out of position. Also check out all screws for tightness.

For protection (above) against bits of cloth and thread, "works" of machine are usually well covered. In this model the bottom plate is held by a single large thumb screw through the center.

The drive motor is mounted vertically in a corner of cast base. Latter is ribbed for rigidity. A plastic cover protects the motor against dust. It comes off easily when two visible screws are removed.

ing contact touches one end of the resistance wire, closing the circuit and causing the motor to turn over slowly. Further pressure moves the contact along the wire to a lower resistance setting. This increases the voltage to the motor, so it speeds up. With the treadle all the way down the machine is at maximum speed.

Anyone who drives a car learns to use this control in a minute, as it duplicates exactly the action of the accelerator.

There are several types of rheostats, some using a compressible carbon pile instead of wire, but the voltage regulating effect is the same.

In the second style of sewing machine

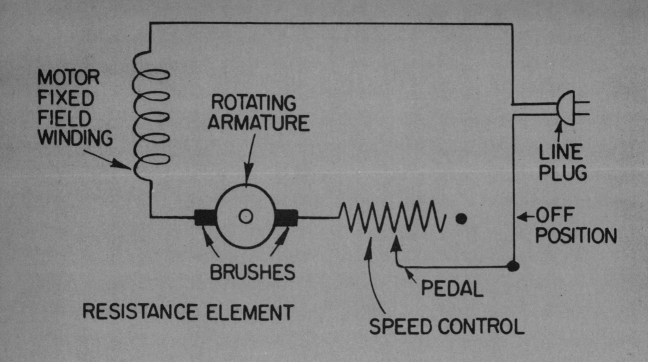

MOTOR
FIXED
FIELD
WINDING

ROTATING
ARMATURE

BRUSHES

RESISTANCE ELEMENT

SPEED CONTROL

PEDAL

OFF
POSITION

LINE
PLUG

Basic wiring diagram of motor section of a typical sewing machine. The speed control might be of the continuously variable or step-adjustable type.

Carbon brushes are in square brass sleeves near the end of the shaft. If they spark excessively they should be replaced. Trick in removing them is to take the tension off the retaining springs.

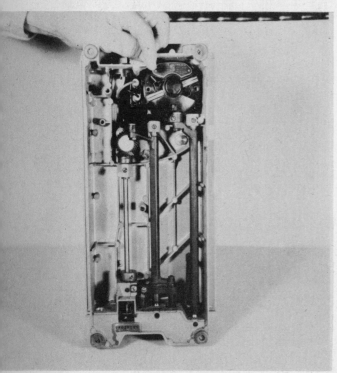

the motor is concealed in the base and drives the needle mechanism through gears and shafts. This is the arrangement found in most modern machines because it lends itself to attractive, streamlined designs. The speed control is the same as before.

Almost universally, the AC line cord and the wires from the foot pedal connect to the back or side of the machine by detachable plugs. When the machine is not in use the cords can be wound around the pedal and the package stowed in the carrying case. Virtually all sewers these days are "portable" in the sense that they can be encased and then stored in a closet.

The motor is rated about 1/12 horsepower, on the average, and is of the "universal" type. This means that it has two small brushes, which will eventually need replacement. Other maintenance is purely mechanical; mostly, it consists of applying small quantities of thin oil to bearings.

The speed control is what needs particular attention because when in use it is constantly jabbed and released; literally, it takes a beating. Check frequently for loose screws and connections and for damage to the connecting cord. A good precautionary measure is to put a couple of layers of black electrical tape over the cord for a distance of about a foot away from the treadle.

The accompanying pictures show representative models of the two styles of machines mentioned herein. •

WORTH KNOWING

Handy Test Light

TEST LIGHT (at right) is useful for determining if circuits are dead or alive. Wire guard is from photolamp; socket is the brass shell type, bulb of any wattage. Wires are soldered to nails taped to wooden dowels.

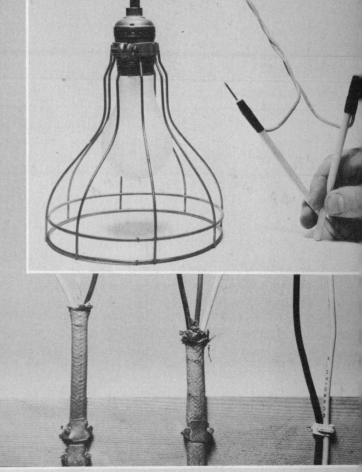

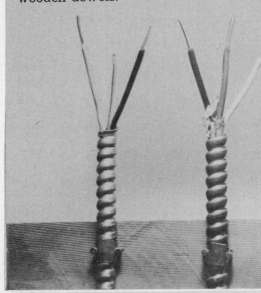

Types of Wire

SOME of the types of wire found in homes (left to right, above) are the two-wire "BX" with bare ground wire; three-wire BX; the two-wire "loom" with bare ground wire; three-wire loom; individual insulated wires usually encased in a thin-wall steel conduit. Usual sizes are No. 14 & No. 12. All wires solid copper.

Safety Extension Cord

ONE OF THE handiest items you will find in shop or garage is a good, long extension cord, at least 25 feet, using three-wire cable, three-prong safety plug and receptacle. Connect the wire with black insulation to the brass colored screws, and the green to the green screw.

ELECTRIC BLANKETS

They're great on cold nights if you keep them dry and in good order.

ELECTRIC blankets and their smaller versions known as "heating pads" differ from other heat appliances such as toasters and irons in that they need much less current. They are always used quite close to the body, so the paramount consideration is safety.

Here is where maintenance is more important than repair. The fact to remember about both blankets and pads is that their heat is produced by thin wires sewn between two layers of cotton, wool or other material. Externally, electric blankets look like any other kind, but because of the wires they must be handled with special care. Pads are less critical only because there's less of them to handle.

Do not throw a blanket into a shapeless heap on the floor or a chair while making a bed, and do not stuff it tightly into a drawer. As much as possible, keep it flat, or at least store it loosely if it is not left on the bed during the day.

By all means save the original box in which the blanket was packed, and use this for summer storage. Follow the lines of the factory folds and the whole cover will then fit the container comfortably.

Cleaning an electric blanket isn't as difficult as it might sound. In the better grades the heating wires are strong and flexible enough to withstand agitation and tumbling in an ordinary home washing machine. Some models can't take this treatment. Play safe by following the manufacturer's recommendations, without deviation.

One answer to the cleaning problem is to minimize it by keeping the blanket clean. Always use a cotton top sheet between the blanket and the bed, and change and wash this frequently to prevent build-up of perspiration and body odors. If the blanket is well aired every morning it may not require actual laundering more than once a year, at the end of the winter season. Consider how often or rather how infrequently an ordinary blanket is cleaned, and then put the electric model on the same timetable.

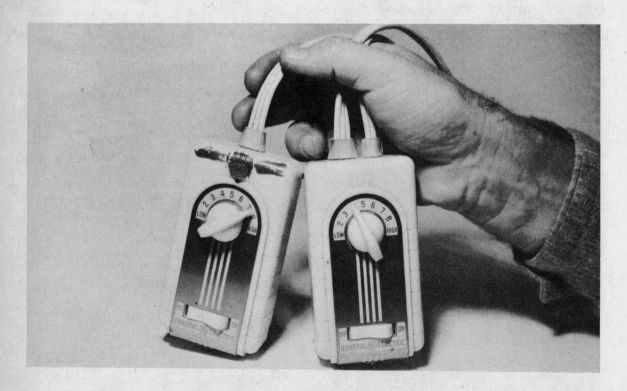

Pair of typical "his" and "her" thermostats for control of two separate electric blankets or for the individual halves of a large double blanket. On-off switches are at bottom. Knobs set the temperature.

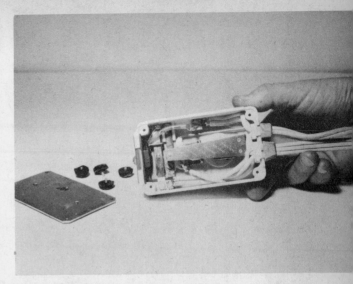

Plastic cases of thermostats have metal bottoms, in this model held by small screws through soft rubber feet in corners. Removal by means of suitable Phillips screwdriver takes only few minutes.

Become familiar with inside of control unit when it is in working order, and then you'll be able to recognize possible points of breakdown. Interior of unit is simple but adjustments are critical.

This control unit for a single electric blanket looks like a small radio set. There didn't seem to be any way of removing knob until closer examination revealed that dial button was removable.

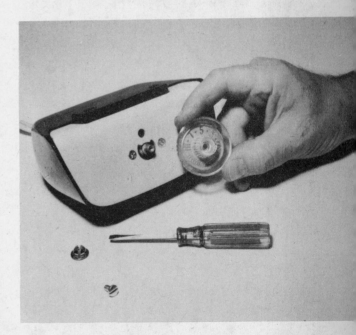

With the dial off, two screws that were previously hidden by it came into view. The hole directly above the shaft permits light from a small lamp inside the case to illuminate the dial's figures.

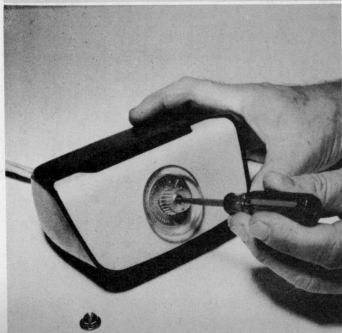

After the button was pried off with knife blade, small screw was found in the center of the heat control shaft. This was removed easily, and then the dial could be pulled off the splined shaft.

The two screws fasten the decorative front panel of the control unit to a sub-panel. When these were taken out the front panel came off completely. To avoid loss, keep the screws in small box.

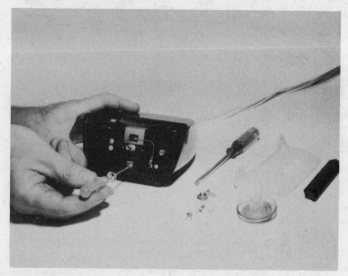

Final disassembly was now completed with removal of one small screw in front panel. Chassis moves out in one piece, grommet, cable follow.

Further disassembly, at left, was delayed because there was no sign of additional screws through the bottom. However, a little poking indicated rubber cable grommet might be involved.

It definitely was. It was very tight, but when its top edge was pushed down with a screwdriver it moved inward and immediately gave the inner chassis a loose feeling. Grommet protects wires.

With eight wires in the cable entering the control unit, it pays to make sure that all connections are secure. If leads are color-coded, make a sketch of their placement, for later reference.

More or less standard type of heating pad is similar in internal construction to the electric blanket, but has two-way heat control instead of variable thermostat. The switch comes apart for checking.

People who suffer from incontinence should be especially careful about using electric blankets, or perhaps they shouldn't use them at all. Not to be indelicate about it, but the fact must be faced that human urine is decidedly acid chemically and a good conductor of electricity. A wet electric blanket certainly poses the possibility of danger.

Heat Control Important

It's easy enough to pass electricity through wires and to make them hot; the trick with electric blankets is to keep the temperature from going too high or dropping off too fast. This control is provided by very sensitive thermal sensors in conjunction with heat-adjusting boxes designed to sit inconspicuously on a night table.

An electric blanket takes a little getting used to. After the first five minutes it feels too hot, so you turn down the control a notch or two. Then it stays cool too long before it comes on again, so you turn the control up. This can go on all night unless you strike a compromise that lets you sleep.

A couple sharing a double bed and one large blanket can have a real problem, because women have a thicker layer of outer tissue than do men and can withstand cold better. A thermostat setting that keeps him warm will have her kicking the blanket off within minutes, and then neither will be happy. Several alternatives are available:

1) Get a blanket with a split heating element, each half controlled by its own thermostat.

2) Use two entirely separate blankets, each with its thermostat.

3) Switch to twin beds and separate blankets.

4) Move to Florida.

Because the current required by a blanket is relatively small (the wires get hot, but they never reach the glowing stage), the element lasts almost indefinitely if not abused, and the thermostat likewise is dependable. Dependable, that is, until a disturbed sleeper winds himself up in the blanket and pulls the entire little control box off the table. If the floor is carpeted it might bounce a bit but continue to work. If the fall is a hard one it might not. The least you can do then is to open it and see if you can spot any fixable damage, such as a loosened wire, a cracked case, etc. The cases are generally molded of plastic, and can often be patched with cellulose cement or any kind of sticky tape.

Heating Pads

About the size of a hand towel, heating pads are intended for localized applications of heat, particularly to treat sore muscles. They do not generally have thermostatic control, but do have low and high switch settings. About the only thing likely to go wrong is the switch itself, because it is snapped on and off a great deal in normal service and its light internal contacts have a tendency to break off. Its two halves are held by screws and can be opened easily for inspection. The two-wire line cord enters at one end, and a three-wire cable emerges from the other and goes to the pad proper. The three wires are part of the heat-control circuit.

Treat a heating pad as you would an electric blanket: keep it clean and dry and refold it neatly after each use. •

ELECTRIC FOOD BLENDERS

They're working properly if they make lots of noise. How to keep them noisy.

Waring blender, an invention of popular orchestra leader, has a heavy base containing drive motor. Rotary switch gives choice of low or high speed. The mixing bowl is readily removable for cleaning.

To check for possible "grounding" of case, a dangerous condition, turn on speed switch, connect VOM in turn from case to prongs of line plug. No reading means that internal insulation is intact.

Make note of internal resistance when appliance is in normal order. Typical readings on blender are zero ohms with switch off; about 30 ohms with switch at low speed setting; and 8 ohms in high.

IN ITS MOST widely used form, the electric blender consists of a small motor that drives a set of metal blades in the bottom of a detachable glass vessel. Screaming around at high speed, the blades can whip up almost any combination of liquids in seconds and can reduce many pulpy fruits and vegetables to thick liquids in less than a minute.

The most vulnerable part of a blender is the glass jar, on two counts. First, it is rather top-heavy and can be knocked over readily. Second, it has a hole in its base through which passes the short axle of the mixing element. When the jar is set over the base of the blender, which contains the motor, this axle engages in a mating hole in the latter's shaft.

Like the propeller shaft assembly of a boat, the opening in the glass must be tight enough to keep liquid from leaking out but loose enough to allow the blades to turn without binding. With average use the packing material at this point should last for several years; with a lot of use the life will obviously be shorter. Removing old packing and installing new is largely a matter of having wrenches of the right size and reach. If the glass jar is nicked from repeated falls, it is sometimes less trouble to buy a new one, complete with blade assembly.

Some blenders have only one speed, high; others have high and low settings, selected by a three-position switch. The third, of course, is "off." Sometimes the machine will groan and refuse to run when the switch is turned from off to low, but will start in high and then run in low when the switch is turned to that setting. This is an indication that the jar is overloaded with too much solid food or that the axle is binding in its packing. The latter is certainly the case if the difficulty occurs with the jar empty.

With this particular blender, knob turns out to have an extension stud, all molded in one piece. Body of switch is mounted to the case of the appliance by a knurled nut, which must be removed.

To prevent marring polished case of the blender, use pliers with thin jaws to loosen the nut of the switch. At this stage of experimenting with appliance, removal of bottom plate is necessary.

Erratic motor operation may be due to dirty or bent switch contacts. To get at switch, look for set screw in knob and loosen. If no screw is visible, pull knob straight off, with tool assist.

of short screws, or held by pull-out clips to which connecting wires are pinched or soldered. Because brush-type motors are generally favored for machines requiring high speed, such as mixers, blenders, vacuum cleaners, etc., replacement brushes are stocked by most hardware and electrical supply stores. It's nice to get exact replacements for a particular appliance, but it's also very easy to adapt larger brushes merely by dressing them down on sandpaper or emery cloth.

Sensibly fitted with screws to facilitate cleaning and inspection, blender's bottom plate comes off easily. Three screws pass through rubber feet. Note if food has splattered here, and sponge off.

With bottom plate removed, the switch can now be pulled out and examined. One case of spotty motor operation was cured by application of hot soldering iron to joints between wires and terminals.

Motor brushes, which may need replacement at some time, are held in metal guides near end of shaft. In this blender, they are released when connector clips leading to guides are pulled out gently.

If the operation of the machine is satisfactory otherwise, don't monkey with the packing, as this can be difficult to get at in some models. It takes only an instant to twiddle the switch from one position to the other.

The motor is generally quite well protected in the base of the blender, but because it undoubtedly uses brushes it should be examined once a year or so. The brushes are actually two little bars of carbon in spring-loaded holders mounted diametrically opposite each other. They bear against the "commutator," a ring of copper strips to which the windings of the rotating part of the motor are connected. Some sparking between the brushes and the commutator is normal, as is brush wear due merely to friction against the relatively harder copper.

The functioning of the brush-commutator assembly can be observed closely if the cover of the machine is removed. The brushes might be secured under the heads

When a clip is removed the brush with its spring attached pops out of its holder. Somewhat soft, carbon does wear down. Brushes should be replaced when they get down to about ⅜ inch.

To prevent its ends from pulling away from connections inside blender, cord is snagged to bottom plate by a small clamp. This is held by screw, removable if cord ever needs replacement.

Excessive oiling is a common cause of trouble in motor-operated appliances that are run only for short periods. A small drop of household oil, once in 6 months, is enough for this blender.

Blenders are run only for short periods and therefore can get by with very little lubrication, or none at all. If there is a hole in the baseplate directly over the bottom end of the motor shaft, resist the temptation to squirt oil into it. Don't even squeeze the can; just let *one* drop leak out of the spout into the opening. Excess oil can readily find its way to the commutator, and since oil is a very good insulator it can literally gum up operation of the motor.

The usual caution against submerging appliances in water to clean them applies to blenders. Any liquid that slops over from the jar can be wiped up readily with a damp sponge. •

FOOD MIXERS

They are easy to keep running with a little attention to lubrication.

Standard pedestal style of food mixer. Speed control is directly under user's thumb, near handle. Motor mount is hinged, so that entire head can be tilted back for mixing blades to clear the bowl.

THE FAMILIAR style of food mixer consists of a heavy cast base, a platform for a bowl, and a motor head on a pedestal. In most models the head can be detached and used free-hand in any loose bowl, but generally it is a bit heavy for this purpose. The lighter and more streamlined hand-held type is favored by housewives and amateur male chefs for whipping up everything from eggs to souffles.

The labor-saving element in all mixers is a small, high-speed motor of the AC-DC "universal" design. The fact that it can work on DC as well as AC is of little importance because DC has disappeared from probably 99.9% of all American homes. However, the expression "AC-DC" seems to appeal to advertising copy writers and it appears in many pieces of sales literature.

A variety of mixing blades can be fitted quickly by means of snap-in chucks, which are on short shafts at right angles to the main horizontal line of the motor. Some blades are made of rather soft metal and are easily damaged if the mixer is put down on a work surface before the motor comes to a complete stop. To prevent this

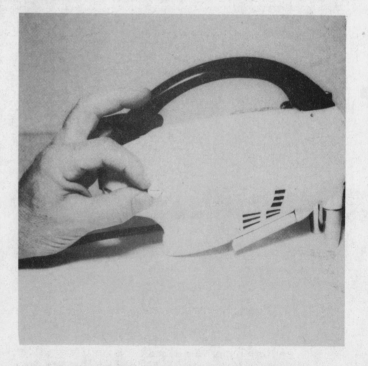

The motor assembly slides easily off the top of the pedestal mount, and stands comfortably on its front twin chucks. The brushes of the motor are at rear end of case. Their caps unscrew quickly.

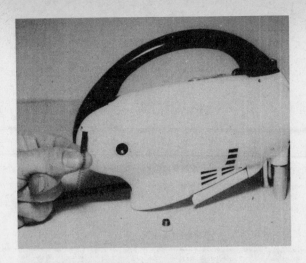

The small brush is of standard carbon type, with a fine wire spring attached. This keeps the end of the brush in firm contact with the "commutator" on the rear end of the motor shaft. Read down.

With the end off you can see that the grease in the gear box has settled well below the two gears connected to the twin chucks, leaving the drive mechanism dry. Shaft is lubricated, gears aren't.

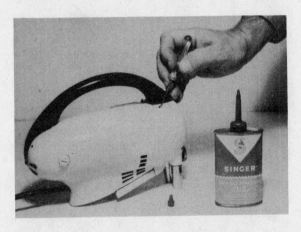

In this mixer, small holes are provided in front and back of housing for lubrication of the shaft. Don't squirt in oil; too much can foul the commutator. Let in one, solitary drop in each hole.

Redistribute the grease thoroughly, putting more of it near the top than at the bottom. This will keep the gears lubricated for another long period before it settles to the bottom of the case again.

Does the front end of the mixer sound grinding, noisy, even after addition of oil? This calls for opening the appliance and making sure that gears aren't stripped, or shaft bent, or just plain dry.

Light weight mixer can be used comfortably with one hand. It has no stand of its own, but when it must be stopped for a moment it can be rested on its heel, just like an iron. Speed control at top.

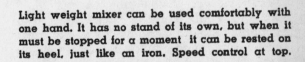

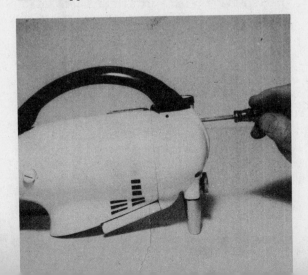

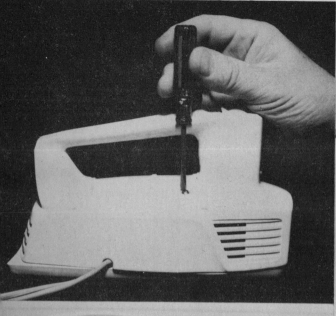

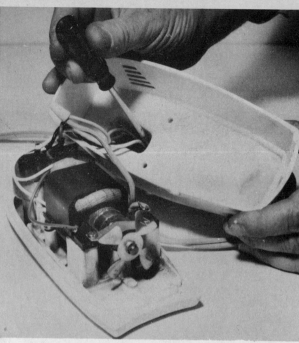

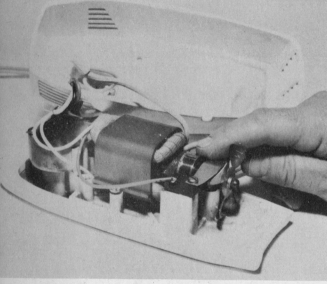

With the mixing blade removed, the portable mixer sits flat on the table, can be mistaken for an iron! Entire body top comes off when 2 screws are removed. The slots are for motor ventilation.

Completely in the clear when the top of the body is folded back, the motor and the gear assembly are easy to examine and clean. Finger points to copper commutator, against which brushes press.

Speed control switch is in handle, cannot be inspected readily. With single mounting screw removed, it drops out. In foreground, at end of the motor shaft, note small fan, for forced cooling.

damage, as well as the annoyance of spattering food all over the kitchen, get into the habit of leaving the blades in the bowl and waiting for the motor to stop after you turn off the switch. This sounds like a rather obvious suggestion, but many people can benefit from it.

Check the Brushes

Maintenance and repair of a mixer is largely a matter of checking the brushes, applying a bit of lubricant to the bearings (but only if the manufacturer's instruction sheet calls for it), and keeping the entire machine clean. In most models the brushes are readily accessible, being held under flat, slotted screws that require only a dime rather than a screwdriver.

One sign of impending brush trouble is

intermittent sparking and sputtering, accompanied by a strong odor; actually, that of ozone. Also, there might be grinding noises in a nearby radio receiver or broken-up pictures in a television set.

By the very nature of its applications a mixture is sure to inhale some of the froth it stirs up. An accumulation of this stuff inside the case can in time certainly affect the operation of the motor, so periodic cleaning is advisable.

If not kept clear of the work area, the cord of a hand-held mixer can sometimes get entangled in the whirling blades, with results that are more often funny than serious. If the user can't get at the switch fast enough the bowl might spill, pudding might decorate the walls, and the cord might acquire a few bruises. The small

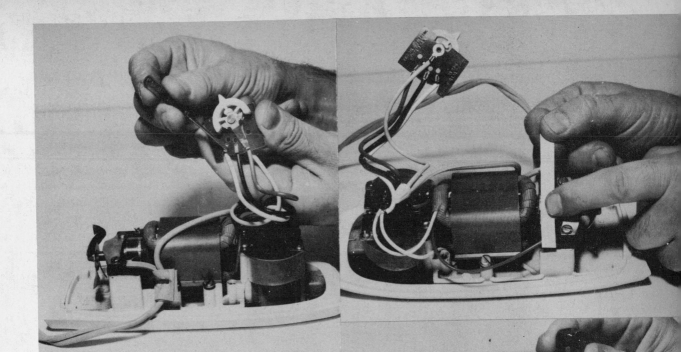

Examine contact surfaces of speed control switch for encrusted food, and scrape clean with small screwdriver or knife blade. Also pull lightly on connections to be sure there are no cold joints.

Motor will run smoothly and without sparking if the commutator is kept shiny. Hold a narrow strip of fine sandpaper against it with one finger, and turn rotor slowly by means of fan at end of shaft.

Check all mounting screws for tight fit. Look for a set screw in stud of small ventilating fan and secure it well. Before reassembly of body of mixer blow out or scrape away all food incrustations.

motor doesn't usually develop enough energy to sever the wire. A layer or two of electrical tape or white adhesive tape should take care of the bruises.

Lubrication of Gears

In all mixers, the right-angle drive mechanism uses gears of some kind. These might or might not be "lubricated for life" at the factory. If the appliance seems to get noisier and noisier with use, possibly the grease has leaked off gradually, or, more likely, has simply been thrown away from the gear teeth by centrifugal force. Fortunately, most mixers come apart easily, and a quick inspection will indicate whether more grease is needed or if the grease already there merely needs to be spread around better.

Speed control is an essential element in mixers, as the requirements of various preparations are different. The pedestal style appliance usually has a wide range of adjustment from very slow to very fast; the hand-held type, at least medium and fast. If the motor runs well at some settings of the control but poorly or not at all at others, the switch contacts are probably encrusted with batter of some kind. Usually, just scratching them clean with a small screwdriver is all they need. Actual breaks in connections are also to be expected, because of the normal vibration of the appliance.

In the accompanying picture sequence two mixers are shown in various stages of disassembly. The job is quite simple and requires only a screwdriver. •

FANS

The most effective place for them is in the attic of a house.

To see if it would really do any good in a hot attic, a large belt-driven fan was mounted temporarily in this manner against an opening in a dormer. It shook a little, but cooled the attic!

Improvement in house comfort was so noticeable that the fan was put on firmer support (top, left) and front edges were taped where they met siding. This eliminated leakage, gave even better draft.

Outer view of installation, above, before it was prettied up. Roof overhang protects against rain, screening against birds and insects. Louvers are better, but more costly. Pole is for TV aerial.

Another good installation of an attic ventilator. Powerful 24-inch fan is enclosed in plywood box, which can be opened for inspection and lubrication of motor. Louvers can be seen through blades.

FOR COOLING

LET'S START with a disclaimer: *fans do not cool.* In some circumstances the heat of their motors might actually raise the temperature instead of reducing it. But fans move air, and air moving through a moist area promotes evaporation, and evaporation tends to cool the immediate vicinity. Since it is high humidity rather than heat that makes people uncomfortable, it is safe to say that fans at least make us feel better.

Sitting in the direct blast of even a small fan is unhealthy. A fan is most effective if it is mounted in a window and can exhaust air from the room or rooms to the outside. There has to be air coming in from another opening to maintain the flow. This can be a window of another room of an apartment, or, best of all, a basement window.

A fan is particularly effective in removing the blanket of stagnant air that is always found in an unventilated attic during the summer. If not disturbed, this is what makes the upper bedrooms of a small house feel like ovens. The bigger the fan the better; for an average five- or six-room house, not smaller than 24 inches in diameter, and larger if it can be gotten in. The technique is to mount this in front of an opening in the side of the house and to leave the attic door or access trap open, so that fresher air from below will push out the stale attic air.

The difference in house comfort produced by this system of forced ventilation has to be experienced to be believed. People coming in from the outside on a summer day, when the temperature is close to 90, will invariably exclaim, "This air-conditioning is really great." It isn't the kind of air-conditioning they think it is, but it's still noticeable. •

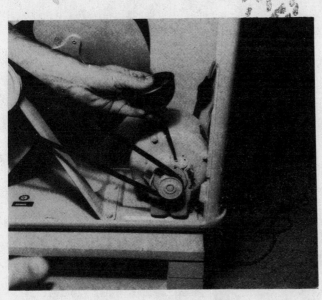

In hot weather the attic fan might be kept running for days on end, so lubrication of motor is important. Look for oil filler caps at both ends.

Bearings of belt-driven fan usually take grease rather than oil. Apply sparingly and often rather than heavily and rarely. Excess grease tends to work out and is spattered around by the fan.

With every lubrication job, check tightness of fan, motor and fan pulleys, belt, motor mounting bolts, and electrical connections. Running all day and night is bound to put some strain on 'em.

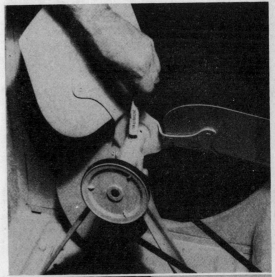

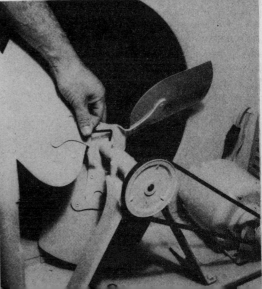

ELECTRIC CAN OPENERS

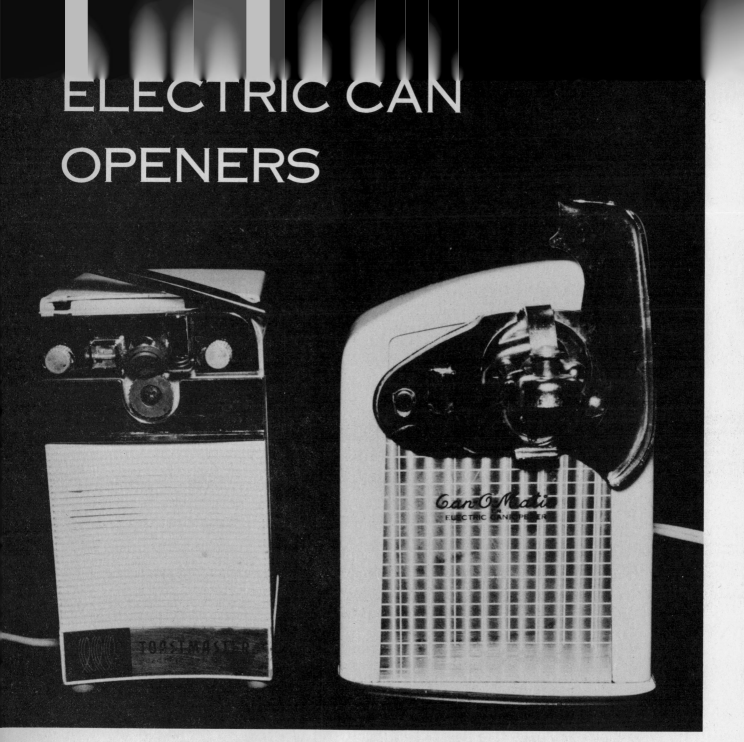

Electric can openers have a characteristic look: A vertical shape, two small angled cutting wheels and pivoted arm to secure the can. Small model at the left can be used on table or hung from wall.

CONSIDERING the number of cans of various kinds found in the American home, it is no wonder that the electric can opener is rapidly becoming one of the most popular labor-saving devices in the kitchen. It ranks high as a gift for newlyweds because it is not only useful but inexpensive.

An electric opener consists essentially of a small, high-speed motor connected to a pair of cutting wheels through a high-ratio reduction gear, usually of the worm type. The cutters develop considerable torque and easily bite their way through the rim of ordinary cans. In doing so they leave smooth edges, which means that the empty cans can be reused for many purposes.

Because this appliance is run for only seconds at a time it can be expected to give long service. Most models are "lifetime" lubricated; some might need a dab or two of light grease on the reduction gear every few years.

If an opener seems to be unduly noisy, perhaps the internal lubricant has settled to the bottom of the case and is not being distributed properly to the gears. As a cure

An opener in working condition does a fast, easy job on cans and simplifies meal preparation for housewife and bachelor alike. Magnet just above cutters holds the lid after it has been severed.

Finger points to major trouble spot in can opener: the junction of the two cutting wheels. Food accumulates here, hardens, and often interferes with operation. The area should be kept clean.

First step in cleaning representative opener is to remove magnet that holds lid after cutting is finished. This usually just pulls straight off, or in some models it might be held by two screws.

Upper cutter is not powered by the motor, but revolves with can as lower cutter turns latter. It is usually held by a hinged tooth, which can be released by a scratch awl or a small screwdriver.

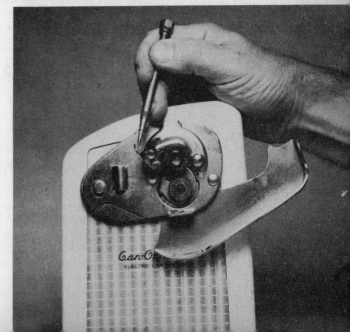

Since cutters dig into a can and touch its contents, food is bound to stick to them. Scrape removable cutter with a knife, and clean out the teeth of the powered wheel with a pointed tool.

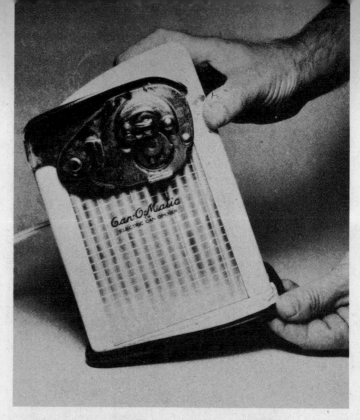

Want to see what makes a can opener work? Disassembly is generally easy, once you find where body screws are located. They weren't in sight on this model until the bumper on base was removed.

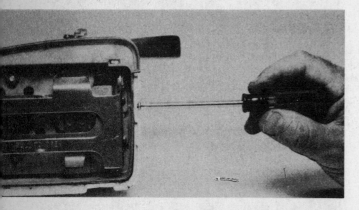

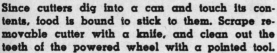

Case of opener is held to base by short screws of self-tapping type. Remove them carefully with well-fitting screwdriver to avoid mashing threads.

Case slides only this far because the line cord apparently is snagged short inside the case by a pinching-type plastic insulator near the bottom.

try the old clock trick of inverting the appliance. You can't very well run it this way, but if it is kept in a warm spot, like a radiator or the top of a gas stove that has a pilot light, the grease will certainly drip down to the gear train. This may not work with all styles of openers, but it is certainly worth trying.

What does require periodic attention is

the exposed cutting mechanism. When a can is being opened, some of the contents is bound to stick to the cutters or to drip over to the magnet that grabs the can's top. If enough of this goo hardens on the metal surfaces it can interfere with the operation of the device. First try brushing with a soapy solution. If this doesn't leave the area clean and bright, scrape with the

Vertically mounted motor, right, is seen to have worm gear on shaft that drives a larger gear at a much reduced rate. The motor switch is in small box, next to shaft. Its cover is being removed.

The trick in loosening the line cord insulator is to squeeze the narrow center part against the rim and at the same time to pull forward. It then slides out of hole along cord; case is now free.

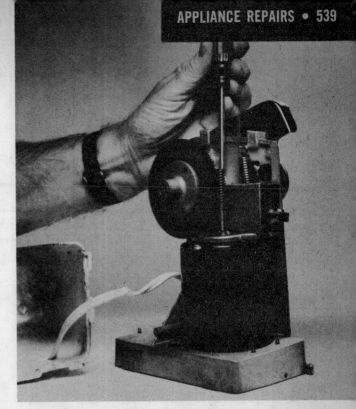

Of single pole momentary contact type, the motor switch has two leads to its terminals. Its snap opening and closing under tension of spring can be observed as opener handle is pushed, released.

Clicktester connected to the prongs of line plug gives loud response if motor and switch of opener are intact and handle is pressed and released several times. No sound is indication of trouble.

blade of a very thin screwdriver or the point of an old knife, and brush again.

The motor of an opener goes on when the handle that clamps the can in place is swung to its closed position. The actual switch is inside the case. Like all switches, it can sometimes stay either open or closed.

The switches in can openers are all of the momentary-contact type. That is, they close to "on" only as long as the clamp handle is kept down to hold the rim of a can. Remember this when checking a switch for its ability to close and open a circuit, either with the Clicktester or a VOM.

One of the openers shown in the pictures stopped working after it had been used only

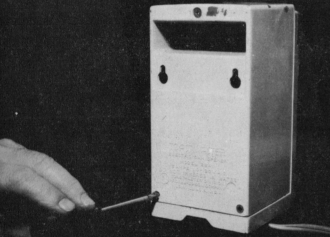

In this can opener, left, above, the upper cutting wheel and the handle are part of a single assembly, which is held by two thumb screws. These can be taken out in a few moments, for inspection.

Handle assembly removed, above, powered wheel is now in the open. The gear-like teeth around its rim are best cleaned with a scratch awl. If this is not available, a large pin will serve.

No trouble finding the screws on this can opener! There are two short ones along bottom edge and one long one at the top. Slotted holes above center line of case are for hanging unit on wall.

Reduction drive in this model consists of double pair of gears, with the motor in the normal horizontal position. A slight application of lubricant (auto grease, Vaseline, etc.) quiets the gears.

a few weeks. A check with the Clicktester hooked to the line plug indicated an open circuit. It seemed unlikely that the motor would go bad so soon, so the appliance was disassembled. When the very last two screws, on the switch housing, were removed, the cause of the failure was immediately obvious; one of the switch wires had worked itself loose. A three-second application of a hot soldering iron fixed it. •

DOOR BELLS

All they need to keep ringing are clean door buttons and some AC.

HOW many times have you visited people to find a sign taped to the front door, "Bell out of order. Please knock"?? Actually, it is very rarely that the bell itself is "out of order." It is operated for a few seconds at a time only a few times each day, and therefore should last forever.

In nine cases out of ten the bell doesn't ring because the bell button outside the door has dirty or corroded contacts. This is not surprising, since it is exposed to all kinds of weather. It is overlooked only because it is such an insignificant little object.

A bell button is held by two screws, which are easily removed, and it has two connections, which are also easily removed. If you touch the bare ends of these wires together and the bell clangs immediately, you know that a new button is all you have to buy. Usually it doesn't pay to spend the time to open the old one.

In the tenth case the bell ringing transformer that you'll find near the electric meter or the fuse box probably has a loose connection or two. How these develop is a bit mysterious. Most likely, the repeated slamming of a nearby garage door or the rumbling of passing trucks is responsible. Anyway, merely tightening the binding posts often gives the bell back its voice. It isn't necessary to turn off the juice; the voltage here is only about 14 or 16.

The exposed brass binding posts of this transformer represent one of two windings called the "secondary." The other winding, the "primary," is connected permanently to the AC line, usually by short wires disappearing into the fuse box. Most transformers of this type feel slightly warm; this is normal, and no cause for alarm. •

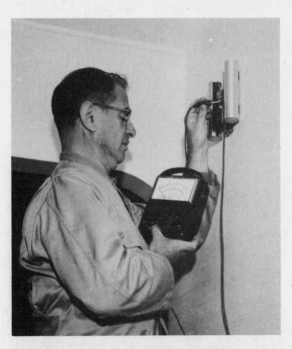

Is low-voltage AC from the transformer reaching the bell? To find out, jam a toothpick into the bell button, set the VOM for low-range AC volts, and touch test prods to binding posts of bell.

The button outside the door is most likely cause of bell failure. When removing it for inspection and probably replacement, pull out wires carefully. They are usually solid and break easily.

Erratic operation of a door bell can be fault of loose connections at the small transformer near the fuse box. First undo them, scrape them clean with knife, and refasten them well with pliers.

VACUUM CLEANERS

The long cords are vulnerable, but their big motors are easy to work on.

The vacuum cleaner probably takes the worst beating of any household appliance because it is used frequently, is dragged around mercilessly by its own cord, and is expected to ingest dust, buttons, string, pins, paper clips, etc., without developing indigestion. It also uses the largest motor, up to ½ horsepower.

In all models, fan blades of some kind are attached directly to the shaft of the motor. They are shaped and directed in such a manner that they draw outside air through the cleaning nozzle and its flexible hose

and into the dirt collecting chamber, a detachable cotton sack or a disposable paper bag. Strictly speaking, the expression "*vacuum* cleaner" is a misnomer. The system isn't really air-tight enough for a real vacuum to develop. It is probably more correct to say that the intake of air at the opening of the nozzle lowers the atmospheric pressure in the immediate vicinity of the latter. The other air in the room is heavier and rushes in instantly to fill the space. Any moderately light object that happens to be in the way is whooshed into the appliance.

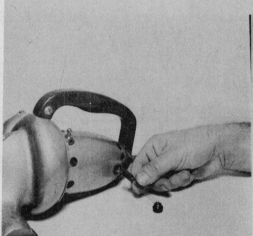

In small hand-held vacuum cleaner, usually used for furniture, brushes are at end of case and are easily removed for inspeciton or replacement. The switch is under handle. Holes are for ventilation.

It Blows Out Too

If the air pressure at the nozzle is negative, in the sense that it is lower than that of the room air, it is very much positive at the other end of the system. Advantage is taken of this situation in many cleaners to provide a powerful blast of air which is particularly useful for operating accessory sprayers. The air by itself is great for dislodging dust, insects, etc., from places that cannot be reached with a regular nozzle. The blower fitting, normally closed by a little trap door, takes the same flexible hose used for vacuuming.

Cleaner motors are of the brush type and therefore require the usual inspection of the brushes themselves. In small hand-held machines the latter are accessible from the outside. In most larger machines the motor is usually enclosed in the case. Accessibility is generally good, because the cases have to open easily anyway for cleaning or replacement of the dirt sack.

A vacuum cleaner does cleaning, but

One reason why this cleaner sounded odd: tangle of string and dirt was caught in blades, could not free itself. Fortunately, entire motor and blower assembly is held by only 4 machine screws.

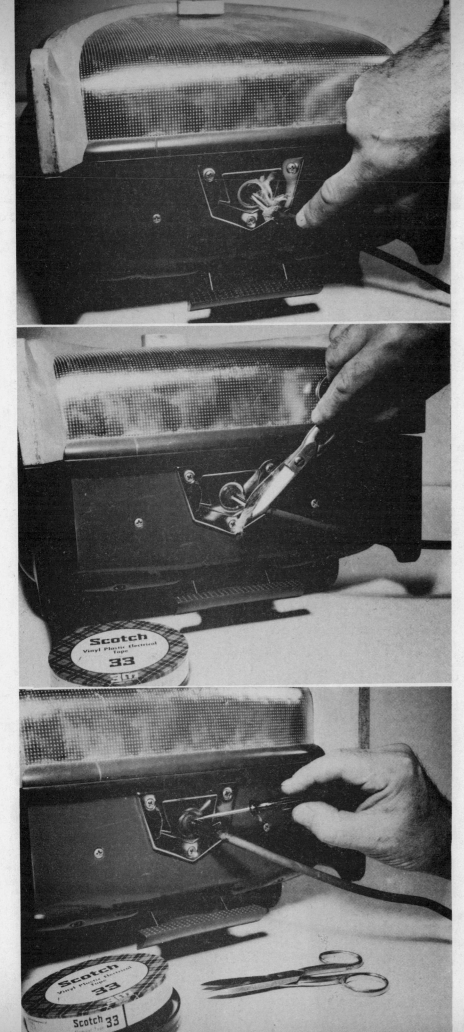

Heavy cleaner was dragged around by its cord; result, outer insulation at point of entrance into case wore away. A little more of this mistreatment and cord would have short-circuited to case.

Wires themselves were intact, so all loose insulation was trimmed away with scissors and thick layer of electrician's tape was wound as close to case as possible. Pedal is on-off foot switch.

Soft grommet in case permitted taped cord to be pushed in with thin screwdriver. This is important; otherwise tape doesn't really protect wires. Often the repair is easier if grommet is removed.

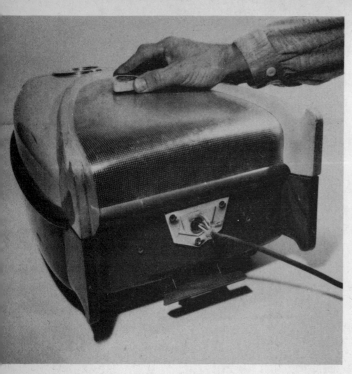

Access to inside of this flat-type vacuum is from top. Decorative knob in center is actually lock. A quarter turn in either direction, top comes off. The cord can be wound around rear "ears" of case.

The first step in inspecting a vacuum cleaner is to open it up. In this typical canister machine the first screws in sight are six through the bottom. Remove screws carefully; avoid stripping.

Motor operation was irregular. Switch was prime suspect, so it had to be removed. Connections to line cord and motor here are by twist-on caps, which are loosened by pliers or by the fingers.

If connections do not yield readily, don't waste time fighting them. It's usually easier to snip them off with side cutters and to resolder them later. The folding clamp secures top of cleaner.

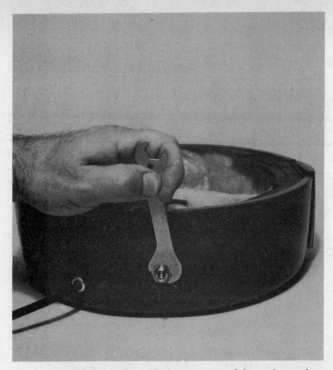

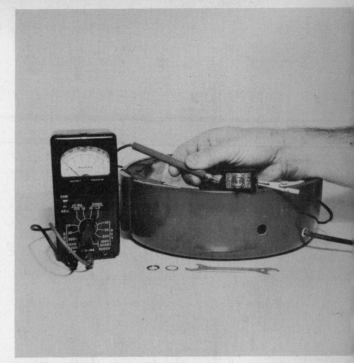

Standard toggle switch is mounted by a large hex nut on a threaded stud. Remove it with a wrench, not pliers. Latter will almost always damage the finish. This "pan" is the bottom of the cleaner.

On-off switch is removed from case for convenience in testing with small VOM. set to read LO OHMS. Jiggling of needle with the switch on indicates bad contacts and need for replacement.

Motor appeared to be mounted in sieve-like cage in bottom of top half of the cleaner. Six more screws around mounting rim could be seen. Some were already loose, probably from motor shake.

Perforated cage lifts out readily and is followed by the motor, which is mounted in an upright position in a shallow metal dish. This area has to be cleaned occasionally; perhaps once a year.

With motor removed from case, top, left, the brushes and the commutator are in view. Here, one of the brush retaining strips is being removed, so that the brush can now be examined for condition.

Spring attached to brush, above, keeps it in firm contact with copper segments of the commutator. Note size of brushes and obtain replacements. Commutator's black from carbon, needs a cleaning.

To restore brightness of commutator, rub gently with small strips of fine sandpaper, NOT emery cloth. Clean surfaces reduce sparking and carbon wear and minimize radio & TV interference.

itself it needs occasional cleaning. Unless a second machine is available in the home, this is best done outdoors with a long-handled brush that can reach into all corners. Check the direction of the wind and keep on the safe side. The fine dust that comes out can be very irritating.

If a cleaner gradually loses some of its early sucking power and a new dirt bag doesn't help, look into the flexible hose. Very frequently this is partially blocked by knots of carpet fuzz and string snared against trapped pins or toothpicks. A little poking with a rifle cleaning rod, a plumbing "snake," or some similar long, round object, usually dislodges the obstruction.

Commutator sparking and hence radio/TV interference are further controlled by "suppressor" unit on motor frame. This is actually a small capacitor. With motor exposed, check it with VOM.

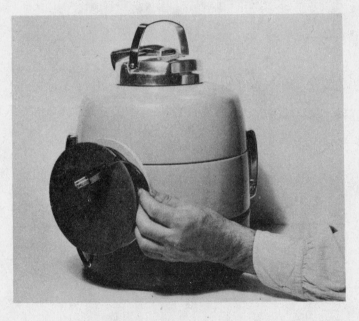

Home-made reel for vacuum cleaner cord consists of two discs of hardboard with center separator. It is mounted loosely to case with one machine screw so that it turns easily. Slot holds plug.

Air leakage in the hose is due merely to cracks. You can locate these easily by running your hand along it. Electrician's tape is fine for patching them, since it's flexible.

The Cord Is Convenient

It's no use telling a woman (or any other user of a vacuum cleaner) not to pull the machine along the floor by its cord, and not to disconnect the line plug by yanking at it. Sometimes the nozzle is a good tow line, but the cord is much longer and is easier to hold. So face it: you must examine the wire often, over its entire length for abrasions and other damage to the insulation, and at its ends for actual breaks. Line plugs of the molded type are quite strong and can take a lot of punishment, but there's a limit. The really weak point is where the cord enters the case of the machine. There is usually a grommet or other kind of ring here. A soft grommet cushions the flexing of the wire, but a metal one merely grinds its way into the insulation. When the latter becomes frayed, it is usually fairly easy to open the case, disconnect the leads, cut off three or four inches of the cord, form new leads, and connect them. If the grommet is big enough, reinforce the cord at the point of entry with tape. Most cords are 15 to 20 feet long, and the loss of a few inches isn't noticeable.

The on-off switch of most vacuum cleaners is foot operated and even the most rugged ones loosen or bend in time. In some models it is only a small toggle switch, but it can be kicked up and down with the toe of a shoe. This type was never intended for kicking and it doesn't last long.

Some cleaners of well-known make have absolutely no provision for storing the long cord. When a machine is put away in a closet the wire is usually left in a heap on the floor, where it is stepped on and otherwise mistreated. As minimum protection, form the wire into a loop about a foot in diameter, flatten it down about half way, and secure the loose ends with a couple of thick rubber bands. It can then be hooked over the handle of the cleaner, or held between the body and a wall.

Probably because they are buried inside the cases of the machines, most vacuum cleaner motors are designed not to require lubrication by the users. Their bearings are usually oversize and may have enough factory-filled grease to last a long time. In general they give very good service; they rarely fail completely. The usual incidental items are what need attention: brushes, switches, cords.

The accompanying picture sequences show three entirely different kinds of cleaners and what might have to be done to them. •

Next stop, the junk yard. Everything valuable or usable has been stripped from this worn-out washing machine, as it should be. The motor was still in good shape and is now running a powerful attic fan.

SALVAGING PARTS

Before discarding that worn-out appliance, search it for useful hardware.

DRIVE on a Monday morning through almost any suburban community in the United States and you'll be struck by an odd sight: here and there, sitting unhappily at the curb, is a partially dismantled clothes washer, or perhaps a dish washer, or an air conditioner, or a mangle . . . down the line to a sprinkling of grills and toasters. It may not be true that appliances, like automobiles, have obsolescence built into them at the factory, but it sure looks that way.

The clothes washer is the commonest discard, probably for the reason that it does more real physical work than any other household device. In a family containing several children the parents are lucky if a washer survives the period from the advent of the first one to the arrival of the second. There are *always* diapers to do!

No Trade-In Value

The trade-in value of used appliances is virtually zero. If you shop around for a new one a dealer will offer you what looks like a generous allowance for your tired washer, and then he'll tell you to junk it. He won't even bother to take it away, unless he has a connection with a local scrap metal yard. He doesn't lose any money by his "generous allowance," because most list prices are highly inflated and are only the starting point for bargaining.

It is a pity just to put an appliance on

the street and wait for the sanitation people to pick it up. (And even that takes a special appointment in some cities!) Even a machine that has stopped working altogether is not valueless. Stripped down to the last removable component, it can yield a rich treasure of useful odds and ends.

Consider the usual clothes washer. Cut off the line cord and you have a fine replacement for use with any electrical device. Trace the internal wiring until the motor is free, and then dismount it. It is usually a ⅓ horsepower unit of rugged construction, ideal for the operation of a grinder, a buffing wheel, a jig saw, a medium-size bench saw, a water pump, an air compressor, an attic fan, a garage door opener, etc. Yet people unthinkingly let it disappear with the garbage!

Motor Can Be OK

Although the motor is the heart of a washer, it does not "go bad" nearly as much as owners believe. Many are equipped with thermal cutouts that open the AC line in case of a severe overload (that is, too much dirty laundry); others simply blow the line fuse if they stall. Much more common are failures of the water control valves; of the clutch mechanisms for fill, agitate, drain and spin; and of the timer that controls these actions. The motor can still be in perfect running condition after all these devices have expired.

The mere mounting hardware in the average clothes or dish washer is worth several dollars if you buy it new. Sturdy bolts and nuts as large as ½ inch, lock washers, springs, brackets, clamps, etc., all will surely be valuable for the repairs that always have to be done around a house.

The timer is nothing more than a geared down clock motor. Remove the cams that actuate the exposed switch levers and you have the basis for a variety of small toys to amuse youngsters.

Of simpler construction than a clothes washer, a dish washer still yields a rich harvest: again a motor, perhaps a little smaller than ⅓ h.p.; a timer; hardware; and often a beautiful propeller of brass or hard plastic. The function of the latter is, of course, to splash the water around the dishes, which are stationary. If nothing else, it makes an odd decoration, a conversation piece, in a den.

"Oh, that?" you'll probably say to guests. "From my wrecked dish washer." They were probably expecting you to say "from my wrecked yacht," so they're bound to laugh.

Air conditioners and refrigerators are not usually good pickings because much of their mechanism is sealed. Of all household appliances they enjoy the longest life. One of the earliest refrigerators was the General Electric "monitor top" introduced in the 1920's; thousands of them are still making ice cubes more than forty years later.

Remove Refrigerator Door!

If you must discard a really "gone" box, do not fail to remove the door before you put it out in the cold. You'll sleep better knowing that no child will suffocate to death after locking himself in any refrigerator that *you* once owned.

Small appliances can be just as rewarding as large ones. Many a hair dryer, vacuum cleaner, food mixer, etc., ends up at the curb only because of some trivial fault: a broken brush in a somewhat inaccessible motor, easily replaced if the latter is dismounted; a heating wire grounded to the case, giving off sparks and frightening the owner out of keeping a dryer; a grease-jammed timer in a table-top grill, preventing the spit from turning; and so on. You can fix the troubles and restore the machines to normal operation; or, if they are too dirty and scarred, you can at least strip 'em for parts. Give boys a couple of wrenches and screwdrivers, and they'll keep busy for hours at this work.

Small Hardware Is Useful

Don't overlook small items such as headless set screws with slotted or hexagonal female ends; ⅜ and ½ inch hex nuts used on the mounting studs of toggle switches; soldering lugs and terminals; shafts, pulleys and bushings; gears and cams; all pieces of insulated flexible wire more than about a foot long; line plugs and similar friction-type connectors; small lamps and pilot lights; fuses, circuit breakers and thermal overload protectors; insulating washers; brackets and clamps; leveling feet; etc. Keep these odds and ends in labeled cigar boxes, and you'll find yourself dipping into them frequently.

Some things like thermostats are not worth salvaging because they are designed to work under specific conditions in particular appliances and are not likely to work satisfactorily in others. But do take off screws, nuts, washers, etc. •

ELECTRIC KNIVES

These are simple motor-operated devices that are easy to keep in order.

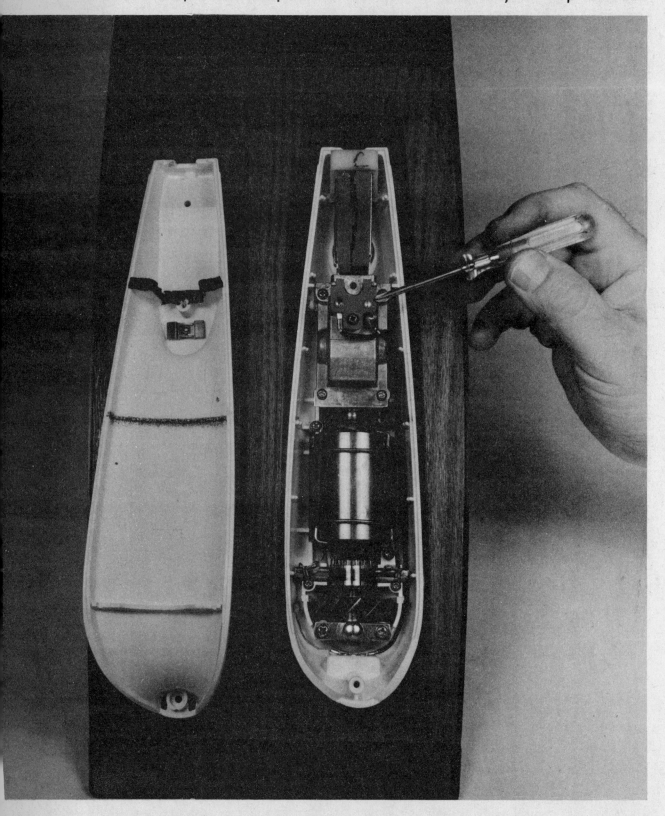

Opened lengthwise like a pickle, the electric knife is seen to have very neat, simple and accessible "works." Screwdriver points to contacts of the switch. Blades fit at top. Drive motor is at the bottom.

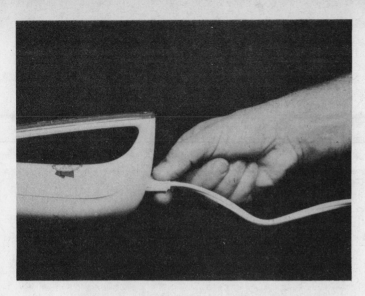

DO. When inserting or removing the line plug of knife, push or pull with a firm, straight motion. DON'T. Don't grab cord and pull or twist. In time this will surely damage both cord and connector.

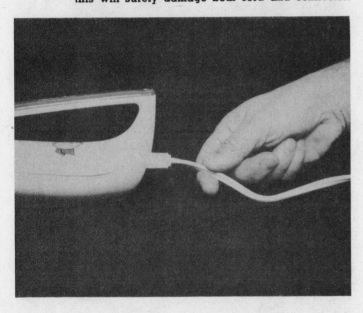

To open the knife, look for body screws. Usually these are of Philips or cross-head type and require well-fitting X-type screwdriver. Turn the latter carefully to avoid damage to the threads.

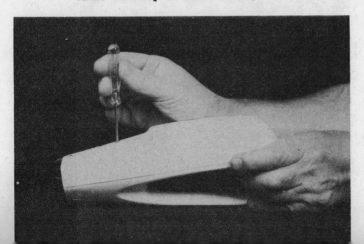

WHEN the electric knife first appeared on the market it was regarded by many people merely as a conversation piece or a status symbol. However, anyone who has owned and used one for any length of time swears by it as a practical addition to the kitchen or the dining room.

Basically, the device consists of a compact but powerful little motor, a gear drive that converts the rotary motion of the motor's shaft to a reciprocating (back and forth) motion, and a knife that is actually a pair of blades. One of the blades is stationary and the other jigs back and forth a fraction of an inch. The edges are serrated, and they bite their way through the toughest meats (and some bones, too!) with surprising ease. You only have to hold the appliance steadily and press down with it lightly.

In a typical knife the motor uses an Alnico permanent magnet field with a conventional armature and commutator. It looks a little small for a 115-volt motor, and investigation reveals that it actually works on about 50 volts DC although it is plugged into a regular 115-volt AC line. The answer to this seeming contradiction is that the circuit includes a tiny rectifier that changes the AC to DC and at the same time reduces the voltage.

The knife shown in the illustrations split conveniently into two sections when the body screws were removed, and the entire mechanism was laid bare. The two brushes that bear on the commutator are readily accessible for inspection or replacement, and the commutator itself can be cleaned in a minute with a small strip of fine sandpaper held against it as it is turned by hand.

In common with other motor-operated appliances that are used only for short periods, electric knives generally do not require lubrication as part of their maintenance. If there are oil holes near the ends of the shaft, apply light oil very sparingly . . . as small a drop as possible.

The control switch on most knives has two positions: On as long as the switch button is kept down with a finger, and on without finger pressure once the button is set about a quarter of a turn to the right.

The line cord is generally loose and plugs in near the back of the handle. A caution: When using the knife, drape the cord behind you, well away from the blades. If the latter hit the cord they most likely will go part of the way through before the dead short-circuit on the wires blows the fuse or circuit breaker in the line. •

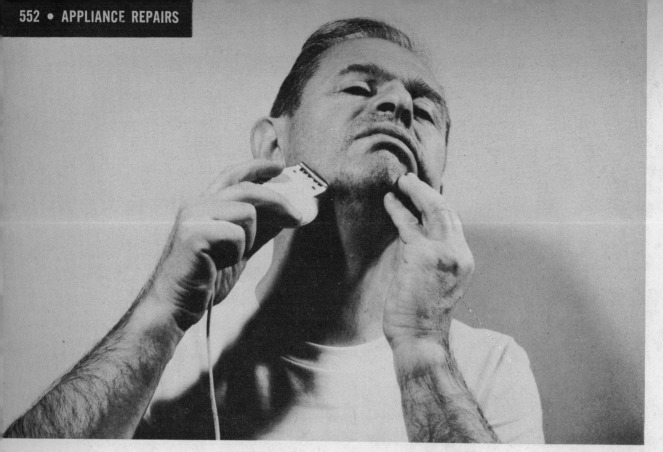

An electric razor cuts hairs closely without gashing the skin. Keep the hands, cord and razor dry.

ELECTRIC RAZORS

They're noisy but effective, and they'll keep buzzing if you keep 'em clean.

IN MANY homes these days the raucous buzzing of father's electric razor is mother's signal to get up and start the coffee. The noise made by this little appliance is probably the only strike against it. It eliminates shaving cream and gashed skin, saves the cost of blades, and leaves the face clean and dry.

By no means an exclusive convenience for men, the electric shaver, in smaller and more delicate designs, has also been adopted enthusiastically by women for removing fuzz from their legs.

These razors use two general forms of motive power: vibrator and motor. The basic vibrator is virtually a refined household buzzer. Alternating current from the house line passes through an electromagnet, near the ends of which is suspended an iron bar called an armature. As the AC varies in strength and direction, it attracts the armature and releases it in rhythm with these changes. The armature is linked to one set of small cutting blades, usually shaped like a comb, which is interleaved with a fixed set. The head of the

razor is pressed against the hair, and this is snipped off as it gets trapped between the movable and fixed blades. The actual range of movement is very small; about a hair's breadth, to use an appropriate expression!

In the second type a small motor might agitate the blades, or it might drive rotary cutters.

Some razors have means of adjusting the depth of cut to suit the beard, the condition of the skin and the appearance the user wishes to obtain.

Keep 'Em Clean

If a man has a heavy beard and shaves daily, little bunches of hair are bound to accumulate in the razor mechanism. They can readily reduce the cutting action to the point where the head of the device merely rubs over the skin. For this reason frequent cleaning, *dry*, is highly important. A tiny brush is packed with most razors; use it! Some heads can be disassembled quickly for a thorough scrubbing; others take a bit of doing.

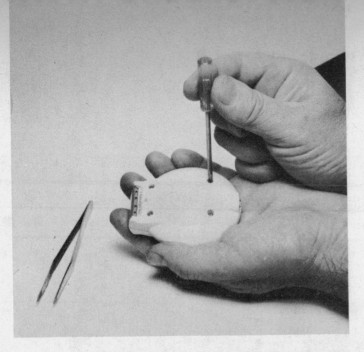

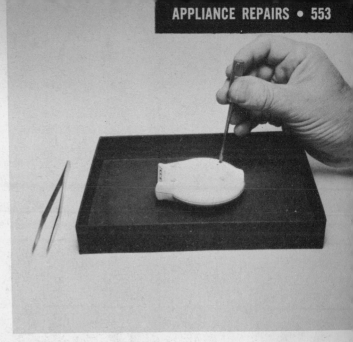

Many razors look like clam shells, and split open like them. As they normally require frequent internal inspection, they are usually constructed to come apart easily. Look for small body screws.

This is one way to keep screws and various other small parts from getting lost: open the razor in a shallow box, preferably of contrasting color. Tweezers (left) are invaluable for replacing parts.

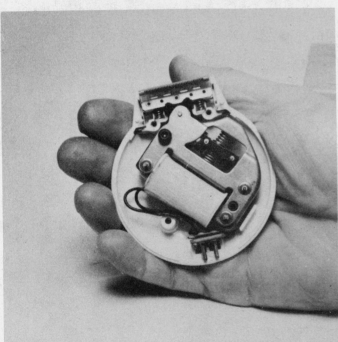

With one half of the clam shell removed, the entire insides of the razor can be examined closely. Small prongs, bottom, are for line connector. Note particularly the fit of armature to cutters.

In this razor none of the components are actually fastened to the body. They merely fit into molded ribs in the two halves of the clam, and become secure only when the latter are screwed together.

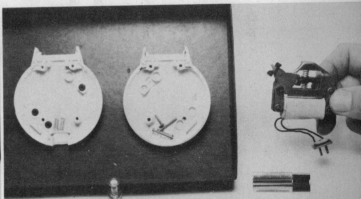

Since all electric razors connect to the 115-volt house line and most shaving is done over or near a sink, which is an electrical "ground," make very, very sure that the hands, the razor and the cord are all thoroughly dry.

Almost all cords are of the detachable type, which makes them easy to roll up and pack with the shavers in their boxes. The connector that goes into base of the razor is usually a rather small, thin one with the wire molded into it. As is the case with heavier cords made for irons, grills and the like, these cannot be repaired. If the small plug becomes damaged, there's no choice but to buy a whole new cord.

Some razors are built like fine watches. If you want to take one apart to see what makes it buzz, remove screws carefully and make mental notes of where the parts fit. •

Dust off the keyboard before and after machine is used and it will stay clean and pleasant to use.

ELECTRIC TYPEWRITERS

Keep a machine clean and lubricated and it will always write well.

ONCE a status symbol for the secretaries of big-shot business executives, the electric typewriter is now just another household appliance. It is probably the most popular—and useful—of all the gifts wished on high-school graduates.

Full-size office machines are very expensive; in the neighborhood of about $500 and up, mostly up. The new portables, however, are much more reasonable, and also more convenient. They are only slightly larger than manual portables but appreciably heavier because of the extra machinery in them. You wouldn't want to lug one around for an hour, but you can carry it in and out of a car or up and down

Keep an unused paint brush near a typewriter and wield it frequently to remove erasures and dust. Turn the machine to this position, so that dirt will fall away from it instead of into the keys.

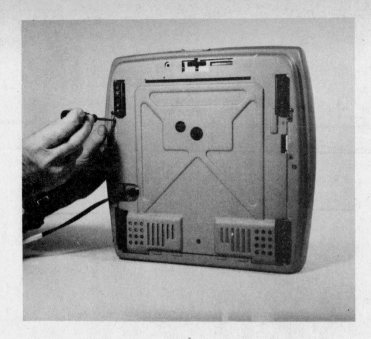

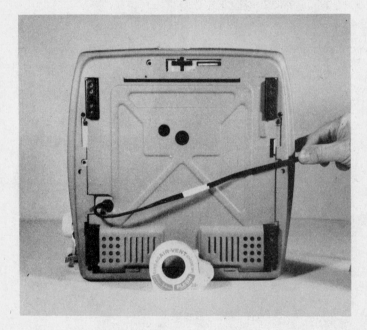

The bottom of typewriter is usually protected by a metal or plastic cover, which unscrews easily. Oblong pieces in the corners are rubber feet. Note how line cord emerges from the lower left corner.

Inside machine should be kept just as clean as outside. Remove fluff with paint brush. Examine drive mechanism for bearings, and use thin oil on them very sparingly. Motor is at lower left.

A damaged line cord can make case of typewriter alive electrically and dangerous to the touch. Ordinary adhesive tape is excellent for covering worn spots. It is strong, and very good insulator.

stairs, when necessary, without any strain.

The electric machine gets its muscle from a small, high-speed motor that turns the equivalent of a compact flywheel. When you touch a key some of the kinetic energy of the wheel is used to release the actual strike bar, the end of which presses the letter to the ribbon and the paper beneath. It doesn't make any difference whether you just flick the key or tromp on it; the impression made on the paper is the same.

The motor mechanism is usually rather complicated, and the best thing to do with it is to leave it alone except for inspection for possible loose screws and for cleaning. Cleaning, in fact, is the keynote to type-writer maintenance, according to the manufacturers. Most trouble is caused by accumulations of bits of paper mixed with rubbings from erasers. The latter are of course abrasive, and in time can raise hob with bearings.

Excessive oil is also bad, because it holds this rubbish. Some lubrication of bearings and joints is necessary, but tiny drops will do a better job than a wholesale spraying.

As in many other appliances, it's the line cord that usually gives trouble long before the typewriter itself develops any. There isn't much bottom clearance on some machines, and the wire can readily be mashed by their weight. •

FLASHLIGHTS & BATTERIES

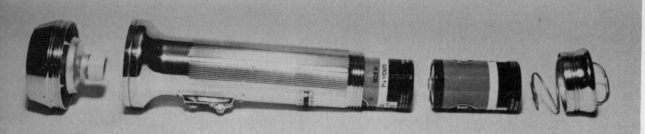

In this style of 2-cell flashlight both ends of the case unscrew. At left is bulb and reflector assembly. At right is opening for the batteries. Spring in cap keeps the latter in tight contact for flow of power.

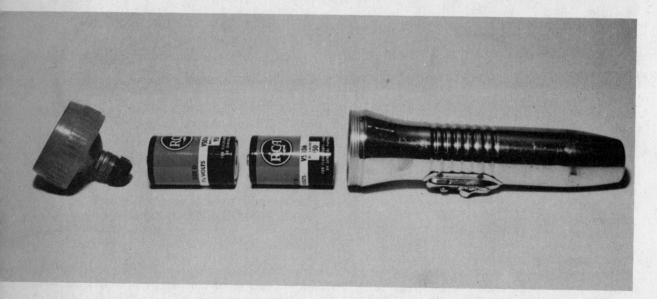

In this style only the bulb assembly comes away from the case; the batteries are dropped into the latter from the top. If they ever bulge because of leakage removal becomes virtually impossible.

IS AN ordinary flashlight considered an electrical appliance? If you're ever caught in the house without one when the electric service fails (for instance, during a storm) you'll learn quickly that it's a mighty useful little "appliance." And it's more than an emergency aid. It's also great for helping to find coins, buttons, jewelry and other small objects that annoyingly roll under furniture or into other dark spots.

If there are children in the house, and a parent wants to go to the bathroom or indulge in a midnight snack in the kitchen without turning on room lights, a flashlight lights the way without awakening anyone.

By far the most widely used flashlight is

the cylindrical type that works on two dry cells of the "D" size. A slightly smaller model uses two "C" cells, which are a bit smaller than the "D." The light from the two are the same, but for about the same initial cost and battery maintenance the larger model is favored because the "D" cells last much longer than the "C."

The secret of long battery life is to keep the light on only when it is absolutely necessary. Conventional dry batteries are intended only for intermittent service, and their voltage drops off rather rapidly if they are kept on too long. However, they have an interesting characteristic; given even short periods of rest, they recuperate quickly. Eventually, the chemicals and other materials in them that generate the electricity will be exhausted, and then replacement is in order.

If batteries are not too far gone it is possible to revive them up, to a point, but for what the "charger" costs you can keep yourself in fresh cells for ten years, without the bother.

Battery Types Compared

For flashlight purposes there is no real advantage in buying the much more expensive dry cells of the alkaline or mercury type. The alkaline is intended for toys and other devices that require much heavier current than that of a flashlight bulb. The mercury is intended particularly for transistor radio sets and other "solid-state" electronic gear that take relatively small currents but are kept on for long periods.

"Dry" cells aren't dry at all, but contain a definitely damp paste-like mixture of chemicals. This goo has a tendency to expand and to leak through the thin zinc body of the battery. When this happens the cells usually become so tightly jammed inside the case of the flashlight that they cannot be forced free without actually wrecking the case.

Most American brand-name batteries have leak-proof cases, but many imported cells lack this feature. They're cheap, but they need to be checked frequently. If they show any signs of a white discharge throw them away, right away.

Any time you open a flashlight to inspect it, brighten up the top and bottom contacts of the cells with sandpaper or emery cloth or any other abrasive that happens to be on hand. Do the same for the center contact of the bulb. This simple treatment often revives a seemingly dying pair of batteries and makes the bulb shine again.

A new flashlight cell measures 1.5 volts;

two in series, as used in a flashlight, thus develop 3 volts. Yet the miniature bulb designed for a two-cell light is rated at 2.3 or 2.4 volts. Why doesn't it burn out quickly? Further, why do most bulbs actually outlast many sets of batteries? The answers lie in the fact that the voltage of conventional dry cells starts to fall off quite soon after a "load" is placed on them; in this case it's the bulb. The reduction is fractional, but it's enough to bring the temperature of the bulb's filament below the melting point.

Most chemical actions are slowed down by cold. Dry cells are definitely affected,

A new cell should measure 1½ volts on low-range DC scale of a VOM. If light dims, check out both cells. Sometimes only one is poor, about 1.1 v., while the other still has lots of energy left.

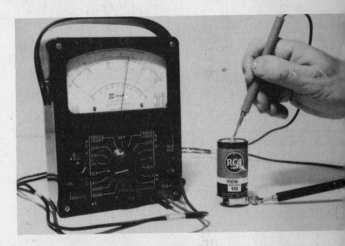

Size comparison of "D" flashlight cell, left, and "C" size, right. Both generate 1.5 volts, but the larger one naturally lasts longer and is a better buy at 18 cents against 13 for the "C" cell.

Before discarding batteries if light grows dark try this simple stunt of cleaning all contacts. It often removes slight chemical corrosion that introduces resistance to the flow of electricity.

In most flashlights bulb has prefocused filament and flanged base and fits in plastic holder that screws over end of reflector. Examine occasionally and clean contacts. Standard bulb is PR-2.

The equivalent of two "D" cells stacked at left, the one-piece battery at the right is a unique storage cell with built-in charger. It produces a steady light and can be re-used indefinitely.

When the top of the storage battery is unscrewed, the insulated end of the case can be seen to have two prongs just like those on conventional line plug. They connect to internal charger and battery.

The battery recharges overnight when it is merely plugged into 115-volt AC outlet. Charge current is small and there is little danger of overcharging. Battery is of the nickel-cadmium type.

Having the same dimensions as two "D" cells, chargeable battery fits accurately in standard flashlight. It is sealed and leakproof and it can be left in flashlight for long periods without bulging.

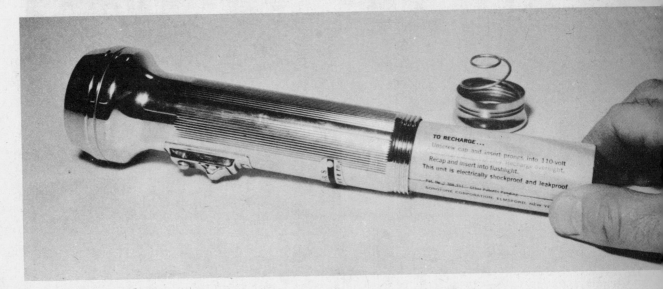

but usually not permanently. A flashlight in a car in an unheated garage during the winter might just about light, but keep it in the house for a few hours and it will come back to life.

Rechargeable Batteries

If you use a flashlight a great deal it might pay to invest in some of the interesting new sealed nickel-cadmium storage batteries in the same size and shape as ordinary batteries. What makes them interesting is that they have their own chargers built right into their cases! Unscrew the top and you find a pair of prongs exactly like those of a line plug. Plug them into any AC outlet and overnight a battery that was all spent is again full of pep. •

SMALL TABLE LAMPS

Using automobile bulbs, they offer good high-intensity illumination.

Fractured, but not a hopeless case. The plastic hinge joining the reflector and the top arm gave way, and the bulb shattered. The whole assembly felt loose; the decision was to open it for a look.

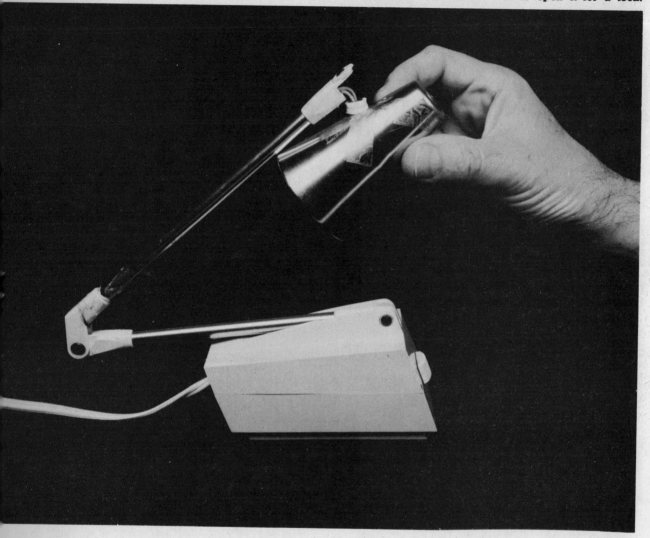

SMALL LAMPS about the size of a tea-cup have become very popular because they concentrate a lot of light into a small area and are therefore effective for reading of books, working on intricate pieces of equipment, etc. What's different about them? Well, ordinary table lamps use screw-base bulbs that work directly off the 115-volt house line. The "minis" use bayonet-base 14-volt *automobile* bulbs that work off step-down transformers in the base of the lamp assembly.

Some lamps have "high-low" switches that give two intensities of illumination. The lamp voltage in "high" is slightly

above normal, in "low" slightly below. The lamp will run cooler and last much longer in low, as might be expected.

A common complaint about the minis is that the bulbs burn out too soon. This is probably due to the desire of some manufacturers to make their lamps seem brighter than their competitors'; they achieve this end simply by boosting the transformer voltage. The bulbs are brighter, sure enough, but at the expense of highly increased temperature and much reduced life.

Keep a few spares on hand. A burn-out is sure to occur just when you are all curled

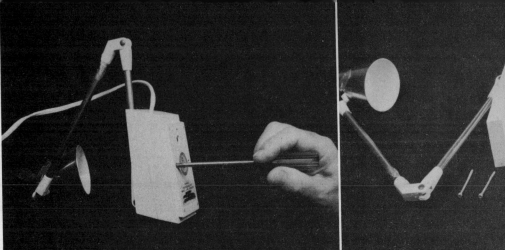

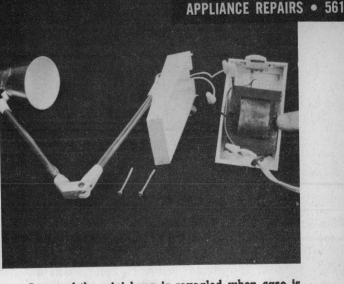

Only fasteners in sight were two screws of the Philips-head type. These were very tight but they yielded to X-point screwdriver that fit snugly. Screws had been threaded directly into plastic.

Secret of the mini lamp is revealed when case is pried open. A transformer (dark object at right) steps house line down to about 14 volts, more or less. On-off switch is in circuit to wall outlet.

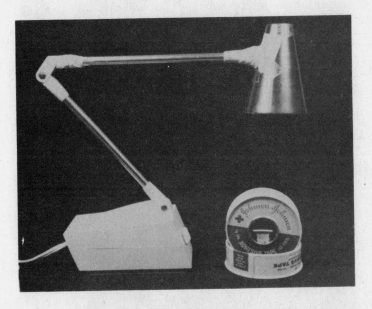

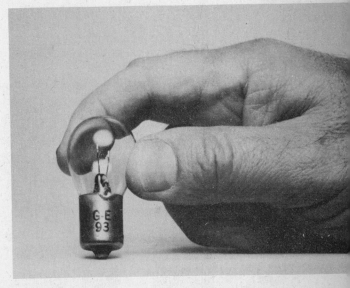

Reassembled and repaired, lamp is as good as new—almost. Reflector is fastened securely to arm with ordinary adhesive tape from family medicine chest. No more hinge action, but plenty of light.

Standard bulb for small lamps is single-contact bayonet base automobile type, General Electric No. 93 or equivalent. Short pins near bottom of base lock it in socket after glass is turned slightly.

up and start to read—so keep them handy.

Automobile bulbs are identified by number. The most widely used one seems to be the General Electric 93.

Most of the troubles that develop with these little lamps is physical. Because they are small and relatively light they can be upset rather readily. The one shown in the illustrations was accidentally pushed off a night table, and the reflector head broke away at the plastic hinge where it joins one of the two adjustable arms. Cement failed to hold the fracture, but a tight bandage of ½-inch adhesive tape restored the lamp to usefulness.

To remove a burned-out bulb, press down on the glass body and at the same time turn it slightly to the left; it will then pop out into your fingers. To install a replacement, put it into the socket and turn it loosely to the right until you feel it drop slightly. Press down and turn a little more to engage the pins in the base of the lamp with the slots in the socket.

In most mini lamps the step-down transformer is sealed in the base and in some models it can get pretty warm after long periods of use. This is no cause for alarm as long as you can touch the base without being scorched. •

HOW TO MIX GOOD

The simple recipe calls for portland cement, sand, gravel, and water

IT ISN'T difficult to make good concrete. All you have to do is follow a few easy rules. The recipe is simple. The ingredients used are portland cement, sand, gravel, and water.

Sand and gravel are often referred to as aggregates. Sometimes other aggregates than sand and gravel are used. The most common alternates to gravel are crushed stone and cinders.

This is what makes concrete tick: When the soft gray powder we know as portland cement is mixed with water it forms a sticky paste. A chemical reaction between the cement and the water makes the paste harden. In hardening, it binds together the

fine and coarse aggregates mixed with it, and it all becomes one solid, rocklike mass.

Note that *portland* cement is not a brand name. It is a *kind* of cement. Cement of other types have been used in building for thousands of years. The Egyptians had a lime and gypsum mortar that they used in building the pyramids. The Romans made cement mortar out of lime and volcanic ash, and they used concrete in making the foundations of the Forum. But cement making became a lost art during the Dark Ages. Then in the 18th century "natural cement" was discovered.

Natural cement is a limestone of special composition. When heated and pulverized,

CONCRETE

it is usable as cement. In 1824, Joseph Aspidin, an English bricklayer, found he could make cement artificially. He did it by burning clay and limestone in his kitchen stove and then grinding the resulting clinker. He called it portland cement because it reminded him of the color of stone on the Isle of Portland, off the British coast.

Manufacture of portland cement in the United States dates back to shortly after the Civil War. In 1902, Thomas Edison invented the type of rotary kiln now used by the cement industry. His invention makes possible the present tremendous production of about 300,000,000 barrels of

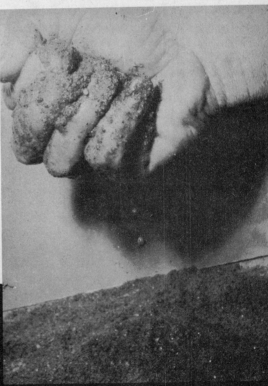

DAMP SAND (photo above, left) contains 1 quart of water per cubic foot. It feels damp to the touch, but it can't be formed into a ball. Wet sand (photo above, right) is kind usually supplied by dealers. It contains 2 quarts per cubic foot, is readily squeezed into a ball. Very wet sand (top photo) glistens, sticks to skin, may drip. It contains about 3 qts. of water per cubic foot. Allow for moisture when mixing concrete.

BASIC SECRET of making good concrete is accurate measurement of ingredients, thorough blending, and addition of minimum of water needed for workability, as the workman shows in the photo on opposite page.

cement a year—a barrel is four sacks.

Today, when we use the word "cement" we generally mean portland cement. Limestone, clay, cement rock, gypsum and other materials go into the manufacture of this powder. It's ground so fine most of it will go through a screen with 40,000 openings per square inch.

Varieties of Cement. Many types of cement are made, of which five are in common use and readily available at most dealers, usually in 94 pound bags (1 cu. ft.). They are:

Standard. Ordinary gray cement. Used for all general construction—footings, foundations, sidewalks, terraces, and the making of mortar. If you don't specify otherwise, this is the kind you'll get when you ask for cement.

White. Similar in every way to regular gray cement except that its white color makes it possible to mix light-colored mortar and concrete. When concrete or mortar are to be colored, white cement will keep the colors cleaner and sharper.

High Early Strength. Hardens and develops strength much faster than regular cement. Permits quick use of walks and driveways, shortens the time concrete must be protected in cold weather.

PORTLAND CEMENT in prime condition is soft and silky to the touch. If it has lumps that don't readily break, cement has absorbed a damaging quantity of moisture.

GOOD GRAVEL or crushed stone should consist of particles ranging in size from ¼ inch up to the maximum size wanted in mix. Variety of sizes makes concrete stronger.

DRY INGREDIENTS are blended thoroughly before water is added. Measure ingredients accurately. Sack of portland cement contains exactly 1 cubic foot, weighs 94 pounds.

Air Entrained. Not as strong as regular portland, but with higher resistance to frost action and to salt. Especially useful where salt and other substances are applied to pavements in ice and snow removal. Concrete made with air-entrained cement won't scale or deteriorate under salt action.

Masonry. A special mixture for use with sand in making mortar. Contains limestone and other special ingredients to increase the mortar's plasticity, water retentivity, and ease of handling.

Other cements include low-heat cements, used in building dams and extremely thick walls where an excess of heat generated during concrete's hardening would cause cracks, waterproofed portland, and puzzolanic portland. This latter variety contains volcanic ash or blast furnace slag.

Aggregates. The bulk of concrete is made up of aggregates—durable inert materials bound together by cement paste. Sand, gravel, crushed stone and blast furnace slag are the aggregates most commonly used.

Fine aggregate, or sand, is material that will pass through a wire screen with ¼-inch meshes. It may include pebbles, bits of stone, tile, and brick. Concrete is stronger if the sand grains are not uniform in size, but vary from fine to coarse. Avoid sands that are predominantly very fine or very coarse. Fine takes too much cement. Coarse makes a rough, unworkable mix.

Coarse aggregate consists of particles from ¼ inch to ¾ inch or larger. The larger the size of the coarse aggregate particles, the less paste (cement and water) necessary to produce a given quality of concrete. Well graded aggregate has a range of particle sizes so that the smaller particles fill up the voids between the big ones. The better this is done, the less cement paste needed to bind them together.

In general, aggregate particles should not be larger than ⅓ the thickness of the wall or slab in which they're used. However, in thick walls and footings, clean stones up to 10 inches or more can be embedded in the concrete in an amount up to half its bulk or more. In reinforced concrete, the size of aggregate particles is best restricted to ¾ inch.

Coarse aggregate particles should be hard and strong, with a minimum of flat and elongated pieces. If flat, elongated or slivery pieces are used, keep them to no more than 15% of the total aggregate.

THE RIGHT MIX

Kind of Work	Cement (sacks)	Sand (cu. ft.)	Gravel (cu. ft.)	Gallons of water per sack of cement if sand is:			Maximum aggregate size
				Damp	Wet	Very Wet	
Footings, foundation walls (not watertight), columns, chimneys, retaining walls, garden walls.	1	3	5	7	6	5	1½"
	1	2¾-3	4	6¼	5½	4¾	1½"
Watertight basement walls, swimming and wading pools, walls above grade, walks, driveways, terraces, tennis courts, steps, floors, septic tanks, storage tanks.	1	2-2¼	3	5½	5	4¼	1"
	1	2½	3½	6½	5	4½	1½"
Subject to severe wear, weather, or weak acid and alkali solutions.	1	2	2¼	4½	4	3½	¾"
Topping for pavement, steps, tennis courts, floors.	1	1	1¾	4¾	4½	4¼	⅜"
Thin construction — 2-4 inches Fence and mailbox posts, garden furniture, tanks, flower boxes, bird baths.	1	2	2	4½	3¾	3½	½"

YOU CAN MIX concrete on any flat, hard surface or platform. Wheelbarrow is convenient for mixing small quantities, as workman shows in the photograph above. Note the use of board to help level tray.

IN USING power mixer, blend dry ingredients first, then add water, as shown. Continue rotating drum for at least two minutes. Don't overload drum.

CONCRETE may be mixed right on the spot where it is to be placed. Professionals can accurately judge water needed by way material handles.

HOW TO FIGURE MATERIALS NEEDED FOR 100 SQ. FT. OF WALLS, SIDEWALKS, SLABS, ETC.

(Quantities given are plus or minus 10%, with no allowance for waste.)

FORMULA	1:2:3			1:2½:3½			1:3:5			
Slab Thickness (inches)	Cement (bags)	Sand (cubic feet)	Gravel	Cement (bags)	Sand (cubic feet)	Gravel	Cement (bags)	Sand	Gravel (cubic feet)	Yards of concrete
3	6½	13	19	5½	13¾	19½	4¼	12¾	21	1—
3½	7½	15¼	22¼	6½	15¼	23	5	15	24¾	1+
4	8½	17¼	25½	7½	18¾	26	5½	17	28½	1¼
5	10½	21¾	32	9½	23¼	32½	6¾	21	35¼	1½
6	12½	26	38½	11	27¾	38¾	8¼	25¼	42½	1¾
8	16	34½	51	15	37	51¾	11	34	56¾	2½
10	21	43½	64	18¾	46¼	65	13¾	42¼	70¾	3
12	25	52	77	22¼	55½	77¾	16½	50¾	84¾	3¾

Aggregate particles that are round or cubicle require less cement and fine material. Avoid shale or any other rock that is laminated or easily broken. Soft or flaky materials, or those subject to rapid wear, are usually not satisfactory. Broken brick and terra cotta can be used where great strength is not important.

The best kinds of rock for aggregate are trap rock, granite, hard limestone, and very hard sandstone, in the order named. Smaller particles of these rocks may be used as sand, but exclude dust.

Bank run or creek gravel can be used in making concrete, but it is usually necessary to screen it to get the right proportions of sand and pebbles. Pass it through a ¼-inch mesh screen to separate fine from coarse aggregate. The saving in cement, and the improvement in the quality of concrete by proper grading of aggregate will usually more than make up for the added effort or expense of screening process.

Gravel cannot economically be washed in any quantity by home methods. If gravel is both dirty and poorly graded, it's usually not worth the effort. A concrete mixer can be used to wash a small amount of gravel. Revolve it in the drum with plenty of water.

Lightweight aggregates make it possible to reduce the weight of concrete from its usual 150 pounds per cubic foot to as little as 40 pounds, but strength and resistance to abrasion are lower. Lightweight aggregates used include burned clay, expanded blast furnace slag, pumice, expanded vermiculite, and hard, clean, vitreous cinders. Concrete of lighter weight can also be made by using an admixture that causes swelling and an increase in volume after the concrete is in place. Follow directions provided by the producer of the product.

Water. The strength, durability and watertightness of concrete is directly related to the quantity and quality of water used in making it.

Generally, water used should be free of acids, alkalis and oil. It should never contain decayed vegetable matter. A safe rule is to use water fit to drink, unless the water is known to contain a large amount of sulfates. According to the Portland Cement Association, seawater produces satisfactory concrete, but with strength up to 20% less. This can be offset by use of a somewhat increased proportion of cement and a decrease in mixing water.

The amount of water used per sack of cement averages about 5 to 6 gallons. Usually, the less mixing water, the better the quality of the concrete. When cement and water are mixed together they form a paste. In good concrete, this paste will coat every pebble and grain of sand and bind them together in one solid, rocklike mass. If too much water is used, the paste is thin and weak and the resulting concrete lacks full strength. The importance of avoiding an excess of water cannot be overemphasized.

More aggregate is used in a stiff, crumbly mix than in a more watery one, and so the stiffer a mix is the lower its cost. However, a mix has to be fluid enough for proper placing. Under average conditions, avoid concrete so stiff it crumbles, or so thin it flows rapidly and segregates.

Consider this: Though a minimum of water produces the best concrete, it may be extravagant to aim for top quality if a more economical mix will fulfill every requirement. Use of somewhat more than a minimum of water will produce a somewhat weaker concrete, but it will permit use of more aggregate and that saves money. However, in no case should you use more than the maximum amount of water recommended for any given concrete formula.

In calculating water requirements, the amount of moisture present in the aggregate must be taken into account. Wet sand—the kind generally supplied by dealers—contains about ½ gallon per cubic foot. Dripping wet sand holds about ¾ gallon. Sand that is only slightly damp contains ¼ gallon. Fine sand holds more water than coarse sand of apparently equal wetness. Damp gravel or crushed rock contains about ¼ gallon per cubic foot.

Formulas. The production of various materials in concrete is usually expressed by three numbers separated by colons. For example, 1:2:4 means 1 part cement, 2

WHAT THEY ARE

CEMENT . . . a powder which, when mixed with water, forms a paste which hardens and has great bonding power. Also, a mixture of portland cement and sand with water, used as stucco, topping for sidewalks, steps, floors, for patching, and in laying up stone.

AGGREGATE . . . fine or coarse materials, such as sand, gravel, cinders, and crushed rock, which are bonded together by cement.

CONCRETE . . . a mixture of cement, sand, and gravel (or other aggregates) with water. Concrete is sometimes incorrectly referred to as cement.

MORTAR . . . a mixture of cement or lime (sometimes both) with sand and water. Used for bonding blocks, bricks, and stone.

GROUT . . . a thin, soupy mixture of cement and sand with water, used in filling cracks and hard-to-get-at spaces.

PREPACKAGED MIXES insure a perfect batch every time, for their ingredients are exactly proportioned. To make concrete, get gravel, mix.

CEMENT readily absorbs moisture, so store it in a dry place. Keep it off the ground. In emergency, protect from rain by waterproof tarp, plastic sheet.

parts sand, 4 parts gravel or stone. The first number always refers to cement, the second to sand, the third to gravel, stone, or other coarse aggregate.

To make good concrete you must measure all ingredients accurately. You can quickly make a bottomless box with inside dimensions of 12x12x12-inches. It will hold 1 cubic foot. Set it on the platform, or in the trough or wheelbarrow where you are doing your mixing. Fill it to ¼, ½ or ¾ level. You merely have to lift the box to dump the contents.

You can mark a wheelbarrow for measuring. Dump a bag of cement in it, level it off and mark it as the 1 cubic foot measure. For small quantities you can get proportionate amounts with any bucket or container. Professionals usually measure with a shovel. Test your shovel to see how many you must take to get 1 cubic foot. Because of the difference in cohesiveness, you'll find that you can get twice as much

MATERIALS REQUIRED TO MAKE 1 CUBIC YARD OF CONCRETE

(Using ¾-inch gravel. For 1-1½-inch gravel, add 10% more sand, 10% more cement, 5% more gravel)

Mix Formula	Amts. Req. (Approx.)		
	CEMENT (bags)	SAND (cu. ft.)	GRAVEL (cu. ft.)
1:1:1¾	10	10	17*
1:2:2	8	16	16**
1:2:2¼	7¾	15½	17½
1:2:3	7¼	14¼	21
1:2½:3½	6	15	21
1:3:4	5	15	20
1:3:5	4½	15	22

* ⅜-inch gravel
** ½-inch gravel

1 bag of cement = 1 cu. ft.
4 bags of cement = 1 barrel
1 ton of sand or crushed stone = app. 22 cu. ft.
1 ton of gravel = app. 20 cu. ft.

portland cement or damp sand in a shovelful as you can get dry sand or gravel.

Make a trial batch in accordance with the table. If it's too stiff, too wet, or difficult to work, alter the proportion of sand and gravel in the next batch to get a more suitable mix, but don't change the amount of water.

Prepackaged Mixes. If you don't want to be bothered with formulas, you can buy prepackaged mixes, such as Sakrete, that contain just the right proportion of ingredients for a perfect batch every time. You need only add water. These prepackaged products are generally available as concrete (or gravel) mix, sand mix for topping and patching, and mortar mix for laying up masonry.

A 90-pound bag of concrete mix makes approximately ⅔-cubic foot of concrete and costs between $1 and $2, depending on the area in which you live. Though this may be four times the cost of concrete you mix yourself, it has the advantages of great convenience when only a limited quantity of concrete is needed and eliminates any guesswork as to how to proportion the ingredients.

Additives may be included in concrete mixes to meet special conditions or requirements. These include hardeners, antifreezes, accelerators (to speed up setting), coloring, bonding agents, waterproofing, and anti-shrink chemicals.

Calcium chloride is most frequently used as an accelerator. It may be dissolved in the mixing water or added to the aggregates. A maximum of 2 pounds per sack of cement may be used, but caution must be exercised so that the cement doesn't harden so rapidly it cannot properly be placed.

How to Mix. Concrete can be mixed by hand on a wood platform (at least 4x6 feet). A platform can be made of tongue-and-groove boards or a sheet of exterior plywood. Also suitable: any flat surface that won't soak up the water or let it leak away. A sidewalk or driveway is fine. Flush it clean immediately after use, and no evidence will remain of the mixing. In some cases, as in putting a topping on a basement floor, the concrete can be mixed right where it is to be used.

For mixing, a hoe with holes in the blade is best, but you can use a garden hoe. A square-edged shovel is better than a pointed one. If the shovel has a long handle it will save bending and extra effort.

Here's one good way to do the mixing: First, spread out the measured sand and add the correct measure of cement. With shovel or hoe mix the two until they are completely blended and the color is uniform. Add the gravel or stone and complete the thorough blending. Each pebble should be coated with cement.

Cut a crater in the middle of the pile all the way down to its bottom and pour in about half of the measured water. With hoe pull the mix up over the outside walls into the water. You can also cut down along the inside rim of the crater, but don't break the wall or allow the water to run over in rivulets for it will carry the cement with it.

When the water is sopped up, pull the walls outward to renew the crater, and add the rest of the water.

In mixing concrete in a trough, tub or mortar box, use the hoe to pull the ingredients back and forth from one end to the other until thoroughly blended. You'll find pulling easier than pushing.

CEMENT is made in gigantic rotary kiln. Supported on huge roller bearings and slightly inclined, kiln rotates so as to move material continuously.

Universal Atlas Cement

If after using the recommended amount of water you find the concrete too stiff, avoid adding water. Instead, on the next batch cut down on the amount of sand and gravel or rock.

Mixing concrete by hand is hard work. For as little as $60 you can buy a mixer that will deliver a thoroughly mixed 2 cubic feet of concrete in two minutes. You can operate it by hand or it will run off a ⅓ HP capacitor electric motor or a 2¼ HP gas engine. These are good for occasional use. Professional, motorized, portable 1-bag mixers delivering 3½ cubic feet of concrete cost from about $375 up. They can be rented.

When using a power mixer, thoroughly blend the dry ingredients first. After water is added, to obtain a thoroughly mixed batch, mixing should be continued for at least two minutes. Don't overload the drum, or try to shorten the mixing period by rotating the drum faster. Wash the machine carefully after each use to prevent hardening of concrete remnants in drum or elsewhere.

Cold Weather Mixing. Avoid mixing concrete when the temperature is under 40 degrees, or if temperatures below 40 are expected within 24 hours. However, with proper precautions concrete can be placed at temperatures under 40 if protected in its first 24 hours from freezing. A heavy freeze during that period will make the concrete crumble.

In cold weather, commercial operators use warm water in the mix. Temperature of the water should range from 150 to 175 degrees, never above. Don't allow the temperature of heated concrete to get over 80 degrees.

About ⅓ can be cut from the setting time of concrete by use of calcium chloride, previously mentioned in the text. This chemical, sometimes called chloride of lime, is the same as is used in combatting dampness in basements. Add no more than 2 pounds per bag of cement. Other chemicals, both liquid and powders, are used to accelerate setting of concrete in cold weather. If both an accelerator and warm water are used, proceed cautiously or you may run into flash-set—the concrete hardening before you can place it.

Never mix concrete when the aggregate is frozen or has ice in it. If necessary, aggregate can be warmed by spreading it over a supported heavy metal sheet and building a fire underneath. Aggregate should not be over 100-degrees when used.

Mixing concrete is only the first step in getting good concrete.

CLEAN OR DIRTY?

To determine if sand is clean enough to use without washing, make this test. Put 2 inches of the sand in a quart bottle or jar, fill ⅔ with water and shake vigorously for 1 minute. Allow it to stand 1 hour. The maximum amount of clay or silt permissible is usually 3%. In other words, no more than ¹⁄₁₆-inch in 2 inches of sand. If more than this settles on the sand, it needs washing.

Organic matter will prevent concrete from hardening properly. To determine if sand is free of organic matter, dissolve a heaping teaspoon of ordinary household lye in a cup of water. Pour the solution over a cup of the sand in a jar. Screw on the jar lid and shake for 1 minute.

If after several hours the liquid is clear or light straw color, the sand is satisfactory. If the liquid is coffee colored, the sand needs washing. Avoid getting the solution on clothing, skin or anything else. Use glass containers only in making the test.

PLACING

LOADED concrete truck may weigh 20 tons or more. Can your lawn or driveway safely take the load? The closer the truck can get in to the delivery point, the less work for you placing its concrete.

START PLACING concrete on the far side of an area, and always dump concrete against loads already placed. Handling pour for even a small slab, and doing it correctly, is not a one-man job.

AND FINISHING CONCRETE

For the very best results, work hard and act fast

PLACE concrete where you want it as soon as possible after mixing, and before it begins to set or harden. In warm weather concrete begins setting in as little as 20 to 30 minutes. Disturbing it after that will impair its strength. The more it has set and the more you disturb it, the greater the damage. Be prepared to act fast and work hard once a batch is ready. In cold weather, ordinary concrete takes several hours or more to acquire its initial set, and speed in placing it is not so important.

Don't add water to a mix that has begun to set. More than the prescribed amount of water will weaken the concrete. If concrete is bought ready mixed, only the dry ingredients will be mixed when the truck arrives at your site. Water will be added as you direct.

Getting Ready to Pour. Your ability to place ready-mix promptly will depend on several factors:

(1) Can the truck move in close to where the concrete is wanted? If it can't, the concrete will have to be wheeled in. Concrete weighs about 150 lbs. per cu. ft. and the average general purpose wheelbarrow won't haul much more than a cubic foot per trip. That means 20 or more trips to handle a cubic yard. A deep-tray contractor's wheelbarrow can cut the number of trips in half.

(2) How much help do you have? Handling even a small delivery of concrete is seldom a one-man job. At least one able-bodied helper is essential.

(3) Is everything ready? Forms must be complete, shovels, wheelbarrows and other tools at hand, help prepared. There is a time charge if a truck is kept waiting or held longer than a normal amount of time for the delivery. Arrangements for concrete deliveries are usually made a day or more in advance. Don't set the time for too late in the day or you may be working long after dark. A concrete job usually can't be interrupted until it's done.

(4) Are you prepared to handle an excess amount of concrete? Even experts can't figure concrete needs exactly, and it's always safer to order just a little more. What if that "little extra" turns out to be $\frac{1}{2}$ yard or more? Can you do something with it? Some contractors have forms for splashboards or stepping stones on hand for such emergencies. Are you planning a future project that will take a concrete footing? Have it ready on a stand-by basis. Once your concrete is mixed it will have to be used, or dumped and wasted.

Forms. Concrete is a plastic material. It will take almost any shape. It all depends on the form or mold you have for it. Forms for concrete can be of earth,

DEEP-TRAY contractor's buggy holds over twice as much as an ordinary wheelbarrow. Even more important, the pneumatic tire makes pushing the load easier, gives concrete a smoother ride.

DON'T DUMP concrete all in one pile and expect it to flow into position. It will segregate. Place it near where you want it—and with a minimum of handling. You'll find shovels and rakes are a necessity.

IN HIGH FORMS, place concrete in layers 6 to 12 inches thick. Start at ends, work toward middle. If excess water appears, make next batch stiffer.

HARDBOARD is useful both as a form liner and as form facing. Its smooth surface permits a large expanse of finished surface unmarked by joints.

BOARDS ½ inch thick are readily bent on a wide radius, particularly if they are first wetted down. Note the substantial bracing and the cross-bracing.

IF FORM BOARDS aren't smooth and joints tight, expect irregularities to show in finished job. "Fins" freshly hardened are ground away on concrete.

wood, hardboard, plywood, metal, or any other material substantial enough to contain it.

Tongue-and-groove or shiplap boards are good form material, for their joints can be made tight enough to keep water from escaping and carrying cement with it. Leakage at joints also creates "fins" which accentuate the joints. Tongue-and-groove boards are usually more desirable than shiplap for their interlocking helps keep them in alignment and prevents offset joints.

Wide boards have a greater tendency to cup than narrow ones. For average work, use 6-inch boards. Use 4-inch or flooring boards for a specially smooth surface. Joint lines are likely to be accented if you use 8- or 10-inch boards. If forms have been exposed to hot, dry weather, soaking will tighten the joints.

Boards should be free of knotholes or other breaks. Rough or cupped boards will leave their imprint on finished concrete, so use smooth lumber where a smooth finish is important, or line the form with form-lining paper or other smooth material. Where the imprint of the wood graining is desired, make the graining more pronounced by wetting the form lumber before oiling, or by spraying it with ammonia. The rough finish thus obtained provides an excellent bonding for stucco.

Hardboard is good form material, especially when a very smooth surface is wanted. With hardboard sheets it's possible to have an area 4x12 feet or more without joint lines. Wood or leather-grained hardboard, on the other hand, offer the means of securing attractively textured surfaces.

Hardboard isn't very rigid. Often it is used as lining for rough wood forms. If used alone it must be exceptionally well-braced. To prevent buckling, leave hard-

board joints open the thickness of a dime. Seal these joints with patching plaster or water putty to balk leaks.

Plywood ⅝ and ¾ inch thick are popular for making forms. Under such trade names as Plyform, it is available in both exterior (waterproof) and interior (water-resistant) grades. The exterior type is especially designed for multiple reuse, although with care the interior type may be reused many times, the glue often outlasting the wood. GPX, a plastic-faced plywood of exterior Douglas Fir, is ideal for concrete forms. It produces a satin-smooth finish and can be continually reused.

Metal forms are a favorite of professional builders. They can be quickly assembled into wall panels in a variety of arrangements. Metal forms are also commonly used in the manufacture of blocks and furniture.

Earth can serve as one or both sides of a form for footings and walls. The earth should be of a type that will stand without caving, especially when wet. Special care must be used in placing and tamping concrete in earth forms. Earth that falls into concrete makes weak and porous spots.

Curves. Hardboard's flexibility makes it useful for forms with curves or bends. Regular boards, ½ inch thick, are also bendable, especially if they are wetted. Plywood ¼ and ½ inch thick may be bent on a 3- or 4-foot radius.

Nailing. The preferred practice is to assemble forms so that they are easy to take apart. Use a minimum of nails. In building forms to be dismantled, box nails are better than common nails for, being thinner, they pull out easier. In building panel forms for reuse, use common nails. They'll take more punishment and abuse.

For maximum strength and minimum marring on removal use two-headed or

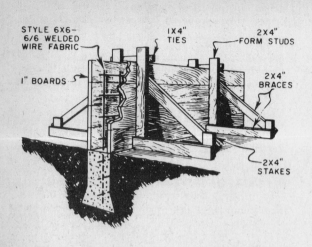

FOUNDATION WALLS above grade may be formed in this manner where earth walls of the trench stand straight and true, and where a wide footing is not required. Most foundations should have a footing, however. In that case the foundation is formed as shown in drawing above, right.

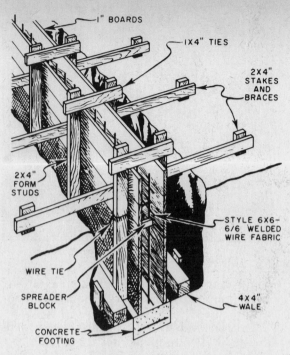

SUGGESTED METHOD of forming for foundations supported on footings, is shown in drawing above.

duplex nails. Use 3d blue shingle nails for attaching hardboard or plywood liners over sheathing, using at least one nail per square foot. For ¾-inch boards and plywood use 6d nails. Clamps and wedges can sometimes be used in lieu of nails.

Ties and Spreaders. Forms must be well-braced and well-tied to keep them in alignment. In building forms for average walls use 2x4 studs spaced on 18- to 24-inch centers to reinforce the facing material against which the concrete is placed. To keep the form from spreading apart, join studs on opposite sides of the form with tie rods, which are available in a variety of types, or with No. 10 or No. 12 soft black annealed iron wire, tightened by twisting.

Ties usually are placed every 2½ feet vertically, closer if more than 3 feet of concrete will be poured in ½ hour. Wires may go either through or around the studs. Alternately, ½-inch bolts may be used. Place 1x2 spacers at every other tie to keep the walls apart when wire is being twisted or bolts tightened. Knock these spacers out as the concrete is placed.

When forms are removed, you can clip off wires close to the surface and drive them back with a punch. Snap ties break off 1 inch back of the surface. Touch up any noticeable marks with mortar. Blend

the mortar with 25 to 50% white portland and the patches won't look darker than the wall. Rubbing the pointed-up spots will also help make them inconspicuous.

To make form removal easier, oil, shellac, or varnish them before use. This treatment also keeps the wood from harmful absorption of concrete moisture. You can compound form oil of 50% light automobile oil and 50% kerosene. Forms must be reoiled before each use.

Walls poured against oiled forms cannot be painted or stuccoed. However, you can buy special form oil (often compounded of paraffin oil and kerosene or benzine) which will not interfere with painting or stuccoing.

If forms aren't oiled or otherwise treated, soak them with water at least 12 hours before placing concrete. If they are extremely dry, apply water more than once.

Handle With Care. The most important single item in successfully placing concrete is to handle the wet material carefully. Take it easy. Rough treatment will separate the coarse aggregate in the concrete from the cement-paste and fine material.

In pouring a slab, don't dump the concrete all in one pile and let it flow into position. The cement paste and fine material will flow ahead of the coarse aggregates. Don't pull the concrete more than you can

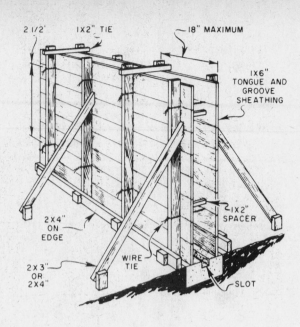

TYPICAL form details for concrete walls (above).

Labels on diagram: 2 1/2" • 1X2" TIE • 18" MAXIMUM • 1X6" TONGUE AND GROOVE SHEATHING • 2X4" ON EDGE • 1X2" SPACER • 2X3" OR 2X4" • WIRE TIE • SLOT

COMMERCIAL OPERATORS often prefer metal forms. They are quickly assembled, require no special bracing, and can be used over and over with minimum maintenance.

help. Pulling, too, encourages segregation. Instead, place the concrete as near to its final position as possible. In pouring a wall, don't drop concrete over 3 feet.

If excessive water comes to the surface of the concrete and the mix isn't an especially moist one, it means you're handling the stuff too rough and too fast.

In pouring into a high form, deposit the concrete in horizontal layers no more than 6 to 12 inches thick, and deposit the material at no greater than 6-foot intervals. Use a spade, a hoe with blade straightened, or a lawn edger, to push rock away from the side forms, to compact the concrete, and to get rid of air pockets. A homemade tool useful for the purpose is a 1x4 board, its end chisel-pointed. Rapping the side of a form sharply with a hammer is also effective in driving rock away from the form and producing a smooth face.

When concrete is placed in tall forms, there will be a tendency toward bleeding —appearance of water on top of the concrete. When this happens, make succeeding batches stiffer and place concrete more slowly.

Pouring Technique. In pouring a wall, do it all in one operation. If you don't, the finished wall will have seams and they may leak. Fresh concrete won't bond to hard concrete without special attention.

SLOT OR KEY helps provide solid joining between footing and wall which are poured separately. To make key, 2x4 is pressed into fresh concrete, removed when concrete has attained its initial set.

GARDEN RAKE held vertically makes good tool for tamping concrete, eliminating air pockets. It also helps in bringing finer material to surface.

WHEN CONCRETE has been poured, it is first roughly leveled off (screeded) with a straightedge that is drawn back and forth across the concrete.

SCREEDING causes concrete to "bleed." After screeding, water may stand on surface. Wait until water disappears before trying final finishing.

This is what to do when a pour must be interrupted: Before the concrete that's in place hardens, rough it up with a pick to expose its coarse aggregate. Next day give this rough surface a coat of grout, or cement paste with the consistency of pancake batter, before resuming pouring. Pour immediately.

Saturate hardened concrete before placing new concrete on it. If the hardened concrete has dried out, it may take several days to resaturate it adequately. There should be no standing water on the old concrete when the new is placed. Certain chemical additives, like Antihydro or Weldcrete, help bond new concrete to old.

Where two separate pourings are to be made, the first for a footing or slab, and the next for a wall, make a key or rebate in the slab or footing with a 2x4. When the concrete has hardened just enough to hold its shape, remove the 2x4. The slot thus made will help tie the two pours together.

In pouring concrete for walls, place the first batches at the ends of a section and then move toward the center. Follow this order as the concrete is built up layer by layer. In a large open area, first place concrete around the perimeter, then move in toward the center. Start at the far end of the area to be covered and always dump concrete *against* concrete just placed. Don't dump it so the flow is *ahead* of concrete just placed.

Special mechanical vibrators are used by professional operators in consolidating concrete in forms. Vibration permits use of stiffer, harsher mixes. The greater stiffness means less water and stronger concrete. Increased harshness means a lowered cement content and greater economy. With vibration it's easier to avoid segregation and bleeding, both of which are characteristic of mixes that are too fluid. Remember this important factor.

Screeding is the name given to the operation of leveling off a concrete pour at its desired height or bringing its surface to a desired contour. Most commonly a 2x4 or 2x6, its lower edge straight or curved, is moved forward across the concrete with a sawing motion. This will level off high places and tend to fill in low places. Additional concrete is shoveled into obviously low spots as screeding proceeds.

If you want a smooth finish on a floor slab, after screeding is complete tamp the surface with a rake. This will help push coarse pebbles down and bring fine material to the surface, but don't overdo it. A wood, cork or other float is also useful in bringing mortar to the surface and for further leveling of high spots and filling in low, but exercise care not to overwork the concrete while it is still plastic.

Troweling. Don't attempt troweling or final finishing of concrete before the pour has begun to stiffen. Wait until all surface water has disappeared and the concrete has lost its sheen. In very hot dry weather, concrete may be ready for troweling in twenty minutes, even less, but more generally this time will be an hour or more. In cold weather, it may be eight or ten hours. When you can pass a trowel in an arc over the surface without its digging in or causing the concrete to bleed, it's safe to trowel. Troweling too soon, or overtroweling, brings too much fine material to the surface and results in dusting and crazing. By delaying troweling, materials remain where they are placed, with hard-wearing coarse particles at or near the surface.

If surface water is slow in disappearing, be patient. Under no circumstance spread dry cement powder or a mixture of cement and sand on the concrete to take up the water. It will result in a finished surface

AVOID

- More than 5 gallons of water per sack of cement.
- Mixes that contain sand, but no coarse aggregate.
- Dusting on fine material to absorb surface water.
- Troweling which brings water or a large amount of fine material to the surface.
- Excessive troweling.
- Quick drying.

WOOD TROWEL or float produces gritty, nonskid surface. For slicker finish, follow floating with steel troweling. Plank helps to get out over a wide slab.

SLAB stiff enough for troweling is not quite stiff enough to support man's weight unless he uses platform or two. Always do minimum of troweling.

that dusts and crazes, and won't take wear.

A wood float will produce a gritty non-skid surface, generally best for sidewalks and driveways. For a smooth, dense surface, best for dancing, shuffleboard, and the application of thin gauge flooring materials, follow floating with steel troweling. Do it only when the concrete has become so hard no mortar sticks to the trowel edge as it is passed over the surface. Hold the trowel in a slightly tilted position; not face-flat.

For a broomed texture, desirable on steeply sloping walks, driveways and ramps, use a fiber pushbroom after floating has been completed. Run the texture counter to the direction of traffic.

Curing concrete consists principally of keeping it from drying out too quickly. Concrete damp-cured for 7 days is approximately 50% stronger. The first two or three days are critical. The first week is important. Concrete does not approach its maximum strength for about four weeks,

and only as long as it is moist can its hardening continue.

To maintain moistness, spray concrete with water at least twice a day for a week to 10 days. Spray wood forms to keep them from drying out. Don't allow concrete to dry out between sprinklings. It may result in crazing or cracking. Shade concrete as soon as possible after finishing. Protect it from the sun and from hot, drying winds.

Covering the concrete while it is curing delays evaporation and preserves moistness. Use canvas, boards, burlap or paper sacking, straw, nonstaining watertight paper, or moist sand. Use bridging boards to keep covers from coming in direct contact with the concrete if this would mar it. An inch of sand will protect new concrete from being pitted by rain. On sidewalks and floors, a small dam of sand or earth around the perimeter may make it possible to keep the surface flooded. Such "ponding" is superior to sprinkling.

Special curing compounds are available.

PROFESSIONALS sometimes use a troweling machine (as shown in photograph above) especially for large areas or for concrete too stiff to handle otherwise. Machine doesn't completely eliminate hand finishing.

Applied right after finishing, they form a protective coating that keeps moisture in. Ordinary liquid floor wax gives good results. Make your own compound by dissolving 5 pounds of paraffin in 1½ gallons of heated light oil or kerosene.

Don't walk unnecessarily on new concrete for 2 to 3 days. Keep heavy loads off it for 2 weeks.

Removing Forms. Leave forms in place at least until the concrete has enough strength to support its own weight plus any load it must bear. In warm weather this may be 1 or 2 days. In cold weather it will probably be 4 to 7 days. Don't remove floor and roof forms sooner than 7 days in warm weather, 14 in cold.

In almost every case it's better to exceed these minimum times. Forms protect concrete against early drying, and so are an aid in moist curing. Further, the longer forms are left on, the more likely the concrete is to shrink away from them, making removal easier. Never remove forms in less than 4 days unless other means of protecting the concrete from losing its moisture are employed.

Though you can use a crowbar or wrecking bar in removing forms, special stripping bars designed for the purpose are available. Never place metal tools against the concrete in prying forms loose. You'll damage it. Use a wooden wedge if it's necessary to wedge between the concrete and the form.

When forms are removed from walls, a final touchup will eliminate joint marks, honeycombs, and other minor imperfections. Work is best done if forms are removed before the concrete has set rock-hard. Rub away form marks with a hard-burned brick, using sand and water as an abrasive. If concrete is hard, use a carborundum block. Point up holes with a 1:2 mortar mix.

Underwater Concreting. You can use concrete successfully in building boat piers and underwater retaining walls. The water should be quiet. Make the concrete mix rich—no less than 7 sacks per yard of concrete. Coarse aggregate should not measure over 1½ inches. Fine aggregate should be 50% of the aggregate total.

An easy way of constructing a pier is to build a box form. Sink the form by filling it with water at the location the pier is wanted. Place the concrete slowly. Don't tamp it.

With care, in quiet water, you can mortar together rocks or other masonry. Both mortar and concrete actually set better and cure better under water.

Cold Weather Precautions. Concrete can successfully be placed in cold weather if care is taken to protect it from freezing and to allow for proper curing. Care is especially needed in doing floors and sidewalks where a large area is exposed to the weather.

Concrete hardens very slowly at 50 degrees, and hardly at all around freezing. If it freezes before it has hardened, it will be damaged. However, it may be frozen once and still be satisfactory.

If freezing temperatures occur only at night, protect concrete from freezing after it has been placed. If temperature is freezing while concrete is placed, it is also necessary to heat water and aggregates. The temperature of concrete when placed should not be less than 50 (preferably 60) degrees nor more than 80. If necessary, heat both water and aggregate to get this temperature.

Don't use mixing water heated above 150 degrees. It may cause flash setting. However, you can pour boiling water over aggregate without danger of flash setting, for the aggregate will cool off the water to below 150 degrees before cement is added.

WHEN CONCRETE is to be topped by flagstone, brick, or a wearing course of concrete, score marks cut in surface help produce bond between base and topping.

FINISHED CONCRETE is covered with paper to help in moist-curing, salt hay to protect it from freezing, and weights to keep paper and straw from blowing away.

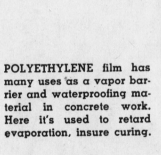

POLYETHYLENE film has many uses as a vapor barrier and waterproofing material in concrete work. Here it's used to retard evaporation, insure curing.

—Visking

Warm concrete will not bond to previously placed cold, hardened concrete. For bonding, new and old concrete should be at approximately the same temperatures.

Don't place concrete on frozen ground. If possible, make excavations before freezing weather and protect the area with straw to keep it from freezing. If the ground is frozen, thaw it out before placing concrete.

After placing the concrete, maintain its temperature at 70 for 3 days, or at 50 for at least 5 days. If high early strength cement is used, richer mixes, or calcium chloride is added, this time may be reduced to 2 days and 3 days respectively. Concrete must be kept moist during this time. In weather when the temperature averages above 40 to 45 degrees, with a brief nighttime low just a little under 40, a tarp placed over fresh concrete is all that is required to keep it at a satisfactory temperature for curing. Cover floors and walks with paper and hay or straw to a depth of 10 to 12 inches. Salt hay is especially effective in warding off frost.

Hot Weather Precautions. Concrete placed in extremely hot weather must be protected from rapid drying and flash setting. Keep aggregates cool by spraying with water. Saturate subgrades some time before placing concrete and spray again just before placing. When possible, keep wood forms soaked.

Avoid placing concrete during the hottest part of the day. Shade the fresh concrete when you do pour. •

STEEL has the won't-pull-apart strength that concrete lacks. Embed steel in concrete and you have a material that can take it from any and every direction.

Wire Reinforcement Institute

REINFORCING CONCRETE

Steel offers the tensile strength that concrete lacks

REINFORCING adds the strength of steel to concrete. Though concrete is a tough, durable material, it isn't flexible and it won't stretch. If unsupported, only a small load can make it tear or break apart.

Steel has the tensile strength that concrete lacks. Embedded in concrete, it can keep the concrete from pulling apart even under tremendous loads. Add that to concrete's ability to take a straight-down load of 2,000 pounds per square inch without breaking or crushing, and you have a material that can take it from any direction.

Adding the sinew and muscle of steel to concrete adds little to its overall cost, but offers big advantages. For example, temperature and moisture will cause a slab to expand. As it expands, its edges push out. What happens when an unreinforced slab contracts? The weight of the slab and its drag on the ground usually means the slab will crack as it tries unsuccessfully to pull back together. Reinforcement counters this tendency to break or pull apart.

Two types of reinforcing materials are in widespread use: rods and welded wire fabric.

Rods. Rods may be plain (smooth) or deformed (with ribs, lugs, or other projections). The strength that smooth rods give to concrete depends upon the bond or adhesion between them and the concrete. Deformed rods on the other hand make

STEEL reinforcing rods come in sizes ranging from ¼ inch to 1⅜ inches, and in plain (smooth) and deformed (with ribs, lugs, or other projections).

YOU CAN have rods cut to required lengths where you buy them. Rods may also be cut with an ordinary hacksaw, or with hammer and chisel.

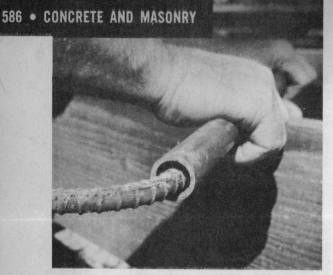

RODS are easily bent by hand into U or L shapes. Bending smaller diameter rods often saves cutting. Hook the end of a rod by using pipe as lever.

RODS are positioned before concrete is poured. In average slab, reinforcement is 2 inches from bottom. In suspended slab, it is 1 to 1½ inches.

RODS must be wired together wherever they cross, whether in a slab, or in a wall. Note rocks used to support rods at proper position in suspended slab.

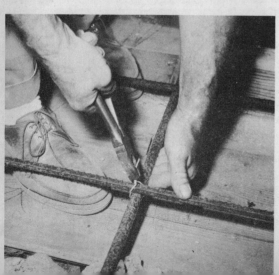

both an adhesive bond and, because of their projections, a mechanical bond. This is highly desirable for it means a deformed rod will bond to concrete even though conditions interfere with adhesive bonding. Plain flat rods have poor adhesive quality and are unsatisfactory.

Reinforcing steel should be free of rust,

Construction of porch floor and steps

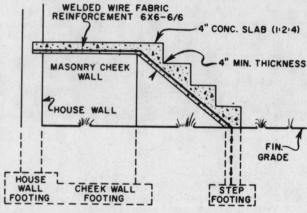

ROD REINFORCEMENT
for step slabs

Slab Length (feet)	Slab Thickness (inches)	Rods, Lengthwise Diameter (inches)	Rods, Lengthwise Spacing (inches)	Rods, Across Diameter (inches)	Rods, Across Spacing (inches)
3	4	¼	10	¼	12 to 18
4	4	¼	5½	¼	12 to 18
5	5	¼	4½	¼	18 to 24
6	5	⅜	7	¼	18 to 24
7	6	⅜	6	¼	18 to 24
8	6	⅜	4	¼	18 to 24
9	7	½	7	¼	18 to 24

for porch or other slab on clear span

Length of Span (feet)	Slab Thickness (inches)	Rod diameter (inches)	Rod Spacing (inches)
4	5	⅜	7½
6	5	⅜	6
8	5½	½	9½
10	6	½	8

for small concrete bridges

Length of Span (feet)	Slab Thickness (inches)	Rod diameter (inches)	Rod Spacing (inches)
6	6½	⅝	8
9	6½	⅝	7
12	7	¾	8
15	8	¾	7

scale, dirt, oil and grease. All these seriously impair their adhesive bonding. From the foregoing it should be clear why old rusty scrap iron, or even most clean, smooth iron of nondescript shape, makes unsatisfactory reinforcing material.

The most popular sizes of rods for average construction are ⅜ to 1⅜ inch diameter in plain or deformed. ¼ inch in plain only. Cost of ½-inch rod is about 13 cents per running foot. Rod suppliers have special heavy-duty cutters for cutting rods to the lengths you want. Some may charge 10 cents per cut. Rods may also be cut with hacksaw, oxyacetylene torch, or hammer and chisel. Smaller diameter rods are

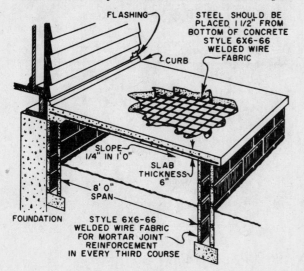

Construction of porch and terrace on clear span

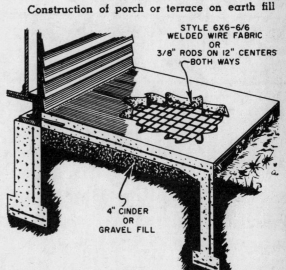

Construction of porch or terrace on earth fill

RECOMMENDED WELDED WIRE FABRIC REINFORCEMENT FOR TYPICAL HOME AND FARM PROJECTS		
Project	Style	Comment
Barbecue Foundation Slabs	6x6-8/8 to 4x4-6/6	Use heavier style for heavy, massive fireplaces and barbecues
Barn, Milk House, and Poultry House Floors	6x6-6/6	
Basement Floors	6x6-10/10	for small area, max. dimension 15 ft.
	6x6-8/8 6x6-6/6	for larger areas or unstable subsoil
Driveways	6x6-6/6	Also use where cars cross sidewalks
Footings	6x6-6/6	In footings 8 to 15-in. thick, place 3-in. above bottom.
Foundation Slabs	6x6-10/10	Use heavier gauge when max. dimension is over 15 ft., or subsoil poorly drained.
Foundation Walls	6x6-6/6	
Garage Floors	6x6-6/6	Position at midpoint of 5- or 6-in. slab.
Hog Wallows and Yards	6x6-6/6	
Porch Floors	6x6-6/6	6-in. slab, 6-ft. span, 1-in. from bottom
	4x4-4/4	6-in. slab, 8-ft. span, 1-in. from bottom
Septic Tanks	6x6-6/6	
Sidewalks	6x6-10/10	average use.
	6x6-8/8	poorly drained subsoil
Steps (free span)	6x6-6/6	Use heavier gauge if more than 5 risers.
Steps (on ground)	6x6-8/8	average
	6x6-6/6	unstable subsoil
Terraces and Patios	6x6-10/10	average
	6x6-8/8	if subsoil poorly drained.
Water Tanks and Feed Bunks	6x6-6/6	

WELDED wire fabric comes in rolls 5 or 6 feet wide, 125, 150, 200, and 300 feet long. Most dealers will also sell fractional rolls, so you'll have no waste.

WIRE FABRIC is easily bent by hand to fit almost any required shape. It is cut as shown. The smaller the gauge number, the heavier the wire.

IN SIDEWALKS, terraces and driveways, reinforcement minimizes cracks. Reinforcement should run continuously, except through contraction joints.

IN SLAB construction, wire fabric is placed over vapor barrier. Where wire sections join they should be lapped one square, or about six inches.

readily bent, and often bending can save cutting.

Welded Wire Fabric. Wire fabric consists of a series of wires welded to other wires crossing at right angles. It has many desirable qualities as a reinforcing material. It can be used effectively in all types of construction. It's easy to form in various shapes, to cut, and to handle. There is never any guesswork about spacing; no chance that reinforcing will be omitted or displaced.

Its strength is attested by these figures: The wire will carry a load of 70,000 P.S.I. (pounds per square inch) before breaking and won't stretch permanently up to a load of 56,000 P.S.I.

Fabric anchors well in concrete because the numerous wires provide a large bonding area, and the rigidly connected cross wires make for a positive mechanical anchorage. Wire fabric will control and minimize cracks caused by heavy loads, shrinking, heaving, temperature and moisture stresses, in much the same manner as does rod reinforcement. It costs about 3 cents per square foot, is readily cut with ordinary wire cutters, or you can use a hacksaw or plane.

Wire fabric is generally available in rolls 5 or 6 feet wide, 125, 150, 200 and 300 feet long. Most dealers will sell fractional rolls.

The size and style of the fabric is indicated by two pairs of numbers, for example, 6x6-10/10 (pronounced six, six, ten, ten). The first pair of numbers refers to the spacing of the wires—6 inches apart each way. The second pair refers to the gauge of longitudinal and transverse wires respectively; in this case both are 10 gauge. The smaller the gauge number, the heavier the wire.

The same size and style of fabric might also be written 66-1010.

Using Reinforcement. Both fabric and rods may be placed in various ways. In a slab, a popular method is to place concrete to half the thickness of the slab and level it off. The reinforcement is then positioned and the second layer of concrete is immediately placed to the full thickness. If rods are used, they must be wired together wherever they cross.

Another method is to support the reinforcement on pieces of brick, or on small piles of concrete spotted every few feet, and place the complete slab thickness in one operation, working the concrete well under and around all reinforcing members. Some prefer to put reinforcing fabric on the subgrade, pour the full slab on top of it, and then lift the fabric up to its proper position in the slab using the tines of a rake.

Either rods or fabric may be run continuously from slabs up into walls. Rods are readily bent into a U or an L. You can hook the end of a rod by slipping a pipe over one end and using the rod as a lever.

In small pools, bend rods into U shapes so the reinforcement of the bottom and opposing walls is continuous. If your rods aren't long enough for this, bend your vertical rods so they lap 18 to 30 inches over the bottom ones. Keep rods 2 inches off the bottom.

Place horizontal rods around the pool's outside walls and wire to the vertical rods. If you have to splice or hook short rods together, do it in the middle of walls, never at corners. Lap 1/4-inch rods 10 inches, 3/8-inch rods 15 inches, 1/2-inch rods 20 inches, and 3/4-inch rods 30 inches. A little extra reinforcing does no harm.

Lap wire fabric at least one space (about 6 inches) at sides and ends. Fabric should clear the sides and ends of any slab by 1 1/2 to 3 inches. In driveways, where concrete is usually poured in sections 25 to 35 feet long with a contraction joint separating sections, stop the fabric 3 inches short of the joints.

In some cases it may be desirable to double the fabric. For example, a 6x6-10/10 mesh is generally satisfactory for sidewalks. However, where vehicles cross the sidewalk, both a thicker slab and a doubled (or 6x6-6/6) fabric is the only safe practice.

Position of reinforcement, whether fabric or rod, should always be well within the concrete. The concrete, sealing out air and moisture, will then protect it from possible rust and deterioration. A minimum cover of 3/4 inch is advisable in all cases. In average use, placement of reinforcement should be 2 inches from the bottom of a slab.

Where a concrete slab is suspended, as between walls in porch construction, steel should be placed 1 to 1 1/2 inches from the bottom of the concrete. Where a slab is cantilevered, reinforcement in the overhanging section should be 1 to 1 1/2 inches from the top of the concrete.

Most local codes will detail requirements both as to reinforcement and its placement. •

Vertical joints in wall are made flush by rubbing the mortar with piece of masonry or block of wood.

Constructing With Concrete Block

If you're interested in attractive appearance and low material cost, plus durability and economical maintenance, concrete block may be a best bet.

THE GREAT usefulness and ever-growing demand for concrete masonry units—blocks, building and roof tile, and bricks of various sizes, finishes and colors —is leading to a newer type of construction in many localities. Lightweight blocks are used, for example, to provide interesting designs in interior walls, thus eliminating the use of plaster. Or the blocks are arranged by various sizes to form a variety of patterns in walls and columns or other areas.

The standard 8x8x16 and 4x8x16 blocks and their variations still dominate the construction field, but you will find many new shapes and sizes. Some blocks are in color or have polished or cut faces to resemble stone. Large and small sizes and shapes can be used to vary the pattern in walls. Lightweight blocks add to the insulating value of walls as well as to their decorative quality. Local supply houses do not always carry all sizes and colors and finishes, so you may have to shop around.

Where standard sized blocks are to be used in a structure, plan the work so that the dimensions of window and door openings fall in full and half sizes in order to avoid loss of time due to cutting and fitting the blocks to odd sizes.

Lintels and jamb blocks for doors and windows can be obtained ready-made, or long blocks for lintels can be cast in place by using a series of shell blocks. These shell blocks are supported underneath, then filled with reinforced concrete, thus eliminating the need to build a complete form for wide spans.

Before beginning any masonry job, it is necessary to make certain that the foundation or footing will be strong enough to support the load of the structure. This foundation or footing should be straight and level. If it is not, then enough mortar should be used in laying the first course so that the top of the first course of blocks will be level. Unless the foundation has been built with forms, it may be necessary to square the corners with chalk lines before starting to build.

The same 2x4 corner guide used for brick work will be useful for concrete block work. (See chapter "How to Lay Brick.") Such a guide must be carefully and strongly braced so that it will not move out of place and will permit the masonry

leads to be built against it. As in bricklaying, corners or leads are built first, three or four courses being sufficient with larger blocks. When all of the corners have been built up, stretcher courses are laid between them.

The first course of a concrete block structure is always laid in a full bed of mortar. A chalk line stretched between the corners will be a guide to the height and straightness of succeeding courses. Where blocks are too high, they are tapped into place with the handle of the trowel.

After the first course, the mortar is placed only on the side of the blocks. This is called face-shell bedding of mortar. The end of each block also is buttered with mortar before the block is placed. Each block should fit snugly against the one preceding it in the course, the block should be level and plumb, and the excess mortar should be scraped off the joints. Trying to adjust the block after it is set will break the mortar bond and may result in leakage

Corners are built up first, several courses high; first you determine number of blocks in a course.

Galvanized hardware cloth strips laid in every other course help bond intersecting masonry walls.

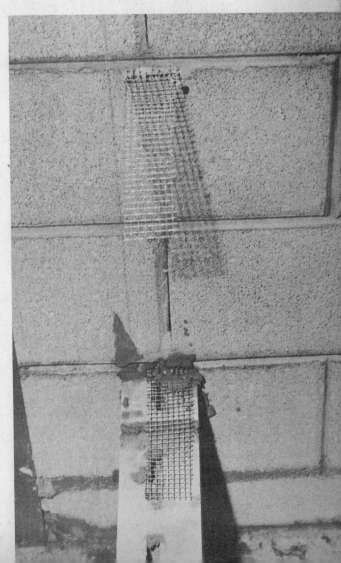

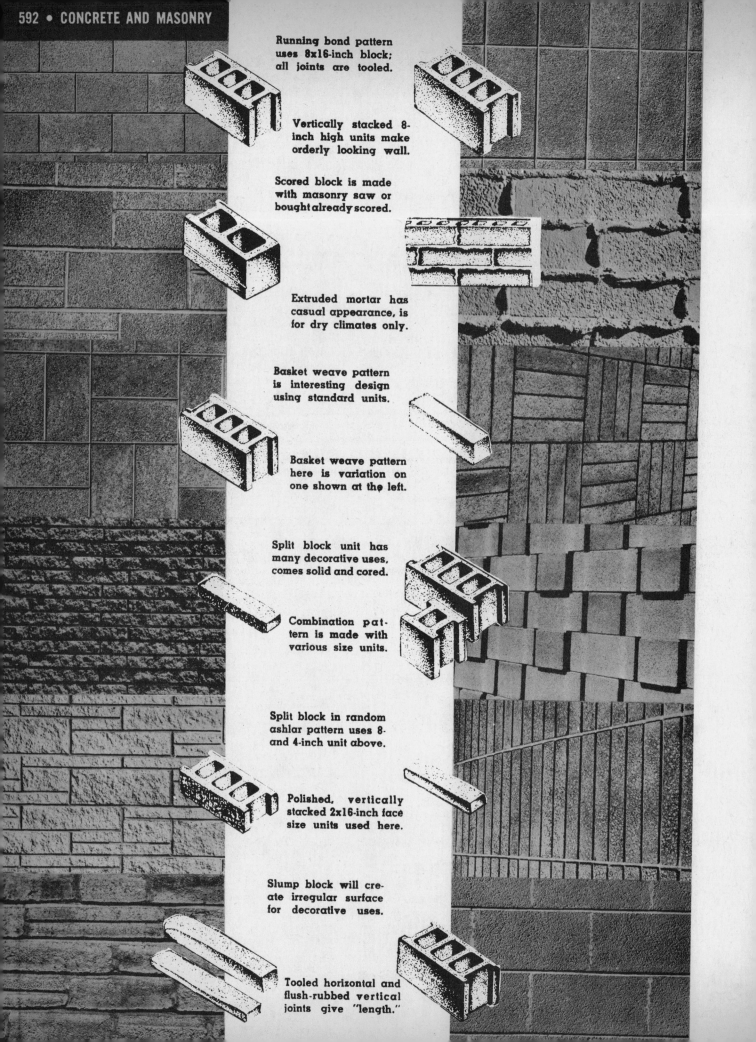

Running bond pattern uses 8x16-inch block; all joints are tooled.

Vertically stacked 8-inch high units make orderly looking wall.

Scored block is made with masonry saw or bought already scored.

Extruded mortar has casual appearance, is for dry climates only.

Basket weave pattern is interesting design using standard units.

Basket weave pattern here is variation on one shown at the left.

Split block unit has many decorative uses, comes solid and cored.

Combination pattern is made with various size units.

Split block in random ashlar pattern uses 8- and 4-inch unit above.

Polished, vertically stacked 2x16-inch face size units used here.

Slump block will create irregular surface for decorative uses.

Tooled horizontal and flush-rubbed vertical joints give "length."

Quantities of Concrete Block and Mortar

Wall thickness in.	For 100 sq.ft. of wall		For 100 concrete block
	Number of block*	Mortar** cu.ft.	Mortar** cu.ft.
8	112.5	2.6	2.3
12	112.5	2.6	2.3

*Based on block having an exposed face of 7⅝ x 15⅝ in. and laid up with ⅜-in. mortar joints.
**With face shell mortar bedding—10 per cent wastage included.

Recommended Mortar Mixes

Proportions by Volume

Type of service	Cement	Hydrated lime or lime putty	Mortar sand (damp, loose)
Ordinary service	1 — masonry cement or 1 — portland cement	— 1 to 1¼	2 to 3 4 to 6
Subject to very heavy loads, hurricanes, earthquakes, severe frost action.	1 — masonry cement plus 1 — portland cement or 1 — portland cement	— 0 to ¼	4 to 6 2 to 3

Quantities of Materials Per Cubic Foot of Mortar

Mortar mixes (volume)			Quantities			
Cement sack	Hydrated lime or lime putty cu.ft.	Sand in damp, loose condition cu.ft.	Masonry cement sack	Portland cement sack	Hydrated lime or lime putty cu.ft.	Sand cu.ft.
1 Masonry cement	—	3	0.33	—	—	0.99
1 Portland cement	1	6	—	0.16	0.16	0.97
1 Masonry cement plus 1 Portland cement	—	6	0.16	0.16	—	0.97
1 Portland cement	¼	3	—	0.29	0.07	0.86

1 sack masonry cement or portland cement = 1 cu.ft.

of water into the wall through mortar joints.

In laying concrete block, as in laying brick, the work is done wherever possible from the inside of a wall, and scaffolding or other supports such as planks on sawhorses or other firm supports are used. Depending upon whether he is right-handed or left-handed, the worker faces the wall in the same direction as he goes around from one lead to another.

After the mortar has become quite stiff, a jointing tool ("sled-runner") is run along the mortar joints to firm the mortar and prevent air spaces or weak spots from remaining. At this time too, the design of the wall pattern can be worked out; for a long wall, you may want only the horizontal joints tooled, with the vertical joints troweled down and smoothed.

Where cross walls and partitions intersect the walls, they should be tied into the main walls. In such cases, every second course of blocks is laid into the outside of main walls by means of three-quarter or other blocks. Metal ties may be used to further secure the walls to each other.

For small door openings, corner block may be used instead of jamb blocks, with ⅜- by 6-inch long bolts laid in the mortar joints, three or four for an ordinary small door. The burrs for these can be countersunk into the door frame and will not show when covered by the door stops.

Unlike brick which should be sprayed with a hose and kept moist or damp during construction, concrete blocks are stored and used dry. This means that they must be placed under cover when they arrive on the job and protected until they are in place in the wall.

Concrete masonry walls should be laid up with mortar composed of one of the proportions given in an accompanying table. All joints should be ⅜ inch thick.

Reinforcing. Ordinarily, it is not necessary to use reinforcing in walls of small buildings, but it is a good practice to place two ¼-inch round reinforcing rods in the horizontal mortar joints between the courses of masonry, just below and just over the windows and in the joint between the two top courses of blocks under the building plate.

Reinforcing bars should be bent around corners, with bar ends lapped 12 to 18 inches and well away from the corner.

Concrete window sills can be cast in place on the job or can be bought ready-made; precast units are increasingly popular.

Cavity wall consists of inner and outer walls separated by air space between.

Rods at such joints also may be wrapped with baling wire.

Sills and Lintels. Concrete sills and lintels can be cast on the job or obtained ready-made. Ready-made lintels are reinforced to carry the weight of walls, floors or roofs over the opening span. Two ⅜-inch rods are used for lintels carrying only wall loads over openings less than 8 feet wide. When lintels carry heavier loads, added reinforcement is required.

Two types of sills are commonly used for wood window frames or metal casements and frames. That for the metal windows has a raised shoulder to support the window frame. Both types project over the face of the wall about an inch and have a groove or drip on the underside of the overhang so that water running off the sill will not run down the face of the wall to stain it or soak it with moisture. Flush sills and window and door frames are not satisfactory.

The Plate. The plate of a building is the wooden 2x6 or 2x8 which is bolted down to the top of the wall, then leveled with pieces of stone or slate or other material to provide the base upon which the roof can be constructed. Bolts holding the plate to the masonry should be long enough to run into the second course of blocks, and should be set in mortar or concrete by putting a piece of metal lath in the core of the block to prevent the concrete or mortar from dropping through. In those portions of the country where heavy winds occur frequently, it may be better if these bolts extend down into the third course of blocks, for extra strength.

Lightweight Blocks. Cinder and other

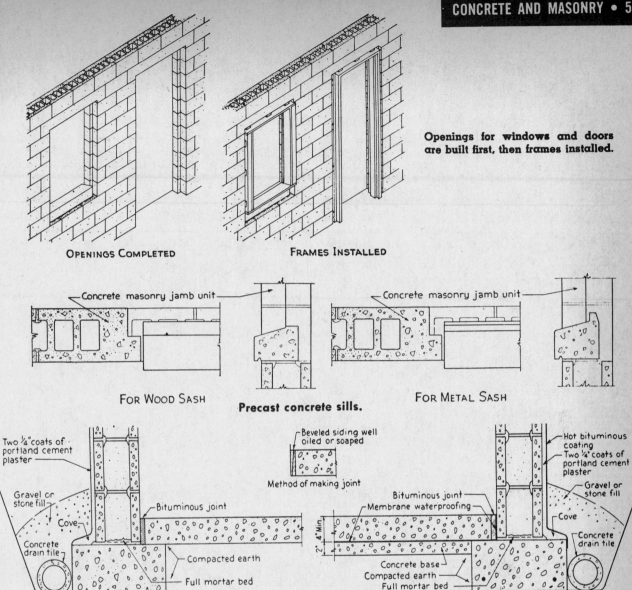

Openings for windows and doors are built first, then frames installed.

OPENINGS COMPLETED

FRAMES INSTALLED

Concrete masonry jamb unit

Concrete masonry jamb unit

FOR WOOD SASH

Precast concrete sills.

FOR METAL SASH

Two ¼"coats of portland cement plaster

Gravel or stone fill

Cove

Concrete drain tile

Bituminous joint

Compacted earth

Full mortar bed

Beveled siding well oiled or soaped

Method of making joint

Ordinary soil

Bituminous joint

Membrane waterproofing

4' Min.

2'

Concrete base

Compacted earth

Full mortar bed

Hot bituminous coating

Two ¼"coats of portland cement plaster

Gravel or stone fill

Cove

Concrete drain tile

Very wet soil

Recommended construction for dry basements.

lightweight blocks are commonly used in combination with brick to form 8- or 12-inch walls, or two rows of lightweight block may be laid with an air space between them.

Such lightweight block walls are tied together with No. 6 gauge metal ties, coated with non-corroding metal or other protection. An air space of 2⅜ inches left between two walls of lightweight block not only adds to the insulating value but tends to prevent outside leaks from penetrating the inner walls.

When loose fill insulation is used inside the face of a block wall or other solid masonry wall, the wall should be painted with a vapor-sealing material in order to keep the insulation from becoming moisture-laden. Two or three coats of aluminum paint will seal the wall surface, or, if fur-

ring strips are used, asphalt paper is used beneath them. Coating the outside walls with portland cement paint helps to make them weathertight.

The moisture or vapor being dealt with in this case is the result of condensation inside the wall, due to the cold air outside or inside meeting the warmer air. This condensation of vapor will moisten the insulation to the point where it becomes heavy, tends to sag, and thus greatly lessens its insulating value.

Watertight Basements. As in any other type of construction, where masonry is used below ground level, a few precautions may eliminate much annoyance and costly reconstruction later on. Footings should always be of poured concrete. The rule is that they should be the thickness of the wall they are to support, and twice as wide.

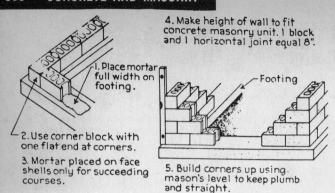

4. Make height of wall to fit concrete masonry unit. 1 block and 1 horizontal joint equal 8".

1. Place mortar full width on footing.

Footing

2. Use corner block with one flat end at corners.

3. Mortar placed on face shells only for succeeding courses.

5. Build corners up using mason's level to keep plumb and straight.

START LAYING BLOCK AT CORNERS

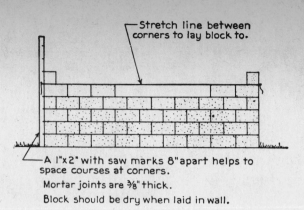

Stretch line between corners to lay block to.

A 1"x2" with saw marks 8" apart helps to space courses at corners.

Mortar joints are ⅜" thick.

Block should be dry when laid in wall.

BUILD WALL BETWEEN CORNERS

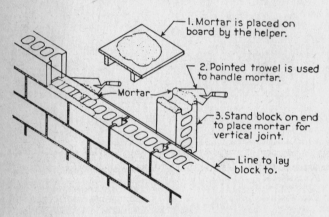

1. Mortar is placed on board by the helper.

2. Pointed trowel is used to handle mortar.

Mortar

3. Stand block on end to place mortar for vertical joint.

Line to lay block to.

APPLY MORTAR IN A DOUBLE ROW

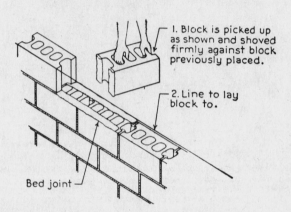

1. Block is picked up as shown and shoved firmly against block previously placed.

2. Line to lay block to.

Bed joint

SET BLOCK FIRMLY IN PLACE

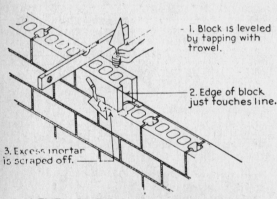

1. Block is leveled by tapping with trowel.

2. Edge of block just touches line.

3. Excess mortar is scraped off.

LEVEL BLOCK AND SCRAPE OFF EXCESS MORTAR

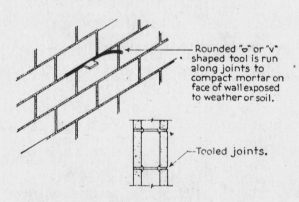

Rounded "o" or "v" shaped tool is run along joints to compact mortar on face of wall exposed to weather or soil.

Tooled joints.

TOOL THE JOINTS TO COMPRESS MORTAR

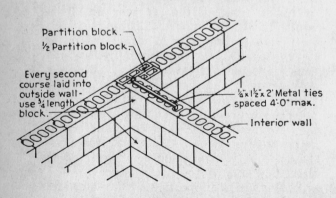

Partition block.

½ Partition block.

Every second course laid into outside wall - use ¾ length block.

¼"x1½"x2' Metal ties spaced 4'-0" max.

Interior wall

BUILD PARTITION WALLS INTO OUTSIDE WALLS

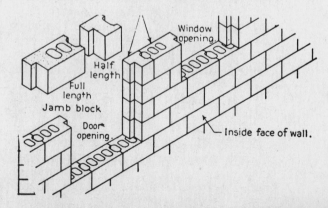

Window opening.

Half length

Full length

Jamb block

Door opening.

Inside face of wall.

USE RECESSED JAMB BLOCK AT SIDES OF DOOR AND WINDOW OPENINGS

Method of building door frames

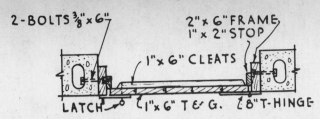

2-BOLTS ⅜"x6"   2"x6"FRAME
                 1"x2"STOP
        1"x6"CLEATS

LATCH   1"x6"T&G.   8"T-HINGE

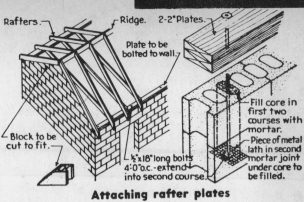

Rafters   Ridge.   2-2"Plates.

Plate to be bolted to wall.

Block to be cut to fit.

½"x18" long bolts 4'-0" o.c.-extend into second course

Fill core in first two courses with mortar.

Piece of metal lath in second mortar joint under core to be filled.

Attaching rafter plates

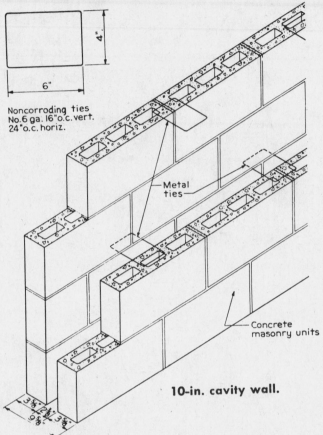

4"

6"

Noncorroding ties No.6 ga. 16" o.c. vert. 24" o.c. horiz.

Metal ties

Concrete masonry units

10-in. cavity wall.

Long beams, lintels, can be built by using beam blocks as below instead of forms for the concrete.

Solid blocks or blocks filled with concrete are used for top course of a floor-supporting wall.

Plastic, workable mortar mix—thoroughly mixed to reduce amount of water needed—is essential.

In all soils, but especially in tight or water-logged soil, drains of 4-inch drain tile should be laid around the outside of a wall and run to a suitable outlet. These drains are then covered with gravel before the soil is shoveled or bulldozed back.

All masonry walls below ground level should be plastered with two ½-inch coats of cement mortar. After these have set, the wall is painted with hot asphalt or bituminous paint, using a heavy brush and making certain that the paint covers the wall thoroughly. These precautions will not prevent a wall inside a basement from sweating during damp weather, but if carefully done, they should prevent leakage through the wall.

Still another precaution is used when laying the floor. A wedge-shaped board which has been well oiled is placed between the wall and the floor concrete. When the concrete has set and dried, this wedge is removed and the space filled with hot tar or asphalt to prevent ground water seepage up through the joint between the floor slab and the wall. •

patching masonry

Find out all there is to know about your mixes before starting any masonry repairs.

THE word "cement" gets quite a kicking around. It is used to designate almost everything connected with masonry construction and patching, from the main ingredient that goes into the mixture to the finished product.

There is an equal amount of confusion about the term "portland cement." That's a type of material, not a particular brand of cement. Portland cement is made by many different companies. It got its name because, when patented back in the early 1800's, it had the hardened appearance of rock quarried on Portland Island in the English Channel.

Cement, therefore, is the principal material from which concrete is made. Concrete is a mixture of cement, sand and a coarse aggregate, gravel or crushed rock, all given the proper consistency with water. When portland cement is mixed with sand and water it is sometimes called a sand mix and sometimes just plain cement, which is where some of the confusion originates. When portland cement is mixed with sand plus hydrated lime, it is called mortar.

Photo above shows a metal trowel used for smooth surfacing and a wooden float for obtaining rough finish. Application of concrete, right, is usually done with a pointed metal trowel, available in many sizes for various jobs.

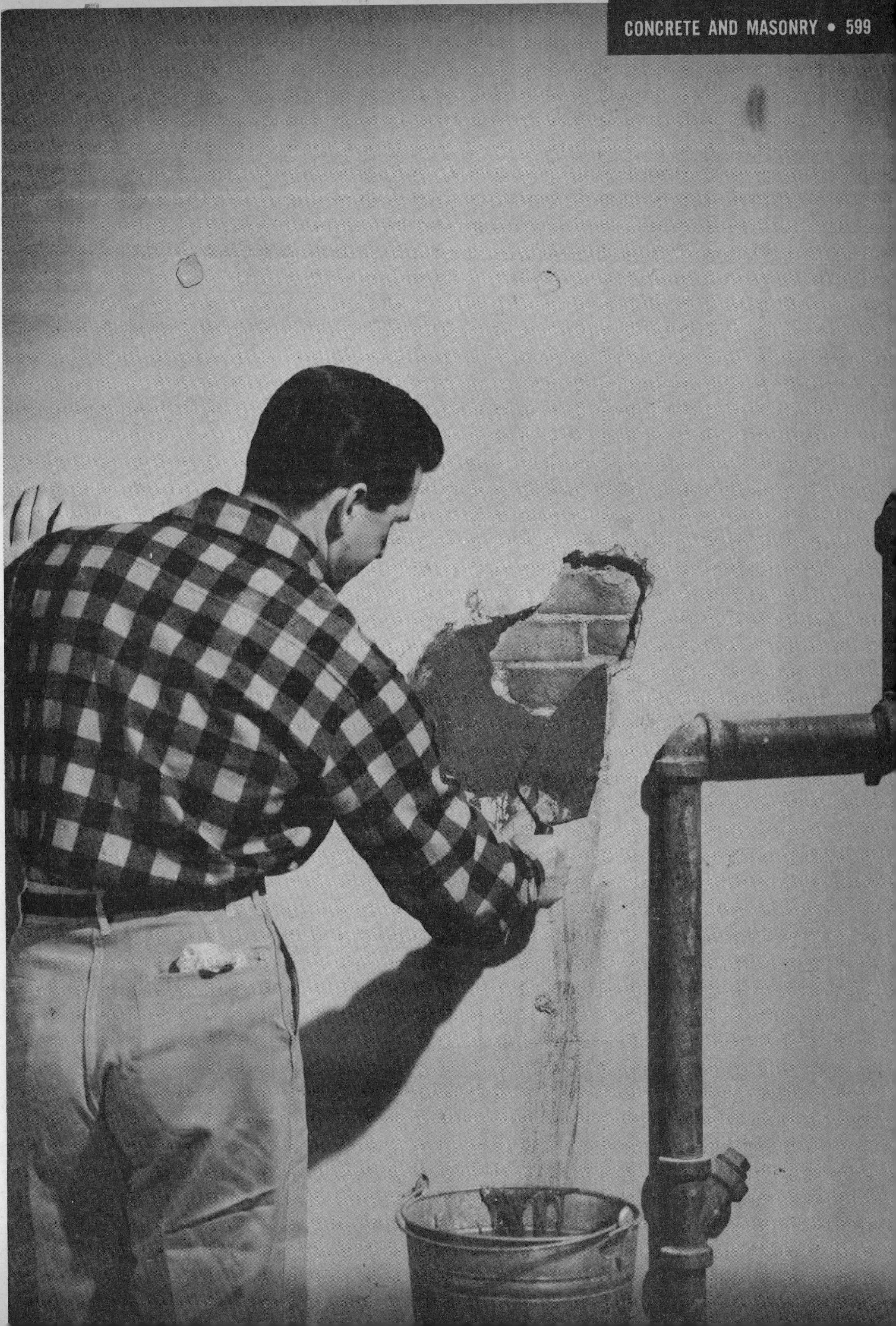

Typical weed-producing crack found in poured side-walks, driveways and patios. If it's small use sand mix; large cracks are filled with gravel mix.

Enlarge the opening by chiseling out the sides. Try to undercut crack so it forms an inverted "V" to increase bonding between old and new concrete.

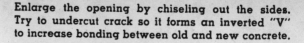

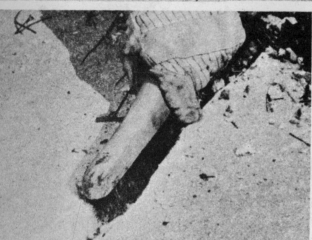

After crack is enlarged and undercut, use a stiff wire brush to clean out all loose particles. Get rid of all concrete chips, dust, dirt and weeds.

Wet area thoroughly to help the new concrete bond to old. Instead of a brush, as shown, a watering can or garden hose can be used to soak opening.

Grout is used to designate any mixture which is extra watery. It may even be just portland cement and water.

You can make all of these mixtures yourself by buying the ingredients separately and adding the right amount of water. You can get large quantities of pre-mixed concrete for use when you're tackling large projects, such as laying foundations or putting down driveways. Or, for small and medium patching jobs around the house, you can buy bags of pre-mixed materials called gravel mixes, sand mixes and mortar mixes, as well as a fourth product where unusual water tightness is essential.

The pre-mixes have everything in a sack except water. When you add the water you have just the right consistency for the particular job at hand. It is true that you pay more for this mix, but you save time

and labor and know that you have the right proportions every time.

Whether you mix your own concrete or buy the pre-mixed variety, bear in mind that you must never use more water than is designated. Too much water always weakens the mixture. Too little water keeps the mixture from being workable and you may find that the various components do not cling together properly. But too much water is far more troublesome since the concrete loses its durability even though it appears to be hardening into a solid, strong mass.

Generally, for small patching, you should use 1 part of portland cement to 2½ parts of fine, clean sand. Where a heavier concrete mixture is desired, what is called a 1:2:3 proportion will get good results. That's one part of portland cement to two

If you have pre-mixed concrete just add water at the rate of five quarts per 80-pound bag. You can do all your mixing on the patio next to crack.

Mix concrete and water thoroughly by turning with a trowel. Start repair when all dry mix has disappeared and is completely saturated with water.

Finished mix is tested by running tip of trowel across it to prove its plasticity. Trowel should leave a smooth, even surface without any bumps.

Apply mixture to crack with a trowel and let stand for about 30 to 45 minutes. Do your final troweling with a steel float to get even, smooth surface.

parts of sand to three parts of gravel. For mortar mixes, usually used around brickwork, a mixture of 1 part of portland cement to 2½ parts of sand, plus about ten per cent by bulk or volume of hydrated lime, is generally recommended. The amounts of water cannot be accurately specified since the water held by the sand itself must be taken into account. The use of wet sand naturally calls for less water. Five gallons of water per sack of portland cement is about right for making concrete when the sand is average in moisture content. With the pre-mixed concrete, one gallon is enough for a 90-pound bag.

Cracked Sidewalks

Sidewalk cracks usually must be made bigger before they can be effectively repaired. It is possible, on occasion, to do

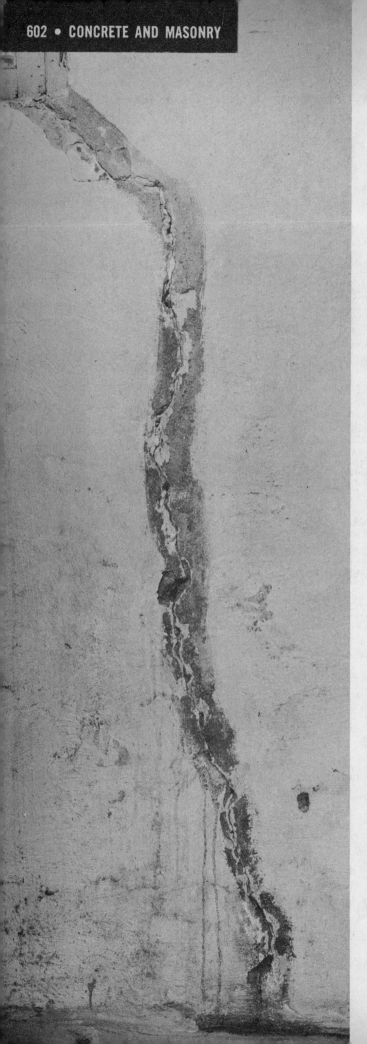

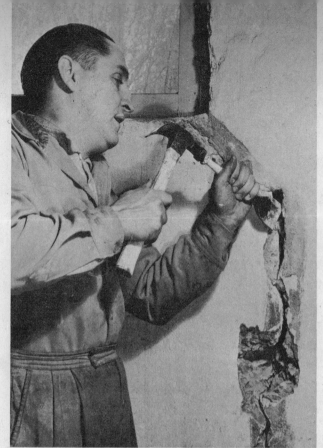

Damp basements often show cracks similar to the one shown at left. Start repair by undercutting and widening the area, using a chisel and hammer.

a temporary job on a hairline crack with grout—a mixture of portland cement and water. But if you want to get lasting results, the crack must be enlarged along its entire length with a cold chisel and a hammer.

The crack must be made wider at the bottom than at the top, a procedure known as undercutting. The undercutting should be done to a minimum depth of one inch. Clean out the opening thoroughly with a brush, being sure you remove any small plant life as well as dirt and pieces of the sidewalk that have been chipped away. Soak the area completely. Fill with sand mix, tamping it tightly, making certain that the opening is completely filled. When the mixture begins to set, smooth it down with a wooden float or a metal trowel, adding more sand mix if necessary. Use the float if you're trying to get a rough surface, a trowel if you want it smooth. Wet down the patch at least once a day for several days.

Patching Concrete Driveways

Repairing a concrete driveway is somewhat similar to the patching of a sidewalk, except that the driveway repair must withstand heavier weights and therefore should be stronger.

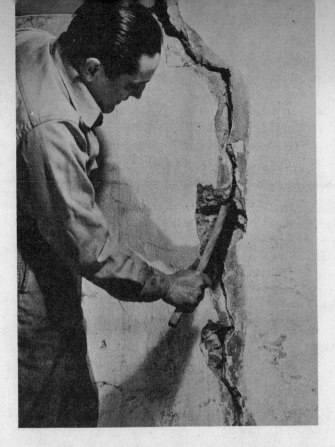

Again, a stiff brush is used to clean out all loose dust and dirt. Don't smooth edges of crack; rough surface helps to bond new concrete to old.

In case of large cracks, above, a garden hose is handy for wetting the area thoroughly. Do this before you start filling crack with the concrete.

Use a gravel mix rather than a sand mix. When the opening has been undercut, cleaned and soaked with water, fill it with the new concrete and level it off. Whereas a sidewalk patch can be walked on after a day or two, it is better to wait at least three or four days before using your automobile on a patched driveway. Again, wet down daily for several days.

A very large driveway patch can be further strengthened by reinforcing it with a piece of metal lath or any other mesh-type wire. Pour about half the gravel mix into the opening, lay the metal into it, then pour the rest of the concrete. Always allow an hour or two for the concrete to set before giving it the final troweling.

Cracks in Stucco

The procedure for repairing cracks in stucco is the same as that for repairing cracks in sidewalks.

Where the crack is large enough so that the smooth finish of the patch will contrast with the finish of the stucco, you'll have to experiment a little to get the right effect.

What is known as a spatter-dash finish is obtained by dipping an old whisk broom into the damp mortar after it's on the wall. Other finishes can be obtained by deliberately leaving trowel marks in the surface.

Mix concrete and apply with metal trowel. Pack the mixture in as hard as possible since it will also add to strength of wall. Smooth with trowel.

On extremely small cracks in walls or patios no undercutting is necessary. After cleaning out dust, wet area and apply mixture to fill the cavity.

Use any method you choose in an attempt to match the patch with the surrounding surface. The principle is to "rough up" the repair while it's still wet.

Patching Brickwork

Under normal conditions, a well-built brick wall is watertight. Should a leak occur, it usually is the result of a shrinkage of the mortar, leaving a space between the bricks.

The re-mortaring of these joints is called tuck pointing or just pointing. Whatever you call it, a lot of future headaches can be averted by doing it at the first sign of the mortar pulling away from the bricks.

A mortar mix must be used for this type of work rather than a mix which does not contain lime. The lime delays the setting of the mortar and thus prevents shrinkage.

Remove all loose mortar with a cold chisel and hammer or an old screwdriver. Work gently since you do not want to dislodge any of the solid mortar or damage the brick itself. Dust out or blow out all particles of loose mortar and then soak the cavity and the surrounding area. The new mortar should be applied with a trowel, the kind that comes to a point and is known as a pointing trowel.

The mortar is thoroughly packed into the opening until it is flush with the brick.

Keep a wet rag or a scrub brush handy to wipe off any mortar that gets on the face of the brick; it is easy to get off while it is wet, difficult after it has hardened. Use the end of the trowel to indent the joints slightly to aid in shedding rain water. Professional bricklayers use several different types of joints between the bricks, but you need not be concerned with them as long as you get a reasonably close match with the surrounding joints. This indenting of the joints should be done a few minutes after the mortar has been applied. Therefore, if you have several bricks close together to work on, fill all the joints; by the time you get to the last one, the mortar in the first will have hardened just enough to get ahead with the indenting.

The patched joints must be wet down at least once a day for several days. While you're at it, wet the surrounding bricks as well, since they absorb moisture from the fresh mortar.

The whitish substance that sometimes forms on brick walls is called efflorescence. It is caused by the soluble salts being washed out of the bricks and mortar. It usually means the wall is not watertight, so any attempt to clean off the whitish deposit should not be undertaken until after the tuck pointing is finished. Sometimes the efflorescence will come off by scrubbing with a wire brush and a little water, but if it has been there for some time, it must be removed with a solution of one part of muriatic acid with from seven to ten parts of water. Scrubbing with a wire brush, dipped in this solution, is highly effective, but the acid solution can be harmful to skin and clothing, so be sure to wear rubber gloves and exercise extreme care. Scrub the brick thoroughly but not so vigorously that you splash the solution. After the scrubbing has been completed, flush the area with water to remove all traces of the acid; easiest way to flush bricks is with a garden hose. In making the solution, use a wooden, glass or earthenware container, never a metal one.

Damp and Wet Basements

A basement which is continually damp or wet is more than just a nuisance. It cannot be utilized for any useful purpose, is a health menace and can also weaken the foundation walls.

Many homeowners who have put up with a damp basement for years have finally discovered, in one way or another, that the trouble all the time was nothing more than condensation. There are several ways to tell whether condensation is the culprit. If the cold water pipes in the basement sweat often when the weather is warm and moist, that's condensation. Take a small mirror and attach or support it close against the wall. If the mirror is wet and foggy after a few hours, that's condensation. Attach a piece of aluminum foil about a foot square to the basement wall. If water appears after a few hours on the surface of the foil, that's condensation. Or, when there is water present on a wall, use an electric fan or a hair dryer and blow

This corner of a concrete porch has broken away from foundation, is sadly in need of repair. Before fixing, study the break to find best approach.

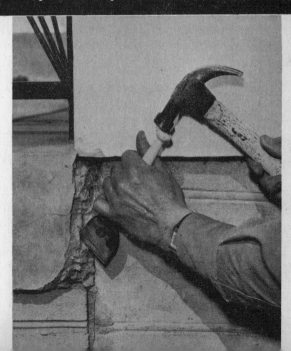

In this break, old concrete must be chiseled away to even up the area. When doing this try to leave a rough surface to give better adhesion of new mix.

To keep concrete in place, a simple form of 2x4 lumber is constructed. Boards shown are slightly oversize, but it's better than a too small frame.

Soak area, including wooden frame, thoroughly with water. This wetting down applies to any concrete, cement, gravel or any other masonry work.

a stream of air against the wall for a little while. If the wall dries up, and stays dry while the air is being blown against it, the dampness was caused by condensation.

Having discovered that condensation is the cause, that little experiment with the electric fan or hair dryer is the clue to the solution: condensation cannot exist where there is a proper circulation of air. You can create such a circulation with a couple of well-placed electric fans or some other type of blower, as well as seeing that the basement windows are always kept open in dry weather.

When condensation is not at fault, you have to find out what the troublemaker is before you can do something about it. Poor drainage conditions very often are responsible. Check carefully to see whether the soil outside your house is banked properly, permitting rainwater to flow away from the house rather than against it. See whether the gutters are doing their job. There may be broken or out-of-line sections which allow the rainwater to flow down the side of the house to the foundation footing. See whether the downspouts are in working order and whether the rainwater coming out of them is flowing away from the house rather than sinking immediately into the ground. The best way to make these inspections is during a rainstorm. It may be inconvenient and uncomfortable to do it that way, but it's a sure-fire method to find out whether anything is wrong.

Should you find that water is entering the basement at a point where a utility pipe is located, go outside and find the spot where the pipe enters the house wall. This may mean digging out the earth around the pipe. Remove all loose masonry near the pipe, working carefully so as not to

damage it. Reseal the joint with one of the waterproof plugging materials. Put the earth back in place, go back to the basement and also reseal the joint where the pipe comes out of the wall.

Cracks and breaks in foundation walls can be repaired with a sand mix—portland cement, sand and water or the ready-mixed type to which only water need be added. Here again, the tried-and-true method of enlarging the opening must be followed, with the bottom of the cut wider than the top. Unless this is done, the new mix will not stay in place. Brush out all loose particles, wet down and apply the mix, being certain that it is packed in thoroughly. Too much water in the mixture will make the patching difficult and reduce the strength of the repair. When the patch begins to set, smooth it off as you press down and add a little more mix if necessary. Keep the area moist for a few days.

Seepage through a basement wall often can be halted—if it is not severe—by an application of portland cement paint. It is important that this paint be mixed and applied in accordance with the manufacturer's directions. Also, the walls must be completely free of all dirt, dust, grease, efflorescence and paint. This may involve a considerable amount of work, so it is usually wise to make a test to see whether the cement paint will be effective. This is done by marking off, during a rainy period, a particular area of a wall where dampness appears. Wait until that area has dried, clean it and apply the paint, using a scrubbing brush and being certain to work the paint into all depressions. When the next severe rain occurs, see whether that painted section becomes damp again. If it does, you know the cement paint will not handle the assignment. If it retards the

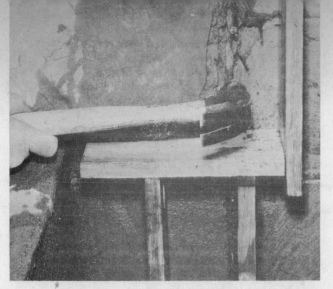

In repair work of this type some reinforcement is necessary to add strength and help bonding. Here, various size nails are driven into crevices.

Concrete should only be mixed after all preparatory work is completed and you are ready to start application. Mix only amount needed for the job.

Stir thoroughly until all dry sand has disappeared. For larger repair work a metal wheelbarrow, as shown, enables you to have mix always close by.

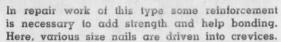

Pack mixture in firmly with a trowel and allow to stand until watery sheen appears, usually 40 minutes, then smooth out with flat metal trowel.

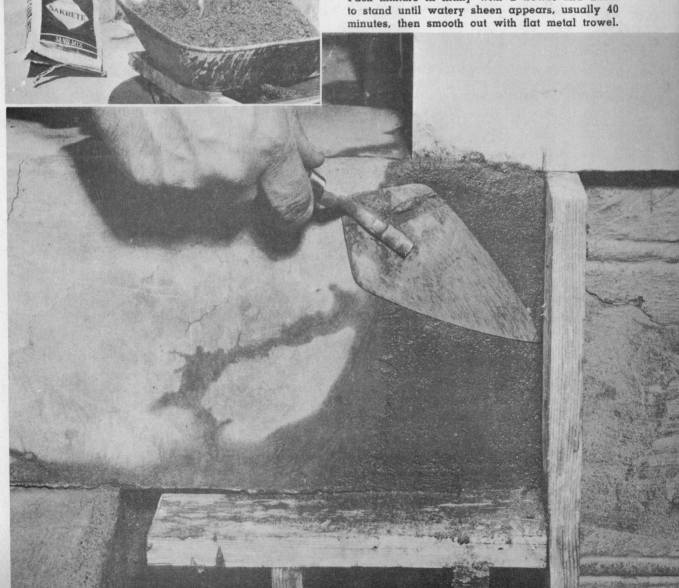

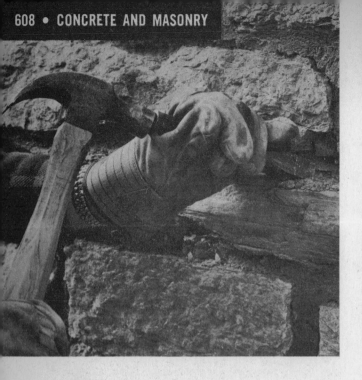

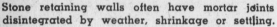

Stone retaining walls often have mortar joints disintegrated by weather, shrinkage or settling.

After all old mortar is chiseled out, use a stiff brush to clean break of any debris, dust or dirt.

dampness, then you can go ahead and do the entire basement with it, using it for decorative purposes as well as to keep out the water.

More severe seepage conditions require the use of waterproofing compound, either a paste or a powder. This compound is mixed with one part of portland cement and two parts of sand according to the manufacturer's instructions. Or you can buy a pre-mix into which the compound already has been added. The preparatory steps for this treatment differ, depending on whether the walls are of concrete, brick or block-type construction. With concrete, the old surface must be roughened with drills, cold chisels or similar tools, leaving holes or openings at least a quarter-of-an-inch deep every few inches. After that, a solution of one part of muriatic acid to ten parts of water is put on the walls with a fiber brush, followed by a hosing down with water. With block-type construction, all mortar joints should be raked out to at least to a depth of half an inch. Whitewash, calcimine, cold water paint and efflorescence are removed with one part of muriatic acid and five parts of water. If the wall has oil paint on it, remove it with a solution of 1½ gallons of caustic soda mixed with one gallon of water; follow with a hosing down with water.

After that, the steps for any type of basement wall are the same. They consist of spraying the entire wall surface with water, applying a coat of grout (portland cement and water) and then putting on the waterproofing mix, which is a kind of cement plaster. This cement plaster is trowelled on the surface to a depth of about three eighths of an inch. The entire wall is then gone over with a broom or wire brush to "scratch" the surface, after which a second coat, ⅜ inch thick, is put on.

The waterproofing or cement plastering treatment also can be given to the floors. Should you decide on this, then the second coat of wall plaster should be carried out on the floor for six or eight inches. The procedure for doing the floor is the same as that for the wall, except that a single thick coat, from one to two inches, will be sufficient.

You will note that in all this discussion of interior waterproofing, whether with cement paint or cement plaster, we have referred only to slightly damp or moderately damp basements. Fortunately, nearly all damp basements fall into one of those two categories. But occasionally, a basement is so damp—wet would be a better word—that it must be waterproofed from the outside. This is the only absolutely certain method of preventing water under pressure from getting into a basement.

Unless you have plenty of help, this outside waterproofing is best left to the professionals. They have all the equipment and know-how. And while it will make a dent in your pocketbook, you'll be glad you didn't attempt it yourself when you see what a job it is to dig to the base of the foundation, entirely aside from the waterproofing itself.

Wet the area to be repaired as well as surrounding surface for better adhesion of new mortar mix.

Curing Concrete

The care and attention given to concrete during the days and weeks when it is hardening is known as curing. This curing, often neglected by the novice, is a vital part of any concrete project, whether it be a repair or an original construction.

Concrete, during its drying process, gets stronger and more water-resistant provided the drying process is retarded. If the drying is not slowed down, the concrete will not be as strong or as water-resistant as it could be. Further, it may develop openings, some on the surface and some which may go right through the concrete. Still another result of improper drying is that the concrete always seems to be dusty no matter how much it is cleaned.

The obvious way to prevent something from drying out too rapidly is to keep it moist. That's what curing consists of— keeping the concrete moist. How moist it should be kept depends on conditions. For instance, newly-laid concrete which is exposed constantly to sun and wind must be kept moist continuously. This is done by covering the concrete with straw, burlap, canvas, sand or anything which will serve as a protection. Whatever the covering is, it should be sprinkled with water periodically. The covering, by the way, is put down after the concrete has hardened a little; a precaution that is necessary to keep the surface from being damaged. This covering is kept on for a week or ten days. When the concrete is not exposed to sun or wind, a covering is not necessary. ●

Use a trowel and your fingers to get the mixture into all crevices. Pack as tightly as possible.

Leo Lemchen, N.S.I.D., designed this kitchen for his own home. Bright red cabinets match built-in Westinghouse appliances including dishwasher, refrigerator and freezer units, microwave oven, etc.

Planning the Kitchen

Your kitchen's the house's busiest room, so plan it with plenty of care.

THE KITCHEN, in many respects, is the most important and most frequently used room in the house. It's not just a place for cooking and serving meals. It's also a congregating place for the family and for friends who drop in. It's the general meeting room for just about any family discussion; it's the family planning center, office, message center, very frequently the laundry center, and a few dozen other things thrown in. There is probably no other room that is used so frequently or for as many different things.

Since everyone, not just the little woman, spends so much time in the kitchen, it certainly stands to reason that it should be designed functionally, efficiently, attractively, and with a certain amount of comfort. Naturally there are certain limitations imposed by the layout of your house and

Well-designed small area provides high-rise units from Hotpoint compactly lining available walls in well-lighted window wall overlooking the terrace.

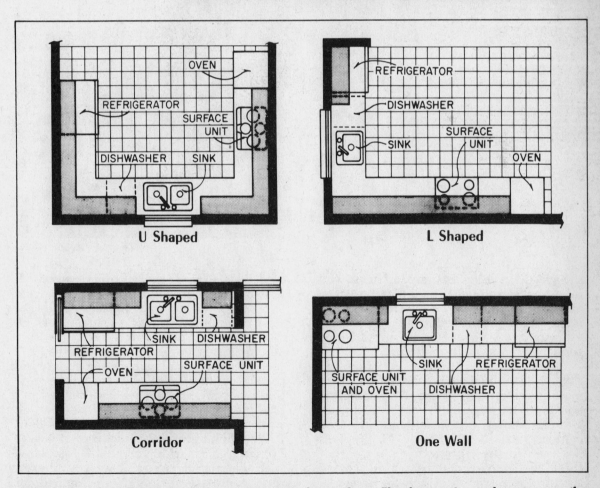

U Shaped

L Shaped

Corridor

One Wall

Other layouts from Hotpoint suggest arrangements shown above. The three major work centers are the refrigerator and food storage center, the cooking and serving center, the sink and cleaning center.

This open country-style design features units set in extended brick wall for a built-in look that is functional and beautiful.

Interesting combination of Pennsylvania Dutch and modern presents a clean but interesting decor for the suburbanite kitchen

General Electric photos

the space available. Sometimes the kitchen may be of an unusual or difficult-to-work shape, or it may just be too small. In older houses the opposite tends to be true, where kitchens are oversized and seem to beg for condensation and streamlining.

Based on its primary function, the kitchen can be broken down into three major work centers. These are: refrigerator and food storage center; the cooking and serving center; the sink and cleaning center.

Taken in their separate parts, each of these particular functions should work as a unit. The refrigerator and the associated food storage cabinets should be grouped together near a convenient working sur-

face that is handy to the other centers. If possible, there should be a logical flow from one center to another, or they should be close enough so the missus doesn't work up a lot of mileage preparing a meal. In a long, narrow kitchen area for example, they can be on opposite walls where she simply has to turn around to reach from one area to the other. With a long-walled kitchen, it's possible to place them side by side so that work moves in a straight, continuous flow.

The cooking and serving center is also treated as a separate unit that is associated with the storage center. The serving area, if at all possible, should be designed for easy access to the dining area itself. Most kitchens have enough room for a self-in-

Large kitchen area has compact L shape for the necessary functions, but leaves rest of the room for work, play and dining.

Marlite photo

This long-aisle kitchen combines food preparation and laundry units along one wall. Cabinets and walls are plastic-coated.

cluded dining area. There will also be a connecting door to a separate formal dining room. This door should not be so far from the cooking and serving area that it becomes an inconvenience, unless you have a platoon of servants to help you prepare and serve meals. The layout and design should keep the travel path as short as possible.

One general rule in arranging the three basic work centers is to keep the sink and cleaning center located somewhere in between the other two centers. A production-line kind of arrangement is always preferable so the work will flow smoothly in one direction.

Ideally, the mistress of the house should not have to walk more than 22 feet maxi-

mum distance between centers. This is an ideal measurement, and while it is not necessarily a hard-and-fast rule, remember that any greater distance between major working areas will help provide you with a very tired wife when you come home in the evening.

There are four basic patterns of kitchen layouts and almost any kitchen can be categorized this way—either as a basic layout or a variation on it. The first type is the U-shaped kitchen which is called the best and most efficient type of plan available. The work centers in this arrangement are joined in a continuous line along three walls. The dining center is usually a short distance from the U itself.

Concave ceiling treatment unifies this oddly-shaped kitchen. Built-in units like surface-cookers and range hood wind around.

General Electric photos

Modern kitchen with Early American theme achieved with severe plankwood cherry cabinetry and the rustic beamed ceilings.

The second basic pattern is the L-shape, and is second only to the U for efficient operation. In this type of arrangement, the work centers are laid out in a continuous line along two walls including one corner. Usually the dining area is in an opposite corner or on a third wall.

The third basic type is a corridor pattern. This is a type of kitchen that is frequently found in small houses and in apartments. This arrangement has the kitchen located on two opposing walls with a narrow aisle between. There is not necessarily a continuous flow from one center to another, but the narrow aisle spacing between the walls reduces the amount of necessary travel from one point to another.

Patterns of this type do not allow any space for a dining area, which must be detached, but should be nearby.

The fourth basic type of kitchen is a single wall. This is certainly the most simplified kind of layout, and the work path is in one continuous line along the wall. This is especially suitable in very limited space, again in very small homes or in apartments.

One additional functional area that can be very important for large and spread-out types of kitchens is the island or peninsula. This can take on the form of a serving counter, a snack bar or a work center that juts out into the center of the room. It can also double as a room divider. Features

Family room adjacent to the kitchen doubles as a dining area and den. The plastic-finished wall material is the secret.

Marlite photo

Turquoise appliances set against a white kitchen background with brick patterned floor is striking.

such as this can draw larger areas closer together, or it can act as a room separator that still provides the conveniences of a larger room.

The general plan for the kitchen evolves from such factors as the size, proximity and location of the various major work centers, windows and doorways and the desired overall kitchen design. The next step is to decide just which appliances are necessary. The three basic items—sink, range and refrigerator—should be located in their respective work center areas. Other appliances that can be added without really requiring any extra space are a range hood, under-the-counter dishwasher, garbage disposal and other small convenience items.

One item that you might want to consider before finishing off the kitchen is a good location for the telephone. This way, you can have the installer put it in ahead of time, hiding the wire between the walls for a custom installation.

An important factor in kitchen design is general lighting, a subject that is covered in more detail in a later chapter. Just remember that lighting will play a very important part in the kitchen's overall appearance and character.

Ventilation is another important feature. While most kitchens are adequately ventilated with exhaust fans, range hoods and so on, the kitchen will still get unbearably hot when the missus is preparing a large dinner or doing any amount of baking. A very worthwhile feature in any modern kitchen is a through-the-wall air conditioner. This type of appliance is recommended even if the house has central air conditioning, since central systems cannot cope with the tremendous amount of extra heat generated in a typical kitchen. The cost of such an air conditioner is modest, and your wife will love you for it the first time she does any real baking in her new quarters. Just bear in mind that an air conditioner in the kitchen is not intended to make the room a haven from summer heat, but just to get rid of the

Storage

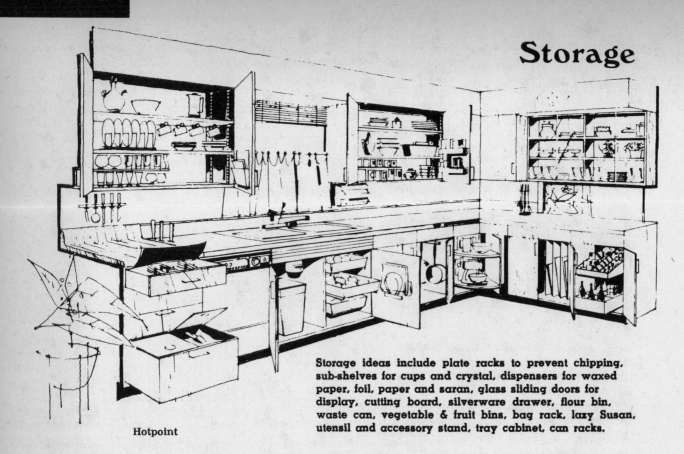

Hotpoint

Storage ideas include plate racks to prevent chipping, sub-shelves for cups and crystal, dispensers for waxed paper, foil, paper and saran, glass sliding doors for display, cutting board, silverware drawer, flour bin, waste can, vegetable & fruit bins, bag rack, lazy Susan, utensil and accessory stand, tray cabinet, can racks.

excess heat generated by a lot of cooking.

Another important consideration are the kitchen cabinets. Ideally, as much wall space as possible should be covered with storage cabinets, both for food and for dishes and utensils. No matter how much storage space is provided, there never seems to be enough, and the kitchen renovation is certainly an opportune time to remedy this. There are several schools of thought where cabinets are concerned. One way to provide additional storage is to run cabinets right up to and flush with the ceiling. This means that there will be a second tier of cabinets for long-term storage that cannot be reached without a step-ladder or stepstool. Actually, this type of cabinet should be used only if additional storage space is at a premium—very sorely needed, no matter what. But if you go ahead with double-tiered cabinets, you can look forward to a lot of ladder climbing to fetch the "whatchamacallit" stored there a year or so ago. If at all possible, the kitchen should have a walk-in pantry near the back door for general and long-term storage of a variety of commodities, soaps, etc. If your present kitchen does not have this, try to arrange to build one in for a touch of storage luxury.

The most conventional way to attach cabinets is to run them up the wall to within two feet or so of the ceiling. Some

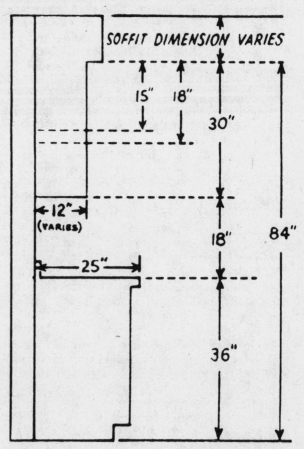

Measure your kitchen area, cabinets, etc., then compare with these standard unit measurements.

Appliance Template

Base Cabinet Template

Wall Cabinet Template

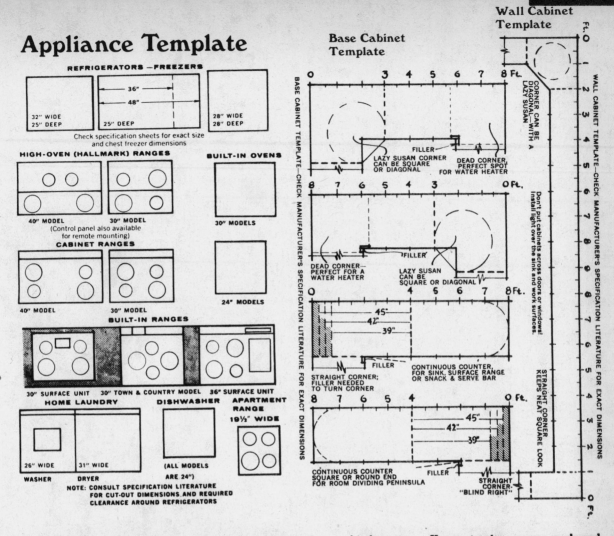

These templates will allow you to start planning your kitchen area. Use a tracing paper pad and trace units in proper place. Try many arrangements before deciding on final plan. Use imagination.

people will just stop there, leaving the tops of the cabinets open as dust catchers and as a general repository for house plants, that huge kettle that's used only once every two months, and that horrible teapot from Aunt Tillie that must be on display whenever she visits. Cabinets installed this way have an incomplete look about them and certainly do little to enhance the attractiveness of the kitchen. If at all possible, try to run a flush soffit from the cabinet top to the ceiling. This is accepted procedure and will give the kitchen a streamlined and finished appearance. Certainly the soffit means that there will be some wasted space above the cabinets, but this space would be wasted anyway. There are a few tricks to using some of this area in several ways, which will be covered in later chapters.

The cabinets can be purchased in ready-made units that fit together like building blocks. Such arrangements are offered by Sears, among others, and outlets of this kind also will provide a complete kitchen planning service free of charge, along with any purchases that you make.

While you are planning your kitchen for efficiency, see if you have room for a full-size upright freezer and possibly a partitioned area for a laundry. The kitchen seems to be gaining favor as a location for these appliances in preference to the basement. There are several good reasons for this, mainly to save running up and down the cellar stairs many times a day. Another important reason is the growing tendency to build a finished recreation and family room in the basement. Naturally, a freezer and a couple of laundry machines occupying basement floor space are just going to get in the way of such plans.

Careful planning of the kitchen layout, its basic design and functions are thus not only essential to the kitchen itself, but as part of the family's entire living pattern. •

Ceiling Treatments

The right kind of ceiling, put up correctly, will do wonders for a room.

A new acoustical ceiling tile has a practical, grease-resistant finish over an attractive texture.
Armstrong Cork Co.

CEILINGS GENERALLY belong to one of four categories. The first type is conventional plaster and lath which should be installed only by a professional. The second type uses gypsum board or other types of wallboard. The third category is the ultra-modern suspended ceiling, which is covered in a later chapter. The particular type of covering we are interested in here is the tile ceiling, and this itself can be subdivided into several categories depending on the kind of ceiling you are covering, what type of tile you plan to use, and the method of fastening.

Ceiling tiles can be anchored in place by one of three methods: gluing, nailing, or stapling. The actual type of fastening arrangement depends on the kind of tile, re-finements the manufacturer has added to the tile's border, and the type of ceiling you're going to cover.

A basic necessity for ceiling tile going on over bare joists is a series of furring strips nailed across the joists. These will provide the nailing or stapling base for the tiles. Some people feel that furring and staples are unnecessary, and that glue is vastly superior. If you belong to this school of thought, first cover the exposed joists with wallboard panels to provide a continuous gluing surface. Of course if you are covering an already existing plaster or wallboard ceiling, there is no problem, and you have the choice of using staples, nails or glue, all depending on how solid the ceiling is.

If you do intend to use staples or nails,

SLIDE TILE INTO POSITION TO MAKE SNUG JOINT; DON'T FORCE OR HAMMER TILE INTO PLACE

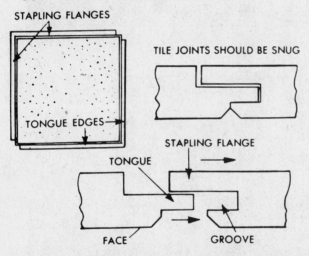

STAPLING FLANGES

TONGUE EDGES

TILE JOINTS SHOULD BE SNUG

STAPLING FLANGE

TONGUE

FACE

GROOVE

MATERIALS FOR EACH 100 SQ. FT.

TILE SIZE	12" x 12"	12" x 24"
½" OR 9/16" STAPLES OR 1⅛" BLUED LATH NAILS*	400	300
8D NAILS FOR FURRING	1.7 LBS.	1.7 LBS.
1" x 3" LATH (LINEAL FT.)	140	140
CARTONS OF TILE	1.7	1.7
COVE MOLDING	PERIMETER OF ROOM PLUS 20%	

*WHERE STAPLES ARE USED, ORDER 50 LATH NAILS FOR FACE-NAILING BORDER

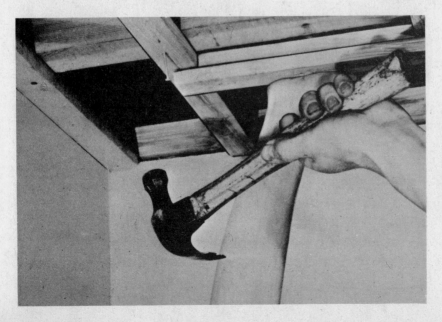

Ceiling tiles are usually installed over 1x3" furring strips which must be firmly nailed to the joists. Spacer jig is shown for quick and accurate positioning of strips.

it's a good idea to install the furring strips anyway, since both plasterboard and plaster have a bad habit of not providing a firm anchor for nails and staples.

The first step is to locate the joists by tapping the ceiling—an unnecessary procedure if you are working on an open ceiling. Once you have located the joists, mark them off with a pencil. Locate the first furring strip either on the center line or six inches to one side, depending on the width of the room. The furring strips must run at right angles to the joists.

If a room is 12 ft. 6 in. wide, every cross course of tile will consist of 11 full (12 x 12-inch) tiles and two 9-inch wide border tiles. Since this is an odd number of full

tiles, the middle tile should be centered on the center line and furring strips should be installed 6 inches on either side of this line. If an even number of full tiles were needed, then a tile joint would have fallen right on the center line, and the first furring strip would be installed there.

Working out from the center of the room, install the rest of the furring strips parallel to the first one on 12-inch centers for standard 12 x 12 tiles. The next step is to find the two intersecting baselines for the border tile. Do this by measuring out from the center line to the wall. Remember that the border tile should be at least a half-tile wide at the ceiling edges. Never permit courses of tile less than 6 inches wide, and

Check level of your furring strips frequently with a straightedge to make sure there are no bumps or depressions to mar the finished ceiling.

Any low spots can be made level by loosening nails and driving thin shims between joist and furring strip. High spots must be trimmed down.

Each border tile should be cut to fit as needed. Don't cut them all at once since the wall itself may be out of line. Here, a backsaw is used on tile.

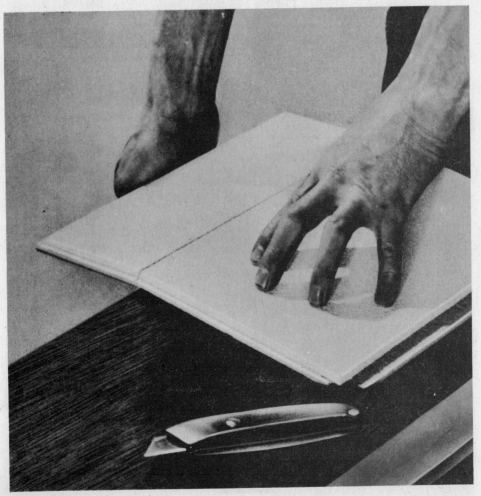

To cut tile with a fiberboard knife, score face of the tile deeply and then break tile over a sharp edge as shown. Trim back of break to finish off.

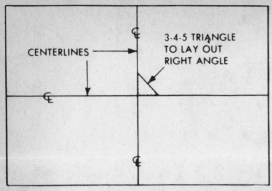

3-4-5 TRIANGLE
TO LAY OUT
RIGHT ANGLE

CENTERLINES

IF ROOM IS perfectly rectangular, you can snap centerlines between midpoints of opposite walls

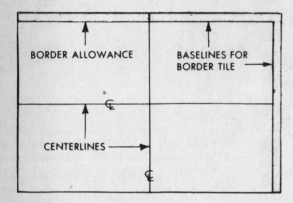

BORDER ALLOWANCE

BASELINES FOR
BORDER TILE

CENTERLINES

TO INSURE baselines being parallel with centerlines, measure out from centerline, not from wall

plan this spacing before stapling the first tile in place.

After nailing up the furring strips, check them for level with a chalk line or a spirit level or both. Any low spots should be shimmed out for an even ceiling surface. You can do this by loosening the nails and driving shims or wedges of wood between the furring strips and the joists.

Next, starting from the established corner where the two major borders intersect, start fastening the tile in place, working out from this corner. Since all of the finishing border tile will have the stapling flanges removed, you will have to face-nail these into the furring strip next to the wall. Be careful to locate these nails close to the wall so you will be able to cover them over with wooden trim molding strips later on.

The tiles interlock forming a straight pattern, provided you keep them even. Be sure to butt each adjoining tile squarely against its predecessor before stapling. Use staples that are at least $\frac{9}{16}$ inch long. If your stapling gun won't handle this size staple, borrow one that will.

Each border tile can be cut with a small backsaw. Even though they are all to be cut to about the same size, don't cut the border tiles all at once, since there may be some unevenness in the wall. Cut them one

When stapling tile to the furring strips, be sure that you maintain perfect alignment with adjacent tiles.

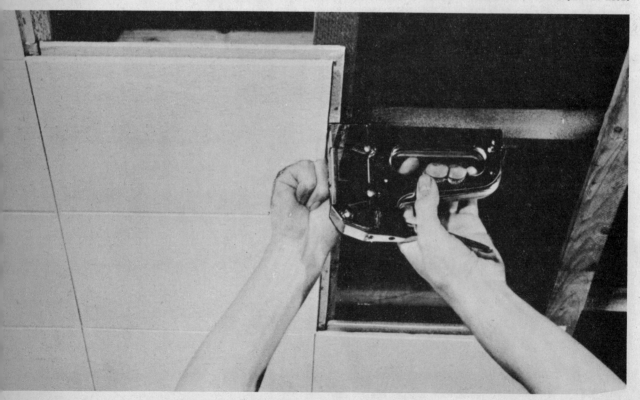

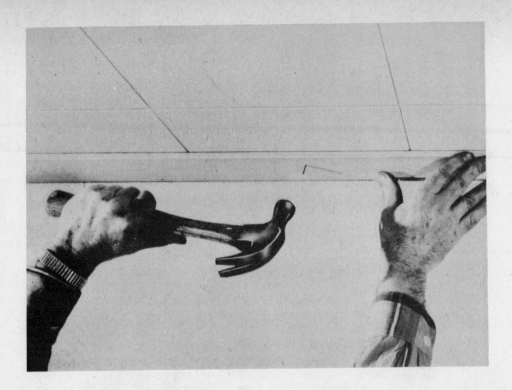

Finishing touch for your new ceiling is provided by cove molding, painted or stained to match the wall below. Finish the molding before installing.

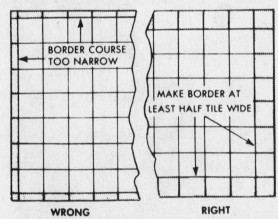

BORDER COURSE TOO NARROW

MAKE BORDER AT LEAST HALF TILE WIDE

WRONG   RIGHT

JOISTS

FURRING STRIPS

BORDER COURSES less than half a tile wide look out of balance. Make them at least 6 in. wide

PROPER SEQUENCE of installing tile is noted above. Border tile are always mounted before adjacent full tile

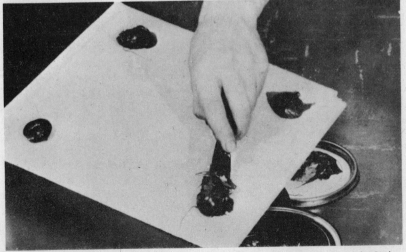

Where the existing ceiling is level and clean, tiles can be installed with an adhesive, either thick or thin, depending on type of adhesive that is used.

Flintkote art and photos

Installation with thick acoustical cement is shown wherein tile is slid into place. Thinner, brush-on adhesive allows tile to adhere flat to ceiling.

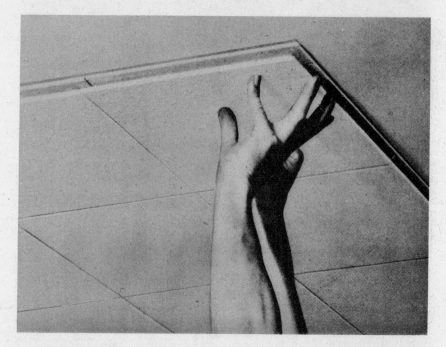

Tiles installed with brush-on adhesive may be stapled here and there to prevent lateral movement. Thick cement leaves some space, so nails are used to prevent breaking edges.

Flintkote photos

at a time as you use them, and mark off each tile before you cut it. When cutting out for odd-shaped obstructions such as pipes and jutting corners, be sure to draw a pattern very carefully on the tile first. Then cut it out with a keyhole or a coping saw. You can also cut tile with a fiberboard knife by scoring the face very deeply against a straightedge and then breaking it over a sharp edge. Trim the back of the break with a knife. The backsaw gives the cleanest cut though, and it is probably the easiest and fastest to use.

After all the tile is up, trim molding that has already been painted or stained to match surrounding wall surfaces can be nailed into place. Use small-head finishing nails and drive them slightly below the surface with a nailset. The shape of the cove molding is up to your individual taste, but it's best (and cheapest) to keep it simple.

There are certain advantages to installing sheetrock or gypsum board on the ceiling before fastening tiles in place. The most important benefit in the sound-deadening effect that it adds to the ceiling. Another feature is that you do not have to worry too much about the location of the furring strips, since you can use adhesive for anchoring the tiles.

There are specific kinds of adhesive for different kinds of ceiling tiles, and the type

Hanging pipes or other obstructions must be boxed in with furring strips to take ceiling tiles, then capped with corner molding as shown at left.

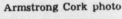
Armstrong Cork photo

If ceiling is high enough, acoustical tiles can be fashioned into a dropped or suspended ceiling using furring strips together with vertical 1x2" hangers.

that you use will depend on whether you are using acoustical tile or other types of material. Even though the proper adhesive will provide enough anchorage to the gypsum board base, it's a good idea to throw one or two staples around the edges of each tile to keep them from shifting. Remember also to apply even hand pressure over the entire tile surface to spread the glue evenly when you push it into place.

When you plan the ceiling, bear in mind that there are certain accessory items that you might want to build in. These could be recessed lighting fixtures, spotlights and ventilators which are available in exact sizes to fill in a one-tile or two-tile hole—

that is, the accessories measure 12 x 12 or 12 x 24 inches and have metal trim plates which cover the edges for a nice custom finish. If you plan to install any of these lighting fixtures or other devices, be sure to run in the wiring for them before you put in the new ceiling. Leave the unconnected cables hanging through the opening at the appropriate point to be hooked up later. Then, when you install the tiles, just leave out the tile or tiles in that spot, nailing around the edges to anchor bordering tiles in place. After the ceiling is finished, the fixture will go in easily, followed by the metal trim plate to finish off your custom ceiling. •

Suspended Ceilings

Newest concept in ceilings is easy to install, can hide a host of evils.

Adaptable for either remodeling or new construction, the suspended ceiling features a combination of incombustible, acoustical lay-in panels and translucent light panels for glare-free illumination.

HAVE A HIGH CEILING in your kitchen? Does it make the room look too big and antiquated? If you're planning on modernizing the kitchen, certainly consider the suspended ceiling—a treatment that is becoming more and more popular.

There are several reasons for this popularity. One is the great ease with which the ceiling can be installed and later modified. Another factor is, of course, the low cost as compared with conventional ceiling covering materials. Also, a hanging ceiling can hide a multitude of sins, such as exposed plumbing, exposed wiring and ceilings that are uneven, or have various obstructions hanging from them. All of this ugliness disappears behind the uniform panels of a suspended ceiling. Plus which the suspended ceiling will never need painting—just an occasional washing.

Several companies supply materials for the ceilings, including Celotex, Armstrong, Flintkote, and Marlite (Div. of Masonite). Different manufacturers offer differing special features, but they all have in common the ease of installation.

If you are considering a suspended ceiling, write to various manufacturers for brochures and information on their products. Celotex, for example, provides not only complete instructions, but a scale grid sheet for planning the ceiling, and a slide-rule type calculator that tells you exactly how many panels, edge molding pieces and Tees will be needed for a particular size room, running the long way and the short way, both for 2 x 4 panels and for 2 x 2 panels. This material estimator is available free of charge from Celotex Corporation, Tampa, Florida 33602, or from dealers.

The first step is to draw the ceiling dimensions on a piece of graph paper as much to scale as possible. This should include any odd-shaped protrusions, alcoves and obstructions. Next find the center line for both major dimensions, and measuring toward the wall on both sides, make a balanced layout with the main Tees 4 feet on center (that is 4 feet between center lines of each main Tee). At this point, measure for wall border rows of equal size lay-in panels. Position the sketch so that the main Tees run *across* (perpendicular to) the ceiling joists. This way you will be absolutely sure of conveniently located existing structural members for fastening the hanging wires.

The cross Tees, which are either 8 feet or 4 feet long on slotted 2-foot centers, alternate top and bottom for assembly to the main Tees. Using the Celotex calculator let's take a typical kitchen measuring 14 x 20 feet. The calculator shows us immediately that this is a ceiling area of 280

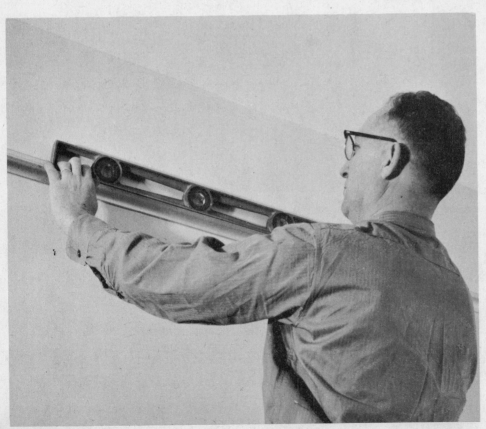

Determine desired height of new ceiling. Allow a minimum of three inches between new ceiling line and height of existing overhead for easy tip in and placement of panels. Attach wall angles around perimeter, using level and carpenter's chalk line.

Celotex photos

Install hanger wires or metal straps, then set the ends of main Tees on wall angles and secure to the hanger straps or wires as shown. Main Tees should be positioned 4' on centers.

Celotex photos and drawings

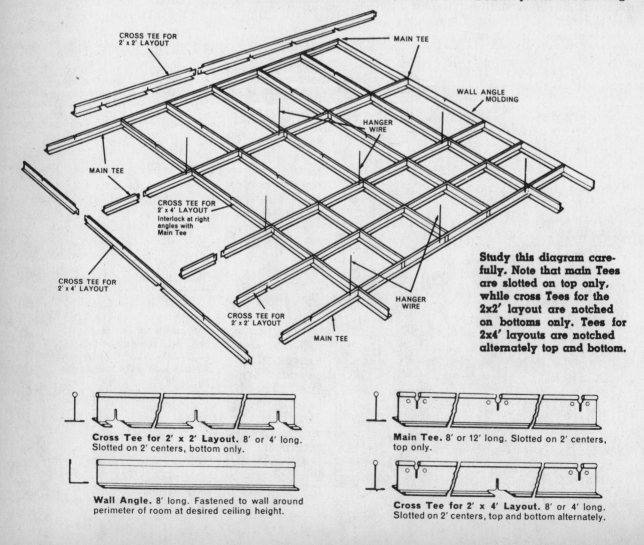

CROSS TEE FOR 2' x 2' LAYOUT

MAIN TEE

WALL ANGLE MOLDING

HANGER WIRE

MAIN TEE

CROSS TEE FOR 2' x 4' LAYOUT
Interlock at right angles with Main Tee

CROSS TEE FOR 2' x 4' LAYOUT

CROSS TEE FOR 2' x 2' LAYOUT

HANGER WIRE

MAIN TEE

Study this diagram carefully. Note that main Tees are slotted on top only, while cross Tees for the 2x2' layout are notched on bottoms only. Tees for 2x4' layouts are notched alternately top and bottom.

Cross Tee for 2' x 2' Layout. 8' or 4' long. Slotted on 2' centers, bottom only.

Main Tee. 8' or 12' long. Slotted on 2' centers, top only.

Wall Angle. 8' long. Fastened to wall around perimeter of room at desired ceiling height.

Cross Tee for 2' x 4' Layout. 8' or 4' long. Slotted on 2' centers, top and bottom alternately.

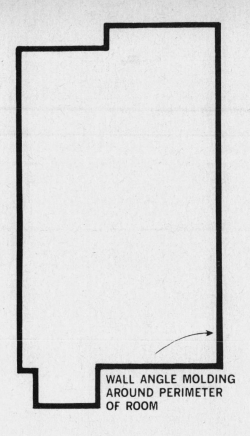

WALL ANGLE MOLDING
AROUND PERIMETER
OF ROOM

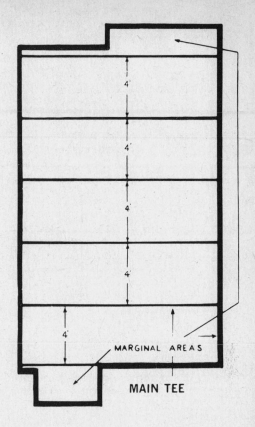

4'

4'

4'

4'

4'

MARGINAL AREAS

MAIN TEE

Diagram for wall molding in a typical room, the height determined by clearance of obstructions.

Complete layout of main Tees spaced exactly 4' on centers comes first. Run these ACROSS joists.

square feet and will require the following parts (if the main Tees run the long way): 68 running feet of wall angle molding; 60 linear of main Tee; 126 feet of cross Tee (for a 2 x 4 pattern); and 40 panels measuring 2 x 4. The estimator also shows required parts for running the Tees parallel to the short wall and alternately for using 2 x 2 panels instead of 2 x 4's.

Once you have lugged the materials home from the lumberyard, you're ready for the actual installation. The first step is to establish the level for the new ceiling. This should be somewhere between the top of the highest window or door frame and the lowest hanging obstruction such as a pipe or duct. You should allow at least three inches between the finished ceiling line (inside measure) and existing overhead obstructions. If you are going to use any luminous ceiling panels, allow at least six inches between the bottom of the fluorescent tube level and the inside of the new ceiling. Attach the wall angle molding around the perimeter of the room at the desired ceiling height, using appropriate fasteners: expandable screws or nails into walls, long wood screws into studs, and

masonry fasteners if you are doing the job in the basement on concrete walls. Use a carpenter's spirit level and a chalk line to make sure that the molding goes on absolutely level.

Using the chart layout that you have already prepared, install hanger wires for the main Tees with, nails, screw eyes or screw hooks into the ceiling joists. Space the hanger wires at about 4-foot intervals (roughly, one per joist); hangers closer together than this will only create problems. After the hanger wires are installed on the joists, rest the ends of the main Tees on the wall angle molding and fasten the hangers to the Tees. Maintain the Tees at true level by using a spirit level and making adjustments by changing the length of individual hanger wires where it's needed. Stand on a ladder next to one wall with your eye level close to the base of each main Tee. Look down the length of the Tee to see if there's any unevenness—it'll show up as a wavy surface in the Tee. Now's the time to correct it.

The next step is to lay in the cross Tees. Start at any convenient location, although the center of the room would probably be

CROSS TEE MARGINAL AREAS

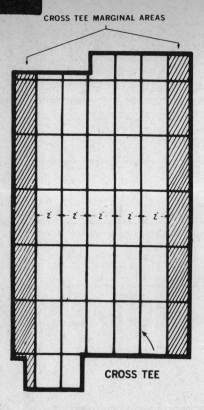

CROSS TEE

Cross Tees for a 2x4' layout, above, are spaced on 2' centers. Marginal panels cut to suit area.

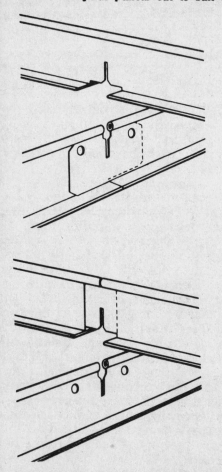

Splicing main Tees, above, splicing cross Tees, below. Ends are butted, end tabs are overlapped.

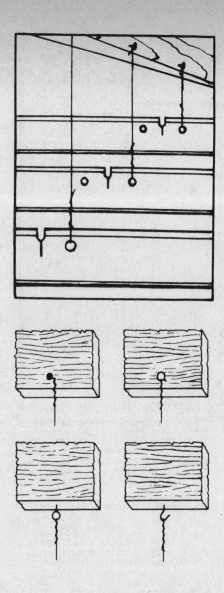

Hanger wires must be firmly nailed to joists or attached to screw eyes firmly imbedded in joists.

the best. Join the cross Tees to the main Tees on their two-foot centers. Lock the cross Tees into position, meshing the slots together with the main Tee slots. Any extra length on the cross Tees can be cut off with ordinary metal nippers.

If 2 x 2 panels are going to be used, install additional cross Tees parallel to the main Tees, interlocking at the center notch of any cross Tees that you've already installed. And that's it. The touchy part is over. Now just install the lay-in panels—fiberboard, mineral fiber or luminous (translucent)—by tipping them up through the openings and lowering them to rest on the flanges of the Tee members. The flimsy-looking Tees and wires will suddenly and dramatically take on the appearance of a finished ceiling.

The last step in the panel installation is to cut and install any irregularly shaped and short-measure border panels next to the wall. The usual hand tools can be used for cutting, since the material's about the consistency of wallboard.

One of the hanging ceiling's special features is the recessed built-in lighting that can be installed in virtually any location. Pick out the areas where you want fluorescent lights, and use translucent panels there instead of the standard opaque boards. The light comes from a 2-bulb fluorescent fixture 6 inches above the translucent panel for precisely located lighting. Another approach is to use nothing but translucent panels for the entire ceiling and to have single-bulb fluorescent channels mounted end-to-end, centered over each panel and running the full length of the ceiling. These can be controlled by a series of switches for modular lighting effects, or can all be turned on at once for an entire ceiling of light. Colored fluorescent tubes, controlled by individual switches, can add the special quality of mood lighting.

For a more flexible layout, the 2 x 2 panels offer an extra amount of versatility. For that matter, if you are working along an irregular wall, you may want to use a couple of courses of 2 x 2 instead of 2 x 4

Cross Tees are shown being intermeshed on 2' centers for a 2x4' panel layout. Use border rows to make up odd-size measurements.

If 2x2' panels are used, position additional cross Tees parallel to main Tees to break up the 2x4' areas for smaller panels.

Once the grid is erected, lay-in panels are installed by simply tipping them up and dropping them to rest on flanges of Tee members. The smaller, 2x2' squares are shown being tipped into place in photo.

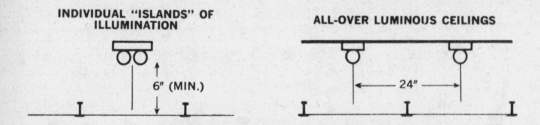

INDIVIDUAL "ISLANDS" OF ILLUMINATION

ALL-OVER LUMINOUS CEILINGS

6" (MIN.)

24"

Drawings, above, show how lights can be used for single-panel illumination or more. Photo, right, shows fixture installation.

Translucent panel is slid into place by removing one of the ceiling panels, tipping light panel up through, sliding it over.

Special box-beam ceilings receive same light treatment, since cross tees are similar to regular tees, have same flange lip.

Box-beam ceilings are put up same way other suspended runners are installed, shape differs.

along the edges to make your life a little easier. Remember though that this will add to the cost of the installation for the extra Tees needed and the slightly higher panel cost per square foot.

A few other finishing touches can also be added. The most interesting is a wood-beam ceiling effect that can be created by using special metal beams mounted directly on the Tees. These are provided with special clips that fasten onto the Tees and the simulated wood beam hooks onto these clips. These beams can be installed either on main Tees or cross Tees, or on both at the same time for a crossed-beam effect. The cross-section measurement of these beams is 2¼ inches wide and 3 inches deep —just enough to give the appearance of the real thing.

One other advantage of the suspended ceiling that is not often mentioned is the fact that it provides an ideal hiding place for air-conditioning and ventilating duct-work, wiring and plumbing. Air-conditioning grilles can be installed in place of some lay-in panels, or a panel can be cut out to accept a ventilating register. Other duct-work that the ceiling can hide includes such items as a vent for an exhaust fan or range hood fan.

This type of ceiling is an ideal medium for many kinds of special effects which can be installed at the same time that you're adding the ceiling. These improvements can be added later on simply by changing or removing one or more panels.

Besides all this, suspended ceilings are the *in* thing these days. •

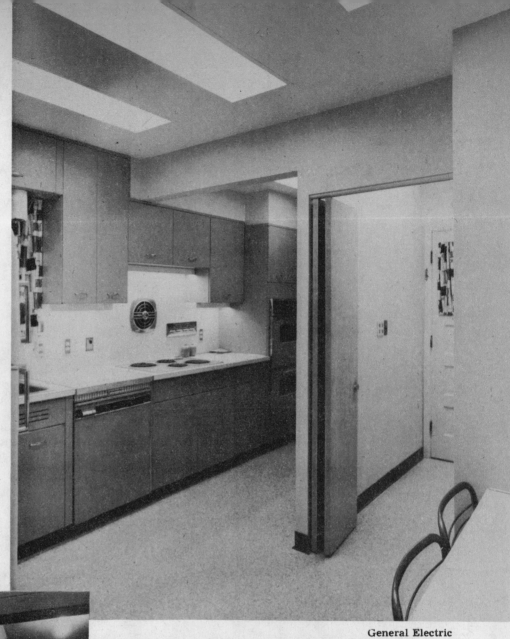

General Electric

The magic of remodeling with only minor basic changes is shown in these before-and-after photos. Good lighting and a roomy one-wall arrangement of built-in appliances provides ample counter and cabinet storage space.

Cabinets and Countertops

Adequate storage space and sleek working surfaces round out the modern kitchen.

PROBABLY THE MOST satisfying single aspect of kitchen remodeling is installing customized cabinets and countertops. The amount of actual work that you put into this installation depends pretty much on how handy you are and how much original cabinetmaking you're willing to do in your own shop. If you're very handy and you have some definite ideas about what you want in the way of cabinets, you can certainly make the beasties yourself. At the same time, if you don't feel that you are skilled enough to do a good job, you can call on a local cabinetmaker who specializes in such work.

The rub is that custom-made cabinets tend to be rather expensive and can boost the new kitchen's cost considerably. Cheapest and easiest way is to buy them ready-made. Spend some time thumbing through a Sears Roebuck catalog and check their cabinet measurements with your kitchen layout. Sears offers a variety of wooden and metal cabinets in standard sizes. The same sizes and units are available in finished birch veneer or in an unfinished knocked-down "ready to assemble" form.

The wood cabinet is probably the easiest to work with and is certainly the most popular in today's kitchens. It can be painted a variety of decorator colors, or finished in its natural wood grain, which will enhance almost any type of kitchen interior. It can be used with plain wooden knobs and drawer pulls, or can be spruced up with a variety of specialty handles and pulls that blend with the kitchen decor.

There are several standard sizes in cabinets as well as several standard utility features. Floor cabinets generally stand 35⅝ inches high and are 24⅝ inches deep.

These measurements are standard, and permit grouping the cabinets and the addition of a continuous countertop working surface. Special cabinets to these same dimensions are made to accommodate sinks. They can be purchased as a large unit or as a simple sink base for design flexibility. If the kitchen has any corners in it, and most do, special corner cabinets make the best use of what would normally be wasted overlap corner space. These contain a three-tiered lazy Susan shelf arrangement that makes even the rear recesses of the cabinet accessible. Since no two kitchens are alike, the cabinets can't be expected to fit exactly. The cabinet manufacturers make trim panels—dummy wood strips with the same finish as the cabinets to fill in the odd spaces against end walls and in odd corners.

When installing the cabinets, try them for a loose fit in the general installation area. Make sure that you leave enough room for major appliances such as the range and refrigerator. Another option is the separate range top and in-wall oven. The range top fits neatly into a sink cabinet for custom mounting.

Installations of this kind are becoming very popular and can provide some additional oven space in what would otherwise be a limited area. It also means that the old kitchen stove no longer has to look the part and can be arranged to blend with original decor and color schemes.

Wall cabinets present another problem. They come in several varieties in two standard heights, 18 inches and 30 inches. The 30-inch unit is the standard wall cabinet that allows access to the countertop working surface with reasonable head-

It's a tight squeeze, so check your sink's fit before doing any irrevocable countertop cutting.

Check alignment and fit of all add-on cabinet doors like this one, which will front sink area.

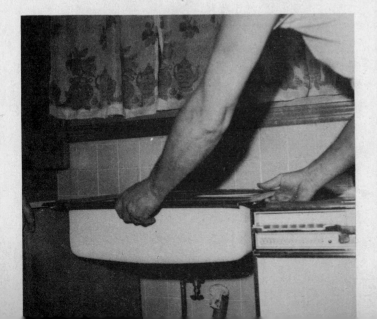

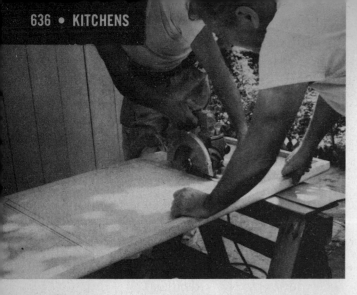

After measuring prefab countertop, marking off outline, cut carefully; use handsaw on corners.

room. The 18-inch cabinet is specifically designed to fit above the range and the refrigerator. This cabinet is also just the right height to hold a range hood.

Countertops raise another choice—prefabricated or custom plastic laminate? The custom prefab is easier to install and represents the latest in modern kitchen design. The Formica plastic laminate is somewhat less expensive, is a lot more work to install, but is much more flexible in special problem installations.

The plastic "sandwich" is installed in two sections—the countertop with 1½-inch plywood base, and the splashboard on a ¾-inch plywood base. The plastic covering itself is available in a wide choice of colors and patterns, one of the main reasons for its popularity.

Measure the plywood for any continuous-run countertop, allowing for overlap and flush wall-butting. Cut adjoining plywood countertop sections to fit flush against the wall and against the first counter section. Use glue and wood cleats to join adjacent plywood sections. Check the plywood top for fit, making final adjustments with hand tools. Next cut the plastic sheets to size; a little oversize is okay, and is even preferable, since this can be trimmed off with a router later on.

Working outdoors if at all possible, spread a generous coat of contact cement on both the plywood and the Formica underside.

Line sink bottom with watersealing putty strips, which are usually packed with the sink hardware.

Sink seated and clamped tightly into place, the countertop is all set for its first trial fitting.

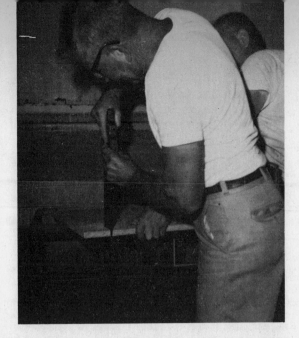

On custom, Formica-topped counters, final adjustments on plywood made "on location" in kitchen.

Coating of 3M contact adhesive goes on the plywood and Formica, outdoors—away from flames.

Apply the cement with a paint brush, paint roller or toothed trowel. If you use a standard contact adhesive such as 3M brand "Fastbond" 10, remember that this cement is extremely flammable and should be used outdoors only. Indoors, this stuff can be ignited by even the occasional electrical sparking of the motor in an electric wall clock!

If you must work indoors, use Fastbond 30 cement. This is nonflammable and is water soluble when it's wet. Disadvantages of the nonflammable variety are its higher price (about twice as much as Fastbond 10, but well worth it) and the longer drying and curing time. Fastbond 10 needs 10 minutes drying time before the plastic can be laid down on the plywood; type 30 takes a half-hour or more.

In either case, the cement must be dry to the touch before the laminate sheet can be installed. Do not let the cement-covered surfaces touch each other at any time before final assembly, as they will adhere instantly. Take the coated plywood into the kitchen and lay it in position on top of the cabinets.

Cover the plywood with a double-thickness (or thicker) of corrugated cardboard. You can use pieces of the appliance and cabinet packing cartons for this. Scrap lengths of 1 x 2 lumber will also do the job. Lay these separator sticks (or cardboards) across the plywood at right angles to the countertop at close enough intervals so they will keep the Formica from touching the plywood when it's laid on top. Then lay the plastic on top of the separators,

Cover dry cement-coated counter with scrap separators, then align cemented Formica on top of them. Removing one separator at a time, press laminate down firmly. Once in place, trim laminate with router.

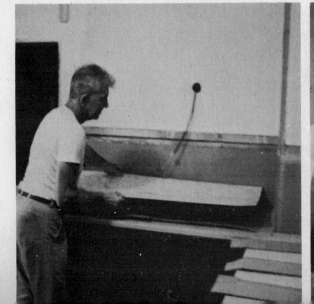

Mark off outline for sink on the plastic countertop being careful not to allow for too much overcut. After cutting out the countertop for sink, line the sink's clamp ring with caulking compound sealer.

again being careful not to let the two cement surfaces touch each other.

Align the Formica edges perfectly with the plywood edges; then while holding the top firmly in position, have your helper (a neighbor, or teen-age slave labor) pull out the first separator at the end of the counter. Press the plastic down at that point. The cement will grab instantly and will hold the top in place. Then work your way down the line, pulling out one separator at a time and pressing the Formica down.

After the plastic top is completely pressed down, trim off any overlap with a router, keyhole saw or backsaw. If there are points where the Formica doesn't quite meet the edge of the plywood, don't worry about it; it will be covered by the snap-on metal edge molding later on.

The splashboard can be made simply by attaching Formica to the wall or by bonding it to ¾-inch plywood sections cut to fit. If you use the latter method, some additional metal edging strips will be needed,

Again, with the hardware provided, bolt down the sink and ring combination to the counter underside. Making the cutout for the flush-mounted range is a ticklish proposition in regard to getting exact fit.

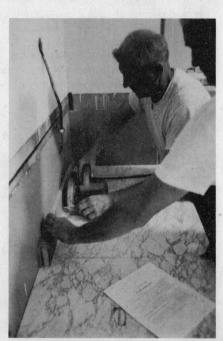

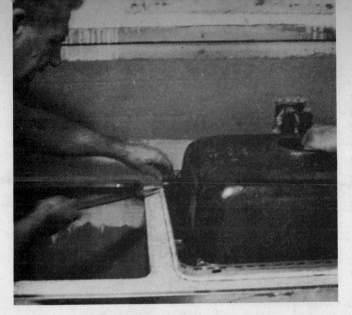

Attach sealing ring to sink with special hardware and clamps supplied. The clamps must be tight. Sink and sealing ring should snugly fit into the countertop hole. Ring covers any irregularities.

along with finishing molding which must be inserted at the junction of the countertop and the splashboard. The splashboard sections must be cut to butt up against the bottoms of the wall cabinets.

An easier installation is possible with prefabricated tops generally available from the same suppliers as the cabinets themselves. These counters are made of a composition board with a plastic covering that has about the same heat- and water-resistant properties as Formica. The

countertop is molded with an antidrip lip on the front edge and an integral splashboard at the rear.

The prefab countertop can be purchased by the linear foot, it can be purchased in prefabricated sections with cutouts for the sink, and there are special corner sections for right-angle turns in the counter. The top has cutout grooves underneath for butting and attaching sections together for a continuous run. This prefabricated counter can be cut with ordinary hand

Final couple of inches of range cutout may be too close to wall for electric saw, so use handsaw. Installing the range in the cutout is the moment of truth—will it fit there or won't it? Planning paid off.

After wall cabinets are hung on studs, bolt them together with countersunk woodscrews at the front.

Screws in front of cabinet hold the sections together, may have to be loosened for alignment.

tools and is relatively easy to work. If you're a little bit unsure of your capabilities with the saw for making sink cutouts, buy the section with the sink cutout already made. This is one case where doing it yourself could be disastrous. If you work with Formica, on the other hand, you *must* do your own sink cutout.

These counters do not require any gluing, but simply bolt onto the floor cabinets themselves. The cabinets, of course, must be bolted into wall studs and fastened to the floor before the countertop is fastened in place. The same is true of the wall cabinets, although they should come later since a supporting brace of the exact height can hold them against the wall while you are working on them.

When hanging a wall cabinet, the one operational guide should be: locate the studs, bore holes in the right places in the cabinets, and hang them directly on the studs. But studs have a habit of not always being available in the right place, and if you run into this problem, use two horizontal furring strips screwed firmly into the studs. These will then form the hanger base for the wall cabinets. Furring strips should be 1" x 3" or 1" x 4". Be sure to anchor them very *firmly* into each stud.

The next step is installing the sink, and for this you just follow ordinary plumbing procedures. One thing to remember before you place the sink on the countertop—seal all of the rim edges with special sealing compound of putty supplied with the sink. This is important, as this seal will prevent leaks under the sink rim and into the cabinet area.

An important finishing touch in the kitchen is the soffit. You may not want to

Finishing touch on the cabinets themselves is addition of the outside hardware to match decor.

Entire photo sequence courtesy of Sears, Roebuck

The soffit, filling in space to ceiling, can be framed with 1x2 or 2x2-in. lumber, making sure the frame provides snug fit.

Cut end supports longer than needed and test length against wall, allowing space for top runner to rest on top of it.

Final phase is nailing the plywood or wallboard soffit into place and it's ready to be painted.

add this immediately, since the soffit can often serve several purposes. This blank panel that runs from the top of the wall cabinet up to the ceiling provides a kind of false partition to give the kitchen a custom-finished appearance. The soffit is just a thin sheet of plywood or wallboard that is nailed onto several vertical braces running from the cabinet tops to the ceiling. These braces should be nailed firmly to the joists and cabinet tops. The soffit is generally thought of as serving no purpose at all, but in real life, it can hide ventilating or air-conditioning ducts or add decorative touches with an occasional cutout for a lighted knick-knack display shelf and perhaps a recessed clock. The clock idea can be especially intriguing but calls for a special faceless clock movement that must be purchased especially for this type of installation. The mechanism is entirely hidden behind the soffit along with any electrical cables and boxes. Only the hands and some tacked-on numbers or symbols show on the soffit itself, and, of course, these must be added after the soffit is painted or wallpapered. The soffit can also house recessed lighting fixtures to illuminate specific areas.

The soffit, of course, should be carried right across open areas that have no cabinets below them, such as the stove or sink under the window. Cases like this, where the bottom of the soffit is exposed, are ideal for recessed fixtures and the good old ventilating fan grille and duct.

There's one use that can make the soffit carry more than its own weight in usefulness—central air conditioning. If you are planning to add central air conditioning to your home and do not have the proper ductwork for it, check your room layout very carefully. The soffit may be the answer to hiding a major duct that can reach through to several rooms in the house—not just the kitchen. In any event, it certainly can accommodate the duct for the kitchen air-conditioning register with plenty of room to spare. •

Marlite woodgrain paneling covers room divider and cabinets, Marlite even provided damp-wipe mural.

Wall Finishes

Paint and wallpaper are fine, but special treatments are very decorative.

THERE ARE MANY KINDS of finishes that you can apply to a wall surface in both kitchens and bathrooms. There are the obvious ones: paint, wallpaper, and various kinds of tile and paneling.

Tile in the kitchen was once thought of as the epitome of modernism, excellence and cleanliness, but today it is quite passé, and certainly will not blend in with the modern kitchen décor. In the bathroom, tile definitely has a place, especially in areas where the wall will be subjected to a great deal of water splashing, such as the shower and bathtub areas. Even here, tile is only

necessary up to a certain level, although a floor-to-ceiling tile in the bath and shower stall areas are appropriate and can be attractive if properly planned.

For some reason, some people still prefer plain white tile, and if this is your cup of tea, read no further in this chapter. White tile has the distinct disadvantage of labeling a house as being old-fashioned. No matter how modern your bathroom is in other respects, white tile is out of order. It also tends to discolor and yellow with age which today's tinted tiles will not do.

If wall tiles are used for wainscoting,

they should climb the wall to a height of about 28 inches, finished off with a capping tile. Tile installed over regular wallboard is fastened in place with a mastic adhesive. In areas where there will be a lot of water splashed, such as in the shower and in the bathtub, a better foundation than wallboard or gypsum board will be called for. Here it's advisable to install metal lath just barely covered over with plaster. Let the plaster dry overnight and then cover this with a plaster brown coat which will provide a good base for the tile mortar. Using mortar instead of mastic adhesive, start the tile with a bottom course and work up.

Tile is easy to cut for odd-size pieces. If you don't have a commercial tile cutter available, simply score the glazed surface with a glass cutting tool, lay the tile face up on a nail or pencil with the score directly over the pencil, and step on it. The tile will break cleanly along the score. When you have to cut irregular patterns in tile for fixtures, nibble away at the edge with a pair of nippers or gas pliers, taking out a small bite at a time. Any uneven cut in the tile will be covered by trim or escutcheon plates on the fixtures later on, so don't be bothered by these irregularities.

After all the tile is in and has dried a couple of days, the final step is grout. Smear the grout on a large section at a time and then rub it off with a rubber squeegee, the type that is used by window washers. Force the grout down into the cracks with a pointed stick. Finally wash the whole area with a damp rag to remove the grout from the tile surface.

Sound like a lot of work? It sure is, and it's an excellent reason why there is a definite trend away from wall tiles in bath-rooms these days. Other surface coverings also available for the kitchen will work just as well.

A material that's a lot easier to install than tile is tile board. It's waterproof and easy to maintain and has the appearance of a genuine tiled wall. Like tileboard, other plastic materials can also be used. They are available in large sheets that go up easily.

More glamorous materials include a variety of waterproof wallboards that are excellent both in the kitchen and bathroom. Some of these boards are available in the Marlite paneling line made by the Masonite Company. The lavatory area can be highlighted by wood grain finished paneling which has a durable and waterproof plastic surface. The paneling goes over existing walls or on new framing, and will not require any painting or refinishing at any time.

Another product that provides attractive wall finishes in simulated wood grain is "Simplank" paneling made by the 3M Company. This material can be cut with a razor blade and goes on with a single adhesive coating around the edges. According to the manufacturer, the little woman can put this paneling up herself in a matter of minutes. It might take more than a few minutes for a gal not acquainted with hand tools and carpenter's rulers, but the emphasis here is on simplified installation.

Of course, there are the usual paints and wallpapers that are available in waterproof finishes to cover these walls, and they should be considered in combination with some or all of these wall materials, since the paint and wallpaper can be replaced periodically for a change of mood or color.

Walls should generally be installed be-

Glass, brick and Marlite-covered cabinets combine to create a bright and youthfully active wall.

More plastic-finished hardboard was used here to create modern grease-free diversion of surfaces.

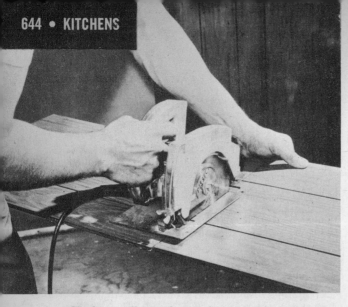

Marlite wall panels can be cut with conventional tools easily and quickly. Power saws work fine.

When installing the paneling over existing walls, spread adhesive to backs with a toothed trowel.

Special clamps supplied with the panel boards are used to lock adjacent sections firmly in place.

Clamps are nailed firmly to studs to hold panels and anchor them to wall. Locate studs with nail.

Marlite paneling should be glued to walls for best results, though it can be placed on new framing.

Planks can be precut to fit around windows and other wall irregularities. Measure; make pattern.

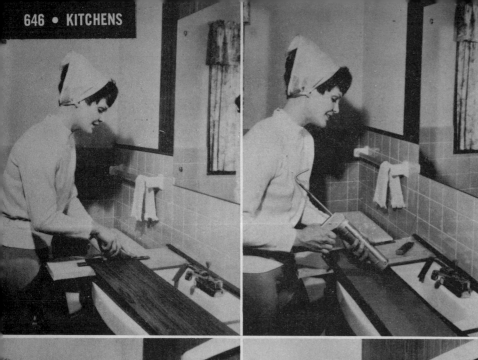

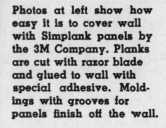

Photos at left show how easy it is to cover wall with Simplank panels by the 3M Company. Planks are cut with razor blade and glued to wall with special adhesive. Moldings with grooves for panels finish off the wall.

fore the major bathroom fixtures go in, with the exception of the bathtub. The tub goes in first; the wall comes later.

In the kitchen, wall materials should be applied behind areas that will be occupied by the refrigerator and the range. It should not be applied behind the sink or cabinet areas since these units will have to be anchored to the wall anyway, and expensive wall covering materials used here will just be wasted. Of course, you will have to be careful to cut the coverings to fit flush against countertops, sinks, cabinets, etc. In many cases you may be able to extend the wall covering an inch or so below the lip of a prefabricated countertop. Be sure to provide a good seal at the edge with putty or other sealing compound.

This whole operation is going to take a

certain amount of planning, and you are sure to have some disagreement with the mistress of the house, when planning and putting the wall coverings up. But compromise on the project. Weigh all of these factors carefully when you choose a material: area to be covered; color schemes; ease of changing color scheme; durability; resistance to water, grease, and other wall destroying agents; ability to be cleaned easily; cost; skill required for installation; ease of installation. Of course, if you are an expert in wall coverings, you won't have to consider these last few factors too long; you will have already made up your mind as to what you want. In either case, remember a wall covering represents a fairly sizable investment and you will have to live with it, so choose carefully. •

Simplank panels were used here to create a wainscoting. Woodgrain fits well with furniture.

Marlite panels, resistant to moisture, are good substitute for tiles in the modern decorator bath.

Marlite, of course, does come in plain colors and in decorative murals for variety of room treatments.

Let your wife help select the pattern, since she will be the one who has to live with the results.

Vinyl Floorings

Set aside an evening and do your kitchen floor a favor with vinyl tiles.

CONGRATULATIONS! You have reached the point where most of the major work has been done in your kitchen or bathroom. The appliances have been installed, countertops are in, sink is flush mounted, cabinets are all in place, and everything looks fine—except for the floor.

Laying vinyl floor tiles is probably one of the most satisfying and frequently frustrating jobs that the home handyman can tackle. It's frustrating if you don't have the patience to do the job correctly or if you don't prepare yourself adequately. The fullfillment is in seeing the finished job well done.

The best time to lay floor tiles is at night when the family is safely in bed and out of the way. Of course, this will probably be an all-night operation, so you should be prepared to do without some sleep or at best, get to bed around five or six in the morning. It's not a job that can be rushed, and certainly will not benefit from any sideline supervision by the wife or anyone else who happens to drop in. Pack your wife off to a movie with her girl friend and make sure to tell her to stop in town for a midnight snack, since the kitchen will be unavailable.

Make sure that you have the entrance to the kitchen blocked with furniture and large hand-lettered signs to keep out would-be trespassers. It's very easy for a bubbling female to come home full of ex-

Make sure subfloor is smooth and free of wax, paint, varnish or oil. Holes or cracks in concrete sub-floors should be filled with crack filler. Cover poor floors with Temboard underlayment or plywood.

Deluxe Temboard underlayment is shown being installed rough side up. Allow thickness of a paper match cover for expansion. Stagger the joints. Green dots are printed every four inches as nailing guide.

uberance and exhiliration after an evening out, completely forgetting what you have been up to. She will unthinkingly breeze into the kitchen for a cup of coffee, walking right through a freshly spread batch of cement. The moral of all this is—keep your family out of the kitchen for the entire evening—and that goes for 3 a.m. raids on the refrigerator, too.

Of course, there should be a certain degree of wifely cooperation in selecting the floor tiles that you intend to put down. This is important, since the kitchen, after all, is where your wife spends the better part of her day, and she will have to live with the tiles much more than you will. Besides, if she isn't 100% happy with the tile design,

she'll forever be finding fault with your installation job, and this can be very unpleasant unless you wear a hearing aid that can be turned off.

When ordering the tile, be sure that you have the floor dimensions exact, and buy enough extra tiles to allow for a few bad cuts and for border tiles that will have to be cut off center with some waste. You will also need some kind of border edging material, if this fits in with your overall floor design. It's perfectly all right for the tiles to go right up to the edge of the floor with no finishing touches at all, but they can look a little bit unfinished in some kitchens.

Finishing "feature" strips can be used along the edges to provide a custom-finished appearance. You can also use vinyl cove base strip along the kick space under the kitchen cabinets. Other materials that you will need will be either some felt paper or one of the special underlay boards such as the Armstrong "Temboard." You will also need an adequate supply of cement for the tiles. You will have quite a load to carry, so be sure the trunk of your car is empty and that you have your roof carrier with you for the board underlays.

The first step is to make the floor surface as even and smooth as possible. Make sure that there is no contaminant on the floor such as wax, paint, varnish, grease or oil. If you're working with a concrete sub-floor, be sure to use crack filler wherever it's needed. Any irregularities or uneven-ness in the floor surface will show up in the vinyl tiles, so take care of these before going any further. On wood floors, plane down any high spots and be sure to nail loose boards back into place.

If you use felt paper, you will need a certain amount of additional cement for laying this down. A much better alternative is the Armstrong Temboard, since this provides an excellent base for the tiles. It's even and provides a certain amount of cushioning effect underfoot.

When laying down the Temboard, leave a small space between adjacent panels—about the thickness of a cardboard match-book cover—to allow for possible expan-

Find the center point of each of the two end walls of the room. Connect these two points with a chalk line. Locate center of line and use a carpenter's square or a tile to mark perpendicular.

Locate points on side walls with straightedge and snap a second chalk line for perpendicular mark. Along chalk lines, lay test row of uncemented tile from center point to one side and one end wall.

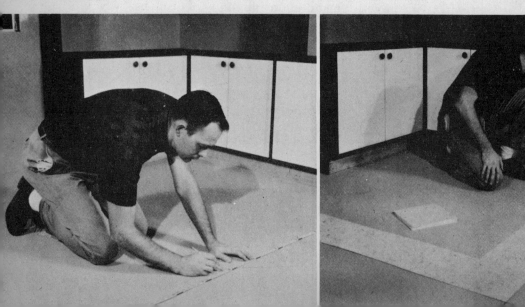

sion. Stagger the joints in adjacent runs of the board in bricklayer fashion, then nail the board with coated or ringed groove nails, at least every four inches along the edges and over the faces of the panels. These boards have green dots printed on them every four inches that are to be used as a nailing guide, so this phase will go quickly and easily.

If you are working on a concrete floor, a certain amount of extra under-preparation is necessary. A 1-inch layer of insulating board should cover the concrete floor, with hot asphalt emulsion as the adhesive. Then a layer of hardboard or Temboard can be laid down, again using hot asphalt as an adhesive. The Temboard is a little more difficult to install this way, but the insulating board will protect it from any dampness or cold coming from the concrete floor. After cementing in place, nail the Temboard or hardboard as you normally would to a wooden underfloor, using nails of an appropriate length.

The next step is to find the center point of the two end walls of the room. These are the short walls. Connect a chalk line between the center points that you find and snap it on the underboards that you have just laid. Next find the center point of the two long walls of the room. Easy way to do this is simply by measuring the chalk line and finding the exact center. Another chalk line should be run across at this point,

Measure the distance between the wall and the last tile. If it is less than 2″ or more than 8″ move the center line parallel to that wall 4½″ closer to that wall and strike line. Same for end walls.

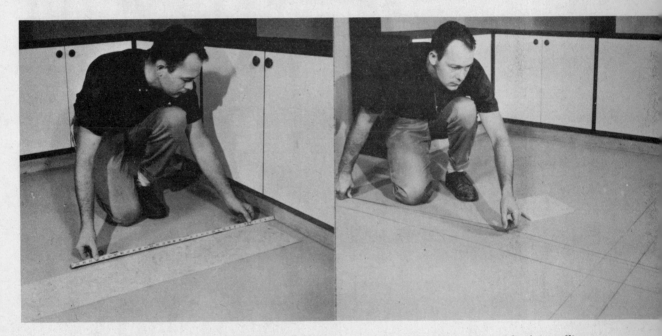

By moving center line closer to wall, additional space is gained that eliminates need of installing too narrow border tiles. Spread brushing cement over one quarter of room but not over chalk lines.

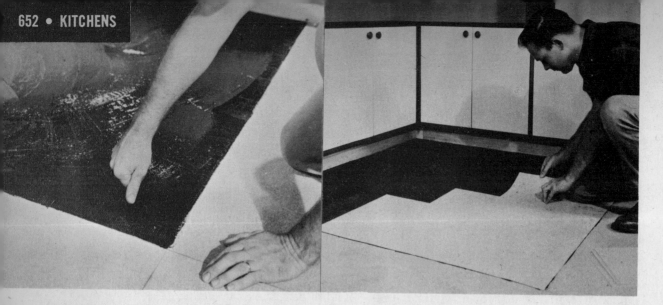

Let cement dry 15 minutes until tacky but will not stick to thumb. Starting at center, place, do not slide, tiles in cement, making sure first tiles are flush with chalk lines and each tile is butted.

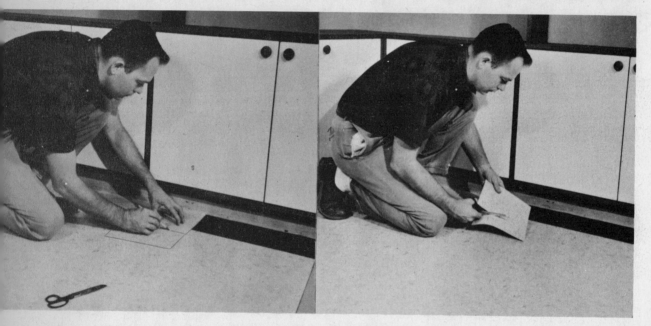

To fit border tiles, place a loose tile "A" exactly over last tile in row. Then place another tile "B" on top of "A" with end butted against wall. Mark tile "A" along edge of "B." Cut with shears.

forming an exact perpendicular to the first chalk line. Find the perpendicular by using a carpenter's square. Next, starting at the center of the room—since it will now be divided into four quadrants—lay a sample course of tiles in an L-shaped pattern from one wall to the centerpoint and then down to the adjacent wall. *Do not* cement the tiles.

Measure the distance between the wall and the last tile in the test row. If the distance is less than two inches or more than 8 inches, move the center line that's parallel to that wall 4½ inches closer to the wall. Do the same for the other course of tiles, then strike new starting lines with the chalk lines. The reason for this is so that

the finishing tiles will be evenly cut all the way around the edges of the room.

The next step is to spread a coat of tile cement over one quarter of the room, being careful not to cover the chalk line. The best way to spread this is with a toothed trowel, provided you are using vinyl asbestos tiles. For certain types of tiles, you can also use a brush.

Let the cement dry for about 15 minutes and then test it for the proper tackiness by touching it very lightly with your thumb. It should feel tacky but it should not stick to your thumb. If it sticks, allow a little more drying time and test it again.

Now, starting at the center, place the tiles on the cement making very certain

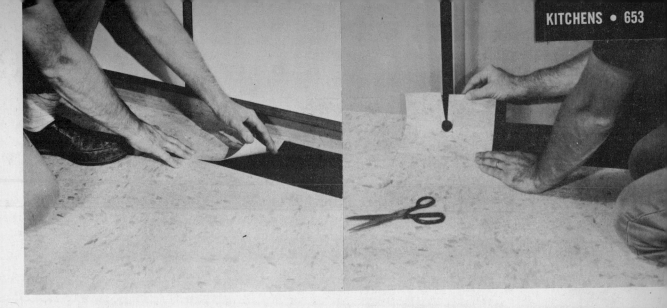

Cut portion of tile "A" will fit exactly into the border space. Make pattern to fit around pipes or obstructions and trace outline onto tile. Cut with scissors. Roll section with linoleum roller.

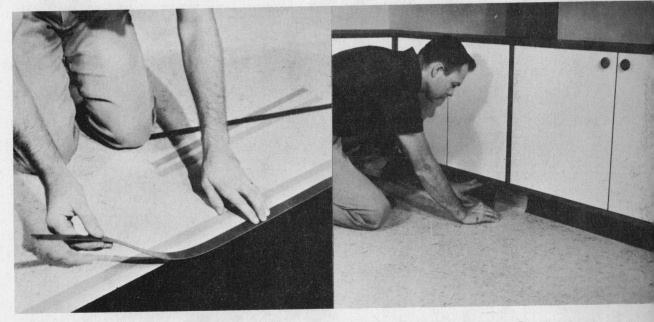

Vinyl-asbestos feature strips can be used to create unusual custom effects on floor. Lay same as tiles. Vinyl cove base is available in a variety of colors, is used to finish off floor at walls.

that the first tiles are exactly flush with the chalk lines and that each tile is butted securely against the previous ones. Do not slide tiles into place, but lay them down.

For the last course of tiles against the wall, mark the tile with a pencil and then cut with large, heavy-duty scissors. These tiles should fit exactly into the leftover space. Where there are irregular obstructions such as the legs of a radiator or a pipe, cut an exact outline of the obstruction, reaching this hole on the tile with a straight-line cut through the tile on the side facing the wall. You may make some mistakes and waste a few tiles at this point, but it's better to spend the few cents per tile extra than to have a sloppy job.

Continue with the rest of the floor in this fashion, working one quarter of a room at a time. When all of the tiles are down, the major part of the work is finished, you can relax, uncork a bottle of champagne or whatever else is handy in the refrigerator. Finishing feature strips and cove base strips can be added now or a week or even a month later if you prefer. These help to create an unusual custom effect and are available in different colors and in interesting patterns. Again, these are laid down with adhesive, but in this case it is a special grade that is different from the adhesive that you used for laying the tiles. It will finish off the floor and will give you the satisfaction of a job well done. •

How to Plan Your Remodeling

Consider space needed, usage, then service needs for light, comfort.

An easy-to-install insulation board ceiling suspended from the rafters turned this attic into a boy's functional bedroom. Suspended ceilings combine sound conditioning with attractive appearance.

Insulation Board Inst.

IN YOUR BASEMENT, if you have one, is an area equal to the area of your whole first floor. And in your attic, if you have one, is a usable area of about half the area of your house. These spaces might be called *your other house.*

How are your basement and attic being used? If you are like most of us, they're just places to stash junk out of sight. You don't show guests through them. You'd be too embarrassed, right? So your family only uses half of the house.

If that's enough, fine. But if you need space for practically any use at all, the cheapest and best place to get it is to expand into your other house—the attic or basement. The floor, wall and ceiling structures are already there. All you have to do is give them some style and utility.

With a fast-growing family and a slow-growing budget, remodeling an attic or basement to gain space for living makes good sense. Don't do it just to increase the value of your home. Most authorities agree that such improvements seldom add as much as they cost. Their real worth is in your use. Design and remodel an attic or basement with that in mind.

The cost of basement or attic remodeling depends largely on how far you go. A family room can be built in the basement for as little as $300 with enough loot left over to kick it off with a swinging happening.

The cost of one such improvement, a do-it-yourself project on a 12x21-foot room, was: furring strips, molding, staples and ceiling tile—$72.67; cork flooring tile and adhesive—$88.30; paint—$15.74; built-in cupboard—$43.41; drapery material—$10; electrical rewiring, ceiling fixtures and other miscellaneous items—$32.28. The total cost was $262.40, not bad considering the usefulness of the room for hobbies, homework, eating, entertaining, reading and relaxing.

A similar professionally designed and built 12x14-foot basement room cost $1500, $300 of it for a bathroom, $500 for other materials and $700 for labor. The inclusion of lots of built-ins boosted the cost.

Completely remodeled basements and attics cost upwards of these figures. Several raised-roof attic remodelings that I know of cost close to $10,000 for three bedrooms and a bath, professionally built.

The first step in basement or attic remodeling is to decide what kind of space you need. Is it more bedrooms? A recreation room? A large room for entertaining? Or small rooms for hobbies.

Next decide where you can best get the needed space. Consider needs for plumbing, electric wiring, heat, storage, accessibility, light and comfort.

Attic

The attic is the best place to remodel—better than the basement—if you hope to increase the value of your home.

The usable space in an attic is limited by the slope of the roof and the height of the roof structure. If the collar beams—

Give spark to your basement or attic by building it to a theme. The big stone fireplace, log-like paneling, guns, trophies and accessories lend a hunting lodge atmosphere to this remodeled basement.
Portland Cement Assn.

Building an attic or basement room can be a family project. The work goes faster if each family member does what he can. Well-made built-ins utilizing the knee wall area of an attic, below, add considerably to the utility of a remodeling project.

Masonite Corp.

Western Wood Products Assn.

horizontal 2x4's usually, that tie the roof rafters together—come across the room too low, it can ruin your chances to use the attic without major structural changes to the roof. There should be about seven feet between the finished attic floor and ceiling.

Some city codes require the 7-foot minimum. If you are not restricted by such a code you should at least consider 6½ feet as a horrible minimum. Good for youngsters, but when your tall friends visit, they will have to remove their heads.

The usable attic space can be increased by building a dormer out one side of the roof. A shed dormer in which the roof is raised for most of its length on one side, does the best job of increasing attic space. Little dormers, which look like overgrown doghouses, are all right for adding light or ventilation to an attic where it is needed. They aren't very practical otherwise, considering their cost.

An attic roof that is too low to be helped, even by a dormer, can be raised and new walls and rooms built under it. The cost can run half as much as another house.

If the floor joists in your attic are 2x4's or 2x6's, they will likely have to be beefed up. (See table.) This may be a job for a carpenter, involving house structure.

Where the attic ceiling and floor get within four feet of each other, *knee walls* are built. These walls run the length of the attic. They are the limit of your usable space. The area behind the knee walls can be devoted to storage.

Armstrong Cork Co.

Plan for adequate lighting throughout your basement or attic improvement. Here a light fixture behind a suspended ceiling is being assembled. The ceiling panel inserted below it will be translucent.

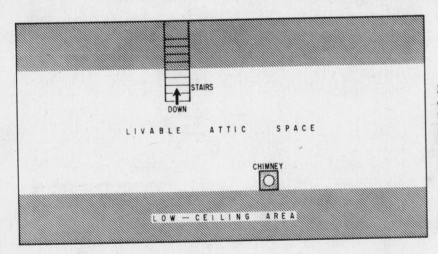

STAIRS

DOWN

LIVABLE ATTIC SPACE

CHIMNEY

LOW—CEILING AREA

Before remodeling, a typical attic with stairs near the center has real possibilities for creating two bedrooms and a bath. The side areas with ceilings lower than 4' are not considered livable.

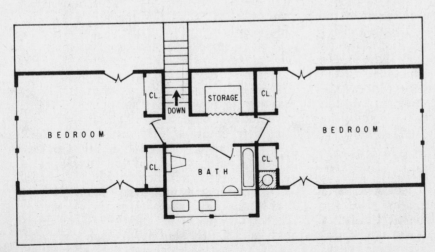

CL.

STORAGE

CL.

DOWN

BEDROOM

BEDROOM

CL.

BATH

CL.

After remodeling, the same attic offers a full bath with lavatory-dressing counter and twin wash basins under an added dormer. A storage closet is loaded with shelves. Windows are placed in the gable ends of the attic to light and properly ventilate it.

The attic is the largest, most useless room in the house until you change it by planned remodeling.

Built-in storage was planned up to the maximum, utilizing the low-ceiling areas and many plywood storage units.

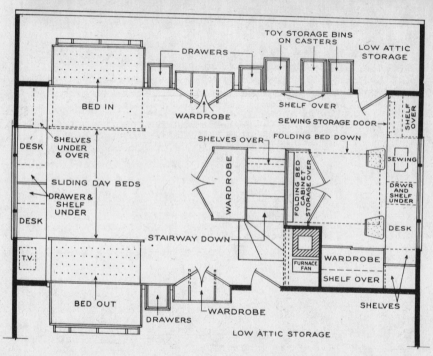

Light and fresh air are important to an attic. Windows should be installed in the end walls of an attic to let in light and for ventilation. Plastic bubble skylights on the roof also can be used to add light where it's needed. A fan can be installed in the gable end of an attic for cooling the house.

Chimneys and pipes running up through the attic's usable space cannot usually be moved and must be walled off. Figure for this in your planning.

Basement

Because of their usual coldness and dampness, basements aren't as ideal for remodeling as attics. Still, beautiful results have been obtained. The most successful designs for remodeled basements work hard at being bright, warm and cheery.

It's done with pleasant wall materials, happy colors, good lighting and a tasteful floor material.

You've got to have a dry basement or you're shot down before you start. See the chapter on drying up problem basements.

The location of the basement stairway has a lot to do with whether people will use a remodeled basement. Often, even family members ignore it. The more "mainline" the basement stairs are the better. Out-of-the-way ones at the back of the house or at the end of a hall are shunned. As part of a basement remodeling, do what you can to make the stairway more attractive. The stairs should be wide—at least three feet—and gently sloping—7-inch riser and 12-inch tread. They should be well lighted.

Often there is a problem in getting sufficient ceiling height beneath all the utilities hung from a basement ceiling. Moving them can be a big project. The ideal is to have enough room to hang a suspended ceiling below the pipes and ducts hiding them. In many basements a compromise must be made and some of the beams or largest ducts boxed out with a dropped ceiling.

Whatever you do, don't emulate one homeowner who was faced with a ceiling height problem. He sawed deep notches in the floor joists. The offending heating ducts were raised into the notches. Fortunately someone straightened him out before the living room ended up in his basement from failure of the weakened joists.

It is possible to dig out the basement floor in a special way that does not remove material needed to support house footings. But is it worth the trouble? Adding on a wing might be just as worthwhile.

There are two ways to design and remodel an attic or basement: do it yourself or hire an architect. If you have the money, by all means use an architect. The ideas and good sense he brings to the project should be worth his fee. But if you're like most of us, you'll have to do the planning yourself.

In either case think long and hard about the kind of remodeling you want. Study the ideas shown in this book and peep through some of the home magazines. Your

neighbors who have been through a remodeling project can be helpful, too. See their improvements and find out what they did and what they would do differently if they had another grab at the remodeling ring.

When you feel you know the score, you're ready to begin drawing plans. Don't let that panic you. Remodeling plans needn't be beautiful architectural drawings, just reasonable sketches indicating what you have in the way of space and what you intend doing with it.

See if you can put your hands on a set of plans for your house. They will help immensely in designing and remodeling an attic by showing where pipes, heating ducts and such hidden home arteries run. Try the contractor who built your house. Or try the local building department. If they don't have a set of plans, probably no one has.

Start your plans by making a drawing to scale showing your existing basement or attic floor plan. It can be done on squared paper, letting ¼ inch equal one foot of space. Your drawing should show all columns, existing partitions, and all obstructions such as furnace, water heater, chimney and supporting columns.

When that has been done, start thinking of where the rooms or areas you need can go, allowing proper space for each. Try to locate rooms with plumbing where there

Remodeled attic is both useful and attractive. A door behind the owner gives access to storage area.

American Plywood Assn. photos

They all look alike, those unimproved basements. Who needs 'em? Substitute your own junk for this architect's basement and it could just as well be yours . . . right? First clean it up and study area.

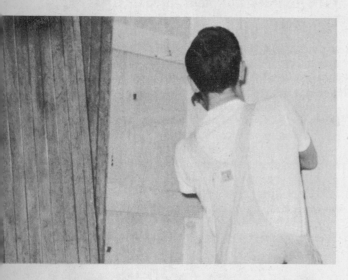

Part of the face-lifting, panels of ⅝-inch prefinished vertically grooved plywood are nailed to 1x4 furring strips on basement wall. Treatment cuts down on refinishing and annoying maintenance.

End walls are covered with ¼-inch A-D plywood. A large panel size makes the basement finishing job go quickly, saves on labor costs. You may, of course, want to use prefinished panels throughout.

MAXIMUM SPANS FOR FLOOR JOISTS

size of member	on 12" centers	on 16" centers	on 24" centers
2 x 4	7'-4"	6'-4"	5'-2"
2 x 6	10'-8"	9'-8"	8'-6"
2 x 8	14'-1"	12'-11"	11'-4"
2 x 10	17'-9"	16'-3"	14'-3"
2 x 12	21'-4"	19'-7"	17'-3"

These are the maximum safe spans for average-strenath joists under a typical 40-pound live load with aouble flooring above and a plastered ceiling below. Many houses are built with provision for expansion into the attic. But if your attic floor joists don't measure up they'll have to be reinforced until they do.

already is plumbing nearby. Plan for all the storage you will need. A good trick is to let a storage wall serve as a partition between rooms.

Most attics will permit two bedrooms IF the stairs go up near the middle of the house. If they go up at one end, about the best you can hope for are dormitory-style bedrooms.

Work with the Plan

Make paper cutouts of furniture and fixtures to approximate scale and arrange them around the areas you've drawn off. Move walls around on the plan if necessary until you have just the area, arrangement and traffic pattern you want for each room. Then draw the walls in for real.

If you use an architect he will take care of this phase based on what you tell him of your needs.

Once you have the plan in mind start

Part of the basement is walled off with plywood-covered storage units and left unfinished as space for the junk in the first photo. Enthusiasts have remodeled themselves right out of junk space.

The total cost of project for labor and materials, including the boys' room and a bathroom, was $1500.

thinking about materials for walls, floors and ceilings. Conduct a search. Visit your building materials dealer and look at the many different products available. Look through catalogs as well as the home magazines and select those that appeal to you while meeting your budget requirements.

Indicate on the plan how heating will be handled, where plumbing will go and where you want electrical outlets. There should be one electrical convenience outlet for every 12 feet of wall. Plan outlets for extension telephone service if that is wanted. Plan for adequate lighting, either by natural light or from electric lights.

When planning any improvement make sure that your house electrical system can handle the extra load. Look at the size of your service entrance box. If you have modern 100-ampere, 220-volt electrical service, it should be adequate unless already taxed to capacity by appliances like an electric range, or electric water heater. Under-powered 30-ampere, 110-volt or even 60-ampere, 220-volt house wiring may call for remodeling right along with your basement or attic job.

Construction

Now you are down to the point of deciding whether to do the remodeling yourself or to have someone else do it. Here are the choices: (1) build it yourself if local codes permit; (2) hire a package remodeler who takes care of everything for one bid price;

(3) get separate bids from the various trades involved, such as carpenter, plumber, etc., and coordinate them yourself; (4) hire skilled craftsmen to work by the hour, buying the materials yourself; or (5) a combination of Nos. 1, 3 and 4.

The big advantage in dealing with a package remodeler is that he takes care of everything. You deal with one person. He is responsible for all the work. If you want to do any of the work yourself, don't go to a package remodeler.

The advantage of hiring out the work yourself is that you save the package remodeler's fee. Watch it, though, because scheduling the various trades involved can be difficult. What's more, the pro's may work on your job last, realizing that it's a one-shot deal.

The best of all, however, is to do what you can yourself and hire retired professionals, if you can find them, to do the rest. Give them time to work at an easy pace. Work along with them as a helper. Set a fair hourly pay that allows them a leisurely pace.

Most home handymen can do such simple work as building walls, floors and ceilings and finishing them. When it comes to the mechanical trades like plumbing, heating and wiring, they'd best get pros to do the work. Moreover, complicated carpentry, such as building in a dormer, requires knowledge that the handyman would either have to get by reading about it or by hiring someone who knows how.

If your basement looks as good as this one before remodeling, you haven't got too far to go. The major additions needed are a ceiling and resilient floor. A few decorating touches can turn it into a family room for the whole household to long enjoy.

Installing vinyl-asbestos floor tile, left, is made easier by an adhesive that can be applied with an ordinary paint brush. Throughout your remodeling try to use simple methods and materials.

You can handle most of the remodeling yourself. Acoustical ceiling tiles are stapled to wood furring strips nailed across ceiling joists. Line up furring strips by blocking out with shims, etc.

Armstrong Cork Co. photos

Ceiling and floor tiles plus masonry paint on the walls finish the job—for less than $300. Indoor-outdoor decor has international flavor through the use of travel posters and carefully selected potted plants.

What to Look Out for

If you hire anyone else to work on your house—make him furnish waivers of lien for all labor and all materials before you pay for the job. This protects you should the contractor buy materials on credit or hire a subcontractor for your job and not pay them. Those who are owed can easily file liens against your property and stick you for the bill. It doesn't make any difference whether or not you've already paid in full for your improvement. Not fair? It's the law and it happens every day. Don't let it happen to you. Most contractors are used to waivers and no reputable one minds being asked. It's good business.

Additionally you should ask anyone who works on your house for proof that he and his helpers are covered by workmen's compensation insurance. Otherwise, if anyone is injured on your job you may be sued.

It can pay you to check with your lawyer on both the matter of insurance and waivers of lien. He should be in on any contracts you sign, too. His fee is good medicine to ward off future ulcers.

Building Permit

Don't get a building permit unless the law requires one for the type of improvement you are putting in. Sounds like kooky advice, but there's a reason. It isn't so much the cost of the permit that hurts, it's the fact that your house is opened to review by the tax assessor. He will surely increase its evaluation to reflect the remodeling you've done. Some cities and counties require building permits only for improvements that extend beyond the house walls. Find out about your code before you goof yourself up with the tax collector.

If you will do the building yourself, you inherit the job of figuring the quantities of materials needed. Make a complete list of all of them.

Use this rough rule of thumb for estimating quantities of materials: Materials that are measured in *square* feet—wall paneling, plywood, flooring and ceiling materials—are figured by calculating how much area there is to cover and adding 20 percent for waste. Materials that are measured in *lineal* feet—moldings, pipe, wire, wall plate and sill lumber—are figured by finding how many feet are needed and adding 10 percent for waste. Materials that are measured by the number of pieces—wall studs, electrical boxes, fixtures, etc.—are ordered by the number needed. Order a few extras if you're not too sure of your estimate.

When you have figured everything and gotten prices from dealers and catalogs, add up the whole tab. This is what your improvement will cost, *minimum*. It's best to figure on extra money for those unexpected extras. Then you're ready to build, all but the hard part—getting the money.

Masonite Corp.

Woodgrain panels brighten up a refurbished basement. As good as most wall materials look when installed, they are not difficult to put up. The bigger the panels, the faster they go up.

Wall Materials You Can Use

There's a large variety of material available to beautify your new rooms.

JUST BECAUSE you want to do the work yourself doesn't mean you can't select from among many materials for wall beauty or wall economy.

If you go the economy route there is plasterboard (often called *drywall*), composition board, fiberboard, hardboard and fir plywood.

If you go the beauty bit, you will spend more for wood paneling, hardwood plywood, ceramic tile, wallcovering of some kind or hardboard, plastic laminated hardboard or gypsum board all with a woodgrain.

Because you choose economy you need not go without beauty. Some of the economical wall materials can be beautiful too. It's all in what you do *with* them and *to* them, most notably painting.

Lath and plaster, since it is neither low in cost, intrinsically beautiful or something you can put in yourself, is easy to leave out of the picture. Still, it's a high quality wall material that's worth considering.

The Wall Materials

Plasterboard—What can you say about gypsum board except that it's used everywhere for its low cost and the smooth wall surface it presents when the joints are filled and taped? Plasterboard started out as a substitute for the then ubiquitos lath and plaster. Now IT is Number 1.

The most commonly used plasterboard thickness is ½ inch. Panels are 4 feet by 8, 10 and 12 feet.

Wood paneling—Popular woods for paneling are redwood, mahogany, fir and pine. Cedar is popular too for closet linings. Not limited to just these woods, you can make paneling out of any wood. The edges may be tongued-and-grooved, splined, butted or they may be set apart with battens behind or on the surface. Patterns may even be milled into the boards or moldings nailed on. Anything goes in creative paneling. What's more, almost all of it looks good.

Less desirable woods such as No. 2 spruce, which is intended for exterior sheathing use, may be stained and finished attractively to make excellent paneling.

Beautiful paneling has been made of old weatherworn barn siding. Paneling can be from ¼ inch to ¾ inch in thickness.

Wallcoverings—It once was called wallpaper. Now there is more than just familiar wall*paper* and all its designs. Take, for example, the vinyl wallcoverings. Or the fabric wallcoverings. And don't forget oilcloth. You can create just about any effect you want with some kind of wallcovering. They're catching on fast.

Softwood plywood—From a plain sanded-surface interior type of boldly textured exterior types of plywood all kinds lend themselves to use on the wall. Some of the more common surfaces are Texture One-Eleven, striated, brushed, kerfed, grooved and rough-sawn.

Plywood for walls may be as thin as ¼

The striking woodgrain swirls of "Chateau" birch set off new hardwood plywood paneling in a basement bedroom. This remodeling combines the cheeriness of a new floor and ceiling with warmth of paneling.

Georgia-Pacific Corp.

inch. Better is ⅜ inch. Panels are made in 4x8, 4x9 and 4x10 feet.

Hardboard—Like plywood, various surfaces of hardboards are available. Many are suited to covering walls. Don't forget to look at the exterior siding types such as Masonite's *Ruf-X-ninety* as well as those intended for indoor use. Usually the ¼-inch thickness is used.

Wood in Large Sheets

The woodgrains—Two types of panels give a woodgrained effect—hardboard and plastic laminated hardboard, such as *Marlite*. Both are ideal for achieving wall beauty and both are prefinished. The laminated products are practically indestructible. All you have to do is put them up. Thicknesses are about ¼ inch. A filigree, a marbletone, pegboards and more than a dozen different hardboard woodgrains are to be had for the buying . . . with matching moldings yet.

Hardwood plywood—If you prefer the

Masonite Corp.

Masonite Corp.

The metal clips that fit into the grooves in one edge of a woodgrain hardboard panel are nailed to the furring strips. Their purpose is to hold the panels to the wall without exposing the nailing.

The next panel, at left, slides over the clips butting against the previous one. The tapered tongue edge fits into grooved edge in other panel leaving a V-joint that looks like others.

Molding shapes show how they are used to trim the corner and top of paneled partition. These moldings were prefinished to match the woodgrain hardboard panels, hiding raw edges.

Masonite Corp.

Small sizes of ceramic tile are sold in ready-to-put-up sheets. A thick layer of mastic is spread directly on the basement wall with a notched trowel and the sheets of tiles are laid in it.

real thing, hardwood plywood is it. Because of its size it goes up faster than wood paneling. Because of its thinner cross section hardwood plywood can bring you the more exotic and expensive woods at prices you can afford. More than 50 domestic woods are made into hardwood plywood. Some exotic foreign woods are used too. Among them are the more common oak, walnut, birch, maple, elm, cherry, pecan, butternut, chocolate, strawberry and vanilla.

The panels all are 48 inches wide and ¼ inch thick. Some are unbelievably beautiful. Buy hardwood plywood prefinished if you like.

Ceramic wall tile—Once ceramic tile was strictly for bathrooms. Not so any more. The quality, colors, sizes and shapes of tile units allow them to be used in every room.

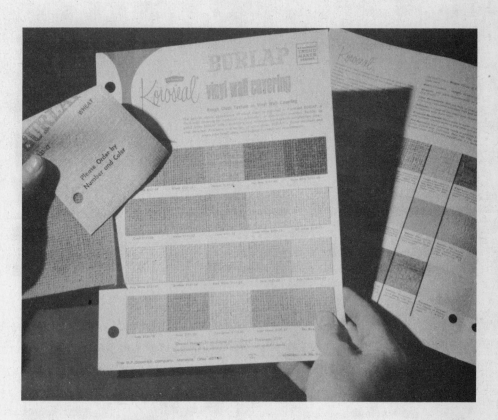

The sample sheet of one manufacturer's vinyl wall covering, in popular burlap pattern, offers a large selection of colors. The folder at right contains more photos of other patterns.

Composition board never had it so good. Shown are a plain board with a dimpled texture, a sand-finished board, a vinyl print pattern, a linen weave in color, a striated board, and a cheery vinyl pattern.

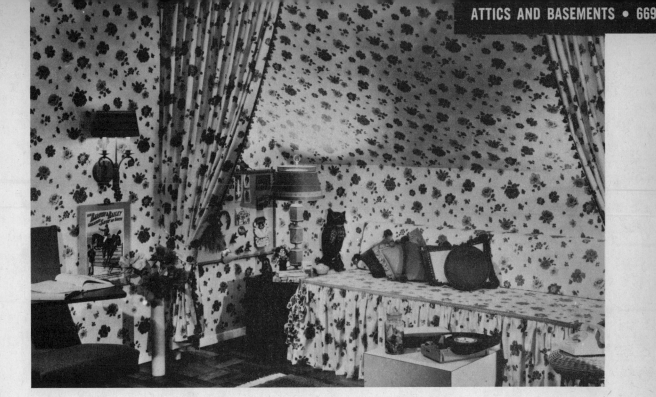

A teenage ivory tower is this colorful room under the eaves of a remodeled attic. The wallpaper and matching fabric are the right background to unify many activities going on in the one room.

In addition to the glazed ceramic wall tile are smaller ceramic mosaic tile, both glazed and unglazed.

Tile colors are those of the rainbow. The smaller tiles often are sold in sheets ready for adhering to the wall.

Ceramic tile may be installed over most sound wall surfaces by troweling on the proper adhesive and placing the tiles in it. Wall tiles are about $\frac{5}{16}$ inch thick. The typical tile measures 4¼x4¼ inches, but there are lots of other sizes too.

Composition board—Made of wood fibers laminated into a good, solid wall material, compo board, as it's been nicknamed, is an old product with some brilliant new faces. In addition to the standard board, you can get panels with linen embossing in varied colors, polyethylene-coated patterns in many designs, panels in vinyl decorator colors, woodgrain patterns and a number of prefinished painted panels. The plastic materials are laminated onto standard compo board making it deluxe all the way.

The board is made in various thicknesses, but the ¼- and ⅜-inch ones are recommended for walls and ceilings. Widths are 4 feet; lengths, 6 feet or more. A number of moldings are available to go with the board.

Insulation board—Also called fiberboard, insulation board is made from wood and cane fibers matted into large sheets of varying thicknesses. It is most familiar as ceiling tile material but insulation board also makes an economical wall material. Wall plank is used for accenting walls, for walls above wainscoting or for entire walls in any room.

One advantage of insulation board besides its low cost is its sound-deadening. Placed under other wall materials, it helps to control sound transmission through walls.

General purpose building board is for ceilings and walls. These panels are 4 feet wide and from 8 to 12 feet long. Thickness is ½ inch. The panels come in plain or prefinished in a number of colors.

Decorative Materials

One especially decorative wall material is made of vinyl to simulate brick and stone. The sheets are trimmed to interlock at the "mortar joints." While the cost is high, the effect is luxurious.

Grilles, doors and panels are made in the most intricate carved wood designs you can imagine. One is real wood in a quilted pattern that stretches across a wall and door. You can get just about any effect that you can pay for. Ask your dealer.

Once you've selected your wall material, get detailed instructions about putting it up from the dealer or manufacturer. These will tell you how to prepare for installation, how to cut the material, how to fasten it to the wall, how to finish it if that's necessary, and even how to care for it once the wall is up. •

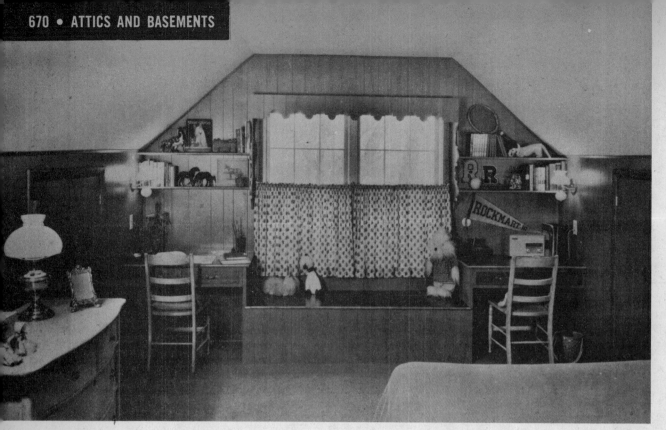

Masonite Corp.

A plain plasterboard ceiling in a room for two high school girls lets the walls and built-ins provide all the luxury while it provides an expansive, light-reflecting color, as shown above.

Ceiling Materials

There is one correct ceiling for every room. Here is a rare opportunity. . .

BEFORE you do your basement or attic ceiling look at some of the exciting possibilities in materials to use. Any of the following would be suitable for a basement or attic. Since the slope of the attic beams means the room is almost *all* ceiling, choose its materials with special care.

Plasterboard—Panels are nailed to framing at the ceiling. The joints are filled, taped and smoothed before painting. Plasterboard, or gypsum board as it is also called, gives a flat, smooth ceiling. It can be coated with texture paint if desired. To install them, the large panels are lifted to the ceiling and secured at one end. Then they're lifted and propped at the other end with a T-bar made from wood. Without the T-bar, is a two-man job.

Fiberboard—Available in large sheets, in planks, in smaller panels or in tile squares, fiberboard also comes in many different surfaces. Included in this category are insulation board and composition board. Some are for painting, others are prefinished. One of the most common is the acoustical surface, with indentations

that absorb sound. Installation of ceiling tile is easy with mastic, staples or clips.

Plastic—Usually fiberglass, plastic ceilings are installed with fluorescent lights behind them for overall room lighting.

Wood paneling—makes a very effective ceiling material when nailed to the framing. The finish can be natural or stained.

Hardboard—While designed for walls, some hardboard patterns make good looking ceilings, even some of the hardboards intended for exterior sidings. Prefinished hardboards such as Marlite are made in wood and marble tones and make great ceiling materials.

Plywood—Textured or plain, plywood is a good ceiling material. The large sheets help the job to go quickly.

There is nothing to stop you from going wild in achieving different ceiling effects. One remodeling used canvas for a basement ceiling. Another made use of floor tile. Wallpaper has been used on ceilings. You could paint the existing ceiling flat black to hide it and leave it with no special ceiling material. That's been done too. •

Stapled to furring strips at the ceiling and around obstructions, 12"x12" acoustical ceiling tiles not only absorb sound but are incombustible.

Fiberboard panels, below, laid on an overhead framework and interspersed with illuminated plastic panels above work areas make a great ceiling.

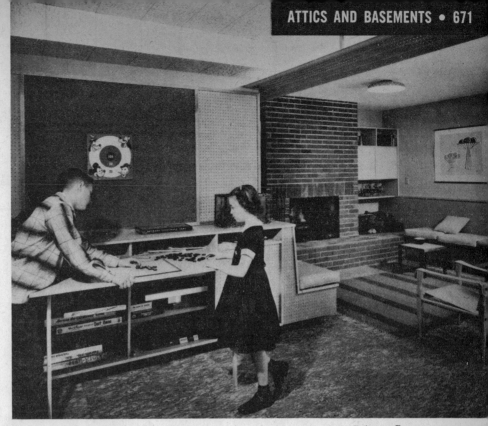

Celotex Corp.

Wood Conversion Co.

Aluminum strips for a suspended ceiling of fiberboard panels is hung from the upstairs floor joists by wires and leveled. This type of ceiling hides pipes, etc., without the trouble of framing and boxing them out.

Masonite Corp.

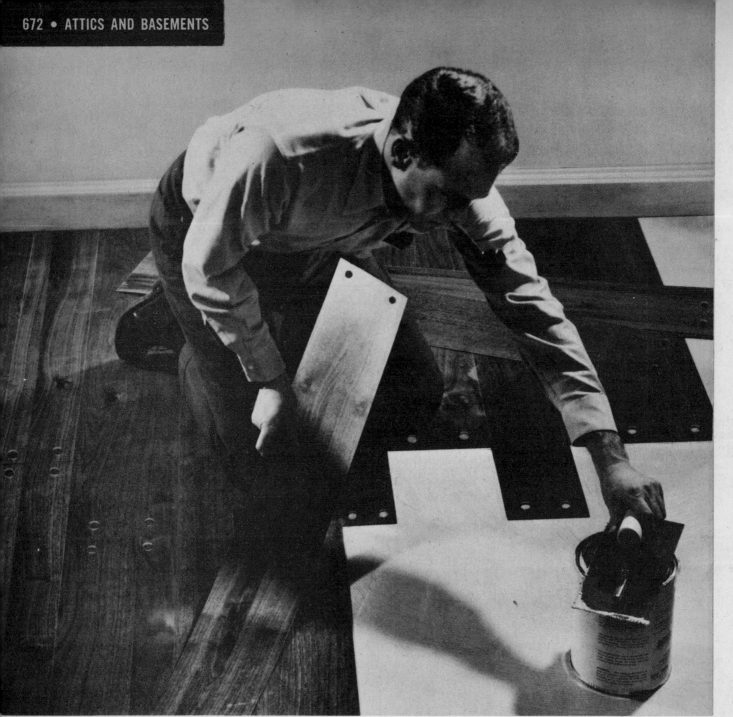

Wood-Mosaic Corp.

Real wood flooring that installs like tile is made of a thin wood veneer bonded to clear vinyl.

Floor Systems You Can Use

Once support is checked out, a variety of covering awaits your choice.

STARTING with a concrete basement floor slab and exposed ceiling joists in an attic, there are a number of choices for finished floors. In the basement you can do nothing and have a usable floor. Not a very pretty one but a usable floor. In the attic, if the joists are exposed, you'll have to do something about building a better floor system.

A floor system comprises the bare support—basement concrete or attic joists—plus any subflooring; any underlayment, if used; a vapor barrier, if used; and the finished floor, the part you see. Since the under-floor must conform to the requirements of the finished floor, select your floor covering first. Then build the floor system to go under it (see chart on page 94).

The first element of a floor system is a subfloor. Many attics already have a wood subfloor built of 1x4- or 1x6-inch boards nailed diagonally to the joists. If your attic has exposed joists, you'll have to put in a subfloor.

While 1x4's and 1x6's can be used as subflooring, plywood presents a more satisfactory surface. For wood and rigid tile finished floors over joists on 16-inch centers buy standard grade 42/20 plywood. Get it in tongue-and-groove, if you can. If not, hardwood strip flooring placed over it should run at right angles to the joists, and wood block or tile joints should not line up with unsupported joints in the plywood subfloor. Group 42/20 plywood will be either ⅝ or ¾ inch thick, depending upon the thickness necessary to win the 42/20 strength designation referring to roof/floor spans in inches.

For resilient tile, carpeting and seamless flooring you'll have to use a better grade of plywood subfloor, one that has knotholes in the inner veneers—as well as in the outer veneers—plugged. Called *underlayment grade, group 1*, it should be used in a ⅝-inch thickness for a 16-inch joist spacing and a ¾-inch thickness for a 24-inch joist spacing. Tongue-and-groove is generally available in this grade. Use it.

Lay the sheets of plywood so that seams between panels are centered over joists. Stagger the rows of panels so that these seams don't run continuously down any joist. Seams running at right angles to the joists need not be staggered.

Nail plywood subfloor panels to the joists using 6d ring-grooved nails. Space the nails 6 inches on centers at the seams and 10 inches on centers through the rest of the panel.

If your nailed plywood subfloor has any joints that aren't smooth across both panels, sand the joint lightly. The easy way is to use a belt sander or oscillating sander.

If resilient tile or carpeting is to be used, cracks between the panels should be filled. An excellent material for this is catalyzed auto body putty, the kind that is used for filling dents in car bodies. Buy it at an auto body and paint dealer or shop. Smooth it into the cracks with a putty knife and sand lightly after set-up.

A basement floor that is dry and in good condition will serve as a subfloor for most finished floor installations. If there is oil, grease, dust, dirt or efflorescence (white powder) on the surface it should be cleaned. Most floor adhesives will not stick to these materials.

Underlayment

The second element of a floor is the underlayment, the part that goes directly beneath the finished floor. If you already have a good ⅝- or ¾-inch plywood attic subfloor, underlayment is not needed there. However, flexible flooring materials used with a 1x4- or 1x6-inch board subfloor need something to smooth out the boards and to prevent expansion and contraction of the floorboards from affecting the finished floor.

For underlayment, use ⅜-inch underlayment grade plywood nailed 6 inches on centers through the panel and 3 inches on centers around the edges. If the floor might get much water spilled on it, use underlayment grade plywood containing exterior glue. Or you can use underlayment grade ¼-inch hardboard. This is nailed the same

New budget-priced, easy-to-install .050-inch vinyl tile offers same easy-care advantages of others.

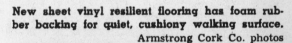
New sheet vinyl resilient flooring has foam rubber backing for quiet, cushiony walking surface.
Armstrong Cork Co. photos

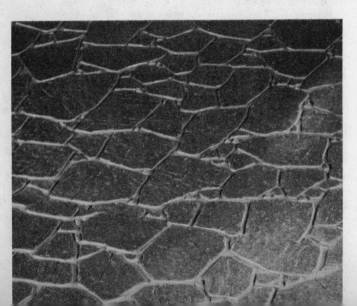

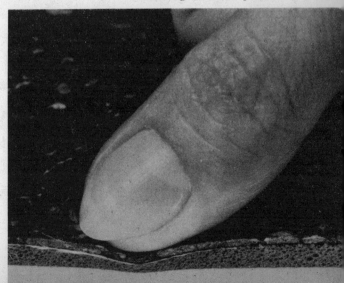

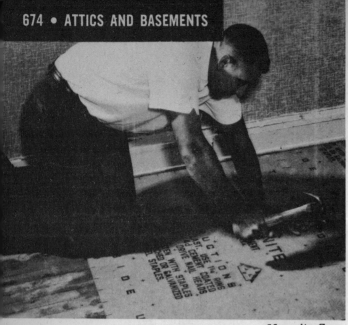

Masonite Corp.

Wood plank attic subfloors need underlayment before most finish flooring materials can be laid. About 1/32" should be left between panels.

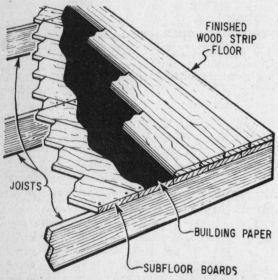

Attic floor system, above, is wood-strip laid at right angles to joists over building paper. The basement floor tile is laid over plastic barrier.

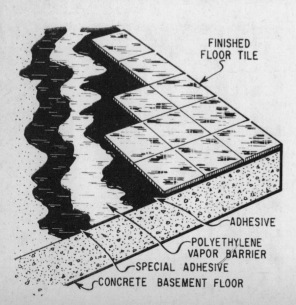

as the plywood underlayment. Don't butt the edges of hardboard underlayment. Leave a 1/32-inch space between panels. Drive nails flush with the surface or slightly below. The surface is then ready for finished flooring.

A basement floor needs no underlayment. However, a vapor barrier is often called for in basement flooring installation. Consisting of a 2-mil sheet of polyethylene bonded to primed concrete with a special adhesive, the vapor barrier prevents moisture from seeping up through the basement floor and ruining your finished floor. You can do the installation yourself.

Types of Finished Floors

There are so many different flooring materials that only a little can be said here about them. Your dealer can give you full information on any that interest you.

Resilient tile—Resilient tiles are laid on a properly prepared subfloor on an adhesive. Asphalt is the cheapest of the resilient tile, costing from 8 to 24 cents per 9x9-inch tile. The cost depends upon the color, lighter colors costing more. While asphalt tile is at home in a basement, it is difficult to care for. Use it upstairs only if you are going cheap all the way.

Inlaid linoleum is better, but it's still linoleum. It's bad news in the basement and you can do better with it in the attic.

Vinyl asbestos is vinyl tile made less costly by adding asbestos. Costing about 17 to 37 cents per tile, it is the most popular tile of all. Care is easy and it wears well. It's an excellent choice for basements as well as attics.

Cork tile is wonderful for its soft, sound-absorbing qualities. The cost is somewhat more than vinyl asbestos, usually. It's not recommended for basement use without a polyethylene vapor barrier over the floor.

Vinyl tile is the ultimate. There are many different kinds, so visit your dealer and compare them. There's also sheet vinyl flooring. The more expensive tiles are available in brick textures, pebbles, marble, wood, etc. And they do look real. The cost is from 30 cents a tile and up to $2 a tile for vinyl cork. Vinyl tile is the easiest to maintain. Either use a vapor barrier for vinyl tile laid in the basement or install it with epoxy adhesive.

Rubber tile makes a floor that looks great. It's a high quality product. For the best job use it in the 1/8-inch or 3/16-inch thickness. With any resilient tile, the thinner the tile the smoother the undersurface must be to end up with a good looking job. A vapor barrier or epoxy adhesive is required for basement use.

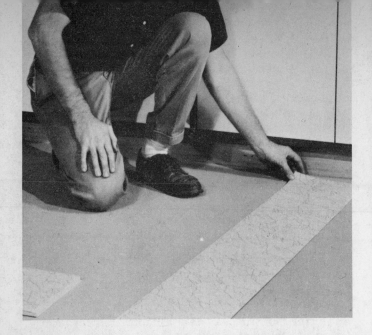

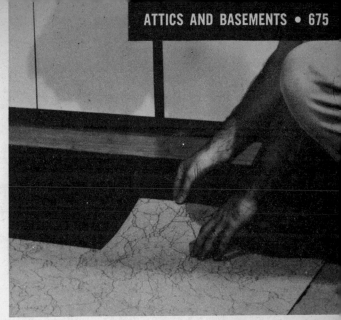

To lay floor tile, snap a chalk line halfway between the center points of two opposite walls. Do the same in the other direction. Then lay test rows of uncemented tile toward the walls in two directions as shown. Spread adhesive for one quarter of the room up to but not over the chalk lines. Place the corner of the first tile where the lines cross. To fit tiles around pipes or other obstructions in a room, make a paper pattern to fit the space exactly. Cut tiles with a scissors.

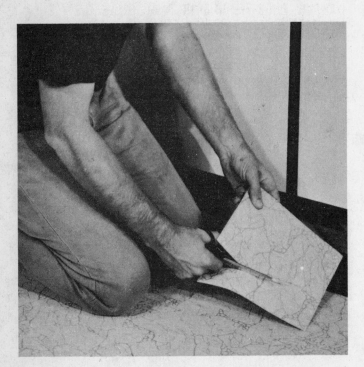

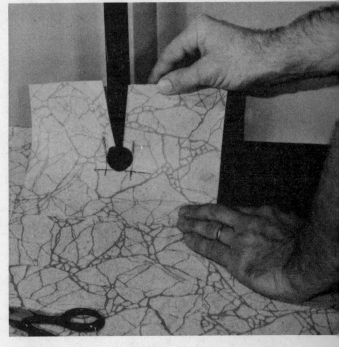

Armstrong Cork Co. photos

Wood—Available in both strip and block, there is something about wood flooring that appeals to everyone. Most types are made with and without a factory-finish. Prefinished is the kind to buy. You can lay it and dance on it the same day. Wood flooring should not be used in a basement with walls that sweat or where condensation is pronounced. In most cases the basement floor should be damp-proofed with a vapor barrier before laying a wood floor.

Strip flooring is usually made in several thicknesses—3/8-, 1/2- and 25/32-inch. Widths are generally from 1 1/2 to 3 1/4 inches or more.

Many woods are used for flooring. The hardwoods—among them red and white oak, maple, beech and birch—produce the longest wearing floors. These woods also cost the most. The softwoods—such as Douglas fir, southern pine, west coast hemlock, western larch and elm—are cheaper floorings for use in areas where the traffic is lighter.

Oak, for one, is available in differing grades: #2 common, #1 common, select and clear. Buy the wood and grade that looks good enough for what you want to pay. Strip flooring is nailed directly to the subfloor or to wood screeds placed in mastic on a concrete floor.

Wood block flooring comes in many patterns that make for beautiful parquet floors. One type of block consists of solid strips glued up. Another type is a plywood block faced with oak veneer.

All sorts of designs are possible with wood blocks. Like strip flooring, blocks are made in varying woods and grades. They're available in unfinished or prefinished.

Carpeting—Most people think of wall-to-wall carpeting as the ultimate in floors. It may be used in attics or DRY basements. Best of all for a basement room would be the new indoor-outdoor type of carpeting.

In the better grades and materials carpeting costs more than wood or resilient tile flooring. If the traffic over it will be light, you can save money by selecting a cheaper grade. Cotton, wool and nylon carpeting, plus various combinations of these, is available in many colors to suit any decorating scheme.

Rigid tile—There are lots of kinds. Ceramic tile, including mosaic, pavers and quarry tile, are generally costly for broad use on floors. Their best use is probably for small areas, such as bathrooms. The variety of colors, shapes, sizes and glazes is almost limitless.

Slate tile and flagstone come from nature and there is consequently much variation in the sizes, shapes, thicknesses, grades, colors and qualities. Because of cost, the uses are limited to small, luxurious areas.

A brick floor can be installed in a basement room if you want to spend your money that way. They would be set in a mortar coat bonded to the concrete floor. Once waxed, these floors are hard to beat for easy maintenance.

Seamless flooring—This relatively new material to the do-it-yourself market seems to have a lot going for it. The installation is as simple as painting. The material goes in basements or attics over a sound subfloor; no cutting or fitting.

One system offers ten different color combinations.

If the floor ever should wear out, another coat of clear plastic would make it like new again, the manufacturer states.

A package for doing 100-square-feet sells for about $58, putting the cost of seamless flooring about the same as pure vinyl tile. At a somewhat higher cost you can contract for a professionally installed seamless floor.

BASEMENT-ATTIC FLOOR SYSTEMS

FINISHED FLOOR TYPE	ATTIC INSTALLATION REQUIREMENTS		BASEMENT INSTALLATION REQUIREMENTS	
	SUBFLOOR	HELD BY	SUBFLOOR	HELD BY
Resilient tile or sheet	Plywood or underlayment over boards	Adhesive	Some go on direct; Some require a vapor barrier; Some not recommended	Adhesive
Wood strip	Plywood or boards covered by building paper	Cut-steel flooring or screw-type nails	2x4 screeds set in mastic over a vapor barrier	Cut-steel flooring or screw-type nails
Wood block	Plywood or underlayment over boards	Adhesive or nails	Requires a vapor barrier	Adhesive
Rigid tile	Either plywood or boards, but with ⅜" underlayment	Adhesive	Goes on direct	Mortar bedding
Carpet	Plywood or underlayment over boards	Adhesive or nails	Requires a vapor barrier	Adhesive
Seamless	Plywood or underlayment over boards	Self-adhesion after being painted on	Goes on direct	Self-adhesion after being painted on

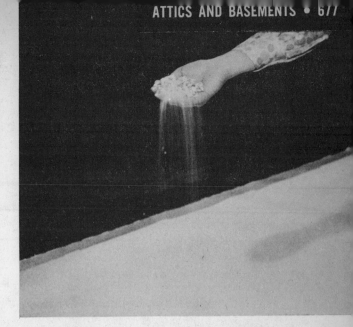

A new seamless floor rolls on over almost any sound floor surface like paint. A full wet coat of laminating plastic is first applied over the white base coat. Next the colored flakes are spread evenly over the wet coat of clear laminating plastic. Plastic is applied and flakes spread until the whole floor is covered. Excess flakes are swept up with a household broom and reclaimed. If there are any areas without enough flakes, they can be touched up at any time, even after the final coat of clear plastic has been applied. Follow the manufacturer's simple instructions.

Types of Adhesives

The adhesive that finished floor materials are laid in not only holds them down, it waterproofs and makes a smooth bedding. Always use an adhesive recommended by the manufacturer of the floor material you're using. This also may depend upon where you are using it. For instance, rubber tile laid in an attic would be set in a different adhesive than if it were laid in a basement. Sometimes a choice of adhesives is offered. Some of the adhesives and their primary uses are:

Asphalt cut back—This is made of "cut back" asphalt that is thinned out enough for good spreading. Use it under asphalt and vinyl asbestos tiles on primed concrete floors.

The primer recommended by the manufacturer should be scrubbed well into the concrete and allowed plenty of time for thorough drying before spreading the adhesive.

Asphalt emulsion—This asphalt adhesive comes thinned to a spreading consistency with water. It can be used for installing asphalt and vinyl asbestos tile either in basements or attics.

Paste—A water soluble adhesive, paste can be used for adhering linoleum, sheet vinyl, rubber and cork tiles in attics.

Wood-floor adhesive—Also called *flooring mastic*, this is used for setting wood block floor tiles.

Ceramic tile adhesive—There are two types, one for walls and one for floors. Un-

The Flecto Co. photos

less you enjoy going the wrong way down one-way streets get the floor type.

Brush-on cement—Specially made for easy installation of asphalt and vinyl asbestos tile, brush-on cement is applied with a paint brush.

Epoxy cement—The catalytic two-part cement is for basement tile installations without a vapor barrier. The parts are mixed before use.

Installing flooring is easy, very pleasant and it goes quickly. When you finish you have something to admire for years. •

Western Wood Products Assn.

A remodeled basement can yield a room of many uses via the compartment system. Space-defining built-out walls and folding doors create an ample kitchen, book and game storage, and a full closet.

How to Finish a Basement

Turn your basement into living space: a party room, den, and guest room.

WHEN YOU THINK of a home improvement, what is the first thing that comes to mind? Be honest now, isn't it a remodeled basement? If you're typical of most homeowners, it probably is.

Basement remodeling is popular because it's easy to do. No complicated jobs are involved, such as building a dormer or snaking plumbing and electrical utilities through walls.

In general the work pretty much follows these lines:

1) Dry up the walls and floor.

2) Install the rough plumbing, wiring and heating, as described in another chapter.
3) Fur out the walls and put in a vapor barrier.
4) Build partitions.
5) Install the wall material.
6) Build the ceiling.
7) Build the floor system.
8) Install the finished plumbing, wiring and heating materials.
9) Build and add storage units.
10) Hang doors and install trim.

Compartment System

With deft remodeling the basement can yield space to meet any need. You may need a party room, guest quarters and a quiet cozy den for TV or reading. All three and more can be built into an ordinary catchall basement without using partitions.

The secret is compartmentalization, making compartments within one room rather than dividing it into smaller spaces. It's a matter of putting built-ins where they'll do the most good.

Built-ins can go on all four walls, encircling the room, to leave free space that becomes the room's dance floor. In one corner goes a food service center, which should include a counter for food preparation and serving, cabinets for glasswear and dishes, and a sink so that washing up can be done on the spot. A range and refrigerator may be used too if needed.

This compartment will be compact. At either end, walls can be built out to a little more than the depth of the cabinetwork and appliances. Folding louvered doors, the closet type, can be hung from the ceiling so that the food center is completely closed off when not in use.

A compartment built next to the kitchen corner will take over as the den. This section of wall is built with book shelves and cabinets. A music system can be included here and the television set can be built into the unit.

Next to the entertainment compartment go closets. Built out to the same depth as the kitchen corner, the book area will appear to be recessed. These closets will form

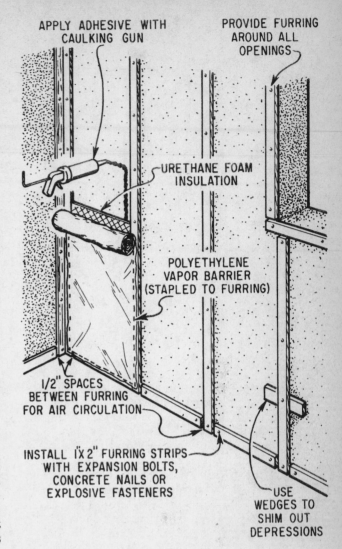

APPLY ADHESIVE WITH CAULKING GUN

PROVIDE FURRING AROUND ALL OPENINGS

URETHANE FOAM INSULATION

POLYETHYLENE VAPOR BARRIER (STAPLED TO FURRING)

1/2" SPACES BETWEEN FURRING FOR AIR CIRCULATION

INSTALL 1"X 2" FURRING STRIPS WITH EXPANSION BOLTS, CONCRETE NAILS OR EXPLOSIVE FASTENERS

USE WEDGES TO SHIM OUT DEPRESSIONS

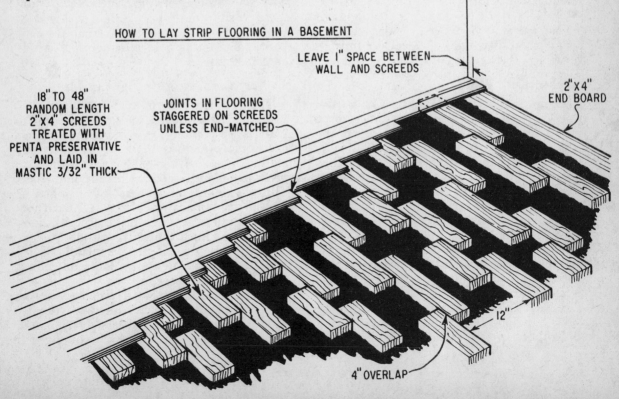

HOW TO LAY STRIP FLOORING IN A BASEMENT

LEAVE 1" SPACE BETWEEN WALL AND SCREEDS

2"X 4" END BOARD

18" TO 48" RANDOM LENGTH 2"X 4" SCREEDS TREATED WITH PENTA PRESERVATIVE AND LAID IN MASTIC 3/32" THICK

JOINTS IN FLOORING STAGGERED ON SCREEDS UNLESS END-MATCHED

12"

4" OVERLAP

BOX-OUT FOR OBSTRUCTION ACROSS THE JOISTS   BOX-OUT FOR OBSTRUCTION PARALLEL TO THE JOISTS

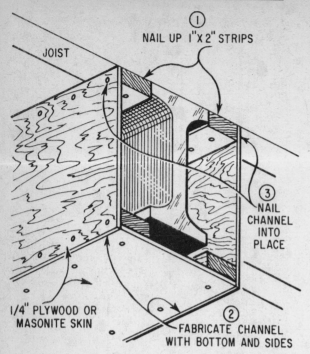

the base for the guest room, but, of course, can also be used for out-of-season clothing storage. Closet doors should match the food center's doors in style.

Complement to the closet can be a sofa or chair, which converts to a bed.

Other walls will yield space for additional compartmentalization. A sewing room can be built in. Laundry facilities also can go behind attractive doors. Hobby equipment of all kinds can be built into various cabinets and closets tailored especially for their contents.

The beauty of the scheme is that you can handle what needs doing. Douglas fir can be used for the built-ins because of its easy workability and the variety of finishes it takes.

Furring Out Walls

No matter what wall material you use practically, the basement walls have to be furred out. If there's a water seepage problem, solve it before you start.

Any plumbing, heating or electrical work that goes into your basement improvement should be installed before the wall materials or furring strips are put on. Don't cover up a wall until you've taken care of the mechanical roughing-in.

Some wall materials call for 2x3 furring. Nail the members up into a framework that will cover each wall. The furring is designed so that its 3-inch face contacts the wall. There should be furring along the top and bottom and both sides. Provide furring on 16-inch centers throughout the wall. If

you're going to panel the wall with ¾-inch-thick boards the interior furring should be placed horizontally to put three rows equally spaced between the top and bottom.

Install the furring framework by tilting it up to the wall. Anchor it to the wall using expansion bolts, concrete nails or explosive fasteners that are long enough to penetrate the furring and into the wall. The easiest method is to rent an explosive stud driver for a few hours. Use great care in handling one of these. It's loaded.

If the wall isn't straight or smooth, you'll have to shim out parts of the furring with wedges of wood. Shingles are fine for this. Do the shimming before fastening the furring to the wall.

Easier and Cheaper Furring Method

The old furring method in which 1x2 furring strips are fastened directly to the wall is permitted for softwood, plywood and some other materials. If properly installed in a dry basement, 1x2 furring is probably plenty good for all the materials. The important thing is to leave about ½ inch of space between joints in the furring strips to allow air circulation around them. The air will keep the wall ventilated. Also, the wall material should be installed with a ¼-inch air gap along the floor and ceiling for circulation.

Furring for large wall panels such as plywood, which are installed vertically, should block under all edges of every panel. There should be furring strips along the

Armstrong Cork Co. photos

To install a suspended ceiling, snap a chalk line at the height of your new ceiling. Attach an edge molding to the wall just below the chalk line by driving concrete nails into the mortar.

Locate the position of the first ceiling runner by measuring the room dimensions to find the width of the border panel (as in a ceiling tile job). Using a string and runner, install a screw eye.

Install first ceiling runner by resting one end on wall molding and fastening the other end to a bent wire. Twist the wire several times. Work along the runner, fastening wires every four feet.

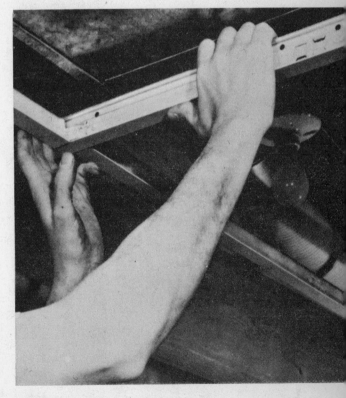

Install four-foot cross tees between the main runners at 24-inch intervals. Simply insert end tab of a cross tee into the runner slot and push to lock, in an Armstrong ceiling. Other makes vary.

With the suspension system now complete, lay the ceiling panels into the grid. Tilt panels upwards and slide them through the opening to rest on the grid flange. Choose from among variety of panels.

Armstrong Cork Co. photos

The finished suspended ceiling combines a modern appearance with acoustical efficiency. Any, or all, of the ceiling panels can be lifted out of the grid system for immediate access to the ceiling.

top and bottom of a wall, at both ends and around all openings. In addition there should be strips every 24 inches on centers for ⅜-inch and thicker panels and strips every 16 inches on centers for thinner panels and panels that are grooved. These strips may run vertically or horizontally.

Shim out depressions in the wall with wedges of wood so that the resulting furred wall is flat and smooth.

If your basement walls tend to get very cold in the winter, cut pieces of ¾-inch-thick urethane foam insulation and stick them in the spaces between furring strips using a good drywall adhesive.

Whether you use the insulation or not, it's a good idea to staple a polyethylene vapor barrier over the furring before putting up your wall material.

Partition Framing

Basement partitions, since they are not load-bearing, can be framed in 2x3 lumber instead of 2x4. There's one exception. Any wall that will conceal a 3-inch copper or plastic drainage, waste or vent pipe should have full 2x4 framing. DWV pipes 4 inches in diameter need a 2x6 wall for concealment.

Follow the same partition framing procedure as outlined in the chapter on attic improvement. Stud spacing should be 16 inches on centers. The single sill can be nailed down easiest with an explosive stud driver. The single plate is nailed to the joists above. If the partition is parallel to the joists, headers are installed above the partition and between the joists. A header is placed every 16 inches.

Double the framing at corners where a partition meets the wall or another partition. The doubled framing is spaced apart with 2x3 blocks to create a nailing face for both wall materials in both directions.

Double the framing around door openings and at corners.

Building a Floor

Your basement floor can be as simple as paint over the existing concrete floor. The next step up is to tile directly over the floor. Resilient tile is easy to install but doesn't provide much insulation to a cold floor. Wood blocks adhered directly to the floor insulate it better.

If you want a level, insulated floor enough to invest quite a bit in it, you can build a wood subfloor by placing 2x3's laid flat on 16-inch centers. Nail wood shims under them every 16 inches as needed to level and support. Use aluminum nails to prevent rusting. Place a 2x3-inch strip

Wood Conversion Co.

Acoustical tile can be stapled to furring strips that are run across the joists above a basement. Simply nail the strips to fall where tile joints will come, and bang away with your loaded stapler.

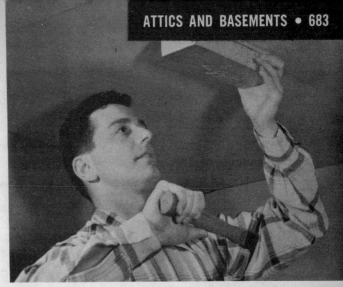

The Upson Co.

Some composition board panels can be installed by pounding them against clips. Nailed to the joists, the clips clinch into the panel back to hold it. Panel edges are nailed and covered with trim.

around the edges of walls and partitions.

Then you can install a polyethylene vapor barrier and subfloor. See the chapter on floor systems. Once the subfloor is in, you can install any finish floor that you like.

If you don't do the whole basement this way, put a door on the finished portion to help people remember to step up every time they enter it. Or build a sloping plywood ramp to ease the transition.

Boxing-Out Obstructions

Turn your attention from the floor to the ceiling. Unless you use a suspended ceiling, unsightly pipes and beams should be boxed-out. An easy way to do this is to nail 1x2 strips to the joists parallel to the obstruction. These aren't necessary if the beam has a 2-inch wood sill resting on it. Then build a channel out of 1x2's and ¼-inch plywood or Masonite. Make it wide enough to fit over the ceiling 1x2's and deep enough to hide the beam. Lift this into place around the beam and have someone hold it there while you nail it.

Boxing-out pipes, etc., running parallel to the joists needs no nailing strips at the ceiling. The sides of the channel are installed first by nailing them right to the joists on either side of the pipe. Then the channel bottom is fabricated by nailing 1x2's along each edge. This is lifted into place between the sides and the sides are nailed to it.

If access must be provided to boxed-out utilities, simply install the bottom piece with screws instead of nails.

Columns are boxed-out easily with a framework of 1x2's and a skin of ¼-inch plywood or Masonite. Fancy moldings can be used on the corners and base moldings

nailed on around the bottom to make the covering look as though it belongs to the club.

Ceiling

If there is ceiling height to build one in your basement, a suspended ceiling is excellent. It not only hides all the uglies at the ceiling, it offers provision for built-in ceiling lighting. Everything you need to make a suspended ceiling can be purchased ready to fit and install. The photos show how to do it.

One problem has been saved for last. If you build a bathroom in the basement and the sewer pipe is not below floor level, you'll have to install the more complex and costly up-flushing toilet.

The same problem affects a basement laundry, although it can drain into a sump pit and be pumped to sewer level with a sump pump. First check your plumbing code on the pumping of water into a sewer. Many do not permit it. If not, you'll have to install a slop sink. Pumped water flows into a funnel-like slop sink and through a trap before entering the sewer by gravity. Thus if the sewer should block up, the pump cannot pump water up and out of upstairs fixtures.

If after it's finished, your remodeled basement tends to be damp, you will need a dehumidifier. The most useful ones have built-in humidistats that turn them on and off as needed to keep the humidity at the proper level. If you have installed vapor barriers on walls and floors, a small dehumidifier should be able to handle a large area. No matter where it is located the humidity will find it and be wrung out of the air. •

Block basement with a water problem. Remodeling a basement like this would be a waste of materials. The hollow concrete block cores fill with water from outside which seeps through inner wall.

Drying up a Problem Basement

Water can enter through cracks, or holes left around pipes in the wall.

AS YOU MIGHT expect, the best way to get a watertight basement is to build it that way in the first place. But that isn't a bit of help to those of us whose houses are built on structural sieves. My own basement is like that—half of it anyway— the half that's built of concrete block.

It happens that my office is in the basement. And right now as I am writing this my feet are in water. About 30 minutes after a rain my office floor is a river between a spot on one wall and the floor drain. Improving a room like this with an attractive wall or floor material would be a waste of time.

There are a host of well publicized methods and compounds for stopping leakage. I've tried them all and I'm here to attest that they don't work, not on a problem basement like mine, at least.

But there are a few methods that DO

work. About a year ago I contacted a professional basement waterproofing engineer, a guy who gets the worst wet basement problems in a whole metropolitan area and solves them. If you think you or I have troubles, you should hear some of the cases HE has had to correct. His firm guarantees the basements they fix to stay dry for something like five years.

I'd been sent to this man by the editor of a top trade magazine for concrete contractors. We collaborated on an article about waterproofing leaky basements. His methods, my words. We presented leakage cures that concrete contractors could use to satisfy complaints. I got permission to share his professional water-stopping secrets with you.

If you need a basement miracle, here it is. I saved my own basement problem just to help illustrate the methods.

Where Water Gets In

Theoretically water should not seep into a basement even though the ground outside is saturated. If the concrete is properly made and placed, a cast-in-place concrete foundation is watertight. Concrete block basements, on the other hand, are not watertight, but the bituminous coating that builders spread on the outside theoretically should keep water out.

In both kinds of foundations, drain tile around the footing outside should pull water out of the earth surrounding a house. A watertight foundation shouldn't even be needed—theoretically.

The theories break down somewhere. The perimeter drains soon fill with mud and no longer function. The block walls develop minor cracks all over. These extend through the dandy bituminous coating. Cast-in-place walls crack, too, and water gets in.

If water doesn't find its way in through a crack, it enters through holes in the wall left by rusting out form ties and around pipes going through the wall. Water even can sneak in through the joint between the floor and the wall. An undrained window well creates a water problem all its own.

Sealing Up a Concrete Basement

Concrete block foundations are by far the worst offenders. Waterproofing them is more difficult too. Comparatively, sealing up a cast-in-place concrete foundation is simple.

One method for eliminating seepage through a crack in a concrete basement wall involves digging down alongside the crack with a shovel and posthole digger. The crack is exposed all the way from grade level to the footing. Then two 1x4 boards are nailed together forming a V as long as the hole is deep. Lowered into the hole, they serve as a form to contain the greatest leak-stopper there is—bentonite.

Bentonite is a special kind of clay. Mined and manufactured by the American Colloid Company, Skokie, Illinois, and found in most big-city *Yellow Pages*. Bentonite costs little but it sure works wonders. Bentonite's magic is in its ability to expand in contact with water. When wet, it swells up to 15 times its original volume. Scoop up a handful of sandy-looking bentonite, form a depression in it and pour in water. Your hand will stay dry, even if you had patience to wait till the pool of water evaporated.

Fill your form with bentonite after backfilling outside the form with earth. When water tries to reach the foundation crack

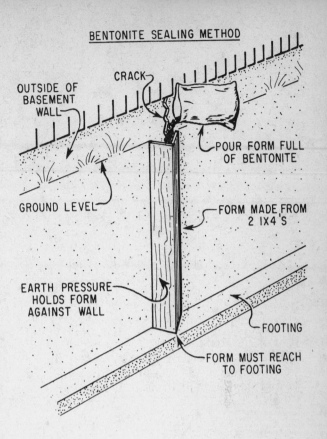

BENTONITE SEALING METHOD

OUTSIDE OF BASEMENT WALL

CRACK

POUR FORM FULL OF BENTONITE

GROUND LEVEL

FORM MADE FROM 2 1X4'S

EARTH PRESSURE HOLDS FORM AGAINST WALL

FOOTING

FORM MUST REACH TO FOOTING

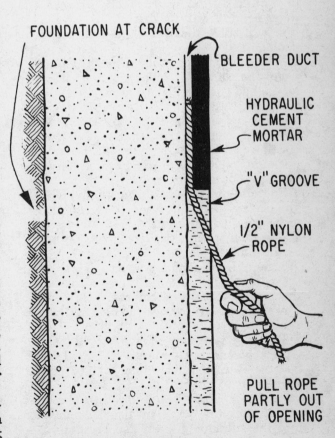

TO MAKE A WALL BLEEDER

FOUNDATION AT CRACK

BLEEDER DUCT

HYDRAULIC CEMENT MORTAR

"V" GROOVE

1/2" NYLON ROPE

PULL ROPE PARTLY OUT OF OPENING

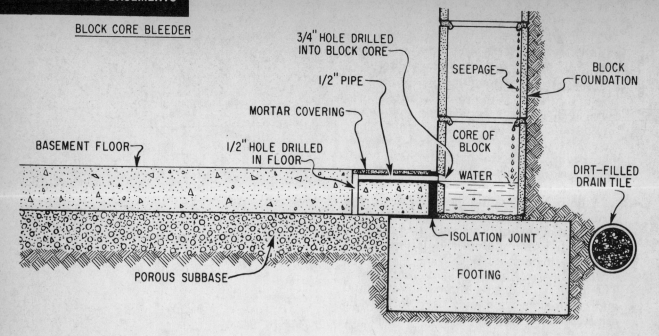

it will be stopped short by the bentonite.

Don't disturb a bentonite waterstopper when it swells up creating a lump next to your foundation. Although it may swell as much as a foot high, leave it as is for several months. After that you can remove any excess bentonite down to within an inch of the crack and fill in with black dirt.

Bentonite will not harm plants or animals.

This method, along with the old standby of putting an extension on the downspout to lead runoff water away from the foundation will solve most cracked-wall leakage problems.

With bentonite, a crack needn't be sealed from the inside. However, if the crack looks bad or if it's so wide that your bentonite merely sifts through from the outside, it will have to be sealed with hydraulic cement mortar or epoxy resin. Use the commercial basement crack sealing formulations of these in combination with bentonite outside.

Foundation cracks in locations where you can't get at them from the outside have to be handled differently. Beneath a stoop is one such spot. A patio or driveway next to the foundation is another.

Although the common approach is to seal these cracks with mortar or epoxy from the inside, these methods rarely last long. The seal soon gives way and seepage starts again.

The only sure way to stop such a leak is with a *bleeder* system. It's called *bleeder* because a duct is left along a filled crack for water to move like blood through a vein. The opening leads to another opening through the basement floor and thence into the subfloor gravel. The bleeder system catches water coming through the wall

and conducts it unseen to where it can be pumped away.

Almost all basement floors are built on a layer of stones, cinders or gravel. This helps the builder to get a level subbase. From the subbase gravel the water soon finds its way to the basement sump and is pumped away by the sump pump. If your basement doesn't have a sump and pump, you'll either have to install one or drain the wall bleeder across a groove chiseled in the floor to the nearest drain. Diverting seepage water under a basement floor that is not drained can be far more disastrous than sweeping dirt under a rug.

If the floortop drain bit seems crude, and you have lots of ambition, you could chisel the groove wide and deep enough to conceal a small pipe. Grout over the pipe with hydraulic cement mortar. Be sure there is provision at the floor drain for rodding out the pipe should it ever clog up.

Making a Bleeder

Before you invest any work in a wall, test to be sure your basement floor has a porous subbase. Drill a ½-inch hole through the floor with a carbide-tipped bit in an electric drill. Locate the hole directly out from the seeping crack half as far away from the wall as the wall is thick, plus two inches. For example, on a 10-inch wall, the floor drain hole should be 7 inches away from the wall. The purpose of this spacing is to miss the footing and drill out into the subbase. If you bore in as far as 6 inches and still haven't broken through, give up and bore another hole two inches farther out. This one should surely clear the footing.

After the drill breaks through, ram a rod through and into the underfloor ma-

WALL BLEEDER SYSTEM

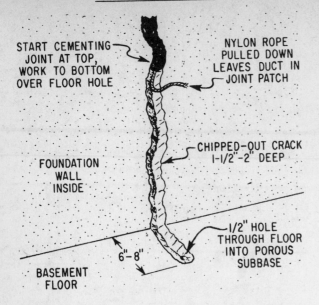

START CEMENTING JOINT AT TOP, WORK TO BOTTOM OVER FLOOR HOLE

NYLON ROPE PULLED DOWN LEAVES DUCT IN JOINT PATCH

CHIPPED-OUT CRACK 1-1/2"-2" DEEP

FOUNDATION WALL INSIDE

1/2" HOLE THROUGH FLOOR INTO POROUS SUBBASE

6"-8"

BASEMENT FLOOR

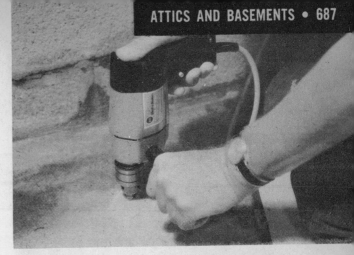

Bore a ½-inch test hole through the basement floor 6 to 8 inches out from a joint in the bottom row of concrete blocks where the seepage is worst.

Chisel a groove from the wall to the hole and pour water in it to make sure that the bleeder is well drained into a porous underfloor material.

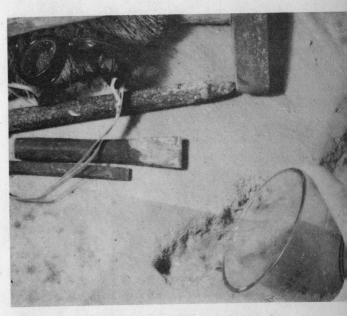

Bore a ¾-inch hole into the block core below the floor level and watch the water flow out. Most foundation blocks have cores at the ends, half and quarter points. Most seepage is at the ends.

terial. You'll be able to tell easily whether the subbase is dirt or gravel. If it's gravel you may go ahead with the construction of a bleeder system.

Chip the wall crack out 1½ to 2 inches deep in a V shape. It need not be the hard-to-make keyed shape they always tell you.

After cleaning out the crack and dampening it, place a 1-foot length of ½-inch nylon rope into the point of the V, starting at the top. Mix hydraulic cement mortar, the fast-drying kind, and pack it into the crack over the rope. While there are several inches of rope still not covered by mortar, stop cementing and let the mortar set. Then pull the rope down but not out of the hole. This leaves the crack filled and flush on the basement side, hollow on the inside.

Continue cementing and pulling until the crack is filled from top to bottom.

Now chisel out a similar groove through the floor to the bored hole and continue making the bleeder right up to the hole. When the hole is reached remove the rope entirely and stuff a wad of bread, *yes bread*, into the hole. This lets you cement the hole over without obstructing the water duct through the newly made bleeder. When the bleeder goes into action after a rain, the bread will dissolve and flush away.

To complete the job, spread epoxy resin over the crack and back an inch on each edge. This is to prevent cracking of the mortar and bleeding of the water through the filled joint.

More Uses for Bentonite

Sometimes water that runs down the joint between a sidewalk or driveway and the foundation can be stopped without the work of inside crack-filling. It's worth a try.

Place a ½-inch pipe in the groove with one end sawed at an angle to cover the drain hole, then fill the groove with fast-setting hydraulic cement mortar, the kind sold for patching wet walls.

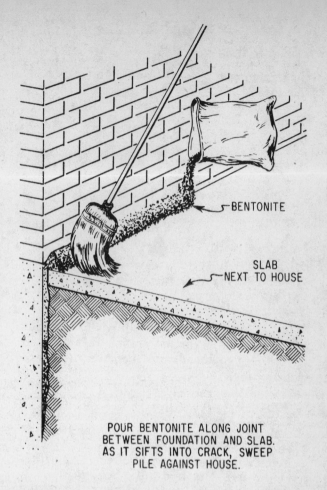

BENTONITE

SLAB NEXT TO HOUSE

POUR BENTONITE ALONG JOINT BETWEEN FOUNDATION AND SLAB. AS IT SIFTS INTO CRACK, SWEEP PILE AGAINST HOUSE.

If the slab-wall joint is too narrow to accept bentonite by sifting, calk it with one of the new elastic compounds that last for years. The calking will let the water drain away on the surface.

If the crack is ¼ inch or wider, a line of bentonite can be spread and allowed to sift down into it. As bentonite disappears down the crack, more may need to be added. Sometimes it's surprising how much material a hungry crack can gobble up. When filled, the excess bentonite may be reclaimed.

If the crack is too narrow to accept bentonite, you can try calking it with one of the new long-lasting elastic calking compounds.

Window Well Problem?

Overflowing window wells that dump water down your wall into the basement during a rain can be dried with a bleeder system. This one is best done with a pipe down the wall. First drill a 1-inch hole through the wall about 2 inches below the sill of a problem window well. Push a 1-inch plastic pipe elbow into the hole. Run a 1-inch plastic pipe from it down the wall to the floor. At the floor, chisel a groove or embed a pipe in the floor to the nearest floor drain.

If there is much flow of water from a window well, it's not a good idea to divert it beneath the basement floor. A torrent of water could create underfloor washouts.

Leakage around deteriorating form ties is the kind you can easily stop, using the epoxies or hydraulic cement mortar.

Seepage that comes up from under the floor, appearing around floor cracks and in the joint between floor and basement wall, calls for an inside drain tile system and sump pit with pump. Putting epoxy or mortar in the cracks won't help. The water pressure will only buckle your floor. Call a professional to install an inside drain system. It entails tearing up the floor clear around your basement to install the tile lines.

The pro's have another trick that can be brought to bear if the wall-seepage-stopping methods outlined here don't work. They have a machine that pumps a slurry of bentonite and water under great pressure into a pipe driven down into the earth next to your foundation. The slurry mixes with soil next to the wall and forms a watertight seal all over the wall. This method won't work on block basements, they tell me.

How about my office after installing the bleeder (see photos)? It's dry for the first time in years even though I've purposely created a lake with a garden hose on the ground above.

Like the man says, it's guaranteed to work.

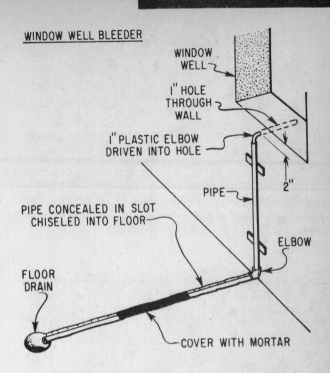

WINDOW WELL BLEEDER

WINDOW WELL
1" HOLE THROUGH WALL
1" PLASTIC ELBOW DRIVEN INTO HOLE
PIPE
2"
ELBOW
PIPE CONCEALED IN SLOT CHISELED INTO FLOOR
FLOOR DRAIN
COVER WITH MORTAR

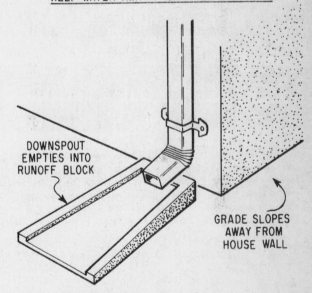

KEEP WATER AWAY FROM THE FOUNDATION

DOWNSPOUT EMPTIES INTO RUNOFF BLOCK
GRADE SLOPES AWAY FROM HOUSE WALL

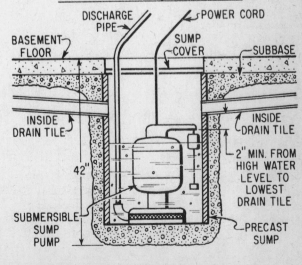

BASEMENT SUMP WITH INSIDE DRAINS

DISCHARGE PIPE
POWER CORD
BASEMENT FLOOR
SUMP COVER
SUBBASE
INSIDE DRAIN TILE
INSIDE DRAIN TILE
2" MIN. FROM HIGH WATER LEVEL TO LOWEST DRAIN TILE
42"
SUBMERSIBLE SUMP PUMP
PRECAST SUMP

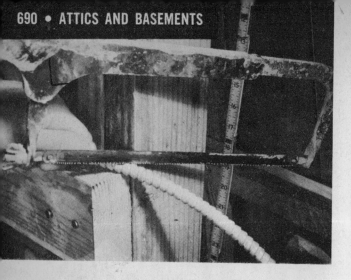
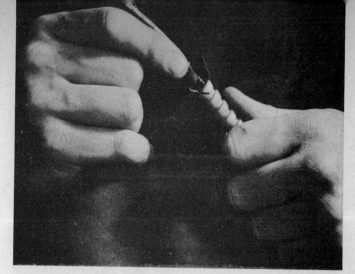
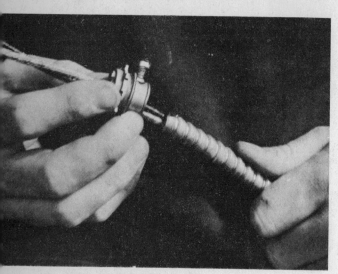
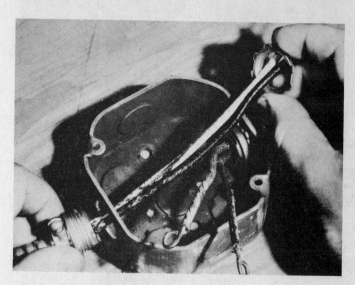

At top, left, armored cable is cut at an angel into one spiral of the armor, about 8 inches back from the end. Don't cut through. Armor can be broken by bending. Top right, strip off paper wrapping from wires and insert a fiber bushing between wires and armor. Bushing keeps insulation on the wires from being frayed by a ragged edge. Bottom left, slip a cable connector over armored cable and secure it to the cable end by tightening the screw. To fasten the armored cable to an outlet box, bottom right, insert wire into a knockout hole, then slip the nut over the wires and tighten.

Wiring an Attic or Basement

Most of the wiring is done while the old and new wall studs are exposed.

NO MATTER what type of rooms you build into a basement or attic, they're going to need additional electricity for lighting and power. This has to come from your house system.

There are two ways you can get the needed electrical power. You can steal it from perhaps already overloaded circuits in the main living portions of the house and suffer the consequence of frequent blown fuses or tripped circuit breakers. Or you can tap the main power distribution center—your service entrance panel. The latter is, of course, best.

If you have a basement the service entrance box is usually located there. This is the big box with fuses or circuit breakers in it. If there is room for adding more fuses or circuit breakers, you can tap the new circuits directly from the entrance box in a basement project. If there are no extras available and it's a circuit breaker panel, you can create them by using the tandem-type circuit breakers and doubling up on some of the existing breakers. This would solve the basement circuit problem.

The entrance panel is too hard to reach by snaking wires through the wall for each attic circuit. The solution there is to snake one large service-entrance-type wire through the walls and hook it to a branch circuit breaker panel in the attic (see drawing). Usually you can get by, breaking through the wall only at headers in order to notch them for the cable. If conduit must be used, you'll likely have to knock out plaster all the way up a wall. The panel is supplied with juice by wiring its service cable directly to the power take-off lugs on the service entrance panel. With this done, you can branch out with from six to 12 new circuits in the attic, no sweat.

First check your present house power. You should not add additional load to your present electrical service if it's already loaded to capacity. A 100-ampere, 240-volt service entrance is considered adequate for houses up to 3000 square feet in floor area. If you have a gas stove and water heater and no major electrical-using appliances such as central air conditioning or electric clothes dryers, you can probably get by with 60-ampere, 240-volt service, even with a remodeled basement and attic.

What Wiring Involves

It would take a whole book to tell you what you'll need to know about installing electrical wiring for an attic or basement improvement. None of it is complicated, but it's very important to know what you're doing. I'd recommend getting a good book on residential wiring. Sears Roebuck has one of the best, *Simplified Electrical Wiring Handbook*, selling for 50 cents. Following directions in the book, you can proceed confidently.

There are two ways of getting the electricity around to where you want it: service cable or conduit. Which you use depends upon the local electrical code applicable to your house. Check the requirements before you order your wiring materials. If the choice is up to you, by all means choose service cable. It's much easier to work with. Cable is available armored or unarmored. I personally prefer the armored type (B-X). It costs more but there's something mighty nice about having a tough wall of metal around all your house wiring.

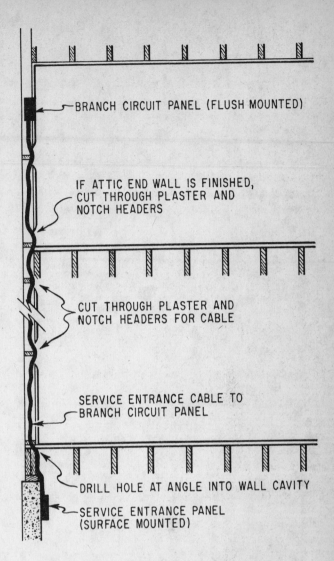

BRANCH CIRCUIT PANEL (FLUSH MOUNTED)

IF ATTIC END WALL IS FINISHED, CUT THROUGH PLASTER AND NOTCH HEADERS

CUT THROUGH PLASTER AND NOTCH HEADERS FOR CABLE

SERVICE ENTRANCE CABLE TO BRANCH CIRCUIT PANEL

DRILL HOLE AT ANGLE INTO WALL CAVITY

SERVICE ENTRANCE PANEL (SURFACE MOUNTED)

To get power in the attic, run a large wire from entrance panel through walls and attach wire to a branch circuit breaker in the attic. The walls need only be broken at the headers in order to notch them to allow the cable to pass through.

Running the wires for a basement remodeling is easy. Everything from the service entrance is exposed and get-attable.

Running the wires for an attic remodeling isn't difficult, but there is the one hurdle of bringing up power from the service entrance panel to the branch circuit panel. It may be necessary to knock out a little plaster here and there, but keep this to a minimum. Take each obstacle as it comes and eventually you'll win out. Once you get the cable above floor level the rest is easy.

A whole assortment of wiring devices is available to help you wire your improvement. They make it easy to do a fast, safe job. •

MAKING THE GRADE

... for pleasing and practical effects

BY T. H. Everett

BEFORE making a lawn or garden consider carefully, and modify if desirable, the contours of the ground. The surface grade is of immense importance in establishing a feeling that the garden is in harmony with its surroundings, that it fits the landscape. This appearance of rightness, of belonging, cannot be attained if grades are wrong.

Many beginners assume that a lawn should be flat and their efforts at grading are directed toward attaining this end. If the location is too steep for this they are likely to attempt a series of flat or nearly flat terraces separated by banks, walls or other devices marking severe changes of grade. That is, they are likely to do this if their pocketbooks permit.

This is all wrong. Level areas of lawn have their useful place in many garden plans but to assume that the more level the turf is, the better, is sheer nonsense. Unless there is good need for a lawn to be flat, every effort should be made to have it otherwise. A perfectly level lawn often indictates lack of imagination.

Flatness is a restrictive landscape feature. It calls for formal or semiformal plantings. It does not permit the easy use of the beautiful and seemingly casual informal planting that goes so splendidly with gentle slopes and flowing contours.

Poorly landscaped, a flat lot can be a horror. Straight lines of paths and plantings cross it without apparent purpose or, worse still, meaningless, silly curves may

O. M. Scott and Sons Co.

A good way to get even grades on slopes or level ground is to sight along T-shaped pieces of wood with cross pieces at right angles with uprights.

be introduced to produce "artistic" effects.

This is not to say that perfectly level panels of well-kept turf are not grand when well located or that flat terraces in the immediate vicinity of the house and at "overlooks," for example, are not in good taste. I merely emphasize that they should be accepted only after careful thought and that in many places contours are preferable. Not any old contours, of course, but those that are practical as well as pleasing. Too-steep grades present their own difficulties and contoured ground, badly landscaped, can be pretty awful, too; but it is harder to do a bad job of landscaping it.

If your lot is not level, develop it in such a way that its natural grades are retained wherever feasible and let any necessary modifications be in keeping with them. Don't buck Nature, work with her.

The surface to aim for should roll or flow in smooth, pleasing slopes that merge imperceptibly without sudden changes of grade or direction. But be practical about it. Arrange the grades so that they present no very special difficulties, as, for example, extraordinary steep ones may do. Let the lawn slope gently away from the house for at least 10 or 12 feet so that surface water drains away (a matter of particular importance when the ground is frozen). Where paths must go arrange minor valleys or, alternatively, let the paths follow natural depressions.

These recommendations are not to be

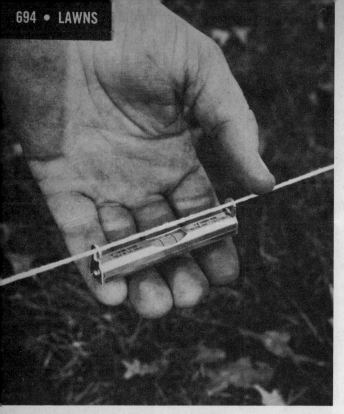

Line or string level is inexpensive instrument for determining levels. Bubble is centered when level.

As one operator determines if bubble in line is centered, the other raises or lowers end of string.

taken to preclude the possibility of having paths leading to high points of vantage; the thing to remember is that they should follow the apparently easiest way to their objectives. Curves or turns made without obvious reason or a hill climbed when an easier way is apparent are bad. Functionalism in landscape grading brings its own beauty as it does in so many forms of art.

If your lot is flat don't regard it as impossible. In flat country it is natural that it should be this way and a perfectly level garden in a naturally flat-land region never looks out of place, as such gardens may do when artificially created in hilly or rolling country.

But added interest can often be given to a level lot by contouring it slightly. The effect must not be extreme. Err by doing little rather than much. No hills or scooped-out depressions, obviously the work of the bulldozer, but the gentlest of rises and barely perceptible hollows, the latter always with outlets so that surface water doesn't collect.

By having the higher land where you will plant trees and tall shrubbery and the lower where free sweeps of lawn and low-growing plants are to be, you will accentuate and improve the effect.

When grading operations are finished there should be an even layer of good topsoil overlying the subsoil. It should be a minimum six inches thick and better eight or more. This even distribution cannot be attained by having a bulldozer, scoop or other implement or tool move the surface soil only. If this is all that is done when

When grades are too severe, lawn is scalped or partly scalped at area "a" or left too tall at area "b."

Grading operations should begin by establishing levels from base of a building or other fixed point.

When using line level without an assistant, weight ends of line and hang them over ends of stakes.

the grading is completed the topsoil will be disproportionately thin in the hollows and thick at the elevations.

To avoid this, strip the topsoil first. Pile it either nearby or where change of grade is to be made. Then grade the subsoil to the desired contours but six inches or more (depending upon the depth of topsoil to be put back over it) below the finish grade.

Topsoil is valuable. Save all you have. It is worth going to considerable trouble to do this. If your house has a cellar you may find topsoil under subsoil against the house or nearby. This is where the builder dumped excavation material on the ground without first stripping the topsoil. It is a common practice. In your grading operations take care to correct this and bring all available topsoil to the surface.

Grades can sometimes be established by eye alone. Where natural rolling effects are the objective, this is often the best way. In critical areas, for example near the house and where the surface is to be reasonably level but drainage in a particular direction must be assured, more precise methods are needed. The eye, unaided, can be very deceiving.

You can establish the grades for a garden of moderate extent with simple tools. If the area is large and distances of more than a hundred feet are involved, it may be desirable to have grade stakes set by someone skilled in the use of a surveyor's level or a transit, although this is not always necessary. To grade without a surveyor's level or a transit (both costly instruments) proceed as follows:

When changes of grade are smoothly curved, as areas "c" and "d," mower cuts grass to even heights.

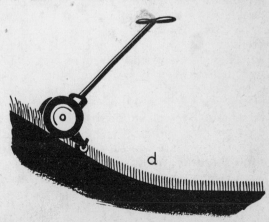

Leveling the ground with a straightedge and a mason's level is a simple and accurate procedure.

Bubble in a small glass tube in center of mason's level indicates whether the straightedge is level.

Take a line (or string) level (obtainable from a hardware store for less than a dollar), a length of mason's twine, a wooden mallet (or a hammer and piece of board) and a number of stout stakes of lengths that allow their tops to stick six inches above finish grade after being driven a foot or so into the ground. Mark each stake clearly, six inches from its top, with a horizontal pencil mark. Begin at some established feature such as the front door step, the sidewalk or road or the base of a large, well placed tree and drive one of the stakes into the ground until the pencil mark is at the level you want the finish grade to be. If you use a hammer for driving the stake hold a board on top of the stake when you strike it to prevent splitting.

Ten to twenty feet away, along the line of the grade you are establishing, drive another stake with its pencilled line (as nearly as you can judge) as much lower or higher than the pencil mark on the first as you wish the fall or rise to be. If you wish a perfectly level grade, set stakes with their pencil marks level with each other.

Now determine exactly the relative levels of the marks by holding the mason's line fairly taut (it need not be stretched tightly) between the stakes, touching the top of each. If you are working alone you can wind the line around a nail set in the top of each stake or weight its end and hang it over the top of the stake, otherwise have

someone assist you by holding the line. Hook the level on at the center of the line. Its bubble indicates which stake, if either, is higher than the other. By raising or lowering one end of the line until the bubble rests at the center of glass containing it, you determine any difference in grade that exists between tops of the stakes. This is the same as the difference in grades between the pencil marks. Raise or lower the second stake until the pencil mark is set where you want the finish grade of the lawn to be.

Use Mason's Level

Follow the procedure described above except in the following particulars. Instead of line level and mason's line, use a mason's (or carpenter's) level and a straightedge. The latter may be a board six to twelve feet long. One edge must be perfectly straight and the center portion of the opposite edge, for at least two feet, absolutely parallel with it. Set the stakes slightly nearer together than the length of the straightedge. To check their relative heights, rest the long straight edge of the straightedge across the tops of both stakes, set the level on the parallel portion of the upper edge. Raise or lower one end of the straightedge until the bubble is centered. Measure the differences in levels (if any) and adjust the stakes so that the pencil marks on them indicate where the finish

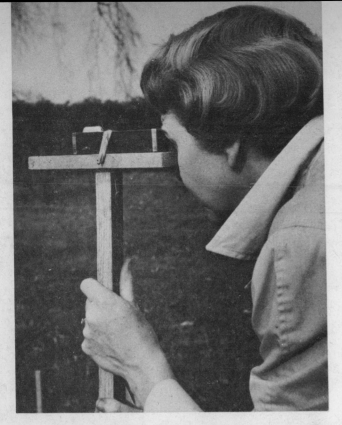

A sighting level makes it easy to determine grades over considerable distances and costs very little.

A surveyor's level, on the other hand, is a more costly and extremely accurate method of leveling.

grade is to be. Do measuring job carefully.

A hand sighting level is an inexpensive instrument that enables levels to be determined over a considerable distance with little effort. Use it with two simple, home-made gadgets: one, a measuring rod, eight to ten feet long, clearly marked in feet and inches (lesser gradations if close work is to be done); the other a stake about an inch and a half square with a six-inch piece of board nailed squarely across its top to form a platform. The length of the stake, plus the thickness of the platform, plus the distance from the bottom of the sighting level to its center line of sight (about half an inch) should be a specific length; four and a half is convenient when leveling grade stakes that stick six inches out of the ground.

Tie the level to the top of the platform with a string fastened to a couple of nails driven on opposite sides into its edges or loop a stout rubber band around level and platform. Have an assistant hold the measuring rod vertically with its end touching the top of one grade stake. Place the bottom end of the stake attached to the platform on top of another grade stake. Hold the platform stake vertically and look through the eyepiece of the level toward the measuring stake. Move the stake you are holding until the bubble you see centers exactly on the center line of the scale that is visible at the same time. The point on the measur-

ing rod held by the assistant that coincides with the center line of the scale you see is then level with it. By reading the height of that point on the measuring rod the difference in levels, if any, between the tops of the two grade stakes is apparent.

Your grading of the subsoil need not be as exact as the finished surface of the lawn but it should approximate it closely. Make sure that no water-collecting hollows are left because these may result in wet swales where it will be difficult to grow good grass. When you are grading provide for good under-drainage. It is relatively easy to do then, more difficult and costly after the lawn is established.

If the subsoil is porous and the water table is low, there will be no difficulties on this score. But if free water stands near the surface or if the subsoil is clayey and more or less impervious you may have problems. In the latter case make sure that all surfaces slope so that water drains from them.

If water stands on or near surface install agricultural tile drains, making sure they rest on a firm well-packed bottom so there is no danger of their sinking or getting out of line after they are installed. These drains will normally be set a foot or more below the top of the rough grade, 18 to 24 inches below the finish grade.

On small plots, grading may be done with a shovel and wheelbarrow; for larger areas

GRADING PROFILES FOR LAWNS

This type of grading requires more soil, provides for nearly level area near house, then long slope.

This provides for nearly flat area near house by creating a terrace supported by masonry wall. Excess soil from below terrace is used above wall.

This provides for a nearly level area near house, then two slopes. New grade is made by cutting and filling, using earth from high area to fill in.

This provides for nearly level area near house, then gently rolling hill which gives lawn feeling of spaciousness. Soil moved from high to low areas.

- - - - - - - original grade
———— new grade

When land slopes toward house, regrade so that a nearly level area slopes from house for drainage.

a bulldozer, scoop or other suitable implement is most practical. Whatever means is employed, if the ground is clayey avoid working on it when it is wet and sticky if at all possible. Unfortunately, this plan of action cannot always be followed if arrangements must be made beforehand for bulldozers, etc., or when such implements have to be used when it is convenient for them to be spared from other jobs. During the grading of the subsoil remove any large stones and builders' debris.

After the rough grading is finished to a predetermined height beneath the finish grade, do whatever you can to improve the subsoil before placing the topsoil over it. Grasses root deeply in agreeable undersoil and deeply rooted lawns survive droughts and other hardships much better than turf with its roots in the upper few inches only. If possible add organic matter such as compost (it need not be well decayed for this purpose) in quantity and, if the soil is acid, a heavy application of ground limestone. A three- or four-inch layer of coarse coal cinders worked into really heavy clay

GRADING PROCEDURE

(Drawing left) Original grade. (Right) If surface is merely leveled, topsoil is unevenly distributed, leaving thin or bare areas where grass will not grow well, and deep soil areas.

(Left) Correct way to grade is to first strip off the topsoil and pile it nearby or where no change of grade is to be made. (Right) Then grade subsoil so it is leveled off.

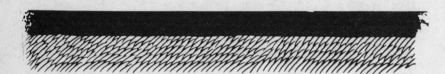

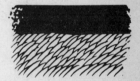

topsoil

subsoil

(Left) After subsoil has been graded and made level, replace the topsoil in even layers. (Right) Key to these drawings.

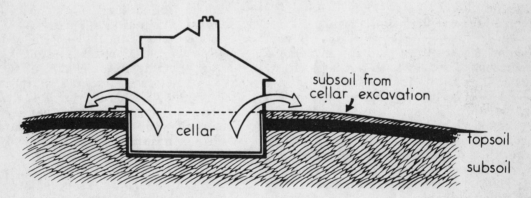

subsoil from cellar excavation

cellar

topsoil

subsoil

Builders often distribute subsoil over topsoil. Prevent this if possible; if not, correct this before making a lawn.

is highly beneficial in opening it up, improving aeration and drainage. Remember, this is the last time you will have opportunity to improve the subsoil. Then spade, or plow or rototill the upper surface to a depth of six inches, mixing thoroughly with the soil the added ingredients and taking care, of course, not to disturb any drains.

Final surface grading is done when the area is raked smooth just before the seeds are sown or the turf is laid, but that consists of very minor adjustments. For all practical purposes the rough grade that re-

sults from the spreading and smoothing out of the topsoil is that of the finished lawn.

First firm the sub-grade by treading it or rolling it, but do not pack it hard. Then rough-rake its surface so that a good bond will be established between subsoil and topsoil. Spread the topsoil to such a depth that after settling it will be at the level you want. Figure a six-inch layer of loose topsoil will sink from one to two inches when compacted, therefore to end with a six-inch depth of topsoil, you must spread a seven- to eight-inch layer of loose soil.

Bulldozers and other heavy mechanical equipment are vital to building activities but pack down soil.

Where heavy machinery has packed down subsoil, it should be loosened before topsoil is spread.

This requires 22 or 23 cubic feet of topsoil for each 1,000 square feet of surface. When you price good topsoil you will understand why I stressed the wisdom of saving all topsoil present on the site. If you don't have sufficient topsoil to insure a good lawn, bring it in from elsewhere or undertake a program of soil improvement and conditioning.

This will take a little time but to attempt lawn making where the topsoil is too poor or too shallow is courting failure.

Where slopes are too steep for the particular garden effect wanted, terracing is necessary. Terraces need not be perfectly level. It is better if they have at least a slight fall and in many places the gradient may, with advantage, be considerable.

Terraces may be supported by solid masonry walls, dry walls (walls built without cement) or by steeply-sloped banks appropriately planted with creeping junipers, cotoneasters, creeping roses, English ivy or other suitable plants. Grass banks are sometimes used but are difficult to maintain if the slope is more than one foot in height for each three feet horizontally.

When grading for terraces try to establish main levels between high and low ground. If this is done the material excavated from the high ground will be available to fill the low places and purchase of fill made unnecessary or reduced. Preserve all topsoil and grade in such a way that when the job is finished there is an even layer over the whole area.

So far as humanly possible preserve all valuable trees. Consider this when deciding what contours the ground shall have. Place substantial guards around endangered specimens during bulldozer and

trucking operations. Instruct contractors and operators to exercise all possible care. Then pray for the best.

Scraping soil from over roots and cutting substantial portions off root systems, seriously injures trees and may result in their death. Cutting roots too deeply and too close to the trunk on one side of a tree may weaken its hold so that it is likely to blow down in a storm.

Adding fill over tree roots should be done with caution. They need air to live. A comparatively thin layer of clayey soil, packed tight, can cut off the supply to the extent that the trees slowly suffocate. It may take a few years for them to die but they surely will if the air supply is seriously reduced. Changes of grade that result in flooding the soil in which tree roots ramify with water is also disastrous; avoid it.

Use Porous Fill

A fill of loose, porous soil (of a sandy or gravelly character) can be put over roots to a depth of about a foot without harm, provided the soil is not heaped around the trunk. To prevent this, build a well wall of stone or brick around the trunk and about 12 inches from it. If you must fill over roots to a depth of more than eight inches with heavy soil or 12 inches with porous soil, take the following precautions. If the depth of fill exceeds those mentioned by no more than three or four inches, cover the area containing the roots and some little distance beyond with a layer of largish stones; over these place smaller stones, gravel or coal cinders to within eight inches of the finish grade, then add the topsoil.

Should you be forced to fill to a depth of 18 inches or more over roots, take spe-

Where fill is placed over roots of tree to be saved, a protective well is built around the trunk.

Trees to be saved should be protected from damage by machinery. Use wood frame, corrugated metal.

cial precautions. Bare the surface roots from the trunk to their farthest extent, usually just beyond the spread of the branches. If the soil is heavy and packed, loosen it slightly with the prongs of a fork but don't spade it over because that breaks too many roots. Apply a dressing of organic fertilizer to the loosened soil.

From close to the trunk to the outer circumference of the roots, lay six (in the case of a very large tree, eight) lines of four-inch agricultural drain tiles. These should radiate from the trunk like the spokes of a wheel. Make sure the drains slope downward as they spread from the trunk at the rate of about one eighth of an inch to the foot. Now connect the ends of these spokes with a circle of drain tiles to form, as it were, the rim of the wheel. This rim encircles the tree at the outermost limit of its roots, ordinarily just beyond the drip line of the outer branches. If there is any danger of the soil being waterlogged, lay another row of agricultural tile from

a spot on the rim where one of the spokes join it in a downward sloping direction to some outlet away from the tree.

Where the spokes connect with the rim, set six-inch glazed tile drainpipes vertically with their tops level with the ground surface and their lower ends opening into the agricultural tiles. Unlike the agricultural tiles, the glazed pipes should have sockets so that the end of one fits snugly into that of the next, and the joints should be cemented. The ends of the agricultural tiles are butted together and are not cemented. The vertical pipes may be filled with rough stones or left open. In either case their upper ends are covered with grids.

The chief purpose of the tiles is to carry air to the roots, but they also serve to drain away any superfluous water and also provide (through the gridded surface openings) a ready means of watering and fertilizing the tree. Watering in droughts, and annual fertilization are helpful, too. •

When the grade is changed, valuable trees can be saved. Tile drains carry off water.

For a house below street level, the soil must be graded up to house so water drains away.

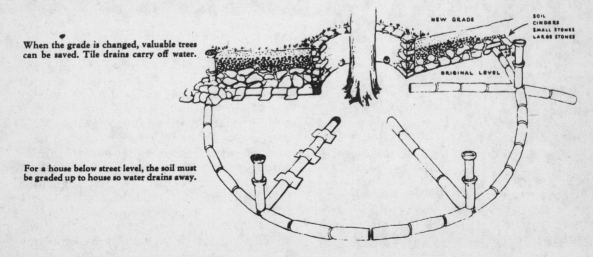

STOLONS, SPRIGS AND PLUGS

... plant them for new grass

SOME GRASSES spread rapidly by creeping stems or stolons. It is quite practicable to establish good turf by planting small pieces of them. These take root and, if planted closely enough together, give rise to plants that soon touch and form unbroken turf. Grasses that may be propagated in this manner are chiefly subtropical kinds such as Zoysia, St. Augustine, Centipede and Bermuda. In addition there is the cool-climate creeping bent.

Creeping bent grass grows readily if the stems it forms so plentifully at or below

(Photo across page) Meyer Z-52 Zoysia is often used as strips of sod, can be cut into plugs by knife or pruning shears. (Photo above) Zoysia set into holes made by trowel.

the soil surface are cut into small pieces and planted. This is the method used by many golf course superintendents to produce perfect turf for putting greens. The turf so formed is extremely uniform. Here's how to go about getting it.

Chop the stolons into pieces half an inch to an inch long and scatter them over soil that has been prepared as thoroughly as it should be for seed sowing. Make sure it is firm and raked smooth before you distribute the stolons. Sow them as you would seed, but not as thickly. The pieces should

be spaced about half an inch apart. One and a half bushels of chopped stolons are sufficient for 1,000 square feet. Make sure they are distributed evenly and press them into the surface by rolling. Spread a covering of fine soil, one quarter to one half inch thick, over the stolons and roll again. An easy way of doing this is to lay a flexible steel door mat over the newly distributed stolons, heap fine soil on it, then, with the back of a rake, spread it level with the tops of the treads of the mat. Remove any surplus soil, lift the mat carefully (a two

Lawn Grass Development Co.
Lawn is plugged by setting up guide lines 12 inches apart, putting plugs along line at one-foot intervals.

person job) and treat the adjoining area in the same way. Repeat this until the whole planted surface is covered with soil. Then roll lightly.

It is very important to water a lawn newly planted in this manner often enough to keep the soil moist.

Where a lawn of a kind exists, and the soil is known to be good to a depth of six or eight inches, it is possible to establish a turf of creeping bent without spading or turning it over. Simply destroy the grass already there. This you may do by skimming it off very thinly with a spade or by applying a very heavy dressing of sulphate of ammonia. Scratch the surface with a rake then sow the stolons and treat as advised above.

Important Considerations

Before beginning a creeping bent lawn consider these facts. It is more costly in labor than making other type lawns from seed. If you have to buy the stolons (possibly you can obtain them from an established lawn without cost) they are more expensive than seed. Lawns of creeping bent require a tremendous amount of upkeep—frequent mowing, watering, fertilizing, top-dressing, etc. They are really for specialists.

One other point. Seaside bent is a kind of bent grass that creeps and can be easily raised from seeds. It produces a turf almost as good as the Washington and Metropolitan strains of true creeping bent which

can only be increased by the use of stolons.

Sprigs are young rooted shoots—pieces of stolon with leaves and roots attached. Lawns of subtropical grasses, Bermuda, Carpet, St. Augustine and Centipede, may be established by planting such shoots at distances of six to nine inches apart. This is called sprigging.

In preparation for sprigging, the soil is made ready as for sowing seed. It is then well watered and the sprigs (each consisting of several joints and shoots) are planted with a dibber (pointed stick) and are firmed in place. After planting, the area is again well watered.

Plugs are pieces of sod, one and a half or two inches or so in diameter, of creeping grasses. When planted, they quickly grow together and cover the ground. They differ from sprigs in that each consists of many rather than few of shoots and includes the soil in which the roots grow (sprigs carry little or no soil with them). Zoysia grasses are the ones chiefly propagated by plugs. They make good turf sooner when grown in this way rather than from sprigs.

Make the soil ready as you would for seeding. Plant the plugs with a trowel, six to twelve inches apart, setting the surface of each level with or very slightly below the soil surface. Make the soil about the roots firm. Water thoroughly after planting. Old lawns may be plugged with Zoysia which will gradually intermingle with established grasses and may take over entirely eventually. •